The Book of Kadam

The Library of Tibetan Classics is a special series being developed by the Institute of Tibetan Classics aimed at making key classical Tibetan texts part of the global literary and intellectual heritage. Eventually comprising thirty-two large volumes, the collection will contain over two hundred distinct texts by more than a hundred of the best-known Tibetan authors. These texts have been selected in consultation with the preeminent lineage holders of all the schools and other senior Tibetan scholars to represent the Tibetan literary tradition as a whole. The works included in the series span more than a millennium and cover the vast expanse of classical Tibetan knowledge—from the core teachings of the specific schools to such diverse fields as ethics, philosophy, psychology, Buddhist teachings and meditative practices, civic and social responsibilities, linguistics, medicine, astronomy and astrology, folklore, and historiography.

The Book of Kadam: The Core Texts

The Kadam school, which emerged from the teachings of the Indian master Atiśa and his principal student, Dromtönpa, is revered for its unique practical application of the bodhisattva's altruistic ideal in day-to-day life. One of the most well-known sets of spiritual teachings stemming from Atiśa and Dromtönpa is a special collection of oral transmissions enshrined in the two-volume *Book of Kadam (Bka' gdams glegs bam)*. The texts presented here include the core texts of *The Book of Kadam*, notably the twenty-three-chapter dialogue between Atiśa and Dromtönpa that is woven around Atiśa's *Bodhisattva's Jewel Garland*. Sometimes referred to as the "Kadam emanation scripture," *The Book of Kadam* is undisputedly one of the greatest works of Tibetan Buddhism. This volume contains (1) Atiśa's *Bodhisattva's Jewel Garland*, (2) the twenty-three-chapter *Jewel Garland of Dialogues*, (3) Dromtönpa's *Tree of Faith: A Self-Exhortation*, (4) *Elucidation of the Heart-Drop Practice* by Khenchen Nyima Gyaltsen (1223–1305), (5) four selected chapters from Dromtönpa's birth stories, (6) two brief verse summaries of *The Book of Kadam*, one by the Second Dalai Lama (1476–1542) and the other by Yongzin Yeshé Gyaltsen (1713–93), and (7) *Sayings of the Kadam Masters*, compiled by Chegom Sherap Dorjé (ca. twelfth century). Although the Kadam school no longer exists as an autonomous lineage within Tibetan Buddhism, its teachings have become fully incorporated into the teachings of all four major schools of Tibetan Buddhism, especially the Geluk school.

THE LIBRARY OF TIBETAN CLASSICS • VOLUME 2
Thupten Jinpa, General Editor

THE BOOK OF KADAM

The Core Texts

Attributed to Atiśa and Dromtönpa

Translated by Thupten Jinpa

WISDOM PUBLICATIONS • BOSTON
in association with the Institute of Tibetan Classics

Wisdom Publications
199 Elm Street
Somerville MA 02144 USA
www.wisdompubs.org

First Edition
13 12 11 10 09 08
6 5 4 3 2 1

Library of Congress Cataloging-in-Publication Data
Bka' gdams glegs bam. English. Selections.
The Book of Kadam : the core texts / attributed to Atisa and Dromtönpa ; translated by Thupten Jinpa.
    p. cm.
Includes bibliographical references and index.
ISBN 0-86171-441-5 (hardcover : alk. paper)
1. Bka'-gdams-pa (Sect)—Early works to 1800. I. Atisa, 982–1054. II. 'Brom-ston Rgyal-ba'i-'byuṅ-gnas. III. Thupten Jinpa. IV. Title.
BQ7670.B58213 2008
294.3'85—dc22

2008012017

Cover and interior design by Gopa&Ted2, Inc. Set in DiacriticalGaramond 10.5/13.5 pt.

Message from the Dalai Lama

THE LAST TWO MILLENNIA witnessed a tremendous proliferation of cultural and literary development in Tibet, the "Land of Snows." Moreover, due to the inestimable contributions made by Tibet's early spiritual kings, numerous Tibetan translators, and many great Indian paṇḍitas over a period of so many centuries, the teachings of the Buddha and the scholastic tradition of ancient India's Nālandā monastic university became firmly rooted in Tibet. As evidenced from the historical writings, this flowering of Buddhist tradition in the country brought about the fulfillment of the deep spiritual aspirations of countless sentient beings. In particular, it contributed to the inner peace and tranquility of the peoples of Tibet, Outer Mongolia—a country historically suffused with Tibetan Buddhism and its culture—the Tuva and Kalmuk regions in present-day Russia, the outer regions of mainland China, and the entire trans-Himalayan areas on the southern side, including Bhutan, Sikkim, Ladakh, Kinnaur, and Spiti. Today this tradition of Buddhism has the potential to make significant contributions to the welfare of the entire human family. I have no doubt that, when combined with the methods and insights of modern science, the Tibetan Buddhist cultural heritage and knowledge will help foster a more enlightened and compassionate human society, a humanity that is at peace with itself, with fellow sentient beings, and with the natural world at large.

It is for this reason I am delighted that the Institute of Tibetan Classics in Montreal, Canada, is compiling a thirty-two volume series containing the works of many great Tibetan teachers, philosophers, scholars, and practitioners representing all major Tibetan schools and traditions. These important writings will be critically edited and annotated and will then be published in modern book format in a reference collection called *The Library of Tibetan Classics,* with their translations into other major languages to be followed later. While expressing my heartfelt commendation for this noble project, I pray and hope that *The Library of Tibetan Classics* will not only make these important Tibetan treatises accessible to scholars of Tibetan studies, but will create a new opportunity for younger Tibetans to study and take interest in their own rich and profound culture. Through translations into other languages, it is my sincere hope that millions of fellow citizens of the wider human family will also be able to share in the joy of engaging with Tibet's classical literary heritage, textual riches that have been such a great source of joy and inspiration to me personally for so long.

The Dalai Lama
The Buddhist monk Tenzin Gyatso

Special Acknowledgments

THE INSTITUTE OF TIBETAN CLASSICS expresses its deep gratitude to Barry J. Hershey, Connie Hershey, and the Hershey Family Foundation for funding the entire cost of this translation project.

We also acknowledge the Hershey Family Foundation for its generous support of the Institute of Tibetan Classics' projects of compiling, editing, translating, and disseminating key classical Tibetan texts through the creation of *The Library of Tibetan Classics*.

Publisher's Acknowledgements

THE PUBLISHER wishes to extend a heartfelt thanks to the following people who, by subscribing to *The Library of Tibetan Classics*, have become benefactors of this entire translation series.

Heidi Kaiter
Arnold Possick
Jonathan and Diana Rose
Robert White

Contents

Preface

THE PUBLICATION OF THIS WORK, *The Book of Kadam: The Core Texts*, which is volume 2 in *The Library of Tibetan Classics*, brings a special collection of Tibet's deeply spiritual literature into the world's literary heritage. The volume contains some of the most important texts of the Tibetan Buddhist tradition translated for the first time ever in any secondary language. Attributed to the eleventh-century Indian Bengali master Atiśa and his principle disciple Dromtönpa, *The Book of Kadam*—the original two-volume Tibetan collection that is the basis of our volume—contains a series of poignant exchanges between two luminaries of Tibetan Buddhism on all the important themes of spiritual awakening. From the basic training in guarding the gateway of our senses and seeking an appropriate environment in which to live to such advanced meditative practices as the sophisticated visualization of the mandala of the so-called sixteen drops, and from somber instructions on how to prepare our mind for death to the detailed contemplations on the twelve links of dependent origination and the cultivation of a compassionate heart, the dialogues reproduced here bring a personal approach to the path to full enlightenment. Sometimes known also as "the miraculous book of Kadam" *(bka' gdams sprul pa'i glegs bam)* because of its origination as a "revealed" text, *The Book of Kadam* is today revered as sacred by all schools of Tibetan Buddhism. One of the major legacies of the book was the embracing throughout Tibet of Avalokiteśvara (the buddha of compassion) and the goddess Tārā (the buddha of enlightened activities) as special divinities connected to Tibet, laying the foundation for what later came to be the institution of the Dalai Lamas.

The present volume contains the core texts of *The Book of Kadam* along with three supplemental texts to help the reader better understand how the collection was historically viewed and practiced.

Two primary objectives have driven the creation and development of *The Library of Tibetan Classics*. The first aim is to help revitalize the appreciation and the study of the Tibetan classical heritage within Tibetan-speaking communities worldwide. The younger generation in particular struggle with the tension between traditional Tibetan culture and the realities of modern consumerism. To this end, efforts have been made to develop a comprehensive yet manageable body of texts, one that features the works of Tibet's best-known authors and covers the gamut of classical Tibetan knowledge. The second objective of *The Library of Tibetan Classics* is to help make these texts part of global literary and intellectual heritage. In this regard, we have tried to make the English translation reader-friendly and, as much as possible, keep the body of the text free of scholarly apparatus, which can intimidate general readers. For specialists who wish to compare the translation with the Tibetan original, page references of the critical edition of the Tibetan text are provided in brackets.

The texts in this thirty-two-volume series span more than a millennium—from the development of the Tibetan script in the seventh century to the first part of the twentieth century, when Tibetan society and culture first encountered industrial modernity. The volumes are thematically organized and cover many of the categories of classical Tibetan knowledge—from the teachings specific to each Tibetan school to the classical works on philosophy, psychology, and phenomenology. The first category includes teachings of the Kadam, Nyingma, Sakya, Kagyü, Geluk, and Jonang schools, of miscellaneous Buddhist lineages, and of the Bön school. The texts in these volumes were selected in consultation with the senior lineage holders of the individual schools. The texts in the other categories were selected based on the historical reality of the particular disciplines. For example, the volume on epistemology contains works from the Sakya and Geluk schools, while the volume on buddha nature features the writings of Butön Rinchen Drup and various Kagyü masters. Where fields are of more common interest, such as the three codes or the bodhisattva ideal, efforts have been made to represent the perspectives of each of the four major schools. *The Library of Tibetan Classics* can function as a comprehensive library of the Tibetan literary heritage for libraries, educational and cultural institutions, and interested individuals.

It has been a joy and privilege for me to undertake this translation project and thus to have the opportunity to offer to the world some of the most precious jewels of the Tibetan tradition. I wish first to express my deep personal gratitude to His Holiness the Dalai Lama for always being such a profound source of inspiration. I would also like to express my sincere respect to my own teacher, the late Kyabjé Zemey Rinpoché, who, for me, always embodies what is most beautiful in the Tibetan Kadam teachings. Numerous individuals and organizations have helped make this translation possible. I express my deepest appreciation and thanks to Barry J. Hershey, Connie Hershey, and the Hershey Family Foundation for their most generous support, without which *The Library of Tibetan Classics* simply would not have been possible. It is their support that also has enabled me personally to work fulltime on translations of key classical Tibetan texts, such as those contained in the present volume, a pursuit that I greatly enjoy and care about.

I owe deep gratitude to several individuals and organizations. The Central Institute of Higher Tibetan Studies in Sarnath provided full access to its library to the Tibetan editors, including myself, who worked on the critical editions of the Tibetan texts translated in this volume. Gene Smith at the Tibetan Buddhist Resource Center helped in obtaining crucial Tibetan texts needed for the editing of the Tibetan texts as well as for my own research. My wife Sophie Boyer-Langri took on with warmth and dedication the numerous administrative chores that are part of a collaborative project such as *The Library of Tibetan Classics*. Finally, I thank my two editors, Amy Miller and David Kittlestrom at Wisdom Publications, whose careful copyediting brought much clarity to the English text, thus making its reading more joyful. It is my sincere hope that the translations offered in this volume will benefit many people. Through the efforts of all those involved in this noble venture, may all beings enjoy peace and happiness.

Thupten Jinpa
Montreal, 2007

Introduction

Tārā proclaimed:
"O Avalokiteśvara, most excellent son,
I will protect your followers.
Take this instruction of mine
And reveal it to those who follow you."[1]
—*The Book of Kadam*

ANY OBSERVANT PERSON who has visited a traditional Tibetan community, whether in Tibet itself or in an exile community in India or Nepal, will notice that among the multitude of deities that form the Tibetan Buddhist pantheon, two figures stand out with respect to people's devotion. They are Avalokiteśvara, the buddha of compassion whom Tibetans reverently call *Chenresik* ("the lord who gazes at beings with his eyes"), and Tārā (*Drölma,* "the savioress"). These two deities are renowned throughout the Tibetan Buddhist cultural sphere—from easternmost Tibet, which borders China proper, to the western regions near Ladakh, Kashmir, and Pakistan, and from Central Asia in the north to the trans-Himalayan regions of the Indian subcontinent in the south. Avalokiteśvara's famous six-syllable mantra, *oṃ maṇi padme hūṃ,* is so ubiquitous throughout the Tibetan cultural sphere that it may be one of the most-repeated strings of letters in human history. The Tibetans' deep devotion to Avalokiteśvara is never complete, however, without their affection for goddess Tārā, his partner in caring for and saving the world. Just as every devout Tibetan knows and recites the famous six-syllable mantra, so, too, most of them know and chant hymns to the twenty-one Tārās. Similarly, where one finds an icon of Avalokiteśvara, one also likely finds an icon of Tārā in her distinctive posture, seated with her left leg folded and right leg extended. With her two hands in the teaching gesture, or *mudra,* she holds in her right fingers the stem of a blue lotus that blooms near her right shoulder.

Inextricably linked with the flourishing of Avalokiteśvara and Tārā worship in Tibet is the story of the Bengali master Atiśa Dīpaṃkara (982–1054) and his interaction with his principal Tibetan disciple Dromtön Gyalwai Jungné (1005–64), the subject of *The Book of Kadam,* or simply "the book."

According to traditional biographies of Atiśa, as conveyed through Gya Tsöndrü Sengé (eleventh century) and, later, Naktso Lotsāwa Tsültrim Gyalwa (1011–64), it was at Tārā's urging that the Indian master finally accepted the persistent invitations of the Ngari rulers in Tibet. It was also Tārā who, according to tradition, prophesized Atiśa's meeting with his spiritual heir, Dromtönpa. As we see in the epigraph above, Tārā also offered her solemn pledge to protect all those who follow Avalokiteśvara, who the book identifies with Dromtönpa himself. These and many other aspects of the story of Atiśa's coming to Tibet—his devotion to Avalokiteśvara and Tārā, and, more importantly, his special relationship with Dromtönpa— left a lasting imprint upon the Tibetan people and the fate of Buddhism in Tibet. Soon after Master Atiśa's death in 1054, and especially after Dromtönpa's founding of Radreng Monastery not far from the Tibetan capital city of Lhasa in 1056, the followers of this Bengali master came to be identified as the Kadam school. The epithet *kadam (bka' gdams)* distinguishes its followers as those who understand the sacred words of the Buddha in terms of Atiśa's instructions.

Perhaps the most important legacy of the book, at least for the Tibetan people as a whole, is that it laid the foundation for the later identification of Avalokiteśvara with the lineage of the Dalai Lama, who continually enacts the solemn pledge of this compassionate deity to accord special care for the people of the "Land of Snows." Although Avalokiteśvara was propitiated in Tibet before the tenth century, and although the designation of the seventh-century Tibetan emperor, Songtsen Gampo, as an embodiment of Avalokiteśvara most probably predates Atiśa's arrival in Tibet, the available textual evidence points strongly toward the eleventh and twelfth centuries as the period during which the full myth of Avalokiteśvara's special destiny with Tibet was established. During this era, the belief that this compassionate spirit intervenes in the fate of the Tibetan people by manifesting as benevolent rulers and teachers took firm root.[2] It is also becoming increasingly clear that Atiśa played a crucial role in the propagation, if not development, of the key elements of these myths. The story of the *The Book of Kadam* is part of that overall story, one that indelibly shaped the self-identity of the Tibetan people and their understanding of Tibet's place in the world.[3]

Master Atiśa and His Teaching Legacy

Atiśa came to Tibet in the summer of the water-horse year, 1042, first to the kingdom of Ngari in western Tibet. For the Tibetans this was an occasion for celebration, as it marked the culmination of years of sacrifice of both personal and material resources aimed at bringing an Indian master of such stature to Tibet. On the Nepalese side of the border, the master was received by a welcoming party of around three hundred horsemen from Tibet, recalling the Tibetan reception of the grand abbot Śāntarakṣita several centuries earlier.[4] By then, Atiśa must already have been familiar with the historical outline of Tibet's conversion to Buddhism: the role of the famous Indian Buddhist philosopher Śāntarakṣita, especially his introduction of the monastic order; the founding of the first monastery, Samyé; and the early Tibetan translators' efforts in transmitting classical Buddhist texts. According to the traditional hagiographical sources, Atiśa was explicitly invited to "revive" and "restore" the Buddhadharma in Tibet in the wake of its "adulteration" with all sorts of misconceptions—both deliberate and out of ignorance—of the scriptures, especially those of the esoteric Vajrayana class.

It is telling that when the Ngari ruler Lha Jangchup Ö requested Atiśa for a formal teaching, as attested in the colophon to Atiśa's *Lamp for the Path to Enlightenment (Bodhipathapradīpa)*, the Tibetan ruler asked for a teaching that would be beneficial for the survival of the Buddhadharma as a whole. According to one source, Jangchup Ö made the following plea: "Instead of some so-called profound or amazing teachings, pray sustain us in the land of Tibet with the teaching of karma and its effects," to which the master replied with great delight, "The law of karma and its effects alone is the most profound teaching."[5] Then, recounting several tales of how even some advanced yogis who had experienced visions of their meditation deities suffered grave consequences as a result of defying the law of karma, Atiśa is said to have consented to nurture the people of Tibet with teachings on karma. In this way, Atiśa came to be known, in addition to his previous appellation as the "teacher of awakening mind," as the "teacher of karma and its effects."[6] Thus began Atiśa's mission in Tibet.

Atiśa is perhaps revered most for his genius in distilling the essence of all the teachings of the Buddha within the framework of a single aspirant's path. His *Lamp for the Path to Enlightenment* organizes the entire corpus of the Buddhist teachings into what he calls the practices relevant to "the persons of three scopes" or "three capacities"—initial, intermediate, and great. This revolutionary approach enabled the Tibetans to understand the heterogeneous literature of the Indian Buddhist sources in their appropriate contexts and to integrate that knowledge meaningfully within meditative practice. Over time an entire genre of literature evolved in Tibet on the basis of Atiśa's seminal works, collectively known as *stages of the path* or *lamrim*. A key feature of the lamrim texts is their graduated approach to the Buddhist path. Within this genre are two broad subdivisions, namely: (1) lamrim proper, the texts that stay close to the three capacities schema of Atiśa's *Lamp*, and (2) *stages of the doctrine (tenrim)*, the texts that emphasize understanding the diverse elements of the doctrine within the larger framework of the Buddha's teaching.[7]

The earliest examples of lamrim texts are notes based on Naktso Lotsāwa's teachings, Potowa's (1027–1105) *Blue Udder* and *Teaching in Similes*, as well as various notes drawn from Neusurpa's instructions.[8] Gönpawa Wangchuk Gyaltsen (1016–82) is said to have composed a lamrim based on the teachings he received directly from Atiśa, and there also appears to have been a lamrim by Ngok Lekpai Sherap (1018–1115)[9] based on Khutön Tsöndrü Yungdrung's (1011–75) teachings. Following Tsongkhapa's (1357–1419) composition of the influential classic, *The Great Treatise on the Stages of the Path to Enlightenment*, not only did the stages of the path become a defining mark of the Geluk school, but the very term *lamrim* came to be almost equivalent to Tsongkhapa's texts on the subject.[10] As for the stages of the doctrine genre, perhaps the earliest work is Ngok Lekpai Sherap's *Six Stanzas on the Stages of the Doctrine*[11] and its commentarial expositions, especially those of Ngok Loden Sherap (1059–1109) and his student Drolungpa (eleventh–twelfth centuries), the latter composing the monumental *Great Treatise on the Stages of the Doctrine*. In addition there are the various notes scribed on the basis of Laksorpa's teachings as well as Naljorpa's (eleventh century) *Instructions on the Entering and Departing Cyclic Existence*.[12]

The second genre of literature that evolved in Tibet from Atiśa's teachings is the cycle of *mind training (lojong)* texts, the most well known of which are Atiśa's own *Bodhisattva's Jewel Garland* (reproduced in this volume), Langri Thangpa's (1054–1123) *Eight Verses on Mind Training*, and the

Seven-Point Mind Training, which is traditionally attributed to Chekawa (1101–75). I have argued elsewhere that the origin of the Tibetan mind training teachings may well have been a compilation of pithy sayings Master Atiśa spoke to different people on different occasions.[13] The focal point of mind training teachings is the cultivation of the awakening mind *(bodhicitta)*, especially in the tradition of Śāntideva's (eighth century) equalizing and exchanging self and others. Furthermore, unlike the stages of the path teachings, mind training emphasizes the use of pithy sayings and a direct approach in dealing with the obstacles to developing the awakening mind. A central element in the mind training teachings is the commemoration of Atiśa's long journey to the Indonesian island of Sumatra and his special reverence for the master he met there, Serlingpa, his principal teacher on the awakening mind.

Early historical and biographical sources also show that Atiśa not only taught important Indian Buddhist philosophical classics, especially Bhāvaviveka's (fifth century) *Blaze of Reasoning*, an exposition of Nāgārjuna's (second century) *Fundamental Wisdom of the Middle Way*, he also composed philosophical works of his own, especially on the subject of the Middle Way doctrine of emptiness. The Indian master's philosophical legacy was ensured when one of his key Tibetan disciples, Ngok Lekpai Sherap, founded Sangphu Monastery, which soon became the most important center of philosophical learning in Tibet. This was followed by the founding of yet another important philosophical center of learning—namely, Narthang Monastery, established in 1153 by Tumtön Lodrö Drak (ca. 1106–66). These two monastic centers came to dominate the study of classical Indian Buddhist learning, especially in epistemology, Abhidharma psychology and phenomenology, the scholastic inquiry into the perfection of wisdom literature, and the Middle Way philosophy of emptiness.

Atiśa also wrote extensively on Buddhist Vajrayana practice, including ritual and meditation texts on the meditation deities Guhyasamāja, Cakrasaṃvara, Avalokiteśvara, and Tārā. He penned evocative tantric diamond songs, some of which echo the metaphors, themes, and emotive tones of the well-known *dohā* cycles of songs attributed to the Indian Buddhist mystic Saraha (ca. tenth century).[14] Today, most Tibetan Buddhist schools have numerous lineages of Vajrayana practice that trace their transmission to Atiśa. Perhaps Atiśa's greatest contribution to Vajrayana Buddhism in Tibet is his personal involvement in the translation into Tibetan of many important Indian Vajrayana texts.[15]

The Blue Annals contains a curious remark regarding Atiśa's Vajrayana legacy purportedly uttered by Tibet's beloved poet-saint Milarepa to his disciple Gampopa (1079–1153): "Although the Kadampas [i.e., Kadam followers] have essential instructions *(dam ngag)*, they possess no oral instructions *(man ngag)*. A demon must have possessed Tibetans' hearts, preventing Master Atiśa from teaching secret mantra, for had he been allowed to, Tibet would today be filled with accomplished adepts."[16] We also find in Chim Namkha Drak's (1210–85) *Biography of Master Atiśa* a passage dealing with this supposed barring of Atiśa from teaching secret mantra in Tibet. In response to Drom's request not to establish a new monastic line of the Mahāsaṁghika order, Atiśa is reported as speaking in exasperation, "I have no authority to teach the secret mantra vows or the *dohā* [cycle of] diamond songs. If I neither have the authority to establish a monastic line, then my journey to Tibet has been pointless!"[17]

In general, I do not think the available textual evidence suggests Dromtönpa prevented Atiśa from teaching Vajrayana; if anything, the sources indicate otherwise. Not only is Drom listed in the lineage of the transmission of several Vajrayana practices stemming from Atiśa, especially those that relate to Avalokiteśvara, Drom also appears to have helped translate some of these Vajrayana texts into Tibetan. It does seem, however, that Drom may have discouraged Atiśa, and especially his immediate disciples, from disseminating too publicly the teachings belonging to the so-called mother tantras. In doing so, not only was Drom following in the noble tradition of the early Tibetan monarchs, who imposed restrictions on the dissemination of the highest yoga class of tantra, but also, more importantly, he may have been keeping vigilant about one of the express purposes of bringing Atiśa to Tibet—to help reform and restore the Buddhadharma in light of the misconstrual and abuse of some Vajrayana teachings, especially sexual practices.

Perhaps the most intriguing set of teachings that traces its origin to Master Atiśa is the collection enshrined in two large volumes known together as *The Book of Kadam,* excerpts of which are translated in the present volume. This cycle of texts, as I've noted, relates Atiśa's special relationship with his spiritual heir, Dromtönpa, and highlights many of the more mystical aspects of Atiśa's legacy in Tibet, especially his veneration of Avalokiteśvara and his propitiation of Tārā. Known as Atiśa and Dromtönpa's "secret teachings" *(gsang chos),* they outline a unique practice called the *sevenfold divinity and teaching.* This teaching is centered on the choice of four meditation deities—(1) the Buddha as the teacher, (2) Avalokiteśvara as the deity of compassion, (3) Tārā as the goddess of enlightened action, and (4) Acala as the protector guardian—and the three scriptural baskets of discipline, knowledge, and meditation. This set of teachings is significant in the ways it creates a shift in focus. For example, with respect to the teacher, the focus of importance shifts from Master Atiśa to Dromtönpa; with respect to land, it shifts from India as the land of Dharma to Tibet as a place of special significance connected with Avalokiteśvara; and with regard to teachings, the focus shifts from the teaching of classical Indian scriptures and treatises to the direct and oral teachings of the masters, especially as revealed in mystic visionary states. Even in the style of language employed, there is a shift from classical composition to a more informal style, with greater use of vernacular Tibetan.

The Kadam Tradition

The Tibetan followers of the Indian master found a locus for their identification as members of a distinct community when Dromtönpa founded Radreng Monastery in 1056, about two years after Atiśa's death. These members came to decribe themselves as the Kadampas, a designation composed of two words covering a wide semantic range—*ka (bka')* refers to sacred words or speech, and *dam (gdams* or *dam)* can refer either to advice and instruction, or to the verbs "to bind" and "to choose." Lechen Künga Gyaltsen, a fifteenth-century historian of Kadam, offers four different explanations.[18] First, *Kadam* may be defined as "those who integrate the essence of the entire three baskets of Buddhist scripture within the framework of the path of the three scopes and for whom all the scriptures of the Buddha appear as personal instructions." This interpretation is said to be based on the following statement attributed to Dromtönpa:

> The wondrous sacred words are the three baskets of scripture,
> Which are enriched by the instructions on [the path of] the three
> capacities.
> This precious Kadam [tradition] is a golden rosary,
> And those who count its beads make their lives meaningful.[19]

According to the second interpretation of the meaning of *Kadam*, the tradition is so called "because the founding father of Kadam, Dromtönpa, chose, in accordance with the sacred instruction of Master Atiśa, the sevenfold divinity and teaching as his principal practice." A third interpretation is that when Master Atiśa was residing at Nyethang, his disciples accorded great authority to his sacred words, so they came to be known as "Kadampas," who hold the sacred words as binding. The final interpretation is that the Kadampas are guided by the three baskets of scripture in their overall Dharma practice and approach Vajrayana teachings and practices circumspectly.

On the other hand, Tsuklak Trengwa, the author of the well-known historical work *A Feast for the Learned,* identifies two meanings of the term and states that both of these interpretations can be found in *The Book of Kadam.* The first is that they are so-called because they uphold the Buddha's sacred words as personal instructions. Second, in that Dromtönpa selected the four divinities as meditation deities and the two awakening minds as the main practice, his followers were called Kadampas.[20]

Atiśa's Tibetan disciples include most Tibetan masters of the period. Among them, three stand out as his principal students in central Tibet. Known as "the trio Khu, Ngok, and Drom," they are, respectively: Khutön Tsöndrü Yungdrung, Ngok Lepai Sherap, and Dromtönpa. Most early sources agree that it was Dromtönpa who, as prophesized by Tārā, became Atiśa's chosen heir and thereby effectively the founder of the Kadam school. Over time Atiśa's other students became Dromtönpa's students as well. Chief among Dromtönpa's students were the "three Kadam brothers"—Potowa Rinchen Sal, Chengawa Tsültrim Bar (1033–1103), and Phu-chungwa Shönu Gyaltsen (1031–1106)—who effectively came to be recognized as "the entrusted holders of the lineage" *(bka' babs kyi brgyud 'dzin).* Potowa became the entrusted custodian of Atiśa's teachings on the authoritative treatises *(gzhung),* while Chengawa became the custodian of the teachings embodied in the essential instructions *(gdams ngag).*[21] Sometimes, Phuchungwa is listed as a third entrusted custodian and is seen as responsible for the "Kadam lineage of oral instructions" *(man ngag)* as embodied in *The Book of Kadam.* Other authors distinguish the following three lineages in the transmission of Atiśa and Dromtönpa's Kadam teachings: (1) the Kadam lineage of authoritative treatises stemming from Potowa, (2) the Kadam lineage of essential instructions stemming from Chengawa, and (3) the Kadam lineage of the stages of the path stemming from Gönpawa.[22]

Potowa's Kadam lineage of authoritative treatises emphasizes the approach of grounding all of Master Atiśa and Dromtönpa's spiritual legacy, especially the study and practice of Atiśa's seminal work *Lamp for the Path to Enlightenment*, in a close study of what came to be called the "six authoritative treatises of Kadam." They are: (1) Asaṅga's (fourth century) *Bodhisattva Levels*, (2) Maitreya's (ca. fourth century) *Ornament of Mahayana Sutras*, (3) Śāntideva's (eighth century) *Guide to the Bodhisattva's Way of Life* and (4) *Compendium of Trainings*, (5) Āryaśūra's (ca. fourth century) *Garland of Birth Stories*, and (6) the *Collection of Aphorisms*, attributed to the historical Buddha. The studies of these treatises are complemented with further Indian Buddhist classics like Nāgārjuna's (second century) *Fundamental Wisdom of the Middle Way*, his *Seventy Stanzas on Emptiness*, and Atiśa's *Entry into the Two Truths* and *An Instruction on the Middle Way*. In contrast, Chengawa's Kadam lineage of essential instructions emphasizes an approach whereby Atiśa's essential instructions, rather than classical treatises, are the key basis for practice. These instructions include the guide on the four truths as transmitted through Chengawa, the guide on the two truths as transmitted through Naljorpa, and the guide on dependent origination as transmitted through Phuchungwa. Finally, the Kadam lineage of oral transmissions as enshrined in *The Book of Kadam* was transmitted through Phuchungwa.

The fifteenth-century Kadam historian Sönam Lhai Wangpo lists the following lineages of Master Atiśa's teachings: (1) Atiśa's teachings as transmitted through his chosen heir, Dromtönpa, based at Radreng, which then branches into the three well-known Kadam lineages of: (i) authorative treatises stemming from Potowa, (ii) essential instructions stemming from Chengawa, and (iii) stages of the path teachings stemming either from Gönpawa or from Naktso Lotsāwa and Laksorwa; (2) Atiśa's teaching legacy as transmitted through Ngok Lekpai Sherap, which branches into two main strands: (i) the Sangphu lineage as transmitted through the famed translator Loden Sherap, and (ii) the lineage of *The Book of Kadam* as transmitted through Sherap Gyaltsen; and (3) Atiśa's legacy as transmitted through Naktso Lotsāwa, whose main successor was Laksorwa. It was through Laksorwa's main disciple, Jayülwa (the founder of Jayül Monastery), that the transmissions of Atiśa's biographical works as well as instructions on the stages of the path flourished. Naktso's lineage also includes transmissions of Atiśa's teachings on the highest yoga class of tantra, such as Guhyasamāja and on various aspects of Avalokiteśvara practice.[23]

In summing up the influence of the Kadam tradition on Tibetan Buddhism as a whole, the author of the influential *Blue Annals* states:

In general, during Master Atiśa's thirteen years in Tibet, a vast number received essential instructions from him and attained higher qualities [of Dharma]; their precise number cannot be calculated. In Tsang is the trio Gar, Gö, and Yöl, while in central Tibet is the trio Khu, Ngok, and Drom. These are [masters] with great fame. Here, however, I have given a broad account of the spiritual mentors whose lineage stems from Drom and [whose names] I have seen myself. Otherwise, in most of the biographies of spiritual mentors who had appeared in Tibet subsequently as well as the yogis who have engaged in the life of an adept, they all appeared to have studied at the feet of a Kadam spiritual mentor. Therefore, Drom was someone whose enlightened activities were extensive and long lasting.[24]

One intriguing issue in the history of the Kadam school is its disappearance. Although more research is needed to confirm this, it seems that by the end of sixteenth century, Kadam effectively ceased to be a distinct school. This may partly be due to the tremendous success of the custodians of Atiśa and Dromtönpa's teachings, on account of which all the key elements of the Kadam teachings became incorporated into the teachings of the other Tibetan schools. Partly, it may be the result of the rapid growth of Tsongkhapa's "new Kadam school," whose followers came to be known as Gandenpa (Gelukpa), named after Ganden Monastery, founded in 1409. We know, for example, that over time the different colleges of Kadam's famous philosophical monastery, Sangphu, came to be run by the Sakya or the Geluk school.[25] In addition, according to one eighteenth-century source, many of the Kadam monasteries had turned into nunneries, although Radreng and Narthang survived as Kadam monasteries.[26]

The Book of Kadam

In its present version, the heart of *The Book of Kadam* is two distinct but interrelated sets of teachings, enshrined in volumes 1 and 2, respectively. The first is the Father Teachings, so called because the teachings contained therein were given in response to questions posed to Master Atiśa by father Dromtönpa, while the second is the Son Teachings, teachings given in response to questions posed by Atiśa and Drom's spiritual sons, Ngok

Lekpai Sherap and Khutön Tsöndrü Yungdrung. On one level, the so-called *Book of Kadam* can be viewed as an extended commentary on a standard Indian Buddhist work, albeit one composed in Tibet. Here I am referring to Atiśa's *Bodhisattva's Jewel Garland*, twenty-six stanzas that ostensibly outline the outlook and practices of a bodhisattva, a buddha-to-be who dedicates his or her entire being to the altruistic ideal of bringing about others' welfare. In fact, the core of the book, both the Father Teachings and the Son Teachings, is framed as instructions, comments, and reflections on specific lines of *Bodhisattva's Jewel Garland*.

For instance, *The Jewel Garland of Dialogues*, the core text of the Father Teachings, consists of twenty-three chapters, each citing a specific section of Atiśa's root text as a conclusion and sometimes as an opening statement as well. The Son Teachings, a collection of stories of Dromtönpa's former lives, is reminiscent of the well-known *Jātaka Tales*, the Buddha's birth stories.[27] Each chapter opens with a citation of a passage from the root text and a request—from Ngok Lekpai Sherap, in the case of the first twenty chapters, and from Khutön, in the case of the last two chapters—on how to relate the cited passage to Dromtönpa's past lives. However, to view the core texts of the book as a standard text commentary would miss the point about these teachings. At best, Atiśa's root text is like a springboard, a literary device to trigger a whole host of issues pertaining to Buddhist thought and practice in Tibet. Of special focus for the Father Teachings is the critical question of how to balance and integrate the foundational Mahayana teachings with the esoteric Vajrayana practices. The Son Teachings, on the other hand, deal primarily with Dromtönpa's identification with Avalokiteśvara and the latter's special affinity with the Land of Snows.

The literary style of the first thirteen chapters of the Father Teachings maintains a consistent eight-syllable or seven-syllable verse with an occasional sojourn into explanatory prose, which often indicates important stages in the dialogue between Atiśa and Dromtönpa. Though retaining a strong oral flavor, these chapters contain some of the most evocative literary verses found in Tibetan literature. They are vibrant, immediate, poignant, and convey a profound spirituality. Often, they are tinged with a wonderful humor and irony. The verses are most evocative when addressing the ever-present theme of the illusion-like nature of reality. The use of puns, iteration, paradoxes, and other literary devices suggests that the verses are authentic creations of a native speaker (or speakers). Chapter 14 begins with an explicit change of voice: "Now the time has come to speak in plain vernacular Tibetan." The chapter then proceeds with rapid verbal exchanges back and forth between Atiśa and Dromtönpa, where most of the exchanges are one-line sentences, a style maintained in both chapters 14 and 15. Chapter 16 is a mixture of verse, one-line exchanges, and repetitive passages in prose giving an idealized image of the landscape around Yerpa, the site where the dialogues supposedly took place. The remaining chapters return somewhat to the original style of eight- or seven-syllable verses. Each chapter ends with Dromtönpa summarizing the exchanges in a series of questions and answers, citing relevant lines from *Bodhisattva's Jewel Garland.*

The literary format for the Son Teachings is very different. Although invoking the Buddha's famous *Jātaka Tales*, each birth story begins with a stanza from *Bodhisattva's Jewel Garland* followed by a request by Ngok (or, in two cases, Khutön) to recount the story of a former life of Dromtönpa in relation to the cited stanza. Although written mostly in prose, the chapters often contain memorable verses as well.

A Summary of the Father and Son Teachings

THE FATHER TEACHINGS

The heart of the meditative practice presented in the Father Teachings is known as the practice of the *five recollections,* an instruction encapsulated in the following verse attributed to Tārā:

> Recall your teachers, the source of refuge;
> See your body in the nature of meditation deities;
> With speech, make your mantra recitations constant;
> Contemplate all beings as your parents;
> Experience the nature of your mind as empty.
> On the basis of these five factors,
> Make pure all roots of virtue.[28]

These five recollections are presented in the book as unfolding as follows: by reflecting upon the enlightened examples of your teachers, profound feelings of admiration and devotion arise from your very depths such that even the hairs on your body stand on end. On this basis, next you, together with all sentient beings, go for refuge to the Three Jewels and ensure that you will never be separated from the practice of the deity yoga whereby you arise as the mandalas of the four divinities—the Buddha, Avalokiteśvara, Acala, and Tārā. Then, on the basis of contemplating all beings as your kind parents, you generate the awakening mind for the benefit of these beings and abide in the meditative equipoise *(samādhi)* of the ultimate awakening mind, wherein emptiness and compassion are fused in nondual unity. In the periods subsequent to the actual meditation sessions, you then culti-vate the perspective of seeing all phenomena, including your own self, as illusion-like, as seemingly real yet devoid of any substantiality.

The book begins in chapter 1 with a string of salutations to the masters of the three principal lineages—the profound view of emptiness stemming from Mañjuśrī and Nāgārjuna, the vast practices stemming from Maitreya and Asaṅga, and the inspirational blessings stemming from Vajradhara and Saraha—up to the key teachers of Atiśa. In chapter 2, Atiśa then specifies his preferred divinities in the context of the second recollection—recalling one's body as divinities—and makes the well-known selection of Buddha, Acala, Avalokiteśvara, and Tārā as the four gods of Kadam. At one point in the text, in the course of conversations between Atiśa and Dromtönpa on the four divinities, Dromtönpa's heart opens up and miraculously reveals progressively the entire realm of the Buddha Śākyamuni, the realm of Ava-lokiteśvara, the realm of Tārā, and finally the realm of Acala. It is here that we also find explicit mention of Avalokiteśvara's famous six-syllable man-tra, *oṃ maṇi padme hūṃ.*

This deity yoga, in its developed form, came to be referred to as the prac-tice of the sixteen drops, which is explained in some detail in Khenchen Nyima Gyaltsen's *Elucidation of the Heart-Drop Practice* (entry IV in part 1 of this volume). The sixteen drops are:

1. The drop of the outer inconceivable array
2. The drop of this Endurance World
3. The drop of the realm of Tibet
4. The drop of one's abode and the drawn mandala
5. The drop of Perfection of Wisdom Mother
6. The drop of her son, Buddha Śākyamuni
7. The drop of Great Compassion
8. The drop of Wisdom Tārā
9. The drop of her wrathful form
10. The drop of Acala, their immutable nature

11. The drop of Atiśa
12. The drop of Dromtön Gyalwai Jungné
13. The drop of the vast practice
14. The drop of the profound view
15. The drop of the inspirational practice
16. The drop of great awakening

The idea of the sixteen-drops practice is fairly straightforward.[29] Like a powerful camera lens zooming from the widest possible angle to a progressively smaller focus and, finally, to a tiny point, the meditation becomes increasingly focused, moving from the entire cosmos to this world in particular, to the realm of Tibet, to the practitioner's own dwelling, and finally culminating within your own body. Within your body, you then visualize inside your heart the Perfection of Wisdom Mother, within whose heart is her son, Buddha Śākyamuni. Within the Buddha's heart is Great Compassion Avalokiteśvara, within whose heart is Tārā, and so on, continuing with wrathful Tārā, Acala, Atiśa, and Dromtönpa. Within Dromtönpa's heart you then visualize Maitreya surrounded by the masters of the lineage of vast practice. In his heart you visualize Nāgārjuna surrounded by the masters of the lineage of profound view; and within his heart you visualize Vajradhara surrounded by the masters of the lineage of inspirational practice.

Finally, inside Vajradhara's heart, you visualize yourself as a buddha, embodying all three buddha bodies, and within your heart is a white drop the size of a mustard seed. This seed increases in size and turns into a vast radiant jewel container at the center of which your mind is imagined as a yellow drop the size of a pea. This, in turn, increases in size and turns into an ocean of drops the color of refined gold; the ocean is transparent, smooth, resolute, vast, and pervasive, and it reflects all forms. You then rest your mind, without wavering, upon this drop of great awakening, fused, and free of any sense of subject-object duality.

In chapter 3, we find the teachings of the three scriptural baskets—the other half of the sevenfold divinity and teaching. Emphasizing the three baskets as the key to understanding the Buddha's teachings, Atiśa shows how the three baskets encompass all the teachings of the Buddha, including secret mantra. He is also reported as stating that the teaching of the three baskets is highly profitable and has minimal risks. After this advice, the text puts this endorsement in the mouth of the four divinities:

Most excellent one, you who care for the common purpose,
Discipline teachings produce the highest divinity of the
  ethically disciplined;
Sutra teachings produce the highest divinity of the noble ones;
Knowledge teachings produce the highest divinity of the
  conquerors.
This is so from the perspective of their principal [functions].
In reality, all three teachings produce supreme conquerors.

These baskets of knowledge teachings lack nothing.
Through excellent instructions revealing the path of the three
  trainings
Emerge innumerable trainees with pure mental streams.
Your choice of profound sacred words is unmistaken, O master.
They are secure throughout all three times—beginning, middle,
  and end.
May all be blessed to possess these three teachings.[30]

The book then goes on, in chapter 4, to explain how joyful perseverance is crucial for success in practicing the three baskets. Chapter 5 presents a series of disciplines whereby the practitioner learns to guard his or her senses against distraction and unwholesome objects, thereby maintaining meditative focus on the themes of the three baskets within the framework of the three levels of practitioners. In his summation of the chapter, Drom calls the approach the "method of contemplating the divinity and the teaching."[31]

Chapters 6 to 11 present various elements of the practice, such as: recognizing that self-cherishing is to blame for all our problems and cultivating the altruistic outlook that perceives others as a source of kindness (chapter 6), the ethical practice of refraining from the ten unwholesome actions (chapter 7), the futility of pursuing material wealth and the need to cultivate the riches of the noble ones (chapter 8), the importance of finding a place of solitude (chapter 9), the importance of cultivating and maintaining deep respect for one's teachers and preceptors (chapter 10), and the way to uphold the sublime beings and their enlightened conduct (chapter 11). This chapter also details how to avoid negative friends, how to rely on one's spiritual mentors, and how to recognize and avoid objects that give rise to aversion and unhappy states of mind.

In some ways, chapter 12 is the heart of the Father Teachings volume, or a text within a text. Unlike other chapters, it begins with salutation verses where homage is paid to the teachers, the Buddha, the Perfection of Wisdom Mother, and all the protectors. It is by far the longest chapter, with two subsections: part 1, with seven *collections (tshoms),* and part 2, with nine collections. Entitled "How to Hoist Your Robes to Cross the Mires of Desire," the chapter opens with an idealized description of a celestial realm that is inside a thousand-petalled lotus and adorned with heavenly lakes. At the hub of this lotus is a five-leveled crystal stupa. This celestial mansion in the shape of a reliquary stupa is occupied by sublime beings endowed with the highest enlightened qualities. Directed to them in the subsequent sections (collections 2 to 4), the text presents the practice of the seven limbs—prostrating, making offerings, confessing, rejoicing, supplicating to turn the wheel of Dharma, appealing not to enter into nirvana, and dedicating. In the fifth collection, the chapter presents a beautiful exposition of the teaching on the twelve links of dependent origination with a lengthy analysis of the nature, characteristics, and functions of the three mental poisons. This is followed, in collection 6, by a presentation on the flaws of attachment and the meditation on impermanence as its principal antidote. Collection 7 outlines the five psychophysical aggregates as well as the sequence of the arising of the twelve links.

In part 2 of chapter 12, composed of nine collections, the central theme is contemplation of emptiness and the illusion-like nature of all things. Beginning with general advice, the text proceeds with numerous reflections on the illusory nature of things with a specific contemplation on the apparent reality and its union with emptiness. There is a memorable section on the process of death and dying (collection 7), followed by a presentation of transference of consciousness at the time of death. This latter collection contains some fascinating comments on the nature of awareness and consciousness at the point of death.

After the marathon-like chapter 12, the book slows down and even loses some poignancy in its use of language. The material in subsequent chapters may well be a later addition, or simply ancillary pieces deemed important to include. Chapter 13 deals with Dromtönpa seeking a heritage, a legacy of a pure way of life, while chapter 14 addresses how you overcome any self-importance that may result from embracing a pure way of life. This is followed in chapter 15 with tools for dealing with adverse situations, such as being criticized. It is in this chapter that we find the famous story of a householder who is magically transported to a totally unknown place where he settles down and starts a family. Following a tragedy that results in the death of his entire new family, the grieving householder suddenly finds himself back at his original home. Much to his dismay, his first wife has not even missed him, for in fact he never left his original home, and his whole experience with a parallel family was nothing more than a magician's deception![32]

In chapter 16 we find an interesting discussion of what constitutes appropriate and inappropriate conduct for a Dharma practitioner, with the following summary admonition to Drom from Atiśa:

> Dwell utterly in solitude, beyond town limits.
> Like the carcass of a wild animal,
> Hide yourself away [in the forest].[33]

It is in this chapter that Atiśa prophesizes the founding of Radreng Monastery. Chapter 17 underscores the importance of being steadfast in the sevenfold divinity and teaching and the need to counter laziness and discouragement by reaffirming your motivation. Chapter 18 discusses how you engage with others, especially through your speech, to help nurture their minds. In these discussions, the text cites various Buddhist masters, including Atiśa's own teachers Serlingpa, Avadhūtipa, Dharmarakṣita, Śāntipa, and Jetāri. Chapter 19 takes the theme of the preceding chapter further and emphasizes the need to constantly pursue others' welfare. Chapter 20 deals with nonsectarianism, and Atiśa emphasizes the importance of being committed to one's own path without denigrating the spiritual orientations and paths of others. This is then followed, in chapter 21, with the dedication of positive karma and purification of negative karma. Chapter 22 is a wonderful exposition of the so-called seven riches of the noble ones—faith, morality, giving, learning, conscience, a sense of shame, and insight. In the final chapter, chapter 23, the entire teachings of volume 1 of the book are condensed into two simple practices referred to as the *two examinations*. They are: examining or guarding your speech when among many, and examining and guarding your mind when alone, as encapsulated in the following two lines in Atiśa's *Bodhisattva's Jewel Garland:*

> Among others guard your speech;
> When alone guard your mind.[34]

THE SON TEACHINGS

As noted above, the second volume of *The Book of Kadam* contains the Son Teachings, which is foremost a collection of birth stories of Dromtönpa's former lives as narrated, according to the book, by Master Atiśa. Each of these birth stories is related in some way to the accounts of Dromtönpa having engaged in a former life in practices described in the root text. Some of these stories make an explicit link between the principal figure of the main story with Dromtönpa and the country of Tibet. For example, we find Prince Asaṅga, a previous life of Dromtömpa, speaking the following prophetic lines in chapter 2 of the Son Teachings:

> O my two parents,
> In the future, in the last five-hundred-year cycle,
> On the crest of snow mountains,
> My father, Prabhāśrī, so-named
> By the ḍākinīs of Udhyāna,
> Will be Drom's father, Yaksher Kushen.
> My mother, the devout Satī,
> Will be known as Khuö Salenchikma.
> I will be born on that crest of snow mountains.[35]

Similarly, in the same chapter, we find the following prophesy being made by a noble one:

> I will be known as Dīpaṃkara,
> Dispelling the darkness of that land.
> You will be a treasury of Buddha's teaching
> Known as Gyalwai Jungné.
> I will be the "great Atiśa,"
> Venerated by the name "the sole god."
> You will be Upāsaka Dharmavardana.[36]
> Venerated as the spiritual mentor Tönpa.[37]

From the perspective of the larger Tibetan tradition, especially the myth of Avalokiteśvara's unique affinity with the Land of Snows, chapters 5 and 19 of the birth stories are the most important. In the former, the longest chapter in the volume by far, we find the following oft-quoted lines:

To the north of Bodhgaya, which lies in the east,
Is a place called Tibet, the kingdom of Pu,
Where there are sky[-touching] pillars of towering mountains,
Lakes of turquoise mirrors in the lowlands,
Crystal stupas of white snow,
Golden mounded hills of yellow grass,
Incense offerings of medicinal plants,
Golden flowers with vibrant colors,
And, in summer, blossoms of turquoise blue.

O Avalokiteśvara, lord of the snow mountains,
There lies your special domain;
There you shall find your devotees.[38]

Also, we read:

In general, he is lord of all beings;
In particular, he will reign in the land of snow mountains.[39]

Chapter 19 of the Son Teachings, the second longest chapter of the volume, is the most elaborate in developing this theme of Tibet as uniquely associated with Avalokiteśvara and of Dromtönpa's place within this scheme. For example, the text tells the story of how, when Dromtönpa was born as Devarāja, a youth prophesized that when the era of degeneration dawns and the Buddha's teaching declines, Devarāja will, at the urging of the bodhisattva Sarvanivaraṇviṣkaṃvin, take the form of a king and establish the foundation for Buddhadharma in the barbarian land of Tibet.[40] He will take birth as a king renowned as an emanation of Great Compassion Avalokiteśvara (namely, Songtsen Gampo) and will invite Tārā (the Chinese princess Wen-ch'eng) and Bhṛkuṭī (the Nepalese princess) to the central region of Tibet. He will thus transform this barbarian borderland into a central land where the Dharma will flourish. The text then goes on to state that a large gathering of monks, all blessed by Dīpaṃkaraśrījñāna, will converge, and at that time people will recite the name of Avalokiteśvara and make supplications to him. They will see the emanation body *(nirmāṇakāya)* of Avalokiteśvara, listen to teachings from him, and be introduced to the tantric practices related to the six-syllable mantra. In brief, great compassion will flourish so widely that the central region of Tibet will resemble the pure land of Potala.[41]

An important element of the story is the presence of Atiśa's former lives in Buddhism's earlier history in Tibet. At one point in the narrative, Atiśa explicitly identifies himself with Padmasambhava, who, the text states, is well known among the mantrikas.[42] Interestingly, the chapter provides a brief chronicle of many of Tibet's rulers. Three of them—Songtsen Gampo, Trisong Detsen, and Tri Ralpachen—are referred to with the now well-known epithet, the "three founding righteous kings," and many of the rulers are said to be emanations of lords of the three Buddha families—Avalokiteśvara, Mañjuśrī, and Vajrapāṇi. It seems that there also evolved among the Kadampas a tradition that identifies Dromtönpa's three principal brother disciples with the lords of the three Buddha families and, more intriguingly, with three famous self-arisen images of Avalokiteśvara.[43]

One of the most interesting aspects of the nineteenth chapter is its close connection with another important Tibetan work of some antiquity that appeared to be a key text in the propagation of the tradition of identifying Tibetan imperial figures with Avalokiteśvara. This is the famous *Kakholma Testament* (literally, *Testament Extracted from a Pillar*), purportedly authored by the seventh-century Tibetan emperor Songtsen Gampo and later rediscovered as a revealed treasure text. According to a tradition dating back to the twelfth century, Atiśa is credited with having retrieved this text in Lhasa toward the end of the 1040s.[44] In fact, in the present redaction of the testament, the text opens with an interesting discussion of Atiśa's visit to the Lhasa cathedral and some miraculous visions he experienced relating to the image of the self-originated Avalokiteśvara icon there. In the text's colophon, Atiśa is quoted as saying that he saw the manuscript of the testament written on a blue silk cloth with gold letters and that there were three versions of the text. He also explicitly states that the text was discovered as a treasure in the cathedral of Lhasa.[45]

The Structure of the Book of Kadam

The two volumes of *The Book of Kadam* contain more than just the Father and Son Teachings. Fifty-four texts altogether were compiled by Khenchen Nyima Gyaltsen (1225–1305), the ninth abbot of Narthang, to create the final version of the book.

Four texts in *The Book of Kadam* are preliminary: Dromtönpa's *The Book's Sealed Command*, his *Self-Exhortation* (entry I of the present volume), and Khenchen's *The Liberating Life Stories of the Lineage Teachers of the Sevenfold Divinity and Teaching* and *Elucidation of the Heart-Drop Practice* (entry IV). These are then followed by Atiśa's *Bodhisattva's Jewel Garland* (entry II), the root text for both the Father Teachings and Son Teachings. As such, it is not listed as a separate text. The core of the Father Teachings, *The Jewel Garland of Dialogues*, appears in twenty-three chapters (entry III) and is supplemented with three additional chapters found in the second volume at the end of Dromtönpa's birth stories. Thus, the Father Teachings are actually comprised of twenty-six chapters. Volume 2 has twenty-two chapters of birth stories (excerpted in entries V–VIII), all of which are part of the main book, and a supplementary chapter that is also considered part of the main book. Therefore, forty-nine texts in total form the main book.[46]

In addition to the main book, redactions of *The Book of Kadam* contain five ancillary texts. The short text *Perfect Array of the Forms of Master Atiśa and His Son,* authored by Khenchen, was written entirely in verse and appears to be a poetic summary of the entire book. Volume 1 also contains four important biographical works: *How Atiśa Relinquished His Kingdom and Sought Liberation,* attributed to Dromtönpa; *The Story of Atiśa's Voyage to Sumatra,* attributed to Atiśa himself;[47] Chim Namkha Drak's *Biography of Master Atiśa;* and *Biography and Itinerary of Master Atiśa,* also attributed to Dromtönpa.[48]

The present volume contains the main twenty-three chapters of the Father Teachings, four chapters from the Son Teachings, and some of the ancillary teachings. I have also included here three additional texts, two more recent compositions in verse summarizing the key points of *The Book of Kadam* to help the reader better understand how the book was viewed and practiced historically, and one of the earliest anthologies of the sayings of the Kadam masters. This last text, compiled by Chegom Sherap Dorjé in the twelfth century, provides the reader with a unique perspective on how richly developed the oral tradition became for the followers of Master Atiśa and Dromtönpa.

The Origins of the "Precious Book"

We now come to the difficult question of the dating of *The Book of Kadam.* There is no doubt the final version of the book was compiled by Khenchen Nyima Gyaltsen. In fact, we have a clear statement by Khenchen that it was on the thirtieth day of the month of Gyal in the Water Tiger year

(1302) that he completed his work.[49] This could mean that the woodblock printing was completed, or it could mean that the final scribing of the manuscript for the blockprint was done on that day. In any case, it was either at the turn of the fourteenth century or toward the final years of the thirteenth century that the present version of the two-volume book was compiled.

But how far back can we trace the origins of the book? In addressing this question, we must first distinguish between two notions of the book—the final version of the book that we have today and an archaic version.[50] It is the archaic version—its date of origin and the personalities involved in its creation—that remains unclear. To understand these we need to look also at the early transmission of the teachings of the book, at least as it is understood by the tradition. Chapter 23 of the Father Teachings concludes with a short colophon that gives an account of the earliest origin of the teachings of the so-called precious book. According to this account, it was Ngok Lekpai Sherap who, at the urging of Mañjuśrī, went to Mount Lhari Nyingpo in Yerpa, where Master Atiśa and Dromtönpa were residing, and requested them to enter into a series of dialogues based upon *Bodhisattva's Jewel Garland.* This discussion takes place over three years, and it is said that Ngok then set these dialogues down in the form of a book.[51] Ngok passed the transmission of the book to Ngari Sherap Gyaltsen (c. eleventh century), who in turn transmitted it to Phuchungwa. From Phuchungwa the transmission passed through Kama Rinchen Gyaltsen, to Shangtön Dharma Gyaltsen, and to Tapka Jangchup Sangpo. Thus, from Drom to Jangchup Sangpo, the book was transmitted through a direct one-to-one lineage of teachers—teachers who Tapka Namkha Rinchen (ca. 1214–86) called the "seven precious beings."[52]

Until Namkha Rinchen, it is maintained, the transmission of the teaching of the book was passed down in one-to-one instruction. However, Namkha Rinchen, following his move to Tapka Monastery after the death of Jangchup Sangpo, spent the rest of his life preaching the "profound meanings of the precious book" to worthy disciples. Namkha Rinchen's public preaching also signals a shift from a so-called "miracle book," which he is said to have hidden in the great reliquary stupa at Tapka Monastery, to a physical scripture.[53]

After Namkha Rinchen comes Drom Kumāramati, who was born in the Iron-Sheep year, most probably 1211 (if not 1271). He met with Namkha Rinchen at a young age, and by fifteen he had already committed the entire

Book of Kadam to memory. Namkha Rinchen was so impressed by this feat that he is said to have remarked, "Now you have exceeded me. Even I do not have the book in my memory in its entirety. Among the previous masters, too, it seems that there were very few who had committed the entire book to memory. Since you have the residue of past good karma, you have the entire book in your memory."[54] Namkha Rinchen then handed over the custody of some religious items of great significance with the transmission of the book. These include, among other objects, a painting of Mañjuśrī drawn by Ngok based on the vision he experienced when he was urged to go to Yerpa to receive the teachings of the book, a small painting of Atiśa and Dromtönpa with Ngok and Khutön done by Ngari Sherap Gyaltsen, and several religious articles that Phuchungwa possessed, such as a lock of Dromtönpa's hair, some relics, and a small hand drum that belonged to Atiśa.[55] It was from Drom Kumāramati that Khenchen Nyima Gyaltsen, the editor of the final version of the book, received the transmission, including the initiation into the mandala of the sixteen drops. One could say that what Khenchen did was to set down in writing what his own teacher, Drom Kumāramati, had stored in his memory from a young age. In fact, the later tradition sees Drom Kumāramati as a reincarnation of Dromtönpa himself and as responsible for the "reappearance" of the precious book as a physical text that subsequent practitioners can benefit from.

So how far back can we trace the archaic version? A number of facts strongly suggest the existence of such a book long before Khenchen's time. In this early, "primitive" form, it seems to be referred to as "the book" *(glegs bam)*, "the precious book" *(glegs bam rin po che)*, or sometimes as *The Jewel Garland of Dialogues.* Let us look at some of the evidence for its earlier provenance.

The first piece of evidence is *The Book's Sealed Command,* the opening text in *The Book of Kadam* attributed to Dromtönpa. Although some would argue that no such book existed at Dromtönpa's time, I see no reason to reject the attribution of this short verse text to Drom. In it, we find an explicit reference to the teaching of the higher qualities of Dromtönpa, most certainly an allusion to his birth stories. Furthermore, we also find mention of *The Jewel Garland of Dialogues* with the statement that it stems from the conqueror (the Buddha), flows to the conqueror himself (Atiśa), and is endowed with the practice of the four immeasurable thoughts. There is also an explicit emphasis on the point that Atiśa's teachings embody all three lineages of vast practice, profound view, and inspirational practice.[56]

At the end of this short work, Khenchen adds: "This [work] resides at the beginning of volume 1 in the format of a smaller text. Stating that one should read this *Sealed Command* prior to giving this teaching, [the teachers] read this text once. In particular, the first six stanzas of this work can occasionally be found inscribed at the end of many of the longer chapters."[57] Since the birth stories of Dromtönpa's former lives are at the heart of the teachings of the book, it makes sense on the part of Drom to insist on a restricted transmission of these teachings, indicating a certain reluctance for this teaching to become widespread—hence, the book's sealed command.

Second, *Liberating Life Stories of the Lineage Teachers of the Sevenfold Divinity and Teaching*, a history of the book's origins as compiled and edited by Khenchen, contains several exchanges between Dromtönpa and Ngok about putting the contents of the book into written form. Drom discourages Ngok by admonishing him to focus on his meditative practice rather than worrying about writing the book down. However, Ngok pledges to write it down to ensure that future generations will have access to it.[58] Since the book "scribed" by Ngok cannot be conventionally seen in public, it acquires the epithet "miracle book." Furthermore, Ngok is reported as saying to his disciple Ngari Sherap Gyaltsen, "Sherap Gyaltsen, you have come. As for this teaching of ours, I have undone the sealed command of my teacher and have committed it to letter."[59] There are many statements like this that relate to a "secret" teaching inherited by Ngok and passed on to Ngari Sherap Gyaltsen. The richness of these sayings are such that they strongly indicate the existence of an oral tradition, going back at least to Ngok and Ngari Sherap Gyaltsen, related to a secret teaching of Atiśa and Dromtönpa.

Third, the sources that Khenchen relied upon in his compilation of *Liberating Life Stories* act as further evidence for the prior existence of an earlier archaic version of the book. On several occasions, Khenchen explicitly names the sources for the various sections of his *Liberating Life Stories* and clearly indicates that he is, at best, the compiler of this historical work rather than its author in the strict sense. For instance, Khenchen attributes a fairly lengthy account of how Phuchungwa received the transmission and passed it on to Rinchen Gyaltsen himself. In addition, the entire text of Khenchen's history is based on a twenty-five-stanza salutation to the masters of the lineage of the book authored by the earlier thirteenth-century figure, Namkha Rinchen.[60] This verse explicitly mentions the twenty-two birth stories of Dromtönpa as well as the statement that all the teachings can be subsumed under the practice of "hoisting your robes to cross the mire of desire," which, in turn, can be subsumed into the seven riches of the noble ones, and which, finally, can be subsumed into the practice of the heart drop.[61] This, in essence, is the heart of the teaching of the Father Teachings volume. For these reasons, I am inclined to conclude that the book, at least the core of the Father Teachings and the Son Teachings, existed long before Khenchen's time.

Perhaps the most important piece of evidence to consider is the existence of a text, attributed to Phuchungwa, that indicates an archaic version of the book's Father Teachings existed as early as the eleventh century. This text is cited in full by Yongzin Yeshé Gyaltsen in his *Rite of the Mandala of the Sixteen Drops of Kadam.*[62] The work begins with Dromtönpa requesting Master Atiśa to reveal a teaching that would integrate all the sacred words of the Buddha into personal instructions; a teaching that is free of the dangerous abyss, uncluttered, free of error, uncontaminated, and supported by authoritative sources; a teaching that is to the point, is easy to implement in practice, possesses a firm foundation, shows the stages of the path as well-ordered, and, finally, presents a path that cannot lead to falsehood.[63] The text then goes on to describe how Atiśa responds to this request by presenting the method of integrating all the teachings of the Buddha within the framework of the three scriptural baskets. Even the profound teachings of tantra, such as the *dohā* cycles of Saraha, are shown to be encompassed by the teachings of the three baskets. Needless to say, the three baskets also include the meditation on emptiness as the ulimate nature of all things. This is followed by a lengthy discussion of the choice of four principal divinities for Kadam practitioners, with a special emphasis on how all the meditative practices of the profound tantric teachings are subsumed under the generation and completion stages of Avalokiteśvara practice. In this manner the master Atiśa presents the profound practice of the sevenfold divinity and teaching to Dromtönpa in the course of a series of dialogues at the retreat of Yerpa. Interestingly, in Phuchungwa's "abridged" version, Atiśa constantly refers to Dromtönpa with the expression "dear son" *(nye ba'i sras)* as opposed to "principal son" *(sras kyi thu bo)*, as found in the final version. Phunchungwa's text ends with the following colophon: "This completes the secret teaching of Dharma king Drom, the sacred words and instruction on the sevenfold divinity and teaching, which was given as a teaching."[64] After this short colophon we find a brief account of the story of the teaching:

The story of its origin is this. The Dharma king renowned as Lord Atiśa came from India to this mandala of Great Compassion [i.e., Tibet], though he had countless disciples…Among the countless joyful feasts of teachings he gave, this instruction on the sevenfold divinity and teaching was set down in writing by the emanation body Ngok Lekpai Sherap, a bodhisattva blessed by Mañjuśrī. Following this, I, the Buddhist monk Phuchungwa Shönu Gyaltsen, one who has been blessed by the conqueror and his son [i.e., Atiśa and Drom] and whose heart has been permeated by their enlightened activities, penned this on the basis of making supplications to my teacher. The spiritual mentor's sealed command is on this, but fearing that this teaching might disappear, I could not bear living alone in the wilderness without putting it in writing.

Whatever shortcomings may be in this,
I request the forbearance of the assembly of noble ones;
Whatever virtues are in this
I dedicate toward great awakening for the welfare of beings.

Thus, throughout all my lives,
May I obtain human existence and be ethically pure;
Remaining at the feet of my teachers,
May I spend my time in learning, reflection, and meditation,
And may all my teachers' aspirations be fulfilled.[65]

Based on the sources available, I am inclined to believe that the present version of the book, especially with its division into Father and Son Teachings (here I am speaking of the core texts—the twenty-three main chapters and three supplementary chapters of the Father Teachings and the twenty-two birth stories of Dromtönpa), is principally the product of three individuals—Namkha Rinchen, Drom Kumāramati, and Khenchen Nyima Gyaltsen, all of whom belong to the thirteenth century. Drops in the form of light circles in the visualization of specific meditation deities is found much earlier in the lineage, but the systematic practice of Kadam's four meditation deities in the form of sixteen drops based on the construction of a mandala appears likely to have been developed by the above three masters. This said, the idea that there are forty-eight sections or "chapters" to the book may preceed even Namkha Rinchen. For example, the encounter between Phuchungwa and Sherap Gyaltsen includes a mention of forty-eight days during which Phuchungwa came to understand each chapter in relation to a drop and how he realized the nature of each to be that of a sphere. It is also stated that Phuchungwa was spiritually nurtured by Sherap Gyaltsen for a period of 290 days, during which he transmitted the entire sixteen drops and abided in the sixteen drops of meditation deities and in the sixteenth awakening drop.[66]

Initially this set of teachings appeared to have been known simply as the *oral instruction on the sevenfold divinity and teaching,*[67] an expression that may even be traceable to Dromtönpa himself. As we noted earlier, Phuchungwa's text not only presents the core teachings of the book but also retains the overall structure of the book—beginning with salutations to the teachers of the three lineages through to the meditation on the four divinities, the presentation of how three scriptural baskets are the framework for the entire Buddhist teachings, how their practice is encapsulated in the three higher trainings, and how the distilled essence of these three is the practices of the persons of the three capacities. Furthermore, the schema of the five recollections as the main medium of meditative practice is presented, as well the intriguing notion of hoisting of one's robes to cross the mire of desire. Interestingly, Phuchungwa's text nowhere mentions the expression "the book" *(glegs bam)* but ends with the concluding statement "This concludes the sevenfold divinity and teaching, the secret teaching of the Dharma king Drom, which has been given as a practice."[68] At some point, Drom's birth stories appeared to have become an additional part of the core teachings of this sevenfold divinity and teaching.

That Atiśa is the author of *Bodhisattva's Jewel Garland,* which became the root text of both the Father and Son Teachings, remains beyond doubt, given its similarites in content, language, and structure to Atiśa's other recorded works. But there is no obvious connection, apart from the relationship of a root text to its commentary, between the instructions on the sevenfold divinity and teaching, centered especially on the meditative practice of Avalokiteśvara, and Atiśa's short text, which on the surface pertains to standard bodhisattva practices. Who then is responsible for relating the two strands of teachings in this unique manner? Apart from the individual texts featured in the book, we have no sources available to help us resolve this question. Perhaps there is something to the fifteenth-century Kagyü historian Tsuklak Trengwa's remark that *Bodhisattva's Jewel Garland* was compiled by Dromtönpa on the basis of Atiśa's oral instructions.[69] If this is true, it is conceivable that an oral tradition connected with Dromtönpa and based on the instructions pertaining to this short work may have evolved fairly early. Given the specific nature of the oral tradition pertaining to the early, "legendary" transmission of the teachings of the book, I am also inclined to accept that the two figures—Ngok Lekpai Sherap and Sherap Gyaltsen, both of whom met Atiśa and Drom—were responsible for the initial development of, or at least the idea of, a special corpus of Kadam teachings centered on Drom as the spiritual heir of Master Atiśa and, more importantly, as an incarnation of Avalokiteśvara. Based on the textual evidence, I would argue that Phuchungwa was perhaps the first to write down this special corpus of teachings. In any case, by Phuchungwa's time, especially after the death of Dromtönpa, the idea that Dromtönpa was an emanation of Avalokiteśvara appears to have already taken firm root in Tibet, at least in the region where Atiśa and Drom's followers were most active.

The Dalai Lamas and the Later Transmissions of the Book

Following the formal compilation of the texts of *The Book of Kadam* by Khenchen around 1302, the transmission of the teachings of this special collection becomes easier to discern. In his records of teachings received, the eighteenth-century Geluk author Longdöl Ngawang Lobsang provides the following transmission lineage: from Khenchen Nyima Gyaltsen to Rinchen Jangchup, then through Jangchup Pal, Rikkyi Dakpoi Pal, Sönam Öser, Sangyé Sangpo, Sönam Sangpo, Paljor Sangpo, Sengé Gyaltsen, who passed it on to the translator Thukjé Palwa, who transmitted the teachings to Gendün Drup (1391–1474), later recognized as the First Dalai Lama. The First Dalai Lama gave the transmission to Panchen Yeshé Tsemo, who passed it on to Gendün Gyatso (1476–1542), later recognized as the Second Dalai Lama.[70] (The present volume features a short verse text by Gendün Gyatso [entry IX] that beautifully summarizes *The Book of Kadam*.) According to later historical sources, it is through the efforts of the First and Second Dalai Lamas that the transmission of the book became widespread in central and southern Tibet.[71] The Fifth Dalai Lama's (1617–82) *River Ganges' Flow: A Record of Teachings Received* provides a similar lineage of transmission from Khenchen up to Sönam Sangpo, at which point the Great Fifth gives two streams of transmission, neither of which contains the First and the Second Dalai Lamas, suggesting several divergent lineages of the book from the fifteenth century onward.[72]

The noted Geluk author Panchen Sönam Drakpa (1478–1554), who was a student of the Second Dalai Lama and a tutor of the Third, states that from Gendün Drup, Mönlam Palwa received the transmission and taught this both at Ganden and Drepung, two of the largest Geluk monasteries in central Tibet.[73] Gendün Gyatso, after receiving the transmission from Panchen Yeshé Tsemo, caused a great rain of the precious book to fall upon many people in the Ü and Tsang provinces in central Tibet, as well as in Nyal, Dakpo, Kongpo, and many other regions far from central Tibet. Furthermore, according to the same source, the bodhisattva Lodrö Gyaltsen (1402–72) received the transmission in Tsang and spread it to western Tibet. The elders Jangyalwa and Sötrepa received this transmission, the latter bringing the teaching to Yarlung.[74] That a transmission lineage of the book is listed by Pema Karpo (1527–96), a principal master of the Drukpa Kagyü lineage, as well as by Taklung Ngawang Namgyal (1571–1626), one of the luminaries of the Taklung Kagyü lineage, indicates that transmission of the book took place within non-Kadam and non-Geluk traditions as well.

Despite its widespread acceptance from its first appearance as a physical text, it seems that even as late as the fifteenth and sixteenth centuries, qualms were being raised about its authenticity. We find, for example, a memorable remark attributed to the Second Dalai Lama, who, in response to the question about *The Book of Kadam*'s authenticity, is said to have replied, "As to how authentic [the ascription of the book to Atiśa is], I do not know. I certainly find it most beneficial to my mind."[75] Similarly, we read the following comment by Tsuklak Trengwa: "These days some who consider it adequate to know only how to discard the Dharma denigrate the book. This is Māra's doing."[76] For Tsuklak Trengwa, *The Book of Kadam* is unique for its presentation of the sixteen drops, the sevenfold divinity and teaching, and the five recollections—in brief, for its presentation of the essence of all the teachings of the Buddha by condensing them into a single practice for guarding one's mind.[77]

Although the first Dalai Lamas and their immediate disciples appear to have been the primary force behind the early dissemination of the book in the Geluk school, later, with Panchen Lobsang Chögyen (1570–1662), some masters of the so-called ear-whispered teachings (*snyan brgyud*) also took deep interest in the book's transmission, especially the initiations into the sixteen drops. Among these masters was Yongzin Yeshé Gyaltsen (1713–93), who composed substantial works pertaining to the book and the meditative practice of the sixteen drops. One of these works, a lucid text in verse presenting the essential teachings of *The Book of Kadam* within the framework of Atiśa's schema for the practices of the persons of three capacities—i.e., the stages of the path approach—is featured in the present volume (entry X).

Although it was only later that a systematic narrative evolved whereby the successive Dalai Lamas were cast as emanations of Avalokiteśvara—a lineage that links the Dalai Lamas with both Dromtönpa and Songtsen Gampo—the identification of Gendün Drup with Dromtönpa was already well established. For example, Gendün Drup's biographer, Yeshé Tsemo, cites the translator Thukjé Palwa as stating, after transmitting the book to Gendün Drup, "Therefore, I am a man of meritorious collection, for I have heard [the book] from Drom and have now passed it on to Drom."[78] Similarly, the fifteenth-century historian of the Kadam School, Lechen Künga Gyaltsen, himself a student of the Gendün Drup, states that although some say Gendün Drup is a manifestation of Nāgārjuna and others say he is a reincarnation of the Kadam master Neusurpa, he is known by most as the emanation of Dromtönpa.[79] By the end of the sixteenth century, authors of other schools also came to refer to the First Dalai Lama as a reincarnation of Dromtönpa.[80] Furthermore, according to some sources, his family hailed from the same ancestral lineage as Dromtönpa's. When Gendün Gyatso was formally recognized as the reincarnation of Gendün Drup, the connection was naturally formed between the Second Dalai Lama and Dromtönpa, and through this relationship to Avalokiteśvara himself.

It was the Great Fifth, however, who created the edifice of the mytho-religious worldview in which the institution of the Dalai Lamas came to have a significance far greater than that of the successive reincarnations of an important historical spiritual figure, namely Gendün Drup. The Great Fifth and his ingenious regent, Desi Sangyé Gyatso (1653–1705), brought about a creative marriage of the two textual sources for the narrative of Avalokiteśvara's direct intervention in the unfolding fate of the Tibetan land and its people.[81] Both the *Kakholma Testament* and Dromtönpa's birth stories in *The Book of Kadam* were already recognized as possessing some mysterious background, one a revealed treasure text and the other literally a "miraculous volume." In his influential *History of Ganden Tradition*, Desi Sangyé Gyatso, in addition to providing copious citations from scripture, interweaves beautifully evocative quotes from *The Book of Kadam* and *Kakholma Testament* to explicitly identify the Great Fifth with Songtsen Gampo, Dromtönpa, the treasure revealer Nyangral Nyima Öser (1124–92), Ngari Panchen (1487–1542), and especially the preceding Dalai Lamas—Gendün Drup, Gendün Gyatso, and Sönam Gyatso.[82] Through efforts like this, the Great Fifth and his regent integrated the myth of Avalokiteśvara's compassionate manifestation as rulers and spiritual teachers in the Land of Snows throughout the ages into a concrete institution that the Tibetans could nurture, preserve, and cherish. For the Tibetans, the mythic narrative that began with Avalokiteśvara's embodiment in the form of Songtsen Gampo in the seventh century—or even earlier with the mythohistorical figures of the first king of Tibet, Nyatri Tsenpo (traditionally calculated to have lived around the fifth century B.C.E.), and Lha Thothori Nyentsen (ca. third century C.E.), during whose reign some sacred Buddhist scriptures are believed to have arrived in Tibet—and continued with Dromtönpa in the eleventh century continues today in the person of His Holiness Tenzin Gyatso, the Fourteenth Dalai Lama.

Technical Note

THE TIBETAN TITLE of the volume translated here is *Bka' 'dams glegs bam las btus pa'i chos skor*, a special anthology of key texts of the Tibetan Kadam school developed specifically for *The Library of Tibetan Classics* and its Tibetan equivalent *Bod kyi gtsug lag gces btus*.

Bracketed numbers embedded in the text refer to page numbers of the critical and annotated Tibetan edition published in New Delhi in modern book format by the Institute of Tibetan Classics (2004, ISBN 81-89165-02-X) as volume 2 of the *Bod kyi gtsug lag gces btus* series.

All Tibetan names in the main body of text are rendered phonetically in accordance with a style sheet developed by the Institute of Tibetan Classics and Wisdom Publications especially for *The Library of Tibetan Classics*. There is a correspondence table at the back of the book where transliterated spellings can be found. Sanskrit diacriticals are used throughout, except for naturalized Sanskrit terms such as *sutra*, *mandala*, and *nirvana*.

Pronunciation of Tibetan phonetics:
ph and *th* are aspirated *p* and *t*, as in *pet* and *tip*.
ö is similar to the *eu* in French *seul*.
ü is similar to the *ü* in the German *füllen*.
ai is similar to the *e* in *bet*.
é is similar to the *e* in *prey*.

Pronunciation of Sanskrit:
Palatal *ś* and retroflex *ṣ* are similar to the English unvoiced *sh*.
c is an unaspirated *ch* similar to the *ch* in *chill*.
The vowel *ṛ* is similar to the American *r* in *pretty*.
ñ is somewhat similar to a nasalized *ny* in *canyon*.
ṅ is similar to the *ng* in *sing* or *anger*.

In the Tibetan original of some of the texts, especially those in part 1, a few annotations were inserted into the main body in small fonts. Most of these appear to be attempts (possibly by a later editor or editors) to identify obscure references, especially to personalities of significance to the Kadam school. I have chosen to reproduce these annotations from the original Tibetan texts in my translation in parentheses. In contrast, additions made to help facilitate the reading of the English translation are provided in brackets.

In the critical edition of the Tibetan volume, which is the basis of the translation, all the texts selected from *The Book of Kadam* were based on the Lhasa Shöl edition of the two-volume *Bka' gdams glegs bam* and were compared against the Tashi Lhünpo edition as well as against the Dergé edition reprinted in modern typeset form by the Nationalities Press, Xining, in 1993. In part 3, the text of *Sayings of the Kadam Masters* in the critical Tibetan edition was based on the Lhasa Phunkhang xylograph edition, a copy of which exists in Kyabjé Zemé Rinpoché's personal library in Ganden Monastery, South India. The text was then compared against the version included in the appendix of Yeshé Döndrup's *Treasury of Gems: Selected Anthology of the Well-Uttered Insights of the Teachings of the Precious Kadam*, reproduced in modern typeset by the Nationalities Press, Kansu, in 1995. In my translation I have referred only to those variations in the reading of the Tibetan texts that significantly affect the meaning of the texts. The referencing of the numerous citations from Kangyur and Tengyur and the works of Tibetan authors has been, on the whole, based on the Institute of Tibetan Classics' new critical Tibetan edition.

Part One
The Father Teachings

I. Tree of Faith: A Self-Exhortation
Dromtönpa (1005–64)

HEREIN LIES Dromtönpa's self-exhortation entitled the *Tree of Faith*.

Out of his great compassion for imperfect spiritual aspirants, [Dromtönpa] the precious teacher for everyone—the embodiment of the four divinities and the three teachings[83]—appeared here in the Land of Snows. In tune with the mental levels [of those he encountered] he displayed numerous deeds, including assuming an appropriate social class and suitable paternal and maternal lineages. In particular, he displayed the deeds of relying on Dīpaṃkaraśrījñāna,[84] who had arrived from India, and receiving from him all forms of knowledge. From the conqueror's arrival in Tibet until his departure to liberation,[85] Dromtönpa lived with the master in the manner of a child with his parents and turned numerous wheels of the Dharma of inconceivable secrets. However, those without clairvoyance failed to perceive this, even though his fame for having pleased the teacher was known to all. Many excellent ordained bodhisattva yogis, like Geshé Gungthangpa, were illuminated by the lamp of the world, but it was our teacher—the perfect spiritual guide, the Dharma king Drom—who was empowered as the conqueror's heir. Following the conqueror's departure to liberation, Drom constructed the prophesized glorious Radreng Monastery, as described in *The Book [of Kadam]*. Dromtönpa upheld the conqueror's untainted liberating life and, in the magical juniper forest, engaged in the four everyday activities.[86] He sustained the qualified seekers who gathered near him with succinct profound instructions rather than numerous public discourses. Although several of his disciples, such as Naljorpa, requested extensive teachings from him, he is said to have made it a point to rebuke them so harshly that it rooted out the afflictions at the very bottom of their minds. In particular, he lived in secluded places and would sing the following songs of self-exhortation, which can, through mere hearing, tame the heart. [4]

Oṃ āḥ hūṃ

O mantras of all peaceful and wrathful deities,
Bless the body, speech, and mind of this man.

In the exalted spiritual palace of Tuṣita
Is the embodiment of the two accumulations, Lord Dīpaṃkaraśrījñāna.
You proclaim the joyful feast of Mahayana teachings
From the uncontaminated space known to all—
Pray sit upon my head as a crown jewel.

Your great mother, O teacher, is the perfection of wisdom;
Mere reflection upon its meaning eradicates
The constricting ulcer of dualistic self-grasping—
Pray let [the perfection of wisdom] ornament my throat.

Your immeasurable love, compassion, joy, and equanimity,
Your union of method and wisdom endowed with the three trainings,
And your scriptures and reasonings all shine radiantly as the sun and
    moon—
Pray let these ornament my heart.

From afar the hollow words [of false teachers] sound wondrously eloquent;
The pretense of these charlatans betrays the teachings of the scriptural
    baskets.
When I see others seek them as if they were the father, the Buddha
    himself,
I dare not part from you, O Father, even for an instant.

Even should one have performed good deeds thousands of times over,
Such teachers would snatch away one's very life for a single error.
When I see others seek refuge in such evil leaders and kings,
I dare not part from you, O most venerable Father.

Though claiming to know all the scriptures and treatises,
The conceited decline to put their meaning into practice.
When I see others rely on such unworthy minds and conduct,
I dare not part from you, O most venerable Father.

Even when continually propitiated, with wasted exertions and goods,
These wrathful, ferocious beings are never satisfied.
When I see others seek them as saviors,
I dare not part from the Dharma that alone is needed.

Though one ceaselessly strives to hoard out of greed,
Grasping at permanence with a view to longevity, one's heart is never
    content.
When I see people depart, leaving all behind,
I long to see you, Teacher—you who are free of attachment.

One's treasury may be filled with thousands of garments,
But when I see, on the day death comes, with wails of lamentation,
That one departs naked, wearing no clothes at all,
I long to see you—you who are swathed in morality.

Though surrounded by sons, daughters, and servants,
One's enemy, the lord of death, subdues one by the neck. [5]
When I see that one travels alone [to death], with no companions at all,
I long to see you soon, together with your divinities.

Those swift-legged ones who ride mounts in the four directions,
If, when chased by the enemy that robs them of their lives,
I see them caught lifeless in their own beds,
I long to see you in an instant, O space-like Father.

At first they unite as if never to be sundered,
Yet at death they part ways while beating their chests.
When I see such misguided friendships arranged through household
    alliances,
I long to see you soon, a true master renunciate.

I, Gyalwai Jungné,[87] whose heart is never satisfied,
O Father, have never countered your aspirations.
So here in this ever-flourishing magical juniper forest,
As I sing these lines aloud with a resounding voice,
Pray seize them with your ears as if hearing them clearly.

The lord of all three realms is the blessed Buddha;
That which brings him into being is the great mother *dharmakāya;*
Those who've achieved this are the wise lords of the ten levels—
I pay respectful homage to the Three Jewels, my refuge.

By relying on the scriptures of my master's advice,
I shall exhort myself, the lazy one, a little.

O noble Three Jewels, most undeceiving refuge,
O precious benefactor who grants the ultimate objective,
O precious physician who heals the illness of the afflictions—
To never be separated from you, I seek your refuge until enlightenment.

From now until the end of cyclic existence,
I will be inseparable from the Three Jewels and the pursuit of others'
    welfare.
Even if threatened, "Forsake others or I will tear your body and life
    apart,"
What use is my own happiness? I cannot abandon my parents.

The beings of this degenerate age are so utterly corrupt:
They sin themselves but place the blame on others;
They seek to profit from the good deeds of others;
With every joke they collect mountains of nonvirtuous karma with
    their speech.

This brings a host of things—greed, hatred, and conflict.
Fearing ill consequences they cover their flaws with their hands;
Fearing other's success they dig deep into other's shortcomings.
When at last things turn back upon themselves, they become livid.

Hoarding wealth for this life, they are kept away from happiness;
On life's other shore they lose [too] and fall into the abyss of lower
    realms.
Those who pursue goals that betray them in both this life and the next,
Yet think, "I am most clever," deceive themselves and spoil their roots
    [of virtue]. [6]

The forces of Māra rejoice and dance with ecstasy;
The forces of goodness, the gods, disapprove and denounce;
Yet these [pretenders] still falsely claim to be Dharma practitioners!
They fail to scrutinize even those charlatans they know to be deceivers
  and ignorantly take them as genuine.

Yet they denigrate and insult the learned and industrious who practice
  Dharma perfectly,
Calling *them* charlatans.
With a character devoid of shame and conscience,
They return harm for help.

When taught Dharma they create negative karma in return.
So many are there who return distortion for kindness.
Even were I to shower them with profound Dharma instructions like rain,
Those with wild negative minds, undisciplined and hardened since
  beginningless time,
Would be difficult for me to tame, for they do not practice the truth.

Even when, once in a million, the shoot of the awakening mind grows
  [in them],
As they are lazy and lack both the foundation of morality and the force
  of antidote,
Fervently pursuing at all times the goals of this life [alone],
Many are snatched by the frost of the five poisonous afflictions.

Without attaining to some degree your own secure attainment,
You cannot lead others to the place of enlightenment.
Therefore, pointing my finger inward,
I will counsel my own mind in words beneficial for all occasions.
Protect me against the frosts of Māra and the hailstorms of the Lesser
  Vehicle;
Bear witness to whatever befalls me, success or failure.

O son of excellent Dīpaṃkaraśrījñāna,[88]
This life of leisure and opportunity is so difficult to find;
Encountering the Buddha's excellent teaching is rarer still;
So squander not this leisure and opportunity so rare.

Why should I not do so? The abyss of lower realms is wide.
Strive to distill the antidote to a lack of moral foundation.

You might appear heroic for having cheated the abyss,
But at this singular juncture, when you've gained a secure footing—
Like someone accumulating a year's provisions in one month—
Remain not idle but apply powerful doses of the remedy.

Life is transient, like a flash of lighting in the sky;
The moment we are born, our lives are marked for disintegration.
I see my own life to be the same;
So do not rest but extract the essence of this body.[89]

Life is transient, like water cascading down a waterfall;
It travels fast and none can seize it.
I see my own life to be the same;
So do not be lazy but practice the sublime Dharma. [7]

Life is transient, like a dewdrop on a blade of grass;
Unable to withstand even the tiniest adversity, it swiftly dries up.
I see my own life to be the same;
So foreswear strong grasping at permanence and meditate upon
    impermanence in four sessions.[90]

Life is transient, like a bee at season's end;
Though hovering now, a slight shift in the weather and it dies.
I see my own life to be the same;
So foreswear strong greed and meditate upon the defects of samsara.

Life is transient, like the rays of the setting sun;
Though brilliant now, they soon will be no more.
I see my own life to be the same;
So foreswear strong hatred and cultivate love and compassion.

Life is transient, like goats and sheep in a slaughterhouse;
Though alive now, with no control, they soon will be dead.
I see my own life to be the same;

So foreswear strong delusion and meditate upon profound dependent
   origination.

Life is transient, like clouds in the sky;
They appear suddenly yet disappear just as quickly.
I see my own life to be the same;
So foreswear strong envy and cultivate the four immeasurable thoughts.[91]

Life is transient, like a cool gust of wind;
It rises in the ten directions and disappears in the ten directions as well.
I see my own life to be the same;
So foreswear strong conceit and cut the root of ego's view.

Life is transient, like a dead bush on a high mountain pass;
Assailed by birth and aging, it has lost its secure ground.
I see my own life to be the same;
So foreswear strong lust for pleasure and embrace hardships.

Life is transient, like people gathered in a marketplace;
Though assembled now, soon they will scatter in the ten directions.
I see my own life to be the same;
So don't offer feeble resistance but practice the powerful remedies.

This body, composed of four elements, is a heap of diseases;
Though it has been dismantled numerous times in the past in this samsara,
It has never been [dismantled] for the sake of Dharma practice
And can still plunge me deep into the mires of cyclic existence.

I am the thirty-two impure substances—puss, blood, and mucus;
I am being devoured by the eighty thousand types of insects.[92]
Viewed from any angle, this heap of suffering cannot rival
The Buddha's body, adorned with the major and minor marks.

Though I have obtained this [body], it means nothing.
Do not cherish it but dedicate it to all beings, both ordinary and noble.
For if I remain miserly, how can I be a Kadampa?
If I am bound by greed, I am not the master's son.
So never indulge in ordinary, crass conduct. [8]

My body is immersed in dream and illusion-like emptiness and
    appearance;
My speech, in the melodious yet empty sound of echoes;
My mind, in the union of clarity and emptiness, method and wisdom.
Bless me Father, most kind supreme Dharma master.
Bless me Dīpaṃkara, lord of all beings.

All phenomena share the reality of impermanence;
Therefore, these metaphors of transience are instructions to myself.
Listen again, Master Drom, son of the excellent teacher.
This teaching from the most sublime mentor of time's impermanence
I see that it serves as an exhortation to my heart.

In the summer, thunder resounds and rain falls heavy;
The forests bloom with dense new foliage;
Countless birds fill the air with sweet songs;
Everywhere the meadows are resplendent with rich turquoise blue;
Yet in autumn, impermanence strikes, and I see the colors change.
This rouses me to virtue, O most kind master.

Golden flowers abound when crops are ripe,
But due to impermanence's push, they change come wintertime.
Even the water becomes crystalline, like glass,
Making the fowl that depend upon it lose heart.
Dejected, they fly away to another place.

This also is transient, for the wind starts to blow.
Gradually the ground warms and new shoots push forth;
Having shed their old leaves, the trees wear new foliage.
Time is a profound and vast treasury of teachings on impermanence.
It resembles the self-enlightened ones who teach Dharma in silence.

When I travel to the barren lands of the nomads in the north,
Violent winds shake the abundant grasses,
Wailing melancholy songs from afar with transient tunes.
The wild animals run pell-mell, with neither aim nor direction.
With no companion at all, I travel everywhere;
With a sad heart, I feel the urge to sing a melodious tune.

My own transience is the best exhortation to practice Dharma.
One discovers teachings even in places such as these.
O Father, as I cannot remain [alive forever] but must depart,
Wherever I travel, I seek a secure ground.

From this moment until the ocean of samsara becomes dry,
May I never be separated from you, O excellent master;
I will teach about this impermanence, the essence of Dharma instruction,
To other sentient beings out of [a wish to] help and benefit them.

Though numerous extremely profound teachings exist,
There are few who contemplate karma and the defects of samsara. [9]
Even among children and grandchildren of the same parents,
One sees that some are boys and some girls;
One sees that some are beautiful and some ugly;

One sees that some are intelligent and some foolish;
One sees that some are rich and some poor;
One sees that some are happy and some miserable;
Yet, on the parents' part, how can there be discrimination?
It's the fruits of past causes ripening upon them.

O listen, you Dromtön Gyalwai Jungné,
Profound Dharma is found even in the most mundane events.
As [the shadow of] karma follows you, commit no evil;
To feel remorse after [the act] is too late, O Dromtön, conqueror's son.

For those beset by the unbearable suffering
Of torments like being cooked and burned in the hells,
It's the fruits of past causes ripening upon them.
When such things happen it is too late, so strive right now.

For those beset by the unbearable suffering
Of torments like the thirst and starvation of hungry ghosts,
It's the fruits of corresponding causes ripening on schedule.[93]
When such things happen it is too late, so strive right now.

For those beset by the unbearable suffering
Of torments like the confusion of animals,

It's the fruits of corresponding causes ripening on schedule.
So seize a secure attainment right now, O conqueror's son.

For those beset by the unbearable suffering
Of torments like the perpetual conflicts of the demigods,
It's the fruits of corresponding causes befalling them.
Do not take on such an existence, O Drom.

If, once in a million [births], you obtain the joys of the gods,
You will rise above this cyclic existence not one bit.
For even in such a realm, self-sustaining suffering is said to exist;
This existence is also a cause of suffering and should be relinquished.

If, once in a million [births], you obtain a human life,
All the analogies of impermanence cited earlier
Will fall upon that human life like a rushing river.

Engaging in virtuous acts is as rare as a star shining during the day;
Your stores of karma and afflictions increase both day and night.
Even if you die this does not change, for you take birth again and again.
Alas, those with evil karma descend to the lower realms.

Therefore, if effects correspond to their causes,
How can an evil act committed be changed into a virtue?
[The shadow of] karma follows you, O Drom, conqueror's son.
Shun nonvirtuous causes as you would a poisonous tree.
Nurture virtuous karma as you would a healing tree. [10]

The Buddha described karma as like a bird and its shadow.
As it follows after, do not say you have not seen it;
As it travels in stealth, do not say you have not heard it.

Since karma is within you, do not seek it elsewhere;
Since it is skilled at fraud, do not comply with it;
Since liberation is impossible if you befriend [bad karma] for too long,
Relate to it like the analogy of a corpse in the sea.[94]

Like a charred log reduced to ashes,
[Bad karma] destroys the limbs needed to traverse the grounds and paths;

Like a contagious disease, it will destroy you without your knowing it.
You can [at least] escape external enemies by running away.

Too many times this evil thieving dog has pulled me down.
Shut the doors [of your senses] well, O Dromtön, conqueror's son.
Purify your interior, O Dharma king endowed with self-knowledge.
Since such is the truth, broaden your commitment to profound karma
And imbue your actions with constant reverence.
As in the dirty white and black rodents analogy told by the emanation
    of Lord Mañjuśrī,[95]
Day and night, time eats away at this human life.

The afflictions deceive us as if granting joy and happiness;
We drink poisonous water as if it were a sweet drink.
O son, do not entrust the lifeline of liberation to Māra's hands,
But rely, day and night, upon the wholesome support of your spiritual
    guide.

Befriend the walking staff of excellent virtuous companions;
Especially, do not cut off your mind from the upholders of discipline;
Read the profound sutras that present karma and its effects;
The realizations of the path will then gradually arise, O Drom.

In particular, from the ocean of the three higher trainings,
You should extract the precious gem that grants all wishes.
Drive out karma and the afflictions with powerful tides [of antidotes].
Hey! If you do this, you will become an excellent person, O Drom.

With such acts you will become the glory of all beings.
Wherever there is a lamp there is illumination;
In the same way, from the presence of a cause, an effect ensues.
Err not with respect to this law and enter the perfect path.

Contemplate the defects of samsara both day and night,
For if you know them you will develop the wish to flee.
With these [lines] the defects of samsara's cause and effect have
    been revealed.

Now to speak of the benefits [of nirvana]—
O Gyalwai Jungné, reflect on the following points:

Like lights shining down through crystals from the space high above,
[Nirvana] utterly dispels the world of darkness, [11]
Illuminating the dependence, for instance, of forms on their visual
    perceptions.
Likewise, from the expanse of nature's purity,
Thousands of lights illuminate samsara and nirvana in their entirety.
Karma and its effects, unreal, are the causes of illusory samsara and
    nirvana.

The hero who sees this and acts accordingly is victorious indeed;
The wise one who understands the words and implements them is
    victorious indeed;
The yogi who is released from samsara and nirvana is utterly joyful;
He who has gained the habit of knowing the mode of all
By realizing the mode of being of one phenomenon,
Joyful is this excellent one, released from all by knowing the one.

Utterly blissful is the intelligent one who understands karma and its ways;
Happy is he whose meditation is pure and unsullied.
The skilled ones are endowed with past virtues that grant wishes.
O all excellent people, such indeed is the power of virtuous karma.

When this fruit of the virtue of all beings—self and others—is born,
One's body becomes adorned with major and minor marks and
    enveloped in light;
One's speech becomes the sound of the sublime Dharma imbued with
    sixty melodies;
One's mind becomes perfect in wisdom and compassion, fully awakened,
    perfecting the two accumulations.
Most excellent are the fruits of nirvana, attained in the past.
This then is a brief [presentation of the] benefits of nirvana.

For the sovereign Dharma king who has gained the ten masteries,[96]
The harvest of his virtues, the force of his supernatural feats, is vast;

His mind expands within one-pointed meditative absorption;
Numerous absorptions are subsumed into one;
This, too, is a union of method and wisdom blissful at all times.

Listen, O Master Drom, the son of our teacher and conqueror.
These are the benefits of transcending the realm of samsara.

Though blissful, do not cling, for [nirvana] will become a source of
  bondage.
Though I sing these profound meanings in a song,
The words are empty echoes, so how can they be real?
If all the points are distilled, only appearances and emptiness remain.

Sounds are echoes with no antecedent and consequent connected stream;
Forms are like bubbles in water and have no essence.
Yet if a beautiful maiden gazes into a mirror,
A vivid face appears, lit up by her tiara of bright teeth.

If she casts her gaze once more into the mirror with a steadier eye,
Since [her image] is a dependent origination it fails to endure;
Though said to exist, it is lost when its source is sought.
Yet to say it does not exist [contradicts] its evident appearance.

Though utterly empty it appears in the great Middle Way;
Though appearing, there is no room to cling to its true existence;
Though false, this stark appearance gives rise to happiness; [12]
So to defy phenomena, saying they are false, is foolish indeed.

Because of this falsehood, when I observe I see diversity;
For if this [perception] were true, the maiden's body would be double,
Or neither of the two [appearances] would exist.
Since such [perceptions] do not cohere, who would take them as real?

When it changes who grasps it to be permanent?
Because it is transient it has lost its self-sustaining power;
Calling it a "shell," an "effigy," and "seedless,"[97]
The conquerors have described it as lacking a core.

In general samsaric things seem to have realities of their own;
Yet how can the noble ones grasp at any of these?
The childish who fail to contemplate this are thus deceived.
Knowing this, I grasp no more but blow [samsaric things] away.

They crash like the falling of the king-like northern mountain;
I see them vanish like the disappearing of the queen-like southern
    mountain;
They fly away like the excellent horse-like western mountain;
I see them seized like the capture of the general-like eastern mountain.

Am I deluded? No doubt, this is the doing
Of an illusionist who is most skilled.
This world of deceptive conventions is a lie;
Since such dreams appear, fall not into slumber.

O Father, untainted Dharma king, in the imperceptible expanse
Such are the facts. How can this be so?
Since these manifestations without existence are [devoid of a core] like this,
If those who assert true existence were indeed correct,
How could these [phenomena] then fit within the expanse of space?

O Father, sever the ropes of such [grasping] conceptions this instant;
Do not send illusions that project appearances but do not exist.

Ah! All things are but mere appearances.
Even should the entire world surround me
And argue against me, claiming phenomena are real,
I, Drom, would find them the greater laughingstock.
What are you saying? Do not extend to others what you falsely perceive.

Do not bend a perfect line, saying it is not straight;
Do not eradicate the true meaning with distorted understanding.
Distill the entire meaning of the two truths—appearance and
    emptiness—
And meditate on them with a single-pointed mind
Until samsara is empty and you fall into [solitary] peace.

Though fully awakened I'll assume the form of a bodhisattva;
I'll fulfill the wishes of sentient beings, my parents.
May I, through the two form bodies, enact the welfare of all beings,
Revealing to each and every one whatever is most suited to his or her
    needs.

This profound teaching, the most precious heart drop[98]
[That lies] inside the innermost chamber of the sacred mind's
    amulet— [13]
By beautifully adorning the environment with a wide array of things,
May I always cherish this [teaching] in my heart and never be separated
From the excellent teacher, the conqueror, the conqueror's mother, and
    her children.[99]

May I, from this point on, throughout the entire universe,
Reveal this [teaching] when I see those with fortunate mental
    continuums,
Displaying affliction-ridden deeds, even when my afflictions have ceased,
As a hidden yogi of profound and vast truths.

May all the aspirations yearned for in unison by conquerors and their
    children
Throughout the worlds of the ten directions, past, present, and future
Be definitely realized in this heart of mine.
May I attain realizations in accord with their aspirations.

This is a self-exhortation entitled *Tree of Faith,* which is the drop of
preparation.[100]

> The sequence [of the practices] appears as follows:[101] (1) Bless-
> ing my three doors by means of the three letters; (2) requesting
> for the teacher's body, speech, and mind to reside at the three
> points of the body; (3) supplicating the teacher, because of [the
> challenges posed by] the diverse perceptions of others [espe-
> cially the more negative ones], never to be separated from one-
> self; (4) requesting the opportunity to see him again soon; (5)
> having seen him, uttering his praises once he resides in the three
> points of the body; (6) taking the pledge; (7) going for refuge;

(8) generating the awakening mind; (9) as for its method or rationale, [reflecting upon] the perspectives of cyclic existence and the difficulty of taming others who have such perspectives; (10) therefore exhorting oneself to first reach a secure attainment; for this, (11) recollecting the witness; (12) then meditating on the difficulty of finding a human life of leisure and opportunity and how it is so easy to lose; thus exhorting oneself to experience the wonder of not falling into the terrifying abyss but securing a firm ground for the future; (13) death and impermanence; (14) karma and its fruits; (15) the defects of cyclic existence; (16) the higher qualities of nirvana; (17) not clinging to these two as [objects of] relinquishment and affirmation but establishing them in terms of the two truths as appearances and emptiness; (18) and [finally] aspiration prayers together with a dedication.

* * *

The teacher of all beings, having laid out simple offerings in front of the Three Jewels, is said to have spoken as follows:

Alas! [Atiśa,] you who rescue us from the negative perspectives [of samsara] and lead each and every sentient being, according his or her fortune, to the cities of higher rebirth and liberation; [14] you who are endowed with the wisdom of knowledge, the great compassion of [deep] kindness, and the activities of enlightened deeds; you who are known as the "guru-deity, the master [embodiment of the] Three Jewels"—hearing of you makes one happy. Those who rely upon you are sustained; those who seek refuge in you are never deceived. Even when you are harmed you bear no hostility. Certainly you are an emanation of Great Compassion. Should I fail to seek refuge in you and fail to take you as my kind master, a sentient being like me will fritter my life away in procrastination and laziness and will fail to touch the secure ground of liberation, let alone become able to lead others [to liberation]. Thus, I seek refuge in you, an undeceiving [savior], and make the pledge, "I will become a lord of all three realms."

In this manner, he performed the following refuge practice:[102]

Countless beings caught in desperation are equal [in extent] to space;
They have no refuge, no friend, and they betray their own well-being.
May they go for refuge to the sublime source of refuge, the precious
　　Teacher;
May they go for refuge to the sublime source of refuge, the precious
　　Buddha;
May they go for refuge to the sublime source of refuge, the precious
　　Teaching;
May they go for refuge to the sublime source of refuge, the precious
　　Community.

May they go for refuge to the sublime source of refuge, the precious
　　Jewels;
May they go for refuge to the sublime source of refuge, the precious
　　Atiśa;
May they go for refuge to the sublime source of refuge, the precious
　　Tönpa;
May they go for refuge to the sublime source of refuge, the precious
　　brothers;[103]
May they go for refuge to the sublime source of refuge, the precious
　　Kadam.

Bless the body, speech, and mind of this affliction-ridden man.
You're the savior and refuge of all beings and the supreme bringer of
　　happiness.
Out of ignorance beings like me are mired in samsara;
Though desiring happiness we have no means [to attain it] and are bereft
　　of wisdom.
Since beginningless time, the burden of unbearable misery has weighed
　　upon us.

Leave us not in pain but rescue us from this cycle of suffering lives.
In particular save us from the agonies of the three lower realms.
O sovereign teacher and the Three Jewels:
Other than you, there is none in whom we can hope, whether in joy or
　　misery.
With your great wisdom, watch us throughout all lives;
With your enlightened deeds, guard us throughout all lives.

For if you do not, in whom can we—beings ridden with evil karma, [15]
Untamed and hard to change—place our hopes as a savior and refuge?
The gods, nāgas, yakṣas, gandharvas, demigods, and Māra's army,
Īśvara, Viṣṇu, and the upholders of extremes—are they our ultimate
   refuge?

Leaving aside future lives, they deceive us even in this life.
Robbing us of our lives, they drag us into an endless cycle of lower
   rebirths.
In the hells is the unbearable suffering of being baked and burned,
   they say;
The hungry ghosts have unbearable miseries of thirst and hunger, I've
   heard.

For the beasts, I've seen their misery of slaughter and servitude.
If today we cannot bear even slight heat, cold, thirst, hunger, and
   beating,
What will we do when this life is no more and we are born in these
   [realms]?
Please raise your army of great compassion now and be our guard.

I am like a flower in the scorching heat of the desert plain—
Due to past [good] karma, I remain unburned and barely alive,
But assailed by afflictions' heat, I'll surely be trampled by the elephant of
   death.
Pray rain down blessing streams from the mountain tops and revive me.

This life is transient and rushes on like a boulder down a cliff;
I cannot seize it even if I try, and it runs downhill without any effort.
Days turn into months and years, and life has no pause.
Alas! My teacher and the Three Jewels, pray be my savior and refuge.

O assembly of dashing young men and gorgeous women:
In the midst of food and drink, resources, wealth, fame, and pleasure,
All procured through the hardships of your kind parents, relatives, and
   servants,
Leaving behind everything—beautiful turquoise, corals, and garments—

When you die alone, naked and crying in lamentation,
All your loved ones will cry, beat their chests, and shout in grief.
With their hair pulled out and their mouths agape, they will shriek your
    name and leap upon you.
What is the use? Nothing can avert death; in fact [such actions] bring harm.

Alas! The flower of youth is destroyed by the frost of time;
The god-like bliss of loved ones is crushed under the mountain of
    suffering.
There is no one that this shameless [death] will not hesitate to slay.
So if all beings will be slain by this [death] with no say on their part,
Alas! Will I alone be spared by him as an exception? [16]

When the time definitely comes for me to die,
O my teacher, meditation deities, conquerors, mother, and her children,
Reside in the center of this destitute being's heart and help ripen it.
Through your blessings [transform] my five aggregates into [the body of]
    a conqueror and my afflictions into supreme wisdom.

Since in the past my body, feelings, perceptions, mental formations,
And consciousness were enslaved by greed, anger, delusion, conceit,
    and envy,
Streams of evil karma flowed into the ocean of the ground-of-all and
    were stored,
Stirring up violently forceful tides of birth, aging, sickness, and death.
At such times I wandered in the wheel of samsara with no refuge or
    friend.

Now master, you alone are everything to me—my friend, savior, and
    refuge;
If you do not act according [to my appeal],
Since we ill-mannered beings so hard to tame tend to procrastinate,
I will not obtain today the higher rebirths endowed with the seven
    attributes.[104]
Since the good fortune of finding the sublime Dharma is so difficult to
    achieve,
You, no doubt, will be a refuge for this blind man astray in
    a desolate plain.

Again, behold me with wisdom and sustain me with great compassion.
Alas! The blossoming body of youth is damaged by dewdrops.
Even in the prime of youth it resembles a butter lamp in the midst of a
    whirlwind.
Like the [empty] core of a banana tree, old age spells the loss of one's
    secure ground.

Alas! I have no power to remain [forever], and so I seek a secure place.
If death cannot be conquered with power, bought off, or run from,
What resourceful, clever, powerful, rich, or fast person can escape it and
    not die?
Which busy and ill-mannered person would it spare saying it is pointless?

Even wild carnivorous animals, such as falcons and wolves,
And ill-fated butchers will have their turn and die powerless.
Even life-robbing demons will definitely die one day.
Even excellent mentors display entering into nirvana for other's sake.

Alas! I, a water bubble, have no power to stay, so please be my savior and
    refuge.
I seek refuge in you, O most kind teacher and venerable Three Jewels.
I supplicate you, O most kind teacher and venerable Three Jewels.
Bless me, O most kind teacher and venerable Three Jewels.

Behold me with wisdom, O most kind teacher and venerable Three
    Jewels.
Lead me on the path, O most kind teacher and venerable Three
    Jewels. [17]
I bow my three doors with reverence at the thousand petals of your
    [lotus] feet.
I prostrate, make offerings, and go for refuge, so grant me your blessings.

Today the conditions and my fortune are excellent, O source of benefit
    and joy;
Today, even if I were to die leaving everything, [it would be] with joy and
    no regret at all.
Together with you and for the sake of all beings, my parents,
I will depart from this world to the world beyond.

I do not care if this insignificant body breaks into a thousand pieces.
To fail [to accomplish] the welfare of my parents is to lose the purpose of
   finding human life,
So from now on, throughout all my deaths and rebirths,
I will thoroughly liberate those beings not yet liberated.

I will thoroughly release those beings not yet released;
I will relieve those beings not yet relieved as well;
I will place within nirvana those beings who have yet to attain nirvana.
May I be a protector for those who lack one and a refuge for those bereft
   of one.

May I be an ally for those who lack one and a country for those who
   have none.
May I enter without obstruction the ten levels
And the paths of accumulation, preparation, seeing, and meditation and
   purify all my defilements.[105]
May I be a leader for the leaderless and a Dharma king, the lord of
   beings.

Until I achieve the status of Dharma king, the lord of beings,
May I, in this and all lifetimes, never be divorced from the noble Three
   Jewels.
May I uphold the sublime Dharma by ensuring its flourishing within me.
May I never be born in the deep and vast ocean of cyclic existence.

May I never be born in the lower realms, which are without limit or end.
May I never be born in states plagued by the absence of the eight
   leisures.
May I be adorned with precious human life in the perfect higher realms.
With perfect birth, paternal and maternal lineages, and retinues,
May I become an excellent Dharma king, supreme among humans.

With a face insatiably beautiful and an excellent body adorned with
   noble marks,
With a voice endowed with sixty melodies whose fame pervades the
   ten directions,
Skilled in loving-kindness, compassion, joy, equanimity, and so on, [18]

May I be omniscient, rich in knowledge and compassion, wisdom and
methods.

Unsullied by the stains of a womb birth and always free of faults,
May I be revered and celebrated by the whole world, including gods and
humans.
May I attain all retentions and absorptions,[106] and realizing the truth of
all things,
May the qualities of the Buddha, the ten faculties and powers, be realized
within me.

The dedications of past, future, and present buddhas and their children,
Hailed as the excellent "aspirations of good conduct,"[107]
Because of the truth of reality's expanse and the Three Jewels—
May all of these be realized within me without obstruction, in
accordance with my aspirations.

May the auspiciousness of all who are auspicious descend upon me
today;
May the auspiciousness of the wish-granting precious jewel prevail;
May the auspiciousness of seven royal emblems, rich in resources, prevail;
May the auspiciousness of the Three Jewels spontaneously accomplishing
others' welfare prevail.

May the auspiciousness of the noble Sangha with three virtuous doors
prevail;
May the auspiciousness of the sublime Dharma, virtuous at all times,
prevail;
May the auspiciousness of the buddhas who have actualized the three
embodiments prevail.[108]

May the auspiciousness of great disciples and self-enlightened ones, pure
in their moral vows, prevail;
May the auspiciousness of bodhisattvas equalizing and exchanging self
and others prevail;
May the auspiciousness of knowledge-bearers, uniting method and
wisdom and generation and completion stages, prevail;

May the auspiciousness of oath-bound guardians with limitless might
and power prevail;
May the auspiciousness of fully awakened buddhas, the perfection of all,
prevail.

In this life as well may the auspiciousness of fulfilling all wishes prevail;
May the auspiciousness of always working for other's welfare through the
four factors of attracting others prevail.[109]

Having sung these lines, [Dromtönpa] engaged in the uncommon preparatory practices [and spoke of the following drops]: (1) the *drop of conventional awakening mind* in terms of the skillful means of the drop of the four
immeasurable thoughts; and at the end, (2) the *drop of ultimate awakening
mind* in terms of the drop of reflecting upon the mind as the ultimate
expanse *(dharmadhātu)*; (3) in particular, the *drop of remembering your
teachers*—the source of refuge—such as those who are endowed with the
three lineages; (4) the *drop of reflecting upon your body as meditation deities*,
such as [Buddha Śākyamuni], who has thoroughly subdued the three doors
and is imbued with great compassion for all beings, [Tārā] the savioress of
the world, and [Acala], who is immutable by either samsara or nirvana; (5)
the *drop of reflecting upon your speech as mantra recitation*, such as the
essence mantras [of these deities] and the three syllables; [19] (6) the *drop
of reflecting upon all sentient beings as your actual or indirect mothers* on the
basis of understanding karma and its effects; and finally (7) the *drop of
reflecting upon the mind as the ultimate expanse*. These are the seven root
drops and, on their basis, the *drop of external environment*, the *drop of inner
sentient beings*, and the method of how to engage in the practice of these
drops, and so forth, emerge.

You should learn these drops, if possible, from the best teacher—a fully
enlightened buddha or someone abiding on the levels and the paths who
is capable of teaching the entire *Book [of Kadam]* from the very drop of his
heart. Learning the instructions from a teacher capable of teaching the
entire book without omitting any of the text is second best. At the very
least, you should learn the instructions from a teacher who is capable of
summarizing *[The Book]* in terms of the sixteen drops on the basis of the
root stanzas. As for the faults and qualities of the disciple-vessel, you should
learn these from the treatises. This concludes the explanation of the preliminary and the main practices.

As a conclusion, you should perform the dedication, recite aspiration prayers, make offerings, take the pledge to be a suitable vessel, and supplicate [the divinities] to enter into the expanse of the drops within the mandala.

Fully ordained monks who have completed their approximation retreats should then make pleas for the divine teaching to be upheld and take the earth and colored sands of the mandala to rivers, mountain summits, or secluded places. Having taken them there, they should guard the secrecy of the secret words. Then, receiving the *Garland of Dialogues* from the mouth of their teacher, they should strive to visualize their teacher and meditation deities in the very drop of their hearts.

This then is the manner in which you extract the essence from this unique dialogue, the instructions for bracing yourself to cross the mire of desire, from all its parts—from the beginning to the end—and undertake its practice within your mental continuum. You should then go to a secluded forest.

This concludes the drop of how to engage in the practice of [the Kadam tradition] endowed with the sevenfold divinities and teachings.

May it be utterly auspicious! *Svasti yana ghathaḥ* [20]

II. Bodhisattva's Jewel Garland[110]
Atiśa Dīpaṃkara (982–1054)

[21] Sanskrit title: *Bodhisattvamaṇevalī*

Homage to great compassion.
(1) Homage to the teachers.[111]
(2) Homage to the faith divinities.

(3) Discard all lingering doubts
And strive with dedication in your practice.
(4) Thoroughly relinquish sloth, mental dullness, and laziness,
And strive always with joyful perseverance.

(5) With mindfulness, awareness, and heedfulness,[112]
Constantly guard the gateways of your senses.
Again and again, three times both day and night,
Examine the flow of your thoughts.

(6) Reveal your own shortcomings,
But do not seek out others' errors.
Conceal your own good qualities,
But proclaim those of others.

Forsake wealth and ministrations;
At all times relinquish gain and fame.
Have modest desires, be easily satisfied,
And reciprocate kindness.

Cultivate love and compassion,
And stabilize your awakening mind.

(7) Relinquish the ten negative actions,
And always reinforce your faith.[113]

Destroy anger and conceit,
And be endowed with humility.
Relinquish wrong livelihood,
And be sustained by ethical livelihood.

(8) Forsake material possessions;
Embellish yourself with the wealth of the noble ones.
(9) Avoid all trifling distractions,
And reside in the solitude of wilderness.

Abandon frivolous words;
Constantly guard your speech.
(10) When you see your teachers and preceptors,[114]
Reverently generate the wish to serve.

Toward wise beings with Dharma eyes
And toward beginners on the path as well,
Recognize them as your spiritual teachers.
[In fact] when you see any sentient being,
View that one as your parent, your child, or your grandchild.

(11) Renounce negative friendships,
And rely on a spiritual friend.
Discard hostile and unhappy mental states,[115]
And venture forth to where happiness lies. [22]

(12) Abandon attachment to all things
And abide free of desire.
Attachment fails to bring even the higher realms;
In fact, it kills the life of true liberation.

(13) Where you see the factors of happiness,
There always persevere.[116]
Whichever task you take up first,
Address this task primarily.

In this way, you ensure the success of both tasks,
Where otherwise you accomplish neither.

(14) Since you take no pleasure in negative deeds,
When a thought of self-importance arises,
At that instant deflate your pride
And recall your teacher's instructions.

When discouraged thoughts arise,
Uplift your mind
And meditate on the emptiness of both.
(15) When objects of attraction or aversion appear,
View them as you would illusions or apparitions.

When you hear unpleasant words,
View them as [mere] echoes.
When injuries afflict your body,
See them as [the fruits of] past deeds.

(16) Dwell utterly in solitude, beyond town limits.
Like the carcass of a wild animal,
Hide yourself away [in the forest]
And live free of attachment.

(17) Always remain firm in your commitment.
When a hint of procrastination and laziness arises,
At that instant enumerate your flaws
And recall the essence of [spiritual] conduct.

(18) However, if you do encounter others,
Speak peacefully and truthfully.
Do not grimace or frown,
But always maintain a smile.

In general when you see others,
Be free of miserliness, and delight in giving;
Relinquish all thoughts of envy.

To help guard others' minds,[117]
Forsake all disputation
And always be endowed with forbearance.

(19) Be free of flattery and fickleness in friendship,
Be steadfast and reliable at all times.
Do not disparage others,
But always abide with respectful demeanor.

When giving advice,
Maintain compassion and altruism.
(20) Never defame the teachings.
Whatever practices you admire,
With aspiration and the ten spiritual deeds,
Strive diligently, dividing day and night.

(21) Whatever virtues you gather through the three times,
Dedicate them toward the unexcelled great awakening.
Disperse your merit to all sentient beings,
And utter the peerless aspiration prayers
Of the seven limbs at all times.[118]

If you proceed thus, you'll swiftly perfect merit and wisdom
And eliminate the two defilements.[119] [23]
Since your human existence will be meaningful,
You'll attain the unexcelled enlightenment.

(22) The wealth of faith, the wealth of morality,
The wealth of giving, the wealth of learning,
The wealth of conscience, the wealth of shame,
And the wealth of insight—these are the seven riches.

These precious and excellent jewels
Are the seven inexhaustible riches.
Do not speak of these to those not human.
(23) Among others guard your speech;
When alone guard your mind.

This concludes the *Bodhisattva's Jewel Garland* composed by the Indian abbot Dīpaṃkaraśrījñāna.

III. The Jewel Garland of Dialogues

Title, Homage, and Preamble

Herein is, from the twenty-six-chapter Father Teachings, the actual dialogue in twenty-three chapters, entitled *The Jewel Garland*.

[25] Sanskrit title: *Bodhisattvamaṇevalī*
[English: *Bodhisattva's Jewel Garland*]

Homage

To the conquerors and their children,
And to the assembly of noble disciples,
I will always pay respectful homage
With my body, speech, and mind.

The Appeal

Once the glorious Dīpaṃkara, the emanation Dharma king, was residing in Yerpa, the great site of the perfected ones that resembles the towering mount Potala.[120] Upon Tārā's right leg was a pavilion made from rainbow light—a [celestial] chamber for shepherd-like bodhisattvas.[121] Inside this perfect celestial palace, whose architectural excellence was beyond imagination, [Atiśa] sat upon a stainless moon disc within a lotus that had been blessed by incalculable buddhas.

As he observed imperfect sentient beings throughout all six times,[122] Atiśa was surrounded by: the seven buddhas who are the refuge of [the beings of] this degenerate era,[123] our teacher Śākyamuni, the buddhas of the ten directions, the eight sons[124] of all these conquerors, the pure appearances of [other] bodhisattvas as described in the sutras—such as in their manifestations as householders, ordained persons, children, and women—and many great disciples together with the self-enlightened ones, constituting an assembly of inconceivable numbers of noble beings. Amid this vast array of perfect emanation beings was the one hailed as Dromtön Gyalwai Jungné.

Drom had performed numerous enlightened activities consistent with the needs of others. In general, [these activities] conformed to the mental states of dependently arisen sentient beings, equal to the expanse of space, who were beyond comparison and measurement, and who possessed their own diverse modes of behavior [26] and diverse aspirations in conjunction with such behavior. In brief, [his activities conformed to the mental states of] the incalculable beings who are subsumed within the six classes, all of whom participate in the causes and effects of karma and the afflictions. He did so by assuming life forms suited to [their needs], adopting suitable languages, and donning appropriate ornaments and attire. He gave teachings appropriate to their contexts; he sought material goods beneficial to them; he promoted the paths suited to their fortunate karma and raised them to ever higher elevations.

Here in the Land of the Snows as well, he assumed successive lives as kings, ministers, and bodhisattvas, thereby leading all [beings] to an abundance of teachings and material wealth. With the knowledge that they are receptive vessels for the ambrosia of the uncontaminated teachings, he led [them] to it. [Looking] into the future, [he had seen that] the people of the Land of Snows will be greedy and expect immediate results. Failing to submit to one another, they will be of a brute nature. Some, in their love of the powerful, will set themselves apart at the top; while some, because of their excessive laziness and procrastination, will segregate themselves at the bottom. Most of the spiritual practitioners will fail to adopt restraint toward the causes and effects of subtle nonvirtuous karma, and proclaiming, "We are pure because karma does not exist," they will defy the subtle norms of karma. Some will defy them knowingly, while some will fail to practice them due to ignorance. Some, while carrying a few words of the Mahayana [scriptures] in their mouths, will denigrate the practice of the profound virtuous deeds at all three stages—at the start, in the middle, and at the end. Some will have the desire to practice Dharma, but remain doomed because they will not know how. A few will take teachings with the wish to understand Dharma, but their masters will lack the capacity [to teach them properly]. Some will fail to find masters who can teach on the basis of combining exposition with [actual] practice. Seeing these numerous instances of decline with respect to comprehensive Dharma practice, [Dromtönpa] took birth in the nomad lands of the north.

The reasons for his assuming the form of a master from the nomads are: (1) his compassion for the unlearned nomads who take life for the sake of food; (2) his compassion for those numerous householders who could not undertake Dharma practice on the basis of the monastic way of life; (3) his wish to help prevent the disparagement of the spiritual practices of nonmonastics, which he feared might arise following his [death] as a result of excessive attachment to monastic life; and, (4) moreover, the need to help vanquish, through compassionate means, the many hostile forces—both humans and nonhumans—who injure the Buddha's teaching; [27] (5) furthermore, the need to help draw others to the daylong precepts and the vows of lay persons by indicating that even someone like Dromtönpa was an upāsaka [lay vow holder] and that these lay precepts are easier to observe and are also a source of great benefit, and then gradually to lead them [on the path]; (6) the need to help expand and perfect the relics and representations of the Three Jewels, even if this were to lead him to take birth in the hells; and (7) on the basis of this, to help ensure the happiness and joy of all beings while developing their faith and respect. Even though he himself had already eradicated all the factors to be relinquished, he assumed the form of a lay upāsaka, thus keeping a low profile.

He had modest desires and was easily contented; he was thoroughly peaceful and disciplined, and possessed a sense of shame and conscience. Skilled in the methods, he had entered the door of Dharma. He was, therefore, outside the ranks of all ordinary householders. In fact, he was taken by them as an object for accumulating merit and as an object of veneration. Because it was easy for them to honor him, he was invited to even the smallest of [feast] offerings. Thus he led [many householders] to the ranks of the fortunate ones [possessing] the daylong precepts and the vows of an upāsaka. Even if there were twenty sponsors at one given time, he did not remain confined to one alone, but would present himself to all of them, even though this was not evident to the others. In this way, he would interact with benefactors equal to the farthest reaches of the sky.

Again, because he did not adopt the saffron robes [of a monk], he would proclaim that he was an upāsaka and would honor with his crown those endowed with ethical discipline. He would honor them by placing on his crown even a patch of cloth from their robes. Even when there was a very young novice monk, he would say "O you monastics, please come first" and would assert that he himself was outside the ranks of the monastic community. Nevertheless, because he himself implemented all [the aspects of] the law of karma and its effects, there was no one whom he advised that would not listen [to his words] and say, "This is true indeed." Furthermore, even if one were to put the entire wealth of Tibet together in one place, this would not rival the wealth given in a day by the great upāsaka to the poor and destitute in China, Nepal, Kashmir, and Tibet. This [fact] is not known by those are fettered [in bondage].

Although in general he performed numerous acts, such as leading [sentient beings] to the six perfections and giving helpful affirmations with regard to their conduct, in particular, he led them to the precious ethical discipline—the basis of numerous higher qualities—and gave high praises [when others gave] verbal affirmations for such wholesome conduct. [28] As for [the story of] how many emanations appeared from him and how they fulfilled the well-being of sentient beings, these will be known later [in the text].[125] In addition, there were diverse enlightened intentions related to his ocean-like wisdom mind that are not presented here, for they are beyond the scope of explanation.

So when the great refuge [Atiśa] was residing amid such an unimaginably perfect setting as described above, the following occurred to [Dromtönpa]:

"At this moment, when the omniscient one is alive, I can cut the [rope of my] doubts pertaining to good and evil. Due to the force of [the negative karma of] his potential spiritual trainees, the conqueror could depart to other realms. Should this happen, it will be difficult for me to request [the teachings]. These days, because of the degenerate nature of the era and because sentient beings have untamed temperaments, even if one reveals to them the profound instructions, they do not practice. They may [in fact] accumulate nonvirtuous karma in relation to the spiritual teachers. So at this time, I would like to request a teaching that most paragons of virtue who will appear after me can rely upon. Today in particular, many celestial youths in the clouds are adorned with various ornaments and carry unimaginable quantities of offerings. Some hoist parasols and victory banners, some raise inconceivable precious banners, and some carry various articles, such as celestial incense, lamps, and so on. Some hold unimaginable collections of musical instruments, like flutes, violins, and so on, [resounding] with melodious tunes. With their bodies half submerged in the clouds, they shower down untold flowers from the skies. With their upper bodies bowed, they seek the gift and honor of the blessing of the two accumulations for those who have gathered to request the teachings."

With the thought, "The power to grant such gifts and the blessing of the two accumulations lies in the most excellent among the teachers, whose very name is blessed. I request the sublime teachers to proclaim these most blessed names," [Dromtönpa] proclaimed:

"O Dīpaṃkara, most excellent of gods,
Unrivalled by any other,
You are the refuge of all beings.
Compelled by wisdom, pray listen to me.

"Today when you, the conqueror, are alive, [29]
You, the Dharma key of benefit and joy,
Reside here because of the fortunate ones.
If I fail to cut [the rope of] my doubts,
Due to [the negative karma of] the trainees, O Dharma lord,
You might depart to other realms.
It would then be difficult, in this degenerate era, to approach you.
At this time when untamed beings whose natures remain wild
Do not put into practice the teachings revealed to them
And deceive the teachers in return for kindness,
I seek from you a teaching that can withstand our trust.

"*Ema!* I see this spectacle of wonder!
Conquerors and their children have gathered in the skies;
Even those who seek peace and bliss have miraculously arrived.
Inconceivable numbers of pure celestial beings
Emit thousandfold lights of numerous colors
[While residing] amid a dense array of lights and clouds.

"They protect with beautiful parasols from above;
They wave beautiful banners from the sides;
They hoist a Meru-like[126] victory banner at the center;
They burn incense made from tens of thousands of medicinal herbs.
The sounds of drums resound vigorously;
When beaten high in the skies the earth shakes [below].
The sounds of thousand-stringed violins,

Which play thousandfold notes,
Resound as words that are virtuous throughout all three times.

"*Ema!* Such a heavenly [image] grips my mind!
The melodies of flutes dispel my sorrow
And evoke the impermanence of sense objects, which I held as enduring.
I generate disenchantment toward what I had held as a source of bliss.
O emanation Dharma king, such a heavenly realm is victorious.

"*Ema!* Such are the fruits of forbearance—
Pristine as conch shells and pure as turquoise,
Like golden seats and emerald stones,
They are clear as red rubies.

"Youthful, soft-skinned, and strong, with no observable veins,
Their waists thin, they are supple and thoroughly agile.
Resplendent and free from illness,
They enjoy the glory of longevity and a wealth of resources.
Like the sun and moon they have arrived in the skies.
May such auspiciousness shower down upon all.

"As I offer this array of offering clouds,
May I enter the path without obstruction
Through the joys of such a heavenly realm.
O teachers endowed with insight, pray attend.

"To enhance the two divine accumulations,
Proclaim all the names that are excellent—
The excellent names that are blessed
And resemble a precious crown jewel:
Avadhūti[127] and Serlingpa,
Śāntipa[128] and Rakṣita,[129]
Jetāri[130] and so on.

"May Sunamānśrī[131] and Ratnacandra,
Suvarṇabhadra and Aśokottama,
Dharmakīrti and Abhijñānarāja,
Vaidurya and the king of the Śākyas[132]—

Who is the fearless teacher—
Always remain inseparable and reside upon my crown.

"I appeal also to the conquerors of the ten directions
And to the bodhisattvas such as the [eight] dear sons,[133]
Pray reside to enhance the conditions of the Dharma. [30]
Even those of you who have vowed to enter peace and bliss,
Having reached your own secure grounds,
Strengthen your forbearance,
And, like me, abide in compassion for a long time
In order to repay the debts owed to your parents.

"Supreme heroes who guard the Sugata's teachings,
Compassionate ones in terrifying guises,
Aflame and wielding weapons, you adopt fearful postures—
Yakṣas, smell-eaters, kumbhāṇḍas, and so on;
In frightening demeanor you shout aloud *huṃ*.
Without violating your oaths,
Pray sustain the [Buddha's] doctrine with compassion.

"For as long as you dwell within this cyclic existence,
Like me, do not be disheartened but wear flames as your attire.
Burn to ashes the firewood of the five poisons[134]
And cast them to the winds of the five wisdoms.[135]
Dissolve them into the space of enlightenment.

"Through whatever manifestations there are of the three buddha bodies,
Through the truth of things' ultimate mode of being,
And through the power of the gathering of indivisible [forces],
May my teaching flourish [like] an ocean."

This concludes the first cluster [of teachings]—namely, the appeal.

The Response

The most excellent treasury of all goodness,
The precious one who is the source of glory,

His eminence, the undefeated teacher,
Extending far his [noble] tongue,
Declared to his principal son:

"O sole friend of all, listen to me.
Your speech is free of error—
The assembly of gods is enveloped in light.
Proclaiming melodies of immeasurable joy,
They carry vast clouds of offerings.
Amid the clouds they all reside
With pure thoughts filled with reverence.

"As for the incalculable sugatas present,
Their eldest son is Avalokiteśvara.
Through the proliferation of countless perfections,
Today we enjoy the first auspiciousness.

"As hosts of goodness exponentially increase,
We enjoy today the first good fortune.
Today an immeasurable assembly of gods is present.
As gods and humans propitiate them,
We enjoy today the first good omen.

"O Avalokiteśvara, eldest among the sons,
You have come here together with the gods.
You have extracted the essence of nectar.
Now, just as it has been stated
Of the gods, nāgas, smell-eaters,
Yakṣas, humans, and kīnāras,[136]
And also countless others respectfully present here,
He who, in order to promote the two accumulations for all [beings],
Proclaims the teachers' [sacred] names, which confers
The beneficial teachings, the doctrine's essence— [31]
His defilements will come to an end.
So propagate wide the teachers' names.

"My mindstream is enriched by the teachings.
All these teachings possess scriptural authority.

How the transmission of these scriptures flow
I shall reveal to the intelligent, both directly and indirectly.
Merely hearing it will bring satisfaction.

"I have said this in response to your plea.
Now I shall reveal the actual names."

This concludes the response.

CHAPTER I

Making Prostrations
to the Distinguished Objects of Veneration

"*Guru sarva nāmaḥ*.[137]
I prostrate to the six kind teachers
Who thoroughly protect all beings—
Mañjuśrī and Buddhajñāna,
The teacher Dīpaṃkarabhadra and Yigepa,
Karṇapa and the abbot Śrījñāna,
[All of] whom conferred upon me [the teachings of] the Common Vehicle.

"Immutable Akṣobhya, lord Amitābha,
Ratnasaṃbhāva, the blessed Amoghasiddhi,
And the great Vairocana, chief among all conquerors—
I prostrate to the peerless vajra-holders,
The unexcelled five buddha families, who have initiated me
Into all the secret mantras in order to plant the seeds of goodness.

"I prostrate to the eight most kind teachers
Who granted me all the secret mantras—
To Nāgārjuna, the lord of beings, and Āryadeva,
To Maticāla and Tilopa, the yogi,
To Catipāla and Mañjuśrībhadra,
To Bodhibhadra and the teacher Śāntipa.

"I prostrate to the five most kind teachers
Who conferred upon me all the secret mantras—
To Buddhajñāna and Gūhyapa,
To Śānta, Kusalī, and Kusalī.[138]

"I prostrate to the ten who granted me the Guhyasamāja
    [teachings]—
To Indrabhūti, Nāgī, and Yoginī,
To Saraha and Nāgārjunagarbha,
To Candrakīrti, Virya, and Maitrīpa,

To Copipa and Lalitavajra,
To Sagep and the peerless Śāntipa.

"I prostrate to the five most kind gurus
Who conferred upon me the Guhyasamāja [teachings]—
To Nāgārjuna, Candrakīrti, and Vidyākaukila,
To peerless Kusalī and Kusalī.

"I prostrate to the eleven who gave me Guhyasamāja [teachings]—
To Buddhajñānapāda and Padmapa,
To the Dharma king Indrabhūti and the lady Lakṣmī,
To Chiwoikyé and Mañjuśrīmitra,
To Buddhajñāna and Kampala,
To Lalitavajra and Sagep,
And to the unrivaled teacher Śāntipa.

"I prostrate to the four most kind teachers
Who granted me all the mother tantras—
To Lohidhakipa and Dharika,
And to my root guru, the brahman Jetāri. [32]

"I prostrate to the two most kind gurus
Who granted me the instructions of Yamāntaka—
To Kamalarakṣita, the supreme among scholars,
And to Kṛṣṇapa, the one who carries the glory of greatness.

"I prostrate to the five who granted me
The instructions of kriya yoga—
To Buddhajñāna and Buddhaśānta,
To Buddhaguhya and Kusulu,
And to the one known as Kusulu [junior].

"I prostrate to the five gurus of the view—
To Nāgārjuna, Candrakīrti, and Vidyākaukila,
And to the Guru Avadhūti brothers.

"I prostrate to those immersed perfectly in the vast practices—
To Maitreya, Asaṅga, Vasubhandu, and Vimuktisena,

To Bhadanta Vimuktisena and the bodhisattva Chogkyi Dé,
To the bodhisattva Vinitasena and to Yakṣaśrī,
To Haribhadra, Ratnabhadra, and Ratnasena,
And to my root guru, the peerless Serlingpa.

"I prostrate to the six most kind gurus
Who granted me the vast practices—
To Mañjuśrī and Akṣayamati,
To Eladhari and Viravajra,
To the bodhisattva Ratnaśrī,
And to my root guru, the lord Serlingpa.

"The eighteen gurus are the chief refuges of the world;
O precious gurus of the [lineage of] vast practices,
Sustain us—myself and my followers—
And keep us united until [we attain] enlightenment.

"I prostrate to the eight kind gurus
Who granted the tantras and the perfection of wisdom—
To guru Nāgārjuna and Āryadeva,
To Candrakīrti and the yogi Tilopa,
To Vidyākaukila and Jñānabodhi,
And to Mañjuśrībhadra and Ratnākaraśānti.

"I prostrate to the eight kind gurus
Who granted the tantras and the perfection of wisdom—
To Nāgārjuna himself and the bodhisattva Āryadeva,
To Matricitra and the yogi Tilopa,[139]
To Catipāla and Mañjuśrībhadra,
And to Bodhibhadra and the teacher Śāntipa.

"I prostrate to the great siddha Mañjuśrībhadra
And to the siddha Śāntipa who out of a kind heart
Grants whatever teachings are most suited
[To the needs of beings] throughout all time.

"I prostrate to the nine great siddhas—
To the preceptor Vajrapāṇi and Padmapa,

To the king Indrabhūti and the lady Lakṣmī,
To Jñānabodhi and Mañjuśrībhadra,
And to my root guru, the peerless Śāntipa.

"I prostrate to the four gurus of the inspirational blessing [lineage]—
To the most compassionate sugata Vajradhara,
To the most holy Tilopa and Nāropa,
And to guru Ḍombhīpa, who possesses the highest blessings. [33]

"I prostrate to the six gurus of the inspirational blessing [lineage]—
To the great scholar and adept Buddhapālita,
To Buddhajñāna and Buddhaśānta,
To Buddhaguhya and the peerless Kusalī,
And to my root guru, Kusalī, the most kind.

"I prostrate to the seven most kind gurus
Who grant the generation of the mind of supreme awakening—
To Maitreya, Asaṅga, Vasubandhu, and Sthiramati,
To the two Kusalīs and the teacher Serlingpa.

"I prostrate to the two heroic gurus
Who grant the uncommon method of mind generation—
To the mahāsiddha yogi, great embodiment of loving-kindness,[140]
And to the one called Rakṣita, who gives away even his own flesh.

"I prostrate to the nine learned among the learned ones,
Who are versed in all philosophical systems—
To Mañjuśrī and Avadhūtipa,
To Dīpaṃkarabhadra and Śākyamitra,
To Riwo Sangpo and Sönyom Shap,
To Kakola and Sagep Shap,
To the great scholar Ratnakāra,
And to the sublime teacher Śāntipa.

"I prostrate to the five precious benefactors
Who grant the treasury of essential instructions—
Nāgārjuna and Nāgābodhi,
Catipa and the teacher Śāntipa.[141]

"I prostrate to the five kind teachers
Who grant the uncommon pith instructions—
To Nāgārjuna, Candrakīrti, and Vidyākaukila,
To the teachers Avadhūti and Serlingpa.

"I prostrate to the six treasuries of instructions—
To Nāgārjuna himself and Āryadeva,
To Candrakīrti and the yogi Tilopa,
To Matisthira[142] and Jñānabodhi.

"I prostrate to the teachers who uphold the hidden conduct
And reside in the invisible expanse:

"To help lead all who have excellently gathered there—
The fortunate ones, gods, humans, and demigods—
You reveal, as if in repetition, the lineage
Of this single river, dividing it into two or three streams.
In the past, throughout all your lives,
You taught the Dharma in person.
Today you appear in space and confer the teachings.
Some of you reveal [the teachings] through emanations.
I prostrate to you, O teachers who choose anonymity
And reside in the expanse of imperceptibility.
O excellent assembly of one hundred and fifty [teachers],
Bless us without interruption.

"As I proclaim the teachings and the excellent names
Of countless scholars and adepts
Who are inseparable from the sugatas,
I, too, am revealed to have an excellent origin.

"Through this may all the beings gathered here [34]
Pass through the presence of the holy teachers
From this instant throughout all their lives
And enhance their two excellent accumulations.
May they attain the ultimate dharmakāya of great bliss
That is within the sphere of the Buddha's form body."

Drom Jé then exclaimed:
"Excellent! O most kind supreme teacher.
Excellent! I have heard the wonderful and noble names.
I have ascertained the wonderful merits of cultivating them.
If summarized well it is thus:

Homage to the gurus!

"Apart from this there is nothing else."

This concludes the first chapter from the *Jewel Garland of Dialogues*, "Making Prostrations to the Distinguished Objects of Veneration."

CHAPTER 2
How Instructions on the Four Divinities Were Conferred

[35] *Deva dharma sarva sapta nāmaḥ.*

[Drom:] "From the clouds of the Sugata's great compassion,
Born from my meritorious collections
Is the peerless Atiśa, the supreme jewel,
The source of all wishes.

"Impelled by the power of your great compassion,
Listen to these resounding words of respect:

"In this degenerate age obstacles are plentiful;
Scarce are the meditation deities who grant higher attainments;
Rarer still are those who receive the higher attainments;
So I request an excellent meditation deity."

The precious jewel [Atiśa] said:
"Listen, you who seek [the fulfillment of] all wishes.
They are Śākyamuni and the inseparable Lokiteśvara,
The protector Acala and Tārā[143]—
Golden, white as a snow or a conch,
Smoky blue, and green—their colors are beautiful.

"Make the *āḥ* at their throats red.
You are the five buddha families and they are you;
You are [also] the five pristine cognitions,
And the five pristine cognitions are you.

"Also the three syllables[144] are you
And you, the three [syllables].
The six syllables[145] are you,
And you are the six syllables as well."

Avalokiteśvara, the source of all wishes,
Victorious excellent Gyalwai Jungné,[146]
Chief among disciples, spoke:

"O supreme jewel, source of all wishes,
King of all wish-granting [jewels], listen to me.
It is great indeed that you have spoken thus.
[Yes] my meditation deities are these four [alone].
Definitely reveal them to me."

The jewel proclaimed:
"The hosts of excellent deities are incalculable;
The teachings of secret mantra are inconceivable, too;
The outer teachings are numerous as well;
Yet [your deities] are the ones with whom you have
    a karmic connection,
So make your choice well today."

The chief among the sons then made an appeal:
"There are no deities who do not protect from suffering;
It is difficult to cross the ocean of cyclic existence
And difficult to endure sufferings as well.

"Since all, including my parents, must be saved,
In order to seek a lasting secure ground,
There is nothing superior to the Three Jewels;
Therefore, I will [seek refuge] in the Three Jewels.

"Because the noble ones, the excellent field, practiced Dharma,
The result, buddhahood of the three bodies, will come about. [36]
The fruit of hardship is the [status of] a conqueror.
Excellent and supreme indeed is the ultimate refuge.

"There is no teacher like the Buddha;
There is no refuge like the Dharma;
There is no fertile field like the Sangha;
So I shall take them as [my] refuge.

"Beneficial in the immediate, they grant happiness in the long run;
Bearing no ill temper, they are pleased when honored;
If you have faith, actualization [of the Three Jewels] is near;
With no procrastination, they always protect.

"[Today] I have done well to find the Three Jewels.
I will nurture the three brothers.[147]
O followers, if you propitiate the Three Jewels regularly,
You will never be deceived; so cut [the thread of] your doubts.

"Of the three, the Buddha is most supreme.
From among the buddhas in this era
There are not more than one thousand conquerors.
Of the thousand [buddhas] it is the king of the Śākyas alone
Who is present in this unruly world.

"I shall make him my sole deity;
I entrust you, O great Sage,[148] with what is good and bad;
You alone are the ultimate refuge."

The master Atiśa said, "This is wonderful;
Make your mental pledge to him firm.
Well done, O most holy Avalokiteśvara!
You, Gyalwai Jungné, are indeed wise in your choice."

Furthermore the son instructed thus:
"The dharmakāya of the blessed ones of all the three times,
[Avalokiteśvara] is the eye of all innumerable sentient beings—
The deity who, like space, pervades [everywhere].
Assuming the ten [bodhisattva] levels, he sustains sentient beings;
His great compassion has no equal;
In particular, he is the deity of Tibet's special destiny.

"*Ema!* Even from the mouth of a five-year-old child
The profound mantra of six syllables issues forth.
Even many who lack complete faculties do not say
'This is beyond me,' but send forth this mantra
And meditate upon it. He is great compassion, indeed.

Highly beneficial, [Avalokiteśvara] liberates one from the ocean of
existence;
Definitely, he is the deity of Tibet's special destiny.

"The six syllables are the six perfections;
Oṃ is *a*, which is the suchness [of things];
This is the unborn perfection of wisdom.
Ma is the word crowning the countless beings,
Who have [all] been our mothers,
Single-pointedly with compassion.
They are endowed also with the four [factors] of perfection.[149]

"The specific sufferings of the six classes of beings
Will also be dispelled by this six-syllable [mantra].
This medicine that relieves all pains is excellent indeed.
I shall also make [Avalokiteśvara] my sole meditation deity.

"You who possess the mind knowing all good and evil—
O Avalokiteśvara, one endowed with untainted cognition,
You, too, are the ultimate of all refuges.
Unrivaled one, have compassion on us!
King of gods, pray listen to me!

"Goddess unsullied by faults
And born from higher qualities alone, [37]
Maiden who is the pristine cognition of the blissful ones,
Savior from the eight dangers who is most needed—
[Tārā] is the deity of our teacher and also the deity venerated
by us disciples.
Thus, I place her upon the crown of my head.

"She is the refuge for all times.
From now on I will seek her never to be separate;
I will make her my sole meditation deity.
Come what may, she is [still] my teacher's deity,
So she can serve also as the deity of his students.
O king of powerful gods, pray listen to me.

"I have seen that, despite regular propitiations,
Some [deities] rob [the person's] breath at the point of death.
Such evil deities are even worse than the demons;
Terminate their propitiation for they deserve to be clubbed.

"In the future, they drag you to the lower realms;
For a single error in your propitiation rite, they destroy you.
So as for Dorlek,[150] Pekar, and so on,
There is no need for such pointless ghostly spirits.

"He who constantly grants higher attainments,
Who has arisen from the bodies of the blissful ones,
Acala, the lord who does not waver in the face of anything[151]—
He is my meditation deity and Dharma protector.

"I request him to accomplish all enlightened activities.
Waver not until the skies become no more
And guard me and the [Buddha's] teachings.
If, despite relying on someone like you, I am led astray,
I fear that even the skies will be deluged with floods.

"*Ema!* I shall make you my sole meditation deity.
These [then] are the four divinities of Drom.
Most excellently, they were given by Atiśa.
Their streams of blessings remain ever present.

"Their compassion's paternal inheritance is indeed powerful;
They are endowed with unobstructed miraculous power and superior
    vision;
They help propagate limitlessly the flowers of the circles [of my
    disciples];
Indeed these four divinities are urgently needed.

"They alone are the outer deities;
They alone are the inner deities;
These four are also the secret deities;
And they are the deities of suchness as well.

"Those who rely on them constantly
Will spontaneously accomplish all goodness."

The jewel declared:
"O eldest among my sons, listen to me.
The [number of] buddhas is incalculable.
Within his children, too, there are the peaceful and the wrathful.
Among them, there are said to be numerous [forms]:
There are the gods and the goddesses;
There are the wrathful males and females;
And there are the heroes and the heroines and so forth.
Will not these four divinities be a little too few?"

The eldest son then appealed:
"O all-knowing sole lord,
Listen to the words of this plea again.

"Though there exist incalculable [buddhas], such as Vairocana,
There are no distinctions among the conquerors;
This indivisibility is, in actuality, the Sage, ·
Who is the precious buddha body encompassing all buddhas.
Adorning my crown beautifully,
May he be seated at the center of my heart.
From him I will receive even the secret mantras.
What need is there to speak of other profound teachings? [38]

"Though there exist incalculable [bodhisattvas], such as the
    eight sons,
There are none outside of the two classes, the peaceful and
    the wrathful.
Though there exist incalculable hosts of great compassion
Who are peaceful and whose great compassion is matchless,
In actuality, they are all Avalokiteśvara.

"*Ema!* He is the father of all conquerors
And the father of all conqueror's children;
He is even the celestial palaces
Of all conquerors and their children as well.

"Even within a single pore [of his body]
Incalculable perfect buddha realms flourish.
Who comprehends the reality of this oneness?
If examined well, however, it appears to be like this:
All the buddhas [endowed with] four buddha bodies
And the [entire] hosts of heroes and heroines—
This alone is the sacred mandala of all.
By relying on this alone, one is saved by all.
The gathering of peaceful deities lies beyond expression.

"Protector Acala, the blessed lord of wrathful deities
Is the celestial palace of the wrathful deities,
Such as the ten ferocious ones, and the heroes, too.
Rely on the assembly of heroes and display wrath.

"This powerful, fierce, compassionate one,
Adorning my crown excellently—
May he again adorn the center of my heart.
From him I will receive even the secret mantra teachings.
What need is there to say of the ocean of other teachings?

"Supreme Tārā defies imagination.
She is the embodiment of all:
The wrathful maidens, the heroines—
The host of peaceful goddesses.
As the supreme celestial palace of all,
Tārā is, indeed, the supreme identity of all.

"*Ema!* If one relies upon this goddess,
What goddess is left who is not contained [in her]?
She is the sole mandala of all [goddesses].
O goddess, to save those who are [within] your sphere,
Be seated upon my crown like a crowning jewel.
Come again as an adornment to my heart.
I will receive from you the immeasurable profound [teachings],
The secret, knowledge, and incantation mantras.
What need is there to say of other [sources of] benefit and joy?

"Thus, may these four perfect and excellent deities,
Who defy the bounds of imagination,
Transform us through their uncommon blessings
For as long as sentient beings remain.

"When I and those who follow in my footsteps
Bow at your feet and make supplications,
At that time, without forgetting,
Bless us with most timely instructions."

Upon being instructed regarding the four divinities,
The soft golden lords of the five buddha lineages,
Emerging from a rainbow tent of soft golden light,
Said to the children on the ten [bodhisattva] levels:

"It is in this manner that the conquerors of all the three times
And the ten directions share the nature of the five buddha lineages.
They are also the king of Śākyas,
Whose skin is like gold.
O Drom, as you are the inner palace of great compassion,
Reveal here your countless manifestations." [39]

Drom Jé's heart opened up,
As if the skies were replete with the five buddha families—
The actuality of our Sage—
And the sky in Drom's heart became filled with the conquerors.
"This is the mandala of the conquerors," he said.

Atiśa said "O most excellent son,
You have made no error in your choice, excellent son.
Such are the fields of the conquerors.
These are the merits of a choice well made.
Certainly this will bring about the welfare of beings.

"From amid a tent of gentle white clouds,
The bodhisattvas shine resplendently like the moon.
Though the children of conquerors are numerous,

None ever deviates from
The [bounds of] great compassion.
So illuminate here your palace within,
Which has no parallel [anywhere]."

Then Drom Jé replied "Okay."
Opening the door of his heart lotus,
He revealed Avalokiteśavara's [pure] realm.

"From amid a tent of green clouds
Hosts of green goddesses [emerge].
Lord Avalokiteśvara, pray listen.
Though incalculable female bodhisattvas exist,
All are embodied in those assembled here.
In turn, they are, in their nature, Tārā,
Just as is the mandala [present] within your heart."

Responding, "Okay," Drom Jé opened
The door of his heart lotus fully
And revealed Tārā's immeasurable realm.

"Amid a tent of gentle smoky blue clouds
Are numerous wrathful deities sharing the same blue hue;
Dancing with legs outstretched or bent, they terrorize Māra's army;
Dancing with smiles and affection, they sing hymns to you, Drom Jé.
Listen, O eldest son!
Though there are incalculable wrathful and heroic deities,
They are all Acala, who has been revealed.
He will guard your teachings and clear away the obstructions,
Just as it is illuminated
In the immeasurable realms [within you]."

Saying, "Okay," Drom Jé laid bare
The doors of his heart and revealed
The wrathful deities' immeasurable realms.

Thus, as [Drom] conferred well the instructions
Of the four inconceivable divinities,

Glorious Dīpaṃkāra was utterly delighted
And exclaimed, "Avalokiteśvara is the embodiment
Of all conquerors and their children!
All the incalculable divinities
Whom we have witnessed here today,
The embodiment of all these is the four divinities.
So let us make four icons.
I shall sculpt and consecrate them as well."

This is the collection on conferring instructions on the four divinities and on
the experience of their visions.

[40] To fulfill the words of his teacher,
The eldest son Drom Jé
Gathered the materials to accumulate merit
In the plains of Yerpa Churi
And ventured forth to create icons of the four divinities.

Atiśa then said:
"Do not create clay sculptures, but draw them,
For if they are too large they will be difficult to maintain."
Protesting, "Do not say such things,"
[Drom] procured excellent materials of varied precious metals
And, preparing clay the size of a small mountain,
Told the master how much clay there was and appealed to him:
"Please construct [the icons] for the benefit of beings."

Then the savior Atiśa sculpted
Sixteen statues resembling himself
And adorned them with various ornaments.
Ordained vajra-holder monks
Gracefully encircled the mound of leftover clay,
While numerous girls in blue and green [attire]
Poured sandalwood water and kneaded the clay.

Before long, icons of the four deities were sculpted
Measuring the height of Maitreya's body.[152]
Immeasurable lights appeared in a dense array,
And [the icons] were enveloped within a tent of five rainbow colors.

Holding various gifts,
Numerous offering goddesses honored them.
Furthermore, incalculable bodhisattvas proclaimed auspiciousness
While assuming the forms of knowledge holders.
The fierce ones with wrathful forms, including Acala,
Were seen expelling the interfering forces.

Our teacher, the [learned] paṇḍita,
Remained resplendent as the great Sage.
In a gradual sequence, the sixteen [replica icons]
Consecrated each of the four statues.

[Seeing] this, the excellent son was amazed.
For an instant he was filled with pure vision.
As he rose from this meditative absorption,
The images of the deities [that Atiśa] built were invisible;
Only the teacher remained seated.
Thinking "amazing!" [Drom] said:

"Our sole undeceiving refuge,
Where has the perfect [assembly] gone?
What happened to the multitude of perfect [divinities]?
They are now only a trace of the mind.
Amazing! This is like a dream—
The instant it is perceived it is no more."

The master then said:
"Since all phenomena are like a dream,
How can the deities born from your labors be real?
They are appearances of the mere gathering of dependent arisings.
If they become empty the instant they are perceived,
How can your divinities be real?

"Since things are dependently originated and transient,
How can [the effects of] your actions be permanent?
I am an ordained monk who is a [mere] apparition,
So how can my conjurations be real,
Based, as they are, upon phenomena that are [themselves] empty?

The divinities created by such an unreal artist—
These falsities of falseness are unsuited to be the divinities." [41]

Drom Jé then appealed:
"How can you utter such grave words?
This is not the context in which to speak of truth and falsity.
I request the divinities that were well constructed.
That they are unreal and formless is absurd.
How can one bear such utterances?
Do not turn this into a sham today."

To this Atiśa responded:
"Your four divinities have gone to Tuṣita.¹⁵³
Those who seek the legacy of good deeds desire fame.
Yearn not for them but remain free of such desire.
Go forth to consecrate this assembly [worthy of] veneration."

Drom Jé then exclaimed:
"Today I have heard sacred words impossible [to believe]!
This makes Tuṣita seem more impoverished than the human world.
Failing to create them for themselves, they have stolen away [our
    icons]—
The four divinities created by [us] humans!
If they have taken away what was not given,
How can [the gods of] Tuṣita be good?"

With a smile upon his face, Atiśa replied:
"Tuṣita is not bereft of divinities;
Nor do they have intentions to steal.
Because the beings of this degenerate era
Would fail to care for the icons with honor,
They have left at Maitreya's invitation."

Drom Jé then spoke:
"Like an ultimatum, your words are harsh.
Saying that future trainees will not care for them,
You say that my meditation deities were led upward.

"Have not the imperfect trainees
Looked after the Sage's teachings?[154]
Ema! Atiśa, I request the divinities from you.
Tuṣita is not bereft of deities.
[Moreover] all the trainees with great devotion
Are circumambulating [us] while exclaiming,
'These are divinities constructed by precious Atiśa and his son.'

"Though the offerings may not be present at all times,
How can the sacred icons suffer from poverty?
Instead, the devout who have gathered here
Shall pay homage and make offerings to the best of their ability.

"If at some point [the icons] become worn or torn,
How can you blame them for this?
In fact, it is the householders who will be difficult to please.
They offered the materials and might therefore inquire after the gods.
But if [the gods] have departed to Tuṣita,
It certainly would be inappropriate to create a set of lies.
Also, how can someone generate faith in them?
If one is let down by those in whom one places great hope,
One will generate wrong views. They [the devotees] cannot be blamed!
What kind of Tuṣita is it that needs mask-like replicas
While excellent natural divinities abound?"

Atiśa then exclaimed:
"O Drom Jé, do not say such things;
Do not make such statements in response.
Alas! Even though conditioned things are impermanent,
Where does that law [of impermanence] exist? [42]
If the law does so exist,[155] this will split open samsara into nothingness."

Then after the passage of some time,
The four wisdom deities appeared in front [and spoke]:
"O Drom Jé, listen to this tale.
Grasp not at the forms as divinities;
Grasp not at the clay as the material cause.
Instead, until the cycle of existence is emptied,

We will be with you without separation;
In particular we will bless you at present.
At dawn, make your choice among the teachings.
Choose that which is most profitable and free of pitfalls;
At that time we will come into your presence again."

In particular, Tārā proclaimed:
"O Avalokiteśvara, most excellent son,
I will protect your followers.
Take this instruction of mine
And reveal it to those who follow you:

"Recall your teachers, the source of refuge;
See your body in the nature of meditation deities;
With speech, make your mantra recitations constant;
Contemplate all beings as your parents;
Experience the nature of your mind as empty.
On the basis of these five factors,[156]
Make pure all roots of virtue.

"Prior to this, execute this incantation.
Its [number] will increase a million fold, the conquerors have said.
O most excellent son, it is as follows:

Oṃ sambhara sambhara bhima nasara mahā jambhava huṃ phaṭ svāhā.

"O eldest son, listen to this as well.
This [mantra] is to advance one to higher levels;
Dedication is supreme for transformation.
By accumulating supreme virtuous roots throughout the three times
On the supreme path of those who are supreme,
Dedicate [your virtues] toward the supreme aim with
    supreme thoughts.
This is the transforming dedication [practice]
And the supreme buddhahood as well.
If you recognize this as empty, [your virtues] will not go to waste;
So purify all three spheres [of your acts][157] without exception."

Atiśa exclaimed "Well said.
When you, Drom Jé, are born into the Tuṣita realm,
Even the constructed divinities will become manifest."

To this the son responded:
"When your thirst is quenched you need not drink.
Having become a refuge yourself, what need is there for one?
Though this is so, if I in any way
Were to violate your words, it would be wrong;
May only goodness reign now.

"Atiśa, you who reveal the path of goodness,
[From you] I have received four inconceivable divinities;
Now goodness reigns throughout all stages—from beginning to end."

This concludes the collection on the creation of the sacred icons.

Thus [Drom summarized]:

I prostrate to the faith divinities.

"Though you have said much, this alone is [the essence]."

Thus, in [Atiśa's] presence Drom Jé summarized all with this [line of verse].
    "You are a wonder, skilled also in summarizing," [Atiśa concluded].

This concludes the second chapter from the *Jewel Garland of Dialogues,*
"How Instructions on the Four Divinities Were Conferred."

CHAPTER 3
How to Choose the Three Sacred Scriptural Baskets

[43] While their wild, untamed minds were being moistened,
The rain of sublime teachings fell without interruption,
Day and night, from thick clouds of great compassion;
Light rays of virtue struck like bolts of lightning.
When thunders of benefit and joy resounded,
A rainbow tent appeared, manifest yet empty,
From the skies of pure reality's expanse.

When gazed upon, one sees a conqueror in a golden hue;
When listened to, one hears syllables auspicious in [all the] three times;
When touched, one's body turns as white as a conch.

Ema! As he experienced such wonder
The longings of the eldest son increased.
At that point he asked his master:

"I, the son of an excellent father,
Have been blessed by four excellent divinities
And remember the excellent teachings, my ultimate aim.
I've gone round [in samsara] for too long, but my longings [still] increase.

"In the large house of samsara bequeathed by many forefathers—
The source of thousandfold suffering—
Since I serve as a host for numerous travelers on the excellent path,
I request [from you] the immeasurable scriptural baskets.
Precious source of all wishes, pray teach these."

The perfect [teacher] taught thus:
"The Buddha's sacred words are limitless.
In the massive house, vast in both width and depth,
These two truths—the causes and effects of cyclic existence—
Propagate the children of existence of the six classes.
They are the honored guests of the awakening mind," he said.

"To entertain them with food of concentration,
We have the radiance of the scriptures.
The scriptural baskets are the Buddha's sacred words and their
    [commentarial] treatises.
The Buddha's sacred words are numerous; the entry points to the vehicles
    are inconceivable.
The treatises protect one from some [harm] and reveal the path to
    happiness;
They turn you away from the abyss of the lower realms.

"That which presents excellently the profound ethical norms
Of what to adopt and what to discard and transforms you into a
    buddha—
The full perfection of abandonment and realization—that, too, is a
    treatise.
O Jungné, generate the buddha whom you most admire
And bond marvelously with him."

Drom Jé then appealed:
"I request an ultimate teaching
That is closest to perfect buddhahood.
May it also serve the welfare of future generations."

Atiśa then proclaimed: "O Drom Jé, what causes are there for [drawing near] this [perfect buddhahood]? [44] If you wish to approach the attainment of buddhahood, commit yourself to the profound secret mantra. In particular, take the dohās into your mind.[158] There is no [way] to buddhahood shorter than this. They are like crops in autumn at the point of ripeness. They are the practice of the great perfected ones. In particular, if you practice all of these dohās, it is possible [to see even] in a barren terrain excellent yogis performing playful dances with the sound of the beating of *damaru* hand drums.[159] For those of highest faculty, the highest teachings are the most suitable. Your entire way of life should accord with the following [song]." He then sang:

"Son, your crown is adorned with a perfect buddha;
Your heart is the palace of the three vehicles;
Your mind is exceptional for it aspires for others' well-being.

Though you have accomplished your ultimate objective,
It has been taught that attaining the final state for the sake of countless
    mothers
Requires a profound final path that brings one closer to the three
    precious buddha bodies.

"Listen! Secret mantra is the apex of all the vehicles.
In particular the profound teachings of the dohās
Were given to me by Master Saraha.[160]
Son, nurture this in the kernel of your heart.

"The mode of engaging in secret mantra is as follows:
The outer is the palace of incalculable divinities;
The inner is the reality of male and female deities.
Yet this is only the generation stage.

"O vajra holder, supreme Drom Jé.
The profound Dharma of primordial emptiness and spontaneity
Is the completion stage, so practice this.

"Though the outer forms may be multiple,
This is a generation stage to the mind of the trainee.
In the profound truth of primordial emptiness,
The outer, the provisional forms, cannot hold up.
Son, if you desire the ultimate, embrace this to be so.

"When there are people like you, barren landscapes will be filled
With the dances of master knowledge-bearers.
Should such a person drink liquor to quench his thirst, it will turn
    into milk;
Should such a person be assailed by demons, they will appear as
    goddesses.

"If this, too, is probed well, [you'll find that] it is the way of adopting
A mind thoroughly perfected in the expanse of transcendent wisdom.
Master knowledge-bearer, supreme Drom,
Even when such a person eats impulsively, the meals turn
    into concentration;

The channels and awareness, the winds and mind, abide in the central
  channel.
This is the essence drop of an excellent mind.
Put these points into practice, supreme Drom Jé."

The son offered the following in response to the song:
"Master, you who are unsullied by the pollutants,
Stainless lord, pray descend upon my crown."

[Then] in the [inner] mind space, empty and blissful,
The glorious, unrivalled [Atiśa] proclaimed:
"O eldest son, you should choose well
This apex of the summit of all vehicles." [45]

[Drom:] "I have now heard the profound [truth], kind father;
I shall nurture this in my heart, master;
I shall spread this good deed to all, master;
I shall hold firm my mind, free of wavering, master;
I shall nurture its experience in secluded places;
I shall roam free in empty terrains unfailingly, master;
I shall make my environment a celestial palace, master;
I shall generate the inner as pure divinities and their [retinues].

"This is the spiritual lineage given by you, my teacher.
Now it is even easier to become fully enlightened.
It is also easier to swiftly lead the innumerable beings.
In this teaching of the Great Vehicle, [I] Dromtön am victorious.
Now I shall cast to the winds concepts of solid objects with mass.[161]
I shall burn the logs of conceptualizing thoughts into flames.

"My wild untamed mind is [now] moistened.
Having traversed the great land of the Buddha's teaching,
I shall depart to the skies of the Sugata's knowledge.

"*Do!* I shall take to heart the apex of all the vehicles.
Hā! is the clear light of unobstructed consciousness.
Do not cling to any Dharma, but pursue the welfare of others.
Have I understood well, savior Atiśa?
Have I contradicted your words, excellent being, king of speech?"

Savior Atiśa then spoke:

"Listen to me, most excellent son.

Son, your activities and conduct are indeed immeasurable.

I had expected such an excellent response.

Though whatever you do is perfect,

Many sentient beings whose minds remain impure—

Having failed previously to accomplish the cause, the two
   accumulations—

Have failed to experience the taste of the three scriptural baskets,

Despite having encountered the teachings of the Great Vehicle.

"They've discarded at will pure ethical discipline, which is the basis;

They've failed to nurture others through resources without clinging;

They've failed to bear that which is hard to endure;

They've failed to take joy in all noble deeds;

They've failed to engage their minds single-pointedly toward
   enlightenment.

We see some deceived by the [Perfection of] Wisdom Mother.

The children bereft of skillful means have lost power and aspiration;

They lack the wisdom that is the all-knowing subject.[162]

"They fail to secure a safe base but expect immediate results;

When nothing is achieved they create anxieties.

They claim to be Mahayanists,

While belittling the profound [law of] karma and its effects;

They consume whatever reaches their mouth at whatever time—

Meat, alcohol, and garlic—a butcher's diet![163]

"Body—They indulge in sports of jumping, sprinting, and wrestling;

Speech—They converse about the meaningless methods of a butcher's
   trade;

Mind—They have brazenly abandoned any show of shame;

Food—They carry unclean human skulls in their hands;

Clothing—They wrap themselves belligerently with foul dog skins;

Name—They call themselves the 'perfected ones,' a hollow name.

"O eldest son, listen to me.

Proclaiming 'I am from the lineage of tantric adepts,' [46]

Bereft, [some] squander their [semen] drops anywhere.

Failing to practice, they are devoid of the generation and completion
   stages.
Yearning for their own well-being, they leave the root precepts in the words.

"O eldest son, listen to me.
[Lesser Vehicle] disciples may be inferior,
But they embrace the four qualities of a virtuous person.
They do not strike back when struck by others;
They do not unearth others' defects when others lay bare their flaws;
They do not return insults for insults;
They do not show hostility when others are hostile to them.

"If the teachings of the disciples are such,
How could one possibly reject the bodhisattvas, the children [of the
   buddhas]?
Though numerous mental streams of sentient beings are perceived,
None among them has not been your mother.

"Even if bodhisattvas are born within the three lower realms,
Their aim is realized if they can lead mother sentient beings out
   [of cyclic existence].
Such is the conduct of the most holy bodhisattvas,
Who wear the armor of great heroism.

"Eldest son Drom, listen to me.
Those [true] great knowledge-bearers of unexcelled [yoga],
[Claiming] 'Below all this is the Lower Vehicle,'
Say that they are the ultimate knowledge-bearers.

"For them the environment of the entire world
Is the pure celestial mansion [of a mandala];
And the entire world of beings within it
Have the nature of gods and goddesses.

"Whatever they eat and drink is a sacred feast;
A la la! It is the five classes of ambrosia.
The sovereign teacher has the nature of the Buddha,
While all fellow practitioners are vajra friends.

"Whichever knowledge-bearers gather, male or female,
They share the nature of divine heroes and heroines.
They are indivisible within a single wheel of time.
All of this is nothing but a pure vision.

"Now, does someone confused think this to be other than a mandala?
Does he err and fail to view them as male and female divinities?
Does he not recognize his teacher as the Buddha?
Does he commit negative karma in relation to his vajra siblings?
Does he proclaim profound secret mantra in the marketplace?
Does he not generate and perfect the mind but instead dwells
     on the ordinary?
Does he not consecrate his food but instead leaves it as ordinary?
Does he not know how to transform food and [hold] it as inherently real?
Does he let his mind be stirred by the winds of conceptualization?
Does he not equalize attachment and aversion toward good and evil?
[If so,] he is not a tantric adept but someone with soiled commitment.
Should he fall to the lower realms it will be hard for him to get free.

"If he guards the practice well without allowing the pledges to
     degenerate,
Before long, he will become manifestly enlightened.
This is the ultimate teaching and the apex of all the vehicles;
This is extremely profound and difficult to safeguard.

"If lion's milk, a wonderful substance,
Is poured into an inferior ceramic pot,
The instant it is poured, the container will break apart.[164]

"O excellent teacher, you who are skilled.
First one trains in [cultivating] pure perception; [47]
Second one gradually cultivates the generation and completion stages;
Third one becomes a vessel of the secret mantra.
At this point a powerless one becomes empowered.
Such a practitioner is hailed supreme as a Mahayanist.

"Eldest son Drom, listen to me.
If the auspicious conditions have converged—

Of excellent spiritual mentor, excellent colleagues, and time—this is
   secret mantra;
Otherwise it would be like a young child nibbling at an animal carcass.

"Son, this is like a person who is feeble
Yet jumps across a cliff because of his greed.
He may possibly arrive faster,
Yet he risks having his body stripped of life
Should he fall down into the abyss.

"Instead, by taking the road that is gentler,
Your body is relaxed now and you are safer in the long run.
If you practice in one sitting the excellent teachings,
The three precious scriptural baskets,
No danger of the lower realms looms; your long-term destiny remains
   bright.

"The teaching of the Buddha is indeed the sublime Dharma.
Those who practice the Dharma properly are the Sangha.
Since this depends on the scriptural basket of discipline,
O son, rely upon Vinaya discipline, the Buddha's sacred words.

"Though you may nurture the secret mantra,
I fear that in the future the fame of 'profound teachings'
Could deceive those tantrikas who have not reached a secure attainment.
It could become the weight that anchors them to samsaric action.
You should [of course] seek the profound secret mantra in your heart,
But with your speech don't mention secret mantra extensively.
For the service of the glorious Buddha's teaching as a whole,
Son, the teachings of the [three] precious baskets are greater.
In the long run they are the most excellent, supreme Drom."

When he heard these words, the following occurred to Drom: "The manner of the sublime teacher's words suggests that for the attainment of buddhahood this Secret Mantra Great Vehicle is indeed an extremely swift
[path] and an apex of all vehicles. If one can succeed in its practice, there
is nothing faster than this. Ordinary beings, chained by all fetters, who are
plagued with a multiplicity of thoughts and who harbor expectations of

immediate results, fail to secure one level yet crave obtaining the second, the third, [and so on]. Failing to reach their own secure base they follow after others' fame and renown. It is indeed a source of great amazement that, despite having heard many profound teachings, they chase after their desire [for more]. They compete to find out which they can do faster— receive [a teaching] or discard it.

"However, if I put this [teaching] into practice and later take a few suitable vessels, such as the three brothers, to an uninhabited region and engage in meditative practice, [wellsprings of] experience will bubble forth, and clear light awareness will be set ablaze. [48] Though the face of the entire earth may become filled with the dances [of heroes and heroines], what good would this do? It is vital to think of the Buddha's teaching as a whole. For example, for a king to reign over his kingdom, having his thirst quenched, his hunger satisfied, and his happiness intact may [actually] be helpful. Since I have to serve the kingdom of the buddhas of the three times, this effort to cover and hide the secret mantra, as one might veil a naked woman's body, requires serving the Buddha's teaching as a whole.[165] So why would I, an old man resembling the setting sun, having become versed in the scriptural baskets, not engage in a practice that is most profitable and victorious—one that can be touched by anyone and observed by anyone? When coming into contact [with the scriptural baskets], one's mouth becomes well fed; when touched, one's hands become softened. One's gains are mountain-sized, even though the risks are only the size of a head.[166]

"Later [I might decide], 'I will make certain to master the dohās and take some [students] such as the three brothers.' So when people will hear the announcements that there are some excellent beings in an uninhabited region, they will say, 'There are some amazing perfected adepts there; we must go receive teachings.' They might bring some material gifts and come to me. At such time, I could reveal [the dohās] to them on the basis of examining whether they are pure receptacles. Some [false teachers], thinking that the presence of one or two favorable conditions is adequate, might feel amazed and exclaim, 'You have accumulated great merits and have thus come to listen to such [teachings of] the Great Vehicle.' And without examining what kind of vessels they are, might pour the contents into them indiscriminately. Or, later, some might assert that this is the tradition of the teacher Drom, and they might consume the profound secret mantra's permitted food [such as meat and alcohol] while not undertaking the requisite rites. Calling it by the name 'ambrosia,' they might drink alcohol without restraint. Calling it 'skillful means,' they might consume meat with no restraint. When actually consuming [the meat], because they have failed to understand death on the basis of other sentient beings, the great tantric adepts, the so-called vajra-holders, would be slaying with their own hands the parents of bodhisattvas and the divinities of tantric practices. At such times, one risks engaging in [deeds similar to] rites of cattle sacrifice!

"Next, calling it a ritual feast, heedless, many would congregate and dance without restraint. Many so-called perfected ones would fall down drunk. Then, pretending to be a buddha in the flesh, he would be delusional from drinking the ambrosial drink of the buddhas and would fight [with others]. [Such a so-called] buddha would say, 'How can you [Drom] and I, if asked, not be equal? I am the son of such and such teacher; I am the nephew of so and so. Who is there that is more powerful than me in this monastery? Who is there in this region that I have not conferred empowerments upon?' [49] Proclaiming that I foresee him or her to be the root of [virtue for] the benefactors, such a person would give titles of 'lama' and 'master' to some young boy or girl who is not even capable of wiping his or her own nose clean. Say that one or two who are ignorant of the [most basic] ethical norms of affirmation and rejection[167] and are fraught with the numerous afflicted forms of meditation practice call this person a teacher, a buddha, they might feel 'I, too, am so and so.' Such a guide may himself be an excellent meditator, but as for the Buddha's enlightened task, he would have failed to lead even a single sentient being [to liberation].

"Furthermore, some, while claiming to be Mahayanists, assert that you cover no ground by means of the lesser meditation practice of the disciples. They label others who adhere to a disciplined lifestyle, such as the teacher Atiśa—who are pure in their morality, modest in their desires, and easily contented, who are outwardly appealing due to practicing the twelve cultivated qualities in places of utter solitude, who are internally endowed with the awakening mind, and whose mindstreams are enriched by the perfect factors of secret mantra—as [practitioners] of the Lesser Vehicle, [calling them] 'disciples' and so on.

"Others, while discarding for the time being the precious ethical discipline as found in the three scriptural baskets—the ultimate foundation of all higher qualities—pretend to enter the Mantra Great Vehicle. Though failing to succeed in its practice, they claim to be tantric adepts, maintain a household, and clad themselves in saffron robes [as well]. With arrogance they go to [sit at the] head of a row. With no shame they call the fruit of their moral degeneration 'noble sons' and seat them at the head of the rows of fully ordained monks of Śākaymuni's order. Thus we have 'discipline norms,' and it only takes one or two [transgressing such norms] to cause the downfall of many.

"[In general] what greater wonder is there than the Secret Mantra Great Vehicle? If you were to become a great glory and savior of beings as described in the tantras on the basis of the auspicious confluence of good karmic fortune and readiness, nothing would be greater. This would indeed be a great wonder. If, on the contrary, you were to commit many acts that undermined the pledges, then there are mechanisms [in the tantra that would result in] epidemics of numerous illnesses across the land. Rains could fail to fall on time, wars and internal strife could proliferate.[168] With no gain at all people could be swept away by dangers.

"To summarize: The profound secret mantra must be concealed well from those who are unsuitable vessels. Since no [path] is hailed more than this for the attainment of buddhahood, it should be revealed to those who are suitable vessels in secluded places. Engage in the three rites of praising, honoring, and hailing, and create the mandala within. No matter how profound it may be, [this secret mantra] is encompassed by the three scriptural baskets. As it is revealed and taught on the basis of recognizing the afflictions' stream-like continuity as the object to be abandoned, [50] one's mental continuum is transformed into a true Sangha Jewel; and since it actually generates one's mental continuum into a Sangha Jewel, it is [in fact] the generation stage.

"Next recognize all sentient beings as your actual mothers and, through the four immeasurable [thoughts], generate this [recognition of others as mothers] as far as possible. Traversing the grounds and paths in their respective sequence through to extraordinary awakening is also the generation stage. Then, investigating the objects of knowledge in terms of their specific and general characteristics by means of the four great logical reasons, recognize all phenomena without exception—unique particulars and generally characterized [phemonena]—as primordially empty, as uncreated by causes and conditions, and as great emptiness, the ultimate mode of being, which is free of conceptual elaborations. This is the completion stage.

"Again, everything is in the nature of mind, the mind is in the nature of emptiness, and emptiness is in the nature of primordial emptiness, devoid of conceptual elaborations. This is transcendent wisdom. Since this is stated to be the Buddha, no divinity is greater than the Buddha. To attain perfection as the ultimate divinity—the great Buddha—is the completion stage. Alternatively, the recognition of all phenomena as dream-like and illusion-like is the generation stage, while the realization of them as devoid of conceptual elaboration and being within the nature of the ultimate truth is the completion stage.

"To summarize: Is tantra encompassed within the generation and completion stages or not? If so, then they are sufficient and you must practice them. There is no need for a tantra that is not encompassed within the generation and completion stages.

"Furthermore, is tantra encompassed within [the teachings on] morality? If so, then it is [part of] the higher training in morality. Since it is the scriptural basket of Vinaya discipline that presents [the training in] morality, [tantra] does not lie outside of discipline. If, [on the other hand] it is not encompassed in morality, a teaching that lacks such a foundation will not endure for long. Who wants a teaching with no foundation!

"Again, is tantra encompassed in the training in mind [stabilization]?[169] If so, since it is the scriptural basket of the sutras that presents [this higher training], tantra does not lie outside the bounds of the basket of the sutras. If [on the other hand] it is not encompassed, a path that lacks activity, [which resembles] the shallow crossing points [of a river], is difficult to traverse.[170] For if you lack excellent activity, which is the crossing point of the path, you will not arrive at the final destination, the resultant state. Cast aside the teaching that has no training in mind, lacks activity and perfect paths, and is devoid of the fruition in buddhahood.

"Furthermore, is tantra encompassed in the training in wisdom? If it is, in which one of the two—contaminated wisdom or uncontaminated wisdom—is it encompassed? If it is encompassed within both, since it is the [scriptural basket of] higher knowledge that presents them, tantra is thus encompassed in the scriptural basket of higher knowledge. [51] If it is not encompassed within the two wisdoms—the contaminated and the uncontaminated—then cast aside that tantra that is not [part of] wisdom. Whichever of the two wisdoms it may be encompassed within, it remains within the bounds of [the scriptural basket of] higher knowledge.

"Thus, in order to set forth the presentation of the training in morality there is the discipline [basket]; in order to set forth the presentation of the trainings in mind and of wisdom there is, respectively, the sutra [basket] and higher knowledge [basket]. These are known as the *three baskets of scripture*. Whether good or bad, these are the three baskets of [the Buddha's] sacred words. Based on these, the treatises [pertaining to the] three baskets came into being.

"In order to summarize the entire discussion, tomorrow the teacher will give a teaching according to which the entire [path] can be practiced together in a single sitting on the basis of subsuming the mental levels of the persons of three categories. Even the teachings of the Secret Mantra Great Vehicle must be [part of] these three trainings. If it is not so and a secret mantra [teaching] is not encompassed within these three [trainings]—that is to say, it is not within morality, it is not within mind, and it is not within wisdom—it is [then] highly flawed. If the tantras, in their entirety, are condensed, none is apart from the three baskets, nor are there three baskets that are not tantra. O great Atiśa, therefore, the following is my opinion.

"By undertaking the Dharma practice of the Sangha, the fruition of buddhahood comes about. 'Sangha' refers to someone who is endowed with ethical discipline. To observe excellent ethical discipline you must have an excellent knowledge of discipline; to observe a middling level of ethical discipline you must have a middling knowledge of discipline; in fact, even to observe the four root precepts, the knowledge of the four root precepts is indispensable. Therefore, since [the survival of] the Buddha's teaching depends upon the Sangha community, the Sangha community depends upon [the survival of] the sublime teachings of discipline, and [the survival of] Vinaya discipline depends upon the discipline upholders, I shall, out of my concern for the Buddha's teaching, take the sublime teaching of Vinaya discipline as one of my chosen Dharmas.

"All profound features—such as the provisional meaning [versus] the definitive meaning, and the ways the buddhas and their children endured hardships in the past [while on the path]—are found in the sutras. Therefore, I will also take the [basket of] sutras to be one of my chosen Dharmas.

"We are not versed in the concealed truths, nor do we possess unobstructed superknowledge. So to present the world of the knowable realm, it is on the basis of [the basket of] higher knowledge that even ordinary beings can have the knowledge of the size and shape of Mount Meru, the four continents, the trichiliocosm, and so on. Therefore, I will also, while focusing on enlightenment, take the higher knowledge [basket] to be one of my chosen Dharmas. [52]

"Whether we call them the *three baskets of scripture* or the *three trainings*, I will give these three teachings on disciplining [the mind] to the future generation of trainees and will [thereby help create so many] with pure ethical discipline that they will cover the face of the earth. I will enhance their mindstreams with the three scriptural baskets and help to completely fulfill the Buddha's teachings."

As Drom reinforced these thoughts and fervently dwelled on them, the four divinities appeared before him. Atisa also said: "O eldest son, your meditation will be enhanced. Practice again and again, for your choice of teachings is most excellent. Just as you have thought, nothing among the entire secret mantras exists that is not encompassed in these [three baskets]. This class of teachings is highly profitable and carries minimal risk. This class of teachings is skilled in means and great in wisdom. This class of teachings leads to success [on the path]."

After Atisa made these statements, the four divinities proclaimed:

"Most excellent one, you who care for the common purpose,
Discipline teachings produce the highest divinity of the ethically
    disciplined;
Sutra teachings produce the highest divinity of the noble ones;
Knowledge teachings produce the highest divinity of the conquerors.
This is so from the perspective of their principal [functions].
In reality, all three teachings produce supreme conquerors.

"These baskets of knowledge teachings lack nothing.
Through excellent instructions revealing the path of the three trainings
Emerge innumerable trainees with pure mental streams.
Your choice of profound sacred words is unmistaken, O master.[171]
They are secure throughout all three times—beginning, middle, and end.
May all be blessed to possess these three teachings.

"Do not doubt but strive in your meditative practice.
You who traverse the path of the final vehicle,
Do not waver with lingering doubts now but strive in meditative practice.
We [who are in] the thoroughly pure celestial palace
Harbor no excessive doubts but strive in our meditative practice.
O son, after thoroughly discarding doubts,
Choose the profound mantra well, O most excellent one!

"'Secret' is not an indication of the teaching's defect;
Though it is hailed for the attainment of buddhahood,
It is difficult for those ordinary vessels to master it.
In perfect consonance with your vessel, O son,
Seek the mandala of secret mantra within."

Speaking these lines they disappeared into the perfectly clear skies.

Again Atiśa spoke:
"Son, have no excessive doubts but uphold the scriptural baskets;
For your ultimate welfare this alone is the most excellent. [53]
Enlightenment is difficult for those fraught with doubts,
[So] engage in meditative practice with a single-pointed mind.

"In the future, thoroughly discard all doubts;
Cherish dearly the cultivation of the points
[Contained] in the Buddha's vast sacred words.
For the lazy, doubts proliferate;
Their pursuit of the ultimate welfare is undermined.
So contemplate the points well, son.
No matter how profound a teaching is, practice is more important.
Now what is called the precious Kadam is excellent indeed!"

Drom replied:
"You have taught many profound teachings;
Were I to summarize well
The most beneficial instructions you have conferred,
What has been wonderfully stated
By the divinities and you, my teacher,
On how all the teachings are integrated
Into the three scriptural baskets as a single taste, it is thus:

> **Discard all lingering doubts**
> **And strive with dedication in your practice.**

"There is nothing other than this."

This concludes the third chapter from the *Jewel Garland of Dialogues*, "How to Choose the Three Sacred Scriptural Baskets."

Chapter 4
How to Strive by Engaging in Activity

[54] On another occasion, Atiśa and his son were staying at Nyethang Or.
As the great Drom lay sleeping early in the dawn, Atiśa addressed him:

"You who are endowed with sevenfold divinities and teachings! Get up!
This human existence of leisure and opportunity is difficult to find;
Encountering the Buddha's teaching is rarer still;
Things are transient and vanish quickly.
Are they not like the ocean waves?
Instruct your mind with one-pointed focus,
And secure a firm base in your mind through [Dharma] practice.

"Sloth and mental dullness have no use.
Since you have found human life with the teaching of the Three Jewels,
Now is the time to seek the ultimate welfare. Do not be lazy!"

Drom Jé responded:
"O Atiśa, teacher of beings,
Treasury granting abundant joy and happiness,
You are right! Behaving like an ignorant person
And sleeping at [all] times resembles a savage.
The fetter of grasping at transience as permanent is great.
How can anyone disregard your sacred words?
This life is but a mere moment.
Can one really afford sleep, dullness, and laziness?
O teacher, bless my three doors
Completely and throughout all times."

Atiśa then instructed:
"Wash your body with the clean waters of retention mantras;
Cultivate the meditative absorption of nonforgetting retention
    mantras;
Place your mind at ease, free of meditative absorption;
Afterward, engage in acts of loving-kindness and compassion;

Return [to your practice] and meditate again on the ultimate mode of
  being."

In response Drom Jé inquired:
"Has not that person lost his purpose,
Who, having found a human life of leisure and opportunity
So difficult to find, falls prey to sleep and mental dullness?"

Atiśa then replied:
"When midday arrives, the fool
Sets aside his work and succumbs to sloth.
At midnight, unable to see anything,
He tries many times to grope for what he had set down.
Though he feels remorse then,
It is too late. His laziness is to blame.
Likewise, ignorant people,
When they have obtained a precious human life,
Fail to view the forms of happiness and misery.
When, due to their faults, they are born in the lower realms,
They fail to feel remorse. Even if they do, it's too late. [55]
Some are tormented by being burned and baked;
Others are afflicted by hunger, thirst, and deprivation;
Some fall under others' power and are killed or enslaved.
Tremendous suffering befalls them;
[They act like someone] groping in the middle of the night.

"Do you understand this? Drom Jé, reflect on this and
Thoroughly discard sloth, mental dullness, and laziness.
No matter what happens in this [mundane] life,
Do not fall prey to its forces.
Sloth has no respect and its loyalty is short,
While laziness chases away all aspirations."

This constitutes the collection on the presentation of the defects of sloth and laziness.

On another occasion Drom inquired:
"Atiśa, savior of all,

If one wishes to attain enlightenment swiftly,
Who are excellent companions to associate with?
How can one, though striving, secure a firm attainment?"

Atiśa replied:
"He who wears the armor of joyful perseverance
Will swiftly achieve ultimate enlightenment.
But if there is no joyful perseverance, you will not see the fruit.

"If you fail to persevere with great efforts
To achieve the level that is secure long-term,
How can you cross to the ocean's other shore?
So put on the armor of joyful perseverance;
Strive for your long-term welfare.

"On the highway of limitless teachings,
Astride the mount of faith,
If you steer with the stirrups of joyful perseverance,
You will arrive at the secure attainment, the [fulfillment of] the two
    welfares.[172]

"My only son, discard pointless procrastination.
Saying, 'I'll do it today, tomorrow, or the day after,' the task is left;
Eventually your life comes to an end,
So pursue [Dharma practice] this very day.

"Alas, My only son!
Heroes are invulnerable to their enemies;
For those with perseverance, obstacles have no edge.
To grasp the secure attainment for all,
If you do not charge with the armor of joyful perseverance,
The hosts of demons' weapons will be sharp;
Hosts of ills will draw nigh your heart—
Though you may discard many [ills], they will befall you like rain.

"In the excellent mansion of the three baskets of scripture,
He who is adorned with the beautiful attire of ethical discipline,
Satiated with the nourishment of blissful concentration,

And well endowed with the light of wisdom—
He who fosters the higher qualities of joyful perseverance,
Should he endeavor on the paths of liberation,
Will, without obstruction and according to his wishes,
Realize his ultimate aim."

In his teacher's presence, [Drom] summarized:
"Indeed, great joyful perseverance
Is what accomplishes it all—higher status and liberation.
May I cast away the evil friends of sloth and mental dullness [56]
And strive never to fall prey to laziness.

"When you sum it up well it is like this:

> **Thoroughly relinquish sloth, mental dullness, and laziness,**
> **And strive always with joyful perseverance.**

"There is nothing other than this."

This concludes the fourth chapter from the *Jewel Garland of Dialogues*, "How to Strive by Engaging in Activity."

Chapter 5
How to Guard the Doors of the Senses
and Hold Your Mind

[57] On another occasion, when Atiśa was staying in Nyethang, Drom said: "We have been born in cyclic existence in general and, in particular, in this unruly world [of the degenerate era]. We have failed to gain mastery over our minds and are easily tainted by the inauspicious forces of evil friends.[173] To rely on a teacher like you, one needs to sit on a single seat and, throwing away entirely the aspirations of this life, to commit with the intention, 'I will realize my ultimate aim today.' It is a joy that you have come from India. [Today] you, a great paṇḍita, have come before this old upāsaka. Many meditation deities have made prophesies and sustained me, an ordinary person, with their compassion. The teachers have also urged me to come here to this place. So now, my spiritual mentor, even from the point of view of thinking of Khu[174] alone, I have no choice but to seek [the realization of] the ultimate aim today. I request, therefore, the methods to accomplish this aspiration."

Then Drom made an appeal:
"In the retreat of Nyethang Orma,
To relieve the upāsaka's sadness,
In the master's presence I make this appeal.
Attend to me, source of benefit and joy.

"Such is the degeneration of this era of strife;
For the sake of powerless beings, out of your great altruism,
You have arrived here from the land of India,
Having been prophesized by deities and teachers.
Grateful indeed am I that you have cared for me.
Now I seek the practices
That will completely unite all ultimate aims.
No matter how you look at it, there is no time for leisure."

Atiśa replied: "Yes, I have a great method. In your practice, relinquish entirely [mundane] aspirations pertaining to this life. Giving excessive expositions and making promises will not accomplish the task. So, as explained earlier, make supplications to the teachers and meditation deities in a secluded place. Integrate the three baskets in their entirety into the [practices of the persons of] the three scopes.[175] Do not allow the māras of sloth and mental dullness to come in. With your three doors [of body, speech, and mind] and, with great joyful perseverance, make elaborate offerings of the seven limbs[176] to the divinities and teachers who have appeared in space before you. Cultivating fervent faith and respect toward them, visualize your teachers and the meditation deities as inseparable, just like the two of us here engaged in conversation. [58]

"Upāsaka, the teachers and meditation deities possess great compassion. The teaching is most potent, and you have the ring[177] of faith and respect. So, as you have just said, discard entirely all lingering doubts, and with resolve, thinking, 'Now even if this body of mine were to be split into a hundred pieces, I will not forsake this meditative practice,' cherish your meditative practice with persistence.

"As for entering into the actual practice, sit upon a comfortable cushion and adopt a good posture. Taking sentient beings as your focus, perform perfectly the practice of going for refuge. For the benefit of others, generate the mind [aspiring] for supreme awakening. Then, while holding fast your mind, [perform the following visualization]:

"In your heart, a white lotus arises from the melting of a white [letter] *paṃ*. Within the center of the lotus, generate a letter *āḥ*, which is a medium-sized drop. When this melts, generate a moon disc that is about the same size. Next, upon the moon disc, visualize *hrīḥ* and *oṃ*, either white or yellow, and generate me as your teacher, indivisible from the meditation deity. Fasten your mind on this single-pointedly. Guard the doors of the eye sense faculty, and do not project it out to external forms. Guard the doors of the ear sense faculty and do not project it out to external sounds. Likewise, do not let your nose, tongue, body, or mind become caught in the conceptualizations of smell, taste, or tactile sensation.

"Through mindfulness, ensure that you do not lose [the visualization of] your teacher; through meta-awareness, make this firm; and through heedfulness, [cultivate] perfect faith and respect [toward your teacher]. Then, hold your mind firmly on [the image of] your teacher, who is the size of a barley grain, and who, brilliant and pure, emits perfectly clear light rays of five or six colors into the ten directions. After mentally paying homage and making offerings to him, make the following supplication:[178]

"'Help me so that the subtlest of subtle defects from beginningless lives in cyclic existence up to the present life become purified.

"'Bless me so that I too can associate with all the conquerors of the ten directions, who, for the benefit of the trainees, never waver even for an instant, but enter the path of wisdom and compassion. Free of attachment and aversion toward them, may I, through exclusively pure perceptions, develop perfect rejoicing. I appeal to [the conquerors] to turn the unsurpassed wheel of Dharma.

"'Bless me so that, the instant I request it, everything that is good throughout all three times—including even material objects like grasses, trees, and caves—reveals the Dharma and turns [the wheel of Dharma]. [59]

"'Bless me so that, the instant I supplicate all the conquerors and their children not to enter nirvana, they appear before each and every sentient being, revealing the teachings to them in accordance with their needs and gradually leading them [to enlightenment] until cyclic existence is emptied.

"'Again bless me so that all the roots of virtue that I have dedicated become free of any conditions causing their exhaustion. By traversing the ten [bodhisattva] levels in their graded sequence, unobstructed by any obstacles, may I become fully enlightened for the sake of all sentient beings.

"'Again bless me so that, whatever aspiration prayers I make for sentient beings come to pass immediately, the instant that I pray them, in accordance with their wishes. Bless me so that I am free of the fetters of self-grasping that obstruct the realization of these [aspirations]. Bless me so that, after pacifying the inner disease[179] of grasping at things and their signs, and after becoming the great middle way [residing] at the heart of the thoroughly nonabiding great middle way,[180] I will abide like the great vajra-holder who is the reality of the Three Jewels and is the buddha body that is free of [all] conceptual elaborations.'

"Make repeated supplications in this manner. Make repeated aspiration prayers, saying, 'May these be realized as [aspired for].' Likewise, motivate yourself through repeated [applications of] mindfulness; be sustained by introspective awareness; and, through heedfulness, conduct yourself in accord [with these supplications]. Similarly, Upāsaka, concentrate your mind entirely not just during the day, not just during the night, but during the three phases of the day and the three phases of the night. At this point, do not search for too many 'profound' [teachings]. At this point, when you are stitching with method and wisdom, do not [sew] with a two-pronged needle. At this point, when you are practicing many profound [teachings] in one sitting in a concentrated manner, harbor no doubts in your mind that split its tip into two. Cherish your persistent effort in meditative practices.

"So, thoroughly abandoning sloth, mental dullness, and laziness, and with great force of joyful perseverance ensuring the perfect confluence of mindfulness, meta-awareness, and heedfulness, hold your mind in this manner throughout the six [phases of] time. Probing your mental continuum as well, see whether there has been a breach in your practice of going for refuge to the teacher and meditation deities; see whether you have cast aside meditative practice because of doubts; see whether you have been swept away by obstacles such as sloth, mental dullness, and laziness; see whether you have severed attachment to your own desires; and see whether your [pursuit of] others' welfare has become partial.

"Of all the thoughts you pursue in this way, the part that has past has no substantial reality, the part that is in the future has no substantial reality, [60] and their present has no substantial reality as well. Abiding in such intrinsic emptiness, the absence of substantial reality—this middle way of intrinsic emptiness—is called *wisdom*. Holding your mind on the teacher and so on is called *method*.

"What is the significance of generating the teacher's body as so miniscule? This has the purpose of holding your mind with clarity such that conceptualizations do not proliferate. It is also easier if you dissolve [the mind] into the ultimate expanse of reality and so on, or into the letters. Upāsaka, this, is the *first drop*.

"Furthermore, it will not suffice to say, 'I will practice when there is more time, more leisure.' What is there that is more important than this [Dharma practice]? If [you think] there is something more important than this, māras have entered [your heart]. So without allowing the māras to enter, visualize your teacher, who is about the size of a barley grain. In the center of his heart, a yellow lotus arises from a yellow *paṃ*. At the center [of the lotus], a moon disc that is approximately the same size arises from a white *āḥ* about the height of a medium-sized drop. Arising from a yellow *oṃ*, the Sage—who is about the size of the teacher as [visualized] earlier— sits upon this [moon disc]. [Meditate on him and venerate him] in the manner described earlier in the context of the teacher.[181] This, then, is the *second drop*.

"Moreover, in the heart of this barley grain–sized Sage, a greenish blue lotus arises from a greenish blue *paṃ*. At its center, a moon disc of about the same size arises from a white *āḥ* about the height of a medium-sized drop. Upon this [moon disc], a greenish blue *taṃ* becomes Tārā about the size of the Sage as described earlier. [Meditate on her and venerate] her also in the manner described earlier in the context of the teacher.

"In the heart of this Tārā as well, a white lotus arises from a white *paṃ*. At its center, a moon disc of about the same size arises from a white *āḥ* about the height of a medium-sized drop. Upon this [moon disc], there is a white *hrīḥ*, which in turn becomes Avalokiteśvara the size of Tārā described earlier. [Meditate on him and venerate] him also in the manner described in the context of the teacher.

"Likewise, in Avalokiteśvara's heart a lotus appears from a *paṃ*, and from an *āḥ* appears a moon disc upon which is a smoky blue *huṃ*. It, in turn, [becomes] Acala about the size of a barley seed. Focus on this and hold your mind. Until cyclic existence becomes empty, engage in the same [practices] as described earlier. Make supplications consonant with such aspirations as continuously safeguarding the Buddha's teaching for a long time and thwarting obstacles presented by the forces of malevolence."

At this juncture, the upāsaka asked, "What hand implements should I adopt?"

"To whom do you make supplications?" Atiśa asked.

"That depends on whatever is most primary [at a given moment]," he responded.

[Atiśa replied:] "In that case, it is okay to visualize each of them as having one face and two arms. [61] Yet, there is no contradiction if you visualize Tārā as having eight arms and Great Compassion [Avalotiteśvara] as having one thousand arms and one thousand eyes, and so on. As for their sitting postures, it is okay to visualize all of them as similar. Alternatively, you can also visualize Tārā in half lotus [position] and Acala with his left leg outstretched and his right leg bent. Also, since this is in the context of [engaging in] meditative absorption, it is stated that if you visualize all of them in the cross-legged vajra [lotus] position, it is a great blessing."

Again Drom asked: "How can I make supplications in the fashion of a destitute person seeking some prosperity?"

Atiśa replied: "You can visualize [the divinities] as carrying alms bowls filled with ambrosia or precious jewels, and so forth. Furthermore, you can also visualize [Tārā] as the savior from eight terrors and so forth,[182] with hand implements and postures just as found elsewhere. Nevertheless, since today's teaching is an instruction on holding your mind, do not engage in excessive elaboration. You can visualize all of them as seated cross-legged and as having one face and two arms. They are small, clear, radiant, and transparent, such that blessings flow the instant you make supplications to them. As for the other [divinities], [their appearances, postures, and hand implements] will be revealed in the context of their individual generation stage [meditations].

"From now on, throughout all activities such as walking, sitting, and so on, unless you are repeatedly reinforcing [in your mind clearly] the five drops[183] referred to earlier, do not act [without deliberation], walking casually and so on. If, however, you wish to do so, visualize the dissolution [of the divinities as follows]: Acala dissolves into his seed syllable and, through a gradual process, he dissolves, together with his seat, into Avalokiteśvara. Continue to dissolve them in the same manner, up until Śākyamuni. When you come to the remaining sole, vivid image of Atiśa, pay homage and make offerings to him.

"Then, as you project your five senses slightly from the objects, think: 'Like a dream, an illusion, and a reflection, objects appear yet cannot be clung to. If everything in this blurred, surreal [world] is, in this manner, false, deceptive, and unreal, then my parents are suffering with no purpose. What a pity! What a pity! It is up to me. I must ensure their happiness; I must ensure their well-being. How I wish they could be swiftly placed within [the state of] buddhahood! How joyful it is that I have the opportunity to work for their welfare, that I have the knowledge of the ultimate mode of being, and that I can make supplications to the higher beings.' Thinking in this way, practice the four immeasurable thoughts. Again, these are the method while the inner meditations are wisdom. Upāsaka, it is important never to be divorced from these two—method and wisdom. [62] This is what I understand to be the meaning of the line 'Divert not your six senses to the objects.'"[184]

To this, Drom replied: "It is most kind of you. Today, I have received an excellent method of meditating on the divine teachings." He then stated:

"Though the teacher has given many teachings,
If I summarize, it is as follows:

> **With mindfulness, awareness, and heedfulness,**
> **Constantly guard the gateways of your senses.**
> **Again and again, three times both day and night,**

Examine the flow of your thoughts.

"There is nothing other than this."

Atiśa replied, "Drom, it is as you have stated. You are skilled at summarizing it all. So, if you were to write a general summary of all the teachings I have given up until today, how would you state this?"

[Drom answered:] "I understand it to be the following:

> Homage to great compassion;
> Homage to the teachers;
> Homage to the faith divinities.
>
> Discard all lingering doubts
> And strive with dedication in your practice.
> Thoroughly relinquish sloth, mental dullness, and laziness,
> And strive always with joyful perseverance.
>
> With mindfulness, awareness, and heedfulness,
> Constantly guard the gateways of your senses;
> Again and again, three times both day and night,
> Examine the flow of your thoughts.

"O teacher, are [all your teachings] encompassed in these [lines]?"

Atiśa replied: "Yes, very well so. I, too, maintain this to be so. When I urged you to do this, you responded that you would do so, and your presentation is excellent."

[Drom said:] "Teacher, up to this point, it appears that [your teaching has] presented how to discard lingering doubts and accomplish your ultimate aim."

This concludes the fifth chapter from the *Jewel Garland of Dialogues*, "How to Guard the Doors of the Senses and Hold Your Mind."

CHAPTER 6
How All Blame Lies in a Single Point

[63] On another occasion when father Atiśa and his son were staying at their residence at Nyethang Or, Drom prostrated to Atiśa and, recollecting the method of holding one's mind and so forth, [stated:]

"Ignorance, craving, and grasping are the causes of sentient beings. Volition and becoming serve as their conditions, while their effects are consciousness, name and form, the six sense fields, contact, feelings, birth, and aging and death.[185] So it is these three—causes, conditions, and effects—that alone turn the wheel of impurity throughout the universe. Covering all our own defects with our palms, we unearth all the frailties of others with our fingers. Students do not implement the teacher's words and sons do not listen to what their fathers tell them. O great Atiśa, a negative era has dawned. Although sentient beings share the experience of the impure cycle of the twelve links of dependent origination, the beings of this degenerate era are partaking individually in what is a common resource. Since it could potentially benefit one or two future trainees, I request you to give a brief explanation of the twelve links of dependent origination."

Atiśa replied, "I shall explain this later when we have to lift our robes because of muddy water."

"In that case, what is the root of bondage?" asked Drom.

Atiśa: "It is the grasping at self."

"What is this grasping at self?" enquired Drom.

"This is something that wants all positive qualities for oneself alone and wants others alone to take on all misfortunes."

"Then please explain this in such a manner so you can say 'This is self-grasping,'" asked Drom.

Atiśa replied: "Where would one find something of which it could be said that 'This is the reified self-grasping?'"

"In that case, please explain to me how it is that [this self-grasping] wants everything and transfers [all] blames onto others."

Atiśa replied, "Upāsaka, why even ask me? This is pervasive in sentient beings. You know this, so what need is there to ask? Even so, I have also seen attachment and aversion labeled as self-grasping."

"Atiśa, there are people who possess such forms of grasping?"

"Where do they exist?" responded Atiśa. [64]

"They are [within] our own mental continuum," replied [Drom].

"Upāsaka, what is one's own mental continuum?"

"It is that which wants everything and grasps [at it all]," replied Drom.

Atiśa: "I, too, would say the same."

"Where does this self-grasping reside?" inquired Drom.

"It is devoid of parts, and I have never seen it myself. There is nothing that abides where there is nowhere to abide. I do not know the colors and shapes of something with no reality," replied [Atiśa].

Drom then asked, "If this is so, how can something so feeble exist?"

Atiśa responded, "Can't one perceive mirage water, a double moon, dream horses and elephants, and so on?"

"Master, these are delusions."

Atiśa said, "I accept this to be so. It is not that he, self-grasping, indulges in attachment and aversion on the basis of being existent. Dogs bark in the wilderness because of an empty container, and our mindstream is greatly perturbed with no ground [at all]."

"Master, if such are the examples, self-grasping seems to be something that never existed at all," said Drom.

"What is this thing that 'seems to be'? It must be real."

"Master, in that case do the forms and functions of the abyss of the three lower realms, the qualities of the higher realms, and the ethical norms of affirmation and rejection [also] exist?"

"There is a dreamer of dreams. Isn't there?" Atiśa responded.

"Master, this is not the same. Dreams are not created by oneself. Though false, they arise [spontaneously]. Birth in the higher realms, lower realms, ethical norms of affirmation and rejection were created."

"Who created them?" asked Atiśa.

"They were created by the mind," replied [Drom].

"I, too, would say the same. Dreams are also created by the mind, Upāsaka, for were they not created by the mind, who created them? Are they created by some other thing? For were they not created by something else or by the mind, Upāsaka, then you have lied about what is itself a lie. The objects of dreams are false; they are devoid of all [characterizations], such as self, other, and so on. In the same manner, even the ethical norms of affirmation and rejection, such as [the causes for taking birth in] the lower realms and so on, are conjured by the mind itself, which then does the affirming and rejecting."

"If this is so, is self-grasping the root of attachment and aversion, and this is one's own mind?" asked Drom.

"What is the color of the mind?" asked Atiśa.

"I have never seen it."

"Then what kind of shape does it have?" asked Atiśa.

"Master, I have never seen it."

"Since it exists with neither color nor shape, [65] and also since it has never been seen with the eyes, this indicates that it does not exist as a form. So empty it of physicality and set it aside. Upāsaka, what type of sound does it have, melodious or unmelodious, loud or muffled?"

"Master, I have never heard it before," replied Drom.

"So since it does not appear as melodious or unmelodious, loud or muffled, and so on, it is not heard by the ears. Given that if it does exist [as sound], it should be audible to the ears, and [given that it is not heard], it does not exist. Now that the mind is devoid also of sound, set it aside. Upāsaka, what type of smell does it have, fragrant or unfragrant?"

"Master, I have never smelled an odor of the mind or mind itself," replied Drom.

"Drom, had it an odor there is no doubt it would have been smelled by the nose. Given that it has never been smelled, this indicates that the mind is devoid of smell. So set aside this emptiness that is the absence of smell. Drom, does your mind exist as some kind of taste, be it delicious or unsavory?"

"All sorts of things seem to emerge from the master's speech. How can there be such a norm[186] [pertaining to] the distinction between a delicious or unsavory taste on the basis of eating the mind?" exclaimed Drom.

"Drom, in that case, does the mind not exist?"

"Master, how can there be the eating of mind, and how can there be the tasting of mind?" asked Drom.

"Drom, this is an indication that your mind is not a taste. For were it a taste, the tongue would experience it. As it is not experienced by the tongue, this indicates that it is not a taste. So set aside that which is devoid also of taste. Drom, what kind of tactile quality does the mind have, soft or coarse?"

"Master, I have never seen the tactile quality of the mind," he replied.

"Drom, why is this so?"

"There is no norm pertaining to observing the tactile quality of the mind," replied Drom.

Atiśa then responded: "Normlessness abounds in sentient beings who are wild. Given that the mind is not an object of tactile experience, this is an indication that it is devoid of tactile quality. So set aside the mind that is also not a tactile phenomenon. Drom, what kind of things exist as the object of mental consciousness?"

"Master, in order for something to appear as an object of mental consciousness, it seems that the senses need to have an immediately preceding condition. For without first becoming the object of the senses, there is no immediately preceding condition that is the object of mental consciousness."

"Fabrications of conceptualization can appear, too," responded Atiśa.

"Master, even fabrications are preceded by their propensities. Furthermore, isn't the entailment, 'Because something is not an object of the five senses, it does not exist as any of the five sense objects' a little too sweeping?"

"Upāsaka, what are you saying? I have not listed all objects to be within these [five sense objects]. I have [only] listed your mind in addition to these [sense objects]. For if the mind exists as any of these [five sense objects], then when you observe it, it should exist as a form, be heard as a sound, and so on. [66] Since it is not perceived as any of these, where does the mind reside? Upāsaka, even ordinary mundane people would give up and shake their hands and exclaim 'I have never seen such a thing with my eyes, nor have I heard it with my ears. I have never smelled its odor, never tasted its flavor, nor does it exist anywhere within [the sphere of] mental consciousness.' You, [on the other hand,] are a person who has been ripened by the pith instructions of the sublime teachers, in whose heart the higher attainments of the meditation deities have entered, and a person who practices the three baskets of the sacred words in one sitting. So you [of all people] should not add meaningless branches and leaves [onto a non-existent tree].

"All of this is the mind. I have realized this nature of mind, for I am a son of Avadhūti. Now even if one's faults are exposed, it is the mind. Even if one is praised, it is the mind. Whether happy or sad, it is the mind. Given that all of these are equal in being the mind, whatever defects arise in your mental continuum wherein self is perceived when there is no self, crush them and let them go. There is no point in concealing such unestablished defects inside a cave that is [itself] not established. There is no point in turning these into poisons and causing illness. There is no reason that the number of illnesses should remain [fixed] at five. There is no need for these to sever the life of liberation and cast one into the three lower realms. Although dreams are unreal, it serves no purpose to dream of suffering.

"Drom, cast out all these false defects. If the sign of having cleansed these defects is positive, this is fine; if it is not, this is fine too. Within this equality of [everything] being the appearance of an unreal mind, if others feel delighted when they are praised, go praise them. Do not search for another's faults, for there is no searcher within you. If something is to be concealed at all, conceal your own higher qualities. The time has now come for this. If something is to be proclaimed at all, proclaim the higher qualities of others. Others will be delighted, and they will not accumulate negative karma on the basis of you. This also has the benefit of dislodging the foundation stones of the afflictions, such as attachment and aversion. Whatever good qualities exist in others, seek out each of them individually and reveal them. Upāsaka, [now] do you understand how everything is the mind?"

"Yes, I do," replied Drom.

"In that case, do you understand the mind's true mode of being?"

"Yes, I do," replied Drom.

Atiśa: "So what need is there of desires for this mind; cultivate contentment. Even though you perceive many sentient beings, all of them are your fathers and mothers who have taken joys in your overcoming of misfortune and [attainment] of good fortune. They have cleaned your runny nose with their mouths, your excrement with their hands, have nurtured you with kingdoms and with gifts, and some, despite having been abandoned [by us], have cared for us again. [67] It is due to the kindness of the teacher that positive qualities are revealed. In general, it is the teacher who has done you the great kindness of granting you your ultimate aim. And it is your parents who are the source of great kindness granting you joy and happiness in this life. You should therefore recognize their kindness and repay their kindness.

"For this, serve the teacher through respectful veneration and meditative practice, and toward your parents, in order to repay their kindness, cultivate immeasurable loving-kindness, immeasurable compassion, immeasurable joy when they are happy, and immeasurable equanimity that is free of discriminating thoughts of near and distant. For the benefit of all—all your mothers—strive as much as possible to attain buddhahood and, discarding lingering doubts, cherish your persistence in meditative practice.

Abandoning all obstacles such as sloth, mental dullness, and laziness, and endeavor with joyful perseverance.

"Drom, although one speaks of 'recognizing the kindness of others and repaying it,' it all seems to pertain to the practice of the four immeasurable thoughts, such as loving-kindness and compassion; the stabilization of the awakening mind; its enhancement from high to ever higher levels; and the definite steering of one's parents with the paddles of [the two awakening minds,] aspirational and engaging. [So] this [recognizing others' kindness and repaying it] refers to a cousin of desire, whereby one has relinquished self-centeredness and generates kindheartedness desiring one's parents [to have happiness] and desiring to repay their kindness."

Drom replied:

"Though the master has given many excellent [teachings],
If summarized, it is this:

> **Reveal your own shortcomings,**
> **But do not seek out others' errors.**
> **Conceal your own good qualities,**
> **But proclaim those of others.**
>
> **Forsake gifts and ministrations;**
> **At all times relinquish gain and fame.**
> **Have modest desires, be easily satisfied,**
> **And reciprocate kindness.**
>
> **Cultivate love and compassion,**
> **And stabilize your awakening mind.**

"There is nothing other than this."

Atiśa responded, "Yes, this is so. When properly condensed, [my teachings] are encompassed in these [lines]."

This concludes the sixth chapter from the *Jewel Garland of Dialogues*, "How All Blame Lies in a Single Point."

Chapter 7
How to Relinquish the Objects of Abandonment and Engage in the Virtues

[68] On another occasion when the two—father Atiśa and his son—were staying at their residence in Nyethang Or, Drom asked: "O great master, what are the objects of abandonment pertaining to all those [practices] I inquired about earlier?"

"You yourself would never commit the five heinous acts[187] or their approximations, so [in this context] it is the ten nonvirtuous actions," Atiśa replied.

"Teacher Dīpaṃkara, I have asked about this not because these negativities might occur in [me], the upāsaka. In my aftermath, there will be all manner of spiritual trainees."

With his palms folded, Atiśa responded, "Yes, my upāsaka is right. There will be one hundred, ten thousand,[188] and twenty-five thousand [trainees]."

"Most glorious one, yes, I am asking about the objects of abandonment for those [people]."

"Upāsaka, if among your sons, nephews, and grandnephews it is rare for someone to engage even in the ten nonvirtuous actions, what need is there to speak of the five heinous acts and their approximations? Furthermore, those who are certain to follow in your footsteps will not engage in the heinous acts and their approximations regardless of whatever situation they confront. As for those who seek your liberating example, they are soiled not even by the ten negative actions. Great compassionate one, listen to me.

"The three nonvirtues of body,
The four nonvirtues of speech,
And the three nonvirtues of the mind—
These are referred to as the *ten nonvirtues.*

"Taking life, stealing or robbing others' wealth,
Indulging in the misconduct of an unchaste act,
Speaking words that are not true
Or telling lies [even] for the sake of humor,
Divisive and frivolous speech—words of affliction,

Harshly inveighing with abusive words,
Covetousness, harmful intent, and wrong views—
These are the ten [acts of] nonvirtue.
Their relinquishment is the reverse, the ten virtues.

"Gyalwai Jungné, since one's father, one's mother, one's preceptor, one's master, a tathāgata, and those with the eyes of Dharma are distinguished objects, if one slays any of them, one will depart without any intermediate state to what all the tantric adepts call *vajra hell,* which in common language is called *unrelenting hell.* According to the presentations of all the Higher Knowledge [texts], it seems to be a place from where there is no chance to escape to a higher state. As for the defects of the hells, [69] I shall explain them tomorrow, when we have to lift our robes [and cross to] the other shores.

"Here, however, it is critical not to fall into the heinous acts. No matter what class of animals one may kill through poison, or weapons, or destructive incantations, the karmic fruition [of such an act] is rebirth in one of the three lower realms. This is a karmic act that does not waver. Furthermore, with respect to all classes of animals, if one either makes others perform the killing or rejoices [in such an act], this karmic act leads to birth in the lower realms. So if one must not kill any being, from [the smallest] insect on a single blade of grass up to a human, what need is there to mention [not taking the life of] the distinguished objects?

"Dromtönpa, if your body were to be pierced by three hundred or so spears continuously over a period of an entire day and not allowed to die, what kind of pain would you experience?"

"Master, it would be unbearable," replied Drom.

"Drom, it is said that this would not measure up to even one hundredth or one thousandth of the least of the lesser sufferings of the hells. Drom, one must, therefore, never take a life; one must never make others kill, nor must one rejoice in killing, for even if one is reborn as a human, one's life will be short.

"Furthermore, one must not take, without being given, material things belonging to others, whether through force, incantations, or subterfuge. It is like this: Do not steal, do not rob, do not engage even in [such acts as] deceitful flattery and insinuation, for if one commits these, just as in the previous case, there is no path other than to the lower realms. Most of [those who commit these acts] are said to take birth as hungry ghosts.

Drom, even if a person *is* reborn as a human, he will be impoverished in resources and remain destitute. He will have obtained a human life, but just barely, with nothing to eat, nothing to be found, and nothing to wear.

"Drom, one must not engage in any way in what is unchaste. One must never defile one's relations, such as one's mother or one's sisters. One must never defile those who observe vows, such as a fully ordained nun. Furthermore, engaging in [sexual acts] during other inappropriate times, or during the day, or with other orifices is called *sexual misconduct.* Since these are causes for departing to the limitless lower realms, together with unchaste conduct one must never ever engage in these.[189] Even if one *is* reborn as a human, one will suffer from grave family problems and experience enormous heaps of suffering. In this context, as well, if one makes others commit such acts [70] or rejoices in them, [the karmic result] is the same as in the previous case [where one performed the act oneself].

"Also, since telling lies [and indulging in] divisive speech, frivolous speech, and harsh words are major causes for taking birth in the limitless lower realms, one must relinquish them at all times and in all forms. Even if a person *is* reborn as a human, he will not be recognized by others as credible. Many will disparage him, his words will carry no authority, and he will become an object of other's ridicule. He will not be harmonious with others, and others will drive a wedge between the individual and his dear friends. He will greatly attract derision, and even those with no reason to will shout abusive words at him, and so on. He will thus be deprived of even the [normal] human joys.

"One must, therefore, learn to seek the seven virtues that are the relinquishments of these seven nonvirtues, and lead others to these seven virtues as well. One should also give compliments to those who cultivate these [virtues]. As for someone like you, Drom, who has secured a firm ground, who does not even care to take birth in cyclic existence, who focuses exclusively on other's welfare, you can engage in the seven nonvirtues by relating them to [the application of] skillful means. Those are [only] similitudes of nonvirtue.[190]

"Drom, toward the possessions of others—should they be the possessions of teachers, of the Three Jewels, of the sick and disabled, and so on— one must never covet with the thought, 'How happy I would be if I had them.' One must not harbor covetousness with such thoughts as 'How I wish I had them; I will try my very best to obtain them.' This is prohibited even for bodhisattvas.

"Also one must not ever harbor any harmful intention, such as gloating when others suffer misfortune, gloating when they experience destruction, or [conceiving] the intent to kill.

"Furthermore, saying that the Buddha [Jewel] is untrue, that the Dharma is untrue, that the Sangha community is untrue, that there are no previous and future worlds, that there is no law of karma and its effects, and using the travails that befall spiritual practitioners as evidence [of such claims]—all of these are what is called *harboring wrong views*. With such karmic acts it is impossible to escape from the lower realms. One must, therefore, relinquish such [acts] in all their forms at all times.

"Drom, I have presented here, by means of an illustrative summary, the ten nonvirtues together with their destructive effects. As for other [aspects], you should read the sutras closely. In the future as well, given that the minds of the ignorant trainees are confused, you should reveal to them this rough type of presentation. If it is too elaborate, it will not benefit the ignorant trainees. So Gyalwai Jungné, take what I have stated earlier as your focus and never be angry or agitated. [71] Never be conceited with pride that impedes success. The instant that anger and agitation arise, crush them with their antidotes. Remain tranquil and disciplined with a demeanor of humility. Never at any time support yourself with ill means but be nurtured throughout day and night through ethical livelihood.

"Gyalwai Jungné, do you know this? Anger destroys the roots of virtue of many eons; conceitedness destroys the young shoots of the cultivation of heedfulness; wrong livelihood causes one to degrade the qualities of a virtuous person. Therefore, Drom, one must never commit any acts that are associated with the ten nonvirtues. This broad presentation [of the ethics of the ten virtues] is part of a dialogue carried out in a casual manner by the two of us. It is not the time for [discussing] the numerous conflicts and connections [between these explanations]. Drom, do you find these [explanations] agreeable to your mind?"

Drom responded: "Even though we would not have the time to engage in an extensive dialogue, it would certainly be fine if you, Atiśa, were to give an excellent explanation that is comprehensive and extensive, that is lucid and substantive on all [the aspects of] the story of these ten nonvirtues. That is why I have brought this up in general terms in our conversation."

Atiśa stated: "Drom, it is not that I do not know how to weave the words together. It is not the case that I have explained things here only in relation to your mind. What would it be like if, say, I had explained in Sanskrit?

This would serve no purpose. None of you Tibetans would understand it then. Furthermore, this approach is like that of a mother teaching her little child how to eat, how to dress, and how to behave. This is not the occasion where one must avoid the flaws of repetition and so on. Drom, if all the people of Tibet were to come in my presence and ask for an instruction that is beneficial to their minds, how would it be if I were to give the following exposition?

"Omniscience and the paths that cultivate it,
Though devoid of any conceptuality, like the king of jewels
Bring to fruition the wishes of those who splendidly seek them.

"Atop the precious tree a flock of birds, the fortunate ones, converge.
Joyful for the branches, they consume the excellent fruits;
With one thousand sunrays, they enjoy immeasurable bliss.
Extending their dual-truth wings, they extract with their loving-kindness
    beaks;
With feet of method and wisdom they're endowed with the seven
    qualities;
These thoroughly pure *garuda* birds are free of attachment.

"Free of the limits of elaboration, the [sacred] syllables are most excellent;
    [72]
The feathers of [principles] concordant with enlightenment are in full
    plumage.
If every single feather is versed in the treatises of the great middle way
And they probe with excellence the two [truths],
Innumerable smaller feathers of dependent origination proliferate.

"Their roots clean and their tips delicately sharp,
Though extremely light these feathers are not blown away by the wind.
Though extremely soft their texture deceives no one.
If you experience this nonconceptuality, the wonders increase.

"*Ema!* Such is the profundity of the truth of the ultimate mode of being.
Like the sun, it fulfills other's welfare without conceptualization;
Nothing within the knowledge mandala remains unpervaded [by it].

"The higher realms well created through afflictions and sexual desire—
Because they damage the drops, the balloon of the afflictions becomes
     inflated.
Since temporary joys and the bliss of prosperity and happiness remain good,
The ultimate aim [becomes] like a flower in the sky.[191]
Amazing indeed it is that the flowers of mundane happiness blossom
And the pleasure-seeking bees of cyclic existence indulge.

"*Ema!* If cloudless clear [skies] do not destroy it,
How can the flower be destroyed by the sun, though hot?
That which is engendered by contaminated bliss is amazing;
It has no end, for the stream of existence flows.
Tight indeed is the interlinked cycle of the twelve links of dependent
     origination;
Great indeed is this base with neither beginning nor end.

"Do you understand this well, all of you here who possess the origins?
Do not be fooled by the fruits of causes that are excellent.
Thoroughly brilliant, they are like a lamp made of straw.
All these bursting bubbles are extremely unstable;[192]
Undertake [Dharma] practice, for [all of this is like] the core of
     a banana tree;
The remnant of past karma resembles a pampered child of a barren
     woman.[193]

"All the young in whom the flowers of contaminants are in full bloom,
You who have attained the ultimate fruit of a youthful body,
Listen, if you seek your ultimate aims.
Joyful will it be if you rob your affliction parents of their lives;[194]
Joyful will it be if you steal the ultimate, which is not given by them;
Joyful will it be if you sexually defile the afflictions;
Joyful will it be you deceive them with lies, for all phenomena
     are unreal;
Joyful will it be if you cause dissension, turning virtues against
     nonvirtues;
Joyful will it be if you utter slander so as to afflict the afflictions;
Overwhelm such divisive speech with abusive harsh words;

The sublime being who indulges thus in these four [nonvirtues of
    speech] is most joyful.
Joyful will it be if you covet the supreme excellence;
Cultivate the good malice that destroys the enemies of the teaching;
Reverse your self-interest and look after supreme liberation;
[Thus] these ten nonvirtues of a misguided path—
Adopt them as ten virtues on the perfect path.

"If you cling to these [practices] as well, this is a great bondage,
So reverse this and cultivate faith in the supreme [objects].
Faith in what, and who is having the faith? They're empty.
The way that faith is experienced [73]—this is the great middle way.

"Do not relapse and harbor anger and pride.
Absence of conceit is the highest humility.
Throw it into the ultimate expanse; ungrasping, let it free.
If you abide in this manner, the distorted will dismantle the distorted.

"How can this deceive you? How will you be sustained?
Ema! Forsake wrong livelihood, and throughout all lives
Be sustained by ethical livelihood.

"Drom Jé, although I have expounded this without any embellishment,
such as composing this in Sanskrit, how will people understand even this
level of composition? Conversation is conversation, and poetry, poetry. You
Tibetans, even if you were to compose for many months, wouldn't be able
to produce this kind of spontaneous verse. You'd think I had memorized
these verses in the past and then recited them!" Saying this, he laughed.

   "As for you, too, Drom, you do not ask about my pith instructions that
are already present. You cause me hardship by asking new and fresh questions, so I'm going to stop listening to you [now]. He who has perfected
the three—learning, reflection, and meditation—need not rely on similes.
All of this is merely a ruse. It is the buddha who is called someone who has
perfected the three—learning, reflection, and meditation. Because of my
fondness for you, I cannot help but be drawn into frivolous speech while
making boisterous statements."

   Drom replied: "This much is fine. Nevertheless, as you yourself said,
Teacher, you must speak in accord with the mental level [of the spiritual

trainees]. If you do not, the ignorant ones will not be guided. It will be like the popular expression 'She calls out like an owl though her mother is a hen.'"[195]

"First, the mother was actually a hen. As for the latter [the ignorant ones], not many guide them in large numbers. It is not that someone like you does not have the latter [ignorant followers]," said Atiśa.

"Master, there is a danger that these [teachings] will be misunderstood," replied Drom. Saying this, he reviewed all of what had been taught before as if Atiśa [himself] were reciting a sutra.

"How joyful it would be if there were in the world many minds like yours! If one were to search I wonder how many would be found?" exclaimed Atiśa.

"Master, how would it be if one were to act in the following way?" asked Drom.

"This life is as transient as the flow of a river;
Swiftly it passes and none can seize it.
Among the incalculable hosts of sentient beings
Not one being exists who has not been our parent.

"Having met the teachings, how can I betray them?
Be they old or young, all living beings are our parents,
And so whatever situation I am in,
I will never kill them; how could I even think it? [74]

"In general, wealth is the cause of so much bondage.
In particular, those things that are not given by my parents,
I have no need for, so why would I take what is not given?
If I have been bound by the chains of cyclic existence in the past,
How can I, knowingly and with defiance,
Engage in sexual misconduct and harbor wrong views?

"Since lies [make] one's life a lie, what use is deceiving others?
If ignorance, attachment, and aversion sever those in harmony,
Alas! Who would knowingly drive a wedge between friends?
The meaningless words of frivolous speech chain everyone;
Why would I knowingly pursue such acts?

"Since everyone is a parent, an embodiment of kindness,
Not relieving their pain with pleasant words but uttering hostile words—
What kind of 'sublime' behavior is this?

"When traversing the path of liberation, free of attachment,
If my own wealth is of no use, what use is others' wealth?
When giving away possessions, one's own flesh and blood, and
     children,[196]
Alas! What point is there in coveting others' possessions?

"When traversing the pure expanse of [perfect] equanimity,
What use are wrong views—Māra's army?
Wise indeed is he who knows this and discards them.
What insane Dharma practitioner, while encouraging others
To relinquish their nonvirtuous deeds, commits them himself?

"When one can give away one's own flesh and blood without
     attachment,
What kind of practitioner is he who eats his parents' flesh and blood?
Will he not feel remorse when his life is demanded constantly in
     retribution?
Alas! Now in order to seek without distraction, this very day,
The well-being of infinite numbers of parents,
Cast aside all ordinary mundane tasks!
Cast aside all afflictions of the three doors!
Pull out and cast away all piercing daggers of conceptualization!
Alas! Would not Drom then become sovereign?"

Atiśa replied: "Yes, you have become, you have become; you are already one from before. You have spoken well. Now, is it possible to summarize what has been said and heard?"

"Teacher, it is as follows," replied Drom.

> **Relinquish the ten negative actions,**
> **And always reinforce your faith.**[197]

> **Destroy anger and conceit,**
> **And be endowed with humility.**

Relinquish wrong livelihood,
And be sustained by ethical livelihood.

"There is nothing other than this.
   "These, in turn, can be related to the six perfections as well."

This concludes the seventh chapter from the *Jewel Garland of Dialogues*, "How to Relinquish the Objects of Abandonment and Engage in the Virtues." [75]

CHAPTER 8
The Riches of the Noble Ones and the *Khakkhara* Staff

On another occasion, when the father Atiśa and his son were staying at their residence at Nyethang Or, many ordained monks of Tibet came and said, "We wish to see the paṇḍita's face and form a spiritual connection [by receiving a teaching from him]."

At that time, Drom Jé stated: "It is said, 'Difficult it is to see one who is accomplished in his conduct.' So now is the time to seek the wealth of the noble ones by means of material wealth. Just as one seeks to accumulate a year's provisions within months, now is the time to seek the long-term ultimate aim in this very life. And our approach is to take our share on a day-by-day basis. [Other than meeting with Dharma,] there is no other purpose for taking birth in a central region. I am delighted that the members of the Sangha have arrived without needing an invitation. This is a sign that the teachings will flourish. [Normally] I sit at the head of the rows when all the benefactors make their offerings; I explain to them the incremental effects of accumulating merit. I give quite a lively exposition. Today, however, I, the benefactor Gyalwai Jungné, have been sent elsewhere, being made to point my finger inward. Since I meditate on impermanence throughout the day and night, I have no leisure to accumulate material things. So whenever the need arises, let's search through the Sangha community's storeroom, take from it, and consume these things." So joyfully and delightedly he entertained and served the teacher and the Sangha well.

At that time, Drom said: "When people gather in a samsaric gathering, satisfy them accordingly with the wealth of material things. Today, however, we have gathered here as an assembly of 'enlightened phenomena.' Thus, we should be enriched accordingly with the wealth of the noble ones. For this, we must relinquish the defilements and thoroughly transcend the qualities of cyclic existence. Free of attachment, we must, for the benefit of others, embrace the way of being of the twelve qualities acquired through training.[198] It is important for you to go for alms and be enriched by the wealth of the noble ones. Atiśa, please speak on these points."

"These words of the spiritual friend are most timely and they inspire our hearts," said the entire Sangha.

Then Atiśa asked all the members of the Sangha to listen to the following essential teaching: [76]

"Material possessions are known as the illusory wealth;
Essenceless, they fluctuate greatly.
[People] sell their own possessions and collect those of others.
Aiming for greater profit,
They forsake happiness while busily chasing wealth.

"Longing for happiness they run about everywhere.
Not sated by sensual objects they take on [more] misery,
Just like a flame at the edge of a forest.
First, do not let it gain ground at the [forest] edge.
Forests have been razed from [flames] at its edge.

"Refrain from the slightest [attachment to wealth], all of you.
Material things are like poisonous flowers,
Young children accept them joyfully, and once befriended,
They fall into their mouths and rob them of their lives.

"Material things are like the salty waters of sea,
The more you happily drink, the more your thirst increases.
Material things are like itchy fungal rashes,
The more you scratch the itch, the itchier it becomes.
Material things are like transient valuables,
Deluded about their benefits, you are robbed by the enemy [death].

"All of these are rooted in the self.
The self chases after the corpse of desire;
Desire, in turn, craves material things.
So as for this wealth of material possessions,
Know that, in the long term, they deceive and have no meaning.

"For refuge, seek well
The supreme objects of refuge—the teachers and the Three Jewels.
Rely on them diligently as the source of refuge.
With excellent faith, longing, and conviction,
Cultivate faith, the great soil of virtue.
This is one of the excellent riches of the noble ones.
Faith brings forth trust and respect;

They, in turn, [bring about] the highest good, supreme
   enlightenment.
Thus, the wealth of faith is secure in the long run.

"So all you faithful ones who have gathered here today,
Guard the morality that upholds the affirmations and rejections,
The source of all higher qualities.
All the trees of virtue with no exception
Grow from morality, the great fertile ground.
Be not too self-centered, but work for other's welfare;
Relinquish nonvirtue and strive in virtue;
Guard against the objects to be abandoned;
This is the noble wealth of ethical discipline.

"Free of attachment, give away all possessions,
Both outer and inner, including your flesh and blood;
This alone is the source of all wishes.
Great indeed is the noble wealth of giving.
So, all of you, without attachment give away material possessions.

"Identifying all objects to be abandoned and their antidotes
And [then] adopting [virtue] and rejecting [nonvirtue] is [true]
   learning.
Through learning, the basis for all-knowing expertise [is laid];
This is one of the riches of the noble ones, so invoke this, all of you.

"Dress nicely in the attire of compunction;
Constantly tighten up with the sash of conscience;
A sense of shame and conscience—
These are excellent riches of the noble ones.
Practice them constantly, all of you gathered here.

"Undivorced from the wealth of insight,
Take everything into the ultimate expanse of enlightenment [77]
And nurture it all within the treasury of great dedication.
Be secured by the hooks of fearlessness and be free of conceit.

"These are the seven riches of the noble ones.
They are hard to achieve by other humans;
In particular they are beyond the purview of the lower realms.
Seek these supreme riches and marvelous will be your long-term fate;
[Even] before then, all humans and gods will honor you.

"*Ema!* Such are the riches of the noble ones.
If you aspire for material things to sustain your body,
To nourish your round body seek the taste of equanimity.

"In such places as [under a] tree, on a rocky mountain, or in a snow cave,
In a cemetery, in the woods, or in the wilderness,
Free of distraction, lay the basis for concentration practice.[199]
If you become attached to this, too, then through nonattachment as the
    condition,
Respectfully uphold the *khakkhara* staff,[200]
The highest symbol of enlightened body, speech, and mind,
Which is undamaged by [the elements of] fire, water, and winds.

"Contemplating the objects of veneration and the offerings, perform
    meditation.
This is the granting of wealth to bring together the enlightened
    phenomena."

Drom responded: "Today in your presence at this residence of Nyethang
Or, Atiśa, were I to summarize in its entirety what you have taught in
response to my request, you seem to be saying this. One should seek places
such as rocky terrains and so on for one's residence. One should be sustained by alms, a food where all tastes are harmonized. And one should
uphold the *khakkhara* staff, the symbol of the Buddha's body, speech, and
mind, which are undamaged by the external conditions of earth, water, and
so on. Since you also seem to be saying that one should contemplate its
symbolism, [namely,] the objects of veneration and the offerings, and
engage in meditation, what are these [symbols]?"

At the residence of Nyethang Or,
The upāsaka of residual [good] karma

Asked Atiśa:
"Wise teacher pray attend to me.

"There is one knot and three sections;
Its mid-pole is pine and its lower body seven-sided;
Its upper part has eight sides and it has four great horns;
It has two reliquaries and a double-rimmed wheel;

"Both rims are hollow inside,
And [it has] twelve rings that are strung together.
In order to clear away my lingering doubts,
Please tell me why is this so."

Master Atiśa spoke:
"That it has [only] one knot
Symbolizes closing the doors to the lower realms.
That it has three sections
Symbolizes the three trainings
Of morality, [concentration of the] mind, and wisdom;
That the mid-pole is made of pine
Indicates that the mind of a virtuous person
Is light, straight, and free of deceit and pretense.
That the lower body is seven-sided [78]
Symbolizes the seven limbs of enlightenment.
That the upper body has eight sides
Signifies the eightfold noble path.
That it has four large horns
Signifies the four noble truths.
That it has two reliquaries
Signifies a buddha's two form bodies.
The dharmakāya, free of conceptual elaborations, is ineffable.
The wheel symbolizes the turning of the wheel of law
Of the four noble truths
By the emanation buddha body at Varanasi
For the five disciples and an assembly of followers.
The hook symbolizes the great compassion
That would lead all beings.
That the upper part is hollow is a symbol

Of the selflessness of phenomena, the absence of inherent existence.
That the lower part is hollow is a symbol
Of the selflessness of persons.
That the upper and lower parts are joined
Signifies [the union of] the two—method and wisdom.
That it has twelve metal rings is a sign
Indicating the twelve links of dependent origination:
Ignorance, volition, and consciousness,
Name-and-form, and the six sense bases,
Contact, feeling, craving, and appropriation,
Becoming and birth, and aging and death.

"This walking staff of the buddhas of the three times and their children
And the assembly of disciples and self-enlightened noble ones
Symbolizes the [precious] reliquaries;
In the sutras it is mentioned clearly as the 'cooler.'"[201]

Again, the upāsaka asked
Master Atiśa:
"How many different traditions are there to this?
How does one go about upholding this [staff]?
What benefits are there for upholding it?
Who are the persons that uphold it?
Are the ones you mentioned earlier the only ones?
What are the tasks of those who uphold it?"

Atiśa replied:
"There are four different traditions to this—
The tradition of the past and that of the future,
The tradition of the present and that of all three.

"During [Buddha] Dīpaṃkara's era,[202] the two truths—
Ultimate truth and conventional truth—
Were symbolized by the two large horns.
This is the tradition of the past Buddha.

"During the era of Maitreya, the single truth,
The sole truth of nirvana,

Will be symbolized by one large horn.
This is the tradition of the future Buddha.

"During Śākyamuni's era, the four truths—
Suffering, its origin, its cessation, and the path—
Are symbolized by four large horns.
This is the tradition of the present Buddha.

"The tradition of all three is the six perfections—
Giving, morality, forbearance,
Joyful perseverance, concentration, and wisdom;
These are symbolized by six large horns.

"Be versed in these four traditions. [79]
In order to do this, uphold the staff in the following manner:
Do not hoist it upright as if holding a spear;
Do not hold it sideways as if carrying a log;
But, like a mother holding her dear child,
Hold it at your heart [with] the training in mind.[203]

"In Kukuraca[204] and so on,
Locations where fear is present,
Whatever one may do, no faults will result.
As for the three trainings and method and wisdom,
Never be divorced from these.

"Uphold [the teachings] with respect, for they are objects of veneration;
Practice them, for they are the indicated teachings.
He who holds this [staff] upholds the higher qualities and the teachings;
Forsaking the eight [conditions of] lack of leisure, he abides on the dry
    shores.

"Wherever this [staff] is upheld is a central region;
In the borderlands, none upholds it,
Nor is it the domain of householders.
Householders are [drowning] in suffering,
Whereas the upholders of [the staff] dwell in happiness;
So depart from your home and uphold it.

"He who is modest in desires, easily contented,
And dwells in utter solitude
Is a person who upholds this [staff];
He who practices the three baskets of scripture
Is [also] a person who upholds this [staff].

"He who carries the Sage's bowl—
Dark, well oiled, and [formed from] perfect measurements—
Is a person who upholds this [staff].

"He who wears the permitted robes,
Saffron-colored, square, and sleeveless,
Is a person who upholds this [staff].
He who lives on food procured through alms
Is a person who upholds this [staff].

"He might wish to topple the container without a handle,
But he fears [the threat of] excessive chores.[205]
He might wish to remove the attire of square clothing,
But he fears [the threat of] excessive chores.
Out of compassion for the deprived
He seeks food through alms,
For he fears [the threat] of excessive chores.

"Bring down Māra's prison, your [attachment to] your native land;
Cut the tethers of karma, the social norms;[206]
Run away from the objects of attachment and aversion, evil karma—
The friends you love and the enemies you hate.

"He has no farms, nor does he have cattle;
He cannot seek wealth, do crafts, or be the leader of others;
Nor can he seek profit or work as a servant;
For he fears [the threat of] excessive chores.

"Shunned from the ranks of humans, he is like a wild animal;
Searching for food only in the present, he is like a bird;
When suddenly standing up, his entire estate is complete;[207]
For he fears [the threat of] excessive chores.

"Not relying on one specific place or location,
Like the sun and moon, he roams everywhere free.
Training his mind through the three [levels of] understanding,
He relinquishes all negative deeds.
Such is the way of life of a Śākya lion,
For he fears [the threat of] excessive chores.

"These are not mere opinions—just read the sutras.
These [qualities] are found in detail there, so take an interest in them.
Free of tasks, abide on the path to liberation.
Journey forth vigorously to the state of omniscience. [80]

"When one upholds this [staff] and goes for alms
Before the doors of the householders,
To symbolize the closing of the doors of the lower realms
With the knot sealing the doors of the lower realms,
You should knock on the lower part of the door
Three times with three knocks at a time.

"Likewise, as a symbol of the opening of the Dharma door
By the buddha body of perfect enjoyment,
Knock on the upper part of the door, hitting the discordant objects of
    abandonment.
In between, ring forth for the householders
The jingling sounds of the twelve links of dependent origination.

"Do not shout lamentations from afar.
Forsake all behaviors abhorrent [to others]
And by abiding excellently in heedful behavior,
Liberate [others] through eloquent words.

"Except for that which is inappropriate,
Accept whatever food is offered, even of inferior quality.
Discarding attachment and aversion to good and bad [qualities],
Dedicate the roots of virtue and make aspirations.

"Embrace the place of the humble and nurture the higher grounds.
Always go for alms with purpose.

Uphold the life of the Buddha so that it does not wane.
Apply analysis that is in accord with the scriptures.
Through this may all please the three buddha bodies."

After he spoke thus, Drom responded: "Great Atiśa, today I have heard a great treatise. I have learned that one must relinquish material things and, while ensuring that one's aims of this life are not lost, one must pursue one's long-term ultimate aim through [the practice of] the seven riches of the noble ones. All of this is elucidated by the *khakkhara* staff. Although you have spoken extensively, if summarized in its entirety, it is this:

> **Forsake material possessions,**
> **Embellish yourself with the riches of the noble ones.**

"There is nothing other than this."

This concludes the eighth chapter from the *Jewel Garland of Dialogues*, "The Riches of the Noble Ones and the *Khakkhara* Staff."

CHAPTER 9
Songs of Perfect Purity

[81] On another occasion when father Atiśa and his son were staying at their residence at Nyethang Or, Drom asked: "You are a great paṇḍita learned in the five knowledge disciplines. So [tell me], in what places should one seek sustenance in the seven riches of the noble ones after having relinquished material possessions? What distractions should one give up?"

Atiśa replied:
"In pleasure gardens and towns,
In places with distractions and diversions,
Stirred by the words of frivolous speech, is the threat
Of being swept away by the māra of material possessions.

"Drom Jé, wherever you may reside,
Hammer down self-centered attachment;
Cling not to mundane pleasures as excellent;
The deceptions of the ordinary world are Māra's acts.

"Failing to secure a firm base for the future,
Yet endeavoring to fulfill this life's aims—
This is like building a house upon water.
You build three ornate stories with no foundation
And decorate them with vibrant colors and patterns,
And with small lotuses and a net of full and half garlands.

"When its basement sinks into the depths of the water,
What point is its majesty? Beware!
Without looking at a vessel's leaky bottom,
You spy the vessel and fill it up.
This is the fault of the foolish person who does not notice the leaks.
Before long [the contents] will trickle out.

"So listen, O excellent Drom Jé.
If, having obtained this human life so difficult to find,

A person fails to rely on the discipline of the three vows
And instead yearns for [worldly] harvests, such a person of mundane aims
Will be bereft of leisure when his life comes to an end.
His hoarded wealth will be of no use.
With no clothes, naked, he will be devoid of food;
With no companions, he will be separated from his loved ones.

"When his consciousness passes through the intermediate state,
He will feel remorse for his past karmic deeds;
He will feel attached to his hoarded possessions;
He will feel resentful toward his loved ones.

"Though he may say, 'Send my things after me!'
People will say 'What's the use? He is dead.'
Seizing his wealth, they will breed conflict.
Those who were closest to him will mourn for a few days.
This is no use, for it is the mourning of those without conscience.
Though they may wail with their chests out and throw dirt in their mouths,
Alas! This will only harm him.
Failing to bring benefits, it will bring [more] harm.

"Then, before too long,
When the deceased is undergoing intense suffering,
The mourning of the conscienceless will turn into laughter.
They cannot see him, nor can they hear him.

"Not only is all his hoarded wealth of no use,
Because of his miserliness, he ends up in the lower realms. [82]
Desperate for hope, heartless, he will have lost his aim.
Drom Jé, seek in your heart the precious wilderness,
[A site] isolated from these effects.

"Many are being swept away
By the mundane aims of this life in a shipless ocean of samsara,
Beaten by [waves of] attachment and aversion.

"Cling not to an essence amid that which is transient;
This multiplies the afflictions, distractions, dwellings, and beddings.

Thoroughly uproot the tree of poisons;
Nurture well the tree of other's welfare,
The sole medicine that brings forth joy.
With a tranquil and joyful mind, seek in your heart
The excellent wilderness, a place of solitude.

"Are you aware of this Drom Jé, excellent son?
The māras are experts in deceit and pretense;
The greedy are betrayed by varieties of wealth;
The practitioners are betrayed by the pretense of Dharma;
The industrious are betrayed by their conceit in seeking goodness;
The learned are betrayed by their inflated self-importance;
The kind are betrayed by being labeled 'He is very meritorious';
The distracted are betrayed by songs, drama, and music;
Most youth are betrayed by a youthful physical body.
Most people are betrayed by beautiful ornaments.

"Listen, seniormost son Drom Jé.
When concentration is increasing, let go of learning;
When learning and reflection are increasing, recall meditation;
When engaged in recitations, let go of concentration.
Ema! This would [certainly] enhance the concentrations.
Leave aside recitations not enforced by concentration.

"When a person climbs a tree,
If he lets go of the lower branches before
Grabbing on to the higher ones, he will fall in between.
Likewise, when engaging in any virtuous activity,
If one undertakes a [second] action
Without finishing the previous task, both will be undermined.

"Listen again, most excellent son.
Ordinary people who fail to secure a firm attainment,
Their antidotes are hollow, and they are carried away by Māra.
Most are deceived by negative friends, their [true] enemy.

"He who, despite forsaking the home life and meditating in the forest,
Is [still] the eldest son beholden to social customs,

Has no chance to abide [peacefully].
'He is dead and she is ill.'
'Come immediately to your native land.'
'If your aged parents are in such [a dire] state,
What is the use of a Dharma practice that demands long effort?'

"'Who among all of mother's sons
Is the best at looking after his parents?'
Unimpressed [with his Dharma practice,] they view it as pursuit of
    [merely] his own happiness.
However much they give to others, they long
For [wealth] themselves and are delighted when their wealth increases.
Shedding tears, they boast of their kindness.
Though claiming to love, in the long run they deceive.[208]

"*Ema!* Drom Jé, listen to me.
Those with little learning and ignorant of Māra's deeds,
Though their wish to do something may be great,
Due to their ignorance, their antidotes are impotent and unformed;
Mistaking them for real [antidotes] they charge after them. [83]
Then, when they see illness, death, and wailing,
Signaling the ending of this life,
Distraught, they are shaken by the winds of distractions.
Even at such a time they do not practice mind training.
Rather, looking at a crying face, they cry themselves.
They then become distracted by diverse chores.
They multiply distractions in a practitioner's wilderness.

"Ah! Do you know this Drom Jé, most excellent one?
Though residing amid such a [worldly] environment,
Saying, 'Such are the manifestations of samsara,'
One should journey alone toward nirvana.

"Ah! May the sufferings of others
Be absorbed into my heart,
And may the joys of this bodhisattva
Increase ever higher and ripen upon others.

"Listen all who have gathered here [and who are caught in] suffering:
The end of birth is death;
The end of meeting is separation;
The end of accumulation is depletion.

"Unaverted by children, wealth, or power,
One is swept away by Māra, the lord of death;
Since nothing can avert this,
At that point entrust yourself entirely to,
And seek refuge in, the Buddha, Dharma, and Sangha.

"Since such is the way of cyclic existence,
Extinguishing aspirations for this life's happiness,
I shall meditate in the solitude of the forest
And turn away from the objects of the senses.

"Now, if you think of me,
Do not wail or engage in frivolous speech.
Contemplate well the defects of cyclic existence.
With your thoughts, firmly go for refuge
To the [Three] Jewels and make supplications.

"'May all collections of negative karma be purified.'
Declare this and purify [negative deeds].
Furthermore guard your speech, a nest of defects.
Harbor no attachments and release them with ease.
Also call out the names of the tathāgatas
And receive the [vows of awakening] mind generation.
In this way, view the defects of samsara in its entirety
And work for the welfare of others.

"Listen to me, Gyalwai Jungné.
Places such as this [samsara] are distractions;
The disciple's wilderness is an isolation of the body;
The bodhisattva's wilderness is an isolation of the mind.
Those sites wherein self-desire is relinquished
And other's welfare [is found] are good. This is [the true] solitude,
Even in a town in the midst of people.

"Cultivate the thought of all as parents;
Nurture them all with compassion, as if they were your son;
Compassion destroys the demon of laziness,
And with perseverance, you accomplish [the aim] in an instant.

"This is just a rough outline;
The compassionate one, a hero among heroes
Who constantly dons the armor of effort,
Whose miraculous powers pervade the universe,
And who abides in isolation no matter where he is, [84]
Such an excellent being is a hero indeed.

"He who is not diverted by distractions but takes them onto the path,
Such an excellent skilled one is a hero indeed.
He who destroys the dense afflictions with their antidotes,
Such an excellent being is a hero indeed.

"He who has no attachment despite living
Amid immeasurable wealth is a hero indeed.
He who contemplates nonconceptuality
Even while surrounded by a thousand wonders is a hero indeed.

"He who remains indifferent while tormented
By one hundred harms is a hero indeed.
He who does not think of joy while showered
With words of praise is a hero indeed.

"He who does not fall prey while entertained
By a million attractive maidens is a hero indeed.
A son of a conqueror, a great hero,
Who remains undisturbed even when entering into battle
And fights with compassion is a hero indeed.
He who does not increase craving and grasping while dining
On one hundred delicious flavors is a hero indeed.

"Listen to me, hero, most excellent son.
The hero remains thoroughly steadfast,
And the hero nurtures the teaching of the heroes.

The hero does not cause the heroes to waver,
But readies the army of heroes [for combat].

"Heroically, the hero rescues his parents
From burning fire pits by flexing his heroic strength.
The hero remains poised in the posture of dancing;
The hero, undistracted by [external] symbols,
Heroically, [performs] the vajra dance of nonconceptuality.

"The hero crushes the distractions to pieces;
The hero casts his fierce glares to the ten directions;
The hero has utterly severed [the chains of] bondage;
The hero, seeking a hero for his teacher,
[Abides] in nonconceptuality within his vajra mind.

"At the celestial mansion of the hero,
Three times the hero dances outside the mandala;
The hero eradicates the lower realms.
Three times the hero dances in the front;
The hero severs all clinging conceptualizations.
Three times the hero shoots up [into the air];
The hero reduces the superior gods to common gods.
Three times the hero strikes the ground;
The hero tames the earth spirits and the irascible nāgas.

"The hero casts wide his eyes, darting back and forth;
The hero perceives the entire expanse of knowledge;
The hero signals with lotus-circling [gestures] to [all] ten directions;
The hero summons the heroes to the lotus seat.
The hero wields the heroic thunderbolt in a spiral;
The hero demolishes the mountain of the egoistic view.
The hero sows joys with beaming smiles;
The hero destroys obstacles with threatening gestures.[209]
The hero beats the skull drum of method and wisdom;
The hero blows the echoing blare of the thigh-bone trumpet;
The hero rings the bell [resounding] pristine melodies;[210]
O hero Drom Jé, there is [such] a celestial mansion. [85]

"O hero, ascend and come to the drops.
To you I shall grant the instruction;
To you I shall confer the great inner empowerment;
To you I shall bequeath the [Buddha's] teaching.

"Ascend, come into the teacher's heart.
Without conception, ascend to the stamen [of the heart-lotus].
O clear light, ascend and come on the moon;
Ascend, Dharma king, come into the tent of light rays.

"Gyalwai Jungné, consume [the food of] concentration.
Thundering the sounds of *hūṃs* and *phaṭs*,
The fierce ones, free of concepts, wear thick flames.
Thundering *hā! hā!* they don beaming smiles;
Thundering *hī! hī!* they are tranquil and disciplined;
Thundering *hū! hū!* they possess realizations;
Thundering *he! he!* they possess joys;
Thundering *hūṃ! hūṃ!* they possess compassion;
Thundering *oṃ! oṃ!* they are the unborn buddha body;
Thundering *āḥ! āḥ!* they are the unborn speech.
They are all of this, and you are the king of all.
You, adorned with armor, are the glory and lord of all.

"Wherever the distractions of this [samsaric] place are absent,
Wherever is utterly free of impurity, is [true] wilderness;
Utter absence of frivolous speech is [true] wilderness;
So guard your outward speech and internally [repeat] *hrīḥ*
And abide in the expanse of nonduality."

Drom Jé then felt satisfied and joyfully
Entered the mandala of his teacher's heart;
With delight upon the lotus stamen, he pressed down
On the moon disc of nonconceptual clear light.
He viewed the assembly of outer, inner, and secret divinities;
He took all conceptualizations into the expanse of the dharmakāya;
He proclaimed aloud conventions as the profound path.

"View: Do not waver toward conceptual elaborations;
Meditation: Place your mind in the ultimate mode of being;

Action: Engage in the excellent conduct of goodness."
Proclaiming thus he enacted these in a dance.

Through the music of method and wisdom,
He [Atiśa] thundered aloud, spreading these [teachings] to all places
    of goodness;
At that time he sang a song of the view:

"O sovereign, unsullied ultimate expanse.
The view devoid of 'I' has vanished into the expanse;
Ungraspable, the object [too] has vanished into the expanse.

"Though perceptions of this and that are infinite,
The source from which they first arose is lost.
What place exists where they can return to at the end?
In the present, they are not related to anything.
As for this law of nature, devoid of [all] three times,
With nothing to see, one is deceived by the objects;
With nothing to remember, one is deceived by oneself.

"In this nondual awareness
There is too much fluctuation, destroying self-composure.
So many bumps and aches exist but, when probed, they perish.
Why are you deluded by something that does not exist?

"Drom, from within a transparent crystal flower
The buddhas, the appearances of unreal buddha bodies, emerge.
This is a positive perception born of auspiciousness and good
    karma. [86]
If you cling to this it casts you far away.

"Ah! All of this is groundless and [mere] effulgence of words;
This [world of appearance] is devoid of the thoughts of clinging
    and the clung.
Awareness that cannot sustain itself and is a mere luminosity;
To what does it cling and how does it do so?

"What is illuminated is conception-free, devoid of substantial reality.
O the world of unexamined diversity may seem attractive;

Hā! How is it that when probed they are no more?
Āḥ! This is so for they are unborn and empty of themselves;
Phaṭ! Now let them be free in natural liberation.

"Drom, this is my way of relinquishing the distractions;
Drom, this is what my wilderness is like.
Contemplate these with joy, my followers.
If among the disciples,[211] I, a Kadampa,
Sing aloud this song of the view of [emptiness],
What do those who claim to be Mahayanists say?"

[Drom:] "In general those who follow father Atiśa,
Who in turn follows in the footsteps of Avadhūti—
What Mahayanist would call them the Lesser Vehicle people?

"That diligence does not slide into ignorance for me
Is due to having nurtured the Dharma, the source of the buddhas;
That scholarship does not impair discipline for me
Is due to having contemplated the profound causality of karma;
That meditation does not impair recitation for me
Is due to having read the profound sacred sutras;
That reading [sutras] does not impair concentration for me
Is due to having digested the sovereign teacher's pith instructions.

"That I know how to practice in one sitting,
Thoroughly integrating all the teachings,
Is due to having endured hardships in Dharma practice.
He who is called 'sovereign Buddha' is all-knowing;
He has perfected abandonment and realization, as well as the two
    accumulations.

"As I aspire for this for the benefit of my parents,
First, through learning, I will cut [the knots of] my doubts;
Second, through reflection, I will cut [the knots of] my doubts;
Third, through meditation, I will cut [the knots of] my doubts.

"Also, each of these three is not pursued in isolation from the others;
When learning I bring reflection and meditation to bear;

When reflecting I bring learning and meditation to bear;
When meditating I bring learning and reflection to bear.[212]

"By integrating all without exception,
I know how to travel by taking Dharma on the path;
As I, a Kadam, have not fallen into a partial approach,
I understand well the entire display, [the world of]
Cause and effect, as optical illusions; this is Kadam.[213]

"I am ecstatic, O most holy Atiśa!
How auspicious it is that the sevenfold divinities and teachings
Are my refuge, the Three Jewels that encompass all.
In general whatever lineage of teachings one may speak of,
[You must check] whether it is encompassed within the Three Jewels of
    refuge.
If it is, then you should embrace it.

"If you harbor attachment and aversion while claiming to be a
    practitioner, [87]
Your practice will not be effective, so it is not the Three [Jewels].
Yet, as for me, even in terms of the future,
The Three Jewels will remain my refuge.
If your practice is effective, whoever you may be, you are excellent;
If you work for other's welfare you are an excellent being.

"Listen, all practitioners who are mindful and intelligent,
Some insane people say such things as:
'All phenomena share the nature of emptiness;
Within that truth there is no karma, no cause and effect.
I eat without discriminating whatever appears at my mouth;[214]
Those who possess judgments suffer downfall.'
I am a person who says the opposite.

"For if nothing exists for you, man,
What need is there to eat whatever untimely meals you find?
A son of a barren woman cannot be hungry!
If, however, things do exist with substantial reality,
Listen, then, you will be eating [food] all the time,

Or 'eating' and 'not eating' will become meaningless.
If they are proven to exist, they cannot cease to be;
If they become nothing, what use will eating serve?

"Ours is the tradition that follows Atiśa;
It is the lineage of the profound view of [emptiness].
Because phenomena lack true existence, diverse appearances arise;
Since [true] referents never were, phenomena arise and pass away.

"Some assert judgments to be as opposed as fire and water.
The reflection of red burning fire is there in the water;
If things are truly real it cannot arise in the water.
The moon, which is fifty yojanas wide,[215]
Can be seen reflected in the water inside an offering bowl.

"I say that this [moon] comes about because in reality it is false.
Without the eyes touching the atoms, forms appear to the eyes;
I say that this is so because in reality it is false.
Also, it is not that it does not exist, for diversities appear.
The contingent is not [truly] existent, or else it could not move.
Within the middle way all sorts of appearances arise.

"Though everything is an appearance of falsity,
Without form how can its reflection come to be?
Though the preceding cause may be false, effects ensue nonetheless;
So do not defy karma but adhere to its practice.
This is the [profound] view lineage of my Kadam [way].

"Though I generate incalculable divinities and their mansions
Within a single drop and make offerings to them,
Toward the teachings presenting the subtle and minute aspects of karma,
I neither exaggerate nor diminish, but implement them in practice.
This is the inspirational lineage of my Kadam [way].

"In the illusory mansion of the appearance and emptiness of phenomena,
Gradually treading the levels and paths to ever-higher stages,
One perfects the cause, the dual collections, and becomes a buddha.
This is the [vast] practice lineage of my Kadam [way].

"Those who challenge this truth are of Māra's camp;
When beings see snow and conch shells as black,
This must be viewed as the defects of the eyes alone.[216]

"Glorious Dīpaṃkara, unrivaled and peerless,
Master, untainted by darkness, you are most radiant; [88]
From your pure mind, the nature of space,
Enjoy this song that I, your son, offer.

"When all the points are condensed, everything is appearance and
    emptiness;
If you listen to the words well, they are empty echoes;
If you reflect upon the meanings well, they are free of elaborations;
In rapture these words slipped from the door of my mouth.

"If errors or faults beset the meanings please bear them;
Even if ramblings have occurred, cast them into the ultimate
    expanse;
Now whatever excellent virtues we may have gathered,
We must obtain a secure level so that none can rob them.
If karma and its causality are true, may these [wishes] be realized.

"Ah, something more is left [to say].
Since all phenomena are but false appearances,
How can karma and its effects be true?
Examine also whether this [causality] is undeceiving.
It is most excellent if finally the three buddha bodies are attained;
So be they true or false, may I attain these [buddha bodies]."

As Drom spoke these lines, Atiśa said, "Drom has played well the game of
the sublime teaching. Today I feel tamed by the Dharma. Now summarize
well all the conversations that took place between us, the master and his
student."

Drom:
"Most sublime teacher, listen to me.
When all the points are condensed it is like this:

Avoid all trifling distractions,
And reside in the solitude of wilderness.

Abandon frivolous words;
Constantly guard your speech.

"It seems that there is nothing other than this."

This concludes the ninth chapter from the *Jewel Garland of Dialogues*, "Songs of Perfect Purity."

CHAPTER 10

Cultivating through Honor
and the Perfect Mode of Seeing

[89] On another occasion when Atiśa and his son were staying at their residence in Nyethang Or, Drom asked:

"Among the teachers who are scholars of great learning,
Though many kindhearted ones exist in the world,
Rare as a day-star are those who possess pure ethical discipline.
Even were those with pure ethical discipline incalculable,
Only one or two among them would be free of self-centered desire."

Atiśa spoke:
"If the attachment of self-centered desire enters one's heart,
One no longer has pure ethical discipline.
For pure ethical discipline helps accomplish
The two perfect purposes."[217]

Drom Jé responded:
"All the kind disciples and self-enlightened ones
Who, on the basis of their own system of teachings,
Possess not even a single affliction—
They aspire for their own well-being;
Is this not diligence in ethical discipline?"

Atiśa then spoke:
"An excellent question, Drom Jé;
Those who have made it to the dry shores of joy,
Where one's body is untainted by the stains—
They are diligent at not being sunk in polluted water;
[Such] an accomplishment of one's own well-being,
That is only [true] diligence."

Drom Jé replied:
"Compared to the bodhisattvas

Are the disciples and self-enlightened ones really diligent?
How can someone who is not in accord with these be diligent?"

Atiśa responded:
"Because the bodhisattvas have all three [qualities],[218]
They cannot be compared with disciples and self-enlightened ones;
They [bodhisattvas] display what appear to be flaws, yet this is a mere
    likeness."

Drom Jé then said:
"So, though many may be diligent,
I say that those who lack self-centered desires are few;
The diligent who are attached to self-centered desires
Are the disciples and self-enlightened ones, sovereign teacher.
The diligent who are not attached to self-centered desires
Are the noble children of the conquerors, master.

"So to these incalculable kind and diligent beings,
Who performs veneration to repay their kindness?"

Atiśa replied:
"It is the teachers, preceptors, and masters."

Drom asked further:
"Who are appropriate friends for them?"

Atiśa responded:
"These are the persons who possess the eyes of Dharma;
They have reached the beginning of the path of accumulation.
As sentient beings on the beginner's stage
Will be blessed subsequently by the buddhas,
They, too, are friends who are appropriate." [90]

Drom Jé then asked:
"When one sees them how should one meditate?"

Atiśa responded:
"Whenever you see your teachers, preceptors, and masters,

Adorn them with respectful venerations;
Mentally pay homage and circumambulate them clockwise
And imagine taking them upon your crown.

"Theirs are gifts of scholarship, diligence, and kindness;
These [qualities] depend upon how much you strive to please them.
Those who are learned in the Dharma and who see the Dharma,
Those who do not defy cause and effect and who sustain others—
Visualize such beings of wisdom and compassion as pure
And call them 'teachers who are my saviors.'

"Though someone may have the mind of a beginner,
He must also be ascertained as a basis of excellence;
He too is a source of benefit and happiness;
So contemplate him as a teacher as well."

Drom Jé then inquired:
"When one sees all [other] sentient beings,
What kind of thoughts should one cultivate?"

Atiśa replied:
"Contemplate all who are older as your parents;
As for those who are in their youth,
Contemplate them as your dear sons or daughters;
As for those who are of equal age,
Contemplate them as your brothers or sisters.

"There is none who has never been your parent;
There is none who has never been your child either;
All are parents, children, and grandchildren with none excluded.

"Draw them forth through the four immeasurable thoughts.
When good occasions arise, reveal the sublime Dharma;
Even if no such fortune arises, this will leave some imprints."

Then Drom proclaimed:
"Paṇḍita, learned and most wise,
Supreme treasury of all well-spoken insights,

Lamp of teaching illuminating the ultimate mode of being,
O supreme teacher, my main refuge.

"Source of glory, most kind,
Sustaining your followers, such as myself,
[You have taught us how to] generate the aspiring and engaging minds—
Call all sentient beings our mothers.

"'How can I attain buddhahood for their sake?'
You should aspire for the attainment of buddhahood.
And from the depths of your heart,
You should engage in the act of giving
Whatever they need, without attachment—
Your sons and daughters,
Your heart, flesh, and bones,
The internal body parts and skin as well,
Your head, limbs, eyes, and so on,
The five precious metals and excellent horses,
Elephants, buffaloes, and wish-granting cows,
Groves and pleasure houses,
Grains, treasuries, and cuisine of one hundred flavors,
Clothes, jewelry, and incense—
Give these if you possess them or through obtaining them.
This, too, [you should do to] bring these beings onto the path.

"Furthermore, satisfying them with Dharma gifts,
Such as the concentrations and so on, [91]
You should, without regard for your own suffering,
Bear hardships and lead your parents.

"So my teacher, listen to me.
You, teacher, have brought into the order
Those who aspire for buddhahood,
Being pulled forth by the chariots of aspiring and engaging [minds].
It is the teacher who illustrates
The excellence of such [deeds].
As I venerate you, please descend to my crown.

"Furthermore, generating myself into a divinity
Through the seed letter and fusing with the wisdom being,
And reaching perfection within the great expanse of reality—
This empowerment [too] is due to the teacher's kindness.
To indicate that this, too, was your doing,
As I venerate you, please descend to my crown.

"'Teacher' refers to these two.[219]
Those who, by turning us away from
The householder's life, which is devoid of heedfulness,
Confer the vows of individual liberation—
They are the preceptors and masters.

"Furthermore, those who grant excellent insights
And correct us from the flawed paths—
They, too, are excellent preceptors and masters.
In order to repay your excellent kindness,
As I venerate you, please descend to my crown.

"Respectfully I pay homage to you through my three doors;
I confess my negative karma and rejoice;
I [appeal to you to] turn the wheel of the Dharma and not to depart;
And I dedicate all my roots of virtue and supplicate you to remain;
Respectfully I shall always make offerings.[220]

"Furthermore, savior Atiśa,
Those who possess the wisdom of learning, reflection, and meditation,
Who are thoroughly trained in the eyes of Dharma—
Such excellent beings are excellent friends [indeed].
Those with the eyes of Dharma, please descend to my crown.
I will venerate you as if you were my teacher;
I will honor you as if you were my teacher;

"Though you may possess a novice's mind,
Since you reveal the excellent [awakening] mind,
I will supplicate to you as my teacher.
Furthermore, I will meditate on my teachers,
As I venerate you at my crown,

Uwavering from kindheartedness, please abide there.
These then are my objects of honor."

This concludes the presentation of the collection on the objects of honor.

"Most excellent teacher, the source of the buddhas,
Born in Bengal you are the supreme son of a Dharma king,
The sole eye of beings, O glorious Dīpaṃkara,
Your peerless intelligence pervades all.

"Though versed in all fields you remain unconceited;
You, the one who engages in the [ascetic] conduct, pray enter my heart.
My parents are being swept away by the enemy of the afflictions;
Caught by enemies, they are utterly submerged in the lake
Of the four rivers of birth, aging, sickness, and death.
O teacher, skilled oarsman of the boat of liberation, [92]
Steer with the paddles of benefit and happiness
And help bring my parents ashore to dry land.

"Most of them are lost in the infinite ocean.
My teacher, you are the nāga with the jewel in your crown.
Pray lead my parents ashore to dry land.
Pray lead them, you endowed with the excellent glory of might.

"Wise one of great compassion, listen to me.
Some of my parents are being burned in flames;
Some of my parents are being dissected with weapons;
Some of my parents are being devoured by insects;
Some of my parents are being eaten by ravens;
Some of my parents are being immersed in boiling lava.

"Unable to bear this, they rush to the plains,
Where they find themselves on a path through a vast land filled with
    razors.
Horrified, as they escape again,
Knives rain down from trees that they confused for cooling shade.
Naked, they are tortured by the cold as well—
In moaning, blistering, and popping blistering hells,

In splitting-like-a-lotus and splitting-like-an-utpala hells.
Such is the fate of my parents today.

"If a person's parents have fallen into a fire pit,
The courageous, unable to bear this, will strive to rescue them.
If this is so, how can I bear my parents' fate?
Alas! Master Drom, do not remain idle.[221]

"My parents suffer the fate of having no clothes.
With no food and straw-thin throats, they have large bellies;
Their limbs are thin and they have no strength at all.
How can you bear this? Drom Jé, do think of this.[222]

"Even if I look at my parents who are delusion-ridden,
Powerless, they are tormented by unbearable suffering.
For many their own flesh becomes their enemy;
For some their hair, skin, blood, and bones rise as enemies;
For some their own strength and kinetic force rise as their enemies;
For some their speed enslaves them and rises as their enemy;
Some, powerless, are assailed by the four elements.
Think, Drom Jé, can you bear this fate of your parents?

"Alas! Even within the so-called happiness of the higher realms,
The body that is born straight becomes bent;
The hair that is black at birth becomes white;
Soft skin of white, yellow, and red tinge, free of wrinkles,
Degenerates into [skin that is] bluish, dry, and furrowed;
[You] no longer [appear] attractive to the minds of all.
Even your own son, nurtured with the tenderest love, glares [at you].
Transient, they all depart to the world beyond;
Can you bear this, Drom? This deserves reflection.

"Though everyone is our parents, children, nephews, and nieces,
We don't regard the other as such and instead assail them.
Can you bear this brute nature? Reflect on this, Drom.
Do not waver from your recognition of them as parents,
As children, and as grandchildren, and lead them with love.
Is there any fault in doing so, Atiśa?

Attend to this well, O wise and compassionate one; [93]
Grant your blessings, O peerless Dharma king.

"Since we cannot afford to be separated [from you],
Please nurture me until samsara is emptied for the sake of [all] my
     parents.
[Now] when I see all sentient beings,
This is the way I will lead them—
Thinking of them as parents, children, or siblings."

This concludes the section on how one should care for them.

Atiśa then exclaimed:
"Your speech is eloquent indeed, principal son!
Yes, maintain such thoughts toward all;
I have nothing more to add."

Drom Jé then responded:
"Though there were many queries and responses,
When all the points are condensed it is like this.

> **When you see your teachers and preceptors,**
> **Reverently generate the wish to serve.**
>
> **Toward wise beings with Dharma eyes**
> **And toward beginners on the path as well,**
> **Recognize them as your spiritual teachers.**
> **[In fact,] when you see any sentient being,**
> **View them as your parent, your child, or grandchild.**

"There is nothing other than this."

This concludes the tenth chapter from the *Jewel Garland of Dialogues*,
"Cultivating through Honor and the Perfect Mode of Seeing."

Chapter 11
How to Nurture Sublime Beings and Their Deeds

[94] On another occasion when Atiśa and his son were on their way from Thangpoché to Nyethang, Drom said:

"Prophesized by our maiden deity,[223]
Sugatas appeared in Atiśa's heart.
Though you work magnificently for the welfare of beings,
As you rest at ease in my dwelling,
O learned Atiśa, I, your son, shall entertain you.[224]

"Are you free from illness?
Conqueror, are your faculties pristine?
Are you enjoying the state of well-being?
Is your physical health without flaw?

"In Buddha Bhaiṣajyaguru's presence,[225]
Inside the garden of medicinal herbs,
I have come to collect some flowers.
Compassionate one, kindly grant me some."

Atiśa replied:
"Lord of Tibet, listen to me.
I have no discomfort whatsoever.
You, Tibet's sublime person, are most excellent;
Compared to you I am inferior.

"Avalokiteśvara, listen to me.
As no excellent virtues come to be
In sites where negative friends reside,
Where can I find a site where good friends reside
That lacks the companions of attachment and aversion?

"Alas! It is better to thoroughly renounce
Negative friends and seek a spiritual friend.

I am like the clouds in the sky—
Seemingly real yet so hard to catch;
I am like a tent of light rays,
Seemingly wonderful yet so hard to catch;
I am like the rays of the sun,
Clear, unveiled by the clouds of defects;
I am like the medicinal tree,
When sought health prevails both now and long term.

"Drom Jé, where is [such] a place of solitude?
Do reflect, I've come here thinking of you."

The great compassionate one responded:
"For you to relieve your sadness, my teacher,
We have Nyethang, a realm of happiness.
In all four seasons of summer, fall, winter, and spring,
It is most pleasant to live there and flowers bloom.

"Hosts of gods will honor you.
This is a great place to relax, great conqueror.
When the seasons of summer and fall approach,
The green meadows on the plain are strewn with flowers;
Tree branches bloom forth with beautiful foliage;
Springs and lakes exude coolness and sweet perfume;
Where beautiful flowers blossom,
Swarms of bees gather and hum melodious tunes.

"An array of lovely birds dwell there as well,
Warbling their melodious tunes. [95]
The earth is fertile, supporting a variety of grains;
With such prosperity, people's welfare flourishes.

"In these countless springs and pools,
Geese, ducks, and waterfowl swim with ease,
Calling forth their melodious songs.
To this place where flowers grow even in winter,
Come, conqueror; there are no negative friends.

"I, too, will renounce negative friends
And rely upon you, a spiritual friend.
Furthermore, I will lead beings to happiness.
O teacher, do come to this open land."

The glorious Dīpaṃkara said:
"My principal son, listen to me.
Discard hostile and unhappy mental states
And venture forth to where happiness lies.[226]

"My principal son, most compassionate one,
Reflect on the karma of all sentient beings.
Lead me to the site of virtue;
Take me to the place free of negative friends;
In such places spiritual activities flourish."

Having said this, without hesitation
The conqueror embarked on the road with his son,
And Drom Jé inquired:

"Who is a negative friend?
What must one do to relinquish such a friend?
Who is a spiritual friend?
What must one do to rely on such a friend?

"What is that object of aversion?
What is that mind of unpleasantness?
How does one travel to the place of happiness?
Teacher, most learned among paṇḍitas,
With an altruistic heart reveal these to me."

The teacher responded:
"He who separates you from liberation's lifeline—
That butcher is your negative friend;
The rope that binds you to the fetters
Of substantial things and their signs is a negative friend.

"He who separates you, the diligent, from morality,
That morally degenerate one is your negative friend;
He who brings the sublime down to the ordinary,
That arrogant one is your negative friend.

"He who presumes to measure the immeasurable,
That presumptuous measurer is your negative friend;
He who, even when death is certain to occur at dawn,
Seeks the mundane aims of this life
And does not contemplate impermanence for even an instant,
That nonchalance is your negative friend.

"He who gives you 'beneficial' advice
With aims concerned with trivial mundane affairs
And definitely destroys your future—
That trickster is your negative friend.

"He who topples the vase of morality,
The excellent soil [from which spring] all higher qualities,
He might seem joyful to the eyes of the morally degenerate,
But all seductresses delighting in this are your negative friends.

"Those rich in sensual objects, songs, and dances,
Beautiful adornments, luxurious clothes, and lavish food, [96]
And boisterous partying with gales of laughter—
All those who indulge in these are your negative friend.

"The one who resides in samsara but remains unmoved
And who, when it comes time to work for others' welfare, seeks
    solitude—
Such a one learned in scholarship is your negative friend.

"One who takes from the hands of those who give without
    possessiveness
And who says, 'A person of no wealth has no happiness,
So do not give away [wealth] but keep it'—
Such a 'kindhearted' person is your negative friend.

"Though others may have no ill will they are let down
By befriending those who do all sorts of ills,
Like the son who slays people and dooms his father—
Those with evil karma are your negative friends.

"Failing to honor the sublime, he nurtures [negative] friends;
Failing to serve his parents, he nurtures a demoness;
Failing to reciprocate kindness, he is swift in retaliation—
He who has no discipline is your negative friend.

"He who is strong in self-grasping, the root of suffering,
And desires for himself all things in the world;
He who disparages others, even the sublime ones—
This 'oneself alone' is your negative friend.

"Ignorant of joyfulness in general and happiness in particular,
They let down the community and yearn for their own happiness;
Those distorted in understanding, who fail to see the true mode of
    being—
All such learned ones are your negative friends.

"He who makes you procrastinate,
Though you aspire to perform virtue, is also a negative friend;
He who dithers with procrastination while something can be
    accomplished right now—
What use is feeling remorse for such a person from the depths of your
    heart?
Such a dull person is also a negative friend.

"Instead of saying, 'No matter how much one reflects,
Nothing else is of benefit, so practice Dharma,'
He says, 'All Dharma practices are easy and comfortable.'
He who draws you closer to suffering is a negative friend.

"My heart-son, excellent Drom Jé,
Be aware of these and forsake negative friends.
For antidotes against them, rely on a spiritual friend.

"Are not ill-suited environments, beds, and so forth similar to a prison?
He who, when observing pure monastic discipline, boasts about the
    'Great Vehicle,'
Yet indulges in luxuries that undermine its very foundation—
He, too, is a negative friend so must be forsaken.

"As for partaking in meat, alcohol, and the like,
Read the *vinaya* discipline texts and the sutras as well,
And if there is a stronger case for permission then it is allowed.
But the sacred words of the Buddha never deceive.
He who consumes that which is not permitted,
Despite engaging in the study [of these texts], is also a negative friend.

"Some insult excellent bodhisattvas who, having forsaken their own
    well-being,
Display diverse activities, consume anything at will as if mentally
    afflicted,
And act with knowledge of the true mode of being.
He who asserts that [such bodhisattvas] 'have no discipline' is also a
    negative friend who must be forsaken.

"He who, [regarding] those who destroy concepts within their natural
    states
And whose generation and completion stages are inconceivable,
Insults them saying, 'They are like dogs and pigs'—[97]
Know that he, too, is a negative friend who must be forsaken.

"In brief, he who hinders your path
To the temporary and ultimate well-being,
Whoever such a person may be—
Know that he is a negative friend and forsake him."

This is the collection on forsaking negative friends.

"Excellent Drom, principal son, listen to me.
Today let us pass the day on this road in Dharma.
This place is wide and barren;
Nyethang is somewhat far from here, too.

"I have not come here from India
For trivial conversations, though.
Speaking of and listening to things that have no benefit
To the heart are false and useless tasks.

"If it benefits the heart it is an instruction;
He who puts it into practice is a suitable vessel.
He who reveals well the qualities of liberation,
He who reveals well the defects of cyclic existence,
He who reveals the norms of affirmation and rejection—
He is a spiritual friend, so rely upon him.

"He who reveals the sublime Dharma of going for refuge
And generating the mind of enlightenment—
Whoever such a person may be,
He is a spiritual friend, so rely upon him.

"He who reveals the very opposite
Of the ways taught by negative friends
Is the most excellent spiritual friend;
So rely upon him as an object of respect.

"He who reveals the six perfections
Associated with the four immeasurable thoughts
Through excellent skillful means and wisdom—
He is a spiritual friend, so rely upon him.
This will have lasting benefit."

This is the collection on reliance upon a spiritual friend.

"Excellent Drom Jé, principal son, listen to me.
Those who have entered the erroneous path of extreme views
Are greatly hostile toward the Buddha's teaching.
They are hostile toward the community that upholds this [teaching].
Such persons are certainly sources of unhappiness.

"Since feelings of unhappiness arise from them,
Discard hostile and unhappy mental states
And depart to a place devoid of them.

"The morally degenerate are hostile toward discipline;
Pledge-breakers are hostile toward the corrective rites.
For the ethically disciplined and pledge-bound,
It is better to discard hostile and unhappy mental states
And depart to a place of happiness.

"Those who are filled with greed cannot tolerate
The fortunate ones who engage in the four means of gathering
    others; [98]
Out of jealousy they relate to them with hostility.
So forsake hostility and its objects and depart to a place of happiness.

"Though in this world what does not accord
With [the ways of] the ignorant is Dharma,
Those endowed with brutish nature,
Who, with [thoughts of] 'me' and 'him,' feel hostility toward others
And are fraught with instinctive attachment and aversion,
They become hostile to anyone who is the 'other.'

"Excellent Drom Jé, principal son, pray listen.
Excellent Drom Jé, a king of armor, pray listen.
Be it at the edge of a town or in the wilderness;
Be it in a cemetery or at the root of a tree;
Be it by the seashore or in a crevice between rocks;

"By residing well in a place of solitude,
If hostility and unhappiness arise no more,
Enhance virtuous deeds and work for others' welfare.
If hostility and unhappiness arise, however,
Depart to a place where you feel most joyful.

"If, having gone there for three days or a week,
Or for half a month, a month, or a year,
Hostility and unhappiness do not arise,
This is a place of solitude, so embrace that site.

"[However] the instant [hostility and unhappiness] arise,
Then, like a rabbit waking up from its sleep,

[Instantly] depart to [another] place of joy.
Listen, excellent Drom Jé, supreme among my sons.

"Be it a dilapidated house with a mere room for oneself;
Be it a shelter that others can barely see;
Be it a donkey shed that even the donkeys don't like;
Be it a shed made of slates or leaves;
Be it a deep cave or a crevice between rocks;
Wherever you reside, there is no end
To honoring the Three Jewels and such objects of honor.
The ethically disciplined who aspire for liberation
Are continuously protected [by the Three Jewels].

"At such time even if you possess many objects of veneration,
Such as icons, they become sources of attachment;
So in the space in front of you generate from a syllable a lotus trunk
And place upon it your teacher, the Three Jewels, and the meditation
    deities.

"Offer them the seven limbs of practice;
Supplicate them thoroughly from your heart
For your temporary and long-term welfare.

"Alternatively, generate within your own heart,
A fire of wisdom [emerging] from a *raṃ* [syllable]
And burn away the hosts of afflictions;
Offer your flesh-and-blood body in a fire rite.

"Then burn entirely in this fire—
Bright, nonconceptual, and utterly clear—
The defilements of other [beings] as well.

"Next, fiercely increasing the power of fire,
Deflate the pride of demons and upholders of extreme views.
By means of giving, ethical discipline, forbearance,
Perseverance, concentration, insight, method, and power,
And by means of aspiration and great pristine cognition,
For the sake of all journeying to enlightenment,

Proclaim the following ten syllables:
Oṃ candra mahārokṣaṇa hūṃ phaṭ.[227] [99]

"As you proclaim these ten spiritual deeds,
Generate a *hūṃ* amid the fire.
This *hūṃ* melts into fire; from this, generate a form
With one face, two arms, and with one leg bent and one outstretched.

"With a dark blue body, he is most terrifying;
He fiercely wields the sword of wisdom in the sky;
With threatening gestures, he warns the army of demons;
He overwhelms the serpent-hooded nāgas.

"Wearing a tigerskin loincloth, he threatens the animals;
His round bloodshot eyes glare in all ten directions;
His charcoal black hair is raised upward.
Generate such [an awe-inspiring] form and cultivate
Compassion, emptiness' true mode of being.
With altruistic thoughts safeguard the teaching.

"When you reside in a place of solitude,
This is an excellent spiritual practice free of attachment.
Be aware of this, principal son;
This is the environment and bedding of sublime beings."

This is the collection on relying upon the environment and bed of true well-being.

Next, Drom said:
"In this age of the last five-hundred-year cycle,
By relying upon your sacred scriptures, sovereign teacher,
I have undertaken the practice of the precious Dharma jewel.
I seek places free of attachment and aversion;
I strive to be free of companions who are objects of attachment and
    aversion;
I constantly rely upon spiritual friends for protection;
I nurture as attendants only those who aspire for liberation.

"In a green meadow strewn with beautiful flowers
I practice the four immeasurable thoughts, leaving deep imprints.
Ultimately, journeying through a series of pure realms,
I will lead all my mothers to the land of jewels."

[Atiśa:] "With your body emerging from the hub of a lotus,
You bring [all] within the fold of your loving-kindness.
Persevere, son, all your [key] followers could
Appear [in this land] in fifty years or more."

[Drom:] "Look at this well, all who are sighted;
This is the crossroads of good, evil, and neutral actions;
This is the time to make your choice.
Those who transcend the force of concepts exceed fifty;[228]
So now, undeceived by the food of shamelessness,
The time has come to advise this rat hole–like mouth.

"Alas, human food is not worth our attachment
When we have the delicious nourishment of ambrosia's essence;
The food of concentration is delectable at all times.

"You are like the water inside a container—
When sought for from the right it spills from the left;
When sought from the left it spills from the right.
Have no excessive attachment to wealth, which has no essence;
Increase the two accumulations, the eternally delicious food. [100]

"These are the suggestions from within me.
These are great instructions for those who have the heart.
Today, I am your companion on the road."

Atiśa replied:
"Excellent Drom Jé, my eldest son,
From this very day auspicious tidings have begun.
It has relieved my exhaustion from journeying.
I have learned that there can be a teaching
That enables everything you do to succeed.

"Those who aspire for liberation,
However they conduct themselves,
They become a resource of Dharma practice alone;
Even in dreams they experience visions of the Dharma.

"Even in terms of the behavior of the childlike worldly ones,
The son of a brahman plays games about the Vedas;
The son of a king plays games about kingdoms;
The son of a butcher plays games about skinning;
The [son of a] skilled musician indulges in song and dance;
And that of a skilled draftsman plays with his drawings.
In brief, whatever activities the parents engage in,
The children will imitate such games.

"Know that all of this is due to imprinting.
Thus, if you thoroughly cultivate the excellent propensities
For learning, reflection, and meditation,
Such [propensities] will follow you throughout all times:
In dreams, in the in-between [waking] states, in birth, and in death,
And during the intermediate state of existence as well.

"Those with the Buddha will become buddhas;
Those with higher births will have higher birth;
Those with clean realms will have clean realms;
Those with the abyss [of hell] will have the abyss;

"For those who are wealthy and give charity,
[The propensities for] this, too, will follow them;
For those who act miserly even though they possess wealth,
Bereft and craving [birth as a] hungry ghost will ensue.

"Those who commit evil deeds will become hell beings;
Those who are close-minded will become animals;
Those filled with hate will experience conflicts and dispute;
Those of strong forbearance will receive excellent bodies.

"Those with perseverance will become Dharma kings;
Those who are ethically disciplined will have higher rebirths,

And in such higher rebirths, joy and happiness will follow.
Therefore, everything follows after its causes.

"Similar things are the progenitors of similar things;
All things follow after their propensities.
Although all propensities are equal in being imprinted,
Imprint propensities that are perfect.

"I will reveal the details when hoisting the robes.[229]
Drom Jé, in the deluded perceptions of others,
'Atiśa and his son are exhausted,' they say;
'The road of this long journey is difficult,' they say;
'There are evil people like robbers about,' they say.
So take me swiftly to our destination."

Saying this, he departed miraculously.
As he arrived at Nyethang Or,
He displayed diverse manifestations
According to the perceptions of individual beings.

Again he said:
"May the flowers of your consent blossom; [101]
Drom Jé, you have displayed the flowers of *na*.[230]
Drom Jé, you're skilled in the provisional meaning;
May the assembly of deities descend to this site.

"May the flowers of the celestial realm rain upon this site.
Emaho! Lord Avalokiteśvara,
Such are the flowers of great compassion.
Drom Jé, look at the [blossoming of these] small [lotuses].[231]

"Strikingly, the petals have opened."
[Drom:] "Their false solid forms remain just about intact."
"Show me the tongue that speaks these words!"
So Drom Jé stretched out his tongue, it is said.

One could see a flower sprouting upon it.
Seeing this Atiśa was pleased.

"Alas! Here indeed is a great wonder!
Drom Jé's tongue is like a meadow with a pond,
Except that the bees have not converged there;
Is it that there is no nectar in his mouth?"

Drom Jé stretched out his tongue again
And upon the lotus was [a miniscule] Atiśa.
As Atiśa saw this he exclaimed:
"This makes me laugh indeed.
Drom has turned me into a honeybee!
I am so small, about the size of a barley seed!"

Then he touched it with his hand.
Atiśa on the lotus laughed at this.
This awoke a laughing monster inside Atiśa;
Repeatedly they both laughed aloud.

Then Drom declared:
"As for this white flower growing in winter,[232]
Be kind and do not turn me into a con artist;
Generally, it is very cold in this barbarian borderland, and
In Uru in particular, much of the ground freezes where water flows.
If a five-petal flower growing on the ground in winter
Pleases you, Master Atiśa, then it doesn't matter if it's unreal,
So it grows on Drom's tongue [as well].
When the bees were asked after, a tathāgata's body appeared.
Initiating laughter, the tathāgata himself laughed—
He laughed like a maiden astonished to see her own face [in a mirror];
He laughed like a goddess who has just revealed herself.
May the auspiciousness of the teacher being pleased prevail."

The most venerable teacher spoke again:
"Drom Jé, reveal to us again the flower on your tongue."
As Drom stretched out his tongue and showed it again,
A miniscule Drom appeared before the teacher,
As he glanced eagerly at the teacher's face with a smile,
The teacher then heard melodious speech in the voice of a child.

The instant he saw this he became thoroughly ecstatic.
"This kind of flower is not found even in India," he said.
"Both the teacher and son are on [Drom's] tongue;
Wondrous indeed is this inner pair!
Drom Jé, do not move your tongue."

As Drom stretched vigorously to relax,
They shook and rocked about, almost falling off. [102]
Laughing aloud [Atiśa said,] "Drom Jé, be gentle.
You are like a child eating chickpeas.
They were rolling on the tongue, a spectacle indeed!
O you two forms, born from the lotus
On a tathāgata's tongue and residing at ease,
Come out! We, too, would like to enter inside."

Drom Jé then responded:
"Lamp of the world, do come inside.
I went there [and found that] both are gone."
As both the conqueror and his son
Went into their chamber of residence,
The assembly of gods was delighted
And rained down countless flowers.

Atiśa then exclaimed:
"Drom Jé, if you are pleased by these excellent flowers,
I'll bless the soil of this region so that
The flowers of the five precious metals will blossom here."

Drom Jé said in response that he would bear this in mind.
Wonderful flowers of gold, silver, and so forth
Filled the entire region of Nyethang.

Then Atiśa spoke:
"I, Dīpaṃkaraśrī, who have been blessed by the teachers,
Have created these blessed flowers.
Through them, may the honor and prosperity of Drom's
    followers flourish."

Then Drom said:
"As for this excellent region, blessed by an excellent being,
May the assembly of all conquerors endorse this [site];
May we spiritual trainees be reborn spontaneously
And purely upon a lotus blessed by conquerors
In the incalculable buddha realms.

"In the myriad realms of the universe in all ten directions,
However many flowers of the five precious materials like this exist,
I offer all of these perfect flowers to the deities.
In this life and throughout the lives of all around me,
May the light of the Dharma shine brightly inside these flowers;
May they be opened and nurtured by the conquerors.

"May my own life resemble the petals of the lotus—
Pure and untainted, may it attain perfection.
May my life resemble a mandala of crystal glass—
Perfectly smooth, refined, and utterly clear.

"May my life resemble a golden reliquary—
May it become a great wonder, ceaselessly captivating.
May my life resemble the mandala of the sun—
Dispelling darkness with no conceptualization.

"From now on throughout all lives
May I uphold my teacher's exemplary life without slackening;
May I illuminate the precious life of the Buddha [103]
And, through pure conduct, spread it to the limits of all directions.

"May everything be excellent at the beginning, in the middle, and at
    the end;
May we be nurtured always by those bound by solemn oaths;
For the sake of benefit and happiness, may we always bring the sixfold
    recollections to mind
With single pointedness and without separating from them."

As he offered these [aspirations], Atiśa said, "Drom, this is most auspicious."

To this Drom replied, "Although you have spoken a lot, the key points appear to converge on a single theme." Atiśa then stated that the time had now come to summarize the [points of their conversation].

So Drom stated:
"Though we entertained numerous questions and answers,
If you summarize it well, it is this:

> **Renounce negative friendships,**
> **And rely on a spiritual friend.**
> **Discard hostile and unhappy mental states,**
> **And venture forth to where happiness lies.**

"There is nothing other than this."

This concludes the eleventh chapter of the *Jewel Garland of Dialogues*, "How to Nurture Sublime Beings and Their Deeds."

CHAPTER 12
How to Hoist Your Robes to Cross the Mires of Desire

[104] *Namo ratnaguru! Guru ratnaguru!*

[Atiśa:] "You who quench the scorching torment of all beings
With cool streams of untainted bliss,
Kind and beneficial lords who are the chief refuges—
To all of you, I bow at your feet.

"You, born from the ocean of the two accumulations,
Compassion par excellence endowed with joyous effort,
The peerlesss king of the Śākyas—
To you, chief of the tathāgatas, I also bow.

"Luminous, unentangled, and excellent at all times,
Mother of noble ones, the source of all well-being,
You never deceive anyone who upholds you—
To you, the mother of four noble beings,[233] I also bow.

"You heroes capable of protecting this [mother perfection]
And all you who cultivate it, such as the irreversible ones,[234]
You who do not fear the waters of cyclic existence—
In order to protect from cyclic existence, I bow to you.

"This breathtaking white lotus is adorned
With hundreds and thousands of petals.
Its roots grow from golden soil;
It is supported by a beautiful crystal stem;
Its stamen is adorned with a Meru-like jewel.
In between the countless beautiful petals
Are the blissful waters of eight qualities—
There are rivers, streams, and pools,
Springs, and wells most sublime.

"These [waters] are adorned with elegant trees that have
Thousands of branches with leaves, flowers, and fruits.

Enjoying these are flocks of magnificent birds.
With [feathers] of gold, silver, crystal,
Emerald, ruby red, and other colors,
Their bodies are most handsome,
And they warble melodious songs.
In this pool of water endowed with eight qualities,
Swans singing heart-stealing melodies play
[Surrounded by] green meadows strewn with flowers.

"At its [lotus] base countless varieties of grain grow
[Symbolizing] the inconceivable resources of the higher realms.
On the lotus petals, there are also
Clear springs resembling dewdrops.
In the winter, crystal reliquaries emerge;
Come spring, turquoise nodes protrude;
In the summer, these transform into blue lotuses
From which grow countless pretty flowers
Adorned with the five precious materials.

"These springs endowed with crystal ladles
Are utterly cooling in times of heat.
They relieve the agony of thirst for anyone who drinks of them.
Waterfowl hover above with delight.
Even the birds there abide with discipline;
The people, too, find peace of mind.

"During the fall, there are golden flowers
Resembling a circle of Śākya [monks]; [105]
The vitality of all these flowers is healthy;
The flowers of the five precious materials
Thrive with beautiful branches and fruits.

"The wealth of [this site] resembles that of a god's realm;
With no threat of impoverishment, everyone is joyful.
Even the [seasonal] transitions follow the same pattern.
In particular, the following events unfold:

"In the summer the lakes, pools, and so forth
Become turquoise mandalas adorned with gold;

In the winter they are crystal mandalas;
In the spring and fall they are beautiful marketplaces.

"Millions of ripples radiate from their centers,
While waves crest at their edges.
Rising from within they dissolve into themselves.
Some teach profoundly without [relying upon] words.

"Inside such an expansive [lotus] stamen
Stands tall a crystal reliquary.[235]
Each level is graced by the noble ones.
Free of folly, they are bound by the sacred words.

"On the first level they go for refuge;
On the second they generate the aspiring mind;
On the third they generate the engaging mind;
On the fourth they view the defects of [cyclic existence];
On the fifth they complete the factors of the enlightened class.

"As for this environment and those who live within it,
Untainted, they are radiant from within and from without.
Action: They perform ethical acts [in accord with] cause and effect;
Clothing: They are dressed beautifully in ethical discipline;
Sash: They tie themselves with a sense of shame and conscience;
Hat: They wear the perfect view [of emptiness];
Food: They are nourished by concentration, the sublime Dharma.

"Their conduct is the unification of method and wisdom;
For companions they seek the gods and the sages;
Their Dharma practice is the three precious higher trainings;
Their father is the great compassion;
Their mother is the nondual perfection of wisdom;
Their son is the natural liberation of conceptualization.

"Whatever they do is a profound Dharma practice;
This sublime Dharma obeys the laws of causal relations;
This relatedness is morality, the foundation.[236]
[The celestial mansion's] faces are guarded by unsullied faith;

Its corners are adorned with excellent immeasurable thoughts;
Its pillars are the countless antidotes;
Its inner sanctum is the fully awakened Buddha;
Its ceilings are the unexcelled teachings;
Its parapet walls are studded with the gems of omniscience;
Its corners are adorned with [the speech] of sixty attributes.
Its length pervades the reaches of sentient beings;
Its height shares the same measure.[237]

"Their son is the precious jewel;
Their servants are diligent perseverance.[238]
The king of giving guards the northern gate;
The king of influence guards the eastern gate;
The king of fame guards the southern gate;
The king of accomplishment guards the western gate.
Such is the inconceivable celestial mansion!

"At the center of an unrivaled lotus,
Enveloped within dense rays of one thousand buddhas,
Inside the chamber of the mother, perfection of wisdom,
A youthful crystal boy holds a staff. [106]
At the tip of his staff he holds a lotus.

"Inside this lotus are the thousand apparition buddhas,
All adorned with the major and minor noble marks.
Each of the thousand petals is adorned with bodhisattvas, who,
In keeping with the prophesies, proclaim the excellent scriptures.

"On the body of this crystal youth
The tathāgatas and their retinues appear radiantly.
What appears on the outside is true also of the inside;
He is [now] not as Drom but as *Bhrūṃ*.[239]

"Do not break the corners[240] but be adorned by them,
For this is the seed of the precious jewel
From which grow countless jewels.
It is called a *conqueror* as well,
And also the very *source*.[241]

This is the supreme ocean also;
The entire great earth is supported by it.
It is the great earth itself as well,
For [the fulfillment of] all wishes come from this.

"Even a single pore of this youth
Cannot be probed by the buddhas,
So how can the noble disciple succeed?
Though the trichilicosm is manifold it is only a single pore;
Such is the conduct of you, supreme Bhrūṃ,
The sovereign of all worlds.

"Whether my own students
Or your followers, their way is excellent;
All those aspirants with eyes of intelligence
Would feel lost were this Bhrūṃ to sink into a mire;
So hoist your robes against those who engender desire
And pull up this Bhrūṃ in whatever way you can.

"As for this white crystal mandala base,
Wash and cleanse it with precious water;
Make supplications, it'll bestow precious jewels.
Oṃ will pull it from the mire."

Having such supreme yearning is
The first collection of "Hoisting One's Robes against the Mires."

* * *

"*Hrīḥ!* Śrījñāna's pristine cognition is radiant.
At the center of one thousand lotuses,
On one great thousand[-petaled lotus] among the thousand,
On a supreme stamen of gold,
Upon a white crystal moon cushion,
A youth appears from melted moonlight.

"*Oṃ!* In the expanse of light from Śrījñāna's
Five pristine cognitions stands the heart mantra.
As one cultivates the pledges single-pointedly,

In the pure expanse of [infinite] space,
There appears a wisdom being in the form of a monk;
Free of attachment he permeates the universe.

"The pristine youth is stainless;
Now pristine cognition [too] is stainless.
I, Dīpaṃ, from Bengal
Will certainly cultivate *ati*[242]
Day and night in the pure ultimate expanse.

"Then, the youth resembling an eight-year-old,
Born from refined moonstones,
Is surrounded by youths numbering double his age
And by an equal number of goddesses.
Four of each of them stand in each of the four directions,
Continuously offering lamps, food,
Incense, perfumes, and so forth." [107]

Then Bhrūṃ Jé proclaimed:
"I respectfully cast one thousand eyes upon you;
Placing my thousand hands upon my crown,
I bow to you with my three doors
And specially offer you this song of praise, so please accept this.
Great pristine cognition, attend with compassion.

"You are like a beautiful and ceaselessly captivating vessel,
Made of unrivaled gold, tested through cutting, burning,
    and rubbing,
With a color of a stainless refined gold.
No matter where it is placed it is matchless.
Though you are the size of a barley seed,
Even ten million seeds cannot match your mass.

"Here barley seeds sustain a human life.
Most precious, you are matchless indeed;
How can even ten million teachers granting
The excellences of the higher realms
Rival you alone, pristine cognition?

"As for your celestial mansion, teacher,
Even though it is ascertained to be Akaniṣṭha,
It is a white lotus adorned with a golden stamen.
Without exceeding its dimensions and not too tall,
You reside upon it, immutable and free of attachment.
Holding your feet to my crown I am victorious.

"Emanating forms equal to the sands on the banks of the Ganges,
You venture forth to [the myriad] realms.
Nevertheless, Bhrūṃ Jé's realm is this central land.
Venture forth into the heart of this lotus tree.
I bow [my] crystal [form] to your body
And offer praise and homage with an unsullied mind.

"As for those with the precious human form
Who have sunk into the mires of desire,
And who, through the force of ignorance, seek to obtain [human form]
    again,
You are victorious for hoisting them up and saving them.
In order to repay the kindness of your buddha body,
I bow my head extolling, 'You have saved my parents.'"

This hoisting of one's robes by means of praise is
The second collection, "Hoisting One's Robes through Knowledge."

　　　* * *

From the trunk of the lotus flower in his hand,
A stem the size of a person emerged,
Lifting up the tathāgata at the lotus hub.
Then, laying down a cushion for comfort,
[Bhrūṃ Jé] made the following offerings:

"In excellent incalculable buddhafields,
Whatever varieties of offerings there are,
Unobscured, they appear here vividly
As lakes, ponds, and pools,
Utterly beautified by the five precious materials
And enriched by the eight qualities.

"Permeated by millions of precious gems,
They are surrounded everywhere by beautiful flowers.
Birds fly joyfully and hover in the skies
Warbling melodious songs—
I also mentally gather these and offer them to you.

"Mount Meru in the jewel realm,
Pure objects in the pure realms—
These offering collections not owned [by anyone], [108]
I mentally gather and offer to you.

"Whatever objects worthy of being offered
That exist within the field of knowledge of even worldly perception—
None is not contained within my offering to you.
Untainted one, collectively accept these untainted offerings.

"These collections of sublime offerings
Unsoiled by mires I offer to you, with robes hoisted.
The mires here are miserliness and expectation of reward."

This is the third collection of "Hoisting One's Robes against the Mires."

* * *

"Then, at his heart, this one of refined [gold],[243]
Collected together in utter clarity
The immeasurable mass of beings' negative karma;
This heap of [negative karma] vibrates forcefully.
Adjacent is a beautiful crystal youth
From whose crystal body flames erupt,
Incinerating the fuel of the defilements.
As the defilements are pressed down once more,
They blaze fiercely as wisdom flames, free of smoke.
For a while, the defilements are exhausted,
And as the youth withdraws the traces of fire,
No ashes are to be found, but only fire crystals.[244]

"Dazzlingly beautiful, they radiantly shine;
The son of fire is utterly bright.

In the past, the brahman Ujjvala
Wisely knew that water crystals and fire
Can coexist without conflict. But [knowing that] if told,
The childish would fear it, he kept it secret.[245]

"Thus, the two—water crystals and fire crystals—
Coexist, adorning the outside and within.
At the center appears a transparent youth.
Today the bodhisattva is free of attachment;
I see him residing in a place free of attachment.
In the past he was endowed with the absence of attachment.

"My faith also remains unshaken
And I am called a 'servant of the Three Jewels.'
Under the refuge of the Three Jewels,
I remain free of attachment due to my firm faith.

"I have purified the negative karma of my parents;
I have journeyed to numerous barbarian borderlands.
To the west of here, because of the greatness of his compassion,
The great compassionate one Siṃhanāda is hailed to be victorious.[246]

"Thus, for a while, I shall go to Tuṣita."
Again in countless barbarian borderlands,
The crystal youth said:

"From this deep spring of mine,[247]
I shall sprinkle some water with flower pistils,
As offerings of the first portion, to the west;
Then, through the meeting of outer, inner, [and in between],
I will declare and purify this collection of negative karma.
For as far as space pervades,
In places where a sentient being
Commits ill deeds directly or indirectly,
I shall gather together here all of these fetters
And, free of attachment, purify them all.

"Ah! You who follow after me, [109]
Declare and purify whatever ills you have

Into the ultimate expanse with repentance and resolve.
Whatever fetter you may have, never even for an instant
Leave it [unchallenged] where it is.

"As for the objects of purification—the teachers and the Three Jewels—
They [perform], in this infinite samsara, the armor-like deeds
Of freeing those so difficult to liberate.
Rejoice [in their deeds] thoroughly [from your depths].

"Request that until samsara is emptied,
[The buddhas] turn the wheel of the Dharma excellently
In whatever ways accord with beings;
Appeal to them to remain unwavering and resolute.
If they wish to go beyond the secure attainment,
There is none among them who cannot do so.
So appeal [to them] to abide here out of compassion
Without losing the ultimate expanse.

"Whatever beneficial virtuous deeds you have performed
Throughout all the three times
Dedicate so that you and all beings
May attain great enlightenment together.

[Pray] "Until I have arrived at such a secure attainment,
May I work for the welfare of [all] beings
With equanimity and without divisions of space.
This, then, is the true state of affairs.
So from now until space is no more,
Pray do not enter into nirvana.
From now on, except for transforming into objects
That beings need on an everyday basis,
Never be in [nirvanic] bliss in the ultimate expanse.

"For as long as samsara has not ceased,
Do not become 'one who has completed his task.'
To preserve the lifeline of the conscientious,
Do not shun your great responsibility.

"Just like the [radiant] white lotus,
Free of stains and vast in dimension,
With blossoming jewel petals and jewel seeds—
May the conquerors raise high the conquerors.

"Just like the sacred crystal reliquary,
May reliquaries raise high the sacred reliquaries.
He who possesses the five pristine cognitions is fully awakened
And endowed with the five qualities."

Not sinking into the mires of negative karma,
Rejoicing and appealing [to the buddhas] to remain—
This most excellent hoisting of the robes against the mires
Is the fourth collection of "Hoisting One's Robes."

* * *

Then from the tongue of Refined Moon,[248]
A white crystal *jaḥ*
Appeared in the form of light,
And touched the [Tathāgata's] body;
Instantly the letter descended to his crown.

Next, a white crystal *hūṃ* appeared
And touched the Tathāgata's heart;
It dissolved into the Conqueror's crown aperture.
Then, a white crystal *baṃ* appeared
Pervading the Conqueror's entire body.
It became indivisible with Great Compassion.[249]
With a crystal *hoḥ*, they are encircled nondually.[250] [110]

This pleased Great Compassion, who emitted
In all directions, both cardinal and intermediate,
Lights in the shapes of hooks,
Lights both white and golden.

The tathāgatas of the ten directions, with complexions like gold,
Appeared in this realm, vivid and real.

Bodhisattvas with crystal bodies also
Filled that world in countless numbers.

With one voice, all the conquerors and their children
Hailed the conquerors' mother;
All the buddha realms were filled with lights;
And heaps of offerings amassed in dense clouds.
Such were [the features of] the inconceivable [world]
Of the excellent four continents, most supreme.

Then from the heart of Refined Moon
Emerged an apparition of a fully ordained monk
Who, in a delightful voice, struck up a conversation
As he stood beside [Drom] in harmonious friendship.
Then Bhrūṃ Jé, Refined Moon,
Offered these words, so beneficial to all,
To the omniscient, apparition monk:

"Wise teacher, pray attend to me.
In this imperfect world of [the beings of] the six classes,
Utterly entangled by the twelve [links],
[Everyone] revolves [in existence] without end.
What is the root of all this?"

The teacher replied:
"Bhrūṃ Jé, it is great ignorance.
On the basis of this [ignorance], eleven [links] come into being;
From these eleven [ignorance] arises as well."

Bhrūṃ Jé then said:
"Were I to ask you to illustrate these twelve,
What would you, O conqueror, say they resemble?"

The teacher replied:
"They are taught in the scriptures as follows:[251]
Ignorance is a blind old woman;
Volition resembles the potter;

Consciousness is like a monkey;
Name-and-form is akin to entering a boat;
Sense bases are like an empty town;
Contact is said to resemble kissing;
Feelings are like being shot in the eye;
Craving is said to resemble drinking alcohol;
Grasping is like reaching for fruit;
Becoming is said to resemble pregnancy;
From this comes existence, the birth of a child;
Aging and death are said to be like carrying a corpse."

As the teacher uttered these words,
Bhrūṃ Jé asked [further]:
"How do they resemble these?
Teacher, explain this to us further."

"As decay is the end of birth for the blind woman,[252]
Though there exist in the outside world incalculable forms
With attractive and unattractive colors and shapes,
Because of her blindness, she fails to see them;
Knocking over utensils and so on, she is ridiculed.
Angry at others, herself miserable, her happiness is lost;
Whatever she does goes wrong.

"Due to aging in samsara for too long, [111]
Those who are bereft of the eyes of insight
Fail to see the virtues and nonvirtues;
They perform all sorts [of actions], such as knocking things over;
Angry at everyone, they destroy their happiness.
So hoisting their robes against this ignorance,
It is better if they can be free from this ignorance.
Human life and morality are the ones to be hoisted [high].
Certainly you are better off free of the mires.

"Just as a potter, through gathering such conditions
As a [mixing] stick, clay, and kneading,
Creates diverse earthenware containers,
The ignorant consciousness brings together

The three [poisons] of attachment, aversion, [and delusion]
And creates the great mires of the six [classes of beings].

"Attachment is the rooster.[253]
Out of ignorance about everything, a person harbors love
For the objects of desire, and thus he is ignorant;
Failing to know what is clean or unclean,
He gives to his friends
Grains, sediment, and nasal mucus;[254]
With no satisfaction, he indulges in these.
Seeking only sensual desires, he gives
Affection to no one but his own spouse.
Though his wife may lack honesty and a good heart,
He works hard to nurture this exclusive friend.
Even when she is far away, he calls aloud to her;
Such a fettered person descends to the lower realms.

"Bhrūm Jé, this is how humans of the degenerate age act.
Utterly confused by the darkness of ignorance,
They are ignorant of virtuous and negative deeds;
Gathering afflictions, they create sufferings.
They do not honor the teachers and the Three Jewels;
They do not look after their kind parents;
They do not give to those who are objects of compassion.
They are sunk in the mires of sensual desire.
If, by hoisting their robes against the mires of desire
And renouncing attachment to all objects,
They go to a place free of attachment, they will be happy.

"The unknowing ignorant rooster
Does not see the abyss with eyes of insight;
It does not see discipline, the skilled rescuer.
Thus, without guarding morality,
Beings sink deep into the mires of desire.
Bhrūm Jé, this is how the lowly outcast acts.
If they hoist their robes against the mires of desire and immorality,
And if they journey with attachment-free discipline, they will
    be happy.

"The hateful are like a venomous snake;[255]
Unable to endure [pain], they devour medicine with their tongues.
To others, they recklessly thrust their venomous tongues;
They seek to rob others of their lives.
The great mire of aversion is just like this;
The root of all of this is self-centered desire.

"Those sunk in desire's mire in the desire realm,
The snake-like ignorant, are also outcasts.
Unable to bear the slightest [pain] themselves,
They strike continuously at others' weaknesses.
And had they power, they would kill.

"They rob others, bind them, and beat them.
In this way they desecrate the entire world. [112]
If they lack power, they burn inside [with anger];
With deceit as their method they sow dissent;
Like a poison or a thief, they destroy others.

"Alas! So it is, Drom Jé.
It is better indeed that the great mire of desire is destroyed;
It is better indeed that they are freed from the great mire of desire;
Hoist high the robes of ethical discipline;
Put on the shoes of forbearance and tolerance;
Join the two hands of method and wisdom;
Escape to a place free of attachment.

"Since the delusion pig is confused,
It turns pristine verdant meadows into burrows;
It is never attracted to the pure [buddha] realms
But lives joyfully and happily in impure fields.
It indulges with relish the dirty swamps of mire.[256]
It assumed similar bodily forms in the past as well;
In one body it makes the sounds of many beasts.
With no thoughts of past and future,
It acts in utter confusion in the present.
The root of this, too, is dark desire.

"So, you with human form and the attire of discipline,
Forsake this mire and, free of attachment, escape.
Do not procrastinate but hoist your robes high!
Furthermore, even as this delusion pig is being slain,
It definitely remains confused about its owner;
Without seeking to escape in whatever way it can,
It heartily consumes the fermented grains of deception.

"Bhrūṃ Jé, although the evil outcast who commits negative acts
Indisputably lets others down, the worldly nonetheless rely on
Evil kings and powerful chiefs.

"Though one may rely on one hundred good people,
One's life can be robbed by a single evil person;
One's wealth may double,
But it can be betrayed by a single [instance of] envy or deceit.
Though betrayed, [the worldly] fail to recognize this.
Again, out of hatred and confusion,
And through desire for revenge, they instead become tormented
And seek another evil chief.
Since he is just the same as the others,
One invokes abundant suffering despite desiring happiness.
It is better to gain freedom from desire's mire;
Do not procrastinate but hoist your robes high;
Forsake desire and, free of attachment, be happy.

"Furthermore, suppose you fail to rely on supreme lasting [sources of]
    refuge,
Such as those with great compassion,
And instead rely upon Īśvara, Viṣṇu, and so on—
Gods who are similar to the [powerful] evil kings—
Then even though your entire lineage propitiates them,
If you fail even once to offer them the first portion of your meal,
Then some local spirit will be displeased, they say.
In return for entrusting your well-being to them, you are robbed
    of your life.
The mire of ignorant desire lets you down.

So do not seek haven in faulty objects of refuge
And toward desire's mire, the root of all faults,
Do not exercise patience but hoist your robes high.

"Moreover, since this delusion pig
Is ignorant of the laws of karma, [113]
It inhales food and drinks, sources of grave defects,
Like heaps of dirt dug out from burrowing.
Those who do not wish to taste even a mouthful of this,
Should [know that] greedily seizing the lives of one thousand parents
For no reason [at all] will cast one to the hells.

"Alas! Bhrūṃ Jé, listen to me.
Though one has just barely taken birth as a human being,
Without even tasting a mouthful [of human life] oneself,
One destroys the entire world;
One robs many parents of their lives;
One deprives many parents their food;
One separates many from clothes and loved ones.
It is tragic indeed, O most excellent son.
The root all of these is the mire of desire.
Harbor no excessive thinking but hoist your robes high;
Excellent is the pure ethical discipline—that which helps one hoist.

"This great fundamental ignorance,
Bringing together the three—attachment, aversion, [and delusion]—
Creates the sufferings of the six realms of samsara;
Thus, volition resembles a potter.

"What is one ignorant of? Of cause and effects
And of the profound thatness [of reality].
By what means is one ignorant? Consciousness.
In what manner is one ignorant? In the manner of blindness.

"The following is how sufferings arise on this basis [of ignorance]:
Like an earthen jar created through composition,
Intense heat and burning is created in the hells;
For the hungry ghosts there is the torment of hunger and thirst;

For the beasts there is confusion, killing, and being abused for labor;
For the demigods conflicts are rife just as for snakes;
For the gods are their many [sufferings], such as the portents of death.

"For humans in the higher realms, here is what happens:
Due to the fruition of past karma
Some are born as boys and some as girls,
Even among the offspring of the same parents.
And among the boys, some are handsome
While others are utterly unattractive.

"Even if it were possible to be equal [in appearance],
Some would be clever and others foolish.
Even if equal [cleverness] were possible,
Some would enjoy wealth and perfect prosperity
While others remained impoverished in numerous ways.
Even [with wealth], one might see equality,
[Yet] some would be resourceful and respected by all,
While others would be powerless and insulted by all.

"While some indulge in negative deeds
And squander even their own well-being,
Some engage in virtuous deeds
And accomplish the well-being of others as well.
They are honored by the gods and respected by the sublime,
While the others are destined for the hells alone.
Extend these [points] to girls as well.

"The two parents are impartial,
So what created differences in their make-up?
All of this depends upon the acuteness of the three poisons
And on which negative actions were most pronounced.

"When sought by the wise, profundity is everywhere.
This [profundity] can be found in the households as well.
For the foolish who fails to see what is right there [in front of his face],
This is like forms in front of a blind man. [114]
So do not procrastinate, but hoist your robes high

In order to cross the great mires of desire
And escape swiftly to a place free of attachment.

"Constantly reminding yourself of impermanence
Exhort yourself to be free from this mire.
Body and mind are like the clouds in the sky—
They gather instantly, yet are gone just as quickly.
Pull up the strings of your conscienceless heart.[257]
Turn inward and upbraid it with derision.

"This life is like the flowers in autumn—
With no time to linger, they are robbed by frost.
So, all you childish ones who procrastinate and are lost,
Wind up the string of your heart.
All ill-natured, pampered children of Māra,
Do not destroy the seed of liberation.
All you youth with the illness of the afflictions,
Do not rob us of our life of happiness.
All the honeybees of evil spells,
Deceive us not with the beguiling seductress,
The shortsighted maiden of impatience.
Deceive not this liberation-aspiring youth.

"Haughty ones conceited with their youth,
Youth is not eternal, and soon remorse will strike.
With tomorrows, the days and the months will go by;
Their collections will turn into years and you will change.
Do not grasp at an essence where there is none.

"With mouth open and fangs bared, [Yama] will ride upon your
    shoulders;
With your eyes wide open, you will be pierced with blades.
You will definitely die, so you who esteem yourselves,
Do not be lazy but discard dejection;
Do not procrastinate, for those with ropes and daggers
May soon separate your body from its life.
Where then will you find a secure ground?
Pity all those devoid of will;

They devour poisonous venom, the effects of conceit.
If they die soon, [in fact] they won't suffer torment [for long]!
The root of this, too, is dark desire.

"Be not excessive in your desires, for they will betray you at death;
Do not grasp excessively at permanence, but turn your mind upward.
Many are those who have been deceived by this mire of desire.
When your horse is caught in mire,
You can neither dismount nor ride the horse—
When the front hooves are freed, the rear ones are stuck;
When the rear hooves are freed, the front ones are stuck.
Even if this process is repeated one hundred times,
It results [only] in sheer exhaustion.
None are freed and all four hooves become mired.
After the horse, the rider will also sink.
At the root, excessive desire is to blame.

"Likewise in this vast mire of desire,
Even for those who pride themselves as practitioners,
Ignorant of the true ways of Dharma
And supposedly cultivating love, desire arises;
Wishing to relinquish attachment, aversion arises;
Wishing to relinquish aversion, delusion arises.

"[For them] foulness meditation is aversion;[258]
Seeming compassion is attachment;
Seeming equanimity is delusion;
Seeming joyfulness is vanity.

"Ignorant of this, the deluded one, when observing morality,
Sinks by grasping it as superior. [115]
When his conduct is good, he sinks by grasping it as superior;
When his view is good, he sinks by grasping it as superior;
When he aspires for good learning, he sinks by grasping it
    as superior.
This is like someone sleeping in winter with insufficient bedding—
When the head is covered his lower body is exposed;
When the lower body is covered his head is exposed.

"Although covetousness may increase in one who is destitute,
It is of no use, for it will sink him into the mire of desire.
This helps not at all, for it dashes his chances for freedom,
So see these defects and pull up the strings of your heart.

"Moreover, a pampered child with turquoise in his ears,
Born to parents of excellent lineage,
Powerful, rich, and bedecked with jewels,
Dressed in the most elegant of clothes,
Which are soft, attractive, and splendidly hued—
A retinue of attentive servants surrounds him.
Called 'chief' and 'master,'
Everyone serves him and rises when he stands.
When seated he is offered refreshments;
Kneeling before him, people join their palms together.[259]

"At that point he might think:
'Who is more important than I?'
'In this world I alone am [supreme]';
'I am worthy of honor by everyone';
'I will not depart from this world.'

"Alas! The lord of death is mightier than he.
Slaying such a pampered child would be piteous.
Snatching him from the midst of his circle, where will you take him?
Separating him from his meals, what will you feed him?
He has no time to rest on a comfortable cushion,
So you will not leave him in his own home.
Alas! Where are you taking this pampered youth?
You cast him away with his fair and soft flesh unclothed.
Who will you dress with his garments and jewels?
Why do you sever his turquoise-adorned ears?[260]
All his dear ones—his parents and those who care for him—
Are wealthy and respected by all.
So where are you sending this scion?
And in sending him, how will you do it?
Will you betray him by dragging him?
How can the conscienceless one thus sever his ties to the future?

"This terrifying reality of death
Happens for others in the same manner.
Furthermore, if such a youth matures,
He is adorned with wealth through considerable hoarding;
Sending off his daughters [as brides], he snatches others' sons;
All admire him and, in comfort and joy,
Excellent mounts convey him when he travels.
When sitting, soft cushions support him.
Dressed in excellent warm clothes,
He is called 'benefactor.'
He delegates his work to his sons,
And, looking after [his own] pleasure, enjoys food and drink.
So, old men and women admired by all, why do you not linger?
What more pleasant place could you be going to?
Having no power yourselves,
You are led away with force by the demon, the lord of death.
Lord of death, you old trickster with no conscience, [116]
Where are you headed with these aged ones?

"Servants cannot follow, so without venerating Jowo[261]
Or the Three Jewels, who are the sources of hope in [times of] despair?
[If you think] these powerless aged ones are sad indeed,
Not so! Rather their kindness is being repaid.
They appear to be being taken away from their joys
In the midst of wealth and children!
Not so! Their life is being paid for another's life.

"The birth of a good son has proven meaningless;
Not scouting out and searching for his parents,
Couldn't he at least afford the leisure of crying and wailing?
Such are the ways of the conscienceless son!
He consumes the wealth accumulated by his parents
Yet sends his parents away naked. How awful!
If this is indeed horrible,
Then giving them away to fire, earth, water, and birds is even worse.

"How can he do this? True indeed it is that the world is conscienceless;
This is so because [the son] has no power.

So where do the powerful take their stand [to combat death]?
None can be found who has overcome [death] through combat.

"Alas! Those who are poor and deprived,
Who are mute, deaf, blind, and crippled,
Will they not be slain by the demon [of death]?
One sees they all must die as well.

"Alas! Who is there that is not slain by you,
[Death] demon, you with no conscience?
You have dragged my parents into the mires;
You have robbed them repeatedly from liberation's lifeline.
Do you yourself not die as well?
If so, you, too, will be condemned.
Will you have a chance to escape?
Whose mire could be worse than yours?

"Alas! If all the parent beings do not hear [about death],
Even when explained in such ways,
Is it because they have no feeling at all?
If they had, they would not be wandering in samsara;
If now they do, they should hear and prepare to leave.
Otherwise how can it be that, though unable to bear suffering,
They do not cross [the mire] but endure [it]?

"Wind up the rope of your heart completely.
O bewildered ones, many things are still [yet to tell].
Are you not reduced to terror by past mires?
It is better to be terror-free than to be in pain.
Whipped and whipped, you will die soon:

"Some die in old age;
Some die when young;
Some die in the prime of youth;
Some die just after birth.
Male or female, intelligent or learned,
Who has seen or heard of anyone who was spared?
Who is that [person]? All die in a mess.

Alas! This is tragic indeed.
Not turning the finger [upon yourself] on hearing this,
What power do you have that you alone will stay on?

"When you hear of everyone dying
And fail to realize that this will happen to you—
Mockingly pointing 'He is dead!'—this is piteous.
Bereft of conscience,
You arrogant ones who 'know' everything,
How long do you think your life will last?
In most cases you cannot count one hundred years.
Soon to be afflicted with sickness,
You are certain to cry out in lamentation. [117]

"What is your destination after death?
You will likely die roped down by undertakers,
Or you will be carried [on the shoulders] of your servants.
Given your [present] conduct,
A horn will likely grow on your head,
Or your hands will turn into wings,
Or you will move about without limbs.[262]
You will definitely be reborn in the beast realm.

"The lazy who do not listen even when told,
Those deluded for as long as space remains,
Remain bowed, expecting things to rain down [on them].
But look at the strength of their miserliness;
Look how attached they are to desire's mire;
Look at the amount of mundane affairs they have;
Look how the monster of envy proliferates within them;
Burning with the fire of hatred in their hearts,
With themselves they are lenient,
But with others they are most calculating.

"They have no beneficial qualities.[263]
The opening of their mouths is small, but their mouths are large inside;
Their necks are thin, but their stomachs huge;
Their legs fail to support their bellies;

What little they eat causes flames in their mouth;
Naked, they fall down in narrow passages.
If they do not fall down,
Due to karma they find neither food nor drink.
Water [appears] as pus and blood.
Even if they see water, it is guarded by foes.
Beyond such perceptions of impurity,
They have no chance for joy. I fear this will happen to you.
Are you confident it will not be so?
Rare it is for cause and effect to violate their law.
For certain, I fear that you will assume such a form.

"If after experiencing all this you retain some measure of joy,
Then it seems it hasn't yet sunk into your heart!
For if you could you would slay everyone;
If you needed something you would just steal it.
You can rationalize all of this;
Even when you don't need to, you steal from others.
You would steal everything if you could.

"Since your behavior and character are like this,
You pursue your mundane goals
Through lies, senseless gossip, and harsh speech, I've heard.
Forsaking morality you accumulate wealth for this life, I've seen.
As for the few thoughts of Dharma you have had,
[Motivated] to gain protection from minor dangers,
Such as [unjust] taxation, labor levies, and so on,
There is not a single [motive] of true renunciation among them.

"Your ultimate aim is thus deficient, is it not?
You have utterly deceived the teachers and the Three Jewels;
You have betrayed your kind parents;
You have destroyed your kindred friends.

"Seeking to accomplish your goal of happiness,
You have striven only at mundane pursuits;
Failing to achieve your wishes, you have fought with all.
Wanting to destroy the other side,

You have injured others.
In the end, these [actions] have always turned back on you.

"You will fall into the fire pit from which it is impossible to escape,
    I fear;[264] [118]
You will be cooked in boiling iron lava, I fear;
Throughout day and night you will have to cross
The thick swamp with no shallow parts, I fear;
You will be entrapped inside a chamber
Of burning iron with flames ablaze everywhere, I fear.

"All of these are but brief illustrations.
If described as in the scriptures they are inconceivable.
So contemplate thoroughly such karmic deeds.
The sufferings of the lower realms are unbearable.

"When you have the leisure today to prevent such experiences,
The time has come to change through the method, powers, and their
    practices.
Those of a foolish nature have great stamina.
What use is this? While change is possible,
How is that you sink still [deeper] into the mires?
So be not lax but hoist high your robes.

"Thus through the convergence of the three poisons,
The sufferings of the six classes are produced."

This is the fifth collection, "Conditioned Things Illustrated."

*　*　*

Then the [crystal-]clear youth
Said these words to the attachment-free deity:

"Supreme teacher, you who liberate
Beings caught in the bondage of fetters
From the deep and vast ocean [of samsara],
You have taught in no uncertain terms:
The root of all that afflicts us
In the mires [of samsara] is desire.

"Attachment robs us of the life of higher rebirths;
It seduces us away from the joys of liberation.
Thus, far away from this great mire of desire,
Meditate single-pointedly upon impermanence.
Hooked by the iron [hook that thinks,] 'Certainly, I will die,'
Yank back the rope of the lasso of your mind.

"Beneficial it is to distance yourself from companions and servants;
Beneficial it is to cut fetters in all their forms.

"Beneficial it is to dismantle all heaps of suffering;
Beneficial it is most certainly to seek a refuge;
Beneficial it is to trick excessive speech with mantra repetitions;
Beneficial it is to trick excessive chores with circumambulations.
Beneficial it is to trick standing and sitting with prostrations;
Beneficial it is to transform sleepiness into meditation;
For those yearning for food, it is beneficial to increase concentration;
Beneficial it is to seek the excellent companionship of Refined Moon.

"Beneficial it is to recognize the root of suffering;
Beneficial it is to cast self-grasping to the wind;
Beneficial it is to carry your enemies upon your shoulders;
Beneficial it is to always banish [all] blames [to their true source].

"Beneficial it is to strike the evil trait with its antidotes;
Beneficial it is to destroy the instant it arrives;
By searching well wherever you reside,
Beneficial it is to destroy it the moment you find one.
Such an aggregate is the [link of] consciousness.

"Sublime teacher, how is this so?
Help shake the root of this unruly one;
Help undo the speed of this evil trait;
Help deprive this evil karma of his life;
Help banish the blames of this morally degenerate one;
Mete out punishments on this violator of the oath.
It deceives on the pretext of 'I am.' [119]

"This source of downfall that needs everything,
He needs profit and victories;
It's not enough to get these, but he wants more;
The grounds for his wants are he himself.

"Sons and daughters, I want;
Farms and houses, I want;
Things and devices, I want;
Clothing and jewelry, I want.
Treasuries and their contents, I want;
Circles of friends and servants, I want;
Fame and praises, I want;
Sacred books and icons, I want.
Retinues and disciples, I want;
Gifts and services, I want;
Residences and retreats, I want;
I am, and I want everything.
I am the best in this world;
Learned and diligent, I alone am;
In family lineage and birth, I excel;
So in this world, it's me, 'I.'
The owner of 'I' who wants everything—
He is [therefore] born in the mires of desire.

"So, Master Atiśa, extract him out;
Extract him, this resourceful one;
Extract him, this clever one;
Extract him, this headstrong one;
Extract him, this aim-ridden one.

"Alas! 'I,' are you not remorseful?
You needed all sorts of things,
Yet you have no conceivable long-term need.
You have lost your retinue and are [now] fallen to the ground.
If caught in the mires you'll have not the strength to rise.

"That you've been let down by the [lack of] antidotes
[Is like] a foolish sheep stuck in the mire—

Your panting is loud but the strength to rise is weak.
Most compassionate one, lift up these beings,
Imperfect and deluded in these ways.
Compassionate one, help end their imprudence.

"Alas! Consciousness, you who engage [and repel] the objects—
If there is an excess of [clarified] butter you rank with the brahmans;
If there is an excess of meat you rank with the wolves;
If there is an excess of alcohol you rank with the ordinary;
If there is an excess of talk you rank with the babblers.
If attracted to forms you hover around the gateway of the eyes;
If attracted to sounds you hover around the gateway of the ears;
If attracted to smells you hover around the gateway of the nose;
If attracted to tastes you hover around the gateway of the tongue;
If attracted to texture you hover around the gateway of the body.
When scheming for goals unable to attain,
At the gateway of the mind you conceive all manner of things.
Alas! What is this old monkey like?[265]
Teacher, please tell us."

The apparition monk then spoke:
"This source of [all] downfalls is like a monkey;
If you place this brainless monkey
In the fortress with six open doors,
Restless, it will run toward all six doors.
One who views [the world] in such a way
Ends up with all sorts of conflicts.

"If the monkey goes to all six doors in full speed,
It feels as if there are six of him. [120]
Furthermore in dense jungles,
If threatened by fire he jumps to the ground;
If threatened on the ground he escapes to the treetops.[266]

"Though seemingly clever, he is foolish;
Likewise, consciousness seems clever
But does not comprehend the final truths.
In the near term it runs everywhere in disarray.
It nurtures the growth of the three poisons,

And one undergoes the sufferings of the lower realms as a result.
Thus it is the great swamp of cyclic existence,
Where [beings are] bound by the iron chains of sense objects.
Nonetheless, if you tame this [consciousness] well,
It will turn into transcendent wisdom.
It will [then] become the root of nirvana."

This is the sixth collection of "Hoisting One's Robes,"
"Hoisting One's Robes High against the Mire of Consciousness."

   * * *

Master Bhrūṃ then asked:
"What are name and form?"

The apparition monk replied:
"Name refers to feelings, discriminations,
Mental formations, and consciousness;
Form resembles a boat.[267]
Feelings are that which experience;
Discriminations grasp distinctions;
Mental formations create through composition;
Consciousness cognizes individual characteristics;
Form is said to be subject to destruction.

"In this great ocean
Of birth, aging, sickness, and death,
Body is like the boat;
Consciousness is like the oarsman;
Virtuous and evil karma are like the oars.
Feelings, discriminations, and mental formations—
These three enter the boat-like body,
Ferried back and forth by the oarsman.

"Consciousness links the mental formations.
Through countless lifetimes past and future,
One repeatedly moves up and down.
Contact refers to the meeting of two things.
From their initial meeting, contact arises;
On this basis feelings of pain and pleasure ensue;

On this basis craving proliferates;
On this basis persistent grasping occurs;
On this basis evil karma comes to pass;
On this basis the negative fruits come into being;
On this basis aging occurs,
On the basis of which sickness arises,
And then sorrows and cries of lamentation.
With fear of death one suffers unhappiness.
Since following a birth it is nature's law to die,
No power can avert it; death will come.

"Second, when the tongue
Comes into contact with a delightful sweet flavor,
Without cognizing reality, through the joining
Of the tongue and the taste and by means of consciousness,
Perceptions of taste are experienced.
Upon such [experiences] one craves and grasps.
On this basis attachment and becoming [come to pass]; [121]
And in dependence upon this suffering arises.
On this basis one decays and dies.

"Third, as for the six sense bases:
One opens the door for the arising of forms;
Another opens the door for the arising of sounds;
One opens the door for the arising of odors;
Another opens the door for the arising of tastes;
One opens the doors for the arising of tactile sensations;
Another opens the doors for the arising of mental objects.
Consciousness rushes toward all these doors.

"It differentiates forms with attachment and aversion;
It differentiates sounds with attachment and aversion;
It differentiates odors with attachment and aversion;
It differentiates tastes with attachment and aversion;
It differentiates tactility with attachment and aversion;
It differentiates mental objects with attachment and aversion.
Pointlessly, it enhances attachment and aversion.

"Therefore, it is like an empty house.
In a house that belongs to someone,
If another person were to break in suddenly,
Insulting [the owner] and causing him harm,
The owner of the house might feel
'Why does he harm me
In my own house for no reason?'
He could expel him or confront him,
And in response the stranger might feel
'The owner of this house is right.'

"But if the owner is slain by the enemy,[268]
No thought of house remains even if the other abandons it;
It is the same with the doors of the six sources.

"So long as 'I,' 'self,' and 'living being' exist,
When someone burns them or attacks with weapons,
Exclaiming 'I' and 'to me,'
Groundlessly, one harbors abundant self-grasping.
Yet when slain by the enemy, death,
And when the six doors are dismantled from their bases,
Who will then have the thought 'I am'?
One is free from self-grasping, the root of unruliness.
The [six sources] are thus illustrated by means of metaphors.

"When the five senses meet with their objects,
This is given the name *contact;*
It resembles kissing, it is said.
On the basis of contact, feelings arise.
From this arise craving for appropriation
And craving for relinquishing unhappiness.
For instance, if an arrow strikes your eye,
It is impossible you won't feel it; this is similar.

"Craving is like drinking alcohol;
Though detrimental in the long run it tastes delicious.
Mistaking it as delicious, one imbibes again and again;
Like plucking fruit [from a tree],

Having tasted the first one, one plucks the next.
In this way one becomes attached to it and craves it.

"Becoming is like the conception of a child
By a whore who engaged in copulation.
When the time approaches,
The child, a source of misery [for her], is born.
On the basis of this [birth], aging occurs,
And in dependence upon this death follows.
Like carrying a corpse, this is the opposite of happiness. [122]

"Master Bhrūṃ, in this limitless cycle of existence,
Those who are sunk again and again
In the mire of afflictions with no escape
Do not understand through the words of the wise.
Therefore, even though I have spoken these challenging words
    to you,
The wise do not criticize the ignorant,
Pouring words into a fool's ears.

"This is similar to [the story of] the infant crawling toward
The edge of a cliff who was not stopped by the truth;
With nothing in hand and merely calling out 'little child,'
The wise one skillfully led the child away.

"Here, too, it is the afflictions, the samsaric phenomena,
Which are the objects of abandonment for the wise."

This is the seventh collection, "On Dependent Origination."

    * * *

[Drom:] "*Hriḥ* Śrījñāna Guru Jé,
What are the deeds of a sublime being?
How does one engage in them to journey to liberation?
How should one view the ultimate mode of being?"

The apparition being said:
"This apparition is endowed with

Echo-like empty words that are most clear;
I am a monk of apparition.
Without grasping at me as substantially real,
Put my instructions into practice.
Pray conjoin appearance and emptiness.

"I am an illusory monk.
Without clinging to me as good,
Put my instructions into practice.
Yoke together appearance and emptiness.

"I am a monk who is the moon['s reflection] in water.
Though seeming to appear, I am devoid of reality.
Because I am empty, I appear as forms;
Because I appear as forms, I am emptiness.

"Apart from this there is no emptiness.
As there is no form other than emptiness,
Do not take the form-like to be a form,
But practice the ultimate nature of form.[269]

"You Bhrūṃ Jé, crystal youth,
Just as you are devoid of flaws and blemishes,
I, too, am a monk of light.
Though appearing, I cannot be grasped.
So without grasping at that which cannot be held,
Place your mind at ease in the naturally free nondual state.

"If you are devoid of what is to be abandoned, you're Bhrūṃ Jé;
If you see that which cannot be seen, this is precious;
If you cognize nonduality, this is the middle way;
If you're free of cognizance, this is the ultimate mode of being.

"I am the rays of the sun;
With no conceptuality, forms are illuminated.
This is illumination alone with no objects to touch.
This natural transparency, vivid, empty, and free of elaborations—
Those with grasping confuse it with the sun.

"What is called *illusion* is unreal;
Unreality is a term for emptiness.
If emptiness is cognized, grasping will end.
This nonduality of object and subject transcends the intellect;
Transcendence of the intellect is the ultimate expanse.

"See this, Bhrūṃ Jé, when you recognize as unviewable
That which cannot be viewed, then the views will end; [123]
When fearlessness is cognized, this is the middle way.
It is profound, so place your mind in the sphere of the middle way.
This, too, is my instruction.

"I, the monk Dīpaṃ, an appearance and empty,
Who emits mist, clouds, and light,[270]
Am born from the heart accomplished by the dual accumulations.
Do not cling to me as substantially real.

"You who don the robes of pure morality,
The conduct of benefit and happiness,
Are not separate from others' welfare; this is profound dependence.
Embrace and practice such conduct.

"I am a monk of untainted virtue.
Uncreated by causes and conditions,
I pacify the disease of substantiality and signs
And spontaneously accomplish great bliss.

"I traverse the paths by means of bodhisattva conduct;
Together with my parents, I journey to liberation.
So without grasping at me through signs,
Put my instructions into practice.

"Yoke together emptiness and compassion.
Though countless instructions like this have been given,
They are like the empty echoes
That resound when someone sings melodious songs
Amid a rocky mountain range.
My words also are empty echoes.

So, without grasping at their signs,
Embrace the corresponding instructions they point to.
Take the empty echoes into the ultimate expanse.

"Though I may seem like a peerless form,
The ultimate nature of form is emptiness.
No analogy corresponds to emptiness,
So practice it in this expanse of no analogy.

"Listen, Bhrūṃ Jé, you who are untainted by stains,
There is nothing to listen to; it is [just] a term.
In their dreams, the youthful
Indulge in pleasure with their beloved friends
And they adorn themselves with beautiful jewels.
Although we all feel attraction to someone,
They engage with such attachments and their objects
Similarly even when they are awake.

"It has been stated in a sutra:
When a young woman sees in her dream
The birth of a son and his death,
She is joyful at his birth but sorrowful at his death;
Understand that all phenomena are like this.[271]

"Listen to this resonant sound again:
On a perfectly clear circular mirror
Appears the face of a beautiful maiden.
Although it is devoid of intrinsic reality,
One feels attraction upon seeing it.
Likewise, as for my pure appearance,
Though it does not exist, it appears as a form.
Thus, even though its giving teachings is an appearance,
Put them into practice as unreal.

"It has been stated in the scriptures:
On a perfectly flawless mirror
The reflection of a form appears
Having no intrinsic reality. [124]
Understand all phenomena in the same manner.[272]

"Similarly, as I, too, share the same nature,
My teachings are also within this nature—
They too are false appearances."

This is the first collection of the instruction on the union of appearance
and emptiness.

* * *

Again on the hub of the lotus
There emerged a radiant white crystal *bhaṃ,*
Which transformed into a white ten-petalled lotus.
A white *bhrūṃ* sat upon it.
Around it like heaps of grain were
Crystals, white pearls, pure silver,
And refined gold—
Victorious, emerging, and abiding.[273]

As white light rays shone forth profusely from this,
They reflected off one another
And expanded out from their source.
They reached out an arms' length in the ten directions
And formed a sphere with their tips converging at the top.
The shape of this resembled a precious [wish-granting] jewel.

From the center of the letter, a single beam
Of golden-hued light shot forth,
Splitting the jewel's tip into three,
[Becoming] a crowning jewel resembling a garuda's head.

From amid the precious letter,
A white *hriḥ* resembling a refined moon appeared and
Instantly turned into a youth.
From his body, coming forth from a fire crystal,
There appeared a halo-like perimeter fence.

This [fence] emitted blue lights rays that
Radiated toward the northeast and disappeared.
Then, after a little while had passed,

A youth [composed] of clear fire crystal
Drew water from the water crystals
And brought it into the celestial mansion.
The clear youth [then] said:

"At the conqueror's retreat called Ra²⁷⁴
There was water, so I went to bring fire [for cooking].
Then I drew forth the water of peace
From the deep spring;
Wherever it touched it brought joy."

After a while, countless streams,
As wide as large horse tails
And inconceivably beautiful, flowed forth
Into all ten directions—above, below, and so on.

Utterly pleased, the principal white youth
Smiled and exclaimed:
"From my deep spring
Countless sources of well-being and happiness issued forth;
They pervade the ten directions—above, below, and so on;
They pervade all pure buddhafields,
Such as the pure buddhafield of Tuṣita.
You who [wish to] perfect my way of life,
Which resembles [a flawless] crystal, pray go there.

"A single beam of light
Divides into two and they depart separately.
They become cooling springs in the central regions
And help increase the sublime beings and their deeds. [125]
When even a cupful of their water
Is brought to the west by some compassionate person,
Beings become untarnished and happy.

"This pure liberating life story
Blossoms like unfolding flower petals.
Thus, as long as the teaching of the Buddha—
Which flourishes everywhere: east, west, south, and north—remains,

"At the conqueror's retreat called Ra[274]

Then even when it is approaching its end,
[This life story] will grant happiness to beings
Through illuminating insight, unimpaired enlightenment, and the
    Dharma;
Through victorious perseverance, through goodness;
And through the sublime deeds of the excellent ones.

"When the sun is about to set in the west,
Then sun mandala resides in the northeast.
Since clouds of karma can veil it,
What will illuminate [things] should this happen?
Tuṣita alone is radiant and stainless.
The *hrīḥs* also exist, scattered here and there;
If probed by the wise, *[hrīḥs]* are uninterrupted."

Then a crystal reliquary–like form,
Resembling in its shape a [wish-granting] jewel,
And possessing five levels,
Appeared—vivid, stark, and tangible.

As light rays shone to the east and west,
Amid the lights, there emerged a monk
Who illuminated the teaching brilliantly.

"My teaching is free of obscurations;
The conquerors' compassion has no interruption;
So how can the sun of the sublime Dharma set?

"Nevertheless, due to their impure perceptions,
People may perceive it as waxing and waning.
The east is resplendent with the moon mandala;
The refined[-moon] youth sends forth emanations
That illuminate the entire world,
Illuminating the [realm of] gods [as well].

"When the Buddha's teaching approaches its end,
The sun mandala resides in the west.
Here, too, the five excellent meritorious names[275]
Will uphold [the teaching] directly and indirectly.

"Not allowing the mandala to be obscured,
They will thoroughly illuminate the sublime buddhafields;
They will illuminate them directly or indirectly.
Though the mandala is devoid of obscuration,
It appears as if veiled by clouds.
When the lights themselves turn into the realm of Tuṣita,
Alas! How indeed will they illuminate the world?

"You companions of the enlightened deeds,
Who possess unwavering concentration and meditation,
Adorn yourselves with the discipline of my way of life,
And, rekindling the fire of the excellent merit
Of honoring the path of the Tathāgata—the highest purpose—
Nurture [the Dharma] with five excellent factors.[276]

"You who alone illuminate the Buddha's teaching,
You have emerged from my long stream
And have illuminated that [stream] as well.
This *hrīḥ* is also a great empty echo."

This is the second collection, "The Miscellaneous." [126]

    * * *

Again the refined-moon youth,
Resplendent and sublimely beautiful,
Appealed to the one with clear and pure ears:

"Jñāna,[277] apparition monk, listen.
Out of habituation to phenomena—
The objects of perception of cyclic existence—
Appearances do not cease even when stopped.
So how should one practice with respect to this?

"All things are disentangled and distinct;
They are adorned with numerous unique characteristics;
They are arrayed with numerous shapes and colors.
How should one meditate upon these phenomena that seem to exist?"

Then the apparition monk differentiated
In clear and unconfused terms:
"You, elegant youth of Kadam,
Behold this wonder of perceived form."

Saying this, he revealed
The radiant crystal mirror *bhrūṃ*.
Bhrūṃ saw the form reflected there.

"Bhrūṃ Jé, practice this as follows:
Within the crystal [mirror] is the crystal form;
Its limbs are in full bloom and have no defects;
Crisp and distinct are its nose and eyes;
Vivid and stark it assumes a smile.
When gesturing it has gestures;
When moving it has movements.
So, too, when standing it has posture,
And when sitting it is seated.
Also when it crosses its legs,
Its legs are half crossed;
It is kneeling when it does so.
Its palms are folded when it folds its palms.

"When spreading its one thousand arms, it has one thousand arms,
And when it displays one thousand eyes, it has one thousand eyes.
Thus its body mandala appears vividly,
As if in the manner of dependent origination.

"As they invariably arise [from their causes] they are dependent
     originations;
If they exist, they do so in dependence.
But if they exist, what need is there of dependence?
And if they do not exist, what depends upon what, for they do appear
     as such?

"In appearance they appear with aspects of form;
It's not that they lack appearance, for they appear as such.
Their appearance is unreal for it's a mere similitude;
The similitude is not the actual, for it has no [intrinsic] identity.

"Emptiness appears as a form;
That which appears is also empty.
Apart from emptiness there is no form.
If one sees one when there is none,
Then the seer is deluded because of an illusion.
This delusion is a groundless fabrication.
Who would grasp through symbols of 'is' and 'is not'?
He who does so grasp is himself deluded.

"Some who are deluded can see the truth.
If there is no seeing, then there is no seer as well.
If one understands this absence, this is the fruit.
Place your mind free in this naturally liberating fruit.

"'To place' is devoid of separateness and oneness.
In emptiness there is nothing to place and no placer,
So implement the first practice of appearance
With regard to phenomena, which appear though are nonexistent." [127]

This is the third collection on appearance, "How, Though Empty, [Phenomena] Are Perceived as Appearances."

    * * *

Bhrūṃ Jé spoke:
"In a dream of pristine clear light,
Within a crystal ocean, there are one thousand wheels.
Upon each wheel are one thousand celestial mansions.
In each celestial mansion are one thousand apparitions,
All engaged in Dharma discourse with one another.
All of these are but mere reflections.

"When one analyzes these reflections well,
The analyzer, too, is dismantled.
The immutable is the ultimate nature of phenomena;
Though the ultimate mode of being is free of elaborations,
In this space-like absence of elaborations,
Clouds appear from the space itself.
Clouds of diverse colors appear vividly;

Radiant and empty wheels spread out to the ten directions.
While spreading out they share the nature of space;
Emerging from space, they dissolve into space.

"Though this site of dissolution has many heaps of clouds,
Since they are multiple they lack reality;
Since they lack reality they disperse everywhere.
That they disperse reveals their impermanence.
This impermanence is also empty.
Those who do not understand emptiness
Confuse what is called *impermanence* with annihilation.
I, the one who recognizes this to be confusion,
Perceive all diverse appearances in this 'no I' expanse."

This is the fourth collection, "Questions and Answers Pertaining to
Appearance and Emptiness."

*   *   *

Again the pristinely pure youth
Said to the apparition master:

"In a person's dreams, there appear
Pleasure groves and trees;
Forests and extraordinary garden houses;
Green meadows with lush green lawns;
Birds and bees hovering in the skies
Warbling joyful melodious songs;
Medicinal herbs and sweet incense;
The shining sun, moon, and stars;
And perfect arrays of food with one hundred flavors.
Thousands of disciplined [monks] read scriptures;
Numerous sugatas reside in space.
Thus, the offerings and their objects are unimaginable.

"Also in the thoroughly beautiful pleasure grove
One thousand crystal youths tend after
Horses, elephants, and buffalos;
Leisurely, they care for their well-being.

"They make excellent offerings,
Such as a wish-granting cow, or a mount.
Though primordially empty, their properties appear.
The unknowing cling to the appearance as excellent; [128]
They confuse the empty refuges with [true] refuges;
They recite that which is devoid of speech and language.
Though devoid of going and coming,
Birds and bees race about here and there;
Elephants run about and the horses as well;
Water buffalos move, and the wish-granting cow goes along.
Such diverse sensations of pleasure vividly appear.

"Though there is nothing to affirm or to reject,
[The thousand crystal youths] discard evil and cultivate virtues;
They reveal the ill consequences and explain the merits.
At that point, even should someone assert 'These do not exist,'
The minds of the deluded ones would not comprehend this.

"'Though all this diversity is real,
You denigrate this and meditate falsely' [they retort].
When you awaken from a dream,
[The images] remain vivid and stark in the mind.
Though this is so, in the same way
Recognize this as yesterday's after-image
And cease clinging at its very root.

"If yesterday someone had said:
'Do not be deluded there is nothing,'
Someone else would have retorted, 'This is denigration.'
Teachers who today reveal the ultimate mode of being
Resemble persons of yesterday;
All phenomena that appear today
Resemble the things of yesterday.
Though numerous objects and subjects exist,
Experienced as the held object and the grasping mind,
Why aren't they the same as those of yesterday?
Later on, they are just like a dream,
So understand all phenomena to be like this."

The apparition monk said:
"Most learned one, listen to me.
All phenomena are like dreams;
All dreams are illusions.
The illusions are one's own consciousness,
For consciousness creates them at all times.
It [consciousness] is devoid of the creator's identity,
The learned do not overuse dreams as an analogy.

"The good and bad of dream objects
Appear as real to the dreaming mind;
Though dreams are devoid of veracity,
The deluded mind confuses them to be true.
Likewise, though all objects
Are devoid of reality, for the mind that grasps
They are confused to be truly real.

"The learned one thus cites dreams as an analogy:
To the mind of the awake,
Though the good and bad of dream objects
Appear most vividly real,
On the basis of this the thought occurs
'No yesterday-objects are found,
So why do I pointlessly grasp at them?'
Still their resonance lingers strongly.

"Then the learned one will think:
'All phenomena are like this.'
One holds as trustworthy that which has no basis for trust;
One grasps as real that which is unreal;
One grasps as substantial that which is insubstantial;
One grasps as signs that which is devoid of signs;
One grasps as elaborations that which is devoid of elaboration; [129]
One grasps as objects that which cannot be held;
One grasps as subjects that which cannot be subjects;
One grasps as dual the nondual subject and object.
This conceptualization cognizes many things;
It constructs numerous baseless characteristics.

"So now even if diversity appears [to the mind],
Since nothing exists, do not grasp at anything.
Even if numerous conceptualizations come together,
Such as [conceptualizations of] joy, pain, and so on,
All of these are but mere appearances.
As for truth, not even its possibility exists;
So experience the appearances likewise.

"Bhrūṃ Jé, mother lode of the precious Kadam,
Behold this expanse, the celestial mansion.
If you find what is unfindable, this is Kadam;
As this relates to the mere appearance
Of the undeceiving apparent karma, this is Kadam."

This is the fifth collection on appearance.

     * * *

Thus the White Lotus[278] spoke:
"Unveiled by the clouds of defilements,
Stainless space, listen to me.
Son of the religious king of Sahor,[279]
Dharma king, you who reign as the regent
Of the sugata Tārā, sole sublime lady, pray listen.

"Pray remove the obscuration to knowledge
That obstructs the ultimate mode of being.
How do the noble ones habituated to nonappearance
Place their minds in the state of nonappearance?

"Not distracted by external objects,
And not dwelling upon their own thoughts as well,
Do they meditate on the appearance of nonduality?
With no cessation and devoid of origination,
With no annihilation and free of eternalism,
Cleansed of the extremes of hopes and fears and of going and coming,
Utterly free of identity and difference,[280]
Do they place their minds in the natural liberation?

"Glorious, excellent Dīpaṃkara,
Dispel what seems like darkness.
Reveal to us the teaching on the ultimate mode of being."

The apparition Dharma king replied:
"Listen to me, crystal youth,
You who are born with a body spontaneously stain-free,
Conceptuality is groundless and free of elaborations;
The ultimate expanse of reality abiding
Within the elaboration-free expanse is devoid of appearances.

"Unproduced by causes and conditions,
Though unconditioned, it is naturally free.
This natural liberation is the great natural liberation;
It is devoid of appearance, O son of space.[281]

"The primordially unborn clear light,
Unborn, luminous, empty, and spontaneous—
This is not the essence, for it is beyond the intellect.
It is the absence of appearances, stainless son. [130]
With no locus it resembles a lotus in the sky.
That which is utterly devoid of shape and color—
This ultimate expanse of the great middle way—
Is devoid of appearance, O clear-light son.

"Devoid of 'from where' and 'where does it cease,'
This sky flower robbed by frost,
As it transcends the intellect of all,
Is devoid of appearance, O dharmakāya.

"The three times are primordially devoid of themselves;
They are [like] three rabbit horns: long, short, and in between.
As they do not appear even as objects of transcendent wisdom,
They are devoid of appearance, O luminous and empty body.

"As the ground-of-all is utterly devoid of the three times,
It is not an object of exaggeration or denigration;
This essential point transcending good and evil
Is devoid of appearance, son.

"As it cannot be increased by the noble ones
Nor decreased by childish ordinary ones,
This ultimate mode of being, free of increase and decrease,
Is devoid of appearance, O pristinely pure body.

"That which is beyond language and thought,
The true suchness of intrinsic nature,
Utterly free from adventitious qualities,
Is devoid of appearance, O pristine cognition body.

"Lacking limits in its depth and breadth,
Devoid of center or margins, it pervades everywhere.
This profound expanse transcends the intellect;
It is devoid of appearance, O appearance and emptiness son.

"Devoid of unity and multiplicity,
That which seems to appear yet has no life,
This natural state that disintegrates when probed
Is devoid of appearance, O one with awareness.

"All norms of affirmation and rejection appear,
Yet when probed they cannot retain their status.
This useless status of one's own being
Is devoid of appearance, O intelligent one.

"Though appearing as if one depends upon another,
When probed things cannot retain this contingent status.
Their initial state breaks down;
They are devoid of appearance, O intelligent one.

"When the root of the origin of birth is cut,
Abiding and going, they cease themselves.
This status of one's being that lets one down when probed
Is devoid of appearance, O intelligent one.

"Existence and nonexistence are displayed as if organized,
Yet when their birth is probed their effects are lost.
This status of equanimity
Is devoid of appearance, O intelligent one.

"You possess levels, eyes, and eyelashes,[282]
Yet when you are analyzed you lose your self-status;
Unstable one who seems to taunt others,
Embarrassing, indeed, it is that you [too] disintegrate.

"If you are defeated with shame, your wanderings will end;
You fail to find the hideaway as well.
This emptiness where the sourceless is found
Is devoid of appearance, appearanceless son.

"Intriguing indeed is the son of nonappearance!
Intriguing indeed are the branches without a root!
Intriguing indeed are the flowers without branches!
Intriguing indeed are the stamens without flowers!
Intriguing indeed is one sitting without a stamen!
Intriguing indeed is the youth when there is no one sitting!
Intriguing indeed are the qualities [of the youth] without a youth! [131]

"Ah, Ah! That the unborn is duality is credible!
That which is credible vanishes into the expanse of nonappearance;
As a mere convention has this absence of appearance been taught.
Do you know this, Bhrūṃ Jé? Meditate on Tārā."

This is the sixth collection, "The Absence of Appearance."

     * * *

Again Bhrūṃ Jé of the Kadam offered
These words to the stainless one:
"By meditating on appearance and its absence,
One attains enlightenment as a result."

The stainless one replied:
"Listen! There is a citation from the profound tantras:
'If, by means of this illusion-like mind,
You meditate upon all illusion-like phenomena
As if they were illusions,
Illusion-like, you will attain full awakening.'[283]
This is the citation on appearance-only meditation.

"Bhrūm Jé, listen to me further:
'If, by means of this space-like mind,
You meditate upon all space-like phenomena
As if they were space,
Space-like, you will attain full awakening.'[284]
This is the citation on absence of appearance.

"Listen further, I have citations on the absence of appearance.
'There are no forms nor is there one who sees;
There are no sounds nor is there one who hears;
There are no odors nor is there one who smells;
There are no tastes nor is there one who tastes;
There is no body nor is there one who touches;
There is no mental faculty nor are there its derivatives.'[285]
This, too, is a citation on absence of appearance.

"I have still more citations on appearance, so listen:
'Form is like a mass of foam;
Feeling is like a water bubble;
Perception is like a mirage;
Mental formations are like plantain trees;
Consciousness is like an illusion';[286] thus it is taught.

"Although all this diversity appears,
Familiarize with it as emptiness;
Even this ultimate empty nature
Is nothing other than appearance,
So meditate on appearance and emptiness as fused.

"Pristinely pure youth, emanation body,
Listen, I have a citation on the fusion of appearance and emptiness:
'That which is conventional is the ultimate;
That which is the ultimate is conventional;
So apart from the conventional truth,
Ultimate truth is not perceived';[287] thus it is taught.

"Therefore, within the apparent world of conventions
Everything, good and evil, appears;

Their effects—happiness and suffering—appear,
Thus the garland of birth and death emerges.
This also does not happen with no cause [at all];
Though they appear as [possessing] causes and effects,
Dependently originating, they disintegrate when probed.

"This initial gathering of causes and conditions
Is easily destroyed by the lord of death demon;
The gods, who are the source of refuge, protect the conditions,
So familiarize [yourself] with the absence of appearance [132]
And hoist your thoughts high from desire's mire,
Which has been prepared by the lord of death demon.
Without obvious grasping at permanence, meditate in four sessions;[288]
Intersperse impermanence and absence of appearance."

Then the naturally pure lotus,
The pristinely pure excellent body
Extended wide his lotus tongue
And offered these words in the master's presence:

"The unborn nature is the buddha body of reality;
The display of appearing bodies is the emanation body;
The perfection of the two accumulations is the enjoyment body.
O Lotus, pray reside at the crown of my head.

"Having taught well the union and the profound nature
Of appearance and emptiness,
In conclusion, appearance and emptiness are indivisible;
And you have taught that all appearances are dependent originations.

"Dependent origination is the gathering of causes and conditions;
From them the garland of birth and death emerges.
Since causes and effects do not deceive,
If you say that this effigy of dependent origination
Is easily destroyed by the lord of death,
As for this perishable body,
What are its causes? How shall one act at the time of death?
What is to be affirmed? What is to be rejected?

Who is the refuge from such danger?
Confer on us relevant pith instructions."

The stainless one replied:
"Pray listen to me, my heart son.
In this inferior body born of four elements,
The intelligence, unobstructed consciousness, inheres.
Due to the power of karma they are connected to each other;
With no secure attainment reached, they are easily divorced.

"As incompatible forces compete, illnesses abound;
Due to propensities, sufferings proliferate.
That terrifying event called death,
Which befalls everyone and cannot be averted,
Strikes like lightning leaving no time to spare.

"This is but a general presentation.
Now the gathering of the parts,
Such as the head, legs, and hands—
This collection is called *the body*.

"Head, legs, and hands,
Fingers and toes, skin and internal organs,
The sense organs such as the eyes, ears, and so on,
Blood, mucus, and so on,
The unclean substances, and the microorganisms—
Eighty thousand of such are gathered.

"Their solidity is produced by the earth [element];
Their moisture is produced by water;
Their heat is produced by fire;
Their mobility is produced by wind.

"In particular, this body assailed by illness
Is engendered from the meeting of wind, phlegm, and bile.
Though [it holds] filth like excrements and urine,
The lord of death demon will devour it.

"You do not want this great impermanence,
But since you have no self-control,
You have to leave when [your body] is stricken down. [133]

"When broken down it divides infinitely;
When probed it shares the nature of emptiness.
Because you are apparent, empty, and subject to disintegration,
When your lifespan becomes exhausted,
You are encircled by the messengers of Yama.
These breath-snatching butchers celebrate,
And the great lord of death presses down on your shoulders.

"Whatever you might eat you have no appetite for;
Powerless, your body's edifice comes undone in the bed.
Crying, those who wish to be close to you support you.
Some with evil karma may consult shamans and astrologers;
The better ones might read scriptures and offer ritual cakes.
Some might become so utterly petrified
That they run around shrieking that a physician should be sought.
Some might sit around you and cry;
Exclaiming, 'How can you die? This is not fair,'
They weep and protest.
Some physicians check your pulse;
Whispering, 'No hope,' they assume certain expressions.
[One physician] says, 'I will treat you like a friend,'
But when the time approaches
He agonizes, 'The patient is going to die.'
At that point a time will come
When you come face to face
With a great expanse of suffering
Against which nothing can help.

"Listen, this is what happens:
When a person is born, he is born in conjunction
With an innate god and a demon,[289]
[Along with] the two—his self and his life force.[290]
The god gathers all favorable conditions
And abandons all adverse conditions.

The god urges one toward all virtuous deeds
And records whatever virtues he performs.
When he is [caught] in nonvirtue or suffering, the god mourns;
When virtuous or joyful, the god rejoices with happiness.
The demon does the opposite.

"As long as the force of his virtue is strong,
And as long as the projected lifespan is not exhausted,
Whatever virtuous deeds he may engage in,
They will hit their mark. The following are such deeds:

"Honoring the Three Jewels in general;
Offering food to the monastics;
Sending ritual cakes to Dharma protectors
And the elemental spirits;
And satisfying the poor with charity.
By taking these as his objects of action,
When he engages in the virtuous activities—
When he performs meditation, recitations,
Or whatever virtuous deeds—
The god proclaims these to the [other] gods
So that the gods, too, perform healing rites.

"At this point the god thinks:
'Effects follow after their causes;
This person has engaged in virtuous deeds, and
He deserves to find their fruit as happiness.
Suffering is pointless, so demon, you go away!
He deserves our protection.'

"Then the demon becomes tormented;
How can he now create obstacles? [134]
Illness free, the person enjoys perfect conditions;
He is adorned with leisure and opportunity.
[He is] admired by all, by both self and others.

"As a result the demonic forces feel:
'Alas! He is [now] beyond our reach;

He is enriching the welfare of both self and others;
[So] let us send him whatever obstacles we can muster:

"'To the aversion-ridden let's send aversion;
To the attachment-ridden let's send attachment,' and so on.
When the person then enters into negative deeds,
[Feeling] hostile toward others and attached to himself,
The simultaneously born innate demon thinks:
'Effects follow after their causes;
Evil ridden, he deserves some suffering, so god, you go away!'

"Then, once the god has become weakened,
The demon robs his life force.
Then, in whatever parts of his body—in the upper or lower,
in such sensory organs as the eyes—
He experiences intense pain.
[The demon] writes down his negative deeds.
When his negative karma increases, his lifespan is extended;
Again he is led to negative karma.

"At that point the god thinks:
'Alas! He is caught in suffering,'
And skillfully leads him to the Dharma.
Both the sick person and the caregiver
Ask for healing rites, and when they engage in
Virtuous activities and offering rites,
His life force is held by the gods as before.
From then on, his life force is well protected;
He recovers well from his illness.
As before, the demon is expelled.

"Alas! Then it will be like this:
Protected by his god, the favorable condition,
And free of his demon, the adverse condition,
The sick person will be cured.
At that point everyone will say:
'Because of performing a healing rite [death] was averted.'
It is due to the meeting

Of past causes with excellent conditions
That virtues performed hit their mark.

"If this were to reverse, the demon would win.
Though he may gather a few roots of virtue,
Though he may have a few healing rites performed,
His past evil karma is severe,
And he engages in negative deeds.
Since the demon obstructs through adversities,
[Death] is not averted by a few healing rites.
The demons taunt the gods;
Saddened, the gods shed tears,
[And] his life force gets lost to the demon.

"He thinks, 'Alas! I will die.'
Without shortening his thought patterns when needed,
He lengthens his thoughts a little,
And when he gives counsel to his own mind,
At that point he'll think: 'O I have failed;
What is called death has occurred.
The hoarded wealth will be of no use;
I have no Dharma practice [to show].
And like removing a hair from a lump of butter,
I will be removed from the midst
Of possessions, resources, loved ones,
And from the midst of my friends.
Alone, my turn has come to leave. [135]
Alas! What I would I do were I to die?'
He rolls back and forth.
What he craves cannot fit into the mouth,
And when he experiences remorse and a despondency,
Then it is actually too late.
At that point nothing can help.
Can his father help? Can his mother help?
Can his son help? Can his daughter help?
Can his wealth help? Can his power help?
Can he outsmart it by hiding? Can he escape it by running away?
Can he outdo it through combat? Can tying himself up help?

It cannot be seduced by a beautiful face;
It cannot be overcome by an attractive physique;
It cannot be seduced by a charming hostess's meal;
So a time will come when there are no means to avert it.

"In his despair he may feel remorse, but it's too late;
It's too late, for the turn has come for the procrastinator.
Surrounded by many beloved ones,
Saying 'There is no way you will die,'
Though [beloved ones] may beat their chests and commiserate,
Who is there that has deceived death?
The time has definitely come for him to die.
This, too, is due to the mire of desire.
It is beneficial to hoist high against blithe grasping at permanence;
It is beneficial to escape to the expanse of the absence of appearance."

This concludes [the discussion] "The Way Dying Occurs";
Brought into a collection, it is the seventh.

*   *   *

"Bhrūṃ Jé, listen to me further.[291]
Now for the separation of the four elements:
First, the earth [element] goes.
One feels that the body is sinking into the earth;
One feels oppressed by one's clothing.
Befogged, one's consciousness becomes dull;
To those who are near
One appeals, 'Pull me up.'
This is first early sign of death.

"Bhrūṃ Jé, pray create good propensities.
It's not appropriate to cry and so forth;
It's not appropriate to ask [the dying] for many deathbed instructions.
The one who, having failed to inquire when the person was not ill,
Now asks at this most critical point and time—
What greater enemy is there than this?
For the person is being thrown into the three lower realms.

"So at that point leave the sick in a solitary place.
With [his body] reclining on his right,
Block his right nostril with dough or something similar;
Recite the names of the Three Jewels;
Cultivate the teachers at his crown aperture;
And perform the activities of the teacher as well.
This is how [one should proceed] when the rite is performed for others.

"For yourself, when the time has arrived,
Mark the three points of your body with the three letters;[292]
Holding your mind on the three letters,
[Visualize] your teacher seated upon your crown;
Your consciousness exits from your crown aperture
And then shoots upward to the teacher's heart. [136]

"Again, Bhrūṃ Jé, listen to me.
At that point, you will perceive
From the east the appearance
Of blessed Vajrasattva the size of a mountain.
[Appearing] his normal color,[293] he is adorned with ornaments.
At this [moment], if your propensities are good,
You will recognize him and experience joy;
If your propensities are bad, you will experience fear,
And fainting, your consciousness will leave.

"Next, the water [element] goes.
In your mouth, dry film forms on your teeth;
Your palate dries and your tongue shrinks.
This is the second early sign of death.

"At that point, you will perceive
From the south the appearance
Of blessed Ratnasaṃbhava as before [like Vajrasattva].
[Appearing] in his own color, he is adorned with ornaments.
If your propensities are good, you'll feel joy upon [seeing]
    the god;
If they are bad, you will experience fear.

"Next, the fire element goes.
The heat from your body is lost;
The luster of your body disappears, as well.
'Now he is dead,' people will say.
This is the third early sign of death.

"At that point, you will perceive
From the west the appearance
Of blessed Amitābha as before.
Recognizing and not recognizing are the same as above.

"Next, the wind element goes.
At this point the wind lifts up your awareness.
As the external air is brought in and exhaled from your chest,
You feel as if awareness is slightly revived.
Mumbling, you will look at others beseechingly.
Due to the wind's action you will feel thirsty and
And ask for some food.
'This fool wants provisions for the cemetery!'
Or 'He has returned!' some will say.
For some there might be no movement at all.
This is the fourth early sign of death.

"At that point, you will perceive
From the north the appearance
Of blessed Amoghasiddhi as before.
Recognizing and not recognizing are the same as above.

"Then, all the heat in your body is lost.
Saying 'He is dead,' everyone prepares to wrap [your corpse].
Alas! Many are taken away by the confused
Before they have time to be dead after having fallen.
It is better if one is left for some days.
Though the external signs are complete,
When all inner breaths are lost to the outside
And the outer breath reaches the inside,
Your consciousness enters deep into the channels.
When it departs to the channels where ḍākinīs reside,

The perceptions of all [these ḍākinīs] will dawn.
If they are not recognized, it is as [explained] before.[294]
If recognized, they will grant powerful attainments and you will be
 happy.

"Furthermore, you will see many deities,
Such as [Buddha] Vairocana.
If you do not recognize them, this will engender suffering;
If you do recognize them, the potential attainments are great.

"In brief, due to good or bad propensities,
When seeing incalculable wrathful deities
In forms that are most terrifying,
Those with bad propensities think: [137]
'Alas! Enemies are after me.'
They conceive that which is excellent in a distorted fashion;
They confuse the source of refuge for their enemy.

"In brief, Bhrūṃ Jé, listen to me.
One will see incalculable peaceful and wrathful deities.
One who is familiar with them will recognize these [deities],
And the [deities] will relate joyfully as an ally and refuge.
Going for refuge to all of them, one will make supplications
And follow all of them.
[In turn], all of the [deities] will reveal the ultimate mode of being.
The teachers will also appear at this site.
At this point make sure that you recognize [them],
And since consciousness is unobstructed awareness,
At best, transfer [your consciousness] to the ultimate expanse;
At medium level, transfer it to the teacher's heart;
At the very least, transfer it to the meditation deity's heart.
I appeal to you to seize a lasting secure ground.

"At that point, the propensities for
Whatever [deities] you have familiarity with will be awakened.
Bhrūṃ Jé, I have given up all chores.
These [events] are certain to occur, so reveal them to all;
And when they occur, definitely recall these [deities].

If you recognize them, birth in the lower realms is impossible.
Those who are unpracticed are let down on account of their confusion.

"When you apply the [practice at death of] transference [of
    consciousness] to others,
Make inconceivable offerings
To the Three Jewels and to your teacher;
Perform the seven limbs extensively as well;
Make supplications to bring about the transference;
Then, at each moment of the [dissolution of] the four elements,
Beginning with the first, call out his name and say:

"'No one is more joyful than you!
Today you've seen the face of the meditation deities.
Look in the east the Buddha has come.
With a blue body he is immense.
He is adorned with perfect ornaments;
He is surrounded by a retinue of bodhisattvas;
He is your savior god, so pray to him;
Without being attached to this body,
Transfer your consciousness to the deity's heart.'"

The [sole] god said:
"The mode of being all phenomena is empty;
Concepts of good and bad do not exist at all.
Without clinging to the extremes of existence and nonexistence,
Enter your awareness into the great middle way.

"Body is like a crystal *ūbhi*[295]
From the crown, clear and transparent,
Eject your awareness and, indivisible with me,
Let us go to the ultimate expanse.

"Bhrūṃ Jé, when this becomes firm,
Let us depart to a happiness that is certain to come;
Even at the crossroads of all that is good and bad,
Success and failure are only four finger widths apart.

"Furthermore, examine people in a gradual sequence:
To those practicing the generation stage, reveal the generation stage;
To those with the completion stage, reveal the completion stage;
To those with pure ethical discipline,
Reveal the aspects of pure buddhafields;
To the immeasurable bodhisattvas, [138]
Reveal the inconceivable rites [of helping others].
In brief, reveal whatever virtuous deeds you do
To those with the firmest propensities.

"Bhrūṃ Jé, as for your sacred lineage,
Since their way of life is pure and they are great in intelligence,
Reveal Tuṣita to them and apply the transference.
The instant this is remembered they will go to that buddhafield.
Why is this so? Because they have no attachment,
Nor do they depend in any way upon this body.
At that point, since consciousness is unobstructed,
Whatever aspect is engendered, [the consciousness] arrives there.
The perceptions of purity appear,
And they will be born in pure buddhafields.

"To whomever aspects of impure [realms] appear,
They will depart without obstruction to the impure realms.
The Middle Way followers who engage in yogic practices
Will go to the middle way in the middle expanse.[296]

"The indication of death is the clear sky;
For those with pure ethical discipline flowers rain down;
For [those with] the awakening mind relics descend;
For those with the generation stage images of deities appear;
For those with pure discipline their bodies remain pure
And they are welcomed by all the gods;
For those on the irreversible stage conches [appear];[297]
For those bodhisattva warriors who have not shunned samsara,
It is said that their heart and tongue will appear.[298]
In general, when a sublime being passes away,
Rainbows appear as a sign from the gods.
The early sign of the ultimate mode is the absence of clouds.

These are the common indications alone;
Their individual signs are inconceivable.

"For some, as explained in all sorts [of scriptures],
The winds have entered their central channel, it is taught;
For them flawless nonconceptuality comes about;
So meditation on the ultimate mode [at death] is most excellent.

"Most ordinary people, however,
Lose consciousness due to the force of unknowing.
Following death, for three days or more,
Or for seven days, they lose consciousness, it is said.

"Some assert that this is the moment
When mother and son ultimate modes meet face to face.
For this, too, there is a flawless scripture.
I appeal to the wise to prolong this moment.
Though this may happen [momentarily] to even a butcher,
Ignorance means [for him] this will end only in a lower realm.

"Alas! Bhrūṃ Jé, listen to me.
Sometimes superior cognitions such as the following appear:
You remember the previous, next, and this life;
You remember where you were born in three previous lives;
You know where you will be born in three subsequent lives;
You know your immediately succeeding life or up to seven lives.
On such occasions the thought might occur,
'In the past, too, I have suffered incalculably;
Alas! Today, like a respite,
I have obtained a human existence,
Yet with no Dharma, and due to many evil karmas,
I am going toward the lower realms. How tragic!'

"Utterly terrified you experience [deep] fear.
Then you lose consciousness for a while;
On awaking, your superior cognition is impaired. [139]
Though you have nothing for a body at all,
You act as if you possess a body.
Standing up suddenly, you think:

'What a desolate wasteland!
Countless terrifying apparitions exist here;
If [even] the appearances are no more,
Why have they come here?'
Thinking this, you run around unobstructed.

"At that point you will be bound by the butcher's lasso—
[Fleeing] as if pursuers are on your trail,
You reach your home, terrified.
You feel that you have gotten free of the butcher
And mimic [the behavior of] the living.
Knowing that you are dead, everyone is grieving—
Wailing and shedding tears.
Though you speak no one responds.
Even your fingers are turned backward;
Your clothes also feel as if they are on upside down.

"Though this is so, if you have virtuous perceptions, the doors
To the lower realms will close and you will go to the higher realms.
However, if those who remain behind do not cultivate virtue,
But cry and wail, then the following will take place:

"You will hear them calling you from a mountaintop.
Yet, when you strive [to get there] and go toward it,
There is nothing there. You hear echoes from the valleys.
Returning, you search, but there is nothing there.
Tormented in this way, you run all about.

"You wander for forty-nine days, it is said.
This is the very least [amount of time you wander];
Until this time you wander for all sorts of time;
For most sublime beings, without any interval
They move upward until [they reach] their secure ground.
Those who have killed their parents and so on
Go straight to the depths of great hell.[299]

"The most evil ones go to the hells;
The attachment-ridden to the hungry ghosts' [realm];
The aversion-ridden to that of the demigods;

The delusion-ridden to that of the beasts.
These [births], in turn, are [subdivided] in numerous ways.
With respect to the beasts, for instance:
The aversion-ridden [are born] as wild beasts;
The delusion-ridden as sheep and so on;
The lust-ridden as donkeys and so on;
If you have all three [afflictions] you are born as a dog and so on.
Extend this to other classes of beings as well.

"To take the hells as an illustration:
It is said that together with your innate god and demon
You are dragged by the executioners
Into the presence of Yama [the lord of death].
He then examines your Dharma and negative karma.
It is said that the demon will show the store of evil deeds,
Whereas the god will show the store of virtuous acts.
If equal, he then looks into a mirror [to probe further].
When he is not sure, it is said he weighs them on a scale.
If the evil [outweighs the virtuous], you will be baked and burned;
For the virtuous this does not happen.

"Bhrūṃ Jé, reveal this much of the instructions to us.
A time will come when we are certain to die. [140]
This is how the four borrowed elements are lost;
This is how the dependent relationship of body and mind is broken.
This is how the hosts of deities will appear;
This is how those with bad propensities are doomed;
This is how those with good propensities win.
The best is to be accustomed to the ultimate mode of being.

"When the time comes for us to die,
This is the instruction and it will certainly help.
There is no one who will not die,
Yet it is extremely rare to find someone who understands this.

"Bhrūṃ Jé, in the bed of a [dying] Dharma practitioner,
Pray do not let a learned person die as an ignorant one!
Do not let a diligent person die as a moral degenerate!
Do not let a kindhearted person die as a charlatan!

"Bhrūṃ Jé, recline [on your right side] and be relaxed;
Do not lie face down like a beast;
Do not lie on your back, [the posture of] lust;
Do not recline on your left, [the posture of] aversion.
Reclining on the right and pressing down on your right veins,
At best, lie down in the great ultimate expanse;
Second best, lie down in the great immeasurable thoughts;
At the very least, lie down with the mindfulness of ethical discipline.
Such are the behaviors for one of an intermediate level.
Otherwise sit cross-legged in meditative equipoise;
And the greater the intensity of your pain,
On top of this, take [upon yourself] entirely
The sufferings of all sentient beings.

These also have no real existence whatsoever;
In truth their nature is free of elaborations,
So in this ultimate expanse devoid of birth and death
Place your mind relaxed and free.
When you perceive forms, visualize them
As your teachers, meditation deities, and Dharma protectors.
[Perceive] them also as unreal and as mere reflections.
[View] sounds as words of the great ultimate mode of being,
And leave these, too, as mere echoes.

"Do not be attached to even an iota of the good;
Harbor no desire to reject the bad.
If conceptualizations arise, destroy them instantly.
When you enter an inferior body,
You are fettered by the 'self' without control,
So, without grasping at selfhood,
Cast yourself into the expanse of no-self.
This is the [diamond-like] vajra conduct;
Cherish the absence of conceptuality at all times."

This is the eighth collection, "The Transference [to Be Effected] When
One Dies."

* * *

Inside the [rainbow] tent of great compassion,
He holds high the bow of great insight
And inexhaustible arrows of skillful means;
Sporting the feathers of the four immeasurable thoughts,
Compassion as the [arrow's] notch pulls hard at the bowstring—
This great arrow of the hero is unhindered,
[Yet] it is bound to the string, the prescriptive antidotes.

This golden son, the hero of the Joyful Realm,
With light rays invoking virtues [in all],
Entirely fills all the world systems, and, [141]
Pulling the bowstring, shoots arrows and hums songs.

His crystal diadem bows and touches
The excellent body of refined gold,
Sprinkling one thousand petals of flowers.
His voice is adorned with words of sixty attributes;
In tunes outshining that of one thousand Brahmas,
He sings praises and pays perfect homage.
One thousand goddesses make hosts of offerings;
One thousand youths declare and purify negativities.
They urge all to rejoice [in the good deeds];
They appeal [to him] not to enter into nirvana.

Then the principal Bhrūṃ Jé
Offered the following [song] to the master's ears:

"The king of death exhorts [us to perform] in easy terms
[The practice of] transference that helps
Us hoist our robes well against the mire of death.
By recognizing [death] through death itself
And by transferring into the immortal expanse,
The halfhearted will hoist high their attitude, master.

"Not seeing desire—this mire of poisonous boiling stew—
As an object of attachment, we flee.
By hoisting ourselves away from attachment and aversion—
Master, please show us such a place to escape.

"Kind indeed is your skillful means, teacher,
Which helps us escape the monstrous fire.
By winding up the long [string of] thought
We can combat this monstrous fire of attachment,
Which cuts short the life of happiness.

"As for the notorious 'mire of rotting corpses,'
The root of this is attachment;
So if one does not cross the basic mire,
The happiness of this 'I' and 'self' will end.

"Sunk in the mire of desire,
One is pecked at by the long beak of 'self'—
The so-called iron worm, desire;
Unbearable sufferings plague us in the mire.

"Alas! This is because of excessive desire;
This is also because of the enemy of self-grasping.
It is close to all afflictions, attachment and aversion,
So roll back halfheartedness, and you will find
The means to travel to the pure buddhafields.

"Desire is like a silkworm—
With the saliva seeping from its mouth,
It binds itself and bars you from leaving;
Likewise, the great mires
That emerge from excessive self-grasping
Bar you from going to the secure ground.
Unbearably, it forces you among the [rotten] corpses.
So by hoisting high against the mire of halfheartedness,
Happier it is to run away, for nothing will help.

"Teacher Bhrūṃ Jé, listen to me.
Human life is like passengers in a ferry—
They'll either reach the dry shore or die at sea.
Between life and death it's [like] the splitting of a barley grain,
For if the ferry and the oarsman are excellent,
It's possible that they will reach the dry shores.

If the two are lacking, however,
It will be the reverse; they will die at sea.

"As for those who rely on the boat of human existence, [142]
If their leisure, opportunity, and teachers are excellent,
They will journey to the other shore of liberation,
But those who lack [such support] die in the ocean of cyclic existence.

"Thus, this [juncture] is the turning point.
So until this juncture is destroyed,
Paddle, O those with the armor of perseverance;
Protect, O teacher, excellent oarsman.
Steer this boat of a human life to a secure ground.
In this life do not let this boat be swept away
By the dangerous waters of illness and miseries.
Bless me so that I will become an excellent oarsman
Who will set all beings free
On the other shore of cyclic existence;
Help me that I may develop true renunciation."

[Drom:] "Alas! Apparition Dharma king, listen.
Born of the merits of sentient beings,
As I, Great Compassion called Bhrūm,
Look more at this cyclic existence,
[I see] that in this uncontrolled cycle of existence,
Sufferings resemble [the patterns of] a water wheel;
Whatever one does brings misery alone.
There seems to be no mechanism at all for happiness.

"As I look at the phenomena of cause and effect,
Seemingly in conflict, they are related;
Assuming this character of a masquerade,
They betray many clever ones. This I see.

"Born of afflictions and karma,
Though their intelligence is sharp, they have lost their aims.
With their mundane affairs more important, they might seem well,
But they turn their backs to their lasting aim. This I see.

"When teaching others they appear learned,
Yet as for their own aims, they are at an utter loss.
In truth they have neither, and in particular, they let [others]
    down;
Smooth-talking, they squander their own life. This I see.

"They are versed in all forms of knowledge and crafts;
Respected by all, they are sources of others' trust.
Yet without seeing the goddesses of the next life,
They are betrayed by the demons of this life. This I see.

"Ethical discipline like a medicinal tree,
Beneficial to both self and others—
Though they mouth it now, they discard it in the long term;
Even the demons ridicule them. This I see.

"Learning, reflection, and meditation
Resembling a king's inexhaustible treasury—
Not seeing this as a source of immediate joy,
They roam through the towns of sense objects. This I see.

"Forsaking the practices that are feasible,
They promise the unachievable buddhahood;
But falling into the abyss of the intermediate state,
They suffer with their head smashed. This I see.

"Abandoning the Three Jewels, which are certain to protect,
Seeking a mighty one, they cultivate Pekar;
The instant they succeed they lose their life.
After death, they roam in the lower realms. This I see.

"Abandoning teachers who reveal the ultimate mode of being,
They consort with negative friends who rob them of happiness;
Not able to see far they are totally blind.
Swiftly they are crushed by elephants. This I see. [143]

"Without examining things, they start a family;
They mate with each other joyfully

And waste both this and future lives.
At death, with no control, they separate. This I see.

"Accumulating all sorts of negative karma for the sake of food,
Even in this life they experience no happiness;
Everyone wishes them dead.
In the long run as well they go to the lower realms. This I see.

"Not relying in their minds and from their hearts
Upon the Dharma, which gives rise to happiness,
They hoard wealth to outshine their enemies,
Even at the cost of death. This I see.

"Though after death they must leave everything,
They hoard and hoard, clinging and attached,
Not daring even to eat and drink;
At death people use [the hoarded wealth] for their rites. This I see.

"Born from your body and nurtured so well,
When grown up and adorned excellently [with jewels],
Saying 'I'm leaving,' [daughters] bring all sorts of misfortune;
They are demonesses who betray their parents. This I see.

"Robbing the wealth in which you have entrusted your well-being,
The nurtured son shuts you up and scolds you;
He brings in a demoness with evil traits
And expels his kind parents far away. This I see.

"Instead of training in this life in the pure visions,
Guarding morality, giving without attachment,
And taking joy in the excellent pursuits,
On account of miserliness, they end up drinking pus and blood.
　This I see.

"Nurturing their enemy within their hearts,
They propitiate this enemy with all that they have;
Yet viewing all external objects as enemies,
They are [tethered] by the demon stakes of false conceptions. This I see.

"Not understanding the great essential point
With which all enemies are defeated collectively,
Opening the way to conceptualization, attachment, and aversion,
They are lost in the traces of such openings. This I see.

"This is the realm of the experience of imperfect beings,
Confused that they possess self-defining characteristics;
These sentient beings, sunk in the mires of the afflictions,
Are certain to be imperfect;
Certain to strike themselves with their own swords;
Certain to drink poisonous water;
Certain to destroy their own lives;
Certain to be their own dead weight;
Certain to doom themselves with their enemies.

"Keeping the butcher enemy inside the house,
They lock the door from the outside with gritted teeth;
They are certain to stand vigil from a distance.
This empty action may appear dignified,
But nothing succeeds from its enactment.

"Though seemingly apparent, things are devoid of reality;
That which is [considered] definitely seen is like a rabbit's horn;
With no thing [as its basis] they catalog its properties.
This is like analyzing the sharpness of [the rabbit's] horn;
[It's like speaking of] a blue son of a barren woman
Drinking poisonous water and glowing with light, [144]
Or having drunk ambrosia, becoming divorced from his life;
They thus carry their own corpse. This I see.

"There is a most courageous lion
With nine heads adorned with striking manes;
Bringing the sky down to the ground,
He wraps it with his manes and throws it. This I see.
Not only do I see these, I have ascertained these facts.

"Alas! The conduct of such [mundane beings] is base;
Do they not circulate like a waterwheel?

They have no reality, for there are many places in which to vanish.
Do they not journey to the field of liberation?
O peerless teacher,
Certainly appearance and absence of appearance can be seen."

This is the ninth collection, "A Concluding Summation."

* * *

If all is summarized, this is the collection on the enlightened class,
which is to understand the absence of birth and death.

The stainless one declared:
"Wherever space pervades,
There your body pervades;
Among the parents who pervade there, too,
Who exists that you would not guide?

"If in even a single pore of your body
There are inconceivable buddhafields
Of incalculable conquerors,
Who can comprehend the arrays of your body?

"Your sugata body is free of attachment to anything
And engages [in activities] without attachment.
You hold back the great mire of desire
Of a person being attached to a thing.
Through your exhortation to [reflect on] impermanence,
You help pull up the strings of grasping for permanence.
As for [indulgence in] pleasure, comfort,
Yearning for happiness, laziness, and procrastination—
You shorten these pull strings.
You, beneficial and joyful one,
O lord, dressed in the armor of perseverance,
Since you are skilled in bringing together
And summarizing all the scriptures,
Pray definitively summarize and reveal them here."

Bhrūṃ Jé spoke in response:

"O excellent teacher, please listen.
If [the scriptures] are summarized it is this:

> Appearance and absence of appearance,
> Good and evil,
> Objects of abandonment and their antidotes—
> No matter which one you are attached to, it will chain you.
> Instead, relinquish attachment to all;
> Hoist your robes against the mire of desire and attachment;
> Go joyfully to the attachment-free expanse.
> If you become attached to the good,
> It will divorce you from liberation's lifeline;
> If you become attached to evil,
> It will divorce you from the lifeline of the higher realms.
> As for the stakes of the conceptualization
> Of grasping at permanence, [145]
> Pull these up high above the mire of desire,
> And, without attachment, go with your followers
> To the unceasing expanse.
> This is the medium-length summation.

"To further summarize:

> **Abandon attachment to all things**
> **And abide free of desire.**
> **Attachment fails to bring even the higher realms;**
> **In fact, it kills the life of true liberation.**

"There is nothing other than this.

"By contemplating and being endowed with
The virtues that arise from learning, reflection, and meditation,
May we proceed through the higher realms and
The ten [bodhisattva] levels and definitely attain full buddhahood.

"This is my, Bhrūṃ Jé's, way of life,
Clear as the crystal youth,
And [dwelling] upon the stamen of the white lotus—

May the auspiciousness of such a perfect life prevail!
May the auspiciousness of the great heroic Sage prevail!
May the auspiciousness of wisdom Tārā prevail!
May the auspiciousness of Great Compassion prevail!
May the auspiciousness of Lord Acala prevail!
May the auspiciousness of pure morality prevail!
May the auspiciousness of the altruistic intention prevail!
May the auspiciousness of excellent method and wisdom prevail!
May the auspiciousness of the realization of suchness prevail!
May the auspiciousness of the confluence of all auspiciousness prevail!

"Without sinking into the mire of desire,
Utterly contemplating impermanence through four sessions,
And, drawn forth by the chariot of aspiring and engaging minds,
May the ultimate vehicle reach [its final destiny]."

This concludes the twelfth chapter of the *Jewel Garland of Dialogues*, "How to Hoist Your Robes to Cross the Mires of Desire." [146]

CHAPTER 13
How the Heritage of the Pure Way of Life Was Requested

Oṃ āḥ hrīḥ hūṃ

O great Sage, wisdom Tārā,
Great Compassion, and Acala—
You four undeceiving lords and refuges,
I place you upon my crown and pay homage to you.

In the realm of the great Sage [Buddha Śākyamuni] in general, inside the lotus tree of Avalokiteśvara in particular, and, more specifically, in the realm of Tārā resembling the stamen [of a lotus], [Dromtönpa] sat upon the vajra seat of Acala inside the teacher's chamber at Yerpa. [He resided] there in the presence of the teacher of beings renowned as Atiśa, he who is the teacher for all beings in general and the lord of India and Tibet, the descendent of the king of Sahor, the jewel among the lights of the world, the one honored at one site by fifty-five learned paṇḍitas, the jewel for all the Sugata's scriptures, the abbot of countless saffron-clad monks, the great custodian of the scriptural baskets who, with a single-pointed mind, upholds all the scriptural baskets on the basis of condensing [their mean-ing] into a four-line stanza, the great vajra-holder of all secret mantras, and the treasury of all types of pith instructions. [Dwelling there,] in the pres-ence of this lord of the Buddha's teaching, [Dromtönpa] is the father of all the buddhas of the three times and the king of all noble ones whose compassion and wisdom equal space. [He is the one] whose deeds and enlightened activities are inconceivable, who voluntarily embraces the suf-ferings of all the beings living in cyclic existence, who can bear unimag-inable penances, and whose heart is never sated by the undistorted meaning of the ultimate mode of being—the profound truth propitious throughout all three times. His body's pores are filled with the incalcula-ble realms of tathāgatas, and the buddha realms in each pore lie beyond analysis for even the bodhisattvas on the ten levels. Even within a single moment he pervades all the sites of the six classes [of beings] with physi-cal emanations that grant to all sentient beings whatever they wish. For instance, to those who are impoverished and deprived, [his emanations grant] food, drink, wealth, clothing, ornaments, horses, elephants, medicine, and physicians. He manifests as savior gods appropriate to the beings of the six classes, such as [manifesting as Avalokiteśvara] Khasarpaṇa[300] in the realm of the hungry ghosts. [147] He subsumes all the teachings into the six perfections, and [the six perfections] into the six syllables. Through the six syllables he closes the doors to birth in the six realms and reveals the Dharma. For the attachment-ridden, he portrays himself as possessing attachment and thus manifests as youthful goddesses who are beautiful and smiling, fair and radiant, with melodious voices and clear words. He manifests in bodies that can engender bliss in the attachment-ridden and lead them to the inconceivable way of life. In the very same way, he portrays himself [appropriately] to the aversion-ridden and others. In brief, he is the peerless teacher, Lokeśvara, our spiritual mentor, the precious wish-granting jewel whose name is blessed by all the buddhas of the three times, the source of all these conquerors, the one who, compelled by [the need of] his destined spiritual trainees, took birth in the paternal lineage of Drom in the north, the upholder of the hidden conduct who is naturally the crown jewel of all yogis, and the being venerated from his [lotus] feet by many millions, thousands, and hundreds of ḍākinīs. This peerless teacher made an appeal:

"Uncontaminated, [this way of life] is the glory of all that is auspicious;
Ceaselessly captivating, it is as majestic as Mount Meru;
Endlessly satisfying to listen to, it is clear and pure;
Incomprehensible when contemplated, it is profound and vast.

"In order for it to be of benefit to all beings,
You have woven this golden garland of queries and answers.
It is like the jewel from which all wishes come;
It grants everything that satisfies one's mind.

"I want to possess this excellent spiritual tradition
Born pure from pure sources—
This way of life thoroughly acclaimed
By all the sugatas of the past,
All the lights who will come in the future,
And all those in the present whose perseverance is unrivaled.

"Now the time has come for desiring my inheritance;
Sole father, lord Atiśa,
In the future, when we are called upon as 'father and son,'
If, in relying upon you—my father Dharma king—
Your heritage turns sour, we both will be ruined.

"[This heritage] is inexhaustible however much one partakes in it,
Stainless from wherever one looks at it,
Bountiful, however one plants it,
Most delicious however one tastes it,
It is like the hub of a thousand-spoked [wheel];
Its cutting edge resembles the [sharp] sides of its spokes;
Its advantage is in excellently gathering the two purposes,
Transferring and transforming from excellence to excellence.
Though it transfers to the continuums of all beings, [148]
Its excellence is never diminished.

"Just as, from one single light,
Lights equal to the sands on the banks of the Ganges come forth,
This single, enduring source illuminates all.
Likewise, although it may be transferred to anyone's continuum,
This [heritage] binds together all favorable conditions
And cuts away all adverse forces.
Both where it travels and that which travels thrive;
It is therefore thought to resemble the waxing moon.

"My qualities, the inner recesses of a white water-lily,
Are hidden and cannot be found by anyone.
Opening it gradually, in the manner of a waxing moon,
[Reveals] noble sages,
Eighty thousand, twenty thousand, and five thousand bodhisattvas,
Brahmans with clear intelligence and learned in all areas,
Whose bodies resemble the seven generations of emanation beings.
Endlessly captivating to whomever beholds them,
One by one, they appear freshly from the depths.
The cooling moon rays cleanse the jasmine flower,
And the juice within is also cleansed.
From pure realm to pure realm we shall go.

"We shall carry the pure propensities in a pure manner,
Clad in pure clothing and [consuming] pure food.
Wonderfully delicious and engendering ultimate bliss,
This is the clothing of discipline and the nourishment of altruism.
In the celestial mansion of wisdom,
The scriptural baskets, the articles of everyday need, flourish;
In particular this [mansion] is beautifully adorned by the seven noble
    riches.
There are servants and retinues of skillful means:
One wears sashes of conscientious character;
One wears shoes that protect beings from the lower realms;
One is dressed in a loincloth of inconceivablity;
One is adorned with a crown ornament of perfect view;
One wears ear ornaments of the common and uncommon
    attainments;
One sports arm bands of powers and fearlessness;
One has a necklace of excellent ethical discipline;
One wears bracelets of immeasurable joy;
One sports anklets of supernatural might;
One possesses a wheel that travels the limits of space;
It is with such resources of the inheritence
That the disciple children must be nurtured well.

"A heritage that is not endowed with these is inferior.
If you conduct yourself in this way, everyone will be nurtured;
If you grant your heritage in this way, it will be good,
O most excellent nondual teacher."

This is the collection on the request.

Then lord Atiśa, through his supernatural might,
Projected [the following] pure vision:
About a full bow-length above [in the sky] in the east,
He created a red rainbow staircase;
About a full bow-length above this,
He created a beautiful green staircase;
Likewise, [he created] blue, yellow, and white ones.

On the top of the fifth staircase, [149]
He built a pure celestial mansion of light.

Then with bodies luminous as light,
The teachers and the deities dwelled inside.
Appearing yet empty, like the colors of rainbow,
They turned the wheel of Dharma, profound and melodious.

He then said to Drom:
"You, who possess the interior of a white water-lily and its juice,
Come hither to the expanse of the cooling moon rays;
Come hither to merit, the path of accumulation;
Come hither to wisdom, the path of preparation;
Come hither to the ultimate mode, the path of seeing;
Come hither to the ultimate expanse, the path of meditation;
Come hither to completion, the path of no more learning.

"This site is the place of great bliss;
This site is the place where the white water-lily opens;
This site is the realm in which to propagate excellent sons.
In this treasury from which one takes the inheritance,
The Kadam father, who is free of all impure stains,
And his son, who has pure propensities, dance and play.

"Climb the staircases in sequence—
The ten staircases on the three paths—and come up here;
You will see to the far reaches of space.
Lead all beings up here,
Whether they are happy or suffering.
If you have excessive distraction, come up here;
You'll see all spectacles without exception.
If your distraction is weak, place your mind,
Naturally free, in the ultimate expanse, the expanse of light.
Whatever you desire, such as clothing,
It is found here, so enjoy it.

"This is the great place of happiness.
So where you see happiness,

Rejoice and go to that realm.
If doubt arises, this is a cause of failure.
Whatever you conceive of first, take it to its end
And gradually everything will be accomplished,
Or else not even one [task] will be accomplished.

"Son of pure conduct,
Such an excellent son as you,
Such an excellent son who upholds excellence,
In your lifetime as well, you are an emanation of the three lords.[301]
At that time [when] you are an emanation of the three lords,
They will uphold your way of life.
Ah! Everyone is your child.
Beautiful and born beautifully in the depth [of a white water-lily],
You are an object of veneration by all, including the gods.
The inside of the flower is also nurtured by the gods.
O my sole son with the pure way of life,
Nurture this at all times, for it is beautiful."

This is the collection on the response.

Then Drom Jé said:
"As for my queries and your answers—
All of this gentle play—
If you summarize it well, it is this:

> **When you encounter the causes of happiness, [150]**
> **In these always persevere.**
> **Whichever task you take up first,**
> **Address this task primarily.**
> **In this way, you ensure the success of both tasks,**
> **Where otherwise you accomplish neither.**

"There is nothing other than this."

This concludes the thirteenth chapter of the *Jewel Garland of Dialogue*,
"How the Heritage of the Pure Way of Life Was Requested."

Chapter 14
Meditating on Perfect Equanimity of Excitation and Mental Laxity through Severing the Root of Suffering

[151] Once again, at that very same place and in the presence of the teacher endowed with the qualities [described earlier], our teacher Drom Gyalwai Jungné spoke:

"Listen, wise one. The people of Tibet need to be tamed. As such, the time has come for me to appeal to you in Tibet's own language—a language that is effective and rich in the vernacular of the uneducated—and in words whose meanings are comprehended the moment that one hears them. What is the root of suffering?"

Atiśa replied, "Drom, it is negative karma."

"Master, what is the root of negative karma?"

"Drom, it is the aggregates, the 'I' or the self."

"Master, now how does the 'I' or the self act as the root of negative karma?"

"Drom, it is by needing everything."

"Master, how does it need everything?"

"It wants oneself to be superior and others to be inferior," Atiśa replied.

"Master, how should one refer to this?"

"Drom, it should be referred to as the 'attachment and aversion ridden.'"

"Master, in whom is this strongest?"

"Drom, it is strongest in those whose [spiritual] practice is weak but whose conceit is strong."

"Master, doesn't one become conceited because one has something?"

"Drom, the fireflies [for example] feel that there are no lights other than their own."

"Master, in their case, too, aren't they conceited because they do possess a flash of light?"

"Drom, the sun and moon are never conceited."

"In that case, master, will conceit lead to success on the path or not?"

"Drom, if one is conceited with the thought 'I will definitely succeed if I work for others' welfare,' this will lead to success on the path. Drom, if one is conceited with the thought, 'I will definitely understand if I pursue the training,' this will lead to success on the path. If one is conceited with the thought, 'I will definitely be capable if I observe ethical discipline,' this will lead to success on the path."

"Master, I wonder if all of these are genuine conceitedness."

"Drom, I am not saying that they are."

"Master, are there forms of conceitedness that do not have its full characteristics?"

"Drom, what kinds of defining characteristics do you need?"

"Master, I seek a definition that can illustrate the definiendum upon its basis."

"Keep quiet, Drom; for if we were to do that, it would not lead to success on the path. That which leads to success on the path is a similitude of conceit."

"Master, are you speaking of a similitude leading to success on the path?"

"In that case, Drom, does not a similitude lead to success on the path?"

"Master, where is [an example] of a similitude leading to success on the path?" [152]

"Drom, all instances in dreams of the recognition that all phenomena are dream-like are cases in point."

"Master, this is, in fact, what is called genuine. [Merely] knowing that heat is the defining characteristic of fire does not lead in anyway to success on the path."

"Drom, is heat not the defining characteristic of fire?"

"Master, in that case are all phenomena permanent and substantially real?"

"Drom, this is not the same. As for being permanent and substantially real, there is no basis."

"Master, so heat being the defining characteristic of fire is real because of having a basis?"

"Drom, you are indeed sharp with words."

"Master, in that case is that fire?"

"Drom, what else would it be?"

"Master, you accept that heat is the defining characteristic of fire."

"Drom, this seems like an instance of knowing something substantially real."

"Master, since there has never been a substantial reality, the only possibility is that it is similar to a substantial reality."

"Drom, are you not being conceited here?"

"Master, if [mere] imputations can lead to success on the path, being conceited is okay."

"Drom, is this a sense of superiority or not?"

"Master, is a sense of superiority an object of abandonment or not?"

"Drom, if one clings, it is an object of abandonment."

"Master, if one does not cling, is it then not an object of abandonment?"

"Drom, a sense of superiority without clinging is a mere similitude."

"Master, how should one deal with a sense of superiority with clinging?"

"Drom, level conceitedness flat."

"Master, what methods are there for this?"

"Drom, recollect the pith instructions of teachers who have practical experience."

"Master, what are [such] teachers' instructions?"

"Drom, having taught [you] ever since the universe began, you are now asking for a teacher's instruction?!"

"Master, we have associated with each other since the beginning of the universe, yet we are still together, aren't we?"

"Drom, that was a joke."

"Master, your humorous retort is as hot as fire."

"Drom, as an answer it is red [as hot fire]."

"Master, if it is timely, it is the [right] answer."

"Drom, in your case, is there such a thing as timely?"

"Master, I am not a sky flower."

"Drom, in that case, who are you?"

"Master, what is the color of white?"

"Drom, you are an expert in waiting for the critical moment."

"Master, he who is expert in waiting for the critical moment is learned."

"Drom, a learned one is quite busy."

"Master, why is this so?"

"Drom, this is because he has to wait for all the critical moments."

"Master, regardless of whether this is so, rushing about is being busy."

The master laughed and said, "Like you Tibetans?"

"Master, just like an Indian mendicant."

"Drom, he bites each grain of rice."

"Master, this will make [the rice to have] an appropriate degree of coarseness." [153]

As Drom spoke these words, a green lady carrying a vase filled with wisdom nectar poured nectar into two crystal ladles—one white and the other yellow—and offered them to Atiśa and his son. She said, "Exchanging jokes is an indication of great thirst. I, too, have heard of your love of humor, which seems to be true. I have therefore come to listen."

Drom replied, "Lady, are you also a mendicant as well? He! He! You had to wander in all the directions accompanying a white youth."[302]

Atiśa inquired, "Why did the white youth experience such haste?"

"Master, he had far too many mothers. Sometimes he was distracted by joy and happiness because they were too happy. Sometimes he had to vigilantly look after them because they were suffering so much."

"How many were there?" asked Atiśa.

"Master, it would be good if there were numbers and limits, but there are none."

"Lady, is space not the limit?" asked Atiśa.

"Master, you measure space then," asked the lady.

Atiśa replied, "I do not know. Ask Drom; he is good at traveling around. He also loves [acts of] elaboration and withdrawal. Also, there must be a limit to space that one can speak of."

"What kind of [acts of] elaboration and withdrawal do I engage in?" asked Drom.

"Drom, you engage in [acts of] elaboration the size of space."

"Master, you have the thought that I do, so please show us the limit of space."

"Drom, what are you talking about? I have never measured space."

"Master is telling a sudden lie. Having said that Drom engages in [acts of] elaboration the size of space, you are now claiming that you have never measured space."

"Drom, I said that you have [elaborations] the size of space, but I did not say that so much is the size of space."

"Master, if you say that Drom has elaborations the size of space, when this analogy is related to the actual fact, you must know both the analogy and fact [that you compared it to]. It is strange that you, a learned man, would make such correlations."

"Drom, you may be right this time. However, if, to say that something were equal to space, one had to comprehend space itself, there would be none who could use space as an analogy."

"Master, is this not a case of doing something while being ignorant? [154] An intelligence that discovers the limit of space is difficult to find indeed."

"Drom, who has measured that space-like ultimate nature of all phenomena?"

"Master, here something measureless is used as an analogy. If space has a measure it cannot be an analogy."

"Drom, how joyful it would be if I were surrounded by people like you who have no conceit and are learned in the Dharma."

"Master, this would be of no benefit. Instead, it would be far more joyful if all sentient beings became human beings like me and were here in your presence to partake exclusively in the Mahayana teachings. However, as with attaining buddhahood on the basis of a female body, this seems to be rare."

As [Drom] made this statement, the blue-green lady appeared vividly in the form of a tathāgatha. Master Atiśa laughed and exclaimed, "What you have illuminated directly [for us] is an excellent form indeed!"

"One who has already become fully enlightened can display any forms, both excellent and inferior. I was speaking of women who possess the fetters of the afflictions."

Then the goddess returned to her own form and asked, "Great Compassion, whose afflictions are greater, mine or a those of a woman with the fetters of the afflictions? I, for one, carry the afflictions of all sentient beings while a woman who is fettered carries only her own share. Without relinquishing the afflictions, one does not become fully enlightened, yet the afflictions are so extensive."

"In that case," replied Drom, "I, too, am greatly afflicted, for I am carrying space."

"Drom, there is nothing to carry of space," [responded Tārā].

"Tārā, there is no carrier either, so cast away everything into equanimity," [said Drom].

"What is it that carries the afflictions?" Drom asked Atiśa.

"Drom, whoever possesses self-grasping."

"In that case, Tārā does not have self-grasping, for she is liberated. As for we who possess self-grasping, how can we relinquish it?"

"Drom, how many times does conceptualization occur in a single day?"

"Master, an inconceivable [amount of] conceptualization occurs."

"Drom, how often does [the realization of] the ultimate expanse arise?"

"Master, being overwhelmed by conceptions, it does not appear to arise."

"For this, Drom, you need the standpoint of my teacher Avadhūtipa."[303]

"Master, do reveal to us that instruction of your teacher."

"Drom, one transforms whatever conceptions arise into reality."

"Master, if all the logs turn into gold, this is what those with greed need. But how can such transformation be brought about?"

"Drom, that is how, on the basis of pith instructions, a base metal is transformed into gold by utilizing the alchemist's elixir. [155] What is needed is to understand the essential point [of the method]."

"Do reveal to us the essential point, master."

"To defeat the enemy, Drom, first you must recognize the enemy."

"What is the enemy?"

"It is conceptualization, Drom."

"How does one destroy that?"

"Drom, destroy it the moment it surfaces."

"How should one proceed to destroy it?"

"Drom, observe where its base is; analyze its shape, color, and so on, and examine its past, future, and so on. Seek where it goes to and where it comes from. At that time, it will not be found."

"Why is this so?"

"It cannot be found because it never was, Drom."

"When it is not found, what should one do then?"

"Drom, this is called 'transforming conceptualities into the ultimate expanse.' If it cannot be found when searched for, this is a sign that it is the ultimate expanse, so place your mind at rest upon this."

"What if it arises again?"

"Then level it out again, Drom."

"Can one skillfully deal with this in a gradual manner?"

"Drom, this wouldn't work, so destroy it by beating it with the antidotes."[304]

"Are there any other objects of abandonment?"

"Drom, harbor no excessive thoughts; concentrate entirely all your aspirations into one."

"Are there other paths or not?"

"A two-forked road will not take you far, Drom, so let go and be single-pointed in your path."

"Are there other aspirations or not?"

"Drom, if you have too many aspirations, you will lose the actual purpose. Do not initiate too many tasks; let go and be single-pointed in your decision."

"Though this is true, nevertheless when adverse conditions happen, such as sickness, it is difficult."

"Drom, what are you saying? There is no better spiritual teacher than these."

"Are they spiritual teachers or what? They are sent by a malevolent force!"

"Why do you say this? Where can one find more excellent buddhas than these?"

"A buddha? But it brings such acute pain?"

"You did not understand, Drom. Sickness is a great broom for negative karma and defilements."

"I do not know whether it is a broom for [cleansing] negative karma and defilements or not. What it does do is to bring great suffering."

"Drom, with respect to this, too, when you do not find it as you search for it repeatedly, then the great effulgence of the ultimate expanse rises."

"In that case, should I be happy when suffering befalls me?"

"Drom, if you are to undertake a genuine Dharma practice, press down on the lid of your happiness-desiring thoughts."

"A cycle of suffering is bound to come."

"Drom, by enduring great hardships, connect suffering with suffering."

"I seek to do this to its end." [156]

"Drom, when you connect them, they get disconnected; this is the essential point."

"Why is this so?"

"This is so, Drom, because one suffers by repeatedly desiring only happiness."

"How should one conduct oneself, master, if one were to summarize all the points?"

"Since self is the root of all negative karma, discard it entirely, like the corpse of one's dead father."

"Master, what are the objects of affirmation?"

"Since helping others is the source of enlightenment, like finding a wish-granting jewel, uphold and embrace it."

"Master, aren't there things that should be left neutral in equanimity?"

"Since both self and others are unborn, let go and discard them with ease in the expanse of the equanimity of nonarising."

"In that case, you accept that. Master, what is the root of the afflictions that must be relinquished?"

"It is this great conceptualization."

"Master, what is the method of destroying this?"

"None other than leveling it out, Drom."

"Master, how is it relinquished by means of its antidote?"

"By means of beating it with no hesitation whatsoever. All paths are traversed by means of this single path, too, and all aspirations are concentrated into this single one as well. Since sickness and so on motivates one to perform spiritual practice, they can compel one to engage in Dharma practice. Therefore, they are excellent spiritual teachers. They reveal the dangers of adverse conditions, such as the malevolent forces, thus [allowing] one to regard those who reveal the means of being protected from [such dangers] as buddhas.

"It is difficult for ordinary beings to see all the buddhas, Drom.

"Drom, all of this is like a mother who disciplines her son and leads him to goodness. True renunciation will arise within, and one will remember the excellent Dharma. One will be closer to the buddhas in heart, so this is excellent," the master said.

"Drom, if one takes on the sickness of all sentient beings every time one is ill, there is no opportunity for negative action and defilements to defeat a great hero.[305] Drom, every time suffering arises, banish the blame to self-grasping, and when you search [for the suffering] you will not find it. Drom, if one hundred conceptualizations, such as [conceptualizations] of suffering, occur because one searches for them one hundred times, there will be one hundred times of not finding. Finding that truth of not finding is the ultimate expanse. In this respect, my teacher Avadhūtipa stated:

> The nature of conceptualization is the ultimate expanse;
> When they arise, it is joyful, for they are an excellent impetus.
> Of what use are they, since they cannot be found?
> They are but the effulgence of the ultimate mode of being.[306]

"Drom, the intention of all the buddhas are found in him. I, too, feel thus: [157]

> Even in a single day, within the realm of self-grasping
> Hundreds of thoughts occur, useful and useless;
> The instant they arise, I search for their antidotes.
> Since I do not find them, they seem to be the ultimate expanse
>   alone.
>
> For if they do exist, out of the great multitude of instances,
> Is there a rule that states that not even a single should
>   be found?"

Drom responded, "Today our conversation has been most enjoyable. The appearance of the goddess has also warmed the teacher's heart, and the teacher's instructions were most profound."

This is the collection on how to recollect the teacher's instructions when conceit and thoughts of superiority arise.

Again, Drom asked: "If this mind becomes too dejected, Teacher, how should one illuminate it?"

"Set it astride the cool blowing wind."

"Master, what should one do once one has thus set it astride?"

"Drom, given the multitude of animals, the attainment of a human life is joyful."

"How should one practice after generating such a thought?"

"Drom, obtaining it is not adequate, for it disintegrates easily."

"What methods can be applied with respect to this?"

"Drom, collect the golden flowers of ethical discipline."

"Where should such a person seek shelter?"

"Drom, seek it in the ocean of uncontaminated teachings."

"How does one abide in such an ocean?"

"Drom, one should abide by consuming rose apple juice and gold."

"I am not asking about how to eat."

"Drom, how can one abide without the resources?"

"One consumes [the food of] meditative absorption."

"Drom, there is no greater food than this."

"How does this help against dejection?"

"Drom, one will think 'How joyful it is that such things will happen.'"

"What is joyful about this?"

"Drom, it is so because one's ultimate aspiration comes about."

"On what basis does dejection arise?"

"Drom, it does so when conditions for negativity are created by others."

"How can the conditions for negativity be dispelled?"

"Drom, think 'They are an impetus for [practicing] forbearance.'"

"What benefits are there in practicing forbearance?"

"Drom, if one aspires for an attractive appearance, [forbearance] is indispensable."

"How does forbearance [lead] to the obtainment of an attractive physical appearance?"

"Drom, [the body endowed with] the exemplary signs and the noble marks."

"Apart from this, is there nothing else achieved from it?"

"Drom, one also attains speech endowed with sixty qualities of perfect melodies."

"The method for dispelling dejection is most excellent. Master, do both mental excitement and laxity arise?" [158]

"Drom, they are in abundance in those who are unruly."

"What methods should one pursue to dispel these?"

"Drom, there is none greater than perfect equanimity."

"What happens if one meditates on compassion?"

"Drom, they can arise, for one can feel dejected."[307]

"Should one meditate on loving-kindness alone?"

"Drom, here, too, dejection can arise."

"Should one meditate on joy alone?"

"Drom, here, too, dejection can arise."

"In that case, should one cultivate equanimity?"

"Drom, here, too, delusion can arise."

"Then there is nothing that can be done."

"Drom, if one recognizes the absence of doing, this is perfect equanimity."

"Though this may be true, does it help at all?"

"Drom, it is not that it does not help. There is no doer."

"Master, isn't this because there is nothing to do?"

"Now you have understood, Drom."

"So how should one practice the immeasurable thoughts?"

"Drom, forcefully and carefully, practice all four."

"Won't excitation and laxity occur?"

"Drom, therefore one practices all four of them."

"Aren't all four more powerful than [just] one?"

"Drom, yet one is the antidote of the other."

"Won't all four cancel each other out?"

"Drom, what reasons do you have?"

"What happens when clay pots attack each other?"

"Drom, what are you saying? How can it be similar to that?"

"Though they may not be similar, still there will be a fault."

"Drom, the head of laxity is kept down by excitation."

"Won't excitation alone arise [then]?"

"Drom, the head of excitation is in turn kept down by laxity."

"In that case, won't one be kept busy with these two?"

"No, Drom; rather, one balances [the two]."

"What happens when they are in equilibrium?"

"Drom, it is like the absence of illness that occurs when the four elements are in equilibrium."

"Can't one meditate on just any one?"

"Drom, practice what you can."

"I am afraid that excitation and laxity might occur."

"Drom, have less doubt in this regard."

"Should one meditate when they do not occur?"

"Drom, one can meditate again and again."

"But if one sinks into laxity, can this [still] become a path?"

"Drom, can one meditate while mental laxity is most pronounced?"

"This will not bring existence to an end, master."[308]

"Drom, I also maintain the same."

"So how does one lay the defects of laxity to rest?"

"Drom, when the faults of laxity are recognized it will be dispelled."

"Master, today's conversation has soothed my mind."

"Drom, I have never indulged in mere [meaningless] chatter." [159]

"Master, there is, therefore, a collection on dispelling mental laxity."

"Drom, there is a collection on dispelling both [laxity and excitation] as well."

"So, though many [teachings], there are three collections.

"Even though there were numerous conversations, with my queries and your responses, if you summarize it, it is simply this:

> **Since you take no pleasure in negative deeds,**
> **When a thought of self-importance arises,**
> **At that instant deflate your pride**
> **And recall your teacher's instructions.**
>
> **When discouraged thoughts arise,**
> **Uplift your mind**
> **And meditate on the emptiness of both.**

"There is nothing other than this."

This concludes chapter 14 from the *Jewel Garland of Dialogues*, "Meditating on Perfect Equanimity of Excitation and Mental Laxity through Severing the Root of Suffering."

CHAPTER 15
How to Train the Mind within the Expanse of Appearance, Emptiness, and Empty Echoes

[160] Again, in the celestial mansion of such a sublime teacher [Dromtönpa], our teacher, the perfect spiritual friend of all, asked the following question for the benefit of future sentient beings whose intelligence is small:

"Master, what is the greatest fault for a practitioner?"

"These afflictions of attachment and aversion seem to be the greatest."

"Master, what is the root of attachment and aversion?"

"It is the things desired by the monks of the monasteries."

"Do I not also have this, master?"

"This can be discerned from the basis and from the strength of self-grasping."

"This self-grasping can easily arise, master."

"Then it will lead everyone to their downfall."

"What should one do if attachment and aversion arise, master?"

"Drom, train in the manner of illusions and apparitions."

"What is the nature of an illusion, master?"

"Drom, it is applied to a base material by means of incantations and medicine."

"In that case, what is an apparition, master?"

"Drom, it is the portrayal of diverse things though being unreal."

"What is the nature of the base [material] of that illusion itself?"

"Drom, it is grasped at as signs though being unreal."

"Do please tell me an example of an illusion."

"Drom, [once] in a town called Śrāvastī,[309]
There was a man named Candrabhadra
Who was skilled in magic.
He had a friend called Śrīman,
Who had a family of three.

"One day Candrabhadra taught magic
To the householder Śrīman.

He told him that this would be useful in the future.
'Candrabhadra, what can I do with it?
I would be happier to own a horse instead,' [replied his friend].
Discerning [the situation], Candrabhadra thought, 'I'll trick him once.'

"Early one morning, while his three family members
Ate their breakfasts, Śrīman spun yarn next to the door;
His wife washed and rinsed [pots, pans, and dishes].

"Then the skilled magician came
Riding up on an illusory horse
And asked Śrīman, 'Do you want to buy this horse?'
Śrīman replied, 'I don't have any money, so I can't buy it.'
'That's alright. You can leave your yarn with me,' said the magician.
Thinking, 'He wants the yarn as the horse's price;
This means I could fool this man!'
Śrīman agreed to buy the horse.
'Well then, why don't you check out how he rides?' asked the magician.
As soon as Śrīman mounted the horse,
The horse sped off, out of control.

"When the sun had set and he had reached an unfamiliar desolate
    region, [161]
He thought, 'I have been doomed by this wretched horse.'
As he looked around here and there,
He saw a house with smoke bellowing [out of its chimney]
And ran fast to the door.
When he knocked on the door and called out for someone,
An old woman came out.
'Wonderful, here is a human being,' he thought.

"'If my luck is bad, she might turn out to be a nonhuman,
And I might get duped by her tonight.
But even if she does deceive me, what can I do?
There is nowhere else to go.

"'I could be devoured by tigers and wolves,
So I had better rely on her instead.'

With such thoughts he asked for a shelter.
'By all means, do come inside,' she replied.

"As he entered the house and looked around,
He saw that she had three daughters.
After she had offered him delicious food and drinks,
The woman asked, 'Who brought you here?'

"Once he told her what had happened earlier,
She replied, 'Now you've got nowhere to go.
This is an island not owned by anyone.
My husband is dead; he is with us no more.
Why don't you start a family with one of my daughters
And become the master of this household?
Even if you leave, you won't get anywhere.'
He felt that he had no other choice.

"So he started a family with one of the daughters.
He lived with them and many years passed by.
He even had three children, two boys and a girl.
One day, while their mother went to collect wood,
The four, the father and his three children,
Went to play on the river bank.
The moon's reflection was visible in the water
And one of the boys jumped in to grab it.
The child was swept away by the water.
When the father jumped in after his son,
Another son followed him and was swept away as well.
Śrīman was beside himself as to what to do.
As he held on to the one behind, he lost grip of the other;
So in the end he caught neither.
On the shore, a tiger carried away his daughter.
He shouted curses at the tiger many times.
Not retrieving all three, he fainted.
Nearly dead, he ended up on the dry shore.
As he woke up from collapsing with grief,
His wife arrived there at the site.

"'What happened?' she asked and he told her the story.
Grief-stricken, his wife plunged herself into the river.
Witnessing the death of his children and their mother,
Śrīman thought, 'What kind of a person am I with such [terrible] merit?
I was separated from some while they were still alive,
And from the latter four I was separated by death.
It would be better if I, too, were to die right here.'

"In his grief, he tore out his hair
[And saw that] all of his hair had turned white.
Anguished, he fled
And, after a while reached his homeland.
When he went to his house and looked around,
He saw his first wife singing a song.
'Are you still basking in the sun?' [she said.]
'I haven't finished washing [the dishes] yet.'
On seeing this, something snapped deep within his heart.
'Oh, how much I have suffered! [162}
I've been lost for so long, and
You didn't even come to search for me once.
Listen to how melodious your song is.
Youv'e not grieved in the least.
Instead of being overjoyed at my return,
You chastise me for basking in the sun!'
As he exclaimed all this, he was enraged.

"Hearing this, the wife thought,
'Is he deluded or crazy, or has he been fooled by magic?
What has happened to him?'
She asked, 'What has happened to you?'
'Wife, I have been separated from you for this long
And you are still unaware of this?' [he retorted].

"'Why do you say such a thing?
Just now you ate your breakfast,
And I still haven't finished washing the dishes.
Look here.' Saying this, she showed them to him.
'What [is going on here]? You may have been tricked by your friend.

Go look at what is left of your spinning.
It's outside; you'll recognize it from its bulk.'

"Then it occurred to Śrīman,
'It seems that what she says is true,
And I have been deluded about all of this.
But it is impossible to be deluded for so many years.
My three children—two boys and a girl—were born.
I saw their death and disappearance!
A year is comprised of twelve months,
And there are three hundred and sixty days.
How can the suffering of a single day
Be felt across such [a span of time]?
Perhaps my wife is deceiving me [after all]!'
With this, he went to check the spinning yarn.
Seeing that it still lay outside the door,
He overcame his doubts.

"After several days passed,
His friend, the skilled magician, came by.
'I haven't seen you for many years.
I felt sad [about this], so I came to see you today.
Where did you go?' he asked.
Once Śrīman had recounted the past events,
The skilled magician replied:

"'All phenomena are tricks of illusion;
Nothing is substantially real.
You never saw your three children and their mother,
So how could there have been even physical contact?
You have never left, with even a single step,
So how could you have reached a far-off land?
Not even a brief moment has passed,
So how could you have suffered for many years?

"'The suffering of samsara is just like that.
Though seemingly real, it is just like your [experience].
Though you have wandered long for eons,

This wandering is like the years you have felt.
Aging is like [the white hair on] your head;
Youth is like the death of your [illusory] children;
Enemies are like that hostile river;
Your friends and family are like the old woman;
Your homeland is like that [desolate] island;
Sunrise and sunset are like your arrival there;
They are like this, grasped as real when they are not.

"'Do not forsake inquiry, householder Śrīman.
This ultimate mode of being, which is primordially empty—[163]
Understand it through hearing your wife's words.
Understand it through your reflections upon seeing your yarn.
Understand it through deep meditation.

"'As for places such as Śrāvastī—
All subjects and objects, without exception,
Are [empty] like this, so analyze them.
Repeatedly reflect on this and you will understand;
Through habituation you will see the truth.

"'In the past you did not believe in the cycle [of illusions];[310]
Yet when searched for, how can real characteristics be found?
Though you wandered for so long,
Not until now have you understood that it's groundless; this is similar.'

"As the skilled magician spoke these words,
Śrīman realized that he had been tricked by an illusion.
He recognized all phenomena to be like this [magician's illusion],
And, losing faith in the factors of cyclic existence,
Became familiar with the truth of the ultimate nature.
Today, he has become Tsültrim Gyalwa.[311]
Seeing the ultimate nature, he is learned in all fields.

"I, on the other hand, am an apparition monk.
For an apparition to create an illusion,
Will even its appearance be possible?
Drom, such is the basis of magical illusion;

Drom, that which is called an apparition is also like this;
Drom, the objects of attachment and aversion are also like this;
So, Drom, continually recognize all things as being the same."

"Master, this analogy of illusion is easy to understand."
  "Dreams are easier to understand, Drom."
  "Master, what is easier for Indians to understand?"
  "We find this illusion most easy, Drom."
  "Master, magical illusions exist in Tibet, too."
  "In Tibet, dreams may be sufficient, Drom."
  "Master, what would happen if one had no dreams?"
  "Then there would be a great wonder."
  "Master, what about poetic words?"
  "One might not comprehend the profound ultimate nature, Drom."
  "I, for one, do not have any dreams."
  "Drom, this is a sign that you have no sleep."
  "As for sleep, yes, I go to sleep again and again."
  "Sleep can be taken [into the path] as reality itself, Drom."
  "Reality itself cannot be taken, master."
  "Therefore you do not experience dreams, Drom."
  "Good omens in dreams are a joy, though."
  "Didn't 'dream' just issue from your mouth, Drom?"
  "These are dreams that occur without sleep."
  "Such things as pure visions can appear, Drom."
  "Master, your conversations are profound indeed."
  "I have never spoken about something not profound, Drom."
  "This is the collection on relinquishing attachment and aversion, isn't it?"
  "You are skilled at questioning as well, Drom."
  "What should one do if one hears insulting words?"
  "Treat them like echoes and let them go, Drom."
  "What should one do if one is being killed?"
  "Recognize that this is in return for taking a life, Drom."
  "Teach us a method that would prevent such things." [164]
  "In that case, Drom, relinquish taking life and let go."
  "This will not avert what happens in this life, though."
  "Generate a deep remorse to fill one's heart, Drom."
  "I need not seek this, for it would not occur to me [to do otherwise]."
  "This is excellent, for it is a sign of having understood, Drom."

"Don't you have [other] methods to speak of besides this?"

"Mentally take upon yourself all sufferings, Drom."

"This is essential for others, but it is difficult to come by."

"Drom, it is true that [embracing others' suffering] does not come about if one does not take them."

"If one takes them all, will that come about?"

"Whatever the case may be, train in this way, Drom."

"What is the purpose of such [a training]?"

"It has been taught that if one desires enlightenment, it is necessary, Drom."

"Which teacher taught this?"

"The teacher Serlingpa taught this."[312]

"Who taught this to Serlingpa, master?"

"Countless [teachers] taught him."

"In that case, master, what is the method of this taking?"

"Drom, draw forth the sufferings of all by means of your breath."

"How should one relate to one's own virtues?"

"Drom, place them astride your breath and give them to others."

"What happens after this?"

"They will become like [the visualization of] emitting [light rays] and withdrawing [them]."

"What happens after this?"

"Buddhahood, the perfect fulfillment of abandonment and realization, will come to be."

"Master, I am hearing some audacious words here."

"This is audacious with a good basis."

"Do please say more, audacious one."

"Drom, whatever happiness comes about, give it to others."

"Say more on this still, master."

"Drom, whatever suffering comes about, take it upon yourself."

"Master, are these not huge boasts?"

"Drom, offer gain and victory to others."

"Most amazing! Do say still more."

"Drom, accept losses and defeats yourself."

"You say so, but are there no dangers?"

"Drom, there is none more wondrous than an enemy."

"Is this not reversing tail and head with respect to a friend?"[313]

"Drom, what if the tail grows on the head?"

"Then it would be a huge hungry monster!"

"Drom, I would also call one's friends the same."

"Can such a norm be viable?"

"Drom, the anchoring burden of the norms of samsara is huge indeed."

"How do you act toward your friends?"

"I shake my head and run away, Drom."

"Master, do you not meet with any friends at all?"

"Once I did meet with one."

"Did you not shake your head [then]?"

"Drom, he ran away due to the effect of my Dharma practice."

"Did you hear what happened in the [Indian] plains?" [165]

"Saying 'the king has arrived' he shed tears."

"Master, they are more polluting than an enemy."

"You've recognized how things are upside down."

"Master, what will happen if one trains in this manner?"

"One will get very close to buddhahood."

"Master, will this purify negative karma?"

"The [negative karma] will become like snow on a hot stone."

"Master, will this [training] serve the purpose of the seven limbs?"

"This will go beyond one hundred limbs."

"Master, how does one extend this to other conditions?"[314]

"By knowing whatever conduct you engage in."

"Master, how should one conduct oneself when eating?"

"There are those who think, 'I am consuming concentration [food].'"

"Master, what else can one contemplate?"

"One is eating only for the sake of others."

"Master, how should one conduct oneself when wearing clothes?"

"Think that one is wearing pure ethical discipline."

"Master, what else should one do?"

"Relate together everything that accords with each other."

"Master, are there no possible pitfalls to this?"

"Drom, if [pitfalls] occur, blame the self."

"Master, if there is no danger, this is highly profitable."

"No, there is no danger of being let down by this practice."

"Master, due to my past karma, I have heard the Dharma."

"There are teachings in the law of karma and its effects."

"Master, yes, there is in this the source of an essential point."

"I've never spoken of something that has no basis."

"Master, if one were to summarize everything, how should one do so?"

"Have faith in the law of karma and its effects, Drom."

"Master, this [then] is a collection on echoes and illusions."

"Drom, bring together all of these well and let it go."

"Though we engaged in many queries and responses,
If encapsulated well, it is this:

> **When objects of attraction or aversion appear,**
> **View them as you would illusions or apparitions.**
> **When you hear unpleasant words,**
> **View them as [mere] echoes.**
> **When injuries inflict your body,**
> **See them as [the fruits of] past deeds.**

"There is nothing other than this."

This concludes the fifteenth chapter of the *Jewel Garland of Dialogues*, "How to Train the Mind Within the Expanse of Appearance, Emptiness, and Empty Echoes."

CHAPTER 16
How He Engaged in the Hidden Conduct and So On

[166] Once again, our teacher, the perfect spiritual friend, was at that very same place and in the presence of the teacher when he asked:

"Master, what is the worst place for a Dharma practitioner?"

"The great prison of one's native land is the worst."

"Master, what kind of company is the worst for a practitioner?"

"Worldly social norms are the great stake that tie one down."[315]

"Master, what is the rope that binds a practitioner?"

"It is loyalty, partisanship, and arrogance."

"Master, what food is worst for a practitioner?"

"Wrong livelihood leads to downfall and excesses."

"Master, do please tell us about other [such foods]."

"This is the food proscribed in the monastic discipline scriptures."

"Master, what is the worst kind of conduct for practitioners?"

"Sprinting and hopping, and eating and drinking while lying down."

"Master, please tell us more about others."

"Check what contradicts the three scriptural baskets."

"Master, who is the worst of enemies?"

"A negative friend, that old source of downfall."

"Master, who is a greater obstacle to the vows?"

"It is women and so on, so forsake them."[316]

"Master, what is the greatest service to one's teacher?"

"The most excellent service is to make everything one does a Dharma practice."

"Master, are not offerings of gifts and ministrations better?"

"Even all the lay people perform these."

"Master, would it be okay if one does not do these at all?"

"It would be an obvious sign of having no respect."

"Master, what are the signs of the degeneration of a monk?"

"It is when he seeks his familial home as his monastery."

"Master, what faults ensue at such a time?"

"Drom, his parents will act as his preceptor, master, and colleagues;
For learning and reflection, he'll enhance wealth and his family line;

A youthful body will enter his heart;
He'll be led away by endearing deceitful words.
For a while he will be called 'the wonderful one.'
Then he'll be robbed of his wealth of the celibate life.
Next he'll be berated as 'you monkish man'!
Then, with no attraction [toward him], everyone will become hostile.
Drom, after death he'll go to the lower realms."

"Master, so where should one take shelter and make one's bed?"
"Take [shelter] beyond the edge of a town or in a secluded monastery."
"Master, in that case, in what manner should one die?"
"You should die like an injured wild animal."[317]
"Master, what manner of death befalls such a person?"
"He will have to bury his corpse himself."
"Master, who will burn and purify the bones then?"[318] [167]
"This is to be done for those who have guarded their ethical discipline."
"Master, they will not be there at such time, though."
"[At that time] they are entrusted to the care of the Three Jewels."
"Master, will the Three Jewels perform [the rites]?"
"Otherwise, what need is there for the Three Jewels?"
"Master, they're our ultimate objects of refuge."
"In that case, they will perform the rites."

"Drom, the first burning and purification is ethical discipline;
Second is the absence of attachment;
Third is arriving at a secure ground;
Fourth is protection within cyclic existence;
Fifth is the completion of abandonment and realization.
Drom, one must create the roots of virtue oneself;
One experiences the grief oneself;
One must know before [death] how to undertake these,
For if one encounters these suddenly, it is too late."

"Master, I have seen practitioners who say
'I seek a teaching for the moment of death;
At that time I might need everything.'
What do you think of these practitioners, master?"

"Drom, all such practitioners are pitiable.
Time—the teachings are required throughout all lives;
Preparation—this must be done when cognizant of what is to come;
'When a practitioner approaches the point of death,
Perceptions from good propensities will dawn,
And he will discard the darkness of ill-natured selfishness.'
To engage in Dharma practice with such hopes
Is to fall into the mundane aspirations of this life.

"You must be victorious in the next life.
When whipped by the iron chain of impermanence,
You'll do anything that is possible.
This is not all there is; still other things will happen.
Even though these things will occur, you will have no fear.

"Happy and joyous, you will ascend upward.
You'll journey to the fields of the pure way of life;
You'll go into the depth of a lotus flower;
You'll journey through the bodhisattva fields;
You'll become accustomed to the cleansing of concepts.

"The behavior of dogs and pigs is [now] no more;
The conduct of cattle has ceased to be;
The sack of filth is torn open;
The tree of harvest-desiring is felled;
The heap of putrid vomit is spread everywhere.

"With no need to meditate you become a deity;
Pure visions have entered your heart;
[Now] there's no danger of separation from the Three Jewels;
The flowered bed of discipline is elaborate;
The jewel mansion of sutras is beautiful;
The wheel of higher knowledge is fixed with spokes;
As you inflict loss on the food of consciencelessness,
You'll attain uncontaminated concentration.

"As you forsake sloth, mental dullness, and laziness,
You'll be enveloped in the light rays of pristine cognition.

Ah! The lotus tree of Kadam is in full bloom.
This is the residence of one thousand sugatas.
It's the place of enjoyment of one thousand bodhisattvas; [168]
It's the ground of happiness for one thousand disciples and self-
    enlightened ones;
It's the object of veneration of all humans and gods;
It's the field of merit, the lord and refuge of the entire world.
The pristine gods touch it with their crowns;
Nine great sages lift it from its base;
This is your inheritance, O Drom Jé.

"It's an inexhaustible mine of millions;
One thousand bathing pools of nectar abound
Containing the three white and three sweet ingredients;[319]
The golden ground is studded with turquoise;
It is filled with millions of apparition birds,
Birds with thick turquoise plumes sprinting about,
Deep turquoise birds hovering joyfully above.
This is the realm of Drom Jé, sovereign of men.

"Your three doors are free of stains;
You honor the stainless conquerors at all times.
Pervading the universe these conquerors fill all of space.
This is your inheritance, O Drom Jé.

"If you indulge in songs and dances, do so in this realm;
You won't fall into the abyss of the afflictions.
If you wear ornaments, pray do so in this realm;
Human ornaments cannot compare with these.
If you indulge in the sense objects, do so in this realm;
They share the nature of the five transcendent wisdoms.

"Ah! Listen to me, Drom Jé.
Having undergone sixty odd pains,[320]
Now happiness increases as its effect.
Having thoroughly trained in the pure propensities,
It is [now] impossible to feel despair and revulsion.
Even if you contemplate impurity, how can they arise?

Drom Jé and his sons shall remain joyous;
Drom Jé and his sons shall enjoy happiness in the long term.
As the fruit of enduring hardships you will find the riches;
The inexhaustibility of the riches depends upon its mine.
Drom, know this and enjoy this realm."

"Master, O paṇḍita learned in the five fields,[321]
Since I have seen this [realm], I conduct myself in this way:
The afflictions are like tasty wine for someone thirsty;
As he drinks, he becomes thirstier and his desire increases;
As he drinks again and again, wild thoughts arise;
He develops the mind to consume anything he finds;
In the midst of many [foul-smelling ingredients] such as garlic,
He indulges in the flesh of his parents and in the sea of blood.
He then resembles a red-eyed ogre in a human form;
Conscienceless and with blunted tail, his body will weigh like an anchor;
He begs, collects, steals, and snatches using his teacher's name.
Like a wild dog charging after [the smell of] blood,
He indulges in such things with unadulterated greed.

"Listen to these words of mine, I, Drom Jé.
Though the [afflictions] may seem joyful, cast them far away;
Though they may seem pleasurable, cut their roots.
These are what lead to birth in the mires of filth;
These are what lead to birth in the impure realms;
These are what make people behave like dogs, donkeys, sheep, and
    wolves.
Though they may have much food to eat, indeed,
Such food is like that of pigs and ravens, alas! [What is the point?]
Has such a person not let himself down?

"In the name of 'no judgment' he needs everything;[322]
His thirst is great and his belly large; [169]
His conduct brute and defiance heightened.
In the case of his own flesh, no one can eat it;
Yet with respect to that of others, he consumes it at all times.
Discard this [conduct] as one would shun a raven.
Not being attracted to the garden of lotuses,

He indulges at will in the midst of impurity.
Making *tongtong* noise he walks [with a] vajra.[323]
Cast this conduct of ravens far away.

"'Nonconceptuality' is the expanse of great delusion;
'All-knowingness' is the expanse of great attachment;
'Nonclinging' is the expanse of great envy;
'Pure vision' is the expanse of great vanity;
'Partiality toward one's own side' is clearly great aversion.
Amid these five powerful masses of flame,
The flowers of ethical discipline will be incinerated.
This will dry out the dewdrops of happiness—the effects [of good
    karma],
And it will throw the ashes to the three abysses.
The winds will blow away [the ashes] reaching everywhere in space.
In observing a sense of shame, he'll be like a corpse;
His corpse will be sunk in the mires of desire;
His body will be devoured by the maggots of afflictions.
Whatever he does will be a source of undoing, *phaṭ!*
Its result will be betrayal, O all practitioners.
Beneficial it is if you discard such distorted understanding.

"If asked, 'In that case, what is the method of
Discarding these? You tell us, Drom Jé.'
Flowers can grow in mire,
[Yet] no flower is soiled by the mire.
The one who discards [the mire] with such knowledge is wise.
Nonconceptual cognition is like a flower.
There is no need for *defiant* nonconceptuality.
Trampling upon conceptualities is deluded;
Instead, please construct this mandala.
In the expanse of nonconceptuality,
Construct a clear-light mansion beyond all measure.
Generate this mandala of clear-light deities,
Naturally free from both clean and unclean.
Through emanations of the omniscient pervading all,
Fill with dances everywhere that space pervades.

"Pervade the entire world with echoes that are
Free of conceptualizations of the eighty-four thousand [afflictions].
If the afflictions—the causes and conditions—are not stopped,
The effects will not be prevented,
So sever their roots and cast them into the expanse.

"The generation stage is the supreme pristine cognition body;
The completion stage is the fulfillment of the two accumulations.
Pristine cognition is equal to the field of knowledge itself;
Compassion is also as expansive as space.

"The seats that appear are a lotus and moon;
Though there are numerous births, this is a spontaneous birth;
The womb is described as the hub of a lotus;
One's companions are the clear-light deities.
In this ultimate mode of being, devoid of letters,
Drom's generation and completion stages are exhausted.

"Make *hrīḥ* the letter of convention;
Make the yellow, of course, with *oṃ;*
Alas! Make the green with *tāṃ;*
The dark blue Acala is *hūṃ* alone. [170]
From these [syllables] is such a celestial mansion created;
It has the nature of perfection.
This is Drom's generation and completion stages.

"Of course, the letters are devoid of letters;
The letters are devoid of change and nonconceptuality;
The lotus, moon, and sun are also devoid of letters.
The peerless, fully awakened Buddha,
Who resides in this mandala and is free of all—
This embodiment of the Three Jewels—I touch with my crown.

"I prostrate to this pristinely pure body,
Free of the duality of homage and an object of homage.
To the gods I offer the collections of pure offerings,
Unsoiled by arising, abiding, and ceasing.

"I confess and rectify the ill deeds [casting me off] a deep abyss
[Performed by] my three doors, devoid of arising, abiding, and ceasing;
As for those who, though empty, display diverse forms,
I rejoice with admiration in these countless saviors.

"Pray turn the wheel in the ultimate expanse
Of the emptiness of wishes and signs;
O dharmakāya, devoid of birth,
Being the nature of spontaneous abiding,
Pray do not depart.

"I dedicate this so that through this virtue
All those of cyclic existence will realize this truth
And be led into such a celestial mansion.
May they experience this secret mantra.

"I dedicate this so that they will immediately
Hail the supreme generation and completion [stages]
Of outer, inner, secret, and suchness,
Upon a seat of a refined moon
On the hub of a thousand-petaled lotus,
Just like the five deities of the action [tantra class].

"This adventitious [world] does not exist
Separate from the ultimate expanse.
May the perfect auspiciousness
Of this perfect absence of separateness prevail.
May the auspiciousness of pristine lineage prevail!
Through purity in the beginning, middle, and end,
May the auspiciousness of unwavering prevail!

"Atiśa, lord of all beings,
My inheritance is excellent indeed.
Paṇḍita, learned in the five fields,
If you say 'Dwell utterly in solitude, beyond town limits.
Like the carcass of a wild animal,
Hide yourself away [in the forest],'

Where will my prospective trainees be?
Show me this place of solitude as well."

After he made this appeal, the master said:
"O supreme lord of the Land of Snows,
There is a prophesy of the Sugata
That when the era of the future dawns,
The conquerors' mother will flourish
From north to further north.[324]

"Thus, to the north of this northern place,
There is a wilderness called Radreng.
Go there, [for] I have consecrated it.
The glorious temple of Radreng
Will be recognized as an equal to Bodhgaya. [171]
That shall be your wilderness;
There, too, your prospective trainees will converge.[325]

"*Ra* stands for freedom from [polluting] dust;
It has been stated that [Radreng] is the door of all Dharma.
This gateway of the Dharma, free of the dust of afflictions,
You will hoist high beyond the summit of cyclic existence.

"It's in the south of the universal monarch;
It's in the southwest of the precious general;
It's in the northwest of the precious householder;
It's in the north of the precious queen;
It's in the southeast of the precious elephant;
It's in the east of the precious jewel;
It's in the southeast of the precious horse.
Bearing each of the seven royal emblems,
The head of the glorious thousand-spoked wheel
Bows at the feet of the supreme conqueror.

"Furthermore, [Radreng dwells] above an eight-petaled lotus,
Below an eight-spoked wheel in space,
In the garden adorned with green meadows and flowers,

On the side of a mountain that exudes perfume,
On the shore of a turquoise lake with swirling svāstikas,[326]
And amid a forest green with lush vegetation and trees.
It is a place where flocks of birds chirp melodious songs,
A terrain where animals roam freely at ease—
Not too close to human habitats,
Nor too remote from them,
Not owned by anyone.
The land there is clean and supports a variety of grains;
It is filled with gods and nāgas who delight in the teachings.

"On juniper trees shaped like icons cast in gold
Grow beautiful eight-spoked branches.
For the humans all this is a mere appearance with no certainty;
For the nāgas it appears as a delightful palace;
For the gods it is a wish-granting tree.

"This is a golden lotus tree;
The buddhas of the ten directions reside upon it,
Emitting light rays in all ten directions.
This is a turquoise blue lotus tree;
The eight bodhisattvas and their eight female counterparts
Reside upon it, bowing to the sugatas.
This is a sign that masters and students possess learning and diligence;
I appeal that many sublime beings converge [there].

"This land has been revealed as perfect.
The perfect sun of the Buddha's teachings shall shine;
This is a sign of excellent long-term prospects.
The river of vast knowledge flows in the front [of Radreng];
I appeal to the learned masters to bow to it.
It obstructs arrows, demons, and upholders of extreme tenets.
Pray associate at once with excellent companions.

"The celestial bodies illuminate the roads;
The four points of the square earth are the four foundations of
    mindfulness;[327]
The four points of the square sky are the four perfect endeavors;

The four points of the square water are the four factors of supernatural feats;
The four sides of the valley are the four immeasurable thoughts;
These are signs that whatever one does will always be virtuous.
Let the antidote of enlightened factors win against the afflictions; [172]
Obstruct the passage of the winds that stir up hostility in the mind.

"I seek such extraordinary omens
That clearly illuminate the blissful and luminous truth.
I seek that brilliant sun with the light of one thousand rays, which,
Descending gracefully on the southern mountain in the front,
Dispels the cause, the darkness of ignorance.
I seek those many [beings] with continuums of [fortunate] karma who
    appear.
Dharmakāya master, though you are free of conventions,
It is due to the merit of many fortunate beings
That a multitude of buddhas arrive there
And consecrate the site. Thus I seek it.

"This resembles the convergence of many fortunate ones
At the feasts of Great Vehicle teachings [conferred by]
The buddhas and their children of all ten directions
Inside the Dharma palace of the Akaniṣṭha realm.

"Vast, high, and majestic,
The northern Mount Meru, king of mountains,[328]
Resembles a king reigning over his kingdom;
Gyalwai Jungné, reside there
And reign over the kingdom of Dharma.

"The northeastern Mount Meru, king of mountains,
Resembles a general embarking on a campaign;
Pray guard Gyalwai Jungné
And defeat the challenges of his opponents.

"The southeastern Mount Meru, king of mountains,
Resembles a householder whose treasury is full;
Pray propitiate Gyalwai Jungné
And relieve the suffering of poverty and depravation.

"The southern Mount Meru, king of mountains,
Resembles a queen sitting cross-legged;
Pray honor Gyalwai Jungné
And propagate many sublime beings.

"The southwestern Mount Meru, king of mountains,
Resembles an elephant stretching out its powerful trunk;
Pray lift high Gyalwai Jungné.
That he may be conveyed steadily, I seek.

"The rocky Mount Meru in the west
Resembles a giant stack of jewels;
Pray help Gyalwai Jungné flourish.
That all his wishes may be realized, I seek.

"The northeastern Mount Meru, king of mountains,
Resembles an excellent saddled horse;
Pray guide Gyalwai Jungné;
That your legs may enact supernatural feats, I seek.

"The vast open plains in the front
Resemble a wheel with one thousand spokes.
They ensure the stability of Gyalwai Jungné.
The defeat of adverse forces as well, I seek.
There are long streams of rivers in the front:
For the teachings to endure for a long time, I seek.
The sun rises so early [in the morning]:
For the students to be gathered soon, I seek.
The sun sets so late [in the evening]:
For the bonds to be guarded for very long, I seek. [173]
The dark junipers proliferate to the far corners:
For the Kadam to flourish in all ten directions, I seek.
It is located amid mountains:
For hosts of excellent students to be gathered, I seek.
There are palaces of nāgas there:
For it never to be wanting for resources, I seek.
The land presses down on the belly of a [giant] turtle:[329]
I ask that the malevolent forces, the enemies, be suppressed.

It is an attractive and most appealing [place] to live:
For it to be the holy place of the buddhas, I seek.

"From the summit of the great Mount Meru
Beam sharp-edged rays of light,
Illuminating the individual vehicles without confusion.
Harbor no excessive thoughts but affirm your stance;
For this to be revealed by the three scopes,[330] I seek.
Toward the mountain's midpoint are light rays of green fields:
For the encompassing antidotes to be powerful, I seek.
At the mountain's base are light rays of forests:
For the great assembly of students to proliferate, I seek.
There are level light rays of open plains:
For work for the welfare of beings to be impartial, I seek.
There are flowing light rays of water:
For the heat of the afflictions to be cooled, I seek.
There are clear light rays of space:
For everything to be sealed by nonobjectifying emptiness, I seek.
There are gleaming light rays of well-oiled things:[331]
For everything to be tamed with boundless grinding, I seek.

"The whitish rocky mountain in the east
Resembles an Indian tiger charging from the air.
It guards against the negative forces to the east:
For the fortunes [of Radreng] to equal the sun, I seek.
The great flowing river in the south
Resembles a dragon with a turquoise mane descending to the earth.
It guards against the negative forces to the south:
For [Radreng's] fame to spread in all ten directions, I seek.
Great medicinal plains fluorish in the west,
Resembling a red bird spreading out its wings.
They guard against the negative forces of the west:
For resources to converge at [Radreng's] hearth, I seek.
As for the great northern Mount Meru—
A turtle supports it on his back.
He guards against the negative forces and gathers conditions:
For him to press down upon my learning seat, I seek.

"Pray attract charms of strength and wealth from the general and house-holder in the east. Though the butter may be golden, pray attract the charms of etiquette and the capacity for transportation from the queen and elephants in the south. Though the barley grains may be excellent, pray attract charms of knowledge and charms fulfilling the wishes of the land of Phenpo[332] from the jewel and celestial horse in the west. Though water is our provision, pray attract charms of the northern oil[333] from the excellent horse and the king in the north.

"Meat, butter, and health are in abundance;
Excellent forests thrive both in the hills and the plains,
Along with one hundred and eight small springs
And eight streams and lakes.
As it is cool in summer and warm in winter, concentration thrives. [174]

"O my heart-like student, you who are a suitable vessel for [Dharma] prac-tice, possessing the eyes of method and wisdom, these are the perfect exter-nal signs. They can be seen even by children. As for those that are the purview of only the noble ones, I shall reveal them to you [now]:

"You, Great Compassion, Jinasāgara,[334]
When you appear in that realm through the force of a supernatural feat,
You will be welcomed by an assembly of thousands of gods.
Emitting light rays in the ten directions, the conquerors will
Empower you, O sovereign among humans.
From you, too, infinite light rays will emanate,
Blessing the entire ground in all directions.

"Listen, O learned one. I will offer you some advice.
Without cutting the gold and turquoise trunks,
Enter inside the trunk of the flowering tree.
Expansive and high, it is supported by one hundred pillars.
Inside this mansion composed of the five precious materials,
The buddhas of the ten directions act.
At its base, release water from the long spring.
This excellent bathing pool of transcendent wisdom
Will be blessed by the conquerors of all ten directions.

"Your hairs, O sublime one,
Shall scatter to all ten directions;
They will grow into twenty-one thousand lotus plants,
Each blossoming with twenty-one thousand petals.
All the conquerors with no exception will appear there.
They will celebrate the feast of the ultimate-nature mother.
Each lotus will have seven layers of skin;
They are clothed in the garments of pure ethical discipline.
Alas! This is the adornment of the clothing of the seven relinquishments.

"The shape of its perimeter is the Conqueror's face;
His head is adorned with the six perfections;
His eyebrows and eyelashes are marked with the Three Jewels;
His two eyes are loving-kindness and compassion.
His two ears are method and wisdom;
His two nostrils are the noble two truths;
His mouth is the door of the eighty-four thousand teachings.
From [his face], the long spring of untainted ambrosia flows.
As the teaching will survive there for a long time, build a perfect
    palace there."

With these [words], the uncommon origin [of Radreng Monastery] was revealed together with advice.

"To the east of the great palace, a lotus tree called *the knowing one* appears. Wide, expansive, tall, majestic, beautiful, attractive, and wonderful to behold, it has eighty thousand branches and petals. [175] Eighty thousand conquerors and their children, bodhisattvas of the eastern direction, sit upon this tree, raining down showers of great compassion. Therefore, it is said:

On eighty thousand crystal lotuses,
Eighty thousand conquerors reside
Together with the bodhisattvas;
They release forth rains of great compassion.

"In front of this, there is a lake endowed with eight excellent qualities called *the knowing one,* which is magically created through the blessing of the eighty thousand conquerors and their children. In the four cardinal directions, there are four most auspicious and pleasurable pools made of precious jewels. Sentient beings who drink from these [pools] have their suffering drawn into the water, rendering them peaceful and freeing them from the lower realms of existence. Therefore, it is said:

> For those who drink this ambrosia of eight excellent qualities
> From the spring and the [surrounding] pools—
> Their sufferings are drawn
> And the lower realms are pacified.

"To the south of the great palace, there is a lotus tree called *the golden one,* which is vast, expansive, tall, majestic, beautiful, attractive, and wonderful to behold. It has eighty thousand branches and petals. Eighty thousand conquerors and their children of the southern direction sit upon this tree, releasing forth the stream of loving-kindness. Therefore, it is said:

> On eighty thousand golden lotuses
> The assembly of eighty thousand conquerors resides
> Together with their children of the southern direction;
> They release forth the stream of loving-kindness.

"In front of this, there is a lake endowed with eight excellent qualities called *the golden one,* which is magically created through the blessing of eighty thousand conquerors and their children. In the four cardinal directions, there are four most auspicious and pleasurable pools made of precious jewels. Sentient beings who drink from these [pools] have their suffering drawn into the water, rendering them peaceful and freeing them from the lower realms of existence. Therefore, it is said:

> For those who drink this ambrosia of eight excellent qualities
> From the spring and the [surrounding] pools—
> Their sufferings are drawn
> And the lower realms are pacified. [176]

"To the west of the great palace, there is a lotus tree called *the copper one,* which is vast, expansive, tall, majestic, beautiful, attractive, and wonderful to behold. It has eighty thousand branches and petals. Eighty thousand conquerors and their children of the western direction sit upon this tree, releasing forth the stream of sympathetic joy. Therefore, it is said:

> On eighty thousand copper lotuses
> The assembly of eighty thousand conquerors resides
> Together with their children of the western direction;
> They release forth the stream of sympathetic joy.

"In front of this, there is a lake endowed with eight excellent qualities called *the copper one,* which is magically created through the blessing of eighty thousand conquerors and their children. In the four cardinal directions, there are four most auspicious and pleasurable pools made of precious jewels. Sentient beings who drink from these [pools] have their suffering drawn into the water, rendering them peaceful and freeing them from the lower realms of existence. Therefore, it is said:

> For those who drink this ambrosia of eight excellent qualities
> From the spring and the [surrounding] pools—
> Their sufferings are drawn
> And the lower realms are pacified.

"To the north of the great palace, there is a lotus tree called *the turquoise one,* which is vast, expansive, tall, majestic, beautiful, attractive, and wonderful to behold. It has eighty thousand branches and petals. Eighty thousand conquerors and their children of the northern direction sit upon this tree, releasing forth the stream of perfect equanimity. Therefore, it is said:

> On eighty thousand turquoise lotuses
> The assembly of eighty thousand conquerors resides
> Together with their children of the northern direction;
> They release forth the stream of perfect equanimity.

"In front of this, there is a lake endowed with eight excellent qualities called *the turquoise one,* which is magically created through the blessing of eighty thousand conquerors and their children. In the four cardinal directions, there are four most auspicious and pleasurable pools made of precious jewels. Sentient beings who drink from these [pools] have their suffering drawn into the water, rendering them peaceful and freeing them from the lower realms of existence. Therefore, it is said:

> For those who drink this ambrosia of eight excellent qualities [177]
> From the spring and the [surrounding] pools—
> Their sufferings are drawn
> And the lower realms are pacified.

"Gyalwai Jungné, though you have constructed a great palace supported by one hundred pillars, the conquerors and their children of all ten directions have transformed it into the following. The great palace is perfectly square. Its eastern part is crystal; southern, gold; western, copper; and northern, turquoise. Its lower part is lapis lazuli, while its upper part is a canopy of exceptional aquamarine stone. Its size is twenty-thousand yojanas to the east, twenty thousand to the south, twenty thousand to the west, and twenty thousand to the north. Therefore, all around it is eighty thousand yojanas, and with its height at twenty thousand yojana, it is perfectly square.

"At its center is a tree with a lotus and an utpala flower, respectively called *the golden one* and *the turquoise one,* a tree composed of various precious substances. It is vast, expansive, tall, majestic, beautiful, attractive, and wonderful to behold with countless branches and leaves. The Great Perfection of Wisdom Mother, whose body resembles the color of refined gold, resides there upon the hub of the golden lotus. With one face and four arms, she is adorned with various jewel ornaments. In her first right arm she holds a sword and in her first left arm, a vajra; in each of her two remaining arms she holds scriptures. Surrounded by her children, the conquerors of the ten directions, she reveals without interruption the meaning of the unborn truth.

"On the hub of the turquoise flower Śākyamuni, the lord of the world, resides. His body resembles the color of refined gold, and his crown is almost invisible to the naked eye. Wearing the [outer] ceremonial robe, the [regular] upper robe, and the lower garment, he upholds a *khakkhara* staff and an alms bowl. As he sits in the posture of an emanation buddha body, surrounded by a retinue of eight bodhisattvas who appear as disciples, he teaches the Great [Perfection of Wisdom] Mother in its extensive, middle-length, and condensed versions.

"In brief, inside this great palace, the incalculable representations of the body, speech, and mind [of the buddhas], who are the excellent saviors and the refuge of the entire world including the gods, come together. Therefore, it is said:

> On countless golden and turquoise flowers
> The Great Mother and her children reside.
> They release forth the long streams [of teachings],
> Excellent in the beginning, middle, and end. [178]

"In front of such a great palace bubbles forth what is known as *the great spring,* which is endowed with eight excellent qualities and is magically created through the blessing of the Great Mother Perfection of Wisdom and her children, the conquerors of the ten directions. Surrounded by eight untainted pools, it sports numerous precious staircases and is scented with the perfume of 108 varieties of medicinal plants. The [seeds of] sufferings of any being who drinks from this spring bring forth [their fruit] into the present lifetime. Some will experience pain in their limbs and some [will experience it] in their secondary limbs. Others will experience [pain] within their internal organs. Phlegm will rise in the summer and bile in the spring. In the winter, wind will rise, while in the autumn, their combination will occur. For those who believe in karma and its fruits, this will catalyze virtuous action. Those who understand the ultimate mode of being of things will be able to purify [these pains] in their very lifetime. Therefore, it has been said:

> The long stream of the Buddha's teaching
> Is surrounded by eight untainted pools;
> Whosoever drinks from this [spring],
> All their sufferings shall be pacified.

"O Gyalwai Jungné, [the long stream] is endowed with such excellent qualities. If it is hard for the imperfect sentient beings to even hear of this, what need is there to speak of their inability to see it? They do not believe in the cause and effect of karma, and they lack the forbearance of the voluntary acceptance of suffering.

"Furthermore, in the eight directions—four cardinal and four intermediate directions—of the great palace, there are three sets of seven precious lotus trees, each with one thousand branches and petals. Eighty and four [lotus trees] emerge there: one in each of the four cardinal directions and two [sets of ten] in each of the intermediate directions. Seated there in the form of youthful men and women, lay bodhisattvas and ordained bodhisattvas, equal in number to the lotus petals, release forth streams of water, perfecting the spiritual trainees. Therefore, it is said:

> In the four cardinal directions and the ordinal directions
> Are eighty-four lotus trees,
> All endowed with one thousand branches and petals.
> Assemblies of youthful bodhisattvas reside upon these,
> Releasing forth streams to fortunate trainees [179]
> And gathering forth immeasurable clouds as well.

"O Gyalwai Jungné, 113 lotus trees of renown will emerge. Before them, three sets of seven springs endowed with eight qualities, such as the 'excellent,' 'endowed with excellence,' 'joyful,' 'endowed with joyfulness,' 'stainless,' 'sweetly perfumed,' will also emerge, [all] magically created and blessed by thousands of youthful bodhisattvas. With one [single] set in each of the cardinal directions and two sets [of ten] in each of the intermediate directions, eighty-four springs will appear there. The sufferings of any being who drinks from this spring are brought forth into their very lifetime and pacified. Therefore, it has been said:

> In all the directions, both cardinal and ordinal,
> There are eighty-four springs of good fortune
> Blessed by the youthful bodhisattvas;
> Whosoever drinks [from them] shall be free from all sufferings.

"And,

> Furthermore, in all the cardinal and ordinal directions,
> There are pools blessed by hosts of youthful bodhisattvas—
> Endowed with eight excellent qualities, most auspicious
> And pleasurable, and scented with the perfume of
> Medicinal plants of 108 varieties.
> Whosoever drinks [from them] shall be free from all sufferings.

"These [pools] are also equal in number to the number of springs. In brief, there are 113 pools.

"Also, in the four cardinal directions of the great spring, there are twenty-four springs—six white-crystal springs, six yellow-gold springs, six red-copper springs, and six blue-turquoise springs. They exist as reservoirs of the six perfections and as a symbol of how all the buddhas of the three times have attained full perfect awakening by means of wisdom and skillful means on the basis of the six perfections. Such water is utilized only by the noble ones, for childish ordinary ones cannot partake of it. In all the cardinal and intermediate directions, there are, in total, a full 113 such springs endowed with excellent qualities. With 108 that the childish ordinary ones can see and five that they cannot see, all of these 113 springs are solely blessed and magically created springs. [180]

"O Gyalwai Jungné, at the site where these 21,000 lotus trees and 226 springs exist, a monastery known as the glorious Radreng will appear as a holy site equal to Bodhgaya in the [kingdom of] Magadha and resembling the Dharma palace of Akaniṣṭha [buddha realm]. It will be vivid, tangible, as striking as a natural mandala of the tathāgatas, as beautiful as a pitched umbrella of peacock feathers, and incessantly attractive. In front of this will be a turquoise lake, the color of deep sky blue, placed in the manner of a water-offering bowl for the tathāgatas. In the summer there will be a meadow of precious jewels abiding like a turquoise mandala that is circular and has a diameter of one yojana. Thirteen varieties of precious flowers will grow upon this. It will be arrayed with boulders ornamented by assorted precious stones strewn in the form of offerings to the tathāgatas. In the fall there will be a golden mandala with a diameter of one yojana upon which thirteen varieties of precious flowers will grow. It will be arrayed with boulders ornamented by assorted precious stones strewn in the form of offerings to the tathāgatas. In winter there will be a crystal mandala with a diameter of one yojana that is arrayed with boulders ornamented by assorted precious stones strewn in the form of an offering to the tathāgatas. In the spring there will be a crystal mandala, marked with rectangular golden lines studded with turquoise jewels, that is arrayed with boulders ornamented by assorted precious stones strewn in the form of offerings to the tathāgatas.

"The seven precious mountains will surround this [mandala of Radreng] and dwell like offerings to the conquerors. On the precious ground, eight lotus petals will support the conquerors and remain there as an offering to them. The precious jewel [with its] eight spokes will be situated there as if pitching a parasol over the tathāgatas. The eight lights—seven natural lights and the light of the sun and moon—will illuminate the tathāgatas and remain there as an offering of light. The mountain of the precious queen will dwell as an offering of food to the tathāgatas. The blue-clad Guardian of Secrets [Vajrapāṇi], composed of diamonds, will reside on the face of the mountains in the manner of a bodyguard of the tathāgatas. In brief, in all the cardinal and intermediate directions will be auspicious substances, [181] auspicious signs, and gods, inconceivable and innumerable, overpowering the earth-bound malevolent forces. The nature [of these deities] will be such that they are perceptible only to the noble ones. The gods will see mountains of precious stones. Some [beings] will see images of the tathāgatas, some will see only the reflections of the symbols like the royal emblems, and some will see flowering trees, wish-granting trees, springs, pools, springs of ambrosia, and bathing pools. In brief, they will see the entire environment—the mountains and the valleys—as that of a celestial abode.

"As for humans, there are two types—those with pure karma and those with impure karma. Of these two, those with pure karma will see, without error: the environment in its directional location, the mountains and valleys as perfectly formed, and the forests of junipers in full flourish. Thus, they will see the lakes, trees, and everything as perfect and as sources of enjoyment. They will also see Mount Meru as vast, lofty, and as having six peaks—three lower peaks on the right and two lower peaks on the left, with the center towering high above [the other peaks]. Below this [they will see] an even wider green valley, beneath which will be three smaller mountains, the right and left of which will be two flat crystal mountains. In the east and west, there will be slightly thinner juniper forests. Slightly below these [forests] will be two springs below which will be a large spring. In front of this spring, they will see a large monastery such as the one [mentioned earlier]. Below this, there will be a long and powerful river, a large valley with many rocks strewn about, and a region with many hillocks, with its upper and lower parts being a bit narrow and its lower base being circular like a roasting pan.[335] They will see that the sun rises early and sets late [in these valleys]. Seeing in such light, everyone with intelligence will praise it.

"O Gyalwai Jungné, construct your monastery there. There your disciples will gather as well. Two yoginīs of ultimate reality itself will serve as its head. Some will be known by a bodhisattva's name, some by an arhat's name, some by the name of loving-kindness (Naljorpa Jampai Lodrö),[336] some by Śākya's name (Khamlungpa Shākya Yönten), and some by the name of Wangchuk (Gönpawa Wangchuk Gyaltsen). Some will be known by the name of concentration, while some will be known by the name of wisdom (Naljorpa Sherap Dorjé). [182] In this way, many [disciples] with meaningful names will converge. All of them will work perfectly for the welfare of sentient beings and will uphold your sacred lineage without degeneration. In particular, there will be three (the three brothers) who will ensure that the blood line of the Three Jewels does not come to an end. One (Putowa Rinchen Sal) will uphold the treatises of the Buddha's teaching; one (Chengawa Tsültrim Bar) will extract the distilled juice of the instructions; and one (Phuchungwa Shönu Gyaltsen) will destroy his inner untamed [ego]. In brief, they will help disseminate the Kadam widely. These are the humans of pure karma.

"The humans of impure karma will disparage your sacred lineage. They will not come to that site and will not see it. They will not discern the law of karma and its effects and will fail to understand the truth of the ultimate mode of being. Therefore, they will not become your prospective spiritual trainees. For if sentient beings lack fortune, even the buddhas [have to] leave them alone.

"Again, Gyalwai Jungné, the obstacles [created by] malevolent demons are numerous. If [such obstacles] were to ever occur there at your site, they could obscure the law of the dependent origination of karma for some disciples who have feeble minds. Some who have drunk from the magically created water and have brought forth [future] sufferings [into the present] might defame the water and not see the bringing forth of their suffering. Failing to understand the subtleties of the law of karma, they might generate wrong views. Failing to carefully guard their ethical discipline, they might go to the lower realms. Before too long, however, this magically created water will help free them."

After these prophesies had been made, Drom spoke:

"Master, though you have said much in response to my queries,
If I were to put in a nutshell it is this:

> Dwell utterly in solitude, beyond town limits.
> Like the carcass of a wild animal,

**Hide yourself away [in the forest]
And live free of attachment.**

"There is nothing other than this."

This concludes the sixteenth chapter of the *Jewel Garland of Dialogues*, "How He Engaged in the Hidden Conduct and So On."

CHAPTER 17
Not Forsaking the Pledges and the Excellence
of the Perfect Spiritual Tradition

[183] On another occasion, at that very same place and in the presence of
the teacher, our teacher [Dromtönpa], the perfect spiritual friend, said: "O
sublime teacher, pray listen.

"The excellent Dharma of ever-increasing virtue—
You've given this to me for a pure liberating way of life.
The Three Jewels, who are the unrivaled divinities—
You've given these to me as ornaments of a pure liberating life.

"Discipline, which is the ground of all excellent qualities—
You've given this to me as the field of a pure liberating life.
The treasury of the mines of inexhaustible Dharma—
You've given this to me as the heritage of a pure liberating life.

"The healing medicinal tree with one thousand branches—
You've given this to me as the medicine of a pure liberating life.
The skill of turning whatever one does always into virtue—
You've given this to me as the conduct of a pure liberating life.
The river stream of profound spiritual teachings—
You've given this as a source of bliss and enjoyment for me, a golden bird.

"The precious ocean of pith instructions is beneficial and [a source of]
    happiness;
The plains on its shores are replete with sands of gold;
Its perimeters are adorned with thousands of beautiful ornaments.
As an object of affection for my Kadam,
You've given me this well-spoken [teaching] holding the mind's goodness.

"O, in the celestial mansions of the Tuṣita realm,
The mighty Indra possesses a great wealth of riches;
He is thoroughly venerated by the lesser Indra-like gods.
Such is the immeasurable pleasure of the heavenly realm.

"Likewise, in the celestial mansion of my Kadam,
The spiritual wealth of the three higher trainings prospers spontaneously.
It is surrounded by numerous sages of pure discipline;
The foliage of the experience of immeasurable joy blooms.

"It is auspicious; O gods of Kadam, come here!
O countless sentient beings, I'll protect you!
Be endowed with the sevenfold divinities and teachings;
You'll be secure in the long term, for this is the field of liberation;
You'll be joyful in the immediate, for this is a teaching free of the abyss;
Your companions will be excellent, for they are all endowed with
    Dharma;
Your purpose will be excellent, for it lacks the corpse of mundane
    pleasure;
Everyone who shares the pure lineage,
Aspire to this Kadam of mine, which is virtuous at all times.

"So cultivate joy, O practitioners!
My teacher Atiśa is most kind indeed.
We've heard numerous accessible teachings that are profound and vast.
Please confer your emphatic advice with respect to these teachings
    now; [184]
We shall never act contrary to your sacred words, master."

It is said that when the principal son had offered these words,
[Atiśa] then replied:
"Drom, you're a profoundly deep and vast ocean;
Though nothing disturbs your depth and extremities,
The surface shows ripples as if being stirred.
Drom, you possess might and are most fortunate.

"Having received the words of sovereign tathāgatas
From the sovereign teachers and their lineage,
I have given to you, my principal son, all that I received.
Now, if you forsake the pledges, you will not be sublime.

"So do not discard the great burden, but make your resolve.
Son, laziness, procrastination, and discouragement—

These arise in those who do not know life's transience.
If such things arise in you who are free of grasping at permanence,
Place the blame on the doings of your enemy, the self.

"Failing to be exhausted by past sufferings,
Will you still follow the trail where you were dragged?
It is this [self] that betrays everyone, starting with one's parents.
Not crushing the head of this self-grasping enemy,
[Trying to] relinquish numerous other factors [individually]—
Such relinquishing is not feasible, so everything remains.
This is so because one has failed to identify the enemy.

"Like a hay bale with one thousand straws [bound together],
It is this bound bale-like self-grasping that betrays us.
How can the objects of relinquishment, which resemble
The thousand individual straws, be like self-grasping?
Most vital it is to pull out the stake that binds the straws together.

"One hundred [different] streams converge under a single bridge.
How can one possibly cross all the hundred streams?
The one who knows this is wise.
Therefore, it is vital to cross the bridge this moment.

"He who knows a banyan tree to be the culprit,
How can he [get rid of the tree] by cutting branches off the top?
It is vital to cut the tree at its root.

"Drom, self-grasping is the source of all downfalls;
Self is the root of samsara and nirvana in its entirety;
He who knows that it is meaningless is renowned as a learned one.
If you cling to this as real you will roam through the hells,
So enumerate its flaws at all times, day and night,
And with effort vanquish laziness and procrastination.

"Drom, this is as it has been taught [by the sages].
Those who place their minds in the conduct of nonconceptuality
[Cannot tolerate] even minute transgressions;
Just like particles in the eye,

They cannot bear them, no matter how tiny they are.
Strive to forsake such karmic acts.

"Ah! As for the final fruits of such conduct,
As you have said, Drom, they will be peerless.
Son, on this stepped jeweled staircase,
Climb in gradual sequence and reach the secure ground. [185]

"Though there are those who speak of a 'one-stroke' [approach],[337]
This is provisional and only understood with respect to the buddhas.
Son, it is difficult to have a quality without the qualified;
Son, it is difficult to have the contingent without what it is contingent
     upon;
Son, it is difficult to have a positing agent without the posited;
Drom, what kind of an effect has no cause?

"Those childish ones who compete with the buddhas—
Drom, how can they immediately become equals?
It is better eventually if one ensures what is best for the long term.
Be cognizant of this and cherish the law of karma,
Without letting your mind be diverted to extraneous pursuits.
Embrace the truth of the sphere of nonsubstantiality, Drom.
This is my emphatic advice."

As he heard these words of his teacher,
With joy, the peerless son
Sat upon the lotus-flower cushion
And recited the sutra of pure ethical discipline.

At that time, a fine man and yogi friend of Drom's
Arrived from the holy place of India;
Saying, "I have come to meet the sovereign teacher,"
He bowed at the feet of the peerless master and said:

"Atiśa, you who are unrivaled in excellence,
For us yogis who have no conceptualization,
Is there any difference at all, in reality,
Between a filthy site and a lotus grove?

"For those of us who have no conceptuality and who nurture carefree
    [conduct],
Karma and afflictions do not arise. How can they?
Though Drom Gyalwai Jungné's words are commanding,
How am I not equal to him, for we are equal as your sons?

"Behold, O compassionate lord of beings.
Between the nourishment of three white ingredients and sweets
And the following things, is there the slightest difference, O Drom?

"Pouring feces into a skull cup,
They stir it with their ring finger and,
Clicking their tongues, proclaim it to be delicious.
Removing their woven cloaks they appear naked;
Their bodies are smeared with stains.

"Drom, in the beginning they are devoid of birth;
Drom, in the end they are devoid of death;
Drom, at present they are devoid of enduring.
I, a yogi who understands this nature [of things]—
How would I roam uncontrollably in samsara?
I am free of attachment to all materiality;
Wherever I live, I make no distinctions between clean and unclean.

"Mine is the vehicle that naturally liberates conceptualizations.
To hold one's mind to be clean would be to conceptualize.
I, a yogi with no conceptuality, am joyful;
I, a yogi with no conceptuality, am clean.
If one delights in immeasurable experience, this is joy."

This is what was said by his supreme yogi friend.
Upon hearing his words, Dromtönpa, the upāsaka, [186]
Revealed his body in the light of a refined moon.
His turquoise mane hair was loose and silky,
And he held up his attractive body, transparent [as a clear crystal],
[Like a] mirror reflecting the sovereign sugatas.
His age was that of a sixteen-year-old youth.
In his right hand he held a small golden bow,

While in his left he had a turquoise fiddle;
His body, seated upon a lotus, was mildly regal.
The thousand beams of his smile radiated in the ten directions.

As the bow struck the fiddle and played it,
It produced eighty-four thousand melodies.
It felt as if the entire earth were being gently shaken;
Everyone felt their bodies tremble slightly,
And showers of light and flowers gently descended.
The pristine gods heard of these omens.
Instantly at this very site,
They made offerings to Drom of the three dairy products and sweets
And followed in the footsteps of Drom's conduct;
Then Drom spoke these excellent words:

"*Hrīḥ*, even though, from the ultimate expanse of unborn nature,
Empty and apparent forms arise like rainbows,
In reality, no self-existence pervades all appearances.
How can this body of such beauty be obscure to anyone?

"Though it is free from the nourishment of sensual objects,
Why should pure nourishment such as this obscure anything?
Within the pure appearance that has no self-existence,
Due to the force of karma and aspirations, [visions] such as these arise.

"I have no conceptualizations that lead to clinging;
However, within the equality of mere appearance,
Clear distinctions exist between this and that vision.
Though the buddhas have no afflictions,
It is better if they induce admiration in the spiritual aspirants.

"When examined well, [one sees that] even the 112 exemplary and
     noble marks
Are devoid of true existence,
[Yet] such a body will indeed be superior here.

"Though the filthy sites are primordially empty,
The lotus grove is indeed superior to such sites.

Though they are equal in being samsaric domains,
How could a god admire the relentless hell realm?

"Though the primordial Dharma is devoid of good and bad,
How could I ever follow the way of the tīrthikas?
Though nourishment is beyond the bounds of true existence,
Who would harbor admiration for such nourishment?

"Though clothes share the empty mode of being,
How can one adopt the conduct of a zombie here?
I [wear] clothes of *pañcalika* silk that are mere appearance;
Master, your crown is adorned with a fully awakened buddha.

"All sites are decorated with varied jewels.
Though you reveal this kind of form, such is your body,
Such is your retinue of disciples, such is their master,
And such are their immediate and long-term fates.

"O friend, pray come here to this site of the lotus tree. [187]
Transform your body of mere appearance a little.
Because I perceive the entire world in pure vision,
Even your body, my friend, resembles a white crystal.

"Never wavering, I shall always partake in this [act].
Though this may seem similar to you it's not so for others.
Though for you gods, pigs, and Amitābha
Are all the same, who are the prospective trainees?

"For those who aspire for the goodness of stacked jewels,
You remain radiant, pure, and most unique.
Nevertheless, as for those who follow in my footsteps,
May their minds not waver from this conduct,
And may they remain like this without interruption."

As Atiśa heard the words of his two perfected sons,
He spoke the following for [both in] common:

"Listen, I, good Dīpaṃkara,
Though I may be learned in the ways of samsara and nirvana,

There is nothing [within them] that is established in reality.
Yet, within convention, everything appears.
It is excellent to cognize the perfect equanimity of all things.
Though in clean and filthy places
There are incalculable good and foul nourishments,
To know the mind without conceptualization is to be victorious.

"In general, at the seat of the Magadha [kingdom],
Numerous buddhas attained their full awakening;
Drom, you will likewise become fully awakened.
Their transcendent mind is not different from yours, Ḍombhi.[338]

"In particular, as for this tradition of Drom Jé,
The savior of spiritual aspirants:
Its meaning has been revealed clearly without confusion.
Whosoever views this truth with a mind of mere appearance
Is worthy to be instructed.

"If the entire meaning is wrapped up completely,
One will not waver from the ultimate expanse for even an instant.
Your service has been great, O two perfected ones;
Continue on in your natural state, just as you are now.
If one's practice is effective, anything is profound;
This is similar to your own example."

When they had heard these words of the excellent master,
The [Indian] son departed into the expanse of the central channel,
And the son Drom Jé, without wavering from his previous state,
Spoke in the teacher's presence:

"O sovereign Atiśa, lord of all beings,
We have been blessed by you, the sovereign sublime master.
Though together with us two disciples
You gave numerous responses to our queries,
If their import is entirely distilled it is just this:

> **Always remain firm in your commitment.**
> **When a hint of procrastination and laziness arises,**

> At that instant enumerate your flaws
> And recall the essence of [spiritual] conduct.

"There is nothing other than this."

This concludes the seventeenth chapter of the *Jewel Garland of Dialogues*, "Not Forsaking the Pledges and the Excellence of the Perfect Spiritual Tradition."

CHAPTER 18
How to Help Guard Others' Minds

[188] On another occasion, at that very same place and in the presence of the teacher, our teacher, the perfect spiritual friend, asked: "Master, what should one do when one sees others?"

"Be peaceful and sincere, and speak truthfully."

"Master, what should one do if they cause harm?"

"Do not respond with wrathful, hostile opposing acts."

"Master, what if they cause harm even when nothing is done in return?"

"It does not matter; always keep a smile."

"Master, this is indeed difficult."

"Because it is difficult, it is greatly meritorious."

"Master, how is it that it is greatly meritorious?"

"This is because such a person understands how to practice."

"Master, how does one speak truthfully with peace and sincerity?"

"Shower whatever praises you can think of. Ha! Ha! There are a lot; don't you know these?"

"Master, yes, I shall indeed do this."

"One should embrace whatever one is asked."

"Master, even the volume of one's speech should be appropriate."

"Yes, strive in this for an extremely long time."

"Master, not much benefit comes from the pleasant interactions of a single day."

"If one strives for a long time, even irons wear out. Drom, Serlingpa said:[339]

> For one who is tranquil, tamed, and wise in speech—
> A bodhisattva, skilled in carrying the burden—
> If even the dark forces of Māra cannot trample upon such a one,
> What wrathful force can perturb him?

"Drom, Avadhūti said:

> It is blissful to hear the words of the bodhisattva
> Who possesses an altruistic heart and is tranquil and tame;

Like a face, the words appear like letters.
If one sees them, it is a cause of happiness.

"Drom, Jetāri said:

No better foundation of excellent qualities is found elsewhere;
[This awakening mind] is the great object of inquiry for all who are
    clear minded;
Even when a brahman is fierce he has no anger;
He always assumes a smiling nature.

"Drom, Rakṣita said:

Even if you are slain by Yama, speak the truth;
If others frown and stir with rage from their depths,
Vanquish retaliation by averting negative acts.
It would be excellent if one were to be tranquil like you, Dīpam.

"Drom, Śāntipa said:

When you see others, [view them] like your parents.
Your conversation should be like that of a new bride;
[Treat others'] frowns as ornaments;
Let [your own] smiles form in the manner of the goddesses.

"Drom, Ḍombhīpa said:

Sounds are like the tunes of a flute; [189]
Why do they not create a melody and communicate tranquility?
Since all things are like the contents of a dream,
What is the use of frowning and grimacing?
Since they disturb the minds of others at all times,
What will you lose [instead] by smiling for a single day?

"Drom, Vidyākaukila said:

Sounds resembling echoes
Are devoid of true existence and clinging;

Therefore, do not grasp at their signs, but let go with ease.
When speaking, do so peacefully, sincerely, and truthfully.

If one frowns and grimaces at others,
One will obtain a repulsive body as a result.
Since this body of mere appearance ages,
Swiftly, one should be like you, Dīpaṃ.

I've conferred the Middle Way empowerment upon you;
No phenomena deviate from the bounds of this [nature],
So implement the practice with no exaggeration or denigration.
This is my instruction.

"Saying this, my teacher departed. Drom, Nāropa said:

However much cyclic existence may stir,
With gentleness and sincerity, do not waver from altruism;
However much you're slain by your parents,
Do not speak words of hostility and anger.
Even toward the enemy who destroys the teaching,
Do not use hostile words and harbor negative thoughts.
It is appropriate to liberate them through great compassion.

Okay it is even if your body is torn down;
Toward the Buddha's teaching this is not the same.
The teaching of the Buddha is to be guarded;
The task of a learned one is to be skillful in means.
This is my instruction, O Dīpaṃ.

"Drom, Prajñābhadra said:

I, Tilo, having remained in the ultimate expanse,
Have never strayed into a false path.
Harbor no resentment against angry words
But practice the four means of attracting others.
The conduct of the sublime ones is to work for others' welfare.
Who will such a person insult or be angry at?

"Drom, though he had many disciples,
It was to me that he gave this [instruction].
This reveals that I, too, am sublime.
I confer this teaching upon you;
I know that you are a sublime being."

"Master, I rejoice in this; you are eloquent indeed. Master, what should one
do if one sees [others] on a regular basis?"
    "Recognize them as embodiments of kindness."
    "Master, how can one repay that [kindness] in a beneficial way?"
    "Give them whatever they wish for without attachment."
    "Master, what is the definition of having no attachment?"
    "It is to give without being miserly."
    "Master, do speak of at least one manner of [such] giving."
    "It is my teachers who gave the following to me.

"If you own [things], give away even a kingdom;
Rejoice when others receive [your gifts].
Give away your homeland, [the source of] charms;
Give away your land, retinue, and possessions.
Give without attachment food, clothes, and medicines; [190]
Give away horses and wish-granting cows;
Give away servants and so on, whatever others desire.

"Furthermore, your head and legs;
Your hands and fingers;
Your brain, skull, and the blood from your heart;
Your intestines, tendons, and liver;[340]
Your lungs, fat, and kidneys—
In brief, with this body of impure substances,
Strive as best as you can to obtain
The supreme body of a buddha
Adorned with exemplary and noble marks,
Most precious and inestimable.

"Giving without attachment is taught to be the key;
Also, during the day and at night,
Please read about the penances of [bodhisattvas]

Such as the one who gave his body to a tigress[341]—
Those [stories] are clearly found within the sutras.

"Drom, Saraha said:[342]

> It would even be okay if this body were to split into one
>   thousand pieces;
> It is important to give it away with no sense of loss.
> Such excellent giving, with no expectation [of reward]
> And no strings attached, is pure [indeed].
> With no clinging to any of the three elements,
> Such excellent giving is acclaimed [indeed].
> The supreme joy at bringing satisfaction
> In others through one's body is [true] generosity.

"Drom, yoginī Nāgī said:

> I've seen supreme heroes who transform
> An inferior body into one with exemplary and noble marks;
> I've seen some who slay all sentient beings,
> Yet no one dies; they experience happiness.
>
> My body is born from the Buddha's teachings;
> He is a kind progenitor indeed.
> To not repay this kindness—
> Who would have a greater debt than this?
>
> How can I not repay this kindness
> And treat this with indifference?
> Therefore, for the benefit of the [Buddha's] teaching
> I will give even my body without attachment.
>
> Also, as they are [all] my own parents,
> I will freely give them whatever they need.
> I will wave the fan of generosity well;
> I will free them by means of eloquent speech.

In essence, adopt a relaxed posture
And speak of the great matter of ultimate well-being.
My teacher says that this is the truth."

[Drom:] "Master, your wisdom is as vast as Lake Himavat;[343]
Its base is inconceivably expansive;
It is inexhaustible no matter where you partake of it.
You are the guide of all beings and father of noble ones.
[Today] I've heard the sacred words of your teachers.

"This life is like the clouds in the sky—
Though densely formed, they dissipate easily.
So whatever class of beings you might see,
Speak clearly with no excess and no omissions regarding
What is peaceful and what is sincere,
What is gentle and what is friendly.
Please explain what is most beneficial."

[Atiśa:] "Do not display anger or volatile moods.
Do not deceive others through smiles and flattery,
But always smile from your very depths.
Though you might see others all the time, [191]
Since they are nothing if not your two parents,
How can you be oblivious to their kindness?
Therefore, through body, wealth, and spiritual teachings,
Satisfy them as if they share your same fortune.
After you have satisfied many beings,
Experience only increasing joy
And do not regret it for even an instant.

"Drom, throughout all lives conduct yourself in this manner.
This is hailed as the most supreme gift."

This concludes the collection on how to conduct oneself when seeing others.

"Master, in these degenerate times,
They assail the lowly with their feet;

They assail the superior with their heads;
They assail their equals with their hands—
With such flawed behaviors as these,
The era of degeneration has dawned.

"The buddhas have displayed [the act of] passing away;
The arhats have also departed elsewhere.
So if you do not illuminate [the teachings],
This country of Tibet shall soon be lost.

"Master, if these three [behaviors] were to arise in me,
How should I relinquish them?"

"Drom, jealousy is the root of everything;
Unable to bear superiors, one denigrates them;
Bereft of compassion, one destroys one's inferiors;
With no sense of shame and conscience, one strikes out at one's
    equals.
If jealousy is relinquished, [other afflictions] will be dismantled.
Cultivating joy is a great method.

"Drom, Candrakīrti said:[344]

> Jealousy destroys one's own roots of virtue;
> If one benefits others, this is the highest self-interest.
> Because the heroes work for the benefit of all,
> Collectively everyone honors the heroes.
>
> This is like the Buddha nurturing his disciples
> And the disciples venerating him [in return].
> Alas, within this world, primordially unborn
> And [comprised] of mere appearance, anything can occur;
> He who does not defy this mere appearance—
> Such a person will embrace the ultimate mode of being.
> Even a king can suffer the decline of his kingdom;
> Through jealousy alone does he suffer
> decline, it is said.

"Drom, Heruka said:[345]

> Jealousy is the basis of numerous afflictions;
> Those riddled with attachment and anger do not see the gods,
> So [for them] the supreme attainment is lost.
> One who knows how to transmute jealousy
> Into the excellent gnosis of discriminative awareness—
> Such a person is a hero indeed.

"This is indeed wondrous," said Atiśa.

"Master, having obtained leisure and opportunity so hard to find,
How can one reduce the wood of liberation to ashes
With the fire of the afflictions?"

"See others as your own parents;
Harbor a sense of wonder toward your equals,
And elevate your inferiors. [192]
If one is meant to strive to help others
Until the entire eon is turned into flames,
Of whom should you be jealous? This is lunacy!"

"Master, I will not engage in the conduct of a lunatic.
Relinquishing envy is hailed as most excellent;
This is the precious instruction.
Atiśa, you have explained this well."

This concludes the collection on relinquishing envy.

"Master, if one were to guard others' minds, how should one go about it?"
   "Relinquish all disputes and let go of them."
   "Master, how does one relinquish disputes?"
   "Bring them to one's own self and say 'It's my fault.'"
   "Master, what if even this does not work?"
   "Place your adversary in the very juice of your heart."
   "Master, how should one respond if the enemy becomes spoiled?"
   "It is taught that experiencing joy in response to [one's] harm is sublime."

"Master, do such things [people experiencing joy in response to harm]
really exist?"

"What are you saying? Sufferings must be embraced."

"Master, do teach us other means of leading [such beings]."

"Make aspiration prayers for the benefit of that being."

"Master, one can pray once, twice, or three times."

"He was driven by his past karma,
To [perform] this negative act [fueled by] impure thoughts.
Even if he causes injury to my body by means of it,
May he never experience retaliatory harm.
May this body of mine bring about its [own] death,
And may this become his last act of killing.

"Drom, one who prays thus and harbors no anger—
Such a person is sublime indeed;
He shall be hailed as excellent among the bodhisattvas."

"Master, even if my body is cut into a thousand pieces,
May I never experience any disturbance.
Now I will don the armor of forbearance,
I will embrace the death of all [afflictions],
And, without breaching my teacher's sacred speech,
I will guard others' minds in accordance with this."

"Drom, you are skilled at summing things properly,
So summarize [this teaching] well and offer it to me."

"Master, though you responded to many of my queries,
If summarized well it is this:

> However, if you do encounter others
> Speak peacefully and truthfully.
> Do not grimace or frown,
> But always maintain a smile.
>
> In general when you see others,
> Be free of miserliness and delight in giving;
> Relinquish all forms of envy.

To help guard others' minds,
Forsake all disputation
And always be endowed with forbearance.

"There is nothing other than this."

This concludes the eighteenth chapter of the *Jewel Garland of Dialogues*, "How to Help Guard Others' Minds."

CHAPTER 19

Constantly Working for Others' Welfare

[193] On another occasion, at that very same place and in the presence of the teacher, our teacher, the perfect spiritual friend, made a plea: "Master, I seek an instruction on how to interact with people."

"Drom, since superficial friendliness and flattery[346] for a day or so is not sustainable, one should carry oneself at all times with a sense of shame and conscience."

"Master, as a foundation for excellent qualities what is more important, noble character or faith?"

"Both are important."

"Master, what is more important when interacting with people?"

"In general, having a noble character is more important; however, in order to bring forth excellence, faith is more important."

"Master, what can one do to ensure a noble character?"

"If you behave like Tibet's 'important people,' you won't develop a noble character. No matter how great you might be with respect to a specific quality, you should not be self-congratulatory but should sit at the end of all three types of people—the higher, the equal, and the lower. Except for actions that are inappropriate, you should do everything you are asked to do with a smile."

"Master, what kind of faith is required to lead one's mind toward higher states?"

"When you see special objects [of veneration], tears will flow from your eyes, the hairs on your body will stand up, and—sighing deeply with rejoicing, hope, and anticipation—you will make supplications to them. Such things will occur."

"Master, how can my faith help lead others' minds to higher levels?"

"Because of your noble character, you will capture the heart of all people. Just as a child cries when her mother cries, others, on account of you, will generate faith as if they have no choice. Drom, if you always act genuinely, whatever you do will be appealing. Even the words you utter will be held as authoritative."

"Master, if this is so, in order to determine [the suitability of] students as vessels [for the teaching], does one also need to examine one's own basic character?"

"Listen, Drom. In general, despite having been born as humans—a higher birth—those who seek the afflictions as their condition have given up their inner mental jewelry. They are betrayed externally by the attire of shame. The golden thread of their long future has been cut short, and their hearts are studded with anger and ferocity. They wear leather boots of thirst-producing [craving]. Let alone being suitable vessels for the divine spiritual norms, these people are not even vessels worthy of [mundane] human norms.[347] Such people will experience only enmity and poverty in abundance." [194]

"Master, what would happen if one were to interact with such types of people?"

"If you practice forbearance, you can interact with them; if you are unable to practice forbearance, they can destroy your virtues."

"Master, it seems that even if one searches everywhere for the pure realms, they are nowhere to be found."

"In this Endurance World[348] of ours, there should be an abundance of this [condition for practicing forbearance]. One can be victorious by means of one's teacher's armor. Pray do not be let down."

"Master, if one practices forbearance, one will obtain an attractive physical appearance in the future."

"Even before your future [life], any forbearance you practice will bring victory here in this very life. In the end as well, it opens the way to be victorious against anger."[349]

"Master, what happens to the person who acts with fickleness?"

"At first everyone he is acquainted with becomes his friend; [but] in the end, they all turn into enemies."

"Master, if this is so, what happens to he who engages in superficial friendliness and flattery?"

"At first, everyone regards him as easy to get along with, but as they come to know his true nature, they become disillusioned and say, 'This person, who is so boastful and quick-mouthed has no substance at all.' So, in the end, he is despised by all."

"Master, is this really so? The so-called humans of the bad era seem to be such that, whatever their character in the long run, if one shows them even some superficial friendliness and flattery in the short run, they seem to help back in whatever ways they can."

"As for such people, Drom, both parties will end up acting in such manner [as you have described]. However, their future will be quite bleak."

"Master, some individuals of the present age have taken birth in the three lower realms in the past. In the future as well, they will take birth in the three lower realms. Failing to realize this, they completely indulge in the mundane concerns of this life alone and fail to undertake anything for the benefit of future lives. Why is this so?"

"Drom, imagine a greedy man is walking across a vast desolate plain carrying a heavy load with nothing to use as a prop to support the load. If he sits down, he will not be able to stand up again; yet, if he does not sit down he will be utterly exhausted. Because it shifts back and forth constantly, the heavy load becomes tilted, yet he is unable to adjust it. As he continues on his journey in immense agony, he finds a rare support to lean upon, so he takes a rest and experiences great pleasure. Becoming attached to the pleasure, he does not rearrange the load, but takes a nap and then resumes his journey, carrying the load as it was. Before he gets far, the thought occurs to him, 'Alas, what kind of person am I? When taking a rest I did not rearrange my load. Now I am struck in this desolate terrain and, if I were to rearrange my load, I would not be able to get up. Yet, I feel so desperate to rearrange it.' He may feel totally lost as to what to do, but by then it's too late. [195]

"Likewise, Drom, in the past these people have suffered in the vast desolate terrain of the lower realms. Without any ease with which to move on, sit down, or rearrange their loads, and after such a desperate experience, they have taken birth as human beings, which is analogous to getting a rest. However, during this period, instead of rearranging their loads, they become attached to the pleasures of hoarding things for this life, to vanity and arrogance, to defending themselves and responding to others' challenges, and to the pleasures of the afflictions of this life. However, having carried the load of suffering continuously, they will die. When a clear consciousness [remembering] up to seven [former] lives arises, they will think, 'What kind of person am I, bereft of any collection of merit? In my past lives I have taken birth in the three lower realms. Yet, even though numerous props came by me, I failed to prepare for the fate of my future lives. So, I am likely to take birth in the three lower realms again.' A time will come when they will be dragged by visions of suffering and will be at a total loss within the three lower realms."

"Drom, now is the time to rearrange your heavy load. The time has come to attain a ground that is secure for all lives."

"Master, this analogy is most appropriate."

"Its meaning is also most appropriate, Drom. Serlingpa said:

People who have no conscience and integrity,
Motivated by self-interest and deceit,
Fool others with their words.
For a few days, they befriend them;
But later, because they have no substantive aims,
They turn even their friends into enemies.
Do not rely upon such people;
They'll deprive you of your initial [awakening] mind generation.
Recognize them as demons and shun them.
Either cultivate compassion [and endure] suffering,
Or strive as best you can to please them.
This is the path of the bodhisattva."

"The teaching given by your teacher is profound indeed."

This concludes the collection on not engaging in flattery and fickleness.

"Master, the minds of imperfect ordinary beings are like this: even if on your part you try your best from all sorts of angles, they distort everything with false conceptualizations. No matter what you do, you can never please them. What should one do about such people?"

"No matter how another person might be, on your part do not allow even a single instance of disparagement. Relate to him instead with an attitude of respect, whether at the preparatory stage, during the actual interaction, or in conclusion. [Then] the gods will not be offended."

"Master, what kind of person is he?"

"It's possible that a good person is being tested by another good person; [196] he could also be someone blessed by Māra!"

"Master, is it appropriate to show respect to those who are blessed by Māra?"

"It is adequate not to allow your afflictions to follow after him. Otherwise, doing whatever makes him happy is a skillful means."

"Master, among the factors that obscure the truth of the ultimate mode of being, what is the greatest obscuration?"

"It is the conceptualization of subject and object that is the greatest."

"Master, given that this is strongest in affliction-ridden sentient beings, how should I go about helping them clear these away and give them instructions?"

"Having an altruistic intention out of compassion is important."

"Master, among all the teachings, aren't compassion and altruism the most important?"

"It is because of this, Drom, that I have asserted [what I said] before, for without them the powerful conceptualization of subject and object will not be vanquished."

"Master, this being the case, if, with the altruistic intention, one goes into the midst of those suffering from contagious illnesses, such as in a plague, will one contract them or not?"

"Drom, if you go to help out of a pure altruistic intention, unsullied by the stains of any self-interested desire, you will not contract [such a disease]. Furthermore, even if you enter into a ring of dark magical spells, into the focal point of destructive mantras of non-Buddhists, into a curse of witches, or into the midst of a battle, no harm can come to you."

"Master, what causal factor is most important for generating this great altruistic intention?"

"Drom, the uncommon forceful compassion is important."

"Master, I would like to request a method for cultivating compassion."

"It is great that you ask, Drom. Go into the presence of a sentient being oppressed by a powerful illness. Then, through your imagination, extend [your attention] to all sentient beings and think, 'Sentient beings have assumed this kind of bodily existence. With such a body, this [kind of] illness appears. On top of leprosy, they get boils; on top of these boils they experience pain, and one pain is followed by another pain. In such a manner, they undergo this kind of agony alone. What a pity! Alas! These [sufferings beings] are not [unknown] to others. These are my parents, who have given birth to me again and again.' In this manner, cultivate compassion to the point that you cannot bear [to see them suffering], as if your actual mother had fallen into a fire pit.

"Likewise, go into the presence of those who are suffering from poverty, deprivation, hunger, and thirst, and who have no clothes, and cultivate compassion in the same manner. Even when remaining at home, reflect vividly upon the sufferings of the hell beings and the hungry ghosts. Meditate upon these [sufferings] up to the point where it becomes unbearable. Then, [counter] mental laxity and excitation by meditating [upon their antidotes] alternately, as presented previously.

"Drom, this is achieved by means of seeking relief from one in the other. [197] Also, this is achieved through alternating with meditations on compassion, the immeasurable thoughts, or impermanence."

"Master, what is the definition of compassion?"

"It is being unable to bear in one's heart the suffering of all sentient beings."

"Master, with respect to the four immeasurable thoughts of my tradition, from where should one begin?"

"Drom, if you experience an unbearable feeling in your heart, the wish to relinquish it arises. For example, if a child falls into a fire pit, his mother's heart cannot bear it. Abruptly discarding all seemingly important tasks, her mind is consumed only with the urgent thought of how to free her child. Usually, Drom, though she has great love for her son, if he is in no immediate danger, she prioritizes other tasks.

"If you possess an unbearable compassion for all sentient beings, Drom, you will drop all [other] tasks and will strive your best to free sentient beings. On the basis of this, you will come to understand all beings as your parents. You will then have no partiality with a sense of either intimacy or distance [toward them]. You will only think, 'How joyful it would be if they enjoyed happiness' and 'How joyful it would be if they enjoyed comfort.' Given that, if they were to attain buddhahood, all other forms of happiness would arise as a byproduct, you will strive your best to lead them to buddhahood.

"Drom, starting with [the cultivation of] great compassion, look at sentient beings and ask, 'Who are these beings that I feel compassion for?' Once you recognize them as your parents, care for them with loving-kindness by striving to help them in whatever way possible. When you have dedicated your loving-kindness, cultivate sympathetic joy with such thoughts as 'How joyful it would be if all beings were happy!' and 'How joyful it would be if all beings attained buddhahood!' When you have dedicated your sympathetic joy, consider all beings with great equanimity, free of any partiality of intimacy and distance, just as you unconditionally affirm your own wish for happiness. Ensure that the pristine cognition of nonjudgment reaches everyone.

"Drom, the root of all altruistic thoughts is compassion. Since it is in dependence upon compassion that all the qualities of the bodhisattva come about, what need is there to speak of [giving rise to] the altruistic intention to help each and every individual being?"

"Master, in that case, how would you teach the actual instruction on [the cultivation of] the altruistic intention?"

"Drom, first go for refuge to the extraordinary objects. In the middle, recognize the pros and cons of samsara and nirvana and generate the supreme mind of awakening for the benefit of others. Then, [explain] how to strive at virtue by means of your body, speech, and mind, and [198] how to exhort [others to engage in spiritual practice] by revealing to them the defects of cyclic existence. Finally, [perform] a dedication together with aspiration prayers. Teaching these out of an altruistic intention to help is called 'the instruction.'"

"Master, though your responses to my queries were numerous,
If the relevant points, in their entirety, are wrapped up, it is this:

> Be free of flattery and fickleness in friendship,
> Be steadfast and reliable at all times.
> Do not disparage others,
> But always abide with respectful demeanor.
>
> When giving advice,
> Maintain compassion and altruism.

"There is nothing other than this."

This concludes the nineteenth chapter of the *Jewel Garland of Dialogues,* "Constantly Working for Others' Welfare."

CHAPTER 20
Practicing the Profound Teaching without Defaming Other Teachings

[199] On another occasion, at that very same place and in the presence of the teacher, our teacher, the perfect spiritual friend, made a plea: "Master, in this world each of the numerous different classes of Dharma practitioners has, in turn, each of the numerous different spiritual traditions; and each of these spiritual traditions has an inconceivable number of diverse methods for implementing these in practice. Not only that, but even with regard to the words of a single teacher, each of his numerous disciples has his own standpoint. All of them speak in terms of 'I' and 'you,' and, between 'our spiritual tradition' and 'your spiritual tradition'; there seem to be many contradictions. Since you are knowledgeable in all [the teachings], master, among these, which ones succeed as the path and which ones do not?"

"Drom, all of these are Buddha's objects of knowledge. You should not disparage any spiritual traditions. Instead, you should cultivate a fervent aspiration [to practice] whatever spiritual tradition you admire most. Through the words of learned teachers, settle all doubts pertaining to your own spiritual tradition. See what is found in the scriptures of the sugatas and use your own reasoning to examine which [traditions] would succeed on the path. In terms of that which is definite to succeed on the path, write it down, venerate it, and so on, and whether it is the ten virtues, the ten perfections, contemplating the defects of cyclic existence, contemplating the benefits of nirvana, actually implementing what is to be affirmed and what is to be rejected, the seven limbs, or dedicating the roots of virtue at the end of all of these, given that the ten spiritual deeds and the ten virtues are the conduct of the sublime ones, you should strive in these without differentiating between day and night.

"Drom, my teacher Vajrāsana said:

> As the hero of ten levels is endowed with the ten spiritual deeds,
> For him the ten virtues increase both day and night;
> Knowing the ethical norms, he performs the seven limbs.
> Sovereign king, cultivate these ten practices of a sublime being.[350]

"Drom, the blessed Nāgārjunagarbha said:[351]

> Strive day and night without reserve in the ten perfections
> And in the inconceivable ten branches;
> This is the conduct of a sublime being.
> Completing the two collections, all will be awakened. [200]

"Drom, Ācārya Vasubandhu said:

> Inscribing, venerating, and giving it;
> Listening, reading, and upholding it;
> Expounding upon it and reciting it;
> Reflecting and meditating upon it—
> He who embodies these ten spiritual deeds
> His body of merit cannot be measured."[352]

"Profound, most profound!
"Master, this citation of Ācārya Vasubandhu is known to be found elsewhere. Where did you hear it?"

"Drom, in the Kaśmiri seats of learning in the north,
As I wandered about free of conceptualization,
Vasubandhu, the supreme among the learned,
Looked intently at me, Dīpaṃ, and said:[353]

> Though you may be learned in the ocean of great treatises,
> If you do not embrace them by condensing them into the ten,
> [All this learning] will resemble only speeches in a play.
> Applying the knowledge of the crafts, inscribe these [treatises] in
>   letters;
> Accept the inconceivable [teachings] as offerings;
> Free of attachment, give [these teachings as] charity at all times;
> No matter how learned you are, strive to learn [more];
> Turn the wheel of reading regularly;
> Distill the essence of everything and take it to heart;
> Expound on the ocean of expository collections;
> In between, engage in recitation at all times.
> Recitations without reflection are mere words;

Yet, if one meditates following reflection, this is hailed as excellent.
Undertake all this within a single sitting.
Write this in four lines and share it with those who desire it;
This is an offering to the sublime beings.

Where there is no guide, listen by reading to yourself;
Uphold the meaning of the words by taking them to heart.
Teach it to all, both visible and invisible.
Through reading, purify the obscurations of speech;
Reflect upon the meaning and meditate again and again.
This is my practice, so adopt this.
He who engages in these ten spiritual deeds
Shall receive immeasurable merits.

"Drom, therefore do engage in their practice."

"Master, since there are so many spiritual traditions, what is the essential point that makes one succeed on the path?"

"It is having the desire to become fully awakened for the benefit of others, relinquishing its obstacle—grasping at the duality of self and others—and being untainted by the stains of attachment and aversion."

"Master, many practitioners have failed to generate such a mind. As for those who have attained temporary happy results there are many."

"Whatever one does is done for one's own sake. As for spiritual practices of body and speech, they may have undertaken [only] about one and a half [deeds]. Such people, who desire the happiness of turning away from cyclic existence, will not arrive at buddhahood."

"Master, does the object of refuge make a great difference?"

"Yes, the object of refuge makes a great difference, Drom. For instance, if you go for refuge to the Three Jewels, fearful and petrified of cyclic existence and by cultivating unswerving faith in the Three Jewels, [201] then, through various means, you will enter a spiritual tradition that you admire most. Then, whatever method of traversing the path you might adopt, ultimately it will lead you to buddhahood."

"Master, excessive talk may not help. Whatever spiritual tradition you follow, whatever outward appearance you adopt, no matter who you associate with for companions, whatever dwellings and beds you seek, and no matter what behaviors you engage in, you must recognize that you have roamed in [cyclic existence] countless times. You have only experienced garlands of birth and death—each death followed by a birth, with each birth requiring a set of parents. Even with respect to one set of parents, you have been born countless times. So if your parents equally encompass the extent of space, so, too, do your parents, children, and grandchildren equally encompass [space]. Think, 'These parents have only indulged in the afflictions, which are the cause; they are experiencing the unbearable sufferings of the three lower realms, which are the fruits. It has fallen upon me to help lead them. They recognize that the law of karma is true; they understand it to be undeceiving and that it must be followed. Though this is true for many, many still remain distorted [with respect to the causes of] happiness and suffering.'

"Contemplating in this way, view the defects of cyclic existence graphically and avidly. [Reflect,] 'How much happiness is there? How much suffering is there?' One does not undergo suffering without having accumulated negative karma; and one does not enjoy happiness without having first performed a virtuous action.

"Master, though your knowledge is vast, there does not appear to be any purpose for instructions that do not benefit the heart. We need to bring together [all the teachings] so that they engage with the self-grasping; otherwise the conscienceless—who, while seeing such defects of cyclic existence, do not make any attempts to help rescue their parents—and the indolent, who indulge in laziness and procrastination, will have no opportunity to attain liberation.

"Master, there are those who have only three excuses for not engaging in Dharma practice over the course of their lives. At first when they are young, they think, 'It is not feasible right now; later when I am older I will practice Dharma.' When they have reached the prime of their vitality, they think, 'I am not too old and I am not too young. At this juncture, when I can do anything, I will accumulate wealth, vanquish my enemies, and protect my friends. When I am older, when my children and grandchildren have grown up and are able to look after me, as an old man, then I will practice Dharma. Right now, this is not possible.' Later, when they are old and decrepit and are not fit for anything, they think, 'Now I am too old. Years before, when I was younger, if I had engaged in Dharma practice it would have been possible, but this did not happen. So you young ones, please undertake [Dharma practice].' Saying such things in hoarse voices, they will need to use all fours just to stand up. At that time their children and grandchildren, the ones in whom they have placed so much hope and expectation, will refer to them with such endearing names as, [202] 'wretched old man,' 'annoying old crank.' Cursing, they might even say, 'It seems it is never this old man's turn to die. Everyone would be better off if he were dead.'

"Master, can such people obtain happiness? If Dharma practice is found in them, a horn has grown on a rabbit's head! There are no stronger means to forsake Dharma practice than these three excuses.

"Master, pray ensure that we do not fall victim to such a fate. When one is young one is vigorous, so it is the time for the young monk to practice Dharma. In the prime of one's life, one can undertake any virtuous activity of the three doors, so that is the time to practice Dharma. If one is old one is worn out; nothing really matters [much] then. Being close to death, one should think of the practices [that can be applied at the] point of death. Thinking, 'I will need provisions for my future life, which is certain to come,' seek the three conditions that help one not to set Dharma practice aside. Even if it hastens death, striving in Dharma practice is crucial. One must help lead one's parents. Thinking, 'I lack the capacity to help lead these unruly parents of mine; I may not be able to do so. I will therefore seek protection, refuge, and support from the Three Jewels.' Since one needs a kind master to protect one from dangers, one should entrust all three—one's mind, heart, and breast[354]—to the Three Jewels and supplicate them, saying, 'Pray protect me and my parents from the sufferings of cyclic existence and the lower realms. Bless me so that I will be fully and manifestly awakened for the sake of my parents.' Go for refuge in this manner. Contemplate the benefits of nirvana, which is the sole antidote against the sufferings of samsara, the object to be relinquished.

"Master, there are two things that I know: the objects to be abandoned must be abandoned and the objects to be adopted must be adopted. One who has accomplished abandonment and adoption is a buddha. Once one has attained buddhahood, one can liberate sentient beings; but without it there is no success. Some may observe a minor aspect of ethical discipline, which is the foundation for obtaining birth in the higher realms. Some are utterly blind; while sufferings of birth, death, and so on fall upon them like rain, they worry, thinking, 'Now I am going to die.' Not only will they die, they will [also] be born. They should think, 'What would I do were I born in the three lower realms?' But, failing to contemplate impermanence even for a single instant, they look here and there and, at times, laugh at things that are dissatisfying and take joy in them. At other times, having to experience even a single suffering or dissatisfaction, they cry out in sorrow and shout lamentations. They don't cry for major [sufferings] but do so for minor ones. They do not cry at the fact that all their parents are suffering but do so if a single [being] is dying. Even in terms of this single being, they don't cry at the fact that the being undergoes constant birth and death; rather, they cry when the being dies once. [203] Failing to see the past and future, they see only the occasional sufferings. Without seeing the long-term consequences, they only see the immediate as the source of problems.

"This [situation] is [like] the so-called 'tale of the bad dog': Once an owner of a dog [needed to hide]. There was an imminent danger from his enemy such that if his dog were to bark, the enemy would discover and harm [the owner]. So he tried to tie the dog with a leash and hide it inside. However, [the dog acted] as if he were being slaughtered and would not obey at all. He wailed while inside [the house] and, unable to bear it any-more, ran outside and began barking. The enemy killed the dog and then [killed] the owner along with him.

"Likewise, as for those who are occupied only with the mundane con-cerns of this life and have nothing to show for their future lives—whether reciting a single line of going for refuge, acquiring a [mere] earful of learning, undertaking a recitation or two, paying respectful homage to a special object of refuge once, circumambulating once, rejoicing once in others' spiritual practice, or at the very least doing something beneficial in this life, such as offering a plateful of doughballs once—without any of this, if someone carries the title of a practitioner and is recognized by oth-ers as a Dharma practitioner, he should be labeled a charlatan. If he is clever with words he will talk; if he is greatly learned in some areas, he won't be even able to support his weight [for he will be full of himself]. Listen instead to the diligent and the disciplined. Listen, [for adding] exposition upon an exposition does not help. A good monk doesn't need a container in which to pour his infractions. He who refrains from what is inappro-priate is known to have entered the ranks of the realized.[355]

"Master, it is beyond question that such an approach is successful on the path. To express it succinctly, a Dharma practitioner needs to be like this: he should be someone who says, 'Relying on teachers in whom all three qualities—learning, discipline, and kindness—are complete, I have settled all doubts pertaining to the treatises and instructions. There is nothing left for me to do but to practice Dharma. If things go well, it is [on account of] the Three Jewels. If things do not go well, it is [also the blessings of] the Three Jewels. My share of correct abiding in terms of study, critical reflection, and meditative practice has not been insufficient. If I do not die [soon], I will continue to gather the two accumulations, step by step. If, on the other hand, I were to die today, I would have no regrets.' Someone like this is needed.

"The actual counterforce should be as straight as the string of a powerful bow; the preparation should be as intense as the heat of a sandalwood fire. He who receives teachings should be flexible like the leather of a musk deer's hide that can be stretched from anywhere. If such an individual happens to be clad in a saffron robe, this is most excellent. Otherwise, so long as he has tamed his mind, there is no fault in whatever way of life he chooses. However, once he has joined the monastic order, [204] he should be such that not even a hundred charming demonesses would be able to seduce him; not even a hundred demons of the dark force should be able to detract him away from the Dharma. It is inappropriate to disparage anyone who is such a spiritual practitioner. There are many ways to pursue [the Dharma]; if one's outlook is not in error, this is sufficient."

After [Drom] had spoken, Master Atiśa replied: "Drom, if you know these things, what need is there to ask me? Anyway, there are no shortcomings in what [you have said]."

"Master, what benefit is there in knowing it for oneself [alone]? There is no fault in repeating things that pertain to others' welfare. I asked you [about these] because you are my teacher. There is the benefit of preventing self-satisfaction more easily later on. There is the benefit of convincing others [as well]."

"Drom, there is no flaw in your [presentation]. I shall give you something whereby all the teachings are succinctly condensed."

"Master, I would like to receive this. Such is needed for Dharma practice. If, [the teachings are] too numerous, one cannot put them into practice. If there are too many excellent teachings, making the choice becomes impractical."

"Drom, sustain the following in your mind:

"Let go of self, embrace others, and reside in a canopy of light;
Undo the basis of appearance and contingence, devoid of essence;
Not finding them when sought is a success on the path;
That is the irreversible path."

"Master, this is a profound teaching."

"Drom, integrate [these teachings] within the immeasurable mode of
  being;
Eliminate from their roots the sufferings of samsara;
This is the irreversible [path].
Cultivate this as long as space remains.

"Drom, though there are numerous traditions, uphold your own;
Do not cling to a tradition but train in others as well;
Forsake exaggeration and denigration of other traditions;
Train in all and integrate them into one.

"Drom, if the soil is fertile, whatever one sows will grow;
For the kindhearted all wishes will come true;
For those who persevere, there are no obstacles;
Those wise in ethical norms journey to liberation.

"Drom, this is it:
Lead the beings by means of appearance;
Restfully sleep in the ultimate expanse of wisdom."

"Master, well said, most learned paṇḍita!
If wrapped up in its entirety, that is it indeed.
Though your responses to my queries were many,
If I summarize them, it is this:

> **Never defame the teachings.**
> **Whatever practices you admire,**
> **With aspiration and the ten spiritual deeds,**
> **Strive diligently, delineating day and night.**

"There is nothing other than this."

This concludes the twentieth chapter of the *Jewel Garland of Dialogues*,
"Practicing the Profound Teaching without Defaming Other Teachings."

CHAPTER 21
Dedication and Purifying Negative Karma

[205] On another occasion, at that very same place and in the presence of
the teacher, our teacher [Dromtönpa], the perfect spiritual friend, made
the following plea:

"O teacher Atiśa,
My spiritual guide who reveals the perfect path,
You who are enriched by the three vows,
Ordained vajra-holder,
Here in this holy site of Tārā's buddhafield,
Indistinguishable from the forest of *khadira* trees,[356]
Like a father at home with his son,
You have leisurely engaged in a jewel garland of dialogues,
Using common terms that are easy to understand
So that it will be suitable for dull-witted beings.

"I have experienced all your higher qualities.
You have conferred upon my mind profound secret empowerments,
Such as the heart drops [of the Kadam tradition];
You have blessed me as a vajra-holder.
Within the primordially empty sphere,
You have conferred upon my mind the profound empowerment,
The sutra teachings on exchanging self and others.

"The lotus grove, sun, and moon of the discipline [basket]
Of those who are learned in ethical norms,
These arise as the supreme foundation for all higher qualities.
I have striven in the six perfections day and night,
Integrating them into study, reflection, and meditation.
Now, it is appropriate to dedicate,
Toward the final supreme enlightenment,
The virtues of my three doors,
Those in which I have endeavored throughout all three times.

"Do not waver, my one god with a smiling countenance.
Though there are countless different languages,
You teach using each of them, without confusion.
You illuminate, in terms of the coarse and minute aspects of infraction,
The subtle aspects of the cause and effect
Of immaculate, pure ethical discipline.
You are my teacher indeed.

"Through your immeasurable power
You do not abandon beings even for an instant;
You engage in the Dharma both day and night.
You are my teacher indeed.

"By uniting all things in appearance and emptiness,
You are most skilled in differentiating generalities and particulars
Without confusing them.
You are my teacher indeed.

"Though your three doors remain immersed in the ultimate expanse,
You reveal everything as bodies of divinities;
You illuminate the generation and completion stages within.
You are my teacher indeed.

"Though you see the ultimate mode of being as it is,
You do not defy the law of karma and its fruits;
You invest your three doors in virtue.
You, the savior, are a teacher indeed.

"Though you have eliminated all misdeeds,
You display [yourself] as a monk dedicated to his vows; [206]
You, the most sublime monk of royalty,
Are a Śākya son and teacher indeed.

"Though you have mastered all [fields of knowledge],
You conceal these [achievements] inside, without displaying them;
You, who are an excellent hidden yogi,
Are a teacher to me, a fortunate person.

"Though day and night you practice the profound tantras—
Interweaving the four empowerments, the generation and completion
   stages,
For you the degeneration and breach of the pledges is impossible.
You, vajra-holder, are a teacher indeed.

"Though all are revealed in one generation and completion stage,
You do not divulge even a single secret.
You are an inconceivable knowledge-holder."

After Drom had spoken these words, Atiśa responded: "Drom
   comprehends, Drom comprehends!"

Drom [then] said, "You are my teacher indeed.
Though always among the five buddha families,
You skillfully display the disciple's form.
Dharma king, embodiment of the five pristine cognitions—
You are the teacher to me, I a Kadam."

Master Atiśa was pleased by this.

[Drom:] "Though you are not hindered in your native tongue,
Some see you are as unversed in Tibetan.
Yet you saw me as someone worthy
To be taught freely; you're my teacher indeed.

"Though there are countless buddhafields,
Having seen my karmic residue of purifyng the buddhafield
And the beings within, you have come north
To this Uru region; you're my teacher indeed.

"*Emaho!* You're an unrivaled buddhakāya;
You're the speech characterized by sixty attributes;
You're the mind encompassing all higher qualities;
You are the Three Jewels and my teacher indeed.

"You are the father of all bodhisattvas;
You are the sovereign of vajra-holders.

Though you embrace the pure way of life,
You take tranquility-seeking disciples and self-enlightened ones as
    teachers.

"To teach in accord with the need is the essence of being learned;
To conceal the profound meaning is the essence of being learned;
To [adopt] the hidden conduct is the essence of being imperceptible;
The subtle cause and effects are the essence of [spiritual] practice—
With respect to these, disciples and the self-enlightened are mentally
    inferior,
And the words of emptiness and the profound secret mantra
Do not fall within the purview of their minds.
Yet, my teacher regards them as most excellent.

"Otherwise, if one were to see the inner nature
Of a Mahāsāṃghika monk,
Though resembling a disciple he could be expelled;
Without rejection, you carry him [instead] upon your crown.[357]

"You, inconceivable teacher,
Are accomplished in inexpressible higher qualities.
If at this moment, when I have found such a teacher this once,
I fail to dedicate [my merits] toward a lasting secure ground,
Then it will be hard to search for a witness,
So please perform the dedications.

"Such cherished objects as my body,
The material things that are of definite need,
And the ultimate aims, together with virtuous roots—
I shall bring them all together and offer them to you.

"Great master, pray listen to me. [207]
I am the master of all secret mantras.
As I am the supreme vajra-holder
Who practices in accordance with the meaning of those [mantras],
I request a dedication that accords with this.
I will also make requests for others in due course."

[Atiśa proclaimed:] "Drom Jé, listen to the essence of Buddha's teaching.
Stainless and beautiful to behold,
Resembling a crystal monument,
Known as the glorious Jinasāgara—
You are my eldest son.

"Like a sun unobscured by clouds,
You are brilliant and unsullied by stains;
You are the sole eye of the teaching in general.
You are my eldest son.

"Though the excellent treasures of secret mantras,
Knowledge mantras, and retention mantras are guarded by the gods,
You manifest as a ordinary person with conceptualization.
You, most profound and expansive, are my eldest son.

"Though, like space, you pervade everywhere,
You are manifest only in this northern region
Where you perform the conduct of a hermit.
You, Avalokiteśvara, are my eldest son.

"Your physical arrays fill the entire world;
Though there are numerous buddhas, they are all you;
You are the buddhafield Densely Arrayed.[358]
You are the eldest among my sons.

"I have conferred upon you all secret empowerments;
You have constructed the mandala within.
Do not sell these as merchandise[359]
But engage with the actual truth. This I bequeath to you.

"I have given you the training in morality;
So, with interest and without transgressing the discipline
Or defying the law of karma and its fruits,
Enjoy the ultimate mode of being. This I bequeath to you.

"I have given you the training in mind;[360]
Set those with good karma to [working for] others' welfare alone;

Though spending time only in pursuit of others' welfare,
Enjoy the ultimate mode of being. This I bequeath to you.

"While seeming to contradict [the teachings] without [actually doing] such,
Endeavor single-pointedly in the practice
Through meaningful study, reflection, and meditation.
This conduct of mere appearance I bequeath to you.

"No matter what fields of knowledge you are versed in,
Do not allow your exposition to deviate from the meaning,
But practice them with a single-pointed mind.
This is what I bequeath to you.

"Now listen, vajra-holder.
The main points of dedication are explained as three:
The preliminaries, the actual [practice], and the conclusion.
The preliminaries are: going for refuge and [striving for] others'
    welfare.
The actual practice is, in turn, composed of three [parts]:
The excellent field, the mental state, and the material.
The field is also explained in terms of three:
There is the field of higher qualities and that of kindness.
Those who are suffering are also excellent fields.

"*Mental state* refers to the purity of the three spheres;[361] [208]
Material refers to those possessions that are worthy of offering.
The meaning of dedication is the following:
What does the dedicating? The mental state.
What is dedicated? The material object.
Toward what is it dedicated (at what is it sealed)? The sugatas.
How is it dedicated? In the form of appearances and emptiness.
The witnesses for this are the five buddha families.
Be free of any division between teacher and meditation deity.
The main part of the actual practice is as follows:

"In the front, from a *baṃ* and a white lotus,
An expansive lotus and moon emerge.
Upon this sits your teacher, who is indivisible from

The meditation deities of the five buddha families.
Having the nature of the five pristine cognitions,
They are inconceivable and abide as witnesses.

"Through excellent method and wisdom,
Gather these apparent and empty virtues of all the three times
And dedicate them in the following manner:

"'O teacher vajra-holders,
As your wisdom and compassion are unobstructed,
Vajra-holders, pray attend to me.

"'Here in this mandala wherein one partakes at all three times
In the empowerments, generation and completion stages, and
    union,
Which are endowed with most excellent method and wisdom,
I dedicate [all these] toward the most supreme of the supreme
In order to fulfill your enlightened intentions.

"'For as long as space is not lost,
May I, together with the vajra-holders,
Thoroughly set in motion the wheel of feasts,[362]
And may I be endowed with the two higher attainments.

"'The external environments are deities' mansions;
The beings within are the gods and goddesses;
No impure perceptions arise.
May I thus abide by the two—method and wisdom.'
All of this is a generation stage;
For the completion stage, reside in the nonobjectified expanse.
This is the supreme dedication."

[Drom then responded:] "Sublime teacher Atiśa,
Vajra-holder, I offer this to you.
Now there have been many who have done
The bodhisattva's exchanging of self and others.
Many have endured penances here at this site;
They have given away this body of flesh and blood many times;

They have transformed this impure body
Into a conqueror's body, a jewel beyond value.

"Mañjughoṣa, as well, pray come to this site;
I will dedicate both aspiration and engagement.
Serlingpa, as well, pray come to this site;
I will nurture your spiritual tradition.
Avadhūti, as well, pray come to this site;
I will make dedications to the expanse of the great middle way.
King of the Śākyas, most compassionate one,
Your lion-like perseverance follows after you.

"You are the sole master of all generation and completion stages;
You are the sole father of all knowledge holders;
O Heruka vajra-holder,
Though you need no invitation, please come here.

"All the deities of the action class,
The mandalas of the pure liberating way of life, [209]
Since you are Avalokiteśvara alone,
With no need for an invitation, encircle my heart.
Alas! All of you encircle my heart.
Divinities with partiality do not exist.

"Maitreya, Asaṅga, Vasubandhu, and Vimuktisena;
Paramasena, Vinitasena, and the glorious Kīrti;
Haribhadra, the two Kusalīs, and Serlingpa—
O compassionate teachers, pray come to this realm.

"Nāgārjuna, Candrakīrti, and Vidyākaukila;
Tārā, the sole eye revealing the ultimate nature—
Pray come here to mark us with a nonobjectifying seal;
Though nonconceptual, reside as the basis of appearances.

"Most compassionate sugata Vajradhara;
Reality-seers Tilopa and Nāropa;
The supreme glory Ḍombhīpa and so on—
All kind teachers, pray come to this site.

"Buddhas of the ten directions, lights of the world,
Together with your children, pray come to this realm.
The four deities of Kadam who are never divorced from me,
All of them are, in reality, indivisible from you,
Like the sandal tree and its perfume—
O most compassionate ones, always reside in my heart.

"Now, all the witnesses have converged;
Seated upon lotus petals they pervade the entire sky.
To you I prostrate and make offerings.
I confess my evil deeds, rejoice, and request [the teachings],
So be seated here and bear witness for me.
Teacher, please perform the dedication."

[Then Atiśa spoke:] "Drom, all the buddhas of the ten directions and
  their children,
Those who are indivisible from the teachers,
O bodhisattvas, pray listen to me.

"I make dedications so that you—
Those who practice, in the three times, the two accumulations
Of the powerful minds of aspiration and engagement—
May, with a single-pointed mind,
Draw forth our kind parents,
Who exist wherever space pervades,
So that they will traverse the ten levels to the [level of] no-more learning
And spontaneously accomplish others' welfare.

"Until they arrive at this stage,
May they, through the blessings of the Three Jewels,
No longer wander in samsara against their will,
But cycle through it by the power of supernatural feats.

"May the desperate find relief;
May those tormented by heat be cooled;
May those tormented by cold be warmed;
May those tormented by hunger be sated.
May those tormented by thirst be satisfied;

May those tormented by sickness be healed;
May those who have died come to life.
May medicinal trees flourish; [210]
May poisonous plants wither and dry out.

"May I be a ship to travel across the seas;
May I be a bridge to cross the rivers;
May I be a mount for long journeys.
May I be a jewel that grants all wishes;
In fact, may I be any resource others desire,
Such as the cow that gives milk at will,
A pleasure grove, or a beautiful mansion.

"May the poor who have no sons be cared for by sons;
May the rich who have no sons bear sons;
May they lead their sons to the Dharma.
May there be no war on this land;
May there be no violation of oaths and no immorality;
May there be no words of the eight dangers—
Enemies, robbers, venomous snakes, and so on.
May the rains fall on time;
May the planets, stars, and so on
Be all excellent at all times."

Once [Atiśa] had spoken, Drom responded: "The witnesses are still present. Master, with respect to morality and the trio of study, reflection, and meditation, I request general and specific dedications."

   "Drom, [here it is:]

"You who abide in the ten directions and fulfill beings' welfare,
Teachers and Three Jewels possessing wisdom and compassion,
With wisdom and compassion, pray attend to those seeking liberation.

"Without leading the three doors astray in mere idleness,
Constantly engaging [in practice], day and night,
Through study, reflection, and meditation upon the conqueror's
   supreme path—

The excellent morality, the basis of all higher qualities throughout the
   three times—
I dedicate this toward [becoming] an excellent savior of all my parents."

[Then Drom said:] "Most excellent witnesses, pray attend to me.
Restraining my three doors well from evil,
I will bind myself to the practice of others' welfare.
I will certainly dedicate toward the great awakening
This accomplishment of the discipline of ethical norms.

"Most excellent witnesses, pray attend to me.
Whatever doubts and misunderstandings I have eliminated
Are based upon what I have heard from my excellent teachers,
By the virtue of this understanding of ethical norms,
May I accomplish abandonment and realization and be free of
   obscuration.

"Most excellent witnesses, pray attend to me.
Through distilling the meaning into a single point
And meditating upon it, after having studied and reflected,
I make this dedication so that beings who have sunk within the seas
Will be led to the dry land of liberation.

"Master, let us set all of these [dedications of the] bodhisattvas apart;
I now ask for a common dedication practice." [211]

"Drom, arhats who possess unobstructed superior cognition
And all noble ones, pray attend to me.
Whatever excellent dual accumulations I might obtain,
Which are virtuous in this life and throughout all the three times,
I dedicate all of it that is beneficial in the present and in the long term
Toward the total fulfillment of others' welfare.

"Until they attain the body of a fully awakened buddha,
May they be adorned with the supreme faculties of higher rebirths;
May they never be assailed by birth, aging, sickness, and death;
And may they always be inclined to the dual accumulations."

"Taking this as the basis, master, please perform a dedication of all disciples and self-enlightened ones."

"Drom, on such an occasion it is necessary to have the noble arhats who have performed their deeds, who have done what needed to be done, who have laid down the burden, who have achieved their personal goal, and who have completely severed the fetters that thoroughly tie one to existence as witnesses seated in the space in front. If the dedicator is a Mahayana practitioner wearing the attire of a disciple, all the witnesses should also be [imagined] as being Mahayanists but having the appearance of the four pairs of personages[363] in the attire of disciples. Doing so is an excellent dedication in the provisional sense. The dedication is [conducted] like this:

> You who free [beings] from great bondage,
> Supreme personages, pray attend to me.
> I make dedications so that, renouncing the mire of the afflictions,
> We may become unbound by the fetters of existence.
> By abiding excellently on the path of tranquility and bliss,
> May we traverse to the supreme tranquility.
>
> Furthermore, through the virtues that make this life meaningful,
> May I dedicate all the virtues of the past
> And whatever virtues there might come to be
> Toward the seeing of no-self.

"Master, let us put aside now all these dedications of the enlightened ones. At this time, when I am running a monastery, have a few students [here and there], and call out others by their Dharma names, when I am creating a place where all the treasures of faith can be housed, some foolish people may misunderstand this. Thus, I request a dedication [practice] that is complete."

"Drom, on such occasions, given that special objects of refuge like the Three Jewels remain present in the space in front of you, you should tell [your students] to visualize them. Revealing the great benefits [of doing this], you should direct their minds [to the dedication practice]. Taking the lead yourself, if you make others repeat after you clearly, this will stabilize their propensities. There is also the benefit that in the future as well, they might request [such a dedication] out of devotion. Then make them say their individual names. If, due to large number, this cannot be done, at the point when one recites 'I who am called by this name...' you can ask them to say their names.

"Drom, these people may not know how to bring together all the virtues of the three times. [212] So you bring them together and help them to verbalize it. Then recite the following:

> All the Guru Buddhas and the Guru Dharma residing in the ten directions, and all those who reside here like the noble Guru Sangha—all of you, my lord and refuge, out of compassion, pray attend to me. I, *who am called by this name*, dedicate all the virtues that I have accumulated, am accumulating, and shall accumulate throughout all three times—all these roots of virtue [born] of my three doors, including: having made offerings to the Three Jewels, having offered gifts and service to the Sangha, and on this basis, having performed the rite of torma offerings,[364] having respectfully cared for my kind parents, having given charity to the poor and destitute, having engaged in the observance of vows such as the day-long vows, having engaged in mantra recitations such as *oṃ maṇi padme hūṃ*, having heard instructions such as these, having reflected upon the joy and sadness of success or failure at bringing about transformation, having [acquired] inconceivable merit through cultivating faith, respect, and compassion, and eventually [acquiring] the transcendent wisdom realizing their ultimate mode of being. I dedicate all such roots of virtue that I have created and shall create to the realization of immediate and ultimate fruits of happiness.

"This is to persuade [others] to cultivate a sense of joy in the fact that, following the attainment of buddhahood, the welfare of all, both self and others, can come about.

> Also, in the meantime, may I through life after life obtain the precious human existence endowed with the seven features. May I adopt the monastic life at a young age, observe pure ethical discipline, engage in the training of all the practices of the Mahayana, and, by traversing the five paths and the ten levels in their proper sequence, swiftly attain full awakening.

"Recite this and make an aspiration prayer.

"Drom, all of this is [only] a seed, though. The person who is accumulating the merits should take the merits he has actually accumulated as the principal focus and, on the side, dedicate those of others as well.

"Drom, if one wishes to dedicate all the virtues collectively there is the following method as well:

> Three Jewels, pray attend to me. May the roots of virtue arising from the six perfections, such as giving; from the sublime and perfect ornaments of the mind, such as study, reflection, and meditation; and from the collection of yogas that are the tools of the mind gradually transform into the highest aim—a fully awakened buddha. [213] May I swiftly dry up the great ocean of the suffering of all sentient beings.

"This tradition [of dedication] exists. There is also the following:

> Three Jewels, pray attend to me.
> Following in your footsteps, my lord and refuge,
> I dedicate the inconceivable and perfect virtues
> That arise from giving charity and observing morality,
> From practicing forbearance and applying perseverance,
> From placing the mind in equipoise and meditating on the ultimate
>   nature,
> From being skilled in the means and diligent through power,
> From having pure aspirations and supreme wisdom.
> I dedicate these toward attaining [the state] of the Buddha, the
>   Dharma king,
> To help lead my parents, whose numbers cannot be counted.

"If you do this as well, it is an excellent method of [dedication according to] the Perfection Vehicle system. Drom, also the witnesses have nothing but witness. So, to condense everything in one fell swoop, one can do this:

> Through the sublime deeds that I have undertaken,
> The [sublime deeds] that I shall undertake until enlightenment,
> And the sublime deeds that my three doors are undertaking at
>   present,
> May I complete the dual accumulations for my parents' benefit."

"Master, this is known as the *repertoire of oceans* dedication.
Now I request for an aspiration in terms of the seven limbs."

"Drom, listen. 'Throughout all lives,
Obtaining a perfect life of leisure and opportunity,
May I honor the Three Jewels with my three doors
Through paying homage and making offerings.

'Purifying nonvirtues with the full presence of the four powers,
May I rejoice in all virtues.
May my exhortations
To have the wheel of Dharma turned be heeded.

'As for those who intend to display passing into nirvana,
May my appeal for them not to do so be effective.
May all my dedications and all that I have aspired for
Be realized the instant that I wish for them.'"

"Master, 'Through such perfect causes and conditions,
For the benefit of numerous sentient beings,
Pray enhance the virtues of my three doors;
Pray also dedicate these toward supreme awakening.'
Does making aspirations in the present
Lead to the attainment of the unexcelled supreme state?"

"Drom, if you do these in the manner described,
Through the mount of the two excellent accumulations,
You will traverse the buddhafields by means of the five paths
And will abide on the path of no-more learning itself.
This is a meaningful human life indeed, well found.
Do put these into practice."

"Master, pray teach us, what are the impediments that prevent the
realization of the dedications and the aims of dedication?" [214]

"Drom, attachment, aversion, and delusion are the *cause;*
This very body, speech, and mind are the *medium;*
The actual [deeds] refer to the ten nonvirtues,
The five heinous acts, and their approximates.

When elaborated, there are the transgressions of the three vows.
Forsaking the Three Jewels, one fails to honor objects of respect,
Such as one's parents, and deceives them.
If summarized, it is being thoroughly fettered
By the [two] great obscurations of afflictions and of subtle knowledge.

"*Objects* refers to one's parents, teachers, preceptors, and masters,
The Three Jewels and one's spiritual colleagues—
They are objects of kindness and of benefit.
Others refers to affliction-ridden sentient beings.
The following lists the occasions, when taking others as the objects,
That actual [nonvirtues], such as killing, arise:
Since beginningless samsara up until the present,
They have committed the most negative acts themselves;
They have compelled others to commit most negative acts;
They have even rejoiced when seeing negative acts done.
For such unruly beings, dedication and its aims are lost."

"Master, pity these unruly sentient beings!
These [deeds] will throw them all into the hells.
They'll experience the unbearable pains of hungry ghosts and beasts,
The conflicts of the gods and the demigods, and the portents of death.
All of those who are powerless and experience such unbearable sufferings
Do so because of their misdeeds in cyclic existence until now.
It's such a pity that they possess no superior cognition.
How I wish they could remember their negative karma for a long time!

"Master, for those who feel intense remorse for having drunk poison,
I request a means to rinse [their afflictions] as with a syrup of beryl fruits;
I wish to know a means to vomit them out with remorse.
As the three poisons have spread, their stomachs are bloated.
Will this not throw them into the relentless hells right now?
Be their ally, O supreme physician.
As they're dying now, what time is there for delay?"

"Drom, understanding the defects of samsara is a means
     of purification;
To a frozen lake, birds are not attached;

To a burnt forest, animals are not attached;
To a demoness in disguise, men are not attached;
To a father's corpse rotten with maggots, a son is not attached.
How can joy arise on a charnel ground?
How can one be joyful living in a prison?
How can a cooling sensation arise amid a fire?
How can joy arise on seeing an enemy?
How can mental happiness arise in the terminally ill?
Who would consider the blazing hells blissful?
Who would confuse the hungry ghosts with the wealthy? [215]
How can the beasts live with freedom [of self control]?
If there were no conflicts, how would the demigods fight?
When early portents of death occur, the gods suffer, too.

"The root of all this is actually the three poisons.
Without these three, evil karma has no platform.
You in whom nonvirtues, the coming together of these forces, are
    manifest;
You conscienceless ones who exploit those who are kind to you;
You, the drowning stones, who put goodness to shame—
Since beginningless time you have chased [these poisons].
Alas! Though you are capable of thinking about this, you still do not
    shun them;
You are shameful, indeed—an imitation of human life!
Though seeing sufferings of such magnitude,
You do not beat your chests with intense remorse.
Will you meekly submit even when your heart is being torn away?
Lunatics, engender feelings of remorse again and again.

"If you do not engender remorse for your past actions,
You'll boil in the three cauldrons of bubbling lava.
Your suffering will be equal to the limits of sky.
If a son were to witness a mighty slayer
Tear out the hearts and devour the flesh and blood of his parents,
Wouldn't he vomit blood and succumb to death?

"Alas! This [tale of] suffering is only half told.
Since your parents meet this fate in samsara repeatedly,

Will you not prevent such sufferings at the level of their causes?
How can you bear this, lunatics?

"Knowing that this is so because of past evil actions,
Will you not seek nirvana as a means to avert this?
Knowing them to be poison, will you not vomit [the three poisons] up?
It is like the ten people who feasted on meat
That they knew was poisonous.
Three felt remorse, but this did not help, and they died.
Three [others] were on the verge of death and feeling deep remorse,
And three more experienced various signs of sickness.
In terror, the following thoughts occured to the last of them:
'Alas! Under the influence of bad companions,
I had the thought to consume this life-robbing meat.
Some have died and some are on the verge of death;
Some have just come down with this terminal illness.
Today such a food has entered my guts.
Now I will die in pain and agony!
O you [ego,] who lack the heart to act with awareness,
Old betrayer, you are always like this!
What pity that no friends and family can aid me.
How can I possibly survive now?
Alas! How can there be one such as me?
Have I only imagined obtaining a human existence?
It does seem I have obtained a human life so hard to find!
Where can I find a physician who can cure my illness
Now that which is called death has come upon me?'

"Thinking in this manner, he will strive to vomit everything out. [216]
Lost and not knowing what to do, he'll try everything.
His loved ones will also run around in a frenzy.
If he is repulsed this much by meat [consumed] previously,
What need is there to speak of him consuming [meat] now?
The mere sight of meat will make him fearful.
He knows that, if he doesn't change his ways, this could spell death itself.
Drom, compared to remorse, the resolve is more precious;
Now perform the confession that resembles vomit-inducing medicine.

"Drom, things are unable to sustain themselves and subject to various
   changes.
For no reason and in sudden bursts,
Causes bring change, like the seed at the time of [producing] a shoot.
Even basic character changes, as when something green turns whitish.

"Time is also transient, as with summer, winter, and so on;
So know that none of this possesses any intrinsic nature.
Their existence does not hold up, while their nonexistence ceases, too.
Like a dream or a river, everything changes and moves on.

"That [things] are not [there] come morning is so because they lack
   intrinsic nature.
Had they existed, how could they change, for they would be just as the
   night before.
The three times, samsara, and the causes and effects of nonvirtues—
With so many arisings and cessations, they are not self-sustained.

"So where are the past evil actions?
What is the nature of things in the present?
Without changing their realities, where would they go?
There is not even an atom of true existence here.

"Nonetheless, since it follows after the deluded mind,
The heart of evil karma that resembles foam on the water
Is unable to bear the touch of its antidote, and thus bursts open easily.
Go for refuge to those who can protect us through the goodness
Of eroding such cleansable karma—the noble Three Jewels—
And gather the dual accumulations.
Confess with deep resolve from your heart,
Expressing in speech the cause, medium, nature, and objects [of your
   actions].

"Confess and purify up to two or three times.
Nurture this antidote like the steady stream of a river;
Ensure its power, like the fire at the end of the world.
Each antidote destroys numerous factors to be relinquished
Upon contact, through encountering them and through constant
   application.

"Then, having turned away from evil and having reinforced [your
    resolve],
Cultivate joy and place your mind in the absence of intrinsic reality.
The mind of awakening is excellent as the principal support,
While the Three Jewels are excellent as witnesses and as the refuge support;
Forceful elimination is excellent as the power of eradication;
The convergence of all remedies is excellent as the power of perseverance;
Not reverting after purification is excellent as the power of resolve.[365]

"Knowledge of the true nature is the mother of all conquerors;
He who is abundant in remorse is a [true] tested hero. [217]
If you know when it is the time, instruct accordingly and rejoice.
To be able to recall [the antidote] is the teacher's instruction.

"Though numerous, all [realms] lie within samsara.
If you journey on the path of liberation you shall be free.
Drom Jé, you've recognized the enemy [now].
Refrain by means of awareness and apply diligence, its antidote.

"Day and night engage principally in virtuous activities.
These are the four powers that destroy evil karma.
They are like a [powerful] tide striking a sand hill;
They are like snow falling on a lake.

"For if even the heinous acts and their cousins can be eroded,
How will the four powers not erode minor acts of nonvirtue?
This is the confession and purification rite for all evil karma.

"You have four precious deities to protect you;
None are not encompassed within these [four].
If you proclaim, 'O guru vajra-holders and so on,
All the conquerors and their children, pray attend to me,'
And appeal to them to bear witness, they will all converge.

"Drom, not deviating from the teacher's instructions,
Purify and dedicate [your merits] through well-composed words."

"If summarized well, it is all subsumed into accumulation and
    purification."

This concludes the collection on purifying the defilements;
It is great as a means to achieve unexcelled enlightenment.

"Master, I, Drom, will add:
Listen, my teacher Atiśa,
As we, respectfully, with our three doors
And with virtuous thoughts throughout all the three times,
Construct representations of the body, speech, and mind
Of the teacher, the sugatas, and their children,
I dedicate these so that we will discard impure body and speech
And achieve the state of an omniscient Dharma king,
With a body adorned with the exemplary and noble marks
And speech endowed with the sixty attributes."

"Drom, this small collection, together with your addendum, is wonderful."

"Master, though your responses to my queries were numerous,
If condensed well it is this:

> Whatever virtues you gather through the three times,
> Dedicate them toward the unexcelled great awakening.
> Disperse your merit to all sentient beings,
> And utter the peerless aspiration prayers
> Of the seven limbs at all times.
>
> If you proceed thus, you'll swiftly perfect merit and wisdom
> And eliminate the two defilements.
> Since your human existence will be meaningful,
> You'll attain the unexcelled enlightenment.

"There is nothing other than this."

This concludes the twenty-first chapter of the *Jewel Garland of Dialogues*, "Dedication and Purifying Negative Karma."

CHAPTER 22
Subsuming [All Higher Qualities] into Seven Riches and Bequeathing Them

[218] Once again, at that very same place and in the presence of the teacher, these profound and vast teachings appeared vividly in Mañjuśrī's heart. At the very moment in which this occurred, he revealed them to his student [Ngok], who was similar to himself. [Ngok], arriving in the teacher's presence as if he had attained the mental state of the first level of concentration, requested the [teachings] given earlier, and our teacher [Dromtönpa] repeated them. Furthermore, the instant he received the oral transmission, he got the following [teaching] as well.[366]

[Drom:] "Master, we've received the joyful feast of Dharma in the past;
Now we request some riches."

"Drom, the wealth of faith draws others through influence,
For if it can attract even all the noble ones,
What need is there to speak of worldly beings?
Faith is the first of the levels.

"Faith is the starting point of the path;
Faith is the shoot of benefit and happiness;
Faith gives forth the harvest of well-being;
Faith undermines attachment and aversion.

"Faith is the sun that lays bare pure vision;
Like a lion-supported throne, it lifts up the conquerors;
Faith is the harvest and resembles a lotus;
It carries upon it all the noble ones;
It enhances the bliss and wealth of the noble ones.

"Drom, faith is the wealth par excellence;
The faithless are like dogs and butchers;
They are like crows and pigs;
Detesting what is joyful, they're ignorant of the good.

"Faith is like the light of a lamp:
Radiant itself, it illuminates others, too.
Dispelling darkness, it reveals forms.
Faith is like nourishment in the desire realm:
After it, one has strength.
Therefore, make your faith firm.
This is the first excellent wealth."

"Master, I who am endowed with the sevenfold divinities and
   teachings
Also need seven riches, and there are still six left.
Bountiful and stable, they are an inexhaustible treasure.
I request that [this treasure], so easy to enlist
No matter how you partake of it, be there in times of need."

"Drom, as the supreme foundation of all that is to be affirmed,
Morality is the most fertile soil.
The excellent pools of eight qualities emerge from it
And grow medicinal trees that create benefit and happiness.

"It is the wide path that is virtuous at all times;
It is the sole path of uncontaminated virtue.
This excellent wealth, an indispensable source
Of all excellent fruits of higher rebirth and liberation,
Is the basis of your enhancement as a noble one. [219]
It is beautiful in your flower garden.
Nurture [morality] as if it were your own life.

"He who has [morality] will be free of all deprivations;
He who has [morality]—his treasury will flourish;
He who has [morality] will gain victory in battle against the māras;
With it, he will travel to the pure buddhafields.

"Drom, this is the second excellent wealth.

"Drom, as for faith and morality alone,
They do not suffice, even for those in the Lesser Vehicle.
One who gives away his entire kingdom is rare;

One who gives away his children and spouse is rare;
One who gives away his head, legs, and arms is rare.
Rarer still is someone who is free of any hopes for a reward.
Thus, to give without attachment is a most excellent wealth.

"During the first innumerable eon,
The hero utterly gave away everything
Until he was free of all hopes and expectations.
Free of attachment, he gave to all who had desire.

"Today he is unexcelled among all beings,
The peerless king of the Śākya clan.
He is the peerless Dharma king;
He has become the perfection of virtue.
Therefore, cherish the wealth of giving as most excellent.

"Drom, give material needs and relieve poverty;
Through spiritual giving, show the excellent path.
Give fearlessness and help remove obstacles.
This is the Dharma of samsara and nirvana in its entirety.
This is the wealth referred to as 'the unexcelled.'
This, then, is the third excellent wealth.

"Drom, even if one observes morality with faith and gives charity,
If one fails to seek the ocean of learning,
It is possible that one may fall through the gaps.
One may not know the levels and the paths oneself.

"Those of the māra class are versed in pretense and deceit;
Disguised as parents, resources, and acquaintances,
As preceptors, masters, friends, and images of the Buddha,
They turn those on the path away from the path.

"In order to analyze faults and benefits,
The wealth of learning is taught to be most excellent.
Through it, the resources of reflection and meditation gather;
Through it, the supreme no-more learning is granted.

"Recognizing all [ills], it is like a physician;
Since this is the most excellent among the riches,
May you, excellent Kadam, embody [the learning of] the great treatises.
As a means for achieving the stage of a conqueror, this is most excellent;
Be nourished by this wealth as long as you live.
This, then, is the fourth excellent wealth.

"Drom, if one has no shame
And does not have the clothes of conscience,
Even in worldly terms he is woeful;
Even his neighbors disparage him.

"If he does not treat his father as a father,
If he does not treat his mother as a mother,
And if he does not respect the elders as elders,
What more wretched [behavior] is there than this?

"Like a lunatic, he would steal, rob, and deceitfully acquire,
Engage in meaningless speech and use divisive words.
A man will sell off all life-sustaining forces of men, [220]
A woman will sell off all life-sustaining forces of women.
Spouses will experience bad conflict;
Neighbors will become resentful.
What greater impoverishment is there than this?

"He betrays his kind parents.
Not repaying their kindness, he leads them to their downfall.
He betrays his masters whom he has served.
He may have performed one thousand beneficial deeds,
But enflamed once, [his shamelessness] will destroy all.
What greater lack of conscience is there than this?

"Even among the worldly, such [behavior] is ridiculed.
Likewise, even though labeled a practitioner,
He repudiates the sublime preceptors and masters;
He detests even their colleagues.

"He betrays the sublime and is completely base.
Having renounced [the world], he collects and hoards;
At a time of detachment, his clinging is strong.
Forsaking his root spiritual tradition,
He grabs for other 'higher' teachings with self-importance.
Disparaging his own center of learning,
He drags down his monastic seat by the feet.
Losing his own standpoint, he fails to find another.

"Not feeling remorse for his own failure,
He blames the teachings and forsakes morality.
As he has no shame, how can he have a conscience?
Under the pretense of being a practitioner, he is sustained by wrong
    livelihood.

"Will he not be let down by the food of depravity?
Will he not turn into a weight [pulling down] to the hells?
Yet he sits in the row of Dharma practitioners;
With the words, 'I am,' he consumes the offerings of the devout.

"This lack of conscience lets others down as well.
Forsaking the seven riches, he seeks things that are not riches.
He has no shame when indulging in deeds contrary to the Dharma,
But in pretense of acting in accord with the Dharma, he says, 'I feel
    shame.'

"You do not call someone who is destitute and has no clothes or food
'Shameful,' but 'deprived.'
In worldly, ignorant beings' sense of shame,
Urine and its pathways are 'shameful,'
But these cannot betray you.

"What is shameful is a lack of conscience.
A lack of conscience leads you to pursue misguided ways.
He who pursues misguided ways goes to the hells.
Drom Jé, forsake all of these;
These are what the civilized call 'shameful.'
The diligent say when they have been inappropriate;

The bodhisattvas nurture this trait of conscience.
If you guard others' minds, you're wise in the sense of shame;
If you honor those worthy of honor, you're wise in the sense of shame;
If you care for those worthy of care, you're wise in the sense of shame;
If you're sharp in repaying kindness, you're wise in the sense of shame;
If you are strong in faith, you're wise in the sense of shame.
Extend these [points] to the ordained monastics as well.

"Carry the teachers and the preceptors upon your crown;
Relate to your colleagues in a way that accords with the Dharma.
Without forsaking your first pledges,
No matter how impoverished you may be of resources,
Exert your three doors in the virtuous deeds,
Help your colleagues, and sustain your seat of learning—
This [ensures] that your trait of conscience will be long-lived.

"If your intelligence is great,
And if a learning seat is being run by a learned person,
Then, applying [the analogy of] a sick person [seeking a skilled
     physician], train at the feet [221]
Of this learned one at this center that accords with the Dharma.
[In this way], nurture your own site."

[Then Drom spoke:] "Master, why are you saying such things?
If harmful clinging is strong, anyone can be let down.
'Our tradition' and 'their tradition' is prejudice;
Too many 'I's and 'you's [leads to] severe unruliness.

"If clung to, whatever you have clung to will cause downfall.
If your prejudice is too strong, you should flee away;
If it seems like clinging, you should forsake it and leave.
Wherever you live, you should guard the precepts.

"Whomever you associate with should not forsake the Dharma.
However you may act, mind training should increase.
If it does not benefit the [Buddha's] teaching as a whole,
What use is there running a small monastery filled with monks
Laden with prejudices? Give them up [so that] you are not let down.

Like snot and phlegm they should be cast away.
Why should one cling like a rooster?
Why should one crave like a wild beast?

"It is better to be free from a place of incarceration;
There is the danger that the monastery will become a prison.
[One can be] like dogs, laden with strong craving and relentless aversion,
Roaming about in an empty temple.

"However, if you have a sense of shame and conscience,
You will travel from happiness to happiness.
Therefore, having a sense of shame is the fifth wealth."

"Drom, I have never delighted in clinging;
If one chases after whatever is pleasant, his trait of conscience will be
    short.
It is most excellent if it benefits the [Buddha's] teachings as a whole,
So be free of clinging and cherish all beings.
From within this absence of clinging, guard the sense of shame;
To have conscience is the sixth excellent wealth.

"Drom, cherish the wealth of insight at all times.
He who possesses excellent wisdom is learned in all fields.
For one who is excellent in wisdom, the well-spoken insights converge.
The fire of wisdom burns away all obscurations.

"The wealth of wisdom is wealth most supreme;
The convergence of all riches is the wisdom mother.
With excellent wisdom one travels to freedom;
Wisdom permeates all areas of the twin aims.[367]

"When wisdom is great, one is skilled in the means as well;
When wisdom is great, one guards ethical discipline;
When wisdom is great, one gives, free of attachment;
He whose wisdom is great seeks [further] learning.

"When one understands, one is adorned with shame and conscience;
With great strength of forbearance, one perseveres;

One skillfully meditates on the one-pointed ultimate nature.
While the mighty hero engages in all activities,
The aspiration horse brings forth transcendent wisdom;
Give this wealth of wisdom to all.
He who possesses this excellent wealth shall be rich indeed!

"[Amid all the preceding] twenty-two dialogues,
There is nothing not contained in this essential point.
This is the most excellent and sublime wealth.
I have revealed this wealth to you with affection;
Do not publicize this in the marketplaces.

"Though this realm is yours,
Not all of them are your people.
If you speak of this to nonhumans, [222]
The forces of Māra, unable to bear it, will rise up
And demolish your chariot.³⁶⁸
Nurture this tradition as [a heart] drop so that it does not decline.
Even though the spokes [of its wheels] may extend up to a yojana,
These nonhumans [malevolent forces] will not uphold their axles;
So these [nonhumans] will denigrate the rim and the spokes.
They'll find no nails [to hold up the chariot] before setting out;
Even when nails are found, they'll not hammer them in;
I fear that this degenerate era might pull apart your chariot.
This is my heart counsel, so listen, Drom Jé.

"If someone were to take this chariot to the crossroads,
The lunatic childish ones will mistreat it.
Not understanding its significance,
They will play with it gleefully and then give it up.
Then, following the mouth of a charlatan,
They will be indifferent to Dharma practice.

"Listen, I will tell you whom to reveal this teaching to.
He is someone who, out of deep [affection] for you and I,
Takes into his heart the essence of the way of life
Of a body adorned with saffron robes.

"In accord with the Discipline [basket] he observes morality;
In accord with the Sutra [basket] he partakes in higher concentration;
In accord with the Knowledge [basket] he enhances higher wisdom.
With no error in the foundation, his morality is pure;
With no error in the path, he journeys to the measureless;
With no error in the fruit, he'll become fully awakened—
Such a person is the one to whom you should reveal this [teaching].
His actions are contrary [to the world];
Shunned from the ranks of humans, he is like a wild animal;
Searching for food only in the present, he is like a bird;
When suddenly standing up, his entire estate is complete.[369]
Such a chore-free person is the one to whom you should reveal this
    [teaching].
Also, such a person will embrace this [teaching] as well.

"Master Drom, all of this is a grave matter.
There could be those who proclaim devotion to you and me
And claim to uphold the lineage of your sacred words,
Who, on the pretext of doing good, harbor wrong views.

"Instead of settling their doubts pertaining to the teachings
By means of learning, reflection, and meditation,
They might exaggerate and denigrate [the teachings]
By citing as proofs what they do not see and hear.
The noble ones disapprove of such people.
This is an insult to them as well.

"Those who have not meditated one-pointedly,
And who lack the [divine] eyes and superior knowledge—
All those unruly ones whose minds are hardened—
Fail to realize the gods and the profound meaning
And [thus] reify and denigrate the hidden facts.

"How can one reveal this [teaching] to such people, Drom Jé?
For if they do not recognize you, Drom Jé, as Drom Jé,
What need is there to speak of [you as] Avalokiteśvara?
Therefore, fearing that those who defame this [teaching]—
The fabricators—might denigrate this [teaching] using Māra's language,

I hammer the nails on you, [chariot] Drom Jé.
Consider well whom to teach and watch the seal.

"As for enemies, you can escape by running away;
It is those who appear in the guise of sons who destroy.
The other spiritual traditions will not engage in this [teaching];
Those who do not see it will not reify or denigrate it. [223]
It is the practitioners who proclaim our own tradition
Who might betray this [teaching], I fear.

"Golden-Ocean Lady and Light-Ocean Lady,
Teaching-Protecting Lady and Mind-Holding Lady,
Mighty Lady and the Greatly Fierce Lady,
Blood-Colored Lady and Smoke-Colored Lady,
Unobstructed Lady and Mighty Lady,
Power-Gathering Lady and Destroyer-of-Karma Lady[370]—
If none of you, the twelve mighty Dharma protectors,
Guard my teachings,
Why, then, do you follow me?

"Do not propagate this dialogue to those who are base;
Do not bring the jewel to the enemies.
One of you depart to the exterior [of the mandala],
While eleven of you go to Bodhgaya.
Guard Avalokiteśvara's teaching.
As for me, I have been called
To be in Maitreya's presence within a year and fortnight;[371]
So receive the supreme attainments from Drom.

"Mighty ones, uphold the ground of ultimate security.
Though you can turn mountains into dust,
If you do not free beings, you serve little purpose."

Then the twelve ladies
Took the conqueror and his son upon their crowns
And exclaimed, "We will follow you, Avalokiteśvara;
We shall destroy the evil-ridden ones
Who reify and denigrate this [teaching].

Some of us are the Tenma goddesses of earth;
Some of us are holders of vajra space.
If angered we bring even the sun and moon down to earth;
If delighted we send even the ocean up to the skies!
Atiśa, the conqueror, the sovereign among humans,
You have brought us from the central land here to a hinterland.[372]
Will you leave us behind and depart to the above?
If we cut off others' breaths, we breach your sacred words.
What else is the nourishment of Dharma?"

Master Atiśa responded:
"You will be sustained by Drom,
So do not transgress Drom's sacred words."

[Then] Drom proclaimed:
"O twelve ladies listen to me.
When placing this gold into a [suitable] container,
Do not harbor enmity or cause disruption.
If it is robbed by someone who is not a receptacle,
Then do not be dispirited and lazy.
Do not take life with Dharma as an excuse.
There are eighty [mighty ones] above you;
As for you eighty [mighty ones], pray do not procrastinate either."

Then the twelve ladies spoke:
"When the essence is poured into the container,
If we, the ninety-two, are not informed,
Feelings of enmity will arise.
Failing to offer tormas, they may [in fact] disparage us.
If they do not venerate the Three Jewels, they are not practitioners.
If they lack compassion, we shall not protect them.
Be cognizant of this and we'll follow your words.
Otherwise, we shall guard them [well].
One who is free of defects is an excellent vessel; [224]
One who does not respect this we shall vanquish;
One whose three doors are disrespectful will soon perish;
We are the appointed Tenma guardians of Tibet."

Later the twelve Tenma guardians exclaimed:
"Conqueror and son, pray attend to us.
The beastly ones who do not practice the sevenfold gods and teachings
Cause disruptions by entering through the cracks;
Isn't it easier if their stirring stick is removed?"

Drom responded to them:
"If you vanquish [them for] many generations, O twelve ladies,
Numerous epidemics may ensue;
So I shall entrust only this much;
Do not release epidemics of illness;
For if you do, you will be acting contrary to me."

Then the two, the conqueror and his son,
Constructed a mandala of Great Compassion.
They turned the wheel of six letters,
The six perfections, in the following manner:
In the east was great Atiśa;
In the south was Great Compassion;
In the west was the Powerful Secret [Acala];
In the north was supreme Tārā;
The eighty white [gods] encircled from the right;
The twelve Tenma guardians came and sat from the left.
Starting from *oṃ* [the mantra] circled clockwise;
Circling four times, [the mantra] dissolved into the two [Atiśa and
    his son].

The teacher was in meditative absorption on loving-kindness;
Great Compassion was in meditative absorption on compassion;
The Secret Name was in meditative absorption on joy;
The Mother abided extraordinarily in all [absorptions].
All of them are heroic bodhisattvas.
Within the expanse of nonconceptuality,
The perfection of wisdom led ahead
And the five perfections followed behind.

Thus, once offerings of realization were made in such a manner,
The Three Jewels were pleased with offerings.

Satisfying the ninety [guardians] with torma rites,
At the time of dedication they departed into the pure expanse.

Then, Drom Jé exclaimed:
"Sublime teacher, pray listen.
If all of these inconceivable [teachings]
Are summarized well it is this:

> The wealth of faith, the wealth of morality,
> The wealth of giving, the wealth of learning,
> The wealth of conscience, the wealth of shame,
> The wealth of insight—these are the seven riches.
>
> These precious and excellent jewels
> Are the seven inexhaustible riches.
> Do not speak of these to those not human.

"Other than this, there is nothing else."

This concludes the twenty-second chapter of *Jewel Garland of Dialogues*, [the chapter entitled,] "Subsuming [All Higher Qualities] into Seven Riches and Bequeathing Them."

CHAPTER 23
The Two Examinations

[225] Once again, at that perfect site and in the presence of the sublime teacher, our teacher [Dromtönpa], the perfect spiritual guide and yogi of hidden conduct, made the following plea: "Sublime teacher, pray listen. This treatise encompassing such vast [themes] is extremely difficult. So please teach us, now, a profound practice that summarizes all the points."

Thus, Atiśa responded:
"Excessive speech is a cause for nonvirtue;
Excessive distraction is a cause for nonvirtue;
Words of praise and words of disparagement,
Pleasant utterances and unpleasant ones,

"Distorted speech and truthful speech,
Explicit statements and implicit statements,
Praise through insult and disparagement through praise,
Hurtful speech and arrogant speech,

"Voicing senseless speech on account of the afflictions,
Speech of attachment and speech of aversion,
Deluded speech and speech of envy,
Conceited speech and speech of untamed views,[373]

"Lies that deceive and humorous lies,
Words wishing to mock others, both wise and foolish,
Ordinary words [aimed at] destroying important people,
'Kill,' 'hit,' and [words] that seek to humiliate,

"Words of superficial friendliness, flattery, and conceit,
Words of deals and aspirations,
Words of battle and of masculine pride—
Even the slightest of these gives rise to strong afflictions.

"Sentient beings are born with the afflictions as the cause.
Because envy and aversion are inborn,

When one person is praised another is angered.
Through needless anger, virtuous roots are destroyed.

"Using foul names they evince bitterness.
With a praise for one, one hundred are insulted.
Through the faults of speech, one attracts enemies;
Through the faults of speech, one loses friends.

"Through the faults of speech, I have heard,
Ploughshares run one thousand times over one's tongue!
Even when pleasant words are abundant,
Distinctions are made through differences in tones!

"When you praise someone only a little,
It strikes at his weakness and creates suspicions.
Praise can turn someone into an enemy.
If an undeserving person is praised,
He will well up with anger even more.
If someone worthy [of praise] is spoken to in measured words,
He becomes angry, as if you have insulted him.

"In general if there are many it's hard to speak;
Harder still is to [speak] to those not kindred in mind;
Harder still is to [speak] to those who are ambitious;
Harder still is to [speak] to those who are small minded.

"The end of a jest becomes a quarrel; [226]
The end of such speech is a conflict between two bodies;
The end of the body is the loss of life;
The end of life is the journey to the lower realms.

"This concludes the *first* examination pertaining to speech.
Not to abandon these despite knowing this is foolishness.

"As for the second [examination], analyze the speech.
With respect to the analysis, first probe the objects.
If they are many, silence is the best;
If there are faithful ones, speak of goodness;

If there are learned people, praise their higher qualities;
If there are disciplined ones, praise their discipline;
If there are kindhearted ones, speak of the practices;
If there are evil-ridden beings, gently avoid them;
If it serves as a remedy, then speak of anything;
Otherwise, refrain from the faults of speech.

"Second when you speak to others,
Bring the voice to your throat [and observe],
Is there an expectation or not?
Is it laden with afflictions, like attachment and aversion, or not?

"Is there attachment of selfish desire or not?
Is there animosity toward others or not?
Do the words become defamation or not?
Is it senseless speech or lying words?

"Is it divisive speech or harsh words?
Will it hurt through insinuation or confrontation?
Will it hurt directly or indirectly?
Is it the word of a noble one or of a childish person?
Is it meaningful or not meaningful?
If so send it to mouth's entrance;
If not dissolve it into the *ah* at your throat.

"Furthermore, when in the presence of one who is absorbed in
    meditation,
Do not engage in recitations;
In the presence of a hardened [Dharma] defamer,
Do not engage in recitations and practice.

"Moreover, proclaiming the Great Vehicle
To a Lesser Vehicle practitioner constitutes a fault.
Though your devotion to your teachers,
Preceptors, masters, and so on might be strong, do not speak
    their praises
In front of those who are laden with prejudice.

"Proclaiming the secret to unsuitable ordinary people
Is a great harbinger of ill effects indeed;
In brief, until you attain superior knowledge,
It is vital to guard your speech in all its forms.

"In particular, be decisive when in the midst of many.
Those who have turned their backs to the Dharma,
The haughty—eloquent in oration and abundant in speech—
They judge all: the high, the middle, and the low.

"When some are praised, others become upset;
By speaking for the benefit of the collective, individuals are upset.
When matters of individuals are spoken of, the collective rises as an
    enemy;
When there is nothing to say, meaningless gibberish is spoken.
One hundred respond to one, one thousand respond to the hundred!
In the end, words destroy your roots of virtue;
The haughty man arrives in the hells!

"Blessed by the māra of distraction,
Amid many one speaks in unceasing chatter.
Though everyone gathered is seething,
Resorting to laughter, he seduces them with praise.
Strike the unruly tongue with [the lashes of] a whip. [227]

"So Drom Jé, analyze your speech;
Cease inferior speech and endeavor in mantra recitations.
Though you may hear pleasant or hostile words,
Remain [still], like a mute person.

"If even the self-enlightened ones guard their speech,
Why wouldn't the excellent bodhisattvas do so?
If you instruct at the right time this is wise;
If your words hit their mark, this is heroic.

"If the words are excellent, it is the sublime Dharma;
If they turn into poetry, they will grab the senses;
If you understand, you'll pay heed to all your speech;
It is vital, therefore, to constantly examine your speech.

"This concludes the *second*, the collection on examining
The objects and the speech, so analyze this."

"Atiśa, most excellent in speech;
Not sullied by defects of speech,
You are proficient in speech, the glory of beings.
Excellent speaker of Dharma, pray listen.

"This is advice for [life among] the multitude.
Now I request a teaching to practice when alone,
The most essential point that encompasses everything,
A teaching for those living in solitude."

"Drom, when alone probe your mind."
"It will be clearer if this is unraveled by means of a teacher's method."
"Drom, with no mind who would grasp at the objects?"
"As there is no grasper they will not be grasped at."
"Drom, with no mind who would speak to whom?"
"As there will be no speaker, why be attached and averse?"
"Drom, such is the nature of subjects and objects."
"What is the foundation and root of the mind?"
"Drom, I haven't found that reality."
"How is it that you have not found this?"
"Drom, because there is no arising, abiding, or ceasing."
"How is it that we perceive diversity?"
"Drom, this is absence of appearance appearing."
"Is not the appearance thatness?"
"Drom, what is it that is called *appearance*?"
"It is the perception of diverse objects."
"Drom, is it the object that is perceived or is the mind itself?"
"It is the mind that perceives the objects."
"Drom, now the time has come to analyze that mind."
"The time has come for the mode of such analysis."
"Drom, show me your preceding awareness."
"What is past cannot be shown here."
"Drom, then show me your future awareness."
"Can the future be here [in the present]?"
"Drom, in that case show me your present awareness."
"There is nothing to point my finger at."

"Drom, why is it that this is so?"

"That is what I am asking *you*."

"Drom, even all the buddhas come to a halt on this point."

"Aren't they versed in everything?"

"Drom, it cannot be that the learned have understood falsely." [228]

"In that case does the mind itself not exist?"

"Drom, they know it as if it exists."

"Who, then, wanders in this realm of cyclic existence?"

"Drom, the 'clever,' essenceless ones wander there."

"Are we not all like this?"

"Drom, you, too, are like a stuffed dummy."

"We grasp at an essence where there is none."

"Drom, this is the behavior of samsaric beings."

"Is it not the case that behavior does not exist?"

"Drom, who is claiming that behavior exists?"

"You just spoke of behavior."

"Drom, trust not in the truth of conventional words."

"In that case were you being a liar?"

"Drom, there is no need for being one, for things are naturally so."

"Can lies become [aspects of] the path?"

"Drom, everything is stated to be illusion-like."

"Is the mind also an illusory mind?"

"Drom, it is a dream, an apparition, a mere luminosity."

"How can one do the generation and completion stages within a mere luminosity?"

"Drom, construct all the mandalas within."

"How does one construct a mandala?"

"Drom, as mere luminosity, as mere awareness, and as mere purity."

"What is the significance of doing such?"

"Drom, so that no disclosure of secrecy will occur and realizations will increase."

"Won't there be obstacles to this?"

"Drom, undetected by Māra, one will become fully awakened."

"Should one practice the method [aspects] after emptiness?"

"Drom, all method and wisdom will increase within."

"What is such a person called?"

"Drom, 'upholder of the hidden [yogi] conduct.'"

"Please wrap all of this up."

"Drom, let go with ease the generated love and compassion, which is luminous."[374]

"How should one examine [the mind] when attracted to a form?"

"Drom, examine the shape and color of that mind."

"How should one examine it when attracted to a sound?"

"Drom, examine whether the mind has a sound."

"How should one examine it when attracted to a smell?"

"Drom, examine whether the mind has a smell."

"How should one examine it when attracted to a taste?"

"Drom, examine whether the mind has a taste."

"How should one examine it when attracted to tactile sensations?"

"Drom, examine its texture."

"How should one examine it when attracted to phenomena?"

"Drom, apart from these [sense objects] what reality-itself is there?"

"Master, there are fabrications of conceptualization."

"Drom, examine the conceptualizations, too, in the same manner."

"How should one examine the examiner itself?"

"Drom, when the body disintegrates where will the limbs be?"

"They arise invariably in relation to [the body]."

"Drom, it is vital to constantly examine in this manner."

"What should one do when, following such examination, [everything] is dismantled?"

"Drom, unable to find anything, they will vanish into the space like a rainbow." [229]

"Is this nonfinding most excellent?"

"Drom, finding and not finding differentiates an ordinary person from a noble one."

"What if, with repeated searching, nothing is found?"

"Drom, one repeatedly sees one's own standpoint."

"Should one place [one's mind] on this nonfinding?"

"Drom, if one releases it with ease this is sublime."

"What is the lineage of this essential point?"

"Drom, it is the conqueror, Tārā, and myself."

"How should I share this with others?"

"Drom, accept those who are suitable vessels into your heart drop."

"Does this accord with the mandala referred to earlier?"

"Drom, the mandala of the mind is more important."

"What are the favorable conditions for this [practice]?"

"Drom, elaborately perform the seven limbs."
"These two examinations are most beneficial indeed."
"Drom, understand them and put them into practice."

"Master, though your responses to my queries were numerous,
When summarized, there are the seven riches;
If further condensed, there are the two examinations.
You have revealed these two examinations in a full chapter.
If the two examinations are summed up, it is this:

> **When among others guard your speech;**
> **When alone guard your mind.**

"On this auspicious point all [instructions] converge.
This is the jewel garland of well-spoken insights!
This is the conduct concealing the sacred seal!"

Your crown adorned by Amitābha, the conqueror,[375]
In whom all jewels of benefit and happiness are stacked,
O lord, we touch [our head] to your feet.

Through such an amiable dialogue,
May all be amiable and flourish.
There is no doubt that this root-like summary
Is the teacher's own words.

[Though] compiled separately, no name was given;
Clearly it is a dialogue on the *Jewel Garland*.
Also, the queries and the answers were not stated there.
Embracing these words of Master Atiśa.
Instantly they were scribed in letters;
The letters were in the Bodhgaya style.

Homage to the sacred teaching of Avalokiteśvara!
May it flourish in all corners not [yet] perceived;
May oath-breaking and moral degeneration cease;
May all latent propensities be destroyed;
May we depart from the land of ignorance;

May we traverse the levels and the paths in sequence;
May there be no obstacles on the path;
May we become omniscient for the benefit of all;
May the Kadam flourish to the farthest corners;
May it remain lotus-like on a lotus;
May it always be with the learned, the disciplined, and the kind;
May I become a lord of all beings without exception;
May I enjoy the mine of dual accumulations;
May all be led to this inexhaustible mine;
May the stream of this river that sustains
The lineage of the Three Jewels always remain. [230]

This concludes the twenty-third chapter of the *Jewel Garland of Dialogues,* [the chapter entitled,] "The Two Examinations."

This completes [the work] composed by the Indian master Dīpaṃkaraśrījñāna.

Maṅgalaṃ bhavantu

Colophon

In the north of Tibet, the kingdom of Pu,[376]
At the sacred place of one hundred and eight perfected ones,
At Yerpa, a place of glory for the glorious,
When the conqueror and his son conversed
In the solitude of the forest of Sangphu,
Lekpai Sherap was immersed in fine analysis
Of the fields of knowledge, their conflicts and interrelations.
At that time, supreme Mañjuśrī came and said:

"Though you are versed in the fields of knowledge,
You have not penetrated the essential points.
Therefore, assigning your assembly of five hundred disciples
To the task of exposition and learning,
Go, unhindered, to the interior of Yerpa.

"There, Dīpaṃkara, the sovereign of Tibet,
And the peerless Gyalwai Jungné,
Having seen the limitless realms of samsara,
Are engaged, day and night,
In a jewel garland of dialogues
Resembling a golden rosary."

Thus referring to the teacher's name
And stating, "They spoke such inconceivable words,"
[Mañjuśrī] revealed the teaching without excess or omission.
Then, within an instant, the deity became invisible.

[Lekpai Sherap] saw wondrous forms and heard teaching sounds;
Lacking the physical ability, he yet longed to fly.
"Before long I will go to Yerpa.
I will listen to words of the conqueror and his son.
As for abiding in morality, learning, and reflection,
These are excellent pursuits and I have performed them.
But I have not excised the afflictions through meditation,

And as I have failed to achieve stability of mind,
I will definitely be brought to maturity at such a site."

Upon thinking this, he experienced surging joy,
And, entering into the midst of his congregation, he exclaimed:
"Today, all of you who have gathered here
Listen to my words and let go of laziness!

"Though in the past we passed our time in exposition,
The pith instructions did not hit their marks.
Therefore, now you must hammer the nails into your heart.
Endeavor in learning and exposition at your own place. [231]

"If it helps the mind, listening and expositions are excellent;
If one is tranquil and tamed, this is the sign of learning;
If afflictions are weak, this is the sign of meditation;
If one sees the ultimate mode of being, this is yoga.

"If scripture and reason come together, one is a true teacher;
If one hits the marks, one is truly learned;
Though one may engage in learning and reflection over a lifetime,
If one does not understand the ethical norms it's a mere chore.

"All elder spiritual friends, wear the great armor
Of exposition; all students,
Practice on the basis of learning and reflection.
For a period of two or three months, I shall behold
The face of the conqueror, listen to his teachings,
And practice at Yerpa, a place of meditative practice.

"So, if you have [urgent] matters speak of them today,
For afterward there is no need for distraction.
Until I am back at this site,
Do not engage in too many pursuits
On the pretext of seeing me or calling for me.
I am now old and concerned for my future,
So, if you have faith and respect, listen to what I've said.

"Now, as for the father Atiśa, the son, and Sherap Gyaltsen,
The tips our minds converge upon a single point.
So, all of you, offer service to me.
Bring over there all my material needs.
Then return to your place and, through spiritual discipline,
Break the neck of the high [conceited ones] and nurture the humble;
Expel the irreligious and honor the practitioners.

"Wealth and high status, they have no purpose.
Negative friends are [like] infected frogs;[377]
Acknowledge only the Dharma practitioners.
If someone says, as if with great purpose, 'Come, see me'
And seduces you, he is a māra, so vanquish him.
Tomorrow at dawn I shall depart to Yerpa."

The learned and disciplined five hundred were confused:
"In the past he was quiet and would never scold us.
Tonight he will be seeking shelter in a forest.
Today wrathful words issued forth from him.
Fearing a delay, he set a deadline [to leave].
It would be difficult now to appeal to him to stay."

Saying this, they did not know what to do.
In whispering voices they spoke in this way.
Some were quietly shedding tears;
Some were consoling and said, "do not cry."
"We cannot bear this! Soon we shall die."
"That he is not passing away is good enough."

At dawn, as the sun rose from the mountaintops,
[And Lekpai Sherap departed], using a single male *dzo* as his mount.
Except for Sherap Gyalsten alone,
No one moved in the direction [of his journey].

As he secretly descended to the plains,
When he encountered other people,
All were confused and asked him,
"In the past you traveled upon an excellent horse

In the company of at least fifty riders,
How is that you are traveling like this today?
Did someone displease you?"

Swiftly they sent messengers to Sangphu.
Then, he arrived at the site of Yerpa. [232]
As before, he met with the conqueror and his son.
He then narrated the story of his coming.
Then, through the excellent medium of his three doors,
He made supplications to never to be separated [from Atiśa and Drom].

The extraordinary twenty birth stories[378]
Were taught by Atiśa to Lekpai Sherap
As the son teachings, which he mastered.
Of the twenty-six father teachings,[379]
Twenty-one were taught in the forest
By Mañjuśrī in their pristine [form].
With no exception he mastered them all.
The instant he arrived, the two [final] chapters [were taught].
Then, during a session of his own teaching,
At the twentieth chapter, he heard the "sacred seal."[380]
Finally, it was completed with the diamond songs.

This concludes the collection on the story of the origins.
With these, the twentyfold Ngok cycle of teachings are complete.

IV. Elucidation of the Heart-Drop Practice
Khenchen Nyima Gyaltsen (1223–1305)

[233] This is the *Elucidation of the Heart-Drop Practice* entitled, "Sun and Moon Drops of Union."

Homage to the sublime gurus!

To the conqueror, his source, and the Sherap pair;[381]
To the three Gyaltsens[382] and the one named Jangchup Namkha—
You who possess the supreme intelligence of four immeasurable
     thoughts—
To you, unrivaled teachers, I pay homage.

As for engaging in the practice of the teaching of the precious Kadam, endowed with the sevenfold divinities and teachings, there are three topics:
    I. Presentation of the defects of cyclic existence preceded by a preface outlining the early origins [of the teachings],
    II. Presentation of the benefits of nirvana by relating these to the definitive ultimate mode of being of things, and
    III. Presentation of the method of practicing the path that progresses to this [state] by relating it to the stages of the rite.

I. Presentation of the Defects of Cyclic Existence Preceded by a Preface Outlining the Early Origins [of the Teachings]

Once, when the conqueror and his son were staying at their residence in Yerpa, a multitude, including many exceptional individuals such as Sangphuwa—an emanation of Mañjuśrī—and many others aspiring for liberation, gathered in their presence to listen to the teachings. As described in *The Book [of Kadam]*,[383] the skies were also filled with teachers and the

buddhas and their children. It is even said that many celestial beings of the
Śuddhavākā realm showered down various offerings from above and sang
melodious songs proclaiming, "The Buddha's teaching is being disseminated in the snowy mountains!" At that time, the gathered assembly, dancing with such excitement that their feet barely touched the ground, made
supplications by shouting aloud, "Lord Avalokiteśvara!" Atiśa responded to
them, saying, "Since this realm is Avalokiteśvara's field, make supplications
to Drom and appeal to him to grant you his attention."

Drom replied, "Taking my teacher and the wise ones as my witnesses,
[234] today I shall expound an instruction that can melt your heart into
drops." Saying this, Drom gave a detailed teaching in accordance with *The
Book*, beginning with death and impermanence and continuing up to the
cause and effect of karma, [including] the sufferings of the six types of
beings, their causes, and so forth. [Hearing] this [teaching], even the great
beings such as Sangphuwa and others, though able to withstand harm from
others and from their own pain, felt extreme fear. Their eyes filled with
tears and, shouting lamentations, they bowed at Drom's feet with intense
devotion, making the following fervent plea: "Pray save us and others from
such sufferings!" Ordinary people also exclaimed, "Alas! If even the great
beings express such things, then what can we do?" Out of an unbearable
sense of sorrow, everyone, both young and old, chanted the following plea:

Bless us father, O compassionate one;
Sustain us with your heart, O compassionate one!

In particular, there was one Kawa Shākya Wangchuk[384]—a physical emanation of the arhat Kālika—who had been an ordained monk in this Land
of Snows for over sixty years, and who, at eighty-two, had a pale [aged] face.
He too felt steadfast devotion for Drom and asked, "How is it that someone like you, a lord of the tenth ground, a member of the Drom lineage
from the north, assumes the form of only a celibate lay upāsaka practitioner
in this imperfect region of snowy mountains? Alas! My age and physical
state have reached such a stage that there is a danger that I might die soon.
Even though we have such a lord as you, how blind and deaf we have been,
clinging to our own individual partisan instructions and failing see or hear
such a clear ocean of instructions as this? What should I do now? Pray bless
my inferior body and speech. Pray tame my inferior mental continuum.
This instruction, so vast and complete, pierces my heart!" Making such
exclamations, he looked into Drom's face and wept.

Atiśa also reacted as if his feet barely touched the ground. Shooting his eyes in all ten directions, he shouted "*Phala! Phala!* If simply by revealing the defects of cyclic existence my upāsaka can place those who have congregated here to the ground of faith in such manner, *Ati! Ati! Ho! Ho!* Still he will pierce their hearts with the iron hook of impermanence and implant the drop of awakening at the center of their hearts. My awareness, too, has improved, so please reveal further the defects of cyclic existence. [235] Lord Serlingpa, pray behold my upāsaka! This upāsaka has snatched away the good heart that you gave me. Teacher Avadhūtipa, pray behold my upāsaka! This upāsaka has taken away the great realization of the ultimate mode of being that you gave me. In this way the upāsaka is highly effective in drawing [others'] mind. In this manner he has led everyone to the ground of faith."

Serlingpa responded:[385]

> Avalokiteśvara, lord of all three worlds,
> For the benefit of others you wear the armor of effort.
> Great compassion endowed with a stainless mandala,
> I pay homage to you, dispeller of beings' suffering.
>
> You encompass the entire world, even unto the limits of space,
> Within the mandala of your body.
> Even the great Buddha Vairocana
> Resides within a single pore of your body.
>
> All the lights of the world from the past, present, and future
> And from all ten directions likewise [reside within you].
> You are the truth body of all the sugatas of the three times.
> To the beings of the six realms you are Avalokiteśvara.
>
> Your eleven faces pervade the universe like space;
> It is blissful indeed to behold the majesty of infinite light.[386]
> Your one thousand arms are the thousand universal monarchs;
> Your one thousand eyes the thousand buddhas of the fortunate age.
>
> Today you have assumed a perfect emanation in the Land of Snows.
> With your hands arrayed in the shape of a thousand petal [lotus],
> Your eyes are filled with moisture trapped in these petals.
> The wheel of the Kadam teaching is like ripples in a lake.

The countless arhats who are born from you
Adorn the utterly beautiful, unblemished golden stupa.[387]
Your body of white crystal, a thoroughly bejeweled Mount Meru,
Sports the levels of ten grounds and five paths in their order.

One thousand lords bless this [crystal body] in actuality;
They subsume all [actions] into four and guard your teaching
    well;[388]
You, Lord Avalokiteśvara, are most industrious.
Displaying forms suited to the individual, you tame each being.

Your legs are crystal poles supporting like gold.
From wherever one views this mandala of your body,
It resembles the seats and lotus petals that are the sources of
    conquerors;[389]
Within the interstices [of your body mandala]
Are unimaginable lakes and ponds
Of compassion endowed with eight qualities.

When the soft breeze of impermanence blows, [236]
It turns the wheel of the three trainings from the center.
With emanations from the center you tame the hinterlands.
Your qualities arise from water and dissolve into water;
Water changes its color due to its container.

Alas! All the sources of benefit and happiness
Arise from your stainless embodiment of great compassion
And dissolve into you, the very lord.
All those to whom your three trainings are revealed
Are taught in accordance with that very individual.

At the center of this lotus with blossoming petals
Within the heart of an utterly pure crystal [dome],
There dwells a white deity emitting thousands of lights.
Adorned with the noble marks, he is endlessly pleasing to behold.
I fold my palms together and bow to you,
Forever smiling and seated upon the blossoming lotus.

Holding a garland of jewels in his right arm,
He displays the spectacle of his pure liberating life.
[Extending] from the tip of his crystal-encircled arm
There is a beautiful lotus with one thousand petals.

Its hub is adorned with the mother, jewel mountain;
She is encircled by all the buddhas of the ten directions.
The [buddhas], in turn, are surrounded by their children.
All are nondual and appear vividly, it is said.

All of their three points are marked with the three letters;
I see them emitting light rays and ripening sentient beings.
Situated upon a lotus seat at the heart of this lord
Is a refined moon disc, fifty yojanas [in circumference].

A beautiful [goddess] stands at each of the four doors in this palace
     of light.
Appearing in the forms of six great mothers,
They are flanked on both sides by [wisdom] mothers and
     [bodhisattva] children.
Thus, I see that gradually the perfection of wisdom, the four
     divinities,

The conqueror and his son, together with the teachers
And the oath-bound guardians, all reside together.
All of their three points are marked with the three syllables;
Their seed letters are the sound of the [six] perfections,
All reverberating in the sound of mantras such as the essence
     mantras.

At the center of the lotus's stamen is an apparition being
Sending Dharma wheels to the ears of the beings of the six classes.
Thoroughly illuminated by lights from both within and without,
His three doors are being blessed, I see.

All beings are aspects of the jewel mind;
The mind is the self-cognizing clear-light dharmakāya.
Free of letters, it disappears into Great Compassion.

Alas! Conqueror and son, listen to me here.
I have given the good heart to the sovereign.
Your good heart has been snatched away by your son,
Yet it's this son who gave me the good heart!
It is Great Compassion who brought me peace; [237]

It is Great Compassion who freed me;
It's to due to him that I became Fame of the Dharma.[390]
This profound truth I offered to you
Has [now] returned to Great Compassion,
Just like water and its ripples, O sovereign.

Please continue to nurture sentient beings
In this manner through the heart-drop [teaching].
This is wondrous indeed, O conqueror Drom!
Today you have led all to the ground of faith.

Many wondrous words such as these resounded from the skies. Then Avadhūtipa spoke:[391]

You are the great nondual compassion;
You are the inconceivable supreme wisdom;
You possess unobstructed supernatural power;
Just as foretold, in this excellent Land of Snows,
Out of compassion and great forbearance, your perseverance blazes;
You have become the lord and glory of all beings.

I received from you whose ocean of knowledge is full
This most profound teaching, resembling space.
I gave this profound truth, devoid of center or periphery, to the
    sovereign;
The sovereign joyfully gave it to you, O conqueror.
Like water and its ripples, this is a dependent origination.
Today you have led all beings to the ground of faith.
Further reveal to them the defects of cyclic existence.
Spark the wish for nirvana in the hearts of those gathered here.

As all these words that had been spoken became manifest in a pure vision, everyone who heard them experienced a deep sense of wonder and looked with reverence at the face of the perfect teacher of all, the spiritual guide [Dromtönpa], who exclaimed: "*Emaho!* O teachers and your children, I do not possess such qualities, so continue to care for me through the force of your compassion." Stating this, he made repeated supplications. In order not to breach the words of the teachers, he taught again, in a sharp and concise form, about death and impermanence, the defects of cyclic existence, and karma and its effects, just as found in *The Book*. Those who had gathered in the assembly all experienced deep revulsion toward cyclic existence. So, for us, too, it is critical to reflect from death and impermanence [onward]. As Atiśa states:

> Constantly reminding yourself of impermanence,[392]
> Exhort yourself to be free from this mire.
> Body and mind are like the clouds in the sky—
> They gather instantly, yet are gone just as quickly.
> Pull up the strings of your conscienceless heart. [238]
> Turn it inward and upbraid it with derision.
>
> This life is like the flowers in autumn—
> With no time to linger, they are robbed by frost.
> So, all you childish ones who procrastinate and are lost,
> Wind up the string of your heart.
>
> Haughty ones conceited with their youth,
> Youth is not eternal, and soon remorse will strike.
> With tomorrows, the days and the months will go by;
> Their collections will turn into years and you will change.
> Do not grasp at an essence where there is none.
>
> With mouth open and fangs bared, [Yama] will ride upon your
>   shoulders,
> With your eyes wide open, you will be pierced with blades.
> You will definitely die, so you who esteem yourselves,
> Do not be lazy but discard dejection;
> Do not procrastinate, for those with ropes and daggers
> May soon separate your body from its life.

If, having obtained this human life so difficult to find,[393]
A person fails to rely on the discipline of the three vows
And instead yearns for [worldly] harvests, such a person of
    mundane aims
Will be bereft of leisure when his life comes to an end.
His hoarded wealth will be of no use.
With no clothes, naked, he will be devoid of food;
With no companions, he will be separated from his loved ones.

When his consciousness passes through the intermediate state,
He will feel remorse for his past karmic deeds;
He will feel attached to his hoarded possessions;
He will feel resentful toward his loved ones.

Though he may say, "Send my things after me!"
People will say, "What's the use? He is dead."
Seizing his wealth, they will breed conflict.
Those who were closest to him will mourn for a few days.
This is no use, for it is the mourning of those without
    conscience.
Though they may wail with their chests out and throw dirt
    in their mouths,
Alas! This will only harm him.
Failing to bring benefits, it will bring [more] harm.

Then, before too long,
When the deceased is undergoing intense suffering,
The mourning of the conscienceless will turn into laughter.
They cannot see him, nor can they hear him.

Not only is all his hoarded wealth of no use,
Because of his miserliness, he ends up in the lower realms.
Desperate for hope, heartless, he will have lost his aim.

O bewildered ones, many things are still [yet to tell].[394]
Are you not reduced to terror by past mires?
It is better to be terror-free than to be in pain.
Whipped and whipped, you will die soon:

Some die in old age;
Some die when young;
Some die in the prime of youth;
Some die just after birth.
Male and female, intelligent or learned,
Who has seen or heard of anyone who was spared?

Because you are apparent, empty, and subject to disintegration,[395]
When your lifespan becomes exhausted,
You are encircled by the messengers of Yama.
These breath-snatching butchers celebrate,
And the great lord of death presses down on your shoulders.

Whatever you might eat you have no appetite for;
Powerless, your body's edifice comes undone in the bed.
Crying, those who wish to be close to you support you.
Some with evil karma might consult shamans and astrologers;
The better ones might read scriptures and offer ritual cakes. [239]
Some might become so utterly petrified
That they run around declaring that a physician should be sought.
Some might sit around you and cry;
Exclaiming, "How can you die? This is not fair,"
They weep and protest.
Some physicians check your pulse;
Whispering, "No hope," they assume certain expressions.
[One physician] says, "I will treat you like a friend,"
But when the time approaches
He agonizes, "The patient is going to die."
At that point a time will come
When you come to face to face
With a great expanse of suffering
Against which nothing can help.

Listen, this is what happens:
When a person is born, he is born in conjunction
With an innate god and a demon,
[Along with] the two—his self and his life force.
The god gathers all favorable conditions

And abandons all adverse conditions;
The god urges one toward all virtuous deeds
And records whatever virtues he performs.
When he is [caught] in nonvirtue or suffering, the god mourns;
When virtuous or joyful, the god rejoices with happiness.
The demon does the opposite.

It is said that together with your innate god and demon[396]
You are dragged by the executioners
Into the presence of Yama [the lord of death].
He then examines your Dharma and negative karma.
It is said that the demon will show the store of evil deeds,
Whereas the god will show the store of virtuous acts.
If equal, he then looks into a mirror [to probe further].
When he is not sure, it is said he weighs them on a scale.
If the evil [outweighs the virtuous], you will be baked and burned;
For the virtuous this does not happen.

Drom Jé, reveal this much of the instructions to us.[397]
A time will come when we are certain to die.
This is how the four borrowed elements are lost;
This is how the dependent relationship of body and mind is
    broken.

Therefore, it is critical to meditate on these aspects of impermanence for
a prolonged period until [these images] arise in your mind with immediacy and vividness. Once, having reflected in this manner, you generate
forceful awareness that you will inevitably die, you will die soon, and there
is no certainty as to when you will die, you then examine where you might
be reborn after death. Since there are only the six realms [in which to be
reborn], no matter where you are reborn there is no hope for happiness.
Atiśa states:

Intense heat and burning is created in the hells;[398]
For the hungry ghosts there is the torment of hunger and thirst;
For the beasts there is confusion, killing, and being abused for labor;
For the demigods conflicts are rife just as for snakes;

For the gods are their many [sufferings], such as the portents of
death.

Dromtönpa also states:

Some of my parents are being burned in flames;[399]
Some of my parents are being dissected with weapons;
Some of my parents are being devoured by insects;
Some of my parents are being eaten by ravens;
Some of my parents are being immersed in boiling lava. [240]

Unable to bear it, they rush to the plains,
Where they find themselves on a path through a vast land filled
    with razors.
Horrified, as they escape again,
The thick green forests shake and rain down knives[400]
Naked, they are tortured by the cold as well—
In moaning, blistering, and popping blistering hells,
In splitting-like-a-lotus and splitting-like-an-utpala hells.
Such is the fate of my parents today.

If a person's parents have fallen into a fire pit,
The courageous, unable to bear this, will strive to rescue them.
If this is so, how can I bear my parents' fate?
Alas! Master Drom, do not remain idle.

My parents suffer the fate of having no clothes.
With no food and straw-thin throats, they have large bellies;
Their limbs are thin and they have no strength at all.
How can you bear this? Drom Jé, do think of this.

Even if I look at my parents who are delusion-ridden,
Powerless, they are tormented by unbearable suffering.
For many their own flesh becomes their enemy;
For some their hair, skin, blood, and bones rise as enemies;
For some their own strength and kinetic force rise as their
    enemies;

For some their speed enslaves them and rises as their enemy;
Some, powerless, are assailed by the four elements.
Think Drom Jé, can you bear this fate of your parents?

Alas! Even within the so-called happiness of the higher realms,
The body that is born straight becomes bent;
The hair that is black at birth becomes white;
Soft skin of white, yellow, and red tinge, free of wrinkles,
Degenerates into [skin that is] bluish, dry, and furrowed;
[You] no longer [appear] attractive to the minds of all.
Even your own son, nurtured with the tenderest love, glares [at you].
Transient, they all depart to the world beyond;
Can you bear this, Drom? This deserves reflection.

Contemplate the defects of cyclic existence just as described here. It is critical you meditate until a forceful wish arises to attain freedom from these. Through such reflection you will recognize that no matter where you are reborn in the six realms, you will be subject to suffering and fraught with misery. Since such [births within cyclic existence] do not come into being without causes, it is crucial to reflect on their causes—karma and its effects—and to forsake nonvirtuous karma. Atiśa states:

This great fundamental ignorance,[401]
Bringing together the three—attachment, aversion, [and
    delusion]—
Creates the sufferings of the six realms of samsara;
Those who have killed their parents and so on[402]
Go straight to the depths of great hell.

The most evil ones go to the hells;
The attachment-ridden to the hungry ghosts' [realm];
The aversion-ridden to that of the demigods; [241]
The delusion-ridden to that of the beasts.
These [births], in turn, are [subdivided] in numerous ways.
With respect to the beasts, for instance:
The aversion-ridden [are born] as wild beasts;
The delusion-ridden as sheep and so on;
The lust-ridden as donkeys and so on;

If you have all three [afflictions] you are born as a dog and so on.
Extend this to other classes of beings as well.

One descends into the depths of great hell. He explained how the sufferings of the lower realms come into being through nonvirtuous karma generated by the three poisons. Furthermore, even in the higher realms, such as the human realms, all the various experiences one has, such as prosperity and misfortune, come about due to karma that extends beyond the previous life. So Atiśa states:

> For humans in the higher realms, here is what happens:[403]
> Due to the fruition of past karma
> Some are born as boys and some as girls,
> Even among the offspring of the same parents.
> And among the boys, some are handsome
> While others are utterly unattractive.
>
> Even if it were possible to be equal [in appearance],
> Some would be clever and others foolish.
> Even if equal [cleverness] were possible,
> Some would enjoy wealth and perfect prosperity
> While others remained impoverished in numerous ways.
> Even [with wealth], one might see equality,
> [Yet] some would be resourceful and respected by all,
> While others would be powerless and insulted by all.
>
> While some indulge in negative acts
> And squander even their own well-being,
> Some engage in virtuous deeds
> And accomplish the well-being of others as well.
> They are honored by the gods and respected by the sublime,
> While the others are destined for the hells alone.
> Extend these [points] to girls as well.

Since they have been taught as the cause and effects of all [sufferings], you should, out of fear, never engage in even a slight negative karma and should, with regret, declare and purify the [bad actions] you have committed in the past. As for virtue, joyfully accumulate even the smallest. It is important to follow [the norms of] what is to be engaged in and what is to be averted without ever becoming complacent.

II. Presentation of the Benefits of Nirvana by Relating These to the Definitive Ultimate Mode of Being of Things

If you were to pursue this kind of striving in virtue with a mind engaged in an unmistaken [understanding of] ethical norms, but you did so only to attain your own liberation and higher rebirth, it would be a loss. [242] Therefore, it is crucial to seek unexcelled nirvana for the benefit of others, for if you attain this, you will become free from all sufferings and a treasury of all joys. Master Atiśa states:

> Like mists, clouds, and light,[404]
> I, the monk Dīpaṃ of appearance and emptiness,
> Am born from the heart accomplished by the dual accumulations.
> Do not cling to me as substantially real.

> You who don the robes of pure morality,
> The conduct of benefit and happiness,
> Are not separate from others' welfare; this is profound dependence.
> Embrace and practice such conduct.

> I am a monk of untainted virtue;
> Uncreated by causes and conditions,
> I pacify the disease of substantiality and signs
> And spontaneously accomplish great bliss.
> I traverse the paths by means of bodhisattva conduct;
> Together with my parents, I journey to liberation.

> Happy and joyous, you will ascend upward.[405]
> You'll journey to the fields of the pure way of life;
> You'll go into the depth of a lotus flower;
> You'll journey through the bodhisattva fields;
> You'll become accustomed to the cleansing of concepts.

> The behavior of dogs and pigs is [now] no more;
> The conduct of cattle has ceased to be;
> The sack of filth is torn open;

The tree of harvest-desiring is felled;
The heap of putrid vomit is spread everywhere.

With no need to meditate you become a deity;
Pure visions have entered your heart;
[Now] there's no danger of separation from the Three Jewels;
The flowered bed of discipline is elaborate;
The jewel mansion of sutras is beautiful;
The wheel of higher knowledge is fixed with spokes;
As you inflict loss on the food of consciencelessness,
You'll attain uncontaminated concentration.

As you forsake sloth, mental dullness, and laziness,
You'll be enveloped in the light rays of pristine cognition.
Alas! The lotus tree of Kadam is in full bloom.
This is the residence of one thousand sugatas.
It's the place of enjoyment of one thousand bodhisattvas;
It's the ground of happiness for one thousand disciples and
    self-enlightened ones;
It's the object of veneration of all humans and gods;
It's the field of merit, the lord and refuge of the entire world.
The pristine gods touch it with their crowns;
Nine great sages lift it from its base;
This is your inheritence, O Drom Jé.

It's an inexhaustible mine of millions;
One thousand bathing pools of nectar abound
Containing the three white and three sweet ingredients;
The golden ground is studded with turquoise;
It is filled with millions of apparition birds,
Birds with thick turquoise plumes sprinting about,
Deep turquoise birds hovering joyfully above.
This is the realm of Drom Jé, sovereign of men.

Your three doors are free of stains;
You honor the stainless conquerors at all times.
Pervading the universe these conquerors fill all of space.
This is your inheritence, O Drom Jé. [243]

If you indulge in songs and dances, do so in this realm;
You won't fall into the abyss of the afflictions.
If you wear ornaments, pray do so in this realm;
Human ornaments cannot compare with these.
If you indulge in the sense objects, do so in this realm;
They share the nature of the five transcendent wisdoms.

Ah! Listen to me, Drom Jé.
Having undergone sixty odd pains,
Now happiness increases as its effect.
Having thoroughly trained in the pure propensities,
It is [now] impossible to feel despair and revulsion.
Even if you contemplate impurity, how can they arise?
Drom Jé and his sons shall remain joyous;
Drom Jé and his sons shall enjoy happiness in the long term.
As the fruit of enduring hardships you will find the riches;
The inexhaustibility of the riches depends upon its mine.
Drom, know this and enjoy this realm.

It has been stated that it is by means of such a liberating life [embodying] the perfect view and conduct that we, the followers of Drom, should partake in the unexcelled bliss of such a perfect field, the residence of one thousand conquerors, free of all sorrows, which has the nature of bliss alone and is free of all forms of impure conduct. Because of this, it is critical we cultivate a great sense of joy for nirvana, a most wondrous fruit. It is important that, out of a fervent wish to attain [nirvana], we practice this very tradition of Atiśa, the path leading to it. Atiśa states:

I am a monk of apparition.[406]
Without grasping at me as substantially real,
Put my instructions into practice.
Pray conjoin appearance and emptiness.

I am an illusory monk.
Without clinging to me as good,
Put my instructions into practice.
Yoke together appearance and emptiness.

I am a monk who is the moon['s reflection] in water.
Though seeming to appear, I am devoid of reality.
Because I am empty, I appear as forms;
Because I appear as forms, I am emptiness.

Apart from this there is no emptiness.
As there is no form other than emptiness,
Do not take the form-like to be a form,
But practice the ultimate nature of form.

You, Drom Jé, crystal youth,
Just as you are devoid of flaws and blemishes,
I, too, am a monk of light.
Though appearing, I cannot be grasped,
So without grasping at that which cannot be held,
Place your mind at ease in the naturally free nondual state.

If you are devoid of what is to be abandoned, you're
    Master Drom;
If you see that which cannot be seen, this is precious;
If you cognize nonduality, this is the middle way; [244]
If you're free of cognizance, this is the ultimate mode of being.

I am the rays of the sun;
With no conceptuality, forms are illuminated.
This is illumination alone with no objects to touch.
This natural transparency, vivid, empty, and free of
    elaborations—
Those with grasping confuse it with the sun.

What is called *illusion* is unreal;
Unreality is a term for emptiness.
If emptiness is cognized, grasping will end.
This nonduality of object and subject transcends the intellect;
Transcendence of the intellect is the ultimate expanse.

See this, Drom Jé, when you recognize as unviewable
That which cannot be viewed, then the views will end;

When fearlessness is cognized, this is the middle way.
It is profound, so place your mind in the sphere of the middle way.
This, too, is my instruction.

Thus, it is stated that as you engage in the implementation of the view and conduct within the sphere of the union of appearance and emptiness, you will become free of the suffering of bewildering false perceptions and attain the sublime dharmakāya, which is the ultimate mode of being, free of grasping and that which is grasped. Practice, therefore, in the manner [thus described]. It is accepted that there are three entrances [to the practice] corresponding to the three lineages of transmission. Drom states:

> Within the middle way all sorts of appearances arise.[407]
> Though everything is an appearance of falsity,
> Without form how can its reflections come to be?
> Though the preceding cause may be false, effects ensue nonetheless;
> So do not defy karma but adhere to its practice.
> This is the [profound] view lineage of my Kadam [way].

> Though I generate incalculable divinities and their mansions
> Within a single drop and make offerings to them,
> Toward the teachings presenting the subtle and minute aspects of
>   karma,
> I neither exaggerate nor diminish, but implement them in practice.
> This is the inspirational lineage of my Kadam [way].

> In the illusory mansion of the appearance and emptiness of
>   phenomena,
> Gradually treading the levels and paths to ever-higher stages,
> One perfects the cause, the dual collections, and becomes a
>   buddha.
> This is the [vast] practice lineage of my Kadam [way].

Thus, our tradition accepts that Drom possessed all of Master Atiśa's teachings, which are encompassed within the three lineages. Although Drom had many followers, he had three spiritual sons, known as the three principal [disciples], who held the teachings of the three lineages separately. Among them, ours is the profound teaching of the *Jewel Garland* tradition, which was transmitted through Phuchungwa, [Drom's] principal [son] in terms of meditative practice. It is within the lineage of inspiration itself that one generates the celestial mansion of the divinities inside a large drop and undertakes the practice in which the generation and completion stages are unified and never separated from the five recollections. [245] Drom states:

> Construct a clear-light mansion beyond all measure.[408]
> Generate this mandala of clear-light deities,
> Naturally free from both clean and unclean.
> Through emanations of the omniscient pervading all,
> Fill with dances everywhere that space pervades.
>
> Pervade the entire world with echoes that are
> Free of the conceptualizations of the eighty-four thousand
>   [afflictions].
> If the afflictions—the causes and conditions—are not stopped,
> The effects will not be prevented,
> So sever their roots and cast them into the expanse.
>
> The generation stage is the supreme pristine cognition body;
> The completion stage is the fulfillment of the two accumulations.
> Pristine cognition is equal to the field of knowledge itself;
> Compassion is also as expansive as space.
>
> The seats that appear are a lotus and moon;
> Though there are numerous births, this is a spontaneous birth;
> The womb is described as the hub of a lotus;
> One's companions are the clear-light deities.
> In this ultimate mode of being, devoid of letters,
> Drom's generation and completion stages are exhausted.
>
> Make *hrīḥ* the letter of convention;
> Make the yellow, of course, with *oṃ;*
> Alas! Make the green with *tāṃ;*
> The dark blue Acala is *hūṃ* alone.
> From these [syllables] is such a celestial mansion created;
> It has the nature of perfection.
> This is Drom's generation and completion stages.

Of course, the letters are devoid of letters;
The letters are devoid of change and nonconceptuality;
The lotus, moon, and sun are also devoid of letters.
The peerless, fully awakened Buddha
Who resides in this mandala and is free of all—
This embodiment of the Three Jewels—I touch with my crown.

In this manner, you will be able to accomplish all meditative practices while maintaining your connection to the five recollections: (1) recollecting your teachers, the source of refuge, (2) seeing your body as the meditation deity, (3) seeing your speech as mantra repetitions and recitations, (4) seeing all beings as your actual mothers, and (5) seeing your mind as the ultimate nature. This is so because when Drom experienced a vision of the four meditation deities once in the past, [the goddess] Tārā declared:

O Avalokiteśvara, most excellent son,[409]
I will protect your followers.
Take this instruction of mine
And reveal it to those who follow you:

Recollect your teachers, the source of refuge;
Your body has the nature of meditation deities;
With speech, make mantra recitations constant;
Contemplate all beings as your parents;
Experience the nature of your mind as empty.
On the basis of these five factors,
Make pure all roots of virtue. [246]

As for the person to whom it is suitable to reveal such an instruction on the practices of the profound meaning: this person should be someone who has first adorned his mental continuum with the morality of the Discipline [basket], who follows in the footsteps of Master Atiśa and his son, who, because of his single-pointed devotion to the two, engages in study, reflection, and meditative practices upon the instructional treatises that are famed as the "Kadam teachings," and who, having been shunned from the ranks of [worldly] humans, has no pursuit other than practicing the three higher trainings. This [instruction] should be taught to such a person. Atiśa states:

Listen, I will tell you whom to reveal this teaching to.[410]
He is someone who, out of deep [affection] for you and I,
Takes into his heart the essence of the way of life
Of a body adorned with saffron robes.

In accord with the Discipline [basket] he observes morality;
In accord with the Sutra [basket] he partakes in higher
    concentration;
In accord with the Knowledge [basket] he enhances higher wisdom.
With no error in the foundation, his morality is pure;
With no error in the path, he journeys to the measureless;
With no error in the fruit, he'll become fully awakened—
Such a person is the one to whom you should reveal this [teaching].

Such a suitable vessel is the one who engages in this practice. In this way, he becomes like Dromtönpa, who was versed in undertaking the practice [of all the teachings]—from the morality of discipline to the teachings of the Secret Mantra Vehicle—in a single sitting, with no contradiction whatsoever. Therefore, he will be a great Kadampa, one whose view is high yet whose conduct is meticulous. The spiritual mentor [Atiśa] himself said:

"O sovereign, unsullied ultimate expanse.[411]
The view devoid of 'I' has vanished into the expanse;
Ungraspable, the object [too] has vanished into the expanse.

"Though perceptions of this and that are infinite,
The source from which they first arose is lost;
What place exists where they can return to at the end?
In the present, they are not related to anything.
As for this law of nature, devoid of [all] three times,
With nothing to see, one is deceived by the objects;
With nothing to remember, one is deceived by oneself.

"In this nondual awareness
There is too much fluctuation, destroying self-composure.
So many bumps and aches exist but, when probed, they perish.
Why are you deluded by something that does not exist?"

"Drom, from within a transparent crystal flower
The buddhas, the appearances of unreal buddha bodies, emerge.
This is a positive perception born of auspiciousness and good karma.
If you cling to this it casts you far away. [247]

"Ah! All of this is groundless and [mere] effulgence of words;
This [world of appearance] is devoid of the thoughts of clinging
    and the clung.
Awareness that cannot sustain itself and is a mere luminosity;
To what does it cling and how does it do so?

"What is illuminated is conception-free, blissful, and empty.[412]
O the world of unexamined diversity may seem attractive;
Hā! How is it that when probed they are no more?
Āḥ! This is so for they are unborn and empty of themselves;
Phaṭ! Now let them be free in natural liberation.

"Drom, this is my way of relinquishing the distractions;
Drom, this is what my wilderness is like.

"Contemplate these with joy, my followers.
If among the disciples, I, a Kadampa,
Sing aloud this song of the view of [emptiness],
What do those who claim to be Mahayanists say?"

[Drom:] "In general those who follow father Atiśa,
Who in turn follows in the footsteps of Avadhūti—
What Mahayanist would call them Lesser Vehicle people?

"That diligence does not slide into ignorance for me
Is due to having nurtured the Dharma, the source of the buddhas;
That scholarship does not impair discipline for me
Is due to having contemplated the profound causality of karma;
That meditation does not impair recitation for me
Is due to having read the profound sacred sutras;
That reading [sutras] does not impair concentration for me
Is due to having digested the sovereign teacher's pith instructions.

"That I know how to practice in one sitting,

Thoroughly integrating all teachings,
Is due to having endured hardships in Dharma practice.
He who is called 'sovereign Buddha' is all-knowing;
He has perfected abandonment and realization, as well as the two
    accumulations.

"As I aspire for this for the benefit of my parents,
First, through learning, I will cut [the knots of] my doubts;
Second, through reflection, I will cut [the knots of] my doubts;
Third, through meditation, I will cut [the knots of] my doubts.

"Also, each of these three is not pursued in isolation from the
    others;
When learning I bring reflection and meditation to bear;
When reflecting I bring learning and meditation to bear;
When meditating I bring learning and reflection to bear.

"By integrating all without exception,
I know how to travel by taking Dharma on the path;
As I, a Kadam, have not fallen into a partial approach,
I understand well the entire display, [the world of]
Cause and effect, as optical illusions; this is Kadam."

Since engaging in the practice of this tradition is so important, relinquish all elaborations upon lingering doubts and undertake this practice with single-pointed faith and reverence. These [teachings] present the causes and effects pertaining to what is to be relinquished and the causes and effects pertaining to what is to be affirmed. Before entering into the rites, you should, therefore, reflect upon them for many days by relating them to their scriptural sources. [248]

III. Presentation of the Method of Practicing the Path that Progresses to This [State] by Relating It to the Stages of the Rite

There are three general points:

    A. The preliminaries
    B. The main practice
    C. The conclusion

A. The preliminaries

The first [section] has two parts: (1) consecrating the trainee's environment and (2) the procedure for creating a mandala to sustain the trainees.

1. Consecrating the trainee's environment

The first, in turn, has two parts, the first of which is the master's exhortation to his own mental continuum. For this, the master should cultivate the five recollections and place the three letters upon the three points of his body. Then, audible to the students, he should recite one, two, or three times, and with full conviction, "The Tree of Devotion" composed by Dromtönpa in the past. The text of this [self-exhortation] is located in a separate [chapter].[413]

Second, the actual preliminary, which must be performed collectively by the master and students, is as follows: for this [rite], arrange whatever offerings you have gathered in front of the Three Jewels. Everyone, both master and students, should then undertake a succinct or elaborate version of the seven-limbs rite. Then, in unison, recite the lines composed by Dromtönpa three times. The text of this [rite] also is located in a separate [chapter].[414]

2. The procedure for creating a mandala to sustain the trainees

When [beginning] the mandala construction, send those who have not received oral transmissions elsewhere. Then, in a room free of unsuitable vessels, you should, while reciting the *oṃ maṇi padme hūṃ* mantra, paint [the room as follows]: make the ceiling white in the aspect of *oṃ;* as for walls, make the east yellow in the aspect of *ma,* the south white in the aspect of *ṇi,* the west blue in the aspect of *pad,* the north green in the aspect of *me,* and the ground white in the aspect of *hūṃ.* The syllables can be merely represented [by being imagined]. Hang a parasol and arrange the three representations,[415] especially those of the four divinities of Kadam. Then fully ordained monks numbering sixteen, eight, twelve, six, four, or two should wear their ceremonial yellow robes and make prostrations to the representations, [saying]:

> Fully awakened buddhas and bodhisattvas,
> O compassionate ones, to help purify evil karma,
> Pray confer upon me
> The sublime rite of rectification.

Make this supplication three times and recite:

> Just as the children of the conquerors did,
> I, too, shall accomplish [others' welfare].

Reciting this three times, perform the rite of rectification [of broken precepts]. [249] Then, having generated yourself as Buddha Śākyamuni, mark the three points of your body with the three letters. Place a clean container filled with pure and scented water in front of you and [visualize that] light radiates from the three letters and dissolves into the water, blessing the water [and transforming it] into the ambrosia of uncontaminated wisdom. Next carry a portion of the water to places in each of the four directions and, as you sprinkle the water, imagine that you are offering ablutions to the earth and water spirits who reside there. Then declare "As I wish to borrow earth and water from this place for the purpose of a spiritual endeavor, with your kind hearts please offer these to me joyfully and embrace this opportunity for [gathering] virtue."

After imagining that they respond, "Please take them with joy," take complete samples of the varieties of earth and water. If you cannot take samples from all directions, you can do so from a single place but from all its directions. When you have returned to your meditation chamber, place these samples in the correct directions without error. Then, making prostrations to all [higher beings], including your teachers and the three representations residing there, recite the following:

> Teachers and sangha members, pray listen to me. As for this great earth that supports everything, those from whom I have taken it are pleased. I have blessed all of them so that they will be endowed with good fortune. As for this water that gathers everything, those from whom I have taken it are pleased. I have ensured that it is free of pollution. Now there are no obstacles and adverse conditions anywhere. So, teachers and sangha members, please construct the celestial mansion.

If only one person brought [the earth and water], one recitation is adequate. If there are four [for example], each should recite this individually, one after the other. Then, at that very moment, all present should chant the following in unison:

Like a golden mountain, you are endowed with all perfect factors;[416]
You are the lord of the three worlds who has relinquished all three
.   pollutants;
You are the Awakened One, whose eyes resemble a fully blossomed
lotus—
This is the first auspiciousness that brings goodness to the world.

That which has been revealed by him, supreme, excellent, and
immutable;
That which is hailed in the three worlds and venerated by the gods
and humans;
The sublime among teachings that creates peace for all beings—
This is the second auspiciousness that brings goodness to the world.

The sublime Sangha is rich in the auspiciousness of spiritual
learning;
They are the objects of giving for gods, humans, and
demigods; [250]
Most excellent assembly, a bastion of self-respect and glory—
This is the third auspicious that brings goodness to the world.

Recite these lines up to three times.

After that, arrange torma cakes and offerings for the four guardian kings
in the four cardinal directions and a torma for the interfering forces as well.
Offer these in their correct order and assign to them their tasks. Then, once
you have engaged in the proclamations and cleansing, expel the interfering
forces as you send the torma for the interfering forces away.[417]

Next, everyone should visualize him or herself as Buddha Śākyamuni
and recite the three syllables *[oṃ aḥ hūṃ]* and the *maṇi* mantra. Then take
the good part of the earth samples that were brought, mix it with water,
including the water that was consecrated earlier, to make clay. Then, [work-
ing] from all four directions, make a platform. If there is an old platform,
then paste it from all four sides. If you are constructing [the mandala] on
a level floor, smear it with [fresh mud paste]. Then, as everyone recites *oṃ
svabhāvaśuddhā sarvadharmāḥ svabhāvaśuddho 'haṃ*, imagine that the
entire environment and the beings within it become empty. From within
this state, generate Avalokiteśvara of the inconceivable external world system. Within his heart generate Buddha Śākyamuni of the Endurance

World;[418] and within his heart generate Avalokiteśvara of the realm of Tibet. Within his heart generate Avalokiteśvara of your own abode, and imagine that it is within his heart that you are constructing the mandala. Then draw the lines in this manner:

Leaving space for the rainbows and lotus,
Draw the Brahmā line [first].
Divide this into four and mark these points;
Also mark a string that is equal to the length of two [parts].

To help find the tip of the Brahmā line,
Add one fourth [of the line] each [to this thread],
And placing the pivot half way to the east and west,
Make bird prints to the south and north.
In this way draw the second Brahmā line.

Then with a length [of string] that is half of the Brahmā line,
Hold the pivot at the tip of the Brahmā line,
And mark the four corners with bird prints.
In this way draw the diagonal and horizontal lines.

Then, over the three main lines,[419]
Draw four long lines and six shorter lines.
Again, just as with the earlier longer lines,
Excluding the middle part of the lines,
On the outside and inside link their two ends.

Of the two central lines, divide the inner into two halves
And the outer into four parts;
Again, just as with the earlier shorter lines,
Divide the first in half, the other half
Into another half, and the second into four parts,
Thus [together] drawing ten shorter lines. [251]

Then, if you wish to construct the fifteen mandalas
Together with their porticos,
Divide all the inner of the outer lines
Into four parts each and the two outer lines

Into half each thus making four;
Excluding the middle part on the outside and inside,
Link their two ends and so on; this is as on the outside.

If you draw the interior with no porticos,
On the inside from the outer lines,
Leaving a space of about one micro unit,[420]
Divide [the interior line] into three parts and the outside line into three.
As for the inside line, leave the middle and link the two ends.
Divide the outer line in half and each of these in half again;
Then, with shorter lines, divide
These into three parts
And divide the middle part in two.
The inside half is divided further by half,
While its outer line is divided into four.

[In] all instances where no space exists for [such size],
Draw [the draft lines] about one third in size, without porticos;
If this also does not fit, examine and draw [an appropriate size].
[Drawing] one, two, three, or four [petals] and so on,
Relate these with the teacher, the four divinities and so on.
The centers of all the four petals are [for the] four divinities,
While the hub is the teacher's celestial mansion.

Draw [the mandala] in this manner:

For coloring [the mandala], the hub of the lotus is white. As for the four petals: the east is yellow, the south is white, the west is dark blue, and the north is green. All those that are to be colored according to their directions should be done in this sequence as well. Place the goddesses in the grids and the four directional guardians at the four doors. On the corners and on the sides, draw numerous white reliquary stupas. On the outer perimeter draw a lotus with one thousand petals or however many petals you can fit. Surround this on the outside with the five colors of the rainbow. As for a [pearl] net of full and half loops, four leveled porticos, the wheel of Dharma, its lotus seat, and a parasol atop the wheel, draw these in accordance with the general custom.

Next, you should place the ritual articles. If enough vases are available, place six vases: one at the center with one on top of it and one in each of the four cardinal directions. Alternatively, you can arrange five vases—one at the center with one in each of the four cardinal directions. You can rely upon only a single vase at the center as well. All of these vases should be adorned with the five sets of vase substances, saffron, milky water, decorating symbols, and a mantra repetition string numbering four or one [corresponding to the number of vases]. Although some perform the rite with tormas and without using vases, it is taught that it is correct to do so with a vase. Then, according to your means, arrange five tormas for the teachers and the four divinities on top of the celestial mansion. Alternatively, arrange one torma for all, without distinction. [252] If this, too, is not feasible, rededicate the four tormas of the four directional guardians from the period of expelling the interfering forces and place these in the four directions. On the right, arrange one [torma] for the Dharma protectors in general, including especially the eight gods of the forces of light, and one for the Tenma protectresses. On the left, arrange one for the beings of the six classes and one for the local spirits. Prepare all of these as retaining tormas enriched with the three dairy products and three sweet substances. Arrange sixteen sets of the five articles of offerings, such as lamps, and place them all around [the mandala]. Arrange [also] in appreciably large numbers [bowls containing] scented water.

Then, however many practitioners there are who have previously received the oral transmission, whether it be a group of four fully ordained monks [or other groupings], they should perform the rite of generating the drops [after] going for refuge and generating the awakening mind. Holding the mantra repetition strings, they should engage in the rite of approximation. They should repeat [the mantras] of Buddha Śākyamuni in the east, of Avalokiteśvara in the south, of Acala in the west, and of Tārā in the north. If it is not possible to do this in all [the directions], repeat the mantras of all four divinities in whatever directions are feasible. However many monks there are who know the sutras and [the methods for] chanting should sing the rites for blessing the ground, the invocation, the praise hymns, the presentation of offerings, and so on.

These are the preliminary rituals pertaining to sustaining the neophytes, a detailed presentation of which is now complete.

B. THE MAIN PRACTICE, THE PRESENTATION OF SIXTEEN DROPS

Next, carrying scented water, a fully ordained monk wearing the yellow ceremonial robe should ask young boys and girls—sixteen, eight, twelve, six, four, or two in number—to wash [their faces and hands].[421] All the boys and girls don attire with the colors of the five buddha families or the colors of the four divinities. Alternatively, have the boys wear white attire and the girls wear green. Teach all the boys and girls how to make the various offerings, such as incense and so on, with all the offering articles facing toward the inside. As all of them see the mandala, ask them to make prostrations and circumambulations, which they perform as they enter [the room]. They should then prostrate three times to the master and, [253] repeating after the master, make the following supplication, reciting three times:

> All buddhas and bodhisattvas residing in the ten directions, pray attend to me. Master, pray attend to me. As I, known by the name…, seek to relinquish this cyclic existence fraught with defects and seek to attain the higher qualities of liberation, O master, reveal to me the path to this [goal].

To this the master should reply:

> You, who are known by the name…, do you desire to hear about the uncommon path that helps you cross the mire of cyclic existence?

After the master has asked this once, the students should then reply, reciting once:

> Yes, I seek this exactly as asked. So master, you who are endowed with a compassionate heart, for the sake of your compassionate heart, allow your heart to be compassionate toward me.

Then the master should respond:

> In the past the Buddha gave countless teachings, and thus there have come to be numerous spiritual traditions. We follow the great Atiśa, the buddha body of emanation. Atiśa possessed all the teachings of the lineages of the three teachers.[422] Although Khu, Ngok, and Drom are renowned as his three principal students, we follow in the footsteps of Drom, who is endowed with all the higher qualities of Atiśa. With respect to [Drom's teach-

ings], as well, there were three lineages that upheld his teachings; of these, ours is the inspirational lineage of practice. Starting with the teacher and his son, this [teaching] has been transmitted from ear to ear and from heart to heart through many great Kadam masters.

Dīpaṃkara and Avalokiteśvara;
Supreme wisdom possessor[423] and Sherap Gyal;
Shönu Gyaltsen and Naljorpa;
Rinchen Gyaltsen and his son;
Dharma Gyaltsen and his son;
Jangchup Sangpo, hailed as supreme—
[All] are hailed as extraordinary and supreme.

Thus, just as stated by Master Namkha Rinchen [in the homage above], this [instruction] has been transmitted through successive lineage holders in such a manner up to this day and is available for practice. Therefore, it is crucial to practice it.

Various procedures for the preliminary rites have already been presented above. In this context, again, with a deep wariness of the defects of cyclic existence and with admiration for the path to nirvana, you should, in accordance with the general procedure, undertake extensively [the practice of] taking refuge and generating the awakening mind. Alternatively, since the methods for training the mind have already been explained in detail earlier, [254] without entering into a long discourse here, [suffice it to say that] you could rely on an existing formula for going for refuge and generating the mind [such as the following]:

All buddhas and bodhisattvas residing in the ten directions, pray attend to me. Master, pray attend to me. All the buddhas and bodhisattvas residing in the ten directions and my master, please help me so that I, known by the name…, can go for refuge to the Three Jewels.

Make this supplication three times.

Again, using the same invocation and specification of timeframe as before, take the common refuge three times by reciting the following before each of the Three Jewels:

I, known by the name…, from this moment until the end of my
life, go for refuge to the blessed buddhas, supreme among the
biped humans. I go for refuge to the Dharma, tranquil and
supreme among those that are free of attachment. I go for refuge
to the noble Sangha, supreme among communities.

Next, make supplications to generate the awakening mind, reciting the following three times:

All buddhas and bodhisattvas residing in the ten directions,
pray attend to me. Master, pray attend to me. Just as the perfectly awakened buddhas of the past—those tathāgatas who
have destroyed the foe—and the great bodhisattvas who abide
in the great levels first generated the mind for perfect and full
awakening, O master, help me so that I, known by the name…,
will also generate the mind for perfect and full awakening.

Next, as for performing [the rite of] special refuge, "From this moment
until I reach the essence of enlightenment" indicates the timeframe. [You
should also make the following substitution:]

I go for refuge to the supreme community, the great Sangha of
noble bodhisattvas who are beyond the stage of reversibility.

Except for these two changes, the rest is the same as in the rite for the common [refuge practice].

Next, in order to generate the awakening mind, say, "Pray attend to me"
as before and [recite]:

Through whatever roots of virtue that I, known by the name…,
have created, encouraged others to do, or have rejoiced in, in
this life and in other lives—no matter whether these roots of
virtue performed were in the nature of giving, [255] in the
nature of morality, or in the nature of meditation—I will, from
this moment forth until achieving the essence of enlightenment, generate the mind for perfect and full great awakening,
just as the perfectly enlightened buddhas of the past—those
tathāgatas who have destroyed their foes—and the great bodhi-

sattvas who abide in the great levels first generated the mind for perfect and full awakening. I will liberate the sentient beings who are not yet liberated; I will release those who have not yet achieved release; I will grant relief to those who are unrelieved; and I will help those who have not yet attained total nirvana attain total nirvana.

In this way, generate the awakening mind three times.

Then, following your master's exposition of the sixteen drops, students should engage in their meditation. Train in them at a leisurely pace and ascertain them in your mind. When you arrive at the point of the mantra repetition, then perform the approximation rite in a thunderous voice. For those with the highest faculties, all sixteen drops are taught in one day; whereas, for those who are below the level of middling faculty, the sixteen drops are taught in a sequential order wherein one entire drop is taught per day.

1. THE DROP OF THE OUTER INCONCEIVABLE ARRAY

First, while reciting *oṃ svabhāvaśuddhā sarvadharmāḥ svabhāvaśuddho 'haṃ,* imagine that the entire world, including the environment and the beings therein, dissolves into emptiness. From within this sphere visualize your own mind [arising] as a white drop, which is bright and free of conceptuality, like a crystal egg or a mass of vivid light. If created it can generate all forms of emanations; if released it dissolves into the natural expanse. As this [light] extends horizontally and vertically, imagine yourself as an enjoyment body Great Compassion who is, in his nature, indivisible from Buddha Śākyamuni. From within this sphere, a white lotus, a lotus pervading wherever space extends, appears in front of you. Upon this generate a white *aḥ*, [from which] a moon disc of similar size appears. Upon this [moon disc] is a white *hrīḥ*. From this generate Avalokiteśvara, who has one thousand arms, one thousand eyes, and eleven heads. [256] His principal hand implements are the same as those within the general [depiction of the deity]. His body pervades wherever space extends. From the three letters at the three points of his body emanate light rays that bring about the welfare of sentient beings. All aspects of the mandala of his body, such as his pores, are filled with inconceivable buddhafields whose limits cannot be fathomed by anyone. Generate a limitless body, such as described in the *Jewel Casket Sutra.*[424] This is also known also as "the drop of the natural ultimate mode of being."

As you venerate this body by means of looking at it with devotion and reverence, he becomes utterly pleased. Imagine that you and all sentient beings, with no one left behind, enter through the wisdom door that has been spontaneously opened at his heart. Imagine this body to be the celestial mansion.

This is the first drop, *the drop of the outer inconceivable array.*

2. The drop of this Endurance World

Inside his heart, a white lotus appears from a white *pam,* and a moon disc cushion appears from a white *ah.* These two form the seat for all those who appear subsequently as well. Upon this [seat], the emanation body Buddha Śākyamuni appears from a yellow *om,* flanked by two attendants. He propounds the teaching of the four truths and, by sending emanations to many places, brings about their welfare. Numerous buddhas, bodhisattvas, noble disciples, and self-enlightened ones entirely fill the space around this palace. As light radiates from the three letters at the three points of their bodies, it touches the three points of the bodies of all beings of the six realms—including yourself—who are gathered there purifying the two obscurations as well as their propensities. All the bodies become unobscured and transparent like a crystal ball. In this place where rainbow tents abound in all directions, generate all other beings into Great Compassion with one face and two arms, holding a precious jewel rosary in their right hands and a lotus flower in their left. Light radiates from the three letters at the three points of each body, and from the tips [of these light rays] emerge uninterrupted masses of offering clouds for [the buddhas], including Buddha Śākyamuni, in particular. Then perform the seven limbs:

> I prostrate to this pristinely pure body,[425]
> Free of the duality of homage and an object of homage. [257]
> To the gods I offer the collections of pure offerings,
> Unsoiled by arising, abiding, and ceasing.
>
> I confess and rectify the ill deeds [casting me off] a deep abyss
> [Performed by] my three doors, devoid of arising, abiding, and
>   ceasing;
> As for those who, though empty, display diverse forms,
> I rejoice with admiration in these countless saviors.

Pray turn the wheel in the ultimate expanse
Of the emptiness of wishes and signs.
O dharmakāya, devoid of birth,
Being the nature of spontaneous abiding,
Pray do not depart.

I dedicate this so that through this virtue
All those of cyclic existence will realize this truth
And be led into such a celestial mansion.
May they experience this secret mantra.

I dedicate this so that they will immediately
Hail the supreme generation and completion [stages]
Of outer, inner, secret, and suchness,
Upon a seat of a refined moon
On the hub of a thousand-petaled lotus,
Just like the five deities of the action [tantra class].

This adventitious [world] does not exist
Separate from the ultimate expanse.
May the perfect auspiciousness
Of this perfect absence of separateness prevail.
May the auspiciousness of pristine lineage prevail!
Through purity in the beginning, middle, and end,
May the auspiciousness of unwavering prevail!

With these words composed by the spiritual guide [Dromtönpa], cultivate a deep sense of conviction. Furthermore, once you have made supplications for the fulfillment of your wishes, until you become weary, place your mind in single-pointed [awareness] and settle upon the deities that are clear and devoid of intrinsic existence. Atiśa states:

It has been stated in the scriptures:[426]
On a perfectly flawless mirror
The reflection of a form appears
Having no intrinsic reality.
Understand all phenomena in the same manner.

> Similarly, as I, too, share the same nature,
> My teachings are also within this nature—
> They too are false appearances.

As stated here, undertake the meditation.

When you become weary from this [meditation], rise by means of the five recollections. [Imagine] that all sentient beings, led by yourself, circumambulate the principal deity and recite *oṃ maṇi padme hūṃ* aloud in unison. Imagine that the obscurations are purified by the emission and withdrawal of lights. This is important. Even if you recite the *maṇi* mantra during all the drops, there is no contradiction. Given that it is this Endurance [World that is being cultivated], generating Buddha Śākyamuni is said to be excellent here. It is taught that there is also no contradiction in generating Avalokiteśvara with one thousand arms or with forty primary arms as the principal deity and reciting the *maṇi* mantra. [258]

Thus, having approximated [the principal deity] and circumambulated him, [imagine that] the principal deity is pleased. He opens the door of his heart, from which he emits a light ray that draws in all the retinue deities as well as all beings of the six realms, including you. As the outer ones dissolve into the hearts of the inner ones, the outer ones transform into a celestial mansion of light, which, in its nature, is the deities themselves, and which appears with colors similar to the [corresponding] deities. The upper part is *oṃ*, the east *ma*, the south *ṇi*, the west *pad*, the north *me*, and the lower part *hūṃ*. It is square, has four doors, and is adorned with four porticos. [It is transparent so that] from the outside the inside is clearly visible, and from the inside the outside is clearly visible. Stabilize this visualization.

Whereas a detailed description has been given here, in the subsequent [drops] the generation stage, with its seed syllable, principal deity and his retinues, and mantra, is different. However, in all other aspects of the rite, from [the generation of] the lotus and moon seats up to the dissolution into the heart, there is no variation from the rite described here.

This is the second drop, *the drop of this Endurance World* in particular.

3. The drop of the realm of Tibet

Inside his heart imagine our mountainous sphere. From a white *hrīḥ* generate Avalokiteśvara either with forty primary arms or with four arms. In this region of ours called Uru[427] [he] has manifested with one face and two arms, so it will a source of great blessing if you were to visualize [Avalokiteśvara] in the same form. In the past, the spiritual guide Rinchen Sal asked the Dharma king Drom himself for a method of visualizing him that is not found elsewhere. Drom suggested that he make offerings to Avalokiteśvara and advised, "Do not visualize him as Drom. I am [actually] like this." Saying this, he transformed [himself] into a *hrīḥ* on a lotus and moon disc, from which he appeared as a white youth in standing position. He had a smiling expression, and his body was slightly bent. His complexion was like polished crystal. His black hair was unbound and draped over his two shoulders. In his right hand he was counting the beads of a precious rosary of jewels, while in his left hand he held a white staff made of crystal. At the tip of this staff was a white lotus with one thousand open petals; upon its yellow stamen was a moon-disc cushion on which sat the Great Mother, holding her usual hand implements. On her right sat the teacher Dīpaṃkara, [259] while on her left sat Buddha Śākyamuni; though identical in nature they manifested distinct appearances. One thousand buddhas and also the buddhas and bodhisattvas of the ten directions sat upon the petals. From the three letters at the three points of their bodies, light radiated and dissolved into the spiritual guide Rinchen Sal. Exclaiming, "You, O man of treatises, have made the precious teaching of the Buddha extremely radiant," Dromtönpa conferred an empowerment upon him, making a great spectacle.

At that instant it occurred to the spiritual guide Rinchen Sal that: "Due to the kindness of my father Dromtönpa, I have received the empowerment of the Three Jewels. I am the principal son of the conqueror and his son. In the future, when father is no more, from whom can I receive such empowerments?" As these thoughts occurred to him, the spiritual guide [Dromtönpa] said: "Rinchen Sal, actual experience is better than [relying on] a future text. Nonetheless, until the root [of this teaching] is exhausted, the youthful bodhisattva upholds my victory banner.[428] You should rely upon him. There is no difference between him and me. Furthermore, though exposition is important, practice is more important, so emanate light from the three letters at the three points of your body, bless the three doors of your parents, and transform their bodies into bodies exactly resembling my own. He [Phuchungwa] also does the same."

Therefore, in this context you, too, should generate yourself as the principal deity with all his features and imagine being surrounded by a great retinue of buddhas and bodhisattvas. Then recite the essence *maṇi* mantra. As for the rest [of the practice of this drop], it is the same as the previous drop.

This is the third drop, *the drop of the realm of Tibet* in particular.

4. The drop of one's abode and the drawn mandala

Inside his heart, visualize your abode as a standing Avalokiteśvara with one face and two arms, as described earlier, who emerges from a *hrīḥ*. Here, too, recite the *maṇi* mantra. The rest [of the practice] is as before.

As a sand mandala is to be created within his heart, perform its rite of generation. The mandala is complete with all sixteen doors. If you wish to be elaborate, you can generate Avalokiteśvara of the external world, [260] Buddha Śākyamuni of the Endurance [World], Avalokiteśvara of the sphere of Tibet, and Avalokiteśvara of your own abode as standing at the four outer doors. Generate these [worlds] gradually in sequence, as before, and enter them. Again, beginning with the Great Mother, gradually enter the twelve remaining drops that are explained later. If, on the other hand, it is [a mandala with] a single door and so on, the outer ones reside inside the heart of the Avalokiteśvara that has been generated in your abode. Within his heart visualize the drop of the Great Mother and so on, as described later on [in the text], up to the drop of great awakening. Entering [the drops] in this manner is most convenient. As for regular daily practice, you should generate yourself into Avalokiteśvara as [portrayed] in your abode, and within his heart visualize the remaining drops, such as that of the Great Mother. The essence mantra is *oṃ maṇi padme hūṃ*.

This is the fourth drop, *the drop of one's abode and the drawn mandala*.

5. The drop of Perfection of Wisdom Mother

Inside his heart visualize the Great Mother, who is yellow and has one face and four arms. With her first right hand she performs the gesture of granting protection, and with her second [right hand] she holds a vajra. Her first left hand is in the gesture of meditative equipoise, and in her second she holds a scripture. Surrounded by a retinue of the buddhas and bodhisattvas of the ten directions, she recites aloud in a thunderous rhythm the sounds of the perfection of wisdom. Visualize this until you gain palpable ascertainment of [all phenomena] as being free of conceptual elaborations.

Here the essence mantra is *tadyathā oṃ gate gate pāragate pārasaṃgate bodhi svāhā*. Recite this mantra. Read aloud scriptures such as the *Perfection of Wisdom* as well. At this juncture you could also undertake the practices of those instructions that pertain to the meditative practice on the profound meaning of the perfection of wisdom, which you need to engage in.

This is the fifth drop, *the drop of Perfection of Wisdom Mother*.

6. THE DROP OF HER SON, BUDDHA ŚĀKYAMUNI

Inside her heart visualize the great Buddha Śākyamuni, who is surrounded only by a retinue of bodhisattvas on the ten levels.

Here the essence mantra is *oṃ muni muni mahā muniye svāhā*. Recite this mantra. At this juncture, if you have any other rites of the means of accomplishment of Buddha's emanation body, undertake their practices here. [261]

This is the sixth drop, *the drop of her son, Buddha Śākyamuni.*

7. THE DROP OF GREAT COMPASSION

Inside his heart visualize Avalokiteśvara with one thousand arms and one thousand eyes. Apart from his [two] principal arms, he holds various hand implements in his arms. He is surrounded only by a retinue of bodhisattvas on the ten levels.

The essence mantra is *oṃ maṇi padme hūṃ*. During circumambulations and so on, [imagine] you enter a pore of that Avalokiteśvara and that you see all the limitless pure buddhafields. Exiting from that [pore,] [imagine] that you again enter another pore and view [the buddhafields] in the same way. Exiting that, too, you glance at the principal deity's face with admiration and engage in circumambulations and so on. At this juncture, if you have other practices pertaining to the cycle of meditative practice of a bodhisattva that you need to undertake as well, you can do so here.

This is the seventh drop, *the drop of his son, the Great Compassion.*

8. THE DROP OF WISDOM TĀRĀ

Inside his heart visualize green Tārā with one face and two arms in accord with her general appearance. She is surrounded by a retinue of countless peaceful goddesses.

Here the essence mantra is *oṃ tāre tuttāre ture svāhā*. Recite this mantra. Praise her by means of the twenty-one-verse hymn as well. At this juncture, if you have other practices pertaining to the cycle of meditative practices of peaceful goddesses that you need to undertake, you can do so here.

This is the eighth drop, *the drop of Wisdom Tārā.*

9. THE DROP OF HER WRATHFUL FORM

Inside her heart visualize a dark green Tārā wearing bone ornaments and the attire of a wrathful deity, such as the skins of tigers, leopards, and humans. Shouting aloud *hūṃs* and *phaṭs*, she holds in her hands a *damaru* hand-drum, skull cup, cudgel, *khaṭvāṅga* staff, and so on. She is surrounded also by a retinue of numerous similarly wrathful goddesses, such as the frowning Bhṛkuṭī. Imagine that all of them are swaying in a dancing fashion.

The essence mantra here is *oṃ tāre tuttāre ture hūṃ phaṭ svāhā*. Recite this mantra. Alternatively, recite mantras of other wrathful goddesses. At this point, if you have other practices pertaining to the cycle of meditative practices of wrathful goddesses that you need to undertake, you can do so here.

This is the ninth drop, *the drop of her wrathful form.* [262]

10. THE DROP OF ACALA, THEIR IMMUTABLE NATURE

Inside her heart visualize a blue Acala with one face and two arms who glares with two bloodshot eyes. In his right hand he holds a sword, and with his left he gestures threateningly while holding a lasso. His right leg is bent, his right leg extended. Wearing a tiger-skin loincloth, he stands amid an army of [dancing] flames and is surrounded by a retinue of numerous wrathful deities.

The essence mantra is *oṃ caṇḍa mahā roṣaṇa hūṃ phaṭ.* Thus [recite] the mantra of the ten perfections. [Recite] *oṃ caṇḍa mahā roṣaṇa,* pray guard the teaching and sentient beings, guard them! *Oṃ sphoṭa sphoṭa mahā krodha chati chate sphoṭaya hūṃ phaṭ svāhā. Oṃ caṇḍa mahā roṣaṇa.* [Strike] the hearts of those who injure the teaching! *Māraya jaḥ jaḥ.* Expel! Expel! Split! Split! Burn! Burn! Grab their hearts! Split open their hearts! *Dhaṃ.* Split open [their] oath samāya! Split open their heart samāya! *Kri hai* strike at their hearts! *Oṃ* sever [the chain of] suffering. *Oṃ sphoṭa sphoṭa mahā krodha chati sphoṭaya hūṃ phaṭ svāhā.* Imagine that the deities and all sentient beings recite these mantras aloud in a thunderous rhythm and that all those who harm the teaching are destroyed en masse. If you have other wrathful deities that you need to meditate upon, you can do so here.

This is the tenth drop, *the drop of Acala, their immutable nature.*

11. THE DROP OF ATIŚA

Inside his heart visualize the lord Atiśa, whose reality is Buddha Śākyamuni, whose nature is the dharmakāya, and whose appearance is that of an enjoyment body adorned with crown ornaments and so on. Giving profound teachings in Sanskrit, he sways elegantly as if dancing. Before him are eight or four Buddha Śākyamunis in the appearance of enjoyment bodies. [Visualize that] there are the same number of Great Compassions to Atiśa's right, the same number of Acalas behind him, and the same number of Tārās to his left. Alternatively, you can visualize one of each of the four deities. In the southeast is Atiśa in the appearance of a learned paṇḍita; in the southwest is Drom; in the northwest Ngok;[429] and in the northeast Khutön.[430] Imagine that all the teachers of Atiśa, especially those of the three lineages, fill the entire space above and around them.

The essence mantra here is *oṃ muni muni mahā muniye svāhā,* or *oṃ maṇi padme hūṃ;* or you can also recite the essence mantra of all four divinities or that of the three buddha families. Here you should also visualize your own root teachers, who are embodiments of kindness, and reflect upon the guru yoga [practice] as well.

This is the eleventh drop, *the drop of Atiśa, the nature of all [deities].* [263]

12. The drop of Gyalwai Jungné

Inside his heart visualize the spiritual guide Drom, the Dharma king, in the appearance of an enjoyment body in dancing pose. His body, which is that of a sixteen-year-old youth, is clear as a crystal in which the Three Jewels are reflected exactly as they are. In each of his four directions are four youths, each emanated by and resembling [Drom]. Above and around him are Atiśa, Serlingpa, Avadhūtipa, and so on—teachers of method and wisdom, who surround him densely, like thick clouds, all reciting the profound words of the Buddha. Countless buddhas and bodhisattvas who reveal the profound teaching appear from their bodies and then, like clear clouds, disappear and depart into the interstices of a rainbow. All of them are engaged in playful dances that resemble the dances performed by Ḍākinī Guhyajñāna when the conqueror, his son, and numerous ḍākinīs gathered inside the heart mandala. Regarding this, read the story of prince Könchok Bang.[431]

For the essence mantra, recite *oṃ maṇi padme hūṃ.* Here, too, you enter into the pores of the emanation bodies, principally the spiritual guide [Dromtönpa], wherein you find numerous beautiful celestial mansions. The conqueror and his son reside there, too, revealing [Drom's] profound past-life stories. View the extraordinary places as Radreng, where extraordinary people who follow the conqueror and his son emanate inconceivable manifestations and are immersed in inconceivable meditative absorptions.

Listen insatiably to the profound teachings and, exiting [from the pores], once again gaze at the principal deity's face and so on.

This is the twelfth drop, *the drop of his son, Gyalwai Jungné.*

13. THE DROP OF THE VAST PRACTICE [LINEAGE]

Inside his heart visualize the conqueror Maitreya, either in his regal form from when he was enthroned as the successor to Buddha Śākyamuni or in the appearance of a fully ordained monk, without the yellow ceremonial robe but bearing the exemplary and noble marks. Everyone who walks in his presence [264] acquires the capacity to enter freely into the meditative absorption on loving-kindness. On his right is the great bodhisattva monk, the elder Gaganāmala, while on his left is the great bodhisattva monk Avalokiteśvara. Both of them are standing in a slightly leaning pose. Everywhere, above and around them, all of the teachers, from noble Asaṅga to Serlingpa, are present in the form of great bodhisattva monks. They recite the profound scriptures of the perfection of wisdom, and, while remaining unwavering in meditative equipoise realizing their meaning, perform the task of leading the spiritual trainees to the unmistaken levels and paths. Thus they engage spontaneously in the three wheels—the wheel of reading by means of study and reflection, the wheel of meditative practice by means of concentration, and the wheel of action by means of the activities. Imagine that they emanate numerous manifestations to the celestial god realms and so on.

The essence mantra is either *maitri* or *pāragate;*[432] it is taught that one can also recite *aḥ* [alone]. In this context, you should reflect upon the lineage of your teachers who teach the profound meaning of the perfection of wisdom; also, you should contemplate any pith instructions you might possess related to meditation on the profound meaning of the perfection of wisdom.

This is the thirteenth drop, *the drop of the vast practice.*

14. THE DROP OF THE PROFOUND VIEW [LINEAGE]

Inside his heart visualize Lord Nāgārjuna in the form of an emanation body with the hand gesture of teaching emptiness, the ultimate mode of being. As a pair of two principal disciples in the form of ordained monks, Atiśa is on his right and Avalokiteśvara is on his left. As for retinues, visualize all the lineage masters of the profound view, from Candrakīrti to Avadhūtipa, all in the form of fully ordained monks. Also at this point, visualize all the teachers who have taught you the meaning of the profound view of the Middle Way. All of these [masters] manifest diverse emanations and then disappear once again into the expanse of nonconceptuality. They reveal the teaching without language. Even when they do so through language, [they proclaim]:

> Free of reification and denigration of "is," "is not," eternalism, and
> nihilism;
> Free of going and coming, hopes and fears, and object and subject;
> Free of self and others, good and bad, and attachment and
> aversion—
> This expanse of drop beyond speech and words,
> This meditation upon the absence of letters,
> Is the meditative absorption of the tathāgatas.[433]

Imagine that the sound of these lines also echoes resoundingly from the environment, the skies, rainbows, lights, [265] lotuses, moon discs, and so on. As these sounds arise, the emanation bodies also depart by disappearing into the ultimate expanse. They reappear in the form of yellow drops, from which they display themselves vividly in the form of their respective bodies. Some manifest as enjoyment bodies and engage in the dance of wisdom. Visualize this.

For the essence mantra, you could either recite *aḥ* or *oṃ maṇi padme hūṃ*. If you have any other meditative practice on the meaning of the profound absence of all extremes, undertake its practice here. As you engage in the meditation and mantra recitation practice in this manner, imagine that Lord Nāgārjuna is pleased. He then exclaims, "Child of the family, as you have completed most of the dual accumulations, do you wish to see the buddhafield in the Akaniṣṭha realm?" Saying this, he opens the door of his heart and draws you into his heart by means of a lightbeam. This is the same as before [in the case of the previous drops].

This is the fourteenth drop, *the drop of the profound view.*

15. The drop of the inspirational practice [lineage]

Inside his heart visualize blessed Vajradhara, who is the embodiment of all secret tantras, all knowledge mantras, and all retention mantras. He is endowed with the inconceivable natures of body, speech, and mind and the enlightened attributes. Blue in color, he is in the form of an enjoyment body. Holding a vajra and bell in his two hands, his body is in a slightly leaning pose with his two legs crossed. He is adorned with various ornaments, such as a crown. At his sides is a pair of principal disciples as [described] earlier, both of whom are in the form of an enjoyment body, supreme heroes holding a vajra and bell in their hands. Visualize all the teachers of the inspiration [lineage], such as Tilopa, Nāropa, Ḍombhīpa, and so on, above and around them; visualize in particular the lineage masters of the *Jewel Garland*. [Visualize] also [that all of space] is filled with the vajra-holders, all of whom recite secret tantras and the profound retention mantras. Creating inconceivable mandalas within a single instant, they, in actuality, confer the four empowerments upon all beings, self and others. In brief, in accord with your mental capacity, conjure immeasurable offerings of meditative absorption; imagine that you please [the higher beings] through your offerings. Recite all appropriate secret tantra and profound retention mantras. Here, meditate also on all [deities] belonging to the enjoyment body class that you would like to practice, [266] and repeat their mantras. Now transform yourself into the nature of a deity and resolve decisively, "Having ceased all ordinary concepts, I will never deviate from the bounds of uncontaminated bliss."

This is the fifteenth drop, *the drop of the inspirational practice.*

16. The drop of great awakening

Again, imagine that, inside his heart, there is an extremely vast celestial mansion, higher than the previous ones, situated upon the lotus and moon seat similar to those [described] earlier. Its form is difficult to comprehend, even by the bodhisattvas on the ten levels. Imagine that all [aspects] of this utterly attractive and beautiful mansion are the inconceivable natures of the Buddha's untangled qualities—the ten faculties, the ten powers, and the four fearlessnesses. As for its nature, its reality is indivisible from the dharmakāya.

At its center, imagine yourself as the dharmakāya buddha endowed with uncontaminated wisdom. In appearance you are an enjoyment body, yellow and seated cross-legged in the posture of meditative equipoise. Immersed in meditative equipoise, not wavering from all enlightened attributes, abide in the great exertion-free sphere of the spontaneous accomplishment of all [aims]. Imagine that, from within this sphere, you manifest numerous emanation bodies and reside in this manner within the celestial mansion.

Then, inside the center of the heart of yourself as the principal deity, visualize a yellow drop about the size of a large mustard seed that is clear and bright as light. As it increases in size, visualize a precious jeweled container that is expansive and extremely high, utterly clear and radiant. Inside this, imagine your own mind, clear and radiant, in the form of a yellow drop the size of a pea. As this light, which flutters about as if [trying to] catch [something], increases in size, it becomes an ocean of drops with the color of refined gold and absolutely smooth. Its base is so stable that it could last until the end of space. It is vast and pervasive like space. It is so pervasive that it permeates every ordinary being and every noble one. Like the surface of a clean mirror, it reflects all forms. Visualize this. [267]

Place your mind in equipoise on this for a long time, and from within that sphere, visualize that the deities of the celestial mansion of the sixteen outer drops transform into drops of their individual colors. Sequentially they dissolve one into another, with the latter ones dissolving into the former ones. Finally, all the drops up to Vajradhara fuse into a single drop that is free of conceptual elaborations and that becomes the size of a pea. This dissolves into the *oṃ* of your crown, the *oṃ* dissolves into the *aḥ* of your throat, and the *aḥ* dissolves into the *hūṃ* of your heart. This in turn dissolves into the drop of [great] awakening. Then, within the sphere of the drop of indivisible emptiness and compassion, which is luminous and devoid of conceptuality, abide in meditative equipoise until you become weary.

When you are weary from [performing] this [meditation], once again, as you have done previously, generate a container from yellow awakening drops the size of mustard seeds and its ocean-like contents from yellow awakening drops the size of peas. From within this indivisibility of emptiness and compassion emerges a white drop that transforms into Avalokiteśvara. He is on the ocean of awakening drops—which resemble the surface of a mandala base made of polished, refined gold—like an ornament placed upon it. Visualize both the ornamented and the ornament as transparent in that each is reflected in the other. Likewise, visualize from one yellow drop Buddha Śākyamuni of the array of this Endurance World. You should also visualize other drops with colors corresponding to the individual deities from which the individual deities who reside [on this ocean] as [described] before appear. Furthermore, all the Three Jewels of the realms in the ten directions also transform into drops of colors corresponding to their individual colors. These are drawn into you through your crown, transform into their respective bodies, and reside on the ocean that is within you. Likewise, all sentient beings are blessed into white drops of enlightened activity; they are drawn into you, whereby they transform into Avalokiteśvaras and reside on the ocean of drops. Although all of them appear in the form of deities, they came into being from, are based upon, and are in the nature of the drop of the indivisible nature of bliss and clarity, which is the single taste of emptiness and compassion. Place your mind in the meditative equipoise [upon this scene] for as long as it lasts.

Again, these deities transform into drops of their respective colors and [268] merge indivisibly with the drop of awakening. Remain in equipoise on this, free of conceptual elaboration. When you become weary from [performing] this [meditation], too, visualize, as before, that they arise as drops of their individual colors from this basic drop. Visualize them as deities and place your mind on [the recognition] that they are apparent yet empty like rainbows. You should meditate in this manner alternating [between equipoise and subsequent practices]. For such an ocean of awakening drop, there is no occasion for requesting their departure; the drops of emanations and the enlightened activities are such that they share the nature of being emitted and withdrawn. However far one might go [in one's visualization], one never deviates from that [final] point.[434]

This concludes [the presentation of] the actual sixteen drops.

Alternatively, when you desire to undertake the practice of all sixteen drops in an integrated manner, as explained earlier, [meditate in the following manner]: from within the sphere of emptiness, upon a lotus and moon that you have generated, visualize your own mind as a white drop that transforms into an Avalokiteśvara of the external arrayed [world]. At his heart, on a moon and lotus cushion, visualize yourself in a meditative posture and seated cross-legged; in reality, you are the dharmakāya, and in appearance you have an enjoyment body. For generating the drops of the environment and the deities within it, do these as in the manner of the preceding [drops]. When visualizing the deities, you should also engage in such activities as making prostrations, offerings, and circumambulations, and reciting the essence mantras. As for the abodes of the deities, you can visualize these in the fashion of one temple complex with numerous smaller chambers with doors facing inward. Most importantly, you should place your mind in equipoise within the sphere of the indivisibility of emptiness and compassion.

If you wish to elaborate on this, you can visualize all the sixteen drops in colors corresponding to that of the deities, which, starting from the interior, emanate outward, as described before. Even if you wish to draw them in, as explained before, you should do so in a sequential order from the outside, with the outer dissolving into the inner. Undertake these two meditations [of emanating out and drawing in] alternately.

In this context when all the sixteen drops are being integrated into one, if you wish to practice guru yoga, visualize at your crown or at the center of your heart the teachers who are endowed with the three lineages or, particularly, the lineage teachers of the *Jewel Garland.* On the ocean of drops, visualize your root teacher. Above him, all the teachers are seated in sequence. Pay homage to them and make offerings. The earlier teachers dissolve into the later ones, [269] and finally even your own root teacher [dissolves] into the drop of awakening. Then place your mind in equipoise within the sphere of the union of emptiness and compassion. This is the supplementary section of guru yoga [practice]. If all of these are condensed, they are but elaborations from and the drawing in of the awakening mind. It is crucial, therefore, to ensure that [all these practices] become meditative absorption on the awakening mind.

Thus, together with the supplementary part, this is the sixteenth drop, *the drop of Great Awakening,* which marks the completion of the entry [into the sixteen drops].

C. The concluding rites

The concluding rites has five parts, of which the first, performing the dedication, is as follows.

1. Performing the dedication

Thus, having completed the meditation practices of the main session well, cease also the approximation [rites] and let the students drink from the vase water and use it for ablutions. Then, offer such substances as the three dairy products and the three sweet substances that are clean and attractive to the teachers, the deities, the Dharma protectors, and all the practitioners as well until they are satiated. After the students have offered whatever flowers they can obtain to the teacher, the teacher leads them in dedicating [the merits] as follows:

O teacher vajra-holders,[435]

As your wisdom and compassion are unobstructed,
Vajra-holders, pray attend to me.

Here in this mandala wherein one partakes at all three times
In the empowerments, generation and completion stages, and
     union,
Which are endowed with most excellent method and wisdom,
I dedicate [all these] toward the most supreme of the supreme
In order to fulfill your enlightened intentions.

For as long as space is not lost,
May I, together with the vajra-holders,
Thoroughly set in motion the wheel of feasts,
And may I be endowed with the two higher attainments.

The external environments are deities' mansions;
The beings within are the gods and the goddesses;
No impure perceptions arise.
May I thus abide by the two—method and wisdom.

All the buddhas of the ten directions and their children,[436]
Those who are indivisible from the teachers,
O bodhisattvas, pray listen to me.

I make dedications so that you—
Those who practice, in the three times, the two accumulations
Of powerful minds of aspiration and engagement—
May, with a single-pointed mind,
Draw forth our kind parents,
Who exist wherever space pervades,
So that they will traverse the ten levels to the [level of] no-more
     learning
And spontaneously accomplish others' welfare.

Until they arrive at this stage,
May they, through the blessings of the Three Jewels, [270]
No longer wander in samsara against their will,
But cycle through it by the power of supernatural feats.

May the desperate find relief;
May those tormented by heat be cooled;
May those tormented by cold be warmed;
May those tormented by hunger be sated.
May those tormented by thirst be satisfied;
May those tormented by sickness be healed;
May those who have died come to life.
May medicinal trees flourish;
May poisonous plants wither and dry out.

May I be a ship to travel across the seas;
May I be a bridge to cross the rivers;
May I be a mount for long journeys.
May I be a jewel that grants all wishes;
In fact, may I be any resource others desire,
Such as the cow that gives milk at will,
A pleasure grove, or a beautiful mansion.

May the poor who have no sons be cared for by sons;
May the rich who have no sons bear sons;
May they lead their sons to the Dharma.
May there be no war on this land;
May there be no violation of oaths and no immorality;
May there be no words of the eight dangers—
Enemies, robbers, venomous snakes, and so on.
May the rains fall on their time;
May the planets, stars, and so on
Be all excellent at all times.

You who abide in the ten directions and fulfill beings' welfare,[437]
Teachers and Three Jewels possessing wisdom and compassion,
With wisdom and compassion, pray attend to those seeking
  liberation.

Without leading the three doors astray in mere idleness,
Constantly engaging [in practice], day and night,
Through study, reflection, and meditation upon the conqueror's
  supreme path—

The excellent morality, the basis of all higher qualities throughout
　　the three times—
I dedicate this toward [becoming] an excellent savior of all my
　　parents.

Whatever excellent dual accumulations I might obtain,[438]
Which are virtuous in this life and throughout all the three times,
I dedicate all of it that is beneficial in the present and in the
　　long term
Toward the total fulfillment of others' welfare.

Recite these [dedicatory stanzas] three times.

2. Performing the aspiration prayer

Until the attainment of the body of a fully awakened Buddha,[439]
May we be adorned with the supreme faculties of higher rebirths;
May we never be assailed by birth, aging, sickness, and death;
And may we always be accustomed to the dual accumulations.

May we spiritual trainees be reborn spontaneously[440]
And purely upon a lotus blessed by conquerors
In the incalculable buddha realms.

In the myriad realms of the universe in all ten directions, [271]
However many flowers of five precious materials like this exist,
I offer all of these perfect flowers to the deities.
In this life and throughout the lives of all around me,
May the light of the Dharma shine brightly inside these flowers;
May they be opened and nurtured by the conquerors.

May my own life resemble the petals of the lotus—
Pure and untainted, may it attain perfection.
May my life resemble a mandala of crystal glass—
Perfectly smooth, refined, and utterly clear.

May my life resemble a golden reliquary—
May it become a great wonder, ceaselessly captivating.

May my life resemble the mandala of the sun—
Dispelling darkness with no conceptualization.

May my life be like a wish-granting jewel,[441]
Fulfilling the aspirations of all beings.
From now on throughout all lives
May I uphold my teacher's exemplary life without slackening;
May I illuminate the precious life of the Buddha
And, through pure conduct, spread it to the limits of all directions.

May everything be excellent at the beginning, in the middle, and at
    the end;
May we be nurtured always by those bound by solemn oaths;
For the sake of benefit and happiness, may we always bring the
    sixfold recollections to mind
With single pointedness and without separating from them.

Throughout all lives,[442]
Obtaining a perfect life of leisure and opportunity,
May I honor the Three Jewels with my three doors
Through paying homage and making offerings.

Purifying nonvirtues with the full presence of the four powers,
May I rejoice in all the virtues.
May my exhortations
To have the wheel of Dharma turned be heeded.

As for those who intend to display passing into nirvana,
May my appeal for them not to do so be effective.
May all my dedications and all that I have aspired for
Be realized the instant that I wish for them.

Thus make aspirations up to three times.

3. PROCLAIMING AUSPICIOUSNESS

The jewel garland is [made] of golden beads;[443]
This utterly beautiful garland is the noble ones' ornament;

It resides in those with pure minds;
May it remain victorious, free of letters.

This is the Sage's path for those who follow me;
It is the supreme jewel unsullied by stains;
Through the three baskets and four divinities,
May it remain victorious and satisfy our mental continuums.

The three scopes and the three divine teachings,
Integrating all these into a single sitting,
Without giving in to mundane aspirations of this life—
May I be victorious on a lasting secure ground. [272]

The lotus ground of ethical discipline,
Encircled by a fence of the four immeasurable thoughts,
Supported by pillars of the six mothers of the conquerors[444]—
May it ultimately be victorious in the long term.

Fortified by levees of the antidotes,
Unharmed by the flames of what is to be relinquished,
And with the shining rays of the sun and moon of dual
    accumulations—
May nonconceptual wisdom be victorious.

In the swamps of this Endurance World's desire,
Most excellent lotus unsoiled by such mires,
Most virtuous, both day and night—
May such pure liberating life be victorious.

On this expansive surface of earth,
May I not fall into the abyss of false views,
Which bring more loss than gain—
May the precious Kadam remain victorious.

From the merits of contaminated virtuous karma,
The foliage of uncontaminated wisdom blooms;
That which gives forth fruits, excellent at all times—
May profound karma and its effects remain victorious.

Without wavering from Perfection of Wisdom Mother,
Unfettered by expectations and greed,
Whatever outer or inner giving I might undertake—
May this most excellent and precious auspiciousness prevail.

Untainted by desire for rebirth and by self-interest,
May the cooling stream of the virtues of my three doors
Always remain uninterrupted;
May this most excellent and precious auspiciousness prevail.

Free of contempt, prejudice, and hostility,
Whatever helps to endure the hardships of samsara,
Whatever heroic armor of compassion I possess—
May this most excellent and precious auspiciousness prevail.

That which instantly advances
All the wishes of mother sentient beings,
The auspiciousness of joyful perseverance—
May the auspiciousness of accomplishing all these prevail.

As for the countless meditative absorptions,
Which are neither meaningless nor useless,
Partaking in these without clinging and obstructions—
May this precious auspiciousness prevail.

Lucidly illuminating all fields of knowledge,
Individually differentiating and integrating them,
Whatever auspiciousness there is in this auspicious truth—
May the auspiciousness of accomplishing all these prevail.

Whatever virtuous acts one performs become successful—
May this precious auspiciousness prevail.
Once one has reached an excellent path, one does not revert—
May this auspiciousness of stability flourish.

May teachings be revealed for the sake of guiding each living
    being—
May this auspiciousness prevail.

Beginning with this conduct of mine,
May whatever deeds I engage in
Become perfect examples for others, and thus,
May the auspiciousness of spiritual companionship prevail.

Beginning from this auspiciousness
Until the ultimate auspiciousness is attained,
May the auspiciousness of spiritual guides
Who lead beings through the four means prevail.

Until cyclic existence is emptied,
May my glory be seen and felt, [273]
And, like space, pervade everywhere—
May the auspiciousness of opening liberation's door prevail.

The auspiciousness in which all auspicious facts have converged,
This [great] ocean of auspiciousness
Is profound, vast, and perfect—
May the auspiciousness of auspiciousness always prevail.

Recite these [verses] many times.

4. PLEDGING NEVER TO DEVIATE FROM SUCH PERFECT DIVINITIES AND TEACHINGS

The students should make three prostrations to the master and, with their palms folded, [recite the following]:

Having protected us from the defects of both cyclic existence and [isolated] peace, you have introduced to us the sevenfold divinities and teachings. Holding us in your heart drop, you have placed us on the path to unexcelled enlightenment and have thus enhanced us. This is most kind indeed. You are the principal son who embodies all the spiritual guides of our tradition, endowed with the three lineages. With respect to divinities, we admire the four deities who are, in their nature, all the conquerors' children. For our teaching, we pursue the meditative practice of the three higher trainings together with their expressions [as embodied in the three baskets]. For our Dharma protectors, we rely on the eighty white guardians and the twelve Tārās. Just as our teacher Dīpaṃkara and his son gave instructions pertaining to [the sevenfold] divinities and teachings in the past, we, too, undertake their practice. We pledge that we shall never deviate from meditating [upon them] at the center of our hearts.

Recite this one time. In response, the master should recite:

O fortunate ones, it is most excellent that you are engaging in practice in this manner. It is important too that, in relation to me, you imagine me as [the embodiment of] the conqueror and his son and, with respect to relating to each other as well, cultivate pure perceptions alone. On my part, I take you all as suitable vessels and as my principal sons and bequeath the sevenfold divinities and teachings to you. Therefore, it is vital that you undertake its practice just as the teacher Dīpaṃkara bequeathed it to Drom in the past.

Master Atiśa states:

Though, like space, you pervade everywhere,[445]
You are manifest only in this northern region
Where you perform the conduct of a hermit.
You, Avalokiteśvara, are my eldest son.

Your physical arrays fill the entire world;
Though there are numerous buddhas, they are all you;
You are the buddhafield Densely Arrayed.
You are the eldest among my sons.

I have conferred upon you all secret empowerments;
You have constructed the mandala within. [274]
Do not sell these as merchandise
But engage with the actual truth. This I bequeath to you.

I have given you the training in morality;
So, with interest and without transgressing the discipline

Or defying the law of karma and its fruits,
Enjoy the ultimate mode of being. This I bequeath to you.

I have given you the training in mind;
Set those with good karma to [working for] others' welfare alone;
Though spending time only in pursuit of others' welfare,
Enjoy the ultimate mode of being. This I bequeath to you.

While seeming to contradict [the teachings] without [actually
    doing] such,
Endeavor single-pointedly in the practice
Through meaningful study, reflection, and meditation.
This conduct of mere appearance I bequeath to you.

No matter what fields of knowledge you are versed in,
Do not allow your exposition to deviate from the meaning,
But practice them with a single-pointed mind.
This is what I bequeath to you.

Saying these [verses, Atiśa] gave instructions for the practices to be primary
and sealed [his instruction] so that it would not be revealed to unsuitable
vessels. Atiśa states:

There is nothing not contained in this essential point.[446]
This is the most excellent and sublime wealth.
I have revealed this wealth to you with affection;
Do not publicize this in the marketplaces.

Though this realm is yours,
Not all of them are your people.
If you speak of this to nonhumans,
The forces of Māra, unable to bear it, will rise up
And will demolish your chariot.
Nurture this tradition as [a heart] drop so that it does not decline.
Even though the spokes [of its wheels] may extend up to a yojana,
These nonhumans [malevolent forces] will not uphold their axles;
So these [nonhumans] will denigrate the rim and the spokes.
They'll find no nails [to hold up the chariot] before setting out;
Even when nails are found, they'll not hammer them in;

I fear that this degenerate era might pull apart your chariot.
This is my heart counsel, so listen, Drom Jé.

If, in such a manner, even an emanation body like Drom, who possessed unobstructed superior cognition, has been instructed with a seal never to reveal [this teaching] to others, how is it that we, on the other hand, should reveal this to others? Therefore, [the master should] admonish [the students] to strive hard only in their own personal practice.

5. REQUESTING [THE DIVINITIES] TO DISSOLVE INTO THE SPHERE OF THE GREAT DROP

All the materials [of the mandala], like the colored sands, [275] should be taken to a clean place, to a river, or to the summit of a high mountain; it is important that no traces remain visible. Sustained by the performance of such a rite, cultivate the essential points of the meditative practice by means of [following a] manual.[447] It is important to expound *The Book [of Kadam]* extensively and relate its profound meanings to meditative practice. Having received the oral transmission of such a meditative practice, it is important to strive in the meditative practice of the drops whenever possible, whether for a single day or more.

Words and conventions are devoid of reality;
Their contents are devoid of real drops.
Since things and their ultimate reality are of a single taste,
This is the drop free of language and meaning.

Therefore, the teachers also cultivate
This profound meaning in the elaboration-free sphere,
In the ultimate expanse without letters;
Likewise, the absence of letters is most supreme.

Today if one is devoid of sound's resonance,
The sound of letters of mere appearance,
The drop of union's ultimate expanse will not be realized;
It is scribed in the great letters of nonduality.

Whatever faults there may be in putting
The hidden ear-whispered meanings into letters,

Out of a pure heart, I seek forgiveness for this
From the teachers and guardians of the sacred words.

Through purification of faults and obscurations,
May I never be divorced, in this and future lives,
From the teachers, deities, and guardians of the sacred words;
Blessed and guarded, may I traverse the paths.

Through this virtue may the bodies and minds
Of myself and all others be encircled
By the precious sevenfold divinities and teachings—
The true teaching and the sovereign [Buddha] himself—
And may we gain victory in the battle against the afflictions.

In the deities' celestial mansions of radiant light,
May we never be divorced from the teachers and deities;
May we abide there with all dear mother sentient beings;
May the auspiciousness of great bliss always prevail!

As for this distilled essence of all the sacred words of the conqueror and his
son, the jewel ocean of the most profound and vast Kadam, an instruction
on how to practice the [sevenfold] divinities and teachings, which is the
principal [teaching] of the three lineages, the method for enhancing the
two awakening minds within the sphere of the great drop—this hand-led
guide to the heart drop, the profound path transmitted through upholders
of hidden conduct alone—all the essential points of the words of the previous teachers as found in the older literature are present within this. It is
a teaching that elucidates the conqueror's approach in terms of its stages of
implementation [into meditative practice] on the basis of relating these to
citations from the teachings of the conqueror and his son as found in *The
Book [of Kadam]* alone. [276] These words entitled, "Sun and Moon Drops
of the Union of Empty Echoes," which illuminate the inseparable abiding
of the land of the fortunate ones within the ocean of drops, have been composed at the glorious Narthang, a space for the precious Buddha's teaching.

Oṃ oṃ maṅgalaṃ kuru oṃ oṃ.
May goodness and auspiciousness prevail!
Ithi!

Part Two
The Son Teachings

V. The Spiritual Mentor's Birth as the Brahman Youth Ujjvala

[277] WHEN ATIŚA and his son were residing in Yerpa on the crest of Mount Lhari Nyingpo, Ngok Lekpai Sherap made the following plea to Drom Gyalwai Jungné: "For three years you, the conqueror and son, have taught the most profound and inconceivable teaching. This uncommon and unique [teaching], in twenty-three chapters, is called the *Jewel Garland of Dialogues*. In it, you state:

> **Discard all lingering doubts**
> **And strive with dedication in your practice.**[448]

"So how did you discard all lingering doubts and strive in meditative practice in the past? Pray with an affectionate heart, do tell me."

In response, Drom replied: "I am a childish ordinary being, chained by so many fetters. How is it possible that I have relinquished all lingering doubts? As I have no supernormal cognition, it is also difficult to reveal to you how I might have dedicated myself to meditative practices in the past. So, although I may not have discarded all lingering doubts and striven with dedication in meditative practices, it is clear that, in general, for those who desire liberation, it is necessary to discard all lingering doubts and strive with dedication in the meditative practices."

As Drom spoke these words, Sangphuwa[449] made three prostrations to Atiśa and appealed: "This Gyalwai Jungné conceals all his higher qualities and does not reveal them, so please, teacher, speak to us about some of his qualities. He does have higher qualities, and you, the teacher, do not resort to exaggerations or denigrations. By hearing his qualities we will cultivate faith and reverence. This could also benefit future sentient beings as well. So, teacher, please do reveal [his higher qualitites] to us."

Atiśa replied: "The entirety of his higher qualities resembles a treasury of precious jewels. His qualities are so great that they are difficult to contain in others' minds, so you should not speak of them to others. [278] For your own retention, I shall explain a few, so listen."

Gyalwai Jungné exclaimed: "Given that there are profound teachings for you to teach that are auspicious in the beginning, middle, and end, what purpose is there, O sublime teacher, in presenting the numerous ways in which I wandered in cyclic existence? Instead, if those future beings who are unruly and whose soil of faith has been blown away by the bellows[450] of false understanding approach you with the expression 'well, in that case,' it is more appropriate for you to reveal the profound teachings, as I have requested before. Please do not bring my heart out into the open."

Ngok interjected: "O spiritual mentor, I am not someone with a big mouth and a small brain. Leaving five hundred monks behind, I have come here to sever [the ropes of] my lingering doubts; so even if you won't tell us, please do not prevent Atiśa from teaching us. Look at my head and my wrinkles as well and sustain me with your heart. Pray, sustain me with your heart!"

Hearing this objection, the spiritual mentor dared not say anything. Then, in a raised triumphant voice, Atiśa said, "Lekpai Sherap, you are right. I have decided to speak. Yet, since this is a heart counsel of us three—father and sons—alone, do not spread this to others." Saying this, Atiśa told the following tale:

"In the town of Kapila, there once lived a brahman named Sujata who was most learned in all disciplines of the brahmanical knowledge of the Vedas.[451] He had a wife called Manoramā to whom a son was born. From an early age, he was intelligent and acted like an adult. The mother exclaimed, 'He behaves like a grownup and he is highly intelligent. Definitely, he must be someone with special karma. It seems as if he naturally deserves his name Ujjvala [the luminous one].[452] He must be taught all the Vedas.'

"So both parents taught him the Vedas, and he learned them without any difficulty. Thus, after seven years had passed, he became a brahman learned in all the Vedas and a source of wonder for everyone. At that time all the brahmans who were well versed in the Vedas gathered in Kapila to debate the Vedas, but no one was able to defeat the brahman youth Ujjvala, so the brahmans inquired, 'How are you so learned in the Vedas at such a young age?'

"The youth replied, 'I have the fully awakened Buddha as my teacher,

[279] the sublime Dharma as my refuge, and the noble Sangha community as my savior. Through the force of being blessed by the Three Jewels, I am convinced of the law of karma. Therefore, I am not plagued with doubts and do not squander the fruits of past actions but strive in the virtues. This is why, even though I am young, I have become versed in the Vedas.'

"As he spoke these words, they concurred, 'Judging by the manner of his speech, he is certainly an emanation. We cannot debate with him.' Saying this, they dispersed and left.

"Then the youth Ujjvala went where his parents were. His parents asked, 'Did you achieve the fame of being versed in the language of the Vedas today?'

"The youth replied, 'Parents, due to the Three Jewels being the dominant condition, yes, this has come to pass.'

"His parents then asked, 'Why is it that you possess the excellent condition of the Three Jewels?'

"The youth responded, 'The Three Jewels are concerned solely with the welfare of sentient beings, and I have conviction in karma and its effects, so these [two] auspicious conditions have come together.'

"His parents asked, 'Who taught you about this profound law of karma?'

"The youth replied, 'Once in this town of Kapila, when the prince known as Siddhārtha revealed himself as the son of Śuddhodana, I was the brahman youth called Prakāśa.[453] One day, as I was standing at the town's gate, the prince, who was surrounded by a retinue of countless ministers, arrived at the gate and we came face to face. The prince then said, "O brahman youth, all effects resemble their causes; none violate this law, so do not stand idle at this gate to the town. Because the mighty [afflictions] were slain by ethical discipline in the past, today you have been born as a human, so be endowed with morality today as well. In the future you will become a brahman youth called Ujjvala who will act wisely in accord with the law of karma. Harboring no doubts with regard to the truth and falsity of karma and its effects, you will undertake the meditative practices and will not deviate from [working for] the welfare of sentient beings."

"The parents, realizing that he was indeed an emanation, asked, 'Will you remain at home and pursue others' welfare? Or will you become a renunciate monk and pursue the welfare of sentient beings?'

"The youth replied, 'O parents, living at home is like [being in] a fire pit. Without finding a secure base oneself, how can one rescue others? [280]

Being a renunciate is like being in a cool chamber; one can rescue others who have fallen into a fire pit. O parents, if I remain at home and am caught in the mires, [it would be as if] no son was born to you. I will fail to find a secure ground myself, and I will fail to rescue you two as well. And if I am unable to rescue other sentient beings, there will be no purpose to my having obtained a human existence. This life of leisure and opportunity would [then] become meaningless.'

"'His parents responded: 'There are two ways of pursuing the welfare of sentient beings: there is the lay bodhisattva and the renunciate monk bodhisattva. Ujjvala, in this town known as Kapila, where there are four different castes and eighteen different categories of crafts, the humans here are blessed by a spiritual king, and thus there are numerous individuals who are wealthy. The foundation of faith is strong, and because of this, there are many fields for accumulating merit. Due to the power of this, there is a great respect toward those who are learned. In particular, those of us with the brahmanical knowledge of the Vedas are pure and excellent. Therefore, Ujjvala, remain here [at home] and pursue the welfare of sentient beings. For protection and refuge, you can seek the Three Jewels. Since you are versed in the language of the Vedas, you are free of ignorance and can, without satiation, enter the path, engage in the perfections, such as generosity, and partake in the experiences of the levels and the paths as well as higher qualities of the other shores.'

"'The son replied: 'What you parents say is true. In general, there are two systems of spiritual practice—that of the insider and of the outsider. As for the outsider's teaching, it should be shunned, though one needs to have the knowledge of it. With regard to the insider's teaching, it is of benefit both to the wider community and to the individual. Its excellence is indicated by [the fact that] it cannot be contained in the minds of outsiders or those who are base. Therefore, the teaching of the insiders must be affirmed, and one needs to have its knowledge. This is twofold: the Great Vehicle and the Lesser Vehicle. The Lesser Vehicle refers to the teachings of the disciples and the self-enlightened ones. Even these two are most profound compared with the teachings of the outsiders. Abandoning the countless parents who have been most kind and abiding principally in the pursuit of one's own peace and discipline reflects little conscience and is shortsighted. However, even though they are to be shunned, they must be known. As for the Great Vehicle, even if one undergoes the unimaginable sufferings of the six classes of births in cyclic existence for the sake of all sentient beings, who have all been one's parents, since one perceives all of them as devoid of intrinsic existence by means of the three levels of understanding, one will never deviate from [the pursuit of] their welfare. He is the son of the buddhas. This is the [true] path. [281] Compared to pursuing the practices of the disciples and self-enlightened ones for an eon, a single instance of this [Great Vehicle path] accrues greater merit. One must affirm this, and, therefore, must have its knowledge as well.

"'This [Great Vehicle] is twofold: the Middle Way and the Mind Only.[454] The Middle Way, in turn, is twofold: the Mere Appearance Middle Way and the Utterly Nonabiding Middle Way.[455] The Mere Appearance Middle Way establishes as false the phenomena that are [actually] false. They present this by means of the eight similes of illusion, such as dreams and so on. Here [too], since both what is being presented and the means by which it is presented are deceptive objects and subjects, they are to be abandoned. However, they must be known. As for the Utterly Nonabiding Middle Way, they state that whether the buddhas appear or not, the ultimate reality of all phenomena is utterly nonabiding. Therefore, one should affirm and know this [school] as well. The Mind Only [view] is twofold: those who propound appearances to be true and those who propound them to be false.[456] Although, compared to the Utterly Nonabiding Middle Way, both of these are mistaken, they must be known nonetheless.

"'Alas! Parents, such is the ultimate mode of being of all phenomena. When analyzed they do not abide at all, so if I remain at home, I will delight in the extremes of elaborations of many arising and subsiding conceptualizations. I will become involved in many chores. This is, in general, the defining characteristic of a samsaric being and, in particular, the character of a householder. O parents, am I not called the brahman youth Ujjvala? If I do not see [things] in this light, I will then be in darkness. Among the householders, those from Kapila [are from] a large town. There are many people and they delight in distractions. There are many who, due to the influence of their friends, have become just like the others. I am young, have an attractive appearance, and have a reputation for having a clear mind. Since both of you parents love me, it would be inappropriate if others were to lead me into the afflictions. Therefore, I seek to sever all lingering doubts that impede accomplishments and strive with dedication to achieve [the state of] Buddha, the lord of the world, which is the most perfect fruit.'

"His parents asked, 'Son, if you are to become a renunciate monk, where do you wish to do so? Which preceptor and master of ceremony do you

wish to receive the vows from? Where will you seek a wilderness in which
to strive for cultivating Buddha, the lord of the world? [282] If, in order to
go to beyond the edge of the town of Kapila, you go elsewhere to a great
distance such as a mountain or a cliff, we two will be deprived of our son.
You are like our eyes; if you stay too far away we will become blind. You
are like our heart; if you go away we will be like the dead. You are like our
limbs; if you go away we will be like the lame. O Ujjvala, since you meditate on all sentient beings as your parents, we are your parents who reveal
themselves in [this] body, so why do you make us suffer?'

"Ujjvala replied: 'You two are right. One's native land is said to be like
the house of Māra. In particular, one's home is like a dungeon in a prison.
It robs you of the life force of happiness. Mundane norms are a massive
chain of bondage; they prevent you from journeying to the place of liberation. Sense objects are like poisons; for the moment they are delicious in
your mouth, yet in the long run, they rob you of your life. O parents, there
is no place here in this town of Kapila for me to dispel doubts and engage
in meditative practices. I will seek a place that will enhance meditative
practice. O my parents, if I am like your eyes, then eyes should look at
forms. If they do not see forms, it is like not having eyes at all. O parents,
having lived at home, I have failed to see the defects of cyclic existence and
the benefits of nirvana. This is like not having eyes at all. Since I am like
your heart I should serve the function of a heart. Since I am like your limbs
I should serve the function of the limbs. Without a heart and limbs, you
will be like a stuffed body with no limbs at all. O parents, I will be the heart
that will keep firm the life of liberation. I will be the limbs that bring forth
the benefits of nirvana. O parents, please be my peerless guides and take
me to a place of solitude, a place where there are spiritual mentors.'

"As he made this request, his parents exclaimed:

> O Ujjvala, you who are like our eyes:
> You have said, 'I will go to a place of solitude,'
> And you have asked us to be your guide and take you
> To a place where there are spiritual mentors
> So that you can strive in meditative practice and sever all doubts;
> In that case, engage in the virtues here. [283]

"As his parents spoke these words Ujjvala replied: 'O parents, however
much I speak I will end up speaking nothing but words of bondage. It is

clear that the excellent purpose is not going to be revealed, so whether it is in the center of Kapila town, in the marketplace, at the town's crossroads, or in the pleasure gardens, I shall, while enjoying the pleasures, ask any person who comes along where the places are where spiritual mentors [can be found] and where the perfect places of solitude are.'

"In response, his mother exclaimed:

> Son, in this joyful town of Kapila,
> Countless emanations of buddhas have appeared.
> They look after those spiritual trainees who have the karma;
> Joyfully, they engage in the Dharma today.
>
> O son Ujjvala, without falling prey to the afflictions,
> And without falling under the influence of evil friends,
> Pray ask them where spiritual mentors reside.
> They, too, will proclaim that they are your parents.

"As she spoke these lines, Ujjvala replied: 'Today the truth of the Three Jewels has been propagated. I have made supplications to the special objects [of veneration] and have made pure aspiration prayers for the benefit of sentient beings as well. Thus, wherever I go, if the emanation beings exclaim, "Your spiritual mentors are your own parents, so discard all lingering doubts and engage in meditative practices right here [at home]," I will then do exactly as you, my parents, have advised. If I am told, however, that my spiritual mentor and my place [of practice] are elsewhere in one of the cardinal or ordinal directions, I will then go to that place. Why? Because the ability of the Three Jewels is potent indeed, and it never deviates from the right moment when the time has come to guide a person of good fortune.'

"One day, in the morning, he went to a lake known as 'the hovering geese,' which lies to the south of Kapila town. There he saw several hundred youth who were enjoying themselves near the lake, who exclaimed:

> O youth, attractive and most beautiful to behold,
> Soft and smooth-skinned, you have a body of gold;
> Serene and intelligent son of a brahman,
> Your body resembles polished gold.

We, an auspicious assembly of several hundred [284]
Young men and women, have come here,
So whatever you desire, O most excellent one,
We will seek it without any obstruction.

Come here regularly for enjoyment.
Here green meadows and colorful flowers blossom;
The birds that sing melodious songs
Flock here joyfully to mate and to honor you.

Many learned ones also come here;
They venerate you with pure words.
From amid dense clusters of clouds,
Numerous gods joyfully emerge,
Carrying varied offerings
And venerating you with devotion.
They live in accord with our way of life.
Before meeting you, they thought nothing of you.

Now, having met you, they are saddened when you leave.
Therefore, we will make real what you say.
We will reveal in words whatever is needed,
So indulge with us in joy and bliss.

"Ujjvala responded:

O you hundreds of young men and women,
Who have [attained] the fruits of past causes of higher birth,
With a joyful presence, here in this place,
You praise me with delight; this is wondrous.

O assembly of youths whose minds are clear and endowed with
    reason,
The playful games of the afflictions,
Which do not turn into the path to liberation, are the debris of
    karma.
Therefore, engage in illusory things, which appear and are empty,
[A pursuit] that benefits the entire world.

Rely on an excellent teacher;
It is happier to associate with liberating friends.
Indulge in playful games in liberation's garden
Where the lotus grove of bliss thrives.

How joyful! O all you youths with clear minds.
What is the joy of gods and humans?
It's enhancing the virtues of the three doors.
What is the most excellent path to liberation?
It's to strive for the sake of others.

What is the conduct of the heroes?
It's to take afflictions into the path.
What is the taking of afflictions into the path?
It's to stir up the objects of abandonment with the antidotes.

What is the most excellent antidote?
It's to directly encounter the objects of abandonment.
What is the direct encounter with the objects of
  abandonment?
It's to destroy them the instant they arise.

"'O youths, the words I have spoken here constitute speech that is virtuous both in the present and in the long term, so, without entertaining any doubts, strive with dedication in the meditative practices. O youth, how many animals are there in the town of Kapila? Compared to them, how many human beings are there? Among the humans, how many do you see who accumulate merit?'

"The young men and women replied, 'O man of high qualities. In this town of Kapila, there are so many animals. [285] Humans are numerous, too, but they number about one twentieth of the animals. [Among the humans,] those who accumulate merit are also about the same proportion. O son of a brahman, what we see is evident to you as well. As we have no supernormal cognition, we dare not say anything other than that.'

"Ujjvala responded, 'O youths, if those who practice Dharma are so rare, will you remain idle? Not only that, will you encourage me to become heedless? O youths, be sure that you make your obtainment of human existence meaningful.'

"The youths asked, 'Where is your home? What are your parents called? Are you familiar to the king's ears?'

"Ujjvala replied:

> My town is to the north of Kapila;
> Born of the brahman caste, learned in all the Vedas,
> [My father,] Sujata, is unrivaled in all fields of knowledge.
> Known as Manoramā, there is a lady with a clear mind,
> Whose learning in all the Vedas is beyond dispute.
> She is my mother, O young men and women.
> Here in Kapila I am famous as a learned one.
> I may be in the king's ears as there are many who bring him news.

> The people of the world follow after renown;
> The world-transcendent engage in the ultimate mode of being.
> O hundreds of youths, you are wise if you engage in this.
> I am going to solitary places to search for a sublime being.

> Do you hear, O hundreds of young men and women?
> If I relinquish my doubts, this will be [the fulfilment of] the true
>   purpose.

"After he had spoken these words, the youths responded, 'Since this town of Kapila is a land of precious jewels, whatever one wishes comes true. Whatever your aspirations are, they come true in this very place, so we, too, will search for a sublime being along with you and shall act in accord with you.'

"Ujjvala replied, 'In that case, go to where your parents are and ask them where might be a place of solitude, good companions, and excellent teachers.'

"The young men and women gazed at Ujjvala. Neither daring to contradict his words nor able to part from him, they remained frozen. At that moment, nine geese, led by one goose, arrived from the south and descended on the lake. The first goose, which looked like a golden vase placed on a turquoise base, faced the brahman youth Ujjvala [286] and warbled various melodious sounds. The young men and women witnessed all of this. Like a turquoise base adorned with golden vases, the eight geese in its retinue sat beautifully in the four cardinal and four ordinal directions.

Many of the hundreds of young people, on witnessing this, experienced a great wonder. As they bowed near the lake and looked at this [spectacle], these geese moved, without breaking their line, to where the youth Ujjvala was seated.

"The youth Ujjvala witnessed this beautiful perfect formation of the most amazing and beautiful geese standing in a row, and as he investigated the melodious sounds they were warbling, he heard the following:

> This town of Kapila is full of distractions;
> The king of Kapila is attached to his subjects as well.
> If you, O youths, remain in this place for long,
> And if the king oppresses you in this town, this will be
>   unbecoming.

"The brahman youth Ujjvala proclaimed:

> Yes, the town of Kapila is full of distractions;
> This king is most attached to his subjects as well.
> Since it would be unbecoming were I to be oppressed at home,
> Show me spiritual mentors and an excellent place of solitude.

"The goose replied:

> O youth of good karma and attractive appearance.
> Here in this lake known as 'hovering geese,'
> Where flowers of pleasure gardens bloom,
> Surrounded by hundreds of young men and women,
> You remain here nurturing joyful experiences.
> As we arrived here from the expanse of the sky gliders,[457]
> We saw a turquoise base, attractive and beautiful to behold,
> Unsoiled by stains and most radiantly clear.
>
> We, the nine geese, who are free of faults of the mind,
> Have descended well and offer you veneration.
> Now listen, for we shall speak our heart advice.
> Go from here to a distance of five hundred krośas.[458]
> In that place, there is a great rocky mountain of solitude.
> The brahman monk Abhayamati resides there.

Receive instructions from him and relinquish your doubts,
And single-pointedly pursue meditative practice, noble son.

This learned one was your spiritual mentor in the past,
And even in the last five-hundred-year cycle as well,[459]
He shall be your lord, so receive the instructions.
O youth, have no doubts but come to that place.

The sublime Dharma is fraught with too many obstacles:
Your parents deceive you and your friends betray you;
You wealth seduces you and your fame chains you. [287]
Do you see this clearly, O renowned one?

"The youth Ujjvala replied:

Here in this 'hovering geese' lake, where lotuses bloom,
Magical golden birds, ceaselessly captivating,
Appeared from naturally pure space in the south.
Free of attachment, wings spread wide, you have descended.

How wonderful! On a beautiful turquoise circular base,
A golden vase is encircled by eight other gold vases,
Arrayed thus, melodious songs can be heard.
Though I am surrounded by hundreds of youths,
My mind does not deviate even slightly
From the joy of seeing you geese.

"When he had spoken these words, the magical goose exclaimed:

In this turquoise lake, unsullied and clear,
In the formation of a golden bird surrounded by eight others,
We speak these many words.
How wondrous! We have beheld the brahman youth.

You have an attractive appearance with a color like refined gold;
We hear that you strive for liberation through heedfulness,
So, with no attachment to anything, depart as soon as you can.
The daughters of Māra smile and dress in attractive clothes;

Speaking in pleasing sounds, as if peaceful and disciplined,
They can delay you and seduce you with their lust.
Therefore, depart for that place swiftly and with perseverance.
The brahman monk will sustain the brahman youth.

"As he heard these words, the following thought occurred to the brahman youth Ujjvala: 'It seems that the brahman monk Abhayamati came here to help me dispel my doubts by manifesting himself as this goose.' As he thought about asking this question, the geese took off and flew to the south. The brahman took this as a sign that there was no time [to waste] and that he, too, must go to the south at once.

"His parents saw that, unlike before, their son had a smiling expression and was filled with joy. They asked, 'Ujjvala, today you are smiling and happy, so, out of affection, please tell us what are the causes and conditions for this?'

"Ujjvala replied: 'I will tell you the causes for this abundance of joy. Please listen.

Today, to the south of Kapila town,
In the great lotus garden,
Nine geese, led by one, stood
Upon the lake called "hovering geese"
After appearing from the vast expanse of the sky.
The lake was like a turquoise base [288]
Upon which were golden vases with bulbous bodies,
Turquoise spouts, and copper bases.
Unmoving, they were tied together like a palm.
Like the hand of a tathāgata, the grip was firm.

In the four cardinal and ordinal directions
Sat golden vases with turquoise spouts and copper bases.
Taking no steps, they swayed and moved about.
Gazing at me they spoke melodious sounds.
As I investigated these [sounds, I heard a goose say to me]:
"This town of Kapila is full of distractions;
The king of Kapila is attached to his subjects as well.
If you, O youths, remain in this place for long,
And if you're oppressed at home, this will be unbecoming.

So go from here to a distance of five hundred krośas;
In that place is a great rocky mountain of solitude.
The brahman monk Abhayamati resides there.
Receive instructions from him and relinquish your doubts,
And single-pointedly pursue meditative practice.
For if you remain too long in this place,
The daughters of Māra might deceive you;
You will be chained by your loving parents.
This is my heart advice for your benefit.
Come what may, depart for that place.
In general, the māras cause many obstacles;
In particular, they undermine the pursuit of others' welfare.
So give up excessive doubts and engage in meditative practice.
This brahman monk Abhayamati
Will sustain you, O brahman youth."

Having spoken in this way, they flew south.
[The goose] said that there is no time [to waste] and so to come
    after them.

O parents, be my guides on the road.
I shall definitely practice the concentrations.
At all times, past and future,
This great fearless brahman [Abhayamati]
Was and shall be my teacher.
I have heard this from the magical golden goose.

O parents, karma and auspicious conditions have met,
So do not cause obstacles, but shun Māra's work.
If I, Ujjvala, born as a brahman,
Engage in the Dharma, this will be meaningful.
Otherwise I will be an upholder of extremes.'

"After he had spoken, his mother Manoramā, a linguist versed in the
Vedas, thought excellently and entered the Dharma. She then declared to
her son the following words reflecting her conviction in the Dharma:

My womb was blessed, for it gave birth to you, Prince.
You are hailed as clear-minded brahman Ujjvala.
There is no doubt that you are an emanation.
Without having been taught, you spontaneously speak the Dharma.

You proclaim the Dharma in clear and eloquent words.
The sun of the 'insider' teaching shines in a most timely way.
Destroying hosts of degenerate ones and upholders of extreme
     views,
You, Dharma Diamond, are indeed a hero.

Straight from this town to the south,
On a rocky mountain five hundred krośas away,
Abhaya, the most learned among all, dwells.
He is venerated as a crown jewel
By one thousand learned brahmans. [289]
Go there! Here in Kapila town,
Though an assembly of learned brahmans
Encircled you and debated with you,
None was able to [defeat you in] debate, O Ujjvala.
It is excellent that you go to receive instructions.
Now, no matter what happens to me,
I will never cause obstacles to your meditative practice.

"His father added:

O clearest among the clear of the brahman caste,
Joyfully you went to the gardens.
There nine magical golden geese prophesized
The glorious Abhayamati, the brahman teacher
[Living] on a rocky mountain in the south,
To be your teacher. This is most excellent!
Certainly if you wish to practice the Dharma,
It is appropriate for you go before him.
If I, too, am delighted by this,
How can I cause you obstacles?

"The youth was delighted with their words and replied to his parents:

Like the stamen of [a lotus], born on a lake,
Opened by a thousand rays of sun,
I am the stamen on the lake of Dharma;
The trunk of my lotus tree is strong.

As you proclaim echoing sounds,
Beautiful and endowed with majesty,
You have illuminated my intelligence.
Just as the cooling moon outshines the stars,

I shall now, outshining the ordinary brahmans,
Swiftly depart to the south.
O Sujata, to live up to your name,[460]
Be Ujjvala's guide and let us start soon.
If you do not wish to go, I will go [alone].

"His parents responded:

Tomorrow when a brilliant, red sun
Shines from the southeast direction and reaches the center,
We shall then depart to the south.
The darkness of extreme-view holders shall be vanquished.

"The youth replied:

Led by the moon and supported by the sun,
The brilliant thousand-rayed one is at the center.
The assembly of stars disperse to the outer limits.
As we journey up to five hundred krośas,
The sun of all suns that is beyond measure
Will be encircled by eight moons[461]
And will radiate rays to the cardinal and ordinal directions.
For those who are obscured by the darkness of unknowing,
Their [darkness] will be dispelled, and they will become free.
Such will be the perfectly arrayed sun.

"After he had spoken these words, his parents replied, 'As you, the clearest of the clear, have suggested, we shall go in the presence of the sun.'

"The next morning at sunrise, they all departed to the forest of solitude in the south and came before the brahman monk Abhayamati. From a distance they saw the brahman monk Abhayamati [290] giving teachings, in an uncluttered and unsullied manner, to eight brahman monks with clear intelligence. There the brahman youth Ujjvala felt great joy, like that of a mother who has just met her only son after not seeing him for many years. Standing between his two parents, he folded his ten fingers together with his two palms joined and placed them at his crown. Chanting the Vedas in a melodious voice, he came before the teacher. He touched the teacher's feet with his crown, made prostrations, and, in accordance with custom, circumambulated [the teacher] three times. Remaining seated in his [teacher's] presence, he made the following plea:

> O light of the world and sole refuge,
> I have heard that in the past and future, at all times,
> You are my lord.
> Out of your compassion, O teacher,
> Pray help dispel my afflictions.

> Many brahmans with limitless intelligence
> Place your feet upon their crowns
> And venerate you as if you were a crown jewel.
> He who venerates you brings suffering to an end.

> Just as the shining rays of the sun
> Destroys the darkness of the realms,
> Likewise, with your light rays, O teacher,
> Pray help dispel my ignorance.

> Even if my body splits into one hundred pieces,
> I will not harbor doubts born of fear
> But will practice your instructions.

> O sole refuge for the ultimate journey,
> I will strive with dedication in meditative practice.
> Pray please also help lead my two parents,
> To whom I owe immeasurable debts of kindness.

"Once he had made this supplication, the teacher responded:

> You, brahman youth Ujjvala,
> It is excellent indeed that you have come before me.
> As effects do not err with respect to their causes,
> Have no doubt, O intelligent one.

> Whatever secure base of liberation there is,
> It is found when cultivated without doubt.
> Whatever mode of being of phenomena there is,
> It transcends the extremes of reification and denigration.
> Whatever mode of being of wisdom there is,
> It transcends the extremes of conceptual elaborations.

> O brahman youth, listen to me.
> If the causes are empty of themselves,
> What effects can they give rise to?
> Due to an abundance of diverse delusions,
> Those with unknowing minds grasp these to be real.

> These [beings] are your parents;
> It is appropriate that you should lead them with your eyes.
> Loving-kindness and compassion are impartial.
> To delight in one's parents happiness,
> To recognize kindness and repay it—
> This is the conduct of the navigators.

> O brahman youth, listen to me. [291]
> These are skillful means and wisdom,
> So without harboring doubts about this,
> Strive with dedication to cultivate them.

> Be seated on a buoyant cushion of meditation;
> Wear excellent garments of pure ethical discipline;
> Consume the nourishment of infinite meditative absorption;
> Put into servitude joyful perseverance;
> Wear the strong armor of forbearance;
> With the weapon of wisdom defeat the enemy;

Assign ministers of skillful means to the ten directions.
This, then, is my instruction.

Now single-pointedly, in this place,
Untainted by the flaws of afflictions,
Such as sloth, dullness, and so on,
Pursue others' welfare with a pure heart.

Though living at home, you are excellent bodhisattvas.
You, Sujata and Manoramā, have given birth to
A meaningful bodhisattva as your son;
You shall be happy throughout all lives.

Thus, without being attached to your son,
Perform others' welfare in Kapila town.
This is my instruction to you.

"After he had spoken these words, the two parents responded:

O supreme teacher, you are the sublime refuge
For us, the community of brahmans.
O teacher, pray reside inside the stamen
Of the lotus of our hearts and be satiated.
Now we shall depart.

"Saying this, they journeyed [back] to the north where their residence was. The brahman youth constructed a small meditation hut. Dispelling all mundane doubts, he took ordination in the teacher Abhayamati's presence and became immersed in a single-pointed meditative practice. At this, the malevolent Māra became unhappy, as if his own son had been snatched away. Assuming a form exactly like that of the teacher Abhayamati, he appeared inside the hut and said: 'Nearly ten years have passed since you joined the life of a renunciate monk, relinquished mundane distractions, and single-pointedly engaged in meditative practice. Now you have eliminated the objects of abandonment, achieved the antidotes, and have become a sublime being. Now living alone will detract you from working for the welfare of others, so emerge from this hut and engage in town life for the sake of others. Partake in pleasures. Now I am granting you my permission.'

"In response the brahman youth said:

O Māra in the guise of my teacher,
With seemingly truthful words, you try to deceive me.
In the past I was seduced by the Māra of distractions.
Now I shall never deviate from this [practice].

O Three Jewels who are unsurpassed as objects
Of paying homage, the sole refuge of the world, [292]
Now, from this day forth
Until you actually appear [before me],
Regardless of what befalls me,
I shall never doubt [in you], even for a moment,
And shall strive even harder in this [meditative practice].
This, then, is my pledge.

"Thus his perseverance increased even more. Then, after a month had
passed, the teacher Abhayamati himself appeared and asked:

Son, did you experience doubts because of Māra?
Did you relapse from single-pointed practice?
Did you mistake Māra for a teacher?
Or did you instead generate even greater perseverance?

"When he had asked this, the youth Ratna Ujjvala[462] replied:

One day as I was meditating single-pointedly,
Māra appeared in the guise of the teacher and said:
'You have engaged in meditation for nine years;
Now you can indulge in anything at your will.'
Not giving rise to any doubts, I persevered even more.
My pledge remains firm and most binding.

"In response, the teacher said:

O sublime being, most intelligent one.
Well done, son of the Three Jewels.
In the future, when the [last] five-hundred-year cycle dawns,

In a barbarian borderland, we two
Shall enjoy the wealth of the Dharma;
Together we shall engage in the welfare of beings.
At that time your mother will have become
A sublime being called Lekpai Sherap.
At that time your mother will request all of today's [tales]—
How you strove in the practice
Without giving rise to doubts and with special effort,
Even when Māra caused obstacles—
And I shall reveal them.
With his propensities awakened, he shall come to know.

"This brahman monk was learned in all worldly and transworldly practices. 'Still,' he blessed and advised, 'you should never waver from this [pursuit] and, for as long as you live, discard all lingering doubts and ensure that you never allow this meditative practice to degenerate.' Saying this, he departed to the pure realms.

"For his part, the brahman monk also vowed, 'Regardless of what obstacles befall me, since I have been blessed as Ratna Ujjvala [Illumination of the Three Jewels], I shall act in a way that is true to the meaning of this name. I shall never deviate, even for an instant, from this practice of meditative concentration.' Thus, for fifty-five years, he discarded all doubts and strove with dedication in the meditative practice.

"O Lekpai Sherap, at that time and on that occasion, I was the brahman monk Abhayamatī; you were Manoramā; [293] and Khutön was Sujata. The brahman youth who received instructions from me and became Illumination of the Three Jewels was Gyalwai Jungné himself."

So Master Atiśa taught.

Thus, from the presentation of the life cycles of Drom Gyalwai Jungné, this concludes the first cycle, the cycle on how he took birth as the brahman youth Ujjvala, which is based on the following lines:

Discard all lingering doubts
And strive with dedication in your practice.

VI. The Spiritual Mentor's Birth as Prince Asaṅga in Kauśāmbhī

[295] ON ANOTHER OCCASION, when Atiśa and his son were residing in Yerpa on the crest of Mount Lhari Nyingpo, Lekpai Sherap came into their presence, prostrated three times, and made the following plea: "O paṇḍita most learned in the five fields of knowledge, yesterday you spoke clearly and extensively on how Gyalwai Jungné took extraordinary births in the past. You have [also] spoken a lot in the form of a dialogue pertaining to the following lines from the *[Bodhisattva's] Jewel Garland:*

> **Thoroughly relinquish sloth, mental dullness, and laziness,**
> **And strive always with joyful perseverance.**

"So today, too, [I would like to ask,] how did Gyalwai Jungné abandon sloth, mental dullness, and laziness and how did he endeavor in joyful perseverance in the past? With a heart of devotion, I wish to hear this. As I am free of any [self-centered] expectations, O Atiśa, please speak of this to me out of a compassionate heart."

Once he had made this request, Atiśa inquired, "Are there any individuals here who are not suitable vessels?"

Drom replied: "Right now there are only three of us: you, father, and your two sons. Later the words might be passed on to the others through the cracks in the walls. Today it seems you are going to speak. You, teacher, do not possess [the flaw of] exaggeration and denigration; and Ngok, you have no conceit based on your learning and knowledge. The foundation of your devotion and respect is great; you relate to your teachers and friends as teachers and friends, and you are skilled in both the spiritual and mundane norms. Therefore, offer a silver mandala adorned with a small white conch to Lord Avalokiteśvara, and, observing the suffering of all sentient beings, cultivate compassion as well. Also, in relation to me, imagine me as an emanation blessed by Avalokiteśvara. Then listen. You, too, O Atiśa, please speak in a way that is consonant with the facts."

As he thus gave his permission, an unprecedented fragrance arose, [296] fresh blue flowers rained down repeatedly, and a melodious voice could be heard exclaiming: "The conqueror and his son have dried up the ocean of attachment and aversion; they have extinguished the flame of false conceptions; they have lit the light illuminating the Buddha's teaching; and they have spoken of the enlightened qualities of the greatness of Lord Avalokiteśvara's body. Because of this, all beings of the region of Tibet shall enjoy happiness."

Drom looked up in the sky and smiled, at which point, Ngok inquired, "Judging by the manner in which you are looking up in the sky and the presence of such a melodious voice and other extraordinary signs, there is no doubt that the assembly of meditation deities is indicating that this [telling of Drom's birth story] is a good thing."

Atiśa responded, "The gods are delighted at the explanation of the enlightened qualities of Lord Avalokiteśvara's body and, carrying flowers and incense in their hands, are making offerings. The goddess Tārā is also making immeasurable offerings of meditative absorptions. Ngok, you, too, should take these [offerings] with your mind and offer them. As Drom has advised, you should also offer in actuality a silver mandala adorned with a conch. This will have great significance."

Ngok replied, "Let alone a silver one, I do not even have a wooden mandala today, so this does not help. If one does not endure some degree of hardship for the sake of receiving profound teachings, this is not appropriate, so I will go to the plains today and search for a silver mandala. I will then return and receive the profound teaching."

"Ngok, do not harbor too many thoughts. All the deities have converged here. It is not possible to send so many gods away because of one human being, so today I will prepare the mandala myself," replied Drom.

Atiśa intervened, "Drom, not that you can't lay out your mandala, but it is Ngok who must perfect his accumulations, so I will give one to him." Saying this, Atiśa took a silver mandala the size of an arm's length from his robes and adorned it with one hundred and eight small conches. He placed this in Ngok's hands and said, "I offer this to you to help fulfill the enlightened aspirations of such kind saviors as Serlingpa. On your part, too, [297] you should offer this to Gyalwai Jungné in order to help perfect your accumulations."

Lekpai Sherap, in turn, offered the mandala to Drom with the statement, "In order to help accomplish my accumulations, I offer this mandala to you." With these words, he sat in Drom's presence.

Atiśa then began in this way: "O Lekpai Sherap, once in a country called Kauśāmbhī there lived a king by the name of Prabhāśrī who had a queen named Satī, to whom two sons were born. They were named Rājyapāla and Asaṅga.[463] Rājyapāla was mentally resourceful, loved wealth and luxury, and was highly possessive of the kingdom and domineering toward his countrymen. Arrogant, he would travel everywhere with a large retinue of young men and ministers as his servants. Asaṅga, on the other hand, was tranquil and disciplined. He did not desire to rule the kingdom, was content with whatever food and clothing he received, and addressed everyone with pleasant words. When he visited pleasure groves and other places, he would bring along many young men who were like him, and, acting as their teacher, he would teach them the Dharma. [When they came to] ponds, he would create a toy ship and ferry many people across to the [other] shore. He would rescue those who had fallen low, and he would indulge in games with highly virtuous symbolism, such as making prostrations, doing circumambulations, and so on. He would give away to others two thirds of the food that his parents gave him. Whenever he saw an ordained person, even if this person were several miles away, he would first be delighted and then, without hestiation, would rush to prostrate to the monk and circumambulate him. He would request, 'Please come to my parents' house. I would like to be within your presence. I aspire to be like you.'

"Because he displayed extraordinary signs of virtue, everyone in Kauśāmbhī, irrespective of their age, bowed to him, exclaiming, 'Such a prince is rare indeed in this world!' His young companions would also point out to the prince whenever they saw an ordained person coming from any direction.

"One day when King Prabhāśrī went to the mountains to hunt, he saw, in a thicket of trees, a monk perfectly clad in the three robes [298] and seated upon a cushion of leaves and straw—a monk whose mere sight inspired perfect veneration. As the king dismounted from his horse and paid homage [to him], his retinue of five hundred also did the same. The king touched the monk's feet with his head and requested the monk to come to the palace for lunch. The monk replied, 'O king, you who are known as the Glorious Light[464] have obtained a human existence, so difficult to find, and among [humans], you have been born into the high caste of royalty. Yet you indulge in such base acts as hunting, making your obtainment of a human life and your royal birth devoid of purpose. In general, all sentient beings are our parents; and in particular, the animals who live on this mountain give us protection. However, you have betrayed them, so there is no way that I can come for lunch at your place.'

"Once [the monk] had spoken, the king thought, 'He is definitely an emanation monk. He knows my name, he is not deferential, and he gives me instruction in the form of a scolding.' Thinking this, he replied, 'Yes, what you say is true. I now confess my wrongs and purify them. I resolve never to commit them in the future, and I will make sure never to be divorced from humility, so please do come for lunch tomorrow.'

"'If I really have to come to your place for lunch tomorrow, you must give me your son named Asaṅga,' the monk replied.

"The king responded, 'In general, a king's dominion must be held by the prince, and that prince should be someone whom everyone respects. Here in Kauśāmbhī, everyone, regardless of their age, reveres my son Asaṅga and takes him to their crown without any rival. Please allow him to rule over my kingdom. Apart from him, O noble one, whatever you may desire, I shall fulfill your wish.'

"'It is because your son has such great qualities that I want him. Otherwise, as I, too, am known as Attachment-Free, I have no need for a youth who is attachment-ridden. Your son Asaṅga was a prince who succeeded in reigning over my kingdom in numerous lifetimes in the past and he will continue to do so in the future until his arrival at the heart of enlightenment. [299] Because he has two parents today, I have asked for him. Besides, even if your son Rājyapāla rules over your kingdom, [Asaṅga] will still remain the prince who will succeed [in reigning] my kingdom. [Rājyapāla] could lead the life of a householder bodhisattva and be allowed to reign over your kingdom. However, if you let Asaṅga rule over your kingdom, your dominion will become no more,' replied the monk.

"Then, the king thought, 'This noble one is definitely an emanation; there is no doubt about it. He revealed the names of both my sons and spoke about their realities.' Wondering why it was that his kingdom would come to an end if Asaṅga were allowed to rule it, he asked, 'Pray tell me, why is it that, if Asaṅga is made to rule, my kingdom will come to an end?'

"The monk replied, 'A kingdom is like a poisonous tree: its branches, leaves, and flowers are most striking and have a sweet and delicious taste, but whosoever consumes it will lose his life. A kingdom is like a burning fire pit: he who goes into it will be burned by the flames of desire. A kingdom is like a prison: one will be surrounded by enemies in the end. A kingdom is like an iron chain of bondage: it will prevent you from walking toward liberation. O king, since this is so, it is impossible for Asaṅga to rule over your kingdom. [For him] being dead is tolerable but falling into the lower realms is not. Will Asaṅga remain heedless at this juncture when he has obtained an existence that is the basis for [attaining] all higher qualities?'

"At these words of the monk, the king became disheartened. 'You, noble one, have described my kingdom to be a source of such shortcomings. You have shown that Asaṅga took birth as my son purely out of great compassion. You have revealed that Asaṅga will recognize the shortcomings of my kingdom and will recognize it as being like a poison tree, a fire pit, a prison, and an iron chain of bondage. You have revealed that Asaṅga will forsake everything and, in accord with the truth, journey to happiness. You have revealed that, even if the prince were to rule over the kingdom, this would be an apparition. I recognize that this will be done in order to tame the householders of Kauśāmbhī. O noble one, just as you have stated, [300] the conduct of Asaṅga is that of a bodhisattva. He gives away to others two thirds of the food we parents give him. All the games he plays accord with the Dharma. When ordained people come, he receives them even from a distance of several miles. He is definitely a person of [great] karma.'

"Thinking there was nothing he could do other than comply with the noble one's request, the king said, 'It is difficult to counter what you say. O noble one, I shall offer Asaṅga to you, just as you have asked. Furthermore, in order to fulfill your wishes, I will offer to you whatever you desire.' Then he implored, 'Please do come tomorrow.'

"The monk replied, 'You, Prabhāśrī, the king of Kauśāmbhī, have now agreed to act in accord with the truth, so today you should return to your land. Tomorrow I will come to your palace. This evening when you return to your palace, you should announce to the entire city that tomorrow a noble one will arrive and everyone who comes to receive him should go for refuge to the Three Jewels.'

"As advised, King Prabhāśrī returned to Kauśāmbhī, where his palace was, and made the announcement as instructed. There, prince Rājyapāla asked the king, 'O sovereign of humans, where are the animal carcasses?' To this the king replied:

In the past I have killed many animals;
But today in the rocky mountains,
I heard it said that they are my parents.
I feel remorse for my past. What else should I speak of today?

"Rājyapāla smiled at this and said:

O sovereign, if you fall prey to other's influence,
How can you hold sway over ordinary people?
This can lead to the kingdom's decline.
O king, your mind is fraught with hesitations.

He who cannot hold his own ground
Will be ruled over by others;
So a hero should shun the caves
And hold his ground firm.

"Then, the king replied:

Today, when I went to that mountain,
I heard that you are someone else's son.
That this will be so in the future, I found in [the monk's] words.
So, without wavering, please rule over the kingdom.

It is the noble one, no one else, who conferred this upon you.
You are an excellent householder bodhisattva.
Through harsh conduct, rule with compassion. [301]
Your younger brother Asaṅga, who is free of attachment,
Will renounce the kingdom and journey to happiness.
He will strive for the welfare of others.
Residing in forests of solitude,
He will shun the kingdom that resembles
A poisonous tree and will journey to liberation.
This will become clear tomorrow, O Rājyapāla.

"Upon hearing this, Rājyapāla felt great delight and replied:

Sovereign king, who revealed this to you?
As he taught, this kingship is
Flawed and has no beneficial qualities.
Sovereign of the people, in order to fulfill your aspirations,
I will rule over the kingdom
And will help all in whatever way I can.
Otherwise, I, too, yearn for liberation.

"The king replied:

I heard these words from a noble one.
Tomorrow he will come to this palace.
Behold his face and drink the nectar of his speech.
However, we shall part from your brother.
Asaṅga will depart to freedom from attachment.[465]

"The prince responded:

Father, I understand what you say. My younger brother,
Asaṅga, will journey to freedom from attachment.
Discarding the poisonous tree, he will embrace the medicinal tree;
Forsaking the fire pit, he will seek a cool chamber;
Renouncing prison, he will journey to freedom.

If today he is revered by humans,
In the future he will be venerated by all.
Asaṅga was born as a brother
Even to an unworthy fool like myself.

Born on one and the same tree,
Many [branches] are crooked and knot-ridden;
Some have flowers with beautiful petals;
Likewise, this is true of us two brothers.

The excellent flower will depart to the forests,
The knot-ridden branch will remain here at home.
Now I will say no more.

"After saying this, he went with a heavy heart to the pleasure garden where his younger brother was staying. There, in the garden, he saw his younger brother surrounded by twelve thousand youths. In the manner of playing a game, he was teaching them the Dharma. As Rājyapāla walked into the garden, he heard his younger brother Asaṅga speaking these words as if in a game:

> In springtime the most striking flowers
> Draw swarms of bees with joyful buzzing;
> A change of season robs their luster and pales them.
> This change in time and in nature is amazing indeed.

> O thousands of youths, you who resemble flowers,
> Today, as youths, you are striking indeed to behold.
> Yet once you have aged—[302]
> Once your nature and time have changed and you have become old—
> Even if they look at you, the bee-like people will no longer be
>   attracted to you.
> Even the eight-year-old gradually becomes fifty.
> The fifty-year-old eventually becomes one hundred years old.
> Life spent, body aged, the young will recoil at you.

> The beautiful and attractive flowers of spring
> Do not last in summer, but change their forms.
> And even the flowers of summer
> Surely turn into something else by autumn.
> In winter who will be attracted to them?
> That which has birth in whatever form
> Is transient and will soon come to an end.

> I am like a beautiful spring flower:
> Undamaged, with an attractive face, I am free of physical defects.
> O youths, you who resemble the swarm of honey bees,
> Drawn toward me, you have assembled here in the garden.

> I, being born, am subject to cessation.
> When I cross beyond the boundary of fifty,
> Like an old flower in autumn I will depart.

As for you, the swarm of honey bees who utter melodious
    tunes—
Your nature will change, too, so do not be attached to me.

Do you know this? O thousands of intelligent youths,
Do not grasp something that is transient as permanent.
Do not cling to an essence where there is no essence.
At a marketplace, countless travelers gather;
Every one returns home in the end and not one remains.

O, gathering of one thousand attachment-ridden youths,
Know that the end of coming together is separation.
In the summer, you are joyfully attracted to
Those splendid grasses growing on a high mountain pass.

In autumn they lose their colors with the frost,
And in winter they dry out completely and decay.
With the blowing winds they flee to wherever they are blown.

Alas! You youths who are drawn toward me,
Being born high as a human you are joyous.
Yet through the accumulation of days and nights,
One day you'll be stolen by the frost, the lord of death.
Therefore, before you are utterly destroyed,
Like the flowers of the Akaniṣṭha heavenly realm
Whose colors never lose their luster, it's time
To seize the secure ground when you've got the chance.

   "On hearing these words, Rājyapāla prostrated to his younger brother's
feet and said:

My flower-like brother is leaving for the forests,
But I, who am like a crooked branch, shall be left behind
    at home,
So how can I remain unperturbed?
If my right hand were left elsewhere,
Would not others disparage me? [303]

Today in the midst of thousands of youths,
I have seen and heard you reveal the profound.
Soon I [too] shall enter the path of liberation.

"After he had spoken, Asaṅga responded:

Today the clear light [of the sun] is about to set;
You, the assembled youths, should also return home.
We two will go to our parent's home.
Pray dedicate all [our virtues] toward the pure expanse.

"Thus they all dispersed and went their separate ways. The two princes also returned to their parents' home. King Prabhāśrī saw his two sons returning home from a distance and thought, 'If I tell Asaṅga today about the noble Attachment-Free's visit here, given that he is not susceptible to sloth, mental dullness, and laziness both during day and night, he might just go to receive Attachment-Free this very night and might possibly never return. Instead, it might be better to occupy him with other topics of conversation and not raise the subject of the noble one.' Thinking like this, he sat down with an animal carcass in front of him.

"Although in the past it was the elder brother who would lead, today it was Asaṅga who was in the lead as they entered the palace. They saw the king there with an animal carcass lying in front of him. [Seeing this] Prince Asaṅga exclaimed:

Those whose kindness to us in the past, since beginningless time,
Cannot be repaid, even if we strive to—
Those parents in the guise of wild animals—
Have you slain some of them?

"The father replied:

I have no power of supernormal cognition;
I doubt whether they are my parents.
Though I have robbed them of their lives,
Pray do not be displeased.

"Then Rājyapāla said:

O great father, please do not pretend.
[The monk] possesses unobstructed supernormal cognition.
Today I saw him teach the Dharma
In front of thousands of youths;
I've heard his sacred words, so difficult to reject.
If he is being revered for no reason
By thousands of youths who take him to their crown,
O sole father, why do you disparage him?
In peace, speak your heart to him.
Though I could tell you the truth,
I might err and cause you to lose heart.

Alas! Great father, keep this in your mind:
You should speak the truth.
In general, lies have only a short life.
You in particular, O king, are an authority.
How can it be appropriate to speak lies
To fulfill your own interests? [304]
If I have erred, however, please forgive me.

"Once he had made this request, the father replied, 'Tomorrow I will collect together all my mistakes and confess them. Since the aspirations of this prince, who possesses supernormal cognition, will be realized tomorrow, today in order not to violate the wishes of your parents, please remain here this night single-pointedly contemplating the welfare of other beings.'

"Asaṅga understood [his father's wish] and was delighted. He walked into the temple of the Three Jewels, and there, with his two legs folded [into meditation posture], his body erect and straight, and his ten fingers and palms pressed together, he spoke in a most melodious voice:

You who save [beings] from that which is so hard to be rescued
     from;
You who lead [beings] from a burning fire to cool [places];
You who transform poisonous sap into medicine—
To you, the Three Jewels, I go for refuge.

Here in this limitless ocean of cyclic existence,
Even though I wander under the power of karma,

O Three Jewels, you who are my unexcelled saviors—
You are my most excellent lamp.

You are the glory virtuous in the beginning, middle, and end.
Even a mere supplication to you helps
Grant the fulfillment of one's wishes—
To you, the Three Precious Jewels, I bow.

Even if hundreds of ill-born bodies crumble,
Never will I transgress your sacred words.

"While he spoke these words, the hair on his body stood on end and his eyes filled with tears. [From then on,] overcoming sleep and mental dullness, he always conducted himself in [such a selfless] manner with great perseverance. When his two parents witnessed this, they both thought, 'If our son, who is so young and has plenty of opportunity to enjoy life, disregards sleep and mental dullness, goes for refuge to the Three Jewels, and makes such fervent supplications with perfect reverence, how can we indulge in sleep and remain in heedlessness?' Thinking like this, and not indulging too much in sleep and mental dullness, they followed their son's example.

"The next morning, as sunrise approached, the noble one entered the palace. Prince Asaṅga went there and touched the noble one's feet with his head. He prostrated to him, made offerings to him, and, once he had arranged a perfect seat, made a request [to the noble one] to be seated:

Though you possess no afflictions, [305]
In order to help liberate these countless parents
From all [categories of] afflictions,
Pray be seated here and attend to me with compassion.

"Once [Asaṅga] had made this request, the noble one sat down with the generation of perfect [awakening] mind for the benefit of all the parents since beginningless cyclic existence, including [Asaṅga's] two parents. Joined by his parents and his elder brother, Prince Asaṅga then made the following supplication:

In the past, since beginningless samsara,
Like maggots infesting a pile of excrement,

I have remained submerged in afflictions' mire;
Thus, I have failed to journey to the place of purity.

Today, most compassionate noble one,
Continuously pour upon us your blessing stream;
Imperfect beings such as us
Are like fish cast onto a dry shore.

In the past, in countless lifetimes,
Though I was sustained by you, the noble one,
The fetters of the afflictions remained undone.
Today, help cut the fetters [of bondage].

In the future, throughout all lives,
Under the kindness of you, O noble one,
I will help lead my most kind parents.
May I become the source of conquerors.

"Thus, with conviction, he made fervent supplications to which the monk replied:

Though there are many jewels in the world,
The Precious Jewel remains a mere possibility.
Though many have obtained a human life,
One endowed with faith is similarly [rare].

Prince, you are most fortunate;
Since you possess the fertile soil of faith—
The foundation of all higher qualities—
The harvests of virtue will increase in abundance.

As for beings endowed with fortune,
You will help them attain excellent happiness.
You are indeed a person of great faith;
To help enhance, at all times, the goodness
That brings excellence throughout the entire world,
The rain of compassion shall fall continuously.
Do not be disheartened, O Asaṅga.
I, too, am known as Asaṅga.

I will help undo your fetters;
I am the one who has reached the secure ground;
I am a friend [to you] at all times;
So look at me with a pure heart.

Unsoiled by any shortcomings,
I am an object of refuge even for the gods.
I alone am the savioress of the world.[466]
In the future, when glorious Dīpaṃkara appears,
You shall be his principal son.

Since you possess no defects,
You display errors just to accord with the world.
Now, relinquishing these stains of errors,
Like darkness when the sun rises,
You should depart to the forests. [306]

"Upon these words of [the monk], Asaṅga, his parents, and the servants, felt deep devotion and reverence. They then prepared meals composed of the mixture of the three dairy products and three sweets, which are appropriate to be consumed by renunciate monks and brahmans. Untainted by unclean substances and prepared in the most perfect clean process, the food was offered to the noble one. On the noble one's part as well, he enjoyed the meal to help perfect the prince, the king and queen, and the prince's elder brother in their accumulation [of merit]. To help ensure that [their merit] would remain inexhaustible, the noble one made a dedication:

Most accomplished sublime beings
With unobstructed eyes and supernormal cognition, pray attend.
I dedicate this merit to the supreme Buddha,
The sublime refuge of all beings.

"As he recited these lines, the prince, together with his parents and elder brother, also joined in the dedication. He then made the following aspiration:

Just as now, I will venerate
The sublime noble one throughout all my lives;

Sustained by [the power of] pure aspirations,
May I journey to the ultimate destination.

"Then Prince Asaṅga rose up. With his palms pressed together, he came before his parents and asked, 'O you two, embodiments of great kindness, you who have given me the light of this world, do you love me?'

"The parents replied, 'So much that we are incapable of being apart from you.'

"'Do you love not being separated for a short period, or do you love not being separated at all times?' the prince asked.

"'The latter,' the parents replied.

"'In that case,' the prince replied, 'I will follow after this noble one and forsake food, drink, clothing, bedding, my palace, pleasure gardens, play-mates, sleep, mental dullness, and all activities of heedlessness. Single-pointedly, I will seek life's final aim so that, from life to life, wherever I may take rebirth, you two can be my parents and we will never be apart from each other. On your part, too, if you two wish never to be separated from me, you should, from the depth of your hearts, entrust yourself to the Three Jewels. Since the causal connections of karma and its effects are profound, refrain even from the slightest misdeeds. Since an ocean of higher qualities can emerge from the accumulation [of merit], collect this even by way of single drops. Since you need a staircase to journey to the place of liberation, observe ethical discipline and make your human existence the foundation. [307] Since profound Dharma can attract māras, constantly strive to venerate the Three Jewels. Since this cyclic existence is subject to suffering, cultivate loving-kindness, compassion, and awakening without interruption. Since [all beings] are our parents alone, do not discriminate in terms of closeness and distance or partialities, and when they are happy, cultivate the good thought of rejoicing. O parents, if you conduct your-selves in this manner, you will have cared for me. This will help fulfill your prayers for being with me throughout all lives. Otherwise, there are so many sentient beings who have been my parents. I, too, have died and taken birth so many times, and there is no certainty that you two alone will be my parents.'

"The two parents asked, 'If we send you, son, our heart, to follow the noble one, is it certain that in the future we two will become your parents and you our son?'

"The prince replied:

O noble one, be my witness.
O my two parents,
In the future, in the last five-hundred-year cycle,
On the crest of snow mountains,
My father, Prabhāśrī, so named
By the ḍākinīs of Udhyāna,
Will be Drom's father, Yaksher Kushen.[467]
My mother, the devout Satī,
Will be known as Khuö Salenchikma.
I will be born on that crest of snow mountains.
At that time I will be sustained by Attachment-Free.
O noble one, is this a delusion?

"The noble one replied:

It is just as you say, supreme son.
In that imperfect hinterland of the foolish,
Since the light of Dharma has not shone,
In that buffer land that resembles darkness,
You, moon-like [light], will take your birth
And dispel the darkness of mind.

At that time I, Attachment-Free,
Will appear there like the sun.
I will bring daylight to many fortunate ones.
Then I will depart to the realm of Tuṣita.
As if possessing attachment, you, Asaṅga
Will reside there and lead the imperfect beings.

"The prince replied:

What will be the teacher's excellent name then?
In what way will I be validated?

"The noble one replied:

I will be known as Dīpaṃkara,
Dispelling the darkness of that land.

You will be a treasury of Buddha's teaching
Known as Gyalwai Jungné.
I will be the 'great Atiśa,'
Venerated by the name 'the sole god.'
You will be Upāsaka Dharmavardana,[468]
Venerated as the spiritual mentor Tönpa. [308]

"When the noble one had spoken these words, the two parents exclaimed, 'O son, if you possess unobstructed supernormal cognition and view householder's life as a source of defects, since there is a danger of undermining the welfare of others, please go to wherever the noble one resides. O prince, if you complete whatever activities you may initiate, then you are truly a sublime person, so now, after having departed to the great forests, do not commit even a single instance of any unethical deed. If you become enamored with sleep, mental dullness, food, drinks, and so on, this would be like the foolish man who, failing to enjoy himself when there was food with hundredfold flavors, collected even the few grains of rice dropped by birds and hoarded them.'

"The prince replied, 'Just as you have advised, I will forsake unethical acts and engage only in ethical activity.'

"The king then rose and, with palms pressed together, said in the presence of the noble one: 'For the benefit of all sentient beings in general and, in particular, to help we two elderly parents perfect our accumulation [of merit], we offer you Asaṅga, who is like our own hearts. Pray accept him out of compassion. I also seek forgiveness from you, O noble one, for the wrongs I have committed by inflicting harm upon the many wild animals I failed to recognize as my parents. From now on, even at the cost of my life, I will never slay any beings who have been my parents.'

"The noble one was deeply pleased with his supplication and made a prayer:

You who are a ruler in the world,
You who were born into the high royal caste,
Together with your queen and sons,
Since you offer your son to me for the benefit of the Dharma,
May you always be cared for by the noble ones as their children,
As well as by all [other] beings.

"Speaking these words and taking Prince Asaṅga along with him, the noble Attachment-Free instantly disappeared from the palace through his supernormal power.

"When Attachment-Free and his spiritual son arrived in the great forest, the noble one gave a hut made of leaves to Prince Asaṅga and said, 'I will be your preceptor and your master of the ordination ceremony. As you possess no attachment, I will bless you as a thorough renunciate. Therefore, until you change this life [for the next], [309] relinquish sloth, mental dullness, and so on—conditions that are adverse to the virtues—and relate to all sentient beings as your parents. Cultivate compassion toward them for their suffering in cyclic existence and develop perseverance in all possible ways so that, ultimately, they will attain buddhahood. You should gain mastery over all these [practices] within the sphere of the absence of substantial reality.' Then he gave the following instruction:

You have taken countless lives in the past.
You were not born to one set of parents alone;
For every birth you've had a set of parents.
Though sentient beings might appear countless,
There is none who has not been your parent.

So if you possess great compassion,
You'll have impartial loving-kindness as well.
You'll rejoice in everyone's attainment of buddhahood.
These are the four immeasurable thoughts. Practice them.

'Parents,' 'suffering,' and 'Buddha' as well,
These are mere words of convention with no reference.
Do not grasp at them as objects of abandonment and antidotes.
Here and now the diverse phenomena are perceived.

Since they are appearances, they are false.
Since they are falsities, they never had reality.
Since they do not exist, they appear as diverse.
For instance, when one experiences a dream,
First one dreams of a horse that turns into an elephant;
The elephant changes into the body of a camel;
The camel then becomes a dog. There is no solidity.

Where did it come from first?
Where does it go in the end? Probe in this manner.
Nothing will be found; when unexamined, diversity appears.
Though the childish ones might be fooled by this,
The noble ones see this as a spectacle.
Asaṅga, practice such unattached acts of giving.

"Asaṅga, the thorough renunciate, exclaimed:

Among countless unreal sentient beings,
There is none who is not my mother.
Binding them together in the four immeasurable thoughts,
I will lead them within the sphere of the ultimate mode
    of being.

"After making this supplication, for thirty-eight full years he thoroughly relinquished sloth, mental dullness, and laziness and continuously pursued the welfare of sentient beings with great perseverance. On the day of the thirty-ninth year, the teacher Attachment-Free came and stated, 'You took my instructions and have made firm my commitments. O thorough renunciate Asaṅga, where are those thousands of youths who used to play with you in the gardens of Kauśāmbhī? What have you determined their future to be?'

"The thorough renunciate Asaṅga replied, [310] 'Some, having switched lives, have gone to the pure realms. Some, although entering through different womb passages due to the power of their karma, will eventually attain happiness. Some, not having switched lives yet, are living in Kauśāmbhī and practicing the instructions I have revealed to them.

O teacher Attachment-Free,
In the future, in the last five-hundred-year cycle,
In a region known as the crest of snow mountains,
The buddhas will shine their lights;
They will bless the land as a pure realm.

I, Lord Avalokiteśvara,
Will display numerous emanations there;
At that time, out of compassion,
You, Attachment-Free, will appear there [too].

Then gradually my sons will appear.
As for those who will be sustained by you, teacher:
Rinchen Salwa (Potowa, Mañjuśrī) will be a supreme son;
Shönu (Phuchungwa, Avalokiteśvara) will hold the banner of the
    teaching;
Tsültrim (Chengawa, Vajrapāṇi)[469] is unsoiled by stains—

These three lords of the buddha families, the lords of beings,
These illuminators of doctrine, most compassionate,
Will create arhats in such numbers—
Full twelve thousands except for three.
Do you know this, O teacher?
The assembly of youths will be sustained by you.
They will be your followers and my sons;
They will appear in that realm without a doubt.'

"Then the teacher Attachment-Free spoke:

O my heart son Asaṅga,
You to whom I gave renunciate vows have become a lord.
Likewise, when the five degenerations rise up and ills become rife,
The thousands of youths
Will reign over your kingdom and nurture beings.

A hinterland will be turned into a central land;
As for the glory of the teaching, the precious garland,
They will care for it like jewels stacked high.
The glorious Mañjuśrī, the lord of the ten grounds,
Will illuminate the precious Buddha's teaching.
Avalokiteśvara, who is accomplished in the ten levels,
Will uphold the victory banner of the doctrine.
Vajrapāṇi, who is accomplished in the ten levels,
Will light the flame of ethical discipline
And will burn away the fuel of immorality.

O principal son, because they will illumninate so brilliantly
The precious Mount Meru of Buddha's teaching,
The texts and treatises that you and I [compose]
Will be well-interpreted like that of Buddha's words.

Alas, the lamps of the entire universe
Are the three lords of the buddha families;
The twelve thousand arhats and those who uphold
The bloodline of the great mendicant,[470]
The countless upholders of ethical discipline,
Like the light of moon on the first lunar day,
Will be known as Gönpawa; [311]
His wisdom immutable; he will be unrivaled.
Beginning with Jangchup Pal,
From the three, [the disciples] will proliferate excellently
[Until there are] twelve thousand and the eighty thousand
    sublime ones.

"Asaṅga responded:

Just as you, the teacher, have stated,
Through the truth of the Three Jewels and
And through the power of the naturally pure expanse,
May everything be perfect as described.

Now I will depart to Tuṣita;
May I never be separated from you, my teacher;
As long as I remain together with you,
I will pursue the immeasurable welfare of beings.

"In this way, he departed, transferring his consciousness to the realm of Tuṣita."

When this [story] was told, Lekpai Sherap stood up and, teardrops flowing from his eyes, exclaimed, "Our lord of the world is such that even when he possesses such excellent qualities he conceals them. In contrast, the teachers of others, when they have a quality the size of a mustard seed, exaggerate it to the size of a banyan tree and proclaim it."

Saying this, he touched Drom's feet with his head and asked, "Why is it that you adopt the conduct of a hidden one and conceal all your higher qualities?"

Drom replied: "Actually, I do not possess that many qualities. Nonetheless, I am not asserting that there is a lot of error in what the teacher has told you. From Śākyamuni, the lord of the world, up to the teachers who are present today, they have all concealed their qualities and have worked for the welfare of sentient beings. If one does not follow in the footsteps of his teachers, he is a corrupt student. In general, if someone possesses excellent qualities within, he will not seek fortune from the outside; rather, he will radiate a natural light. Foolish people might not see this, but the wise will. If someone possesses a [wish-granting] jewel at home, even if he does not proclaim outside that he has one, naturally it will bring benefit to both self and others."

Then Ngok responded, "In that case, who were the parents and so on at that time?"

Atiśa interjected, "This is the remainder of my narrative. I will tell you. As for the two parents, this should be clear from prophesies made earlier. Rājyapāla is the great Khutön, Attachment-Free is myself, and what need is there to say that the thorough renunciate Asaṅga is Dromtönpa himself. O Lekpai Sherap, it is in such a manner that this Gyalwai Jungné thoroughly reliquished sloth, mental dullness, and laziness, and continuously pursued the welfare of others with perseverance." [312]

Thus, from the presentation of the life cycles of Drom Gyalwai Jungné, this concludes the second cycle, the cycle on how he took birth as Prince Asaṅga, which is based on the following lines:

> **Thoroughly relinquish sloth, mental dullness, and laziness,**
> **And strive always with joyful perseverance.**

VII. The Spiritual Mentor's Birth as the Youth Saṅghavardana in Magadha's Lotus Region

[313] ONCE AGAIN, at Yerpa, on the crest of Mount Lhari Nyingpo, Master Atiśa, his son, and Kawapa[471] gathered together. When all the benefactors, except for the family of the three Shakgönpa brothers, had converged, Ngok led at the head of all the students and performed the seven limbs, such as prostrations to Atiśa and Lord Avalokiteśvara. In particular, Ngok decorated the round silver mandala with a white conch shell and offered this to them. In the perimeter, beyond [these students], fifty-six young maidens made offerings of fifty-six mirrors. Then Ngok pressed his palms together and appealed [to Atiśa] to teach, just as he had requested on the previous day.

Atiśa replied, "Do you, the benefactors, have some [specific] questions to ask?" at which point, Sengé, the benefactor of Yerpa, rose and responded, "Since the day before yesterday, we have been experiencing numerous signs, such as great tremors in the earth, light rays, melodious tunes, and so on. What is the significance of these?"

"Ask your father Dromtönpa. Why do you ask me?" inquired Atiśa.

Sensing that the teacher possessed supernormal cognition, everyone experienced perfect devotion. Then the benefactor Sengé responded, "There is no difference between you two, teacher, father and son."

Atiśa replied, "The benefactor is eloquent in speech. For several days, I have spoken about how your father Dromtönpa took birth as the extraordinary kings and ministers of Tibet, how he helped benefit sentient beings many times. Because of this, many who share in the positive forces of the gods and the Dharma were joyous, and intense light rays came forth. Due to the power of the auspiciousness of interdependence, phenomena such as tremors occurred. In the skies as well, numerous melodious tunes resounded. These are great omens."

It is said that the benefactors shouted lamentations, saying, "We did not hear what was taught on the previous days." [314] Atiśa responded, "It is as if you have heard them. Today, just as Ngok has asked, you, too, shall hear the profound teaching, so listen.

"Once in the country of Magadha in an area called the Lotus Region, there lived a wealthy householder named Śrīgupta who had deep religious faith. His wife was called Karabha, and she gave birth to a son named Saṅghavardana. All the townspeople had great affection for the householder and, upon hearing that a son was born to him, they brought excellent clothes, food, and beverages and gathered together. Not long after his birth, the son sat up cross-legged on his mother's lap, looked at everyone with eyes wide open, and smiled. This greatly surprised everyone. They said that in the future he would create many ordained ones and would become a spiritual teacher for the town. When he reached age six or seven, he asked his parents to bring his three robes.

"'What are the three robes?' his parents asked.

"'They are the lower robe, to cover the sites of shame; the upper robe, to help engage in heedfulness; and the patched [yellow] robe of excellence,' he replied.

"His two parents responded, 'All of these are clothes of renunciate monks, and patched robes are garments of a fully ordained celibate monk. Son, you cannot obtain these clothes yet.'

"The son replied to them, 'He who no longer makes the afflictions in the home of the afflictions is a renunciate monk. He who refrains even from minor and minute misdeeds by his three doors is a fully ordained monk. These three [robes] are his clothes. I, too, am a renunciate monk, fully ordained, who has seen the defects of cyclic existence, who has perceived the benefits of nirvana, who relinquishes the poisonous sap–like cycle of existence, and who embraces medicine-like nirvana. I have taken birth here in the lotus of the higher realm in this sphere of the mire of desire in order to repay your kindness, my two parents, and to help lead those with whom I have connections of good karma to good actions. Since it is easy to be soiled by the mire, in order to ensure that the lotus is not soiled, I will distance myself from the town, which is a mire of afflictions. I will discipline my mental continuum, [315] wear the clothes of ethical discipline, and tie my robes with the sash of the antidotes of a sense of shame and conscience. To guard against the rough terrain of nonvirtue I will wear the boots of the view of the ten virtues. I will nurture the conduct of the skillful means of helping others. I will reside in the victorious ground, free of people, free of the enemy of the five poisons, and free of the inferior natural inclination of pursuing one's own self-interests. I will use the clean bed and bedding of a brahman unsoiled by the stains of particular afflictions, such as attachment, aversion, and [selfish] expectations. I will adopt the conduct of someone with shame and conscience who gives away both outer and inner articles without possessiveness. I will reside in a dwelling that is free of the residences of a high-caste and important householder. I will not reside in a wilderness that is not pure.'

"Upon hearing his statements, his parents exclaimed:

> Alas! If we have been made joyous like the shining sun,
> How is it that this sun is setting the moment it has shone?
> Why do you wish to relinquish this luxurious and auspicious
>   dwelling
> And live as a homeless person, like an animal carcass?
> Alas! It is one thing to be abducted by an evil enemy,
> But why do you wish to bury your own self?

"The son replied:

> If sunlight did not illuminate beings,
> Then wouldn't it be the same as midnight?
> I fear the terror of samsara's sufferings
> But will be happy in solitude with heedful living.
>
> My heart-enemy is the evil self-grasping,
> So if I myself do not bury my own self,
> What future enemy could be greater than this [self]?
> No weapon-wielding foe can cast me into cyclic existence.
>
> In fact, he teaches the Dharma and perfects the fruits of
>   forbearance,
> So it is happier to be like an animal carcass, free of attachment.
> It is better to hide oneself and become invisible.
> Parents, do not cling to me, but let me go.

"Unhappy and carrying their son, the two parents went to the center of town, where the townspeople asked: 'O two precious householders, what is wrong?'

"'We have heard that we will be separated from our son,' they replied.

"'Leaving your kind parents behind, where do you wish to go?' the townspeople asked the son.

"'Fearing that I will be separated from my kind parents for too long, I wish to go and seek the means to prevent such a separation,' the son replied.

"'If there is such a method, you can implement this while living here,' the townspeople responded. [316]

"The son replied to them:

> In the filthy mire of a hometown,
> How can a blue lotus grow?
> In a hometown resembling a [coreless] banana tree,
> How can a beautiful flower garden thrive?
>
> In a hometown resembling a fire pit,
> How can the bliss of cool arise?
> In a hometown resembing a prison,
> How can joy and tranquility arise?
>
> If, together with my parents,
> I endure pain in prison,
> Together, our lives will cease—we will not survive long.
> [In such a situation] how can one save the other?
>
> Therefore, I will go to a place of happiness;
> I will empty the fire pit–like [dwelling].
> I will lead my parents to a place of joy.
> This is [certainly] better, O householders.

"After he spoke, an emanation-monk appeared and said, 'If one fails to cut attachment to self-interest, places such as those beyond the town limits will not be places of solitude. Therefore, forsake your self-interests and, pursuing the welfare of others excellently, enjoy your dwelling, bedding, and so on [in a place of solitude].' Proclaiming this, he became invisible.

"The parents then exclaimed, 'We have heard such excellent words and feel assured. Now it is tolerable to be separated from our son for a while. That it will be auspicious in the end is for the best. Still, until you reach maturity, you could be devoured by dangerous animals. So for the time being, do not let this human life, so difficult to obtain, become wasted.' These words resonated with those of the townspeople as well, and they felt reluctant to let him go to the wilderness beyond the town limits.

"One day, Saṅghavardana went beyond the edge of the town. Out of concern, the townspeople followed him. They saw him cut pieces of flesh from his body to feed a hyena. With compassion and with tears falling from his eyes, he was saying, 'Ah! You have assumed a bodily existence and have nurtured my body many times. Today eat this transient body that cannot be relied upon.'

"'Alas, such a sight we have seen!' exclaimed [the townspeople], and some fainted with terror. Others chased the hyena away and collected the pieces of Saṅghavardana's flesh and bones and placed them inside a cloth. On reaching the town's crossroads, they were encircled by other people from the town. Many cried aloud, shouting, 'How dare an evil beast like that jackal destroy such a son who is like the heart of a flower?' Then the face of the earth was filled with light, rainbows and clusters of light gathered in dense formations, [317] and from the skies a host of gods issued forth the sounds of 'emaho!'

"A red rainbow arched forth from the youth's blood, while a white rainbow appeared from his bones. A yellow rainbow appeared from his body, and a blue rainbow formed at his heart. Also, excellent multicolored rainbows were formed on his various joints. At that moment, his parents, who were at home, felt their hearts tremble. His mother exclaimed:

> This youth who is so like the sun—
> When he said that he would go beyond to the west,
> My heart sank and I begged him to postpone [his journey].
> Without violating my words, he obeyed me.
> Today, however, I hear wailing
> And see incalculable rainbows and clusters of light;
> In particular, I see five rainbow tents
> Arched above the town square.
>
> Alas, my one true heart—
> Has he been devoured by a dangerous beast?
> Has he been felled by a venomous snake?
> Has he been shaken by an evil person?
> Has he been possessed by a devil?

Alas, the veins of my heart throb [violently].
O Śrīgupta, stay not here, but go at once to the crossroads.
Our son is not in the house!

"By the time they reached the town's crossroads, the youth resembled someone endowed with exemplary signs and noble marks. The lumps of flesh remained behind, however, and the townspeople were agonizing and shouting lamentations. Seeing this, the parents fainted in the town square.
    "At this point, the youth said:

My kind parents are sad;
All-permeating awareness is empty.
This ill-born body of mine is a source of pain—
First it is the soil that nurtures suffering;
In the end, through decay it assumes its present [suffering] state.
What use is this [fruit of] contaminated karma?

Through the perfect purity of my mind
And through the truth of the Three Jewels,
May my body be restored as before
In order to dispel my parents' pain.

"As he spoke these words, his body was revived to its previous state. Then, placing his hands on his parents' heads, he said:

Do not be sad, my two parents;
Undamaged, my excellent body has become well.
If the lights reveal such an appearance,
Why withdraw your thoughts?
O seeds of you, the conceptualizing mind,
Be awakened and behold me.
Karabha, do not be dejected. Rise up!

"The two parents regained their consciousness and rose up. Then, immediately, the youth said:

This ill-born body, so quick to disintegrate,
What can it do? I have seen it bring a secure base. [318]

In the past it has bound me, so I am like this [today];
If it were to bind me still, I would remain the same.

"The parents replied:

Alas, our sole eyes, alas!
Though you see your past wrongs,
Will you commit wrongs in the future?
Definitely, we fear that this body will be lost.

So that we will not be deprived of a son,
O son, do live for a long time.
Wherever you live, do so with calmness.
We will not impede your spiritual practice.

"The son replied:

I welcome the words of my parents!
To repay your kindness,
I will go to a place beyond the town limits.
May the Three Jewels be my preceptor and master.

"The moment he spoke these words, he instantaneously transformed into a renunciate monk who was ceaselessly captivating. About five hundred youths who were present there experienced a sense of wonder and exclaimed, 'If you seek the dwelling and the beds of wilderness, why shouldn't we do the same?' They appealed to him to ordain them. The emanation monk Saṅghavardana asked them, 'Ask your parents for their permission. It is important for them not to create obstacles.'

"The youths asked their parents and the parents responded, 'O youths, if Saṅghavardana, who is like the eyes of the town, is becoming a renunciate monk, why shouldn't you lesser ones become renunciates as well?' The youths then went to the emanation monk Saṅghavardana and informed him of their parent's response.

"Saṅghavardana replied, "You are fortunate indeed. We will now meditate and make our dwellings and beds in the wilderness. Make sure that each of you achieves your own secure base of birth in the higher realm. In the future, in order for us to perfectly lead many fortunate beings in the

Land of Snow Mountains, to do our part to help sever [the root of] their numerous misdeeds, to help enhance the treasury of perfect higher qualities, and to help defeat many who are immoral and degenerate in their commitments, we will utterly reveal within our mental continuums the three teachings and the four divinities inside the hub of the golden lotus of Kadam. Emanating buddha bodies, we will pursue the immeasurable welfare of sentient beings.'

"In this way, with great joy and delight and without any obstacles, everyone became renunciate monks. Then, everyone lived equally in dwellings beyond the bounds of human habitats, [319] such as in places of extreme solitude that are five hundred yojanas or five hundred krośas away from any town. During all these periods, they shunned thoughts of gain and fame or of gifts and services. They did not indulge in the enjoyment of praise, eulogies, or flower adornments. Just like wild animals, they ensured that their dwellings were beyond the towns. Just like the carcasses of dead animals, they remained free of preconceptions and interacted with all things with no sense of attachment. They lived there, untainted by negative friends and unsoiled by all the conventional norms of townspeople. They were propitiated and revered by all the gods, nāgas, and yakṣas. The rains fell on them at the appropriate time, no one ever heard any news of droughts, and [everyone] enjoyed good health, free of illness. Even the ordinary people of the towns were led to the Dharma."

Then Master Atiśa said, "Lekpai Sherap, I myself was the emanation monk who exhorted [others] to sever their bondage to self-interest and go to the forests; Drom Gyalwai Jungné was the emanation monk Saṅghavardana; and you were the householder Śrīgupta. Karabha was Kawa Śākya Wangchuk, and the five hundred youths who joined the renunciate order and lived in the wilderness will appear gradually in this northern country."

Thus, from the presentation of the life cycles of Drom Gyalwai Jungné, this concludes the twentieth life cycle, the cycle on how Drom Gyalwai Jungné took birth as the youth Saṅghavardana, which is based on the following lines:

> Dwell utterly in solitude, beyond town limits.
> Like the carcass of a wild animal,
> Hide yourself away [in the forest]
> And live free of attachment.[472]

VIII. The Spiritual Mentor's Birth as Prince Śaraṇadatta in the Town of Sukhavat

[321]⁴⁷³ ON ANOTHER OCCASION when the conqueror Atiśa, his son Gyal-wai Jungné, and Lekpai Sherap of Sangphu were residing upon Tārā's right knee,⁴⁷⁴ Khutön Tsöndrü Yungdrung came before them and, just as before, having made all the offerings such as the silver mandala, asked Atiśa: "Just as it appears in the remaining part of the *[Jewel] Garland of Dialogues*, I ask you to tell us, as you mentioned yesterday, the story of our spiritual mentor's past birth that could lead to great laughter."

Atiśa replied, "Shall I tell the one about a sharp beak, or about his birth as someone kind, most kind? Or shall I tell one that can withstand the test of time?"

"How many births were there when he was kind, most kind?" inquired Khutön.

Atiśa replied: "Many times he was learned; many times he was disciplined; later he was many times born kind; and many times he was born as a great king. As for all the other life stories, even the Buddha would be unable to count them."

The spiritual mentor interjected, "Tell the story of how I once dug up an elephant's corpse." Atiśa agreed and told the following story:

"Once, in the past, in a town called Sukhavat, the great Drom was born as a religious king named Śaraṇadatta. You, great Khu, were born as his minister Samudācāra, and my great Amé⁴⁷⁵ was born as the queen Asaṅga-koṣa. She was devout in venerating the high Three Jewels, compassionate in caring for lowly, ill-mannered beings, and for those in the middle, she donned the garments of shame and conscience. She cared for everyone as if they were her children.

"At the center of this town was an extremely wide and deep well. [322] One day, an elephant fell into this well. Despite their efforts, no one could rescue the elephant. As its body laid there, decomposed and rotten, all the nāgas, who were so concerned with cleanliness, ran away, and so the well dried up. As everyone in the town suffered from the lack of water, it occurred to King Śaraṇadatta, 'The townspeople are suffering due to lack of water. With the power of the blessed buddhas who are endowed with great compassion, I will extract the elephant's carcass and lead all these beings to happiness.' Thus, both the king and his minister went to the well, where the king commanded his minister, 'Look after my body so that no harm comes to it. I will enter the elephant's carcass with my consciousness and bring it out.'

"Issuing this command, he went to the bottom of the well. The minister, however, left his own body, entered the king's body, and maimed his own body with lacerations. After the king had entered the elephant's body and brought it out of the well, he noticed that his own body was now gone and only the maimed body of his minister was left behind. Seeing he could not enter the minister's body, he [spotted] the corpse of a parrot's body with no injuries and entered it.

"At that time, a large number of merchants were converged in a [nearby] garden. At night [the parrot] would help round up the caravan animals that had gone astray. He would sing comforting lullabies and give solace to the merchants by encouraging them to sleep with peace. He would sing wondrous songs like the following:

> Human life is so difficult to find.
> With sun-like faculties free of darkness,
> You [now] pursue your mundane aspirations,
> But on the day you die,
> All the possessions you acquired with such effort will be left behind.
> If you journey alone and naked,
> Seek the lasting garment of morality;
> Think that nothing else is meaningful.
>
> When self-grasping attachment enters your heart,
> You'll deceive even your father, who is worthy of respect.
> 'Though one [the father] may look after many [children],
> The many [children] cannot carry the weight of the one';
> Unreliable, false thoughts increase in them toward their kind one.

You have failed to see karma and its long-term effects.
Even if you engage in minor virtues
That grant some partial joys,
If you fail to prevent the subtle obstacles,
You'll say, 'The Dharma is not true either, for such things occur.'
With no means of escape, you'll go to the lower realms. [323]

Alas! All you merchants who have gathered here,
One day death will definitely come;
Do something profitable so that you'll be happy then.
Even though you continue to aspire for them,
Wealth and possessions only increase your pain.

The pain of searching for what you do not have,
And the pain of guarding what you do have—
You have harbored these over one hundred lifetimes.
Listen, O most eager merchants,
Beneath each possession is an enemy;
Each enemy brings a suffering,
All of which are then hung around the owner's neck.
If you fall prey to thirst for pleasure and wealth,
You will experience a great mass of suffering in return.
Recognize this and put it into practice.

"The merchants felt a deep satisfaction, and the chief merchant adopted the parrot. One day the parrot flew over his [old] palace and observed what had happened there. He saw that his own body had been assumed by his minister. His queen also looked sad and was given to sighing; the palace and the servants within it had lost their luster. Even the auspicious music was nowhere to be heard, so [the parrot] inquired:

In the past the king, queen, and their retinue
Lived in harmony and enjoyed wealth and spirituality;
The palace was filled with joyful music.
These days, however, even you, the queen, look dejected.
The king also appears to be a coward.
O queen, be at peace and speak to me.

"Hearing the parrot speak, the queen felt some peace and replied:

O learned bird, listen to me.
Though such prosperity existed here in the past,
Today, a demonic force has robbed us of our joys;
Into the depths of the well from which countless drank
A careless elephant had fallen,
So the well dried up, placing all of us in misery.

Unable to bear this the king went to extract it.
Although his minister accompanied him in order to assist,
He did not return; the lord alone [returned].
Unlike before, he has become sharp-tongued.
Even the kingdom has lost its majesty;
With no musicians, songs and dances are no more.
Since then no objects worthy of veneration have appeared.
It must have been due to the minister's good fortune that we had
    these in the past;
Now that the minister is no more, perhaps they, too, are lost.
Unless, of course, the king suffered a tragedy;
Do you know anything [about this], O learned bird?

"In response, the parrot spoke:

Listen well, Asaṅgakoṣa,
I am King Śaraṇadatta.
When, out of concern for beings,
I was extracting the elephant from the well, [324]
I entrusted my body to my companion Samudācāra
And my consciousness went to the bottom of the well
And entered the elephant's corpse.
When I returned to the surface, the minister's body lay injured
And the king's body was nowhere [to be found].
Seeing no point in entering the minister's body,
I entered this body that I found.

For days I have been living in the garden
Amid the transiently gathered merchants;

Sincerely I have taught them the Dharma and made them happy.
Today when I returned here and saw you,
Though joyful, I felt unhappy and was saddened [to see you
  unhappy].

Go to the merchant today.
Buy me and joyfully bring me home.
Then, when the king is having his meal,
I will lie in a pile of earth, and as I get up,
I will flap my wings and fill his meal with dirt.
He will then beat me and I will die.

Then cry aloud, 'My parrot!
Tell me a beautiful story!
Flap your wings about with joy!'
Uttering such words, you should weep.
Then the king will say, 'Don't cry. I will revive the parrot!'
Leaving his body in the palace, he will enter
The parrot's body and speak to you,
And as you respond with expressions of joy,
I will then enter the king's body.

"The instant the queen heard this [plan], she was delighted.
Immediately she went to the merchant and asked,
'Please sell me your bird.'
The merchant refused to comply.
'No, I wont sell. I need it myself,' he replied.
In response, the parrot said:

Please do sell me to this queen,
For if the winged creature escapes into the sky,
It will be of no value and you will lose the merchandise itself.
Now I will set price for my own self;
O queen, trade me for three animals:
One riding horse and two buffaloes.

"Having traded in this way, she returned to the palace.
The parrot spoke in metrical verses,

And the queen responded with joy.
One day, as [the parrot] executed what they had planned before,
The king hit the parrot with a club and killed him.
Then, as the queen reacted in the ways described before,
The king, saying, 'Don't cry. I will revive the parrot,'
Went inside [his body] and revived the parrot.

"As he spoke and flew around,
The king then entered his own body.
The palace interior became filled with light;
The entire palace became most radiant.
Like with the shining sun, people felt their minds refreshed.
Then the king revealed his hidden treasures.
Showing them to the bird, he declared:

> By deceiving the one who has rendered you kindness,
> O minister, you have now become an animal.
> Had you not violated your own body,
> I would have worn the minister's armor;
> I would have rendered you my service; [325]
> Yet with a distorted mind, you destroyed your own body.
> With no better body I became a bird;
> With a king-like body you failed to rule.
> Without merit, the body [alone] is of no use.
> Though I have no need for the kingdom,
> Since you cannot sustain the land,
> I will assume my own body and work for others.
> Be happy, O lady Asaṅga.
> Gather merit, you who are forceful in giving;
> Nurture well your retinue, O most sincere one.

> Birth in the higher realms is a royal palace;
> You've found the excellent island of a precious human life,
> So in this ship sailing across to the other shore,
> Without being trapped by the tides that press down
> On the ocean of birth, aging, sickness, and death,
> Travel in peace and with happiness.

"As such sounds of the Dharma echoed,
The queen's thoughts were filled with the Dharma,
And on the basis of firm one-pointed meditation,
She placed her mind, without wavering, on the ultimate mode.

"In a subsequent experience of clear awareness,
[She saw], in the future, an emanation of a sugata
Taming countless beings in a central land and in the hinterlands.
[She saw that] at that time there would be countless yogis with excellent
   qualities
All aspiring for awakening.
Having found the supreme hidden conduct,
[The sugata] would thoroughly suppress the tides of hinterlands.

> May I be not separated from this sugata-emanation,
> Traveling across India and Tibet.
> May I bow at your feet, O Dharma king,
> And venerate you in the ultimate expanse of reality.

> Again, in front of the seven Mount Merus,
> Inside the glorious royal palace,
> Where the scriptures radiate with brilliance,
> May I meditate upon the ultimate nature
> On a turquoise lake with one thousand swirling spokes,
> In the presence of numerous golden lotus trees.

> May the minister with a parrot's body
> Transform his misdeeds as well, and,
> Even if he becomes a learned one among the learned,
> May he bow at your feet[476]
> And propagate Dharma wealth and auspiciousness.

> [The minister:] Listen to me, O emanation master,
> By bowing at your feet
> How will I become a learned one among the learned?

"The master then replied:

In the future, about twenty generations from now,
Many who will bow at my feet.
Twenty most learned ones will emerge in succession,
Learned in various fields of knowledge.
In the end, too, just as you have prayed for,
I will tame you in the hinterlands
And venerate the sugata emanation;
And may we then depart to the place of goodness. [326]
May your aspirations be fulfilled just as you wish.

"Ah, out of compassion, the sovereign
Created an attractive body with magical eyes,
Clad in most attractive garments,
And made the minister's consciousness enter it.
At mealtimes he reverted into a parrot.
He applied himself to spiritual activities;
With remorseful heart he purified his misdeeds.
With resolve he venerated others with devotion.

"One day an undamaged corpse
Of a youthful brahman man was found.
The sovereign washed it with perfumed water
And summoned the minister's consciousness into it.
He taught him the various well-spoken insights.
Thus, among those who were learned,
He excelled in linguistics, logic, and the arts.
Then he trained him in the apparent phenomena,
Insubstantial, resembling magical and optical illusions.
In composition and exposition of eloquent works,
Thus did he attain the status of a supreme scholar.
He also became skilled in healing the sick.

"Then an emanation-monk appeared
In the space above the king and spoke to Samudācāra:

O brahman youth, become a renunciate.
Place yourself in the solitude of forests;

Discipline your mind, and in all your lives
We two shall care for you.

"Then the emanation[-monk] conferred the vows upon him;[477]
The minister, having prepared his provisions,
Lived a satisfying [life] in the forest.
Asaṅga[kośa] vanished into space;
Śaraṇadatta's pursuit of beings' welfare was uninterrupted.
Never discouraged, his forbearance was great;
Having led many beings to the Dharma,
Attachment-free, he departed to the ultimate expanse.

"O great Khu, your end was excellent. This was also the auspicious condition that allowed us both to sustain you. Given these reasons, one who is known as Gyalwai Jungné is indeed endowed with the inconceivable qualities of enlightened deeds and activities. Since you two—Khu and Ngok—have asked for it, I have given you the full narration of this list of stories without omission on how, with no sense of despair, Dromtönpa worked for others' welfare on numerous occasions. As explained before, after Gyalwai Jungné, many ordained renunciates will appear. They will bow at his feet and revere him, and they will make aspiration prayers for the future. Although I could say a lot of things, such as how they are [all] his own emanations, how they are directly blessed by that deity, what [specific] individuals they will become in the future, and what shall be their names and so on, Drom has repeatedly sealed me from speaking about these. [327] Nevertheless, since it is possible that, within the minds of the spiritual trainees of special fortune, naturally arising letters can appear, a book could appear. However, given that it is difficult for those who follow the path by means of faith to uphold the book, read it, reveal it extensively to others, comprehend it within their minds in its entirety, or sustain it with perfection, it is not in the form of conventional letters. Even if it were, there would be inconsistent [editions]. Therefore, to help you ascertain [the stories], and on the basis of drawing from various beneficial activities, I have given you, here, a very rough outline that you can fathom. Now, do not preach this in places where people lack faith and are heedless. Do not teach this to ordinary beings who do not share the same spiritual tradition. This, then, is my seal."

[Atiśa continued,] "Again, those who have faith in Kadam, those who practice Kadam, whose minds can contain it, who have conviction in it, who practice it as their heart drop, and who have deep admiration for their teacher's higher qualities should explain this. Moreover, there are those who, despite having respect for the teacher, view him as an ordinary upāsaka; those who make judgments about greater and lesser teachers; those who think in terms of [such judgments as,] 'He has this much knowledge,' 'His name is this,' 'He was born at such a place,' 'He performed such activities,' or 'He relied upon six teachers and then passed away'; and those who assert, 'Such and such a person committed evil karma.' As for these many people, who, while having respect [for their teacher], grasp at limited judgments, you should definitely teach them this [book] by showing them what constitutes the tradition of Kadam.

"Again there could be regions where the following occurs: masters are conceited because of their position; the greedy are conceited because of their wealth; the powerful are conceited because of their authority; the civilized are conceited because of their births; the haughty are conceited because of their strength; or the youth are conceited because of their beauty. You should not teach this [book] to such conceited ones.

"Why? Because they do not value the source of precious jewels as such but treat it as a heap of rubbish. [Furthermore,] even if you are a sublime being, if you are not recognized as valid by all, your teaching may not be recognized as perfect because of [lack of esteem for] you. You risk having your teaching derided.

"As for the teacher, he should be like this: he should be a spiritual mentor revered by all, a bodhisattva who is respectful toward all beings, and a person who is held as authoritative by others. [328] On the part of the individual himself [or herself], he should neither exaggerate nor denigrate, but should examine the suitability of the vessels just as explained in *The Book.* Such a person should teach *[The Book].*

"Furthermore, if there is an opportunity to turn a person with wrong views away from such views you should teach this. If there is an opportunity to enhance virtues such as faith, you should teach this. If you have the text, visualize the text as the spiritual mentor and, imagining yourself as Avalokiteśvara, recite the words of the *Jewel Garland.* If you have no text, seek apology [for possible omissions and errors], but teach *[The Book]* nonetheless."

After [Atiśa] had spoken, Lotsāwa[478] commented: "In a certain part of India, a paṇḍita once [had to climb] a staircase thirteen times, and so on. [...][479] Once, when Nāgārjuna and King Decö Sangpo were alchemically producing gold on the basis of a corpse,[480] the king went to Śativana cemetery thirteen or up to twenty-one times to [try and] bring back a corpse. The master commanded, 'Until you have brought me the corpse, do not look back, do not speak, and do not rest, for if you do any of these you will fail to bring back the corpse.' However, because the corpse told stories like these [ones I've mentioned (e.g., the paṇḍita and the stairs)], the king would fail in his mindfulness and exclaim, 'What a wonderful story!' Saying, 'You cannot keep secret what is meant to be kept secret,' the corpse would then get lost and would not be retained.

"This corpse also told a story about two birds. Finally, the corpse asked, 'On each of the thirteen steps on a staircase, there are thirteen birds, and in each of the bird's beaks there are thirteen grains of barley. How many grains are there?' Before he could complete the calculation, the king reached the master's presence. Then, three nights later, [they] applied alchemy to the zombie, which is said to still exist in India, transforming it into gold. I heard all of these stories most clearly from an Indian paṇḍita. He would count the golden hills to be thirteen or up to twenty-one."

Atiśa observed, "This translator has heard all sorts of things! Keep in your mind this story of how, failing to heed his master's command, the king lost the corpse [so many times] and seal your mouth tight. Secrecy is important.

"In closing, Khu, irrespective of where he took birth, this Drom never defamed the Dharma, he admired whatever teachings he found most affinity with, he strove both day and night in pursuit of the ten spiritual activities, [329] he dedicated the virtues of the three times for the benefit of all sentient beings, he was never divorced from the seven limbs, and, recognizing defective forms of speech, he ensured that he was free from the faults of mind."

Thus, from the presentation of the life cycles of Drom Gyalwai Jungné, which have been made complete to Khu, this concludes the twenty-second life cycle, the chapter on how [our spiritual mentor] took birth as King Śaraṇadatta, which is based upon the following lines:

Never defame the teachings.[481]
Whatever practices you admire,

Up to:

**Among others guard your speech;
When alone guard your mind.**

With these, from among the twenty-two Son Teachings, the two teachings for Khutön are complete.

PART THREE
SUPPLEMENTARY TEXTS

IX. Summary Points of The Book of Kadam
Gendün Gyatso, Second Dalai Lama (1476–1542)[482]

I

[331] Crown of the Śākyas, supreme savior whose speech is incomparable,
Dharma sovereign Maitreya, the Buddha's regent,
Mañjuśrī, transcendent wisdom of all the buddhas—
I supplicate you. Behold me with your eyes of compassion!

2

Excellent teachers of the vast practice,
Profound view, and inspiration lineages,
And the assembly of Atiśa's one hundred and fifty teachers—
I request that you reside inseparably upon my crown.

3

Though already fully awakened for countless eons,
Never forsaking the beings of this degenerate era,
You perform, without fear or attachment,
Such apparition dances as the Lotus-Born Vajra[483]—
I bow to you, O great Atiśa.

4

Lokeśvara, the father of all conquerors,
Creating countless emanations such as Könchok Bang,[484]
Depa Tenpa, and the successive religious kings of Tibet—
I bow to you, O sovereign Dromtönpa.

5

Though, as Mañjuśrī, you perceive all objects of knowledge,
Lifting high the lotus feet of the conqueror and his son,

You requested and compiled the peerless sublime teaching
Of the precious book, O Lekpai Sherap.

6

O Śākya Wang, great pillar of arhats,
Naktso Lotsāwa, whose kindness is unparalleled,
Khutön, who is in actuality the fierce blue-clad [Vajrapāṇi]—
I bow to you, the immediate disciples of Atiśa and his son.

7

Shönu Gyaltsen, who is Lord Avalokiteśvara,
Potowa, master of the Kadam teaching,
Tsültrim Bar, accomplished in learning and realization—
I bow to you, the principal sons of Dromtönpa.

8

The four Gyaltsens, who are supreme among conqueror's sons,
Jangchup Sangpo and Namkha Rinchen,
Shönu Lodrö and the one bearing the name of "heat rays"[485]—
I bow to the teachers of the lineage of this teaching.

9

As I recall the liberating lives of these sublime teachers,
Supreme refuges, the hairs on my body stand up with devotion.
We, my kind parents in the six realms and myself, [332]
Go for refuge so that we will never be separated from the Three Jewels.

10

The king of the Śākyas is, in actuality, all buddhas;
Avalokiteśvara is the identity of all peaceful bodhisattvas;
Lord Acala is the embodiment of all wrathful deities;
Tārā is the embodiment of all wisdom goddesses.

11

I will never part from the deity yoga whereby
I myself appear as myriad circles of the four divinities,
And, remembering all beings as my kind parents,
I will generate the supreme awakening mind for their sake.

12

Constantly abiding in equipoise on the ultimate awakening mind,
The oneness of emptiness and compassion
Whereby the world appears as illusion-like in its aftermath—
May I never part from the five recollections.

13

Most profound and expansive awakening mind,
The supreme source of all the buddhas,
He appears constantly in the myriad perfect and imperfect worlds—
This is the eleven-faced Avalokiteśvara Jīnasāgara.

14

The buddhafields present in his thousandfold arms and eyes
And in each and every pore in his body cannot be analyzed
By the disciples, self-enlightened ones, or bodhisattvas—
May I achieve the state of the inconceivable array
Of the mother of the buddhas of all three times.

15

May I instantly transform into the forms of the Śākya king,
Equal in number to the atoms of the hundred billion worlds,
And by manifesting the twelve enlightened deeds,
May I become a savior for beings pervading all of space.

16

Avalokiteśvara, Dromtönpa of the refined moon—
In his right hand there is a jewel rosary, while in his left
There is a thousand-petaled lotus upon a blazing crystal.
At its center are Perfection of Wisdom Mother, Śākyamuni, and
    Dīpaṃkara.

17

The thousand petals are adorned with the thousand buddhas of the
    fortunate eon;
Buddha Amitābha resides upon Dromtönpa's hair,
While the bodies and the fields of the buddhas of the three times
Appear constantly on his body, like reflections in a mirror—

May I meditate upon the drop of the Land of Snows and the drop of
    one's own abode
As inseparable within my heart.

18
Their external appearance is that of the deities' bodies;
Inside they are rainbow-like celestial mansions
Marked with six-syllable [mantras] in the six directions.
I visualize them throughout all stages.

19
In their center is the Perfection of Wisdom, mother of all buddhas;
In her heart is her principal son, the chief of the Śākyas;
Upon the stamen of his heart is Lord Avalokiteśvara;
Upon his lotus heart is Lord Acala;

20
In his heart is the supreme goddess of enlightened activities,
In peaceful and wrathful forms. As I visualize these in sequence—
The six drops of meditation deities contained within—
May I constantly practice the yoga of contemplating them. [333]

21
During these occasions, when I embrace the practices
Of the yoga of recitation and the meditation of individual deities
Associated with one of the four classes of tantra,
May I receive the small, medium, and great attainments.

22
Within the noble lady's heart, just as before,
On a sun and lotus seat upon a lion throne inside a mansion,
The glorious Dīpaṃkara, chief of all realized knowledge-bearers, resides;
He is in the appearance of a "vajra-holding monk."

23
The four divinities reside in the four directions [around] him, in a
    manner expressing the nine dances;
While in the four intermediate directions,

Atiśa as paṇḍita and the trio—Drom, Ngok, and Khu—reside.
I visualize them in sequence and in the skies above him.

24

I visualize the three lineages and the hundred and fifty [teachers];[486]
I accumulate merit by means of the seven limbs.
Taking the four empowerments of meditative absorption,
May my heart be filled with streams of blessings.

25

In his heart is the conqueror Maitreya;
Majestic as a golden mountain, he is encircled by [the masters of]
The [lineage of] vast practice, and within his heart is Lord Nāgārjuna,
Who dons the gesture of dependent origination.
[Lord Nāgārjuna] is encircled by the lineage of the elaboration-free view.
As I accumulate merit in sequence and make supplications as before,
May I become a vessel for the stages of the path, profound and vast.

26

Nāgārjuna states, "O child, you have accomplished
Most of the dual accumulations. Within the excellent Akaniṣṭha realm,
As Vajradhara, you will enter into union with Vajramañjarī
And will be encircled by the teachers of [the lineage of] inspiration.
As the principal figures of all three lineages,
There are Atiśa father and his son."

27

Again, like before, as I accumulate merit and make supplications,
And as I embrace the profound practices of the generation and
    completion stages
Associated excellently with the father and mother tantras,
May I attain the supreme state of eight proficiencies[487]
By transforming birth, death, and the intermediate state into the
    three buddha bodies.

28

Again, as I enter into [Nāgārjuna's] heart,
The immeasurable mansion arises. In its nature it is the unexcelled
    qualities

Of the fully awakened buddhas, the eighteen undefiled attributes:
The ten powers, four fearlessnesses, and four perfect discernments.

29
Within its center I become the nature of the truth body,
Appearing in the form of countless enjoyment bodies
And emitting clouds of emanation bodies.
Within the heart of such an indivisible union of the three buddha
    bodies,
The indivisible awakening minds of the two truths abide in the form of
    a drop.
May I meditate upon this inseparably at all times.

30
When this is elaborated upon, the inexhaustible wheels of the three
    buddha bodies [emerge] from this
And pervade the entire world—both the container and its contents. [334]
When withdrawn, may the sole drop that is the actuality[488]
Of emptiness and compassion remain unwavering in my mind.

31
Conquerors pervading space have revealed
Ways of teaching pertaining to the causal and resultant vehicles
To countless sentient beings
In perfect accordance with their inclinations and mentalities and in their
    own tongues.

32
Though [the scriptures] cannot be captured in numbers or
    measurements,
The twin methods of seeking higher birth and definite goodness[489]
Encompass everything for the trainees without omission;
As for all the scriptures pertaining to methods of achieving higher
    rebirth,

33
Their themes are encompassed in the paths of initial scope;
While the subject matter of all the diverse teachings

Pertaining to methods of seeking liberation
Are encompassed in the paths of intermediate scope.

34

The method of cultivating the state of omniscience—
All the secrets of the exalted speech pertaining to
The two great vehicles of the causal and resultant stages—
Is encompassed in the paths of the great scope.

35

Therefore, as for all the scriptures of the buddhas:
Their expressions are encompassed within the three baskets;
Their contents are [encompassed] within the three precious trainings;
And their practices are [encompassed] within the [paths of the] three
   scopes.

36

This pure lineage of the sacred words of the great sage [Buddha],
To which the epithet "Kadam" has been conferred,
May I practice this by masterfully bringing them together within [the
   framework of]
The sevenfold [path of] the four divinities and the three teachings.

37

When this tradition of the instruction
Of glorious Atiśa, father and son, suffered extreme decline,
Atiśa himself emanated most excellently as Tsongkhapa
And [revitalized] the tradition of the Kadam teaching.

38

In particular, [he revived] all hidden tantras and their commentaries,
Such as those of the glorious Guhyasamāja,
And the scriptural and realizational Dharma of the old and new Kadam—
May they flourish in all directions and throughout all times.

39

Glorious cudgel-wielding wisdom lord,
O Mahākāla and the twelve Tārās,

And the assembly of eighty white guardians—
Please assist us unwaveringly to help us realize these aims.

This aspiration prayer summarizing *The Book of Kadam* and all the essential points of the stages of the path of sutra and tantra was composed by the monk Gendün Gyatso, who sits in the last rows of Kadam [practitioners]. It was requested by the noble savior of beings, master of ten canonical treatises, Ato Sherap Gyaltsen, with extensive offerings of gifts from Dokham. [335] The master of the fields of knowledge, the glorious Lodrö Sangpo, also made a [similar] appeal. It was written at the great learning seat of glorious Drepung with Chökyi Paljor Lekpa as its scribe. Through this endeavor may the precious Kadam tradition flourish in all directions and throughout all times.

Maṅgalaṃ!

X. Heart-Instructions of The Book of Kadam
Yongzin Yeshé Gyaltsen (1713–93)[490]

[337] THIS IS THE HEART-INSTRUCTIONS of *The Book of Kadam* entitled "An Excellent Vase of Ambrosia."

I. Supplicating the Lineage Teachers and Properly Relying on One's Spiritual Mentor

Namo guru muni Indrāya

1
Amid the myriad celestial bodies of saviors,
The body of your excellent courage remains most complete;
This beauty is enhanced further by the various patterns of compassion—
I bow to you, O peerless teacher, you who resemble the radiant moon.

2
Though following in the footsteps of this supreme teacher,
With the eyes of intelligence closed, I did not see your body of noble
    marks;
With the legs of morality injured, I failed to traverse [the path].
Pray sustain me, a desperate one, with your great compassion.

3
Sovereign of Dharma Maitreya, the Buddha's regent,
Asaṅga and his brother, the two Senas,[491] and so on,
O the assembly of teachers of the lineage of vast practice,
Pray bless my mental continuum.

4

Mañjuśrī, who embodies all the wisdom of the buddhas,
Noble Nāgārjuna, Candrakīrti, and so on,
O assembly of teachers of the lineage of profound view,
Pray grant me the excellent path of the Middle Way.

5

The all-pervading lord Vajradhara and Vajrapāṇi,
Saraha, Tilopa, Nāropa, and so on,
O assembly of teachers of the lineage of inspiration,
Pray bless my mental continuum.

6

In the presence of Buddha Ratnagarbha,
Having upheld the supreme mind that is the shoot of buddhahood,
You have traveled beyond the deeds of the bodhisattvas;
I supplicate you, O stainless conqueror.

7

Having extracted the distilled essence of the scriptural ocean of the
    Supreme Vehicle,
This ambrosia of the Supreme Vehicle,
You satisfied all in India and Tibet who had the fortune to practice the
    Supreme Vehicle;
I bow to you, the initiator of the chariot way of the Supreme Vehicle.[492]

8

To disseminate the Buddha's teaching, you performed
Deeds akin to a second Buddha throughout India and Tibet,
You are unrivaled in upholding the teaching of the Buddha;
I bow to you who are a light to the Buddha's teaching.

9

Especially for the desperate beings of the north;
You restored life with the nectar of precious awakening mind;
You are a great bodhisattva who is foretold in prophesies; [338]
I bow at your feet, O Dīpaṃkara.

10

Because of their compassion, none of the buddhas and their children of
　the myriad worlds,
Are able to bear [the suffering of] the utterly ignorant beings
Of this country, which is encircled by thoroughly white mountains.
I bow to you who emanated [in this land] as a crystal youth.

11

Not even the most compassionate peerless Teacher himself
Could tame the beings of this northern country.
O compassionate lord, you who especially care for them,
I supplicate you, most holy Holder of the White Lotus.

12

All the beneficial factors and happiness of beings pervading space,
All of these definitely depend upon your force.
Hailed as the sole source of the ocean of conquerors,
I bow to you who are praised by all the buddhas.

13

Through inconceivable manifestations of skillful means,
You brought the glorious lord Dīpaṃkara
And dispelled the darkness of the land of Tibet;
I supplicate you, O spiritual mentor Dromtönpa.

14

In upholding the profound and secret ear-whispered lineage
Of the exemplary lives of Dīpaṃkara and Gyalwai Jungné,
You have realized the power of the ocean of waves of aspirations;
I supplicate you at your feet, O Lekpai Sherap.

15

In the garden of pure discipline of true renunciation,
From the unfolding of one thousand petals of the precious awakening
　mind,
You satisfy all fortunate trainees with the ambrosia of vast practice;
I supplicate you, O Potowa Rinchen Sal.

16

You hoist the supreme wish-granting jewel of the Kadam ear-whispered
    teachings
Atop excellent victory banners of meditative practice
And spontaneously accomplish the twin purposes of self and others;
I supplicate you at your feet, O Shönu Gyaltsen.

17

Through the maturation of the power of familiarity for many life cycles,
Right from childhood you were blessed by meditation deities.
You thus became a treasure of quintessential instructions;
I supplicate you, O Chenga Tsültrim Bar.

18

Your light of knowledge shines upon all the scriptures;
You vanquish egoism with the thunderbolt of equalizing and exchanging
    self and others;
You train in cherishing others more than your own self;
I supplicate you, O Kadam teachers such as Chekawa.

19

Your fame as the most courageous among all compassionate buddhas is
    renowned in the myriad worlds of the ten directions;
Though you have perfected all fields of knowledge, you give away even
    your body and life without possessiveness in the quest for knowledge;
Though finding the Conqueror's state, as a youthful bodhisattva [339]
    you show the excellent unmistaken path to beings of the degenerate
    age;
I bow from my heart to the compassionate gentle lord[493] who is famed as
    the second Buddha in disseminating the Buddha's teaching.

20

You bring all sacred words and their commentarial treatises
Together as the stages of practice
Of a single person of good fortune and impart their instructions;
I supplicate you, most kind teacher. Pray bless my mind.

21

All the excellences of samsara and its pacification
Are definitely dependent upon your power;
O spiritual mentors who show the unmistaken excellent path,
Bless me so that I am able to rely upon you correctly.

22

Even with respect to a one-day guide to a dangerous place,
We need to examine whether he is reliable,
So how can just anyone be acceptable
As our guide on the path to enlightenment?

23

Viewing such a spiritual mentor, endowed with all the qualifications,
Perfectly as the embodiment of all the buddhas,
I will generate, at all times and in all situations,
Uncontrived admiration and respect [for him],
And I will strive to please him by implementing his words.

24

If I see charlatans, full of bravado,
Who toss together a mélange of Dharma and non-Dharma themes,
Deceiving the devout, I will shun them like mucus;
Even in my dreams will I never engage in such contamination.

25

The sublime spiritual mentors who lead me
On the path that pleases the buddhas—
Never will I forsake them, even at the cost of my life;
By delighting them through the three ways of pleasing,
May I perfect the pure exemplary life of Kadam.

Thus, from the practices of the innermost essence of the heart instructions
given by our sole lord, the great Atiśa Dīpaṃkara, to the Dharma king
Dromtönpa, wherein the key points of all the scriptures and their commentaries as encompassed within the three baskets of scripture and the four
classes of tantra are entirely summarized and instructed, this is chapter I,
which is of definite importance at the beginning, the section on *supplicating*

the teachers who are endowed with the three lineages and properly relying upon the sublime spiritual mentor, who is the root of all excellence.

II. Exhorting Oneself to Make This Human Existence of Leisure and Opportunity Meaningful

1

Having gathered merit in past lives, I have obtained a human existence;
I have met with a spiritual mentor who reveals the unmistaken excellent
    path. [340]
At this juncture, when all outer and inner conditions have converged,
I will make sure I am never deceived by my own self.

2

Since beginningless time in this samsara of the three realms,
I have wandered everywhere with no respite at all;
Most of that time I have been in the depths of the three lower realms.
At all times I have suffered hundreds of unbearable pains.

3

Even when I have obtained a human life from time to time,
I have not heard even the name of the Three Jewels
But have been born in the dark realms, devoid of leisure;
I was nothing but a beast with the body of a human.

4

Even when I have been born in an era of light,
Because my propensities for past habits were so strong,
I craved contaminated bliss and I accumulated karma,
So once again I spiraled down and down.

5

Even when I had the opportunity to encounter the sublime Dharma,
Since I was bereft of the flawless eyes of reasoning,
I failed to distinguish between what is Dharma and what is not;
Deceived by fictitious Dharma, I let myself down.

6

Even if I know various categories of teachings,
If I do not have the instructions of a teacher of the lineage,
I will fail to recognize what practice is most suited
To my natural inclination and mental faculties.

7

Repeating others' words like echoes
And not comprehending the enumerations or sequence of the paths,
Even if I place my hopes in my heartfelt efforts alone,
The only fruit of this labor will be exhaustion.

8

Not sustained by a sublime mentor of the lineage,
If I lack the power to examine the treatises with reasoning,
Then, like a blind man caught wandering in a desolate plain,
With no sense of direction, I will fall into the abyss of falsity.

9

Many are deceived by nonvirtuous teachers
And evil friends who [propagate] fictitious Dharma.
Discarding all boundaries of the precepts of the three vows,
They boast of instantaneous recognition of the mind's nature.

10

"All practices of the method aspect are conceptualizations;
Not engaging the mind with anything is the most supreme."[494]
There are many who are deceived by such false views that defy dependent
    origination,
And they return from their human life empty-handed.

11

If one is not endowed with the instructions of a teacher of the lineage,
Even if one might read numerous categories of teachings,
One will fail to know how to practice that is most in tune with one's
    mind;
There are many whose efforts will thus become fruitless.

12

Therefore, Atiśa, master of Buddha's teaching,
Stated to Dromtön Gyalwai Jungné:
"Since it's vital to understand the essential point
Of how to integrate all the teachings embodied within

13

The three scriptural baskets and the four classes of tantra
Within the single framework of one's own practice,
The definitive heart-advice of the entire assembly [341]
Of teachers who possess the three lineages is this:

14

'From the stanzas [of the discipline basket] to the glorious Samāja,[495]
Their integration into a sequence of practice for a single person,
The stages of the path of both sutra and tantra,
I will reveal this to you, so cherish it well.'"
In this way, he imparted this essential instruction.[496]

15

As for the most excellent way of making human life meaningful,
Called the "profound instruction of Dharma,"
The stages of the path of the three scopes are required for this;
Be it a fortunate rebirth or definite goodness, whatever one seeks
Is achieved by means of this approach of the path of the three scopes;
Nothing cannot be realized through this.

16

As for the various instructions that appear Dharma-like,
Even if, without relying upon this stages of the path [instruction],
I might train in these, I will fail to succeed in my practice;
Even if I practice them, my aims will not be realized.

17

Like leading someone who wants to go from east to west,
Like taking the talisman to the western gate
While the evil demon lies at the eastern gate,
There are many whose pursuits become mostly futile.

18

If you pursue this [instruction] of the path of the three scopes,
There is no aspiration you cannot realize;
So if, fearing a future in the lower realms,
You seek an existence in a fortunate realm,
You can achieve this through the path of the initial scope,
In which the collection of conditions [for this] is complete and error free.

19

If, disenchanted by cyclic existence of the three realms,
You wish to obtain the state of liberation,
This can be achieved through the path of the middling scope,
In which the collection of conditions [for this] is complete and error free.

20

If you wish to achieve the state of buddhahood
In order to free all sentient beings pervading space in its entirety,
This can be achieved through the path of the great scope,
In which the collection of conditions [for this] is complete and error free.

21

Without relying upon an excellent instruction such as this,
Do not place your trust in numerous teachings,
Systems boasted as "excellent" and "profound."
So many people suffer doom
By failing to make the right choice
Between a wish-granting jewel and an ordinary one.

23

Atiśa and the conqueror Tsongkhapa—
The heart of their instructions is complete and flawless.
Since it will be hard to find such instructions in the future,
I will not forsake them even at the cost of my life.

24

To all the teachers endowed with the three lineages,
To my teacher Munindra Vajradhara,[497] who embodies
All meditation deities, buddhas, and their children,
I supplicate you; pray bless my mind. [342]

Thus, from the practices of the innermost essence of the heart instructions given by our sole lord, the great Atiśa Dīpaṃkara, to the Dharma king Dromtönpa, wherein the key points of all the scriptures and their commentaries as encompassed within the three baskets of scripture and the four classes of tantra are entirely summarized and instructed, this is chapter II, the section on *exhorting oneself to make this human existence of leisure and opportunity meaningful.*

III. Training the Mind in the Path Common with the Person of the Initial Scope

1

Embodiment of the compassion of myriad buddhas,
O my root teacher, Munīndra Vajradhara,
Pray reside on my crown upon a lotus seat,
And bless me that my mind may turn toward the Dharma.

2

This human life, so hard to find yet so valuable,
Will definitely cease, yet there is no certainty when this might happen;
At death nothing other than Dharma is of benefit,
So I pledge to practice sublime Dharma until my life's end.

3

Though there is no guarantee that I will not die this very day,
I make plans and preparations to remain forever;
What kind of monstrous demon has possessed my heart?
Bless me that I may expel this malignant demon of self-grasping.

4

After death I cannot choose where I might be reborn;
If I am reborn in the regions of the lower realms,
How will I bear the pains of heat, cold, hunger, and thirst?
Who will be my savior and refuge at that time?

5

So today, when I have freedom in my hands,
I will go for refuge to the undeceiving Three Jewels,

The refuges that save me from all the terrors of the lower realms;
I will ensure that the precepts of going for refuge never degenerate.

6

If, on my part, I do not go for refuge,
Even if the power of all the buddhas and bodhisattvas were pulled
     together,
This would not rescue me from the abyss of the lower migrations;
So I will never let myself down.

7

Whatever happiness and suffering there are in this cyclic existence,
Since all of it is due to one's own karma,
At all times and in all contexts I will guard my three doors
And strive to relinquish evil and to acquire virtue.

8

I will forsake all base thoughts and actions,
Such as pursuing material gain and honor out of attachment to self,
And I will embrace the hosts of thoroughly white actions,
Such as giving charity and [observing] discipline out of altruism.

9

If, due to the afflictions, I indulge in negative actions,
Terrified and alarmed, I will instantly relinquish them
As if a venomous snake has touched my body,
And, through the four-powered confession, purify them
     immediately.

10

O most kind teacher Munīndra Vajradhara, [343]
Behold me, a destitute one, with compassion;
Bless me so that in the future I will be free from the lower realms
And so that I will obtain an excellent existence in the higher realms.

11

Obtaining an existence endowed with the eight special attributes,
May I be free from all obstacles, and may all favorable conditions

Be present to cultivate the thoroughly perfect path;
May I reawaken the potency of the seed of the Supreme Vehicle.

Thus, from the practices of the innermost essence of the heart instructions given by our sole lord, the great Atiśa Dīpaṃkara, to the Dharma king Dromtönpa, wherein the key points of all the scriptures and their commentaries as encompassed within the three baskets of scripture and the four classes of tantra are entirely summarized and instructed, this is chapter III, the section on *training the mind in the path common with the person of the initial scope.*

IV. Training the Mind in the Path Common with the Person of the Intermediate Scope

1
Unexcelled teacher Buddha Munīndra
And the assembly of teachers of the three lineages,
Pray bless my mental continuum
And lead my thoughts toward the path to liberation.

2
If, having gone for refuge to the undeceiving Three Jewels,
I correctly practice discarding evil and cultivating virtue,
I will be saved from the abyss of unfortunate migrations in the lower
   realms
And will be able to obtain a fortunate migration.

3
Yet if I fail to generate the thought of pure renunciation,
My mind will fall prey to the power of karma and afflictions.
Once again I will plunge below and will wander continuously;
Therefore, I will cultivate renunciation toward cyclic existence.

4
From the peak of existence down to the relentless hells,
No matter where I am born in this cyclic existence of the three realms,
I will remain bound within the suffering of pervasive conditioning,
So I will develop revulsion and disenchantment toward all of existence.

5
Though existence in the fortunate realms is positive in samsara,
Birth in the fortunate realms is also within the bounds of
    suffering,
For when one takes birth with a human body,
The sufferings are incalculable, it has been taught.

6
With one's mind under the dominion of attachment,
It enters the two fluids of the parents,
And, like a worm in an fetid, dark, and filthy environment,
One dwells in the womb, experiencing pain.

7
When, after a full nine months have past, one is born in the tenth
    month,
One is squeezed tightly between the bones of the womb's entrance;
One experiences pains more acute and unbearable
Then being reborn in the hell realms, it has been taught.

8
After birth, one's body is assailed at all times [344]
By various outer and inner harms, like sickness and malignant
    forces;
With a proliferation of afflictions, one engages in negative acts,
So I will recognize that birth is cyclic existence's fortress.

9
Since the reality of conditioned things is their impermanence,
The sufferings of sickness, aging, and death,
Arise sequentially like ripples on a lake,
So I will generate the wish to be free from cyclic existence.

10
Furthermore, one must soon part,
Unwillingly, from loving family and friends,
And one's enemies cause numerous undesired harms,
So what reliability is there in such a transient reality?

11

What comes together separates, and what is amassed gets depleted;
The end of high status is decline, and all that is born dies.
Everything shares the nature of the conditioned suffering;
Contemplating such truth, I will generate the wish to be free.

12

That I must undergo sufferings of such an unbearable magnitude
Is due to the monstrous demon of self-grasping.
I will let go of the attachment to my own self, which brings my downfall;
I will practice the path of freedom that leads beyond the world.

13

If you wish to achieve the state of sublime liberation,
Rely on the sublime mentor who shows you the path;
Let go of the base thought that is attached to your self,
And practice the three trainings, the opposite of the afflictions.

14

Since it is taught that among the three trainings
The foundation and the root is the morality of individual liberation,
Bless me so that I may make the individual liberation [ethic]—
The root of the Buddha's teaching—my heart practice.

15

You possess compassion greater than all the buddhas,
Most holy teacher Munīndra Vajradhara,
Pray always reside as my crown ornament
And bless me so that my individual liberation [vows] remain pure.

Thus, from the practices of the innermost essence of the heart instructions
given by our sole lord, the great Atiśa Dīpaṃkara, to the Dharma king
Dromtönpa, wherein the key points of all the scriptures and their commentaries as encompassed within the three baskets of scripture and the four
classes of tantra are entirely summarized and instructed, this is chapter IV,
the section on *training the mind in the path common with the person of the
intermediate scope.*

V. *Training the Mind in the Awakening Mind*

1

Most precious teacher embodying all three objects of refuge,
Pray reside on my crown upon a lotus and moon;
Bless me so that the supreme awakening mind,
The essence of all scriptures of sutra and tantra, will arise within me.

2

Seeing the three worlds as a massive pit of blazing fire
And spurred by revulsion and disenchantment toward them, [345]
If I engage well in the three pure trainings,
I will be able to gain freedom from cyclic existence.

3

Nonetheless if I lack love, compassion, and the awakening mind,
I will not be able to acheive the state of buddhahood;
Nor can you fully accomplish the dual aims of self and others,
So I will strive to generate the supreme awakening mind.

4

If I divide [others] with labels of "enemies" and "friends,"
The supreme mind of equanimity toward all will not arise,
So I will let go of attachment to myself and toward other beings
And practice equanimity, equalizing the mind toward all.

5

My parents, who have been kind to me since beginningless time,
Are shackled by karma and afflictions in the prison of samsara;
They undergo hundreds of most unbearable sufferings.
Repeatedly thinking of this, I will develop compassion for beings.

6

As for me and all beings equal to the extent of space,
That which has chained us in this cyclic existence,
From beginningless time until now, is the demon of self-grasping;
I will strive to tame this monstrous demon of self-grasping.

7

Reflecting on how this monstrous demon of self-grasping
Has caused harm from beginningless time to the present,
I will let go of this thought cherishing my own well-being
And practice the thought cherishing others more than my own self.

8

Urged by powerful forces of loving-kindness and compassion,
With no hint of possessiveness
I will give my body, possessions, and roots of virtue
To my kind destitute parents, whatever they desire.

9

Like in the exemplary life of our teacher Munīndra,
I will contemplate the benefits of cherishing others;
And all the nonvirtuous karma and sufferings of others
I will take upon my mind and purify.

10

Just as the peerless teacher Munīndra
Practiced giving at all times, as found in the Jātakas,
Such as when he was born as Maitrakanyaka,
I will practice giving and taking in all my deeds.

11

All the joys of cyclic existence of the three realms
And even the bliss of unexcelled liberation—
All of these ensue from the thought cherishing others more than myself;
I will endeavor to practice equalizing and exchanging self and others.

12

As for my most kind parents who are wandering in cyclic existence,
To view them as wish-granting jewels from which emerge all wishes,
Or as meditation deities who grant higher attainments,
And to cherish all sentient beings—
This is the way of life of the great beings of Kadam.

13

Contemplating in this way, through the power of practicing giving and
taking, [346]
The potency of the seed of the Supreme Vehicle becomes ever more
enhanced;
Thus I will cultivate the altruistic resolve and courage [making the
determination]:
"I alone will liberate all beings without exception."

14

Drawn forth by the force of this altruistic resolve,
I will generate the irreversible supreme awakening mind, [thinking,]
"I will definitely attain complete enlightenment,
The fulfillment of all the aims of self and others."

15

When this precious supreme awakening mind arises,
At that very instant you become a child of the buddhas;
All the buddhas will consider you as if you were their only child;
Accepting you as their sibling, the bodhisattvas will nurture you.

16

Be it vast learning, superior cognition, or supernatural feats,
Even if you do not possess these other qualities,
Because of your mind generation, the place where you reside becomes
An object of veneration for all beings, including the gods.

17

Brahma, Indra, and the four guardians of the world,
Even great beings such as the disciples and self-enlightened ones,
Pay homage to the practice of love, compassion, and the awakening
mind,
And honor them in all possible ways.

18

Be it constructing representations of Buddha's body, speech,
and mind,
Giving charity, or accumulating any sort of expansive virtues,

If such [actions] are not reinforced by the precious awakening mind,
After bearing their fruits, they will cease.

19
The practice of love, compassion, and the awakening mind, however,
Is like an excellent tree with wonderful fruit;
As it bears fruit, it flourishes all the more.
So I will practice the supreme mind at all times.

20
As for this precious supreme mind cherishing others more than myself,
I will generate it during all six phases of the day and night;
And, in order to help increase that mind, I will strive to gather
The dual accumulations, such as by venerating the Three Jewels.

21
Beings of the degenerate age are inconsistent within and without,
Yet even if I am betrayed by their deceit and pretense,
I will never abandon them, but will increase my compassion further
And cultivate the altruistic thought: "When will I achieve their welfare?"

22
So that my awakening mind will not degenerate even in future lives,
I will discard the four negative factors, such as deceiving a preceptor or
    master,
And constantly cultivate the four positive factors,
Such as offering respect to the bodhisattvas.

23
The essential point of all the scriptures of the Great Vehicle,
The sole heart-practice of all the bodhisattvas,
This precious awakening mind cherishing others more than myself—
May I be blessed so that this soon arises within me.

Thus, from the practices of the innermost essence of the heart instructions
given by our sole lord, the great Atiśa Dīpaṃkara, to the Dharma king
Dromtönpa, wherein the key points of all the scriptures and their commentaries as encompassed within the three baskets of scripture and the four

classes of tantra are entirely summarized and instructed, this is chapter V, the section on *training the mind in the awakening mind,* which is the gateway of entry, the foundation and the root, the heart and the life itself of the path of the person of great scope.

VI. Training the Mind in the Bodhisattva Deeds in General

1

Embodiment of the compassion of all the buddhas and their children,
O teacher, I supplicate you who embody the reality of all buddhas;
May I be able to train in the deeds of the bodhisattvas,
The road trodden by all the buddhas.

2

All who have been my kind parents since beginningless time—
Unable to bear their desperate fate in cyclic existence,
I have pledged, "I will free all destitute beings";
Now I will fulfill this pledge as promised.

3

Since a buddha's enlightened attributes are inconceivable,
The multitude of their causes is also inconceivable;
Still, I will train in that which encompasses the essential points of all
    bodhisattva deeds—
The six perfections and the four means of attracting others.

4

I will let go of my tight grasping of avarice
Toward my body, material possessions, and so on;
I will practice the generosity of giving everything to others—
My body, my possessions, and my collections of virtue.

5

I will discard all negative deeds that violate
The precepts of the awakening mind out of attachment to self;
I will practice the three ethical disciplines of the Supreme Vehicle,
Such as avoiding the acts and their bases that are harmful to others.

6

I will let go of hostile thoughts and not tolerate
The adverse conditions that are contrary to my wishes;
And, like the example of the Forbearance-Preaching Sage,[498]
I will not hurt others but will practice forbearance.

7

I will let go of wasting my entire life
In procrastination due to craving for my own happiness;
Instead, through the wish to benefit others, I will practice
The bodhisattva deeds with perseverance steady as a stream.

8

I will let go of this wasteful life
Wherein my time is consumed by laxity, torpor, and distractions;
I will practice meditative concentration aspiring to help
All other beings, which are equal in extent to space.

9

I will let go of this wandering in cyclic existence,
Seduced by the monstrous demon of self-grasping;
I will practice the wisdom of discriminative awareness
On the transcendent path of the noble ones.

10

If, having enhanced my mind, I aspire to work for beings' welfare,
I should let go of this arrogance that craves self-importance; [348]
With the wish to help all beings equally,
For the welfare of others I will practice the four means of attracting
    others.

11

In particular, if I do not search for the perfect view,
I will fail to cut the root of cyclic existence,
And I'll fail to tread the noble paths of any of the three vehicles;
I will, therefore, search for the Middle Way view.

12

It's this demon of self-grasping that has fettered me
In the prison of samsara since beginningless time,
So I will let go of this thought grasping at self
And practice the view of helping others.

13

Whatever objects appear in the field of my six senses,
I will probe them with the reasoning of profound dependent arising;
Viewing them as mere appearances, I will cut the root of grasping at
    the real.
"All phenomena are devoid of intrinsic identity," taught the Buddha.

14

Though all phenomena come into being through dependence
And reliance upon their respective causes and conditions,
If perused through critical analysis probing their ultimate mode of being,
Not even a particle can be seen [that possesses substantial reality].

15

The apparent world of undeceiving dependent origination
And the emptiness of not finding when analyzed—
If you understand that these two arise as free of contradiction
And are complementary, you have succeeded, the most excellent one
    said.[499]

16

If I understand this excellent path of the union of the Middle Way,
Whereby the ascertainment of dependent origination as infallible
Can excise the root of the delusion grasping at substantial reality,
Then I will not revert to any other erroneous views.

17

If, spurred by the intention of the awakening mind,
I integrate within my mind the infinite mode of being,
The sufferings of samsara will be excised from their roots;
This is the path of irreversibility.

18

As long as space remains,
I must seek the excellent path that is the union
Of the awakening mind and the Middle Way view
And help liberate all beings, Atiśa said.[500]

19

Just as found in [the series of] dialogues engaged in
By the most excellent one and Gyalwai Jungné,
May I remain resolute in liberating sentient beings
Throughout all times and for as long as space remains.

Thus, from the practices of the innermost essence of the heart instructions given by our sole lord, the great Atiśa Dīpaṃkara, to the Dharma king Dromtönpa, wherein the key points of all the scriptures and their commentaries as encompassed within the three baskets of scripture and the four classes of tantra are entirely summarized and instructed, this is chapter VI, the section on *training the mind in the bodhisattva deeds in general.* [349]

VII. Training the Mind in the Resultant Vajrayana

1

The convergence of all buddhas into a single embodiment,
You are the nature of all-pervading Vajradhara himself,
I supplicate you, O most precious teacher;
Pray bless my mental continuum.

2

Having trained in renunciation, the awakening mind, and the perfect view,
As my courage increases ever greater,
And when I can no longer wait to help liberate beings,
I will then enter the short path of Vajrayana.

3

If I wish to enter the unexcelled Diamond Vehicle,
I will search for with great effort and please
The qualified vajra master, who is the most excellent root
Of all attainments, both common and supreme.

4

Having pleased the vajra master,
I will enter a mandala inside a vajra fence and tent,
Completely enveloped within five-colored light rays,
And be enhanced through the four pure empowerments.

5

At that time, just as I give my promise,
Calling upon the buddhas and their children as witnesses,
I will guard the pledges relating to diet, safeguarding, and
    observances,
[Holding them] dearer than even my life.

6

As the cause for swift attainment of two resultant bodies,
I must practice the yoga of two profound stages;
Thus I will ripen my mind through the first stage
And be freed through the practice of the second stage.

7

It swiftly completes the great waves of merit;
It's the supreme method for realizing the form body;
I will behold and cultivate the deity body, the appearance aspect,
Enveloped within a halo of beautiful five-colored light.

8

When the action winds and conceptualizations that are the roots
Of karma and afflictions chaining us to samsara are excised,
And when they cease to flow through the sun and moon channels,
Clear light dawns amid the expanse of duality-free space.

9

This is the utterly secret essential point,
Elucidated most clearly in this region of snowy mountains
By Atiśa and the conqueror Tsongkhapa.
I will find firm conviction that this is free of error,
And I will extract the essence of this human life.

10

Teacher Vajradhara, you who embody all refuges,
Pray always reside in the stamen of my lotus heart,
And with the ambrosia of the complete stages of the path,
Pray help satisfy my mind swiftly.

Thus, from the practices of the innermost essence of the heart instructions
given by our sole lord, the great Atiśa Dīpaṃkara, to the Dharma king
Dromtönpa, wherein the key points of all the scriptures and their commentaries as encompassed within the three baskets of scripture and the four
classes of tantra are entirely summarized and instructed, this is chapter VII,
[350] the section on *training the mind in the resultant Vajrayana*.

VIII. Training the Mind
in the Heart-Drop Instruction of Kadam

1

O assembly of teachers endowed with the three lineages,
O four supreme meditation deities of Kadam—
Respectfully, I supplicate you from the depth of my heart;
Pray bless my mental continuum.

2

Having trained in the stages of the path of the three scopes,
And having entered the gateway of Vajrayana,
Those who wish to awaken most swiftly
Should search for the heart instructions of Kadam.

3

From a sublime spiritual mentor upholding the Kadam tradition,
One endowed with the instructions of the three lineages,
I will receive the heart-drop [instruction]
Upon entering a celestial mansion enclosed within a rainbow tent.

4

In a celestial mansion of inconceivable form,
Entering the innermost space of the infinite knot

Of the secret heart of Great Compassion Jinasāgara,
I will receive the four pure empowerments.

5
Through the determined thought of equalizing and exchanging self and
    others,
I will lead all my parents, all sentient beings; gradually entering
The secret door of Jinasāgara's heart, I invoke the blessings
Of the buddhas and their children and cleanse the two
    defilements.

6
Beholding the glorious wheels of wisdom's natural resonance
Of conquerors, their consorts, bodhisattvas, and peaceful and wrathful
    deities,
I will swiftly complete great waves of merit
Through meditative absorption perceiving everything as pure.

7
Having successfully recognized the two truths
Through the power of guruyoga endowed with the three lineages,
I will swiftly cut the root of all illusions, self-grasping,
The source of doom for all, both self and others.

8
I will adorn my body with Kadam's four supreme divinities;
I will adorn my speech with the jewels of the three baskets of
    scripture;
And adorning my mind with the three higher trainings,
I will swiftly cultivate the state of union.

9
If, through conduct utterly free of conceptual elaborations—
The most excellent immediate cause of that state of union—
I always abide by sleeping in the expanse of the wisdom
Of the ultimate mode of being, dualistic illusions will be cleansed.

10

Lead all beings [to buddhahood], advised Atiśa,
And cultivate the Buddha's form body appearing in all possible guises
Through the power of practicing the yoga of the nonduality of the
    profound and the luminous
With the skillful means of perceiving [everything] as illusion-like.

11

Thus, from reliance on a spiritual mentor up to union,
This [instruction on] the stages of the path [351]
Is the ultimate distilled essence of the pith instructions
Of Atiśa and the gentle lord [Tsongkhapa], it is said.

12

Those who wish to practice instructions such as this
Should forsake this [mundane] life and, in the solitude of the
    mountains,
With no enemy and no friend, with no master and no servant,
With no sadness and no fatigue, concentrate all their efforts.

13

In order for such a practice to be successful until its end,
It is vital that all adversities appear as favorable conditions,
So whatever perceptions arise—be they pleasant, painful, good, or bad—
Transform them into the path of the fourfold practice.[501]

14

Since the mentalities of the beings of the degenerate age are so diverse,
There are accordingly numerous traditions of spiritual practice;
Do not adulterate [the teachings], but uphold your own tradition
Of the sevenfold divinities and teachings, Atiśa said.[502]

15

Differentiating well, through reason, between perfect truth and its
    facsimile,
Enter the path that will please the conquerors;
If instead you harbor blind attachment based on "mine" and "others,"
This will doom both self and others.

16

Therefore, without being attached to the way of the ignorant,
Learn all systems, both your own and others',
And relinquish defaming other traditions;
So the stainless one advised the Conqueror's son.[503]

17

Learn all the instructions of the four schools;
Integrating them within a single body of the stages of the path,
Ensure that you discipline your own mind;
So the learned paṇḍita told the crystal youth.[504]

18

Just as any crops can grow when the soil is fertile,
In a good heart all higher qualities arise as wished for;
Whatever you do must be enforced by the awakening mind;
So stated Atiśa to the spiritual mentor Dromtönpa.[505]

19

One whose mind is stable and diligent has no obstacles;
One who is versed in what is allowed and what is proscribed goes to
    liberation.
Thus, learning, discipline, and kindness must complement each other;
This is most important, said the most excellent lord.

20

In brief, be it engaging in the practice of the three general points
Or ensuring one's possession of the three inseparable conditions,[506]
It is vital to understand all these practices of the commitments and
    precepts of mind training
And to engage in their practice.

21

Bless me, O most holy teacher, so that I may perfect
The pure causes, the pure paths, and the pure results
By taming my mind through the pure Kadam way of life
Of the sevenfold divinities and teachings.

Thus, from the practices of the innermost essence of the heart instructions given by our sole lord, the great Atiśa Dīpaṃkara, to the Dharma king Dromtönpa, wherein the key points of all the scriptures and their commentaries as encompassed within the three baskets of scripture and the four classes of tantra [352] are entirely summarized and instructed, this is chapter VIII, the section on *training the mind in the heart-drop instruction of Kadam.*

Colophon

Thus I proclaim:

This most profound secret of dialogues
Between Lord Dīpaṃkaraśrījñāna
And the source of the ocean of conquerors,[507]
How can it be an object of a child's mind?

Just as if a little child were
To measure the sky with his fist,
Or an ocean with his palm,
What could be more comical?

Similarly, for an ignorant child like me
To make definite statements of this and that
In relation to the ways of heroes on the high levels,
This saddens the learned and the sublime.

Nonetheless, since, due to the kindness of my teacher, Lord Maitreya,[508]
I received the instructions of Kadam,
I have penned some of my thoughts into a pattern
With the thought that this, too, could be of benefit.

Any shortcomings in this are due to my failure to explain,
Due to false explanations, or due to revealing secrets [inappropriately].
I declare them from my heart to all the compassionate ones;
Pray help cleanse all these defects together with their causes.

I dedicate whatever virtues I have received from this endeavor
So that the instructions of Kadam—

The essence of the Buddha's teaching most complete and flawless,
The sole foundation of life for all beings—will endure for a long time.

May I be inseparably cared for by sublime mentors
From now on throughout all my lives,
And may I be able to tread the levels and paths step by step,
Living the pure life of the sevenfold divinities and teachings.

In what is known as *The Book of Kadam*, the root verses of the *Bodhisattva's Jewel Garland* and the twentieth chapter of its commentary—a teaching [born of the] dialogues undertaken by glorious Atiśa and Dromtön Gyalwai Jungné for a period of three years pertaining to the theme of how to integrate the key points of all the scriptures and their commentaries as encompassed within the three baskets of scripture and the four classes of tantra into the stages of practice of a single person—Atiśa states:[509]

> "I will give you something whereby all the teachings are succinctly condensed. [353] This is what is needed for that which is called Dharma practice. If [the teachings are] too numerous, one cannot put them into practice. If there are too many excellent teachings, making the choice becomes impractical. Sustain the following in your mind:

> "Let go of self, embrace others, and reside in a canopy of light;
> Undo the basis of appearance and contingence, devoid of essence;
> Not finding them when sought is a success on the path;
> That is the irreversible path."

> "Master, this is a profound teaching."

> "Drom, integrate [these teachings] within the immeasurable mode
>   of being;
> Eliminate from their roots the sufferings of samsara;
> This is the irreversible [path].
> Cultivate this as long as space remains.

> "Drom, though there are numerous traditions, uphold your own;
> Do not cling to a tradition but train in others as well;
> Forsake exaggeration and denigration of other traditions;

Train in all and integrate them into one.

"Drom, if the soil is fertile, whatever one sows will grow;
For the kindhearted all wishes will come true;
For those who persevere, there are no obstacles;
Those wise in ethical norms journey to liberation.

"Lead the beings by means of appearance;
Restfully sleep in the ultimate expanse of wisdom."

Jedrung Lobsang Dorjé, the elder brother of the sovereign conqueror and the savior of all,[510] has eyes of intelligence cast widely over myriad treatises. He requested a comprehensive yet easily accessible explanation of the instructions on how to practice the condensed essential instruction presented [by Atiśa in the above citation]. It is at his urging that this heart instruction of *The Book of Kadam* entitled "An Excellent Vase of Ambrosia" was composed by the monk Yeshé Gyaltsen, an upholder of the instruction of Kadam and a vagrant in the Sukhāvatī chamber of the great Potala Palace.

XI. Sayings of the Kadam Masters
Compiled by Chegom Sherap Dorjé (ca. twelfth century)[511]

[355] HEREIN LIES the scattered sayings of the sublime masters of Kadam.

Respectfully I pay homage to the sublime teachers.

I. Sayings of Master Atiśa[512]

Once when the great master Atiśa, the sole lord, visited central Tibet, his three disciples Khutön, Ngok, and Dromtönpa[513] asked the following question: "Atiśa, in order for a practitioner to attain liberation and the state of omniscience, which is the more important of the two—the sutras and their commentarial treatises or the teachers' essential instructions?"

Atiśa replied, "Essential instructions are more important than the treatises."

When asked, "Why?" he replied, "Even if one can recite the three scriptural baskets by heart and is versed in the definitions of all phenomena, at the time of actual meditative practice, if one lacks the application of the [essential instruction of the] teaching, the teaching and the person will remain separate from each other."

They then reported, "If one were to thoroughly condense the application of the essential instructions of the teachers, it appears to be abiding in the three vows and striving in the virtues through one's three doors. Is this not so?"

Atiśa responded: "Even if you abide in accord with the three vows and remain pure, as long as your mind is not disenchanted with the three realms of cyclic existence, you will create the conditions for turning the wheel again. [Also,] even if you strive through your three doors in the virtues both day and night, if you lack the knowledge of how to dedicate them toward full awakening, they will be eroded through some distorted conceptualization. Even if you are a learned scholar, a disciplined [practitioner], a teacher, or a meditator, if you fail to turn your thoughts away from the eight mundane concerns, whatever you do will be [directed toward] the goals of this life, and you will fail to find the path to the future."

* * *

Again, Khutön, Ngok, and Dromtönpa asked Atiśa, "Of all the teachings of the path, which is the best?" The master replied:

> The best learning is realizing the truth of no-self.
> The best discipline is taming your mindstream.
> The best excellence is to have great altruism. [356]
> The best instruction is the constant observation of your mind.
> The best antidote is the recognition that everything is devoid of intrinsic existence.
> The best conduct is being at variance with the mundane world.
> The best higher attainment is the lessening of your mental afflictions.
> The best sign of higher attainment is a decrease in your attachment.
> The best giving is the absence of possessiveness.
> The best morality is a tranquil mind.
> The best forbearance is to uphold humility.
> The best joyful perseverance is to be able to let go of the endeavor.
> The best concentration is the uncontrived mind.
> The best wisdom is to make no identification of "I am" with any thing.
> The best spiritual teacher is to challenge your weaknesses.
> The best instruction is to strike at your very own shortcomings.
> The best friends are mindfulness and introspective awareness.
> The best motivating factors are your enemies, obstacles, illnesses, and sufferings.
> The best skillful means is to be free of apprehensions.
> The best beneficial deed is to help [someone] enter the Dharma.
> The best help given is to turn [someone's] thoughts to the Dharma.

* * *

Dromtönpa asked, "What is the most final of all teachings?"

"The most final among all teachings is the emptiness that is endowed with the essence of compassion," Atiśa replied.

He continued, "For example, in the world there is a medicine called 'the powerful single remedy' that counteracts all illnesses. In the same manner, like the powerful single-remedy medicine, if you realize the truth of emptiness, which is the [ultimate] nature of reality, this becomes an antidote against all afflictions."

When asked, "If this is true, why is it that all those who claim to have realized emptiness have failed to minimize their attachment and anger?" Atiśa replied:

"These [people] have arrived at mere, empty words, for if you have genuinely realized the truth of emptiness, then your body, speech, and mind are like a cotton cloth that has been [softened by constant] pressing down under the feet or like [hot] barley soup into which butter has been thrown for seasoning. Master Āryadeva states that even if you develop a mere doubt as to whether the ultimate mode of being of things is empty, this will shred cyclic existence to pieces.[514] Therefore, if you have realized the truth of emptiness without error, this would resemble [the finding of] the powerful single-remedy medicine. Thus, all the teachings of the path are encompassed within it."

* * *

"How is that all the teachings of the path are encompassed within the realization of emptiness?" asked Dromtönpa. [357]

Atiśa replied: "All the teachings of the path are embodied in the six perfections. And if [practitioners] realize the truth of emptiness without error, they will be free of deep desire and grasping attachment; hence, there is the uninterrupted perfection of giving. Since those who are free of grasping and attachment are not soiled by the stains of nonvirtue, there is the uninterrupted perfection of ethical discipline. Since they are devoid of anger from grasping at 'I am' and 'mine,' there is the uninterrupted perfection of forbearance. Since they are endowed with joy at the truth that has been realized, there is the uninterrupted perfection of joyful perseverance. Since they are free of distractions grasping at phenomena as substantially real, there is the uninterrupted perfection of concentration. Since they are free of conceiving anything in terms of the three spheres,[515] there is the uninterrupted perfection of wisdom."

* * *

"If this is so, for one who has realized the truth, is it through the view of emptiness and its meditation alone that one becomes fully enlightened?" asked Dromtönpa.

The master replied, "Nothing in this world of appearance and [every-day] convention does not come into being from one's own mind. The mind, too, is an empty awareness, and the recognition of it [i.e., the empty mind] as the nonduality of awareness and emptiness is the *view*. Abiding in this continuously with mindfulness, free of distraction, is the *medita-tion*. The gathering of the two accumulations from within such a state in an illusion-like manner is the *action*. When one can accomplish this in one's immediate experience through one's practice, this will become possi-ble in dreams [as well]. When this becomes possible during dreams, it will [then] be possible at the time of death. When this becomes possible at the point of death, it will [then] become possible during the intermediate state [as well]. And when this happens during the intermediate state, one is cer-tain to achieve the supreme attainment [of buddhahood]."

* * *

Once when Master Atiśa was residing at Nyethang, the three teachers Shang Nachung Tönpa, Gyura Tönpa, and Lhetsang Tönpa asked him about the tenets of the [Indian] logico-epistemological schools.[516]

Atiśa said: "There are many philosophical systems of both non-Buddhist and Buddhist schools, all of which are but garlands of conceptualization. Conceptualizations are beyond calculation and they have no use. As there is no time to spare in life, now is the time to seek what is most essential."

Shang Nachung Tönpa then asked, "How does one seek what is most essential?"

Atiśa replied: "Train your mind to cultivate loving-kindness and com-passion toward all sentient beings, who equal the expanse of space. [358] For their sake, strive to gather the two accumulations and dedicate all roots of virtue that arise from this toward the full enlightenment of all sentient beings. Be sure that you recognize the nature of all of these as empty and their characteristics as being like dreams and illusions."

* * *

When Master Atiśa first visited Ngari he lived there for two years. There he gave many essential instructions to those headed by Lha Jangchup Ö.[517]

[Once] he was intending to return to India, and as he was about to take to the road, Lha Jangchup Ö once again requested personal advice. When Atiśa responded that what had already been given in the past should suffice, Lha persisted with his plea. The master then gave the following instruction:

Emaho!

O friend, you whose knowledge is high and whose mind is utterly clear,
Though it is inappropriate for me, one of low intelligence and lacking in accomplishments, to offer any advice,
As you, my excellent friend who is so dear to my heart, have exhorted me,
I, a childlike one with small intelligence, offer this suggestion to your heart, my friend.

As one requires a teacher until the attainment of enlightenment, rely on a sublime teacher, O friend.
As one requires learning until the ultimate mode of being is realized, listen to your teacher's essential instructions.
As the mere knowledge of the teachings does not lead to full enlightenment, put it into practice, for knowing alone is inadequate.
Distance yourself from those objects that afflict your mind and always reside in places that increase virtue.

As distractions cause harm until one has attained stability, seek solitary forests.
Forsake friends who give rise to afflictions, and seek those who enhance virtue and respect their wishes.
As there is no end to mundane chores, discard them and abide with natural ease.
Throughout day and night dedicate your virtues and always guard your mind.
As you've received essential instructions, whatever you do, be it meditation [or other activities], do so in accordance with your teacher's words.

If you pursue this with great respect, you will reap its fruits
before long.
If you act in accord with the Dharma from your heart, both
provisions and support will be attained as by-products.
O friends, sensual desires are insatiable, like drinking salt water,
therefore cultivate contentment.

Despise all thoughts of haughtiness, conceit, and arrogance and be
tranquil and tamed. [359]
As distracting pursuits referred to as "merit" are obstacles to
Dharma practice, relinquish them.
As offerings and honor are Māra's lasso, measure them carefully like
the weights of a scale.
As words of praise and fame are tricksters, cast them out like spit
or snot.

Though today happiness, good fortune, and friends may have
converged, since this is only momentary, leave them behind.
Since the future is longer than the present, hide well your resources
in treasure as provisions for the future.
As you must depart by leaving everything behind, there is no use
for anything, so do cling to nothing.
Cultivate compassion toward the weak and abandon mocking and
disparaging them.

Have no prejudice of clinging to and recoiling from the classes of
friends and enemies.
Have no jealousy toward the learned ones, but respect them and
receive knowledge from them.
Do not scrutinize others' faults, but probe your own and discard
them like poisoned blood.
Think not of your virtues but of others' and, like a servant, show
respect for all.

Cultivate recognition of all beings as your parents and love them as
if they were your own children.
With a smiling face and loving heart, always speak what is true
without hostility.

Since excessive pointless conversations cause confusion, engage in appropriate measures of speech.

Since excessive pointless chores disrupt your virtuous deeds, discard non-Dharma pursuits.

Do not strive too hard in meaningless pursuits, for this is wasteful hardship.

Come what may, do not die with attachment; since the other shore is born of karma, it is better to rest your mind at ease.

Alas! If you become despised by the sublime beings, you are as good as dead; so be honest, not deceitful.

Since the sufferings of this life arise from past karma, do not blame others.

Since all happiness is the teachers' blessings, repay their kindness.

Since you cannot tame others' minds while your own mind remains untamed, first discipline your own mind.

Since you cannot enhance others if you lack superior cognition, strive well in your meditative practice.

Since you are certain to depart leaving your accumulated wealth behind, commit no negative karma for its sake.

Since this wealth of distractions is without essence, give charity adorned with gifts.

Since it beautifies this life and leads to happiness in the future, always observe pure ethical discipline.

Since hatred proliferates in the degenerate age, put on the armor of forbearance free of anger.

Since you might be left behind because of laziness, ignite the flame of joyful perseverance like a [blazing] fire.

Since it is on the road of distraction that one exhausts one's lifespan, the time has now come for the endeavor of concentration.

Due to wrong views [360] one fails to realize the ultimate mode of being, so inspect well the perfect truth.

O friends, there is no joy in this mire of samsara, so depart to liberation's dry shores.

Practice well the teachers' instructions and drain the lake of
   samsara's suffering.

Keep this [advice] well in your hearts and listen to this suggestion,
   for this is not mere mouthing of words.
If you do this, I'll be happy, and both you and others will enjoy
   happiness.
O listen well, dear friend, to these words of advice from an
   ignorant man.

Thus the master Atiśa, the sole lord, advised Lhatsün Jangchup Ö.

* * *

Once when Atiśa was residing in the rocky mountains of Yerpa, he gave the
following instruction to Ölgöpa Yeshé Bar:[518]

"Homage to blessed Ārya Tārā! Homage to the sublime teachers! O
noble son, reflect well on these words of mine.

"In general, the lifespan of human beings in this degenerate age is short
and, as far as the fields of knowledge are concerned, there is a great diversity. Furthermore, as you cannot have any certainty as to how long you
might live, seek to accomplish swiftly what you most aspire for.

"Do not say, 'I am a fully ordained monk,' while consorting with activities of mundane livelihood, such as [acquiring] material possessions.

"Do not say, 'I am a hermit monk,' while harboring the pain of having
your mundane pursuits undermined—or the fear of this happening—even
though you are residing in the wilderness.

"Do not say, 'I am a hermit monk,' while your mind remains not
divorced from an admiration of this life's sensual pleasures and of harmful
intentions.

"Do not say, 'I am a hermit monk,' while not relinquishing association
with the worldly even though you are residing in the wilderness, or while
continuing to expend your time in frivolous chatter, or in conversations
pertaining to a householder's life, with whosoever happens to be around.

"Do not say, 'I am a bodhisattva monk' while being incapable of bearing even the slightest harm to yourself caused by others or while doing even
the slightest benefit to others.

"If you continue to say so, despite [such actions], you are telling a great
lie to the world. Even though you might be able to make such claims to

the world, you cannot do so to those who possess the divine eyes, unobstructed at all times. Second, you cannot make such claims, for the law of karma and its effects follows after you. Third, you cannot do so to the beings who possesses the eyes of the Dharma. [361] Furthermore, remember what you have pledged in the presence of the meditation deities and the teachers when you generated the awakening mind.

"When you encounter things that try your patience, do not become despondent or exclaim, 'O this is difficult!' and fail to practice forbearance. Remember that even though [this may be] difficult, you have no choice but to face it. Hesitation born of such thoughts as whether something is difficult or not is relevant only to the period prior to taking the vows and making the pledge. After you have taken the vows and made the pledge, if you undermine them, this constitutes deceiving the meditation deities and the teachers. Therefore, even if it is difficult, remember that there is no choice but to practice forbearance.

"Also, the purpose of residing in the wilderness is to forsake association with the worldly and to relinquish clinging to friends and family. As you relinquish these, this ensures the cessation of all causes and conditions of distraction and conceptualization, such as yearning for sensual objects; thus, you look [only] at the precious mind of awakening, so never, even for a single instant, follow after the thought that worries about mundane pursuits.

"Because of failing to engage correctly in the practice of Dharma in the past, and because of the weak habituation of your mind to [such practice], mundane conceptions arise frequently, and they also remain powerful. Therefore, if you fail to apply special antidotes against them, residing in the wilderness will be pointless, for then you will be like the birds and the wild animals that live there. Do not think that, since it is too difficult at present, you will engage in the practice later on, for if a blind person loses hold of a precious jewel, he will not find it again.

"When you undertake the practice, do not measure in terms of years and months; rather, analyzing your mind, assess the level of your realization on the basis of the depth of your habituation [to the practices]. Examine whether or not the afflictions are diminished. Constantly watch your mind. Do not inflict suffering upon yourself; do not deceive yourself; do not deceive the meditation deities and the teachers; and do not do things that spell doom for both self and others.

"Even if the pursuits of this mundane life are undermined, [this is good, for] that which must be undermined is becoming so. For example, if there is a mass of filth in front of you, you have to clean it with a broom and throw it away. If someone were to help you do this, wouldn't you be delighted? In the same way, whatever conceptualizations there are pertaining to the affairs of this life must be relinquished with all available antidotes, and if your teachers and special friends help you do this, won't you be delighted? [362]

"Having made the pledge in the presence of meditation deities and the teachers, do not discriminate among the objects of your giving. Although differences do exist among the objects, as far as training your mind in the awakening mind is concerned, there is no difference [among them].

"Do not be angry toward those who perpetrate harm, for if you get angry about those who cause harm, when will you practice forbearance? Whenever afflictions arise, it is necessary to remember their antidotes. What point is there in a Dharma practice that allows the afflictions to roam free? So when looking at the precious awakening mind, do this without giving a single opening to loss of mindfulness, for when a gap is opened due to degenerated mindfulness, the māras of afflictions will enter, and if they do, they will create obstacles for the awakening mind. When this happens, remember that this will undermine others' welfare, and for yourself, too, there will be no choice but [a birth in] the lower realms. Even though you might have the thought, 'I have practiced Dharma,' this will be meaningless, and you will go empty-handed.

"O noble son, when you finally die, be sure you do not cause your teachers and your special friends to feel sorrow and disappointment. Do not cause the worldly people who are interested in Dharma to become disappointed and doubtful.

"If you do not probe again and again by comparing your own mind with the sacred scriptures, even though you might feel, 'I have practiced Dharma,' the practice and the person will remain far apart. And if, when you die, instead of experiencing the signs of having trained your mind in the awakening mind, you experience the signs of the lower realms, others will have no option but to feel disappointment and sorrow. Therefore, giving up entirely the practice tainted with the vain thought, 'I have spent my entire life in Dharma practice,' ensure that at the point of death you will not be empty-handed.

"In brief, even if you reside in the wilderness, if you fail to let go of mundane pursuits and fail to avert your mind from yearning for sensual objects, then the Dharma has failed to benefit you. This is called 'not having done

one's task.' If you hope to conduct yourself in such a manner that both this life and future lives are not undermined, then Dharma practice has become [only] a hobby for you. Such a hobby will remain nothing but a Dharma practice of words, food, and pretense.

"Therefore, rely on special friends; do not associate with negative companions; do not reside in fixed locations; and do not stay at one place and hoard contaminated possessions. Whatever you do, do so by relating it to the Dharma. Ensure that whatever you do becomes an antidote to the afflictions. When you conduct [yourself] in this manner, it becomes perfect Dharma practice, so put effort into this. [363] If higher qualities arise in you, do not become inflated with conceit, for you will fall prey to Māra.

"While residing in places on the limits of town, ensure that you yourself are pacified and tamed. Be modest in desires and learn to be content. Do not focus on your own [good] qualities or seek out others' shortcomings. Do not be afraid and apprehensive. Do not have too many preconceptions. Cultivate a good heart. Do not be distracted by misguided ways, but contemplate the Dharma on a regular basis. Adopt humility; accept losses; give up trumpeting [your good deeds]; let go of deep desires; cultivate affection; and have moderation in all things. You should be someone who is easy to please and easy to nurture. Run away from the worldly like a wild animal.

"If you do not relinquish mundane norms, you are not a Dharma practitioner. If you do not relinquish the four pursuits, such as farming, you are not a monk. If you do not discard sensual objects, you are not a fully ordained monk. If you lack loving-kindness and the awakening mind you are not a bodhisattva. If you do not let go of [mundane] pursuits, you are not a meditating yogi.

"Do not become a servant to sensual desires. In brief, while residing in the wilderness, ensure that you have few chores and that you undertake only the practice of the Dharma. In this way, ensure that when death approaches you will have no regrets."

Again Atiśa said:

> Now, in this age of degeneration, is not the time for bravado; it is
> the time to expose the bones of your heart.[519]
> Now is not the time to claim the high ground; it is the time to take
> the ground of humility.

Now is not the time to seek retinues and servants; it is the time to
seek solitude.

Now is not the time to measure your students; it is the time to
measure yourself.

Now is not the time to cling onto words; it is the time to
contemplate their meanings.

Now is not the time to travel around; it is the time to remain
settled in one place.

II. The Sayings of Dromtönpa

The three brothers[520] who were the disciples of the spiritual mentor Dromtönpa requested of him a method to condense the [essential] points of all
the aspects of the path to omniscience.

Dromtönpa stated: "For an individual practitioner to attain the buddhahood of omniscience, [364] inconceivable numbers of precepts can be
the entries to the path. As for what is to be cultivated within, however, there
is only one thing. What is this single point? It is emptiness endowed with
the essence of compassion.

"To distinguish its [aspects] further, *empty* refers to the ultimate awakening mind; it is the ultimate mode of being of all phenomena realized as
primordially unborn. *Compassion* is the conventional awakening mind,
which is the generation of great compassion toward those sentient beings
who have failed to realize this [unborn nature]. Therefore, Mahayana practitioners for whom [the two awakening minds] have not yet arisen should
first strive to generate the two awakening minds. In the middle, while training in the two awakening minds that have already arisen in their mental
continuums, they gain certainty they will actualize their ultimate results—
the Buddha's truth body and form body.

"Although there are many methods for generating the awakening mind
where it has not yet arisen, when summarized for practice, there are only
three root methods and nine principal divisions. First the three roots are
subsumed into (1) training the mind, (2) gathering the accumulations, and
(3) seeking the meditative absorptions.

"Their nine principal divisions, which are their branches, are [as fol-
lows]: First, although there exist numerous methods for training the mind,
the three principal ones are: (1) meditation on impermanence, (2) cultivation of loving-kindness and compassion, and (3) meditation on the two

selflessnesses. Among the methods for training the mind, these three are the greatest and, moreover, all other methods are encompassed by these three.

"Although there are numerous methods of gathering the accumulations, the three principal ones are: (1) making offerings of material things and service to the teachers, (2) making offerings to the Three Jewels, and (3) making offerings of material things and service to the spiritual community. Among the methods of accumulating merit, these three are the greatest and they also encompass [all other methods].

"Although there are numerous ways of seeking meditative absorptions, the three principal ones are: (1) observing pure ethical discipline, (2) making supplications to the lineage teachers, and (3) seeking both physical and mental solitude. These three alone are the greatest, and they embody the methods of seeking the meditative absorptions of tranquil abiding and penetrative insight.

"Thus, as a result of practicing these nine points in a concentrated manner, the two awakening minds arise in your mental continuum with the force of spontaneity. The moment the ultimate awakening mind arises, the realization of all external and internal phenomena as free of dualistic elaborations—as empty and unborn—will spontaneously arise [as well]. At that time, one will have found within oneself a joyful state of mind. [365] The moment the conventional awakening mind arises, feelings of loving-kindness and compassion toward the sentient beings who have failed to recognize this [truth of emptiness] will arise especially. Your sole task in life will become working for the welfare of sentient beings. At that point, whatever activities you engage in will become beneficial to other sentient beings.

"You will thus combine these two [awakening minds] into a union so that at the very moment [when the realization of] emptiness [is present], compassion for sentient beings will grow especially, while at the very moment of compassion, you will not observe a substantial reality of oneself and [other] sentient beings. Thus, by recognizing [all] appearances as empty and like illusions, when these two [minds] arise in union, you have entered the unmistaken path of the Great Vehicle. As you become trained in this [union], and when your habituation to this becomes perfected, you will attain the perfect dharmakāya and the perfect form body. From the ultimate awakening mind you attain the dharmakāya, while from the conventional awakening mind—i.e., compassion—you attain the form body.

And, from the mastery of the indivisible union of these two, you attain the indivisible nature of the dharmakāya and form bodies."

* * *

Again, the three brothers asked Dromtönpa, "Of the two—view and action—which is more important for the perfection of one's own interests and others' welfare?"

Dromtönpa replied, "In order to perfect the welfare of self and others after entering the door of the Great Vehicle, you need to combine perfect view and perfect action. One in isolation [from the other] cannot accomplish this [aim]."

"If so, what constitutes perfect view and perfect action?" they asked.

Dromtönpa responded: "*Perfect view* refers to the recognition that all phenomena are, from the point of view of their ultimate nature, devoid of existing in any substantial mode of reality and free of all extremes of eternalism and nihilism, and the recognition that from the conventional perspective, all external and internal phenomena are like dreams, illusions, and apparitions. You recognize them simply as expressions of your own mind, and you thus never place your trust in any thing or chase after any objects.

"*Perfect action* refers to respecting the law of karma and its effects, understanding that on the dream-like, illusion-like level of conventional truth, the positive and negative karmas do not fail to give rise to their effects. Out of great compassion, you strive for the welfare of the sentient beings who fail to recognize this truth.

"Such perfect view and perfect action arise naturally for someone in whom the two awakening minds have arisen."

"If this is so, what flaws arise when view and action are in isolation [from each other]?" they asked. [366]

Dromtönpa replied, "If you do not respect the law of karma and its effects and let your behavior become degraded, you will be incapable of working for the welfare of both self and others, so your view will also become misguided. If you possess perfect action but fail to realize the ultimate mode of being [of all phenomena], you will be incapable of working for the welfare of both self and others, so your conduct will become misguided. Therefore, if you do not combine view and action, you will fall into error; it is necessary [therefore] to train in the union [of the two]."

* * *

Again, the three brothers asked Dromtönpa, "Of the two—practicing in solitude and benefiting other sentient beings through teaching—which has a greater impact?"

Dromtönpa replied: "If a beginner who does not have the slightest experience of realization within his or her mental continuum were to help others through teachings, this would have no benefit. This is like pouring blessings from an empty container: there are no blessings to pour out. The essential instructions [of such a teacher] would be like beer made of grains that have not been well covered: there is no taste and vitality to such essential instructions.

"A person who has attained the [stage of] 'heat'[521] but not its stability will not be able to bring about the welfare of other sentient beings, for this is like pouring blessings from a full container: when the other [container] becomes full, it itself becomes empty. The essential instructions of such a person would be like passing a torch from one hand to another: when the other [hand] is illuminated, one's own becomes darkened.

"Once one has attained the bodhisattva levels, one should, as much as possible, engage in the activities of bringing about the welfare of sentient beings. Here the blessings are like the higher attainments flowing from an excellent vase: even when all others are enhanced, it never becomes empty. The essential instructions of such a person resemble a source lamp: even when all other [lamps] are lighted, it itself does not become obscured.

"Therefore, during this age of degeneration, for ordinary beings, it is the time to familiarize your mind with loving-kindness and compassion in solitude. This is not the time to actually benefit sentient beings. It is the time to guard against the afflictions within your mind. This is analogous to the period when it is more appropriate to guard the fledgling shoot of a medicinal tree than to cut it."

* * *

Once a teacher from Kham asked Dromtönpa about the meaning of the two selflessnesses.

Dromtönpa replied, "If you were to probe with your mind and search from the top of your crown aperture to the bottom of the soles of your feet, [367] not a single entity is to be found that is called the 'self.' That nonfinding is the selflessness of persons. Recognizing that the searching mind, too, is devoid of intrinsic existence is the selflessness of phenomena."

* * *

A woman named Salo Tsomo of Drom from the Tré[522] region of Phenpo made an offering of forty bags of barley [to Dromtönpa] and asked the following question: "My brother Dromtsik sent me to give you a message, O spiritual mentor. All the monks here have gathered for the purpose of attaining the omniscient state of buddhahood. We two siblings seek the same attainment. Spiritual mentor, since you possess the essential instructions of Master Atiśa, the sole lord, as if poured from one full vase into another, today we request that you confer on us, keeping nothing hidden, the essential instructions for the attainment of buddhahood."

The spiritual mentor Tönpa replied, "First contemplate extensively death and impermanence and the law of karma and its effects, and ensure the purity of all the vows that you have pledged to observe. Cultivate loving-kindness and compassion extensively and stabilize the awakening mind. To this end, gather the two accumulations by means of various methods. Purify negative karmas through various means. While maintaining the non-objectification of the three spheres with regard to all phenomena, dedicate all your roots of virtue toward the attainment of full enlightenment by all sentient beings. If you conduct yourself in this way, you need feel no sorrow for not having met Atiśa. There is no greater teachings than this for becoming fully awakened. In the future one need not feel saddened for not meeting me, the old man of Drom, for there is no greater teachings than this."

* * *

Once an upāsaka asked the spiritual mentor Dromtönpa, "If one remains undivorced from loving-kindness, compassion, and the awakening mind, is this not, directly or indirectly, always the cause for the fulfillment of others' welfare?"

Dromtönpa replied: "Without question, this is the cause for the perfect realization of others' welfare; this will become the cause for the perfect realization of your own welfare as well, for if you remain undivorced from loving-kindness, compassion, and the awakening mind, it is impossible to be reborn in the three lower realms of existence. Starting right now you can become an 'irreversible' person. If, however, due to past grave negative karmas and powerful adverse current conditions, you were to take birth in the lower realms, [368] a mere single instance of recollecting loving-kindness, compassion, and the awakening mind would, that very instant, free you from that lower-realm birth. You would be certain to achieve the status of the extraordinary form of a human or celestial existence. For example, the *Guide to the Bodhisattva's Way of Life* states:

> Whatever suffering is in the world
> Arises from wishing for one's own happiness;
> Whatever happiness is in the world
> Arises from the wish for others' happiness.

> What need is there to say more?
> The childish pursue their own interests,
> While the buddhas act for the welfare of others;
> Observe the difference between these two.[523]

"Therefore, loving-kindness, compassion, and the awakening mind are the causes for accomplishing the great purposes of both self and others, it has been taught."

* * *

Again, once at Radreng,[524] an elder was circumambulating the outer perimeter. Dromtönpa asked him, "O elder, performing circumambulation may be satisfying, but wouldn't it be better if you practiced the Dharma?"

The elder felt that, compared to performing circumambulations, perhaps it would be more effective if he were to read the Mahayana sutras, so he [sat down to] read the sutras on the temple's veranda. Dromtönpa told him, "Reading the sutras might also be satisfying, but wouldn't it be better if you practiced the Dharma?"

Thus, [the elder] took this as a signal indicating that, compared to reading the sutras, engaging in meditative absorptions is more profitable, so he abandoned reading the sutras and sat down with his eyes closed. Again, Dromtönpa said, "Meditating might also be satisfying, but wouldn't it better to practice the Dharma instead?"

After failing to find any other method, [the elder] asked, "O spiritual mentor, if this is so, what kind of Dharma practice should I undertake?"

"O elder, give up [attachment to] this life; give up [attachment to] this life," replied Drom, it is said.

In this way, Dromtönpa stated that, so long as we fail to forsake attachment to this life, whatever [practice] we undertake does not become

Dharma practice, for such an act will remain within the bounds of the eight mundane concerns. By contrast, if we let go of attachment to this life, we will remain untainted by the eight mundane concerns, and [only] then will whatever we do become a path to liberation.

* * *

Once Potowa asked the spiritual mentor Dromtönpa, "Where is the line between Dharma and non-Dharma?"

Dromtönpa replied, "If it is a remedy against the afflictions, it is Dharma; if not, it is not Dharma. If it is at variance with all worldly people, it is Dharma; if it is in accord [with the worldly], it is not Dharma. If its trace is positive, it is Dharma [369]; if not, it is not Dharma."

III. Sayings of Other Masters of Kadam

The spiritual mentor Gönpawa[525] said:

> The root of omniscience lies in the two accumulations.
> The root of the two accumulations lies in the awakening mind.
> The root of the awakening mind lies in loving-kindness and
>   compassion.
> The root of the precepts of all of these [practices] lies in the six
>   perfections.
> The root of giving lies in the absence of grasping attachment.
> The root of ethical discipline lies in reliance on good companions.
> The root of forbearance lies in upholding humility.
> The root of joyful perseverance lies in contemplating death.
> The root of concentration lies in seeking solitude.
> The root of wisdom lies in observing your own mind.
> The root of blessings lies in admiration and respect.
> The root of higher attainments lies in the vows and commitments.
> The root of higher qualities lies in learning, reflection, and
>   meditation.
> The root of others' welfare lies in the absence of selfish desires.
> And the root of both self and others' welfare lies in meditative
>   practice.

* * *

Yerpa Shangtsünpa[526] said: "If we aspire from the depths of our heart for liberation, we must, while continually contemplating death and impermanence, abide in the four natural attributes of a noble one in both our thoughts and actions.

"The four natural attributes of a noble one are: (1) being content with modest clothing, (2) being content with modest food, (3) being content with modest bedding, and (4) being content with modest facilities for subsistence, such as medicine for illness. Alternatively, they are: (1) being modest in one's desires, (2) having the ability to be content, (3) being easy to nurture, and (4) being easy to fulfill.

"*Being modest in one's desires* refers to not having a deep desire for good facilities and for abundance, and to giving up all material possessions. *Having the ability to be content* refers to being content with few and modest material things. *Being easy to nurture* refers to [370] being able to subsist on modest clothing, bedding, and food. *Being easy to fulfill* refers to being satisfied with minimal and modest offerings, material gifts, and services.

"Since all the factors of enlightenment reside in the mindstream of the person who abides in the four natural attributes of a noble one, they are known as 'abiding with the four natural attributes of a noble one.' As all negative karmas, which are the causes of cyclic existence and the lower realms of existence, reside in the mindstreams of those who are motivated by the mundane desires of this life and who thus do not abide in the four natural attributes of a noble one, so they are known as 'abiding with the natural attributes of Māra.' Therefore, if we fail to relinquish desire in this life, we will fall prey to the power of desire in our future lives as well, so we must relinquish all mundane desires pertaining to this life and abide within the four natural attributes of a noble one. To relinquish mundane desires of this life, it is critical to constantly meditate on impermanence, which is their antidote, for if you fail to meditate on impermanence one morning, by midday you will be someone who is concerned with the mundane affairs of this life."

* * *

Again, Yerpa Shangtsün said: "If you aspire to attain omniscient buddhahood, you need the three untainted factors: (1) your virtues must not be tainted by mundane conceptions pertaining to this life; (2) your actions of body and speech must not be tainted by the afflictions; and (3) your meditative practice must not be tainted by [the mindset of] the self-enlightened ones. In brief, your action must [illustrate] perfect realization.

"What is the measure of a perfect realization? It is flexible when it should be, so it must be flexible in terms of the view. It is strict when it should be, so it must be strict in terms of conduct. It is heroic when it should be, so it must be heroic in applying the antidotes against the afflictions. It is humble when it should be, so through the achievement of forbearance, it must be humble when provoked by others and so on."

* * *

Once the spiritual mentor Potowa[527] was asked by an upāsaka, "To engage in a single-pointed practice of Dharma, what is most important?"

Potowa replied: "To engage in a single-pointed practice of Dharma, the contemplation on impermanence is most important. For if you contemplate death and impermanence, in the beginning it will cause you to enter the Dharma. In the middle, it will act as an impetus to engage in virtuous actions. Finally, it will act as a complement to realizing perfect equanimity of the ultimate nature of reality.

"Again, if you contemplate impermanence, first [371] it will act as a cause for enabling you to let go of attachment to this life. In the middle, it will act as a condition for averting clinging to all aspects of cyclic existence. Finally, it will act as a complementary factor for entering the path of nirvana.

"Again, if you contemplate impermanence, and its realization arises in your mind, first it will act as a cause for cultivating faith. In the middle, it will inspire joyful perseverance. And finally, it will cause wisdom to arise.

"Again, if you contemplate impermanence, and its realization arises in your mind, first it will act as a cause for inspiring armor-like joyous effort. In the middle, it will act as a condition to inspire the joyous effort of actual application. And finally, it will act as a complementary factor to inspire irreversible joyful perseverance."

* * *

Once Kyangtsa Dortsül[528] asked the spiritual mentor Potowa for an instruction. Potowa replied:

"Contemplate impermanence repeatedly, and when the thought that death is inevitable arises, you will arrive at a point where there will be no hardship in abandoning negative karma and engaging in virtue.

"In addition, repeatedly cultivate loving-kindness and compassion, and when they arise in your mental continuum, you will arrive at a point where there will no longer be any hardship in working for the welfare of sentient beings.

"In addition, repeatedly meditate on emptiness, which is the ultimate mode of being of all phenomena. And when this [realization] arises in your mental continuum, you will arrive a point where there will no longer be any hardship in eliminating the delusions."

* * *

Again, Potowa gave the following teaching to his assembly of disciples in general:

"In general, the blessed Buddha, taking into account the existence of eighty-four thousand classes of sentient beings or categories of afflictions, taught as antidotes to these, eighty-four heaps of teachings. All of these, when condensed in words, are embodied in the three precious baskets of scripture. In terms of their subject matter, they are embodied in the three precious higher trainings.

"Of the three precious higher trainings, first, it is on the basis of the higher training in morality that the higher training in meditation arises. On the basis of [the higher training in meditation], the higher training in wisdom arises. This, then, eradicates the afflictions from their roots, thus leading to full awakening. Therefore, since the first of the three higher trainings, the higher training in morality, is the foundation of all, [372] those at the beginning stage must take morality as their principal practice.

"Attachment is the factor that is contrary to morality; furthermore, attachment is the root of all afflictions, for it is on the basis of attachment that all afflictions arise. Through it, negative karma is accumulated and one wanders in cyclic existence. To eliminate attachment, its antidote—the meditation on foulness—is taught.

"There are five different methods for this meditation on foulness.[529]

1. First *visualizing the object as one's mother, as one's child, or as a sister* is as follows: when the image of an object of attachment, such as a woman, becomes manifest, if you experience lustful attachment for a woman older than yourself, cultivate the thought of her as being your mother. If you experience lustful attachment toward a woman who is equal to your age, cultivate the thought of her as being your sister. If you experience lustful attachment for a woman younger

than you, cultivate the thought of her as being your daughter. By meditating in these ways, your lustful attachment will be averted.

2. If, despite engaging in such meditations, your lustful attachment is not overcome, second, *contemplating the effects of having a sense of shame and conscience* is as follows: generate the thought, 'If I entertain such improper thoughts in my mind, the buddhas and bodhisattvas, who posses the wisdom eyes of unobstructed sight, will come to know and see this. They will be displeased and I will not be protected. If I engage in unbecoming conduct, the gods of earth and skies will proclaim this to others; in this life my infamy will spread everywhere. In future lives, too, I will depart to the lower realms.' As you practice a sense of shame and conscience by recalling such thoughts at all stages, from beginning to end, attachment will cease.

3. However, if, despite such meditations, your lustful attachment does not cease, third, there is *visualizing the image of [the object] as being foul and [bearing] a foul odor.* The first part of this, meditating on its foulness simultaneously, is as follows: visualize the woman's body[530] as being a container of thirty-two foul substances and a city of eighty thousand classes of worms, just like the example of a dog's corpse infested with maggots, lying rotten in the summer.

    The gradual meditation is as follows: first, visualize the woman's body as being discolored, then as festering, then as bloated, as cut up, as infested with worms, as gnawed, and finally, as a skeleton.[531] Through these [visualizations], your attachment will cease. [373]

4. However, if this also does not avert your attachment, fourth, *meditating [on the object] as an enemy or a slayer* is as follows: reflect, 'This woman is my enemy, for she undermines the thoughts that are in accord with Dharma practice.[532] She is the slayer of liberation's lifeline. She is the hailstorm destroying the harvest of positive karma. She is the thief that robs away all factors that lead to perfection. She is the demon that obstructs all roots of virtue. She is the prison guard that prevents me from escaping the suffering of cyclic existence. She is the troublemaker that gives impetus to all the afflictions. Like the furnace chamber of the hells, she is the source of all sufferings.' As you meditate on these certainly your lustful attachment will come to cease.

5. Fifth, *visualizing [the object] as the trick of an illusion* is as follows: [reflect,] 'A magician, for example, tricks many people by conjuring numerous creatures, such as men, women, horses, and elephants,

with most attractive appearances and features. Likewise, through their attachment and clinging to things, all of which are false, deceptive, and devoid of intrinsic existence like such illusions, sentient beings undergo suffering in the cycle of existence. In particular, this false, deceptive body of a woman, which is of little benefit and a source of enormous faults, has deceived me uninterruptedly at all times in the past, and it will do so today.' By meditating this way, your lustful attachment will come to cease.

If, despite meditating through all these methods, you fail to overcome attachment, the māras have entered [your heart]. Therefore, you must strive to receive some means for overcoming the māras from your teacher."

* * *

Spiritual mentor Chengawa[533] gave the following teaching to the assembly of his disciples in general: "In general, if you were to condense all the teachings—all three scriptural baskets and the two vehicles—they would be embodied in the two: refraining from harming others and helping others. To put these two into practice, forbearance is critical, for without forbearance, you will retaliate against the harm that [others] inflict upon you, and when this happens, you do not turn away from causing harm. Without this [forbearance], there is no helping others, so to succeed in your Dharma practice, forbearance is essential.

"There are four methods of practicing forbearance: (1) practicing it in the fashion of putting up a target for shooting arrows, (2) practicing it by means of [cultivating] loving-kindness and compassion, (3) practicing it in the fashion of a master and his pupil, [374] and (4) practicing it by means of [understanding] the nature of reality.

1. First, *practicing [forbearance] in the fashion of putting up a target for shooting arrows,* is as follows. If you don't place a target, it cannot be hit by an arrow; it is only because the target has been hoisted that it can get hit by the arrow. In the same manner, if you had not hoisted the target through your past karma, the arrows of harm would not have hit it in this life, so the arisal of harm perpetrated by others is due to your accumulation of negative karma in your past lives. It is not appropriate, therefore, to become angry toward others. The *Guide to the Bodhisattva's Way of Life* states:

So if I do not wrong them,
No one will wrong me in return.[534]

Previously I, too, have caused such harm
To other sentient beings;
Therefore, this befalling of harm upon me—
I who have harmed sentient beings—is just.[535]

Not only that, even in terms of this life, you will reap the effects of having inflicted harm on others in the early part of your life in the later part of your life. Likewise, you will reap last year's [harm] this year, last month's harm this month, and yesterday's [harm] today. Even in this very moment, if you post the target by [using] painful words toward others and by [engaging in] negative behavior, right away, the arrows of painful words and so on will fall upon you. Therefore, recognize that it is because you put up the target that the arrows of harm from others have befallen you. With such awareness, refrain from being angry toward others. This is what Chengawa taught.

2. *Practicing forbearance by means of loving-kindness and compassion* is as follows. If, for example, a lunatic were to harm someone, others who are sane would not challenge the insane person; rather, they would say, 'poor thing, what a pity,' and would not retaliate against him. In the same manner, [reflect that] those who perpetrate harm against you are deeply insane and possessed by demons with forceful afflictions. Thinking, 'how tragic,' cultivate compassion toward them. In a way, the lunatic who is possessed by a malevolent force is less insane and, therefore, the harm he inflicts is of a lesser degree, for he harms only someone's body and life. As his insanity is confined to a few years, months, or few days, it is shorter in duration. In comparison, when a human being who possesses a 'sane' mind inflicts harm on animals, it is a graver insanity. Since he has been under the power of afflictions since beginningless cyclic existence until now, the duration [of his insanity] is longer. Because of his unrestrained indulgence in nonvirtue through his body, speech, and mind, which gives rise to the sufferings of the three lower realms, the impact of his harm is greater. [375] In contrast, having compassion instead is greater in terms of its effect, so cultivate loving-kindness

and compassion toward those who perpetrate harm toward you, and do not harbor anger toward them. The *Guide to the Bodhisattva's Way of Life* states:

> If, when they are under the power of the afflictions,
> They kill even their own dear selves,
> How could it be that at such times [when afflicted]
> They do not cause injury to others' bodies?

> Thus, under the power of the afflictions,
> There are those who engage in such acts as killing themselves;
> Even if you feel no compassion,
> How could you be angry at them?[536]

3. *Practicing forbearance in the fashion of a master and his pupil* is as follows. If there were no preceptor to confer the precepts, for instance, there would be no vows, and if there were no master to give the teachings, there would be no knowledge [of the scriptures]. In the same manner, if you had no enemies to harm you, you would have no forbearance. Thus you should recognize others who threaten you with verbal abuse and so on as teachers who grant you the gift of forbearance; and, practicing sympathetic joy and repaying the kindness, view yourself as a student seeking to learn forbearance, and do not be angry toward them.

4. *Practicing forbearance by means of [understanding] the nature of reality* is as follows. On the ultimate level, all the factors—myself, who is the object of harm, the other, who is the agent of harm, and the act of harm itself—are emptiness, the ultimate nature of reality. All these perceptions, such as me being attacked, are the apparitions of a deluded mind and therefore resemble dreams and illusions. Thus it is inappropriate to be angry toward them. The *Guide to the Bodhisattva's Way of Life* states:

> Thus with respect to these empty things,
> What can be obtained, what can be lost?
> What can be disliked, what can be liked?
> Who can be humiliated as well?[537]

One does not remain angry toward a dream enemy after awaking from sleep and recognizing his lack of intrinsic existence. Likewise, the enemies of the present are, on the ultimate level, devoid of intrinsic existence, just like a dream. So instead of being hateful toward them, you should practice forbearance." This is what Chengawa taught.

* * *

Again, the spiritual mentor Chengawa said: "To attain liberation and omniscience you must train in a practice that is at variance with all worldly people. For instance, the worldly cherish the buddhas more than sentient beings; they cherish themselves more than others; [376] they cherish those who help them more than those who cause them harm; and they cherish pleasure more than hardship.

"Given that we must act in a reverse manner, we must cherish sentient beings more than the buddhas. Why? Because toward the buddhas, [normally] not even the slightest disrespect will arise. There are [in contrast] four reasons why we must cherish sentient beings. (1) We must cherish them on the grounds that all beings of cyclic existence are our parents; (2) since our parents are suffering in cyclic existence, we must cherish them by offering our help; (3) we must cherish sentient beings on the grounds that by helping them our own welfare will be secured as a by-product; and (4) we must cherish them on the grounds that by helping sentient beings we make offerings to all the buddhas and bodhisattvas and please them.

"Also, worldly people cherish themselves more than others. We, on the other hand, must cherish others more than ourselves. Why? Since beginningless time, we ourselves have caused our own sufferings; nobody else has made us suffer. We say at present that it is the afflictions that cause us to suffer; yet between afflictions and self there is no real duality, so self is the enemy that has made us suffer in cyclic existence since beginningless time. It is necessary, therefore, to inflict as much damage as possible upon this enemy. As for others, we must cherish them. Why? Since it is in relation to other sentient beings that we accumulate merit, all the happiness in the world arises from them; thus we must cherish them. Since it is on the basis of sentient beings that we can cultivate the two awakening minds, it is from them that all higher qualities of nirvana come into being. We must, therefore, cherish sentient beings.

"Worldly people cherish those who help them more than those who cause them harm. We, on the other hand, must do the opposite. Why? In worldly terms one's parents are the greatest source of benefit. Parents give their children an estate, land, a house, gold, turquoise, horses, cattle, a wife, servants, and so on. From the point of view of Dharma practice, however, there is nothing more harmful than this, for on the basis of having been given these objects of attachment, karma and afflictions increase tremendously, [377] thus leading to their accumulation, and this eventually becomes a factor for casting one to the hells. Although one's parents of this life may seem beneficial in the present, since they ultimately lead one to suffering, [in one sense] there is no greater enemy.[538] Therefore, we must cherish those who cause us harm more than those who bring us benefit. Why? Due to the enemy's infliction of harm, we cultivate forbearance and thus obtain immeasurable merit. Because of our enemy's harm, we step up our efforts and traverse higher and higher levels. We thus achieve all higher attainments, so we must cherish those who inflict harm upon us.

"Worldly people cherish pleasure more than hardship. We, on the other hand, must do the opposite and cherish hardship more than pleasure. Why? [Worldly people] are attached to the pleasures of going to bed, sleeping, sex, laziness, clothes, and food, and these all cause suffering. We, on the other hand, must cherish hardship because, through the pains involved in serving teachers and members of the Sangha, performing ascetic practices of ethical discipline, and engaging in virtuous activities, our accumulations will be completed and obscurations purified. We will thereby attain the state of great bliss." Therefore, [Chengawa] said that we must cherish [hardship]. He said that since it is on the basis of physical illness and mental pain that one experiences disenchantment toward cyclic existence and generates true renunciation, we must cherish hardship.

Therefore, according to [Chengawa], if you possess these four practices that are at variance with the worldly, then, like the accurate divination of an oracle, you need not do anything else. If you lack these four, then, like a bad fortune teller, nothing you do will be of any benefit.

* * *

Again, the spiritual mentor Chengawa said: "At present, even the Dharma practices of the best practitioners are mixed with [the concerns of] this life.

First, fearing weakness, one latches on to the coattails of every group.
Fearing abduction by ghosts, one does retreats on wrathful deities.

Fearing starvation in some future life, one hoards possessions.
Fearing ill repute, one adopts all kinds of affected behavior.

"You may wish to attain buddhahood amid such [pursuits], but it cannot happen. It is as if you want from the same sheep both a bag for carrying water [378] and a sheepskin that can barely be lifted. It is not possible.

"If so, how should you act? We practice forbearance instead of retaliation when someone harms us, and so a person with a harsh mouth cannot torment us. Since the principal [response to] a harsh mouth is the practice of forbearance, you need not latch on to a group," Chengawa said.

"If enemies and obstacles seek opportunities [to harm] us, we recognize the self to be nonexistent even on the conventional level, like the horns of a rabbit. And since we have already given away our body to the ghosts, even the gods and demons of the trichilicosm cannot harm it. Foremost among counterforces is the realization of no-self; hence you need not undertake mantra recitation of wrathful deities.

"Although we may have no possessions and provisions, we commit the core of our mind to Dharma practice, commit the core of our Dharma practice to [the life of] a beggar, and commit the end of this [life of a] beggar to death. Therefore, all those with faith honor us. Foremost among possessions is the absence of attachment; hence you need not hoard material things.

"If others disparage us, since we have ensured our minds to be free of pretension, we will become, in the end, an object of admiration by all. Therefore, since the basis of fame and renown is flawless thoughts and behavior, there is no need at all to adopt pretentious behavior [anyway]," said Chengawa.

* * *

Again, the spiritual mentor Chengawa said: "In general, it is on the basis of [grasping at] the self-existence of persons and the self-existence of phenomena that all the afflictions and distorted thoughts proliferate. In particular, for us, it is the [grasping at] the self-existence of persons alone that causes harm. Therefore, it is the self-existence of persons that is to be attacked and eliminated through the three [levels of] wisdom—the understanding derived from learning, from reflection, and from meditation. However, in our case, even while engaged in learning, reflection, and meditation, our [grasping at] self expands, the strength of our forbearance is weaker than a deer calf, and our temperament is more edgy than the ghost of Tsang.[539] These are signs that our understandings derived from learning, reflection, and meditation have gone wrong. If we view external appearances as somewhat empty, yet our inner self remains intact, without even a scratch, this is like shooting an arrow far away when the target is directly in front of us. This is like searching for the footprints of a thief in the meadow when he ran to the forest, or sending ritual torma to the northern gate while the ghost is at the eastern gate."

* * *

Spiritual mentor Phuchungwa[540] said: "We have obtained this utterly fragile human existence of leisure and opportunity. [379] Although we have obtained this, we don't have the power to stay long, for we must [all] die. At the time of death, we have no power to retain all the mundane thoughts regarding this life and the mundane beauties, not even a fallen petal of a flower. Nothing can accompany us. At that time everything will be revealed starkly, the level of our intelligence, the strength or weakness of our ability, and our skillfulness or its lack in the pursuit of our goals.

"If, at the time of death, one can remain joyful and rest in a warm glow, then the level of one's intelligence is high, one's ability is strong, and one's pursuit of goals is skillful. Such a person is called 'competent.' But if, at that time, vivid visions of Yama's form and the aspects of the lower realms appear, one has not been skilled in the pursuit of goals and has thus failed to be competent. In the case of most of us, many travel mistaken paths because of continual reinforcement of the planning for this life.

"It is impossible that the fully awakened perfect Buddha would speak falsehood. It is also impossible that the [great] authors of the treatises, such as Master Nāgārjuna, would speak falsely. It is also impossible for the sublime teachers to speak falsely, so the question is, 'Who then puts us on the wrong paths?' It is our desires pertaining to this life that have led us to the wrong paths, so we should constantly contemplate death and, by recalling death, ensure we never remain attached to our selfish interests. We should meditate on the defects of cyclic existence in its entirety and, by bringing disenchantment to mind, ensure we never become attached to any part of cyclic existence. We should meditate on emptiness—the ultimate mode of being of all things—and, by recalling no-self, ensure we never become attached to things and their signs."

* * *

Again, the spiritual mentor Phuchungwa said: "If you are practicing Dharma seriously, you should be like a writing board with holes in it. Just as a writing board with holes cannot be used for inscribing taxes, you should be someone who cannot remain together with those who are concerned only with this life.[541] Excessive befriending and appeasing of others will lead you to be abducted by the māras, so not appeasing others is something to be desired. Because he is not pleased, he does not come; and because he disparages you, others do not come either. In such situations, though you may have only a single *shogang* coin[542] for your provisions, while it lasts, your mental state will remain joyful and you will be able to engage in virtuous activities. When virtuous activities increase, higher qualities come about naturally. Then, even the welfare of others will come about spontaneously." [380]

* * *

Again, the spiritual mentor Phuchungwa said:

> Greater is the bliss of eliminating sensual desires than the bliss of
> indulging them.
> Greater it is to know a single meaning than to know many words.
> Greater are the benefits of giving teachings than the benefits of
> giving many material things.
> Greater is the fear of the suffering of future lives than the fear of
> this life's sufferings.
> Greater it is to resolve doubts within one's mind than doubts about
> outer meanings of words.

* * *

Spiritual mentor Nyukrumpa[543] said:

> Those who wish for [birth in] higher realms and the definite
> goodness of enlightenment should cultivate the recognition of
> cyclic existence as a prison.
> They should cultivate the recognition of their body and life as
> bubbles in water.
> They should cultivate the recognition of evil friends as an enemy's
> henchmen.

They should cultivate the recognition of their teachers as wish-granting jewels.

They should cultivate the recognition of afflictions as venomous snakes.

They should cultivate the recognition of negative karma as deadly poison.

They should cultivate the recognition of sensual objects as fire buried in ashes.

They should cultivate the recognition of fame and renown as echoes.

They should cultivate the recognition of gifts and honor as snares or nets.

They should cultivate the recognition of evil friends as a plague.

They should cultivate the recognition of positive friends as a fortress.

They should cultivate the recognition of all sentient beings as fathers and mothers.

They should cultivate the recognition of giving as a wish-granting cow.[544]

They should cultivate the recognition of morality as a precious ornament.

They should cultivate the recognition of forbearance as an excellent armor.

They should cultivate the recognition of joyous effort as a heavenly horse.

They should cultivate the recognition of concentration as a great treasure [vase].

They should cultivate the recognition of wisdom derived through learning, reflection, and meditation as a lamp.

* * *

Spiritual mentor Khamlungpa[545] said:

Since it is extremely hard to obtain a human existence of leisure and opportunity, guard morality as you would protect your own eyes.

Since there is no knowing when this illusory aggregation might come to an end, strive in spiritual activities through body and speech.

Since all conditioned positive karmas are [ultimately, insignificant and] neutral, make extensive aspiration for the benefit of the sentient beings. [381]
Since everything is transient and illusory, grasp at no thing as substantially real but let go of clinging.

* * *

Spiritual mentor Benjakpa[546] proclaimed the following as a counsel to his own heart:

Since you lack even the power over today's lifespan, do not plan for a permanent stay, O monk.
Cling not to this illusory aggregation as a self, O monk.
Grasp not as dual that which is by nature nondual, O monk.
Cultivate loving-kindness and compassion for those who have failed to realize this, O monk.
Since you must plant the seeds of your ultimate goal in this very life, summon courage and joyful perseverance, O monk.

* * *

Once when spiritual mentor Kharak Gomchung[547] was visiting Chenga [Monastery], the teacher from Gyal, Yeshé Sung, asked, "I would like to request from you, O spiritual mentor, a method for engaging in spiritual activities."

The spiritual mentor Kharakpa replied, "There are three levels to the method of engaging in spiritual activities. The lowest level of spiritual activity is to avoid harming sentient beings; the middle level of spiritual activity is to help sentient beings; and the highest level of spiritual activity, since both self and sentient beings cannot be objectified, is to meditate on the unborn nature."

* * *

Again, the spiritual mentor Kharakpa said:

Since no aspects of higher qualities grow in a person who lacks faith, seek a spiritual mentor and read the sutras.
Since no aspects of higher qualities grow in a person who lacks joyful perseverance, contemplate death and impermanence and shun laziness.

Since no aspects of higher qualities grow in a person who is vain,
lower your head and adopt humility.

"If you possess these three practices, you will be a suitable basis for the disciple's path, a suitable basis for the bodhisattva path, and a suitable basis for the secret mantra path as well. In brief, you will be a suitable basis for all higher qualities."

* * *

Again, the spiritual mentor Kharakpa said:

Since attachment prevents you from transcending cyclic existence,
you err if you do not view it as a flaw.
Since aversion destroys virtues from their root, you err if you do
not view it as a flaw.
Since vanity prevents growth of extraordinary higher qualities and
weakens the roots of virtue, you err if you do not view it as a
flaw. [382]
Since generosity brings forth the perfect resources of gods and
humans, you err if you deride giving.
Since morality brings forth the extraordinary existence of the higher
realms, you err if you deride morality.
Since compassion is the root of all Great Vehicle teachings, you err
if you deride compassion.
Since the bodhisattva vows are an extraordinary method for cultivating omniscience, you err if you deride the bodhisattva vows.
Since swift attainment of common and uncommon higher
attainments depends upon secret mantra, you err if you deride
the commitments of secret mantra.

* * *

Again, the spiritual mentor Kharakpa said:

The ultimate view is to be free of all standpoints.
The ultimate meditation is to be free of all mental engagements.
The ultimate action is to be free of all norms of affirmation and
rejection.
The ultimate practice is to be free of all experiences.

* * *

The spiritual mentor Drakgyapa[548] said: "If we wish from our heart to act in accord with the Dharma, we should regularly meditate on death and impermanence and turn our backs on the mundane aspirations of this life. For even if we were to achieve all three—joy, happiness, and fame—in this life, if our thoughts are not turned toward the Dharma, these will all be tricksters. Swiftly we must shun them so that we have no connections with them. They are to be discarded one day anyway, so if we let go of them today, it will be worthwhile.

"Even if we are renowned as a learned one, a disciplined one, a teacher, and a meditator, if we fail to give up [attachment to] this life, we will pursue only the means for achieving greatness in this life. In this way, we will need to cover the entire earth with our restless pursuits, and through this, naturally and forcibly, we will become saturated with negative karma, increasingly at odds with the Dharma. Continuing to think 'I will not die,' we will die with clinging and attachment, with the chores of this life left unfinished. For us there is nowhere to go but to the lower realms. If, on the other hand, the [realization of] death and impermanence has arisen in our minds and we have forsaken [attachment to] this life, we may not have been renowned in the past as a learned one or as a disciplined one, but we will accomplish all the aims without others' being aware of it. Such a person, no matter when he dies, because of having made exclusive preparations for death, will be able to die happily and joyfully, free of any attachment or clinging to something. [383]

"Therefore, our approach should be like this. Keeping death and impermanence in your heart, examine whether all the things you have done in the past, all that you are doing now, and all that you intend to do in the future are mixed with [the mundane aims of] this life. If they turn out to be mixed with [the mundane aims of] this life, they have become mixed with the afflictions, so relinquish all the afflictions and negative karma [falsely] construed as Dharma practices. To relinquish these, persistently and repeatedly apply the vigilance of mindfulness, the observation of introspective awareness, and the restraint of heedfulness. You may have made many efforts driven by [attachment to] this life, but on the morrow of death, you will have to depart naked and empty handed, so take death for your pillow instead and engage in a Dharma practice untainted by thoughts of this life.

Given that between tomorrow and the next life no one knows
which will come first, to implement this [ideal], starting now
and before tomorrow arrives, offer all your material possessions
toward the accumulation of merit, declare and purify whatever
remorse you harbor in your heart, train your mind toward all the
objects [of mind training], strive to the best of your ability in
whatever Dharma practices you know, make all imaginable
aspiration prayers for the benefit of the sentient beings, and so
on. Act as though you have no choice but to do these things.

Given that between the next month and next life no one knows
which will come first, starting now and before next month
arrives, act as though you have no choice but to do this.

Given that between tomorrow morning and the next life no one
knows which will come first, starting now and before tomorrow
morning arrives, act as though you have no choice but to do this.

Given that you have no control over even this evening's lifespan,
this very day, offer your material possessions toward the
accumulation of merit, declare and purify any remorse in your
heart, make extensive aspiration prayers, engage in meditative
absorptions, and so on. Act as though you have no choice but to
do these.

"Right from the morning of our birth, the only [definite] thing in front of
us is death. There is also no certainty as to when this death will strike, so
we must consistently behave as if we were likely to die this very evening."

* * *

Spiritual mentor Neusurpa[549] said:

Since conceptualization of enemy and friend will not lead to
buddhahood, recognize all sentient beings equally as your
mother.

Since conceptualization of ordinariness will not lead to
buddhahood, [384] recognize all sentient beings equally as
meditation deities.

Since conceptualization of signs will not lead to buddhahood,
recognize all phenomena as equal in their emptiness, the
ultimate nature of reality.

* * *

Spiritual mentor Langri Thangpa[550] said:

> Since one person cannot fathom the measure of another, do not
>   denigrate anyone.
> Since all teachings of the Buddha bring results, do not engage in
>   them while distinguishing good ones from bad ones.
> Since the welfare of sentient beings is a Mahayana practitioner's
>   only task, ensure that your armor of working for others' welfare
>   is not weak.
> Since without attaining a secure ground for yourself you cannot
>   lead others, strive hard in the meditation practices in solitude.

* * *

Spiritual mentor Sharawa[551] said:

> Since [attachment to] women is the root of afflictions, do not seek
>   them where you are.[552]
> Since alcohol is the root of afflictions, do not drink it even under
>   threat of death.
> Since traveling is the root of afflictions, do not engage in excessive
>   travel.
> Since the hoarding of things is the root of afflictions, relinquish
>   grasping attachment.

* * *

Spiritual mentor Jayülwa[553] said:

> Since it is the foundation and the basis of the path to liberation and
>   omniscience, observe pure morality.
> Since it is the axle of the path to liberation and omniscience, train
>   in the awakening mind.
> Since it is the staircase of the path to liberation and omniscience,
>   strive constantly to gather the two accumulations.
> Since he is the navigator on the path to liberation and omniscience,
>   always rely on the spiritual mentor.

* * *

Again, the spiritual mentor Jayülwa said:

> Subject and object are like sandalwood and its scent.
> Samsara and nirvana are like water and ice.
> Appearance and emptiness are clouds and the sky.
> Conceptualizations and the nature of reality are like waves and the
> ocean.

* * *

Spiritual mentor Tölungpa[554] said:

> If you aspire for liberation from your heart, follow after the
> disciplined rather than the learned;
> Follow after the practitioner rather than the preacher;
> Follow after the humble rather than the high;
> Follow after the friend with faith rather than the friend with
> intelligence.

"We are not pitiful because we lack the knowledge of the teachings; we are so because of befriending people who do not act in accord with the Dharma."

* * *

Again, the spiritual mentor Tölungpa said: [385]

> Grasp not at the appearances of constructs as substantially real.
> Place not your hope in conditioned phenomena.
> Grieve not over the dismantling of illusions.
> Weaken not the antidotes against desire and the afflictions.
> Embrace not the eight mundane concerns.
> Prolong not your association with negative friends.
> Harbor not excessive love and affection in your relation with loved
> ones.
> Weaken not your faith and respect for your teachers and the Three
> Jewels.
> Be not attached to your body and possessions.
> Weaken not your dedication to learning, reflection, and meditation.
> Shower not with special praise the distractions of gifts and honor.

Weaken not your resilience against hardships entailed in [Dharma]
   practice.
Weaken not your altruistic compassion free of clinging.

* * *

Spiritual mentor Nambarwa[555] said:

If you fail to feel disenchanted with cyclic existence of the three
   realms, your mind will not engage with liberation, so meditate
   on the defects of samsara in its entirety.
If you do not radically terminate attachment and clinging, your
   bondage to sensual objects will not be cut, so forsake material
   possessions as if they were gobs of spit.
If you do not possess the substantial causes, the blessings of
   spiritual mentors will not enter you, so cultivate the recognition
   of your teachers as buddhas.
If you do not meditate on impermanence on a regular basis, you
   will be confined to this [mundane] life, so cultivate [awareness
   of] the lack of time in your mind.[556]
If you fail to train the mind within, you will not be sustained
   always by altruistic resolve, so train in the awakening mind.

* * *

Once, a tantric practitioner requested the spiritual mentor Chimphupa[557]
for an instruction. He responded:

This [world of] appearance is an illusion; grasp it not as
   substantially real.
The body is flesh and blood; grasp it not excessively as self.
Material goods are [fruits of] past karma; exert not too much
   effort.
Whatever you do is suffering; have not too many chores.
The cycle of existence is suffering; embrace it not.

"As for other essential instructions, I will give them to you later when there
is a long day."

* * *

Spiritual mentor Shawo Gangpa[558] said: "Today, at this juncture when we have obtained a human existence of leisure and opportunity, met with a spiritual mentor, and encountered the Mahayana teachings, we should strive our best to prepare the bed for our future lives and plant the feet of liberation and omniscience.

"First, to strive our best to prepare the bed for our future lives, we must eradicate the ten negative karmas from their roots and embrace the ten virtues. For this, we need to forsake [attachment to] this life. To attain liberation we must avert our thoughts from every part of cyclic existence. [386] To plant the feet of omniscience we must train in the awakening mind within our mental continuums.

"To generate these three thoughts, we must accumulate merit, for without gathering the merit, we will not be able to understand the teachings. Even if we do understand the teachings in some instances, their realization will not grow in us. Even if some fragmented realizations grow in us, they will evaporate and will be of no benefit. Therefore, the reason we wandered in cyclic existence in the past was because of our failure to accumulate merit and our collecting of demerit. Even in this life, our failure to have things as we wish is due to our failure to accumulate merit and to eradicate negative, nonvirtuous karmas from their roots. Thus, the root of all teachings can be subsumed into the following two—accumulating merit and purifying negative karma."

* * *

Again Shawopa said: "As for us, the desires of this life are what bring the sufferings of this and future lives, so we should shun the things that attachment to this mundane life craves. When the objectives of this life's desire are extensive, our mind lacks peace; we wander everywhere, and in the course of this, all three factors—negative karma, suffering, and ill fame— strike simultaneously. We must, therefore, relinquish this multipronged mind of desire. When we succeed in turning away the mind of desire, that is when joy and happiness starts.

> We seek happiness in this and throughout all lives, and so, as a sign of this, neither crave for anything in your heart nor hoard anything.
> When you do not crave for gifts, this is the best gift.
> When you do not crave for praise, this is the best praise.

When you do not crave for fame, this is the best fame.
When you do not crave for retinues, this is the best retinue.

"If you would practice the Dharma from your heart, point the tip of your mind to [the life of] a beggar. Ensure [this life of a] beggar to the end by being able to enter death.[559]

"If you are able to cultivate this kind of attitude, it is certain you will not be susceptible to distress caused by any of the three—gods, ghosts, and humans. If, [on the other hand], you seek to quench the thirst[560] of the desires of this life, things like the following will happen: you will disgrace yourself; you will create your own miseries; others will ridicule you, while you yourself will be miserable; and, in the future, you will depart to the lower realms.

"Therefore, if you abandon broadcasting [the good deeds you have done], adopt humility, relinquish desire, forsake all non-Dharma activities, and strive well in the meditative practices, the following things will happen: you will be happy and others will admire you, and in the future, you will attain enlightenment. In brief, if on our part, we initiate all kinds of endeavors, know all sorts of things, engage in all kinds of deeds, and however much we might say, [387] as long as our thoughts are not turned away from the desires of this life, we have no means of gaining the happiness of both this and future lives. If our thoughts are turned against all forms of desire, we no longer need to search for happiness."

* * *

Again, the spiritual mentor Shawopa said:

> Be not like those who, while failing to gain autonomy themselves,
>   seek to control others;
> Not like those who, while lacking higher qualities within their
>   mental continuums, aspire to be others' master;
> Not like those who, despite possessing great faith, fail to refrain
>   from negative karma;
> Not like those who, while admiring emptiness, possess excessive
>   self-grasping;
> Not like those who, despite having great intelligence, fail to
>   recognize what is Dharma and what is not Dharma;

Not like those who, despite having sharp intelligence, fail to understand the teachings;

Not like those who, while refraining from slight negative deeds, fail to shy away from grave ones;

Not like those who, while having great altruistic motives, fail to avoid harming [to others];

Not like those who cannot live alone and are incapable of being in the company of others;

Not like those who, while desiring to be disciplined, have little endurance;

Not like those who, while being very generous in the short term, have little flexibility deep down;

Not like those whose teachings are high but whose realizations are low;

Not like those whose masters are excellent but whose behavior is bad;

Not like those who, while delighting in the study of the teachings, dislike implementing them;

Not like those who, while desiring solitude, delight in associating with others [socially];

Not like those who, while desiring excellence, remain beset with extreme greed;

Not like those who, while aspiring for liberation, have whatever they do slide into the eight mundane concerns.

* * *

Again, the spiritual mentor Shawopa chastised himself:

You confounded one—who yearns for the high teachings for his inferior mentality!

You old mind—who hopes for improvement to occur while he does not improve himself!

You heartless one—who acts as if the Dharma were important for others and negative karma for himself!

You distorted one—who assigns appropriate acts to others and innapropriate conduct to himself!

You who resembles a steep slope of clumps of earth[561]—who has greater negative growth than positive growth!

You expert in contraction—who is elaborate in his promises but
brief in implementation!

You of wrong livelihood—who seeks the afflictions and pretends to
apply their remedies!

You who are laden with hopes and fear—who hopes others see his
qualities and fears others seeing his faults!

You who seeks victory over Dharma colleagues while accepting loss
from relatives!

You who seeks victory over the antidotes while accepting loss from
the camp of the afflictions! [388]

You who seeks victory in this life while accepting loss in the future
lives!

You who seeks victory from those who perpetrate harm while
accepting loss from those who bring benefits!

You who fails to understand that causing harm to others also causes
harm to yourself!

You who fails to understand that helping others also helps yourself!

You who fails to understand that harm and suffering are conditions
favorable to Dharma practice!

You who fails to understand that desire and happiness are obstacles
to Dharma practice!

You who, while proclaiming the importance of Dharma practice to
others, does not act in accord with the Dharma yourself!

You who, while despising others for committing negative acts, fails
to curtail your own ongoing [negative] deeds!

You who, while failing to detect your own grave shortcomings,
detects even the slightest faults of others!

You who curtails your altruistic deeds when no reward is
forthcoming!

You who cannot bear to see other practitioners being offered gifts
and honor!

You who loves the high and is hostile toward the weak!

You who dislikes tales pertaining to the next life!

You who loses your temper when others correct your flaws!

You who, while hoping others detect your virtues, does not allow
others to become aware of your negative karma!

You who is content when your external behavior is good even when
your inner thoughts remain base!

You who regards the pursuit of material things and objects of desire
   as joy and happiness!

You who, while failing to search for happiness within, searches for it
   on the outside!

You who, while having pledged to follow in the footsteps of the
   Buddha, follows after those of the worldly!

You who, while consulting the bodhisattvas, treasures merchandise
   [for sale] in the hells!

You who, while dedicating your body, resources, and virtues of the
   three times to sentient beings, fails to let go "I" and "self"!

You who fails to understand that the affection of negative friends is
   the precursor of doom!

You who fails to understand that the anger of virtuous friends is a
   source of benefit—

Because you'll waste so much time on "what is" and "what is not,"
   do not indulge in chatter with others.

Because it will lead to the proliferation of craving, do not reign over
   a kingdom in your mind.

Because there is greater risk than profit, do not delight in making
   promises.

Because this will necessarily undermine your virtuous activities, give
   up excessive chores.

Relating these chastisements to his heart, Shawopa offered such counsel.

* * *

Among this heart advice of the sublime masters of Master Atiśa's lineage, a
few of the sayings of the Kadam masters, which once remained scattered,
have been collected and compiled [here] by the monk Chegom. [389]

IV. Supplement 1: Sayings of Kharak Gomchung [562]

Homage to the sublime teachers!

I present here [the sayings] by summarizing into six sets of three, six sets of
four, eight sets of five, five sets of six, and a set of seven.

A. *Six sets of three*

1. The first set of three, the three necessities, is:
   a. First, it's necessary to fear death.
   b. In the middle, it's necessary to have no remorse even if you were to die.
   c. Finally, it is necessary not to fear death.

2. There are three things to be abandoned:
   a. Abandon your place of birth.
   b. Abandon home and family.
   c. Abandon activities and chores.

3. There are three things to be embraced:
   a. If you embrace a teacher, essential instructions will flow.
   b. If you embrace meditation, experience will grow.
   c. If you embrace meditative absorptions, realizations will increase.

4. Make sure you do not commit the three confusions:
   a. A Dharma practitioner and pretender are likely to be confused.
   b. The view and words are likely to be confused.
   c. Meditation and intention are likely to be confused.

5. There are three methods of meditation:
   a. First, meditate on the words.
   b. In the middle, meditate on the combination of words and their meaning.
   c. Finally, meditate on the truth of the mind.

6. There are three things you must not be apprehensive about:
   a. Do not be apprehensive about being hungry when old.
   b. Do not be apprehensive about losing support.
   c. Do not be apprehensive about being despised by the world.

B. *Six sets of four*

1. Of the six sets of four, there are four best facts:
   a. If the rope of mindfulness is not cut, this is the best meditation.
   b. If cyclic existence is recognized as impermanent, this is the best recognition.

    c. Gaining control over body and speech is the best vow.

    d. The flourishing of virtuous activities is the best retreat.

2. There are four "are not"s:

    a. If you do not refrain from negative karma, you are not a Dharma practitioner.

    b. If you are devoid of vinaya discipline, you are not a monk.

    c. If you are devoid of commitments, you are not a tantric practitioner.

    d. If you fail to let go of grasping, you are not a sublime person.

3. There are four roots:

    a. If you delight in alcohol and women, this is the root of misdeeds.

    b. If you delight in activities and chores, this is the root of distractions.

    c. If you grasp material wealth, this is the root of bondage.

    d. If you are vocal with your mouth and quick with your action, this is the root of negative karma.

4. There are four areas of error:

    a. If you don't relinquish subject-object duality, you don't go beyond the surface, so this is an error.

    b. If you don't relinquish the afflictions, you are a yogi in name only, so this is an error.

    c. If you don't relinquish bias, your conduct is a mere pretense, so this is an error.

    d. If you don't let go of activities, you remain a mere ordinary person, so this is an error.

5. There are four resemblances:

    a. If you teach Dharma to others yet fail to practice it yourself, this resembles a lay person playing the role of a protector in a dance. [390]

    b. Selling tantra as a commodity resembles exchanging medicine for poison.

    c. Failing to discipline your mind while possessing great essential instructions resembles having a jewel but remaining poor.

    d. Being attached to home after having forsaken the worldly norms resembles being caught in a snare after having escaped from the swamp.

6. There are four necessities:[563]

    a. You need to ensure that you do not turn your spiritual teacher into an evil friend.

    b. You need to ensure that you do not turn your meditation deity into a demon.

    c. You need to ensure that your meditation on emptiness becomes an antidote against the afflictions.

C. *Eight sets of five*

1. There are five difficult passages:

    a. The difficult passage of cyclic existence so hard to escape

    b. The difficult passage of discrimination, deviating from the Dharma

    c. The difficult passage of Māra, remaining by oneself alone

    d. The difficult passage of learning, being satisfied with essential instructions

    e. The difficult passage of malevolent forces, one's conduct being unheedful

2. There are five misplaced things:

    a. Pursuing learning in order to become superior to everyone else is misplaced.

    b. Giving teachings to others in order to receive material gifts and fame is misplaced.

    c. Engaging in meditative equipoise with no instruction on meditation is misplaced.

    d. Observing morality with an expectation of receiving material gifts and honor is misplaced.

    e. Giving charity in order to bring everyone under your influence is misplaced.

3. There are five slippery slopes:

    a. If one is highly intelligent, vastly learned, and reputed to have accurate divinations, one can slide into becoming a busy preacher with no time for meditation practice.

    b. If one is sharp-minded and cares greatly for material things, one can slide into becoming a ritual master or a merchant chief.

    c. If one is powerful and has great skills, one can slide into becoming a guarantor or a security [in financial transactions].

d. If one is eloquent and quick to act, one can slide into becoming a chief or a treasurer.

e. If one remains ignorant and is weak in persistence, one can slide into ordinary conduct and have no time for meditation.

4. There are five principal things:
   a. Principal among views is the belief in the law of karma and its effects.
   b. Principal among virtuous activities is restraint from harming other sentient beings.
   c. Principal among meditative practices is ensuring your commitments and vows do not degenerate.
   d. Principal among pledges is being able [to fulfill them].
   e. Principal among actions is cultivating the approximation of deities.[564]

5. There are five autonomies:
   a. Autonomy due to: Gaining mastery over the essential instructions
   b. Being capable of overcoming circumstances through antidotes
   c. Having awakened your natural inclinations through faith
   d. Possessing an ethical discipline free of hypocrisy
   e. Being capable of dispelling even the slightest harm caused by obstacles

6. There are five "is"s:
   a. Freedom from desire is bliss.
   b. Freedom from objectification is emptiness.
   d. Freedom from any locus is nonconceptuality.
   d. Freedom from exertion is the nature of reality.
   e. Cessation of desire is the fruit.

7. There are five questions of Atiśa, the sole lord:
   a. If one has realized the view [of emptiness], is it necessary to meditate or not?
   b. In order to become a buddha, [391] is it necessary to combine method and wisdom or not?
   c. For the bodhisattva vows, does one need to have the individual liberation vows as its basis or not?
   d. With regard to the wisdom-knowledge empowerment, can it be

conferred by celibate [practitioners] above the level of upāsaka or not?[565]

8. There are five contexts when ingesting human nourishment is not appropriate:
    a. Consuming dangerous poison
    b. Utilizing what is given [to others]
    c. Enjoying a consort
    d. Enjoying funds borrowed as debts
    e. Consuming burning flames[566]

D. *Five sets of six* [567]
1. There are six types of foolishness:
    a. To delight in and have affection for this mire of cyclic existence, which is the root of suffering, is foolish.
    b. To render extravagant care on this transient body, which is like a reflection, is foolish.
    c. Even if you are poor, to hoard your possessions without regard to negative karma is foolish.
    d. To pay attention to [the concerns of] this life alone despite the uncertainty of when the great suffering will strike is foolish.
    e. To think you'll be able to endure the sufferings of the lower realms following your death when you can't even endure the slightest suffering at present is foolish.
    f. Failing to practice the profound and vast teachings and creating suffering for yourself is foolish.

2. There are six inappropriate things:
    a. Though aspiring to be disciplined and realized, not averting your thoughts from cyclic existence is inappropriate.
    b. A fully ordained monk not entering the Buddha's teaching [through actual practice] is inappropriate.
    c. The intelligent not comprehending Dharma is inappropriate.
    d. The learned scholar not respecting the law of karma and its effects is inappropriate.
    e. The devout being soaked in negative karma is inappropriate.
    f. The virtuous departing to the lower realms and hells is inappropriate.

3. There are six ways of being deluded:

    a. Instead of searching for excellent instructions, learning about meaningless conventional topics is deluded.

    b. Instead of roaming the wilderness of the mountains, building the dark dungeon of cyclic existence is deluded.

    c. Instead of reflecting on the truth alone in solitude, lecturing on Dharma in large congregations is deluded.

    d. Instead of meditating in absorption on no-self, being distracted by indulgence in material wealth is deluded.

    e. Instead of giving charity without possessiveness, hoarding food and [sustaining] a wealth of avarice is deluded.

    f. Instead of practicing the Dharma properly, appeasing others by adhering to worldly norms is deluded.

4. There are six shameful things:

    a. Having the gateway of sublime Dharma, which resembles a shining sun, yet performing destructive rites is indeed shameful.

    b. Having taken pledges in front of the lord of the world,[568] yet indulging in heedless behavior is indeed shameful. [392]

    c. Having generated the mind of supreme awakening, yet denigrating others is shameful.

    d. To excessively scrub and cleanse this body adorned with foul substances is also shameful.

    e. To be devoid of wisdom and compassion while proclaiming to be a Mahayanist is also shameful.

    f. Having entered the profound secret mantra, yet not observing the commitments and being lazy is also shameful.

5. There are six recognitions:

    a. Recognizing the teacher as the source of mundane and supermundane higher attainments

    b. Recognizing the commitments as a foundation

    c. Recognizing your body as the mandala of the deities

    d. Recognizing sentient beings as buddhas

    e. Recognizing the world of appearance and existence as like dreams and illusions

6. There are six perfect essential instructions:
   a. Observe whether or not the enemy of the five poisons is being pacified from within.
   b. Observe whether or not you are free from the illness of cyclic existence.
   c. Observe whether or not you have vanquished the forces of the four māras.
   d. Observe whether or not your meditative equipoise and subsequent realizations are equal.
   e. Observe whether or not you are abiding in the [stage of] manifest movement.[569]
   f. Observe whether or not you have met with the innate path.[570]

E. *One set of seven*

There is one set of seven, the seven useless things:
   a. You may have taken all the vows, from going for refuge to the secret mantra, but if you fail to avert your thoughts from worldly norms, this is useless.
   b. You may regularly give teachings to others, but if your vanity is not pacified, this is useless.
   c. You might show progress, but if you lose the entry-level [practice] of going for refuge, this is useless.
   d. You might strive in virtuous activities day and night, but if they are not reinforced by the awakening mind, this is useless.
   e. You may define the *imputed nature,* the *dependent nature,* and so on,[571] but if you fail to recognize things as illusion-like, this is useless.
   f. You might know the three baskets of scripture, but if you lack admiration and respect for your teachers, this is useless.
   g. You may meditate on emptiness, but if this does not become an antidote against the afflictions, this is useless.

These scattered exhortations, the essential instructions of Kharak Gomchung—instructions set down in writing by the spiritual mentor Lhopa[572]—are complete.

V. Supplement 2: Sayings of Chegom

Nāmo guru!
(Homage to the teachers!)

The precious father Chegom said: "If you recognize the world of appearance and existence as the mind, [393] realize the mind itself as empty, and have no grasping at the superiority of your realizations—this is the ultimate view.

"To be held by the glue of nondistraction, having placed your mind in the uncontrived state, and to be devoid of objectification and grasping at this or that object—this is the ultimate meditation.

"To turn adversities into the path, to sever [the rope of] clinging at favorable objects, and to be devoid of adoption and rejection or affirmation and negation—this is the ultimate conduct.

"To recognize everything that occurs as devoid of substantial reality, to be devoid of rejection and acceptance with regard to good and bad, and to let go of everything at will—this is the ultimate removal of interfering forces.

"To have your perceptions dissolve into an inchoate mass, to have your delusions dismantled, and to have your clinging quickly cease—this is the ultimate sign of heat.[573]

"To loose the hitching post of self-grasping, to exhaust desires through realizating everything as devoid of self-existence, and to sever the rope of expectations—this is the immediate fruit.

"On this basis, to purify your awareness, to uphold the natural ground of the dharmakāya, and to engage selflessly in the welfare of others—this is the ultimate fruit.

"Actually, even with regard to these ultimate facts, there is no ultimate enjoyment or abandonment [of mind]; they are ultimates only in their relative contexts.

> Therefore, since the basis is empty like an echo, do not grasp this
> empty echo as real.
> Since the illusory path is a construct of the mind, with respect to
> such mental constructs, do not engage in affirmation and
> negation.

Since the resultant three buddha bodies are empty names, with
respect to such empty names, do not harbor any hollow
expectation or suspicion."

Nāmo guru!
(Homage to the teachers!)

"The ten perfect factors are:
1. Having conviction in the law of karma and its effect is the perfect
   view of the initial level of mental facility.
2. Realizing all external and internal phenomena as a union of the
   four—appearance and emptiness, and awareness and emptiness—is
   the perfect view of the middle level of mental facility.
3. Realizing the indivisibility of all three—the object viewed, the
   viewer, and the realization [itself]—is the perfect view of the highest level of mental faculty.
4. Abiding in a single-pointed meditative absorption is the perfect
   meditation of the initial level of mental facility.
5. Abiding in meditative absorption on the union of the four factors is
   the perfect meditation of the middle level of mental facility.
6. Abiding in the sphere of nonobjectification of the three—the object
   of meditation, the meditator, and the experience [itself]—is the perfect meditation of the highest level of mental facility.
7. Observing the law of karma and its effects as you would guard your
   eyes is the perfect action of the initial level of mental facility. [394]
8. Engaging with all phenomena as if they were dreams and illusions is
   the perfect action of the middle level mental facility.
9. Not engaging in anything is the perfect action of the highest level of
   mental facility.
10. The progressive diminishing of self-grasping, afflictions, and con-
    ceptualizations is the perfect sign of heat of all three levels of men-
    tal facility—initial, middle, and highest. These are the ten perfect
    factors."

These are the words of Chegom.[574] May the welfare of sentient beings
flourish.

Table of Tibetan Transliteration

PHONETIC SPELLING	WYLIE TRANSLITERATION
Akya Yongzin (a.k.a. Yangchen Gawai Lodrö)	A kya yongs 'dzin
Amdo	A mdo
Ato Sherap Gyaltsen	A kro Shes rab rgyal mtshan
Ben Gungyal	'Ban gung rgyal
Benjakpa (a.k.a. Ben Gungyal)	'Ban 'jag pa
Changkya Rölpai Dorjé	Lcang skya Rol pa'i rdo rje
Chakpa Mepa	Chags pa med pa
Chaksorwa (a.k.a. Laksorwa)	Phyag sor ba
Chegom Dzongpa	Lce sgom rdzong pa
Chegom Sherap Dorjé (a.k.a. Chegom Dzongpa)	Lce sgom shes rab rdo rje
Cheka (monastery)	'Chad ka
Chekawa Yeshé Dorjé	'Chad ka ba Ye shes rdo rje
Chenga Lodrö Gyaltsen	Spyan snga Blo gros rgyal mtshan
Chengawa Tsültrim Bar	Spyan snga ba Tshul khrims 'bar
Chenresik	Spyan ras gzigs
Chim Namkha Drak	Mchims Nam mkha' grags
Chimphupa (a.ka. Rok Chimphupa)	'Chims phu pa
Chiwoikyé	Chi 'o'i skyes
Chökyi Paljor Lekpa	Chos kyi dpal 'byor legs pa

Chökor Gyal (monastery)	Chos 'khor rgyal
Chöphel	Chos 'phel
Decö Sangpo	Bde spyod bzang po
Depa Tenpa	Dad pa brtan pa
Dergé	Sde dge
Desi Sangyé Gyatso	Sde srid Sangs rgyas rgya mtsho
Dharma Gyaltsen	Darma rgyal mtshan
Dingpopa	Sdings po pa
Dokham	Mdo khams
Dölpa Sherap Gyaltsen (a.k.a. Ngari Sherap Gyaltsen)	Dol pa Shes rab rgyal mtshan
Drakarwa	Brag dkar ba
Drakgyapa (a.k.a. Jolek)	Brag rgyab pa
Drakmarwa	Brag dmar ba
Drepung (monastery)	'Bras spungs
Drip Tsechok Ling (monastery)	Sgrib tshe mchog gling
Drojé Denpa	Rdo rje gdan pa
Drolungpa	Gro lung pa
Dromtön Gyalwai Jungné	'Brom ston Rgyal ba'i 'byung gnas
Dromtönpa	'Brom ston pa
Drukpa Pema Karpo	'Brug pa pad ma dkar po
Dungkar Lobsang Trinlé	Dung dkar Blo bzang 'phrin las
Ganden	Dga' ldan
Gandenpa	Dga' ldan pa
Gampopa	Sgam po pa
Geden	Dge ldan
Gedenpa	Dge ldan pa
Geluk	Dge lugs
Gendün Drup (First Dalai Lama)	Dge 'dun grub

Gendün Gyatso (Second Dalai Lama)	Dge 'dun rgya mtsho
Geshé Lhaso	Dge bshes Lha bzo
Gezé Jangchup	Dge mdzes byang chub
Gö Lotsāwa (Shönu Pal)	'Gos Lo tsā ba (Gzhon nu dpal)
Gönpapa	Dgon pa pa
Gönpawa	Dgon pa ba
Gönpawa Wangchuk Gyaltsen (a.k.a. Gönpapa or Gönpawa)	dGon pa ba dBang phyug rgyal mtshan
Gugé	Gu ge
Gungthangpa (a.k.a. Naktso Lotsāwa)	Gung thang pa
Gyal	Rgyal
Gyalwa Gyatso	Rgyal ba rgya mtsho
Gyergompa	Dgyer sgom pa
Gyura Tönpa	Gyu ra ston pa
Ja Dülzin	Bya 'dul 'dzin
Jamgön Amé	'Jam mgon A med
Jampel Gyatso (Ninth Dalai Lama)	'Jam dpal rgya mtsho
Jangchup Gyaltsen	Byang chub rgyal msthan
Jangchup Namkha	Byang chub nam mkha'
Jangchup Nangwa	Byang chub snang ba
Jayül (monastery)	Bya yul
Jayülwa Shönu Ö	Bya yul ba Gzhon nu 'od
Jolek (a.k.a. Drakgyapa)	Jo legs
Jowo	Jo bo
Kadam	Bka' gdams
Kagyü	Bka' brgyud
Kakholma	Ka khol ma
Kangyur	Bka' 'gyur

Karma Kagyü	Karma Bka' brgyud
Karmapa Rangjung Dorjé	Karma pa Rang byung rdo rje
Kawa Shākya Wangchuk	Ka ba Shā kya dbang phyug
Kham	Khams
Khamlungpa Shākya Yönten	Khams lung pa Shā kya yon tan
Kharak Gomchung Wangchuk Lodrö	Kha rag sgom chung Dbang phyug blo gros
Kharakpa	Kha rag pa
Khedrup Norsang Gyatso	Mkhas grub nor bzang rgya mtsho
Khenchen Nyima Gyaltsen	Mkhan chen Nyi ma rgyal mtshan
Khuö Salenchikma	Khu 'od Bza' lan gcig ma
Khutön Tsöndrü Yungdrung	Khu ston Btson 'grus g.yung drung
Könchok Bang	Dkon mchog 'bangs
Kushen Yaksher Phen	Sku gshen yag gzher 'phen
Kyangtsa Dortsül	Rkyang tsa rdor tshul
Kyirong	Skyid grong
Laksorwa (a.k.a. Chaksorwa)	Lag sor ba
Langri Thangpa	Glang ri thang pa
Langthang (monastery)	Glang thang
Lechen Künga Gyaltsen	Las chen Kun dga' rgyal mtshan
Lha(tsün) Jangchup Ö	Lha (btsun) Byang chub 'od
Lha Lama Yeshe Ö	Lha bla ma Ye shes 'od
Lhasa Shöl	Lha sa zhol
Lha Thothori Nyentsen	Lha Tho tho ri gnyan btsan
Lhetsang Tönpa	Lhad tshang ston pa
Lhopa	Lho pa
Lodrö Sangpo	Blo gros bzang po
Longdöl Ngawang Lobsang	Klong brdol Ngag dbang blo bzang
Lungshö Nyukrum (monastery)	Klung shod snyug rum

Milarepa	Mid la ras pa
Nakpa Tsering	Nag pa tshe ring
Naktso Lotsāwa Tsültrim Gyalwa	Nag 'tsho Lo tsā ba Tshul khrims rgyal ba
Naljorpa	Rnal 'byor pa
Naljorpa Amé Jangchup	Rnal 'byor pa A mad byang chub
Naljorpa Sherap Dorjé	Rnal 'byor pa Shes rab rdo rje
Nambar (monastery)	Rnam 'bar
Nambarwa	Rnam 'bar ba (also spelled Gnam 'bar ba)
Namkha Rinchen	Nam mkha' rin chen
Namri Songtsen	Gnam ri srong btsan
Narthang (monastery)	Snar thang
Nechung	Gnas chung
Neusurpa	Sne'u zur pa
Neusurpa Yeshé Bar	Sne'u zur pa Ye shes 'bar
Ngari (monastery)	Mnga' ri
Ngari Sherap Gyaltsen	Mnga' ris Shes rab rgyal mtshan
Ngaripa	Mnga' ris pa
Ngok Lekpai Sherap (a.k.a. Sangphuwa)	Rngog Legs pa'i shes rab
Nyatri Tsenpo	Gnya' khri btsan po
Nyethang Or(ma)	Snye thang 'Or (ma)
Nyingma	Rnying ma
Nyukrumpa Tsöndrü Bar	Snyug rum pa Brtson 'grus 'bar
Ölgöpa Yeshé Bar (a.k.a. Shangtsünpa)	'Ol rgod pa Ye shes 'bar
Pabongkha Dechen Nyingpo	Pha bong kha Bde chen snying po
Panchen Sönam Drakpa	Paṇ chen Bsod nams grags pa

Pawo Tsuklak Trengwa	Dpa' bo Gtsug lag phreng ba
Pehar	Pe har
Pekar	Pad kar
Pema Karpo (a.k.a. Drukpa Pema Karpo)	Pad ma dkar po
Phagmo Drupa	Phag mo gru pa
Phen yül (a.k.a. Phenpo)	'Phen yul
Phenpo	'Phen po
Phuchungwa	Phu chung ba
Phuchungwa Shönu Gyaltsen	Phu chung ba Gzhon nu rgyal mtshan
Poto (monastery)	Po to
Potowa Rinchen Sal	Po to ba Rin chen gsal
Pugyal	Pu rgyal (also as Spu rgyal)
Radreng (monastery)	Rva sgreng
Rampa Lhading (monastery)	Ram pa lha sdings
Rinchen Gyaltsen	Rin chen rgyal mtshan
Rok Chimphupa	Rogs 'Chims phu pa
Sakya	Sa skya
Salo Tsomo	Za lo 'tsho mo
Samten Ling (monastery)	Bsam gtan gling
Samyé (monastery)	Bsam yas
Sangphu (monastery)	Gsang phu
Sangphuwa (a.k.a. Ngok Lekpai Sherap)	Gsang phu ba
Sera (monastery)	Se rva
Shang Nachung Tönpa	Zhang Sna chung ston pa
Shangtsünpa (a.k.a. Ölgöpa Yeshé Bar)	Zhang btsun pa
Sharawa (Yönten Drak)	Sha ra ba (Yon tan grags)

Shawogang (monastery)	Sha bo sgang
Shawo Gangpa (a.k.a. Shawopa)	Sha bo gang pa
Shawopa (Pema Jangchup) (a.k.a. Shawo Gangpa, Shawowa)	Sha bo pa (Pad ma byang chub)
Shawowa (a.k.a. Shawopa)	Sha bo ba
Sherap Gyaltsen	Shes rab rgyal mtshan
Shigatsé	Gzhis ga rtse
Sönam Lhai Wangpo	Bsod nams lha'i dbang po
Sumpa Khenpo (Yeshé Paljor)	Sum pa mkhan po (Ye shes dpal 'byor)
Taklung Ngawang Namgyal	Stag lung Ngag dbang rnam rgyal
Tapka (monastery)	Stabs ka
Tapkapa	Stabs ka pa
Tashi Khyil (monastery)	Bkra shis 'khyil
Tashi Lhünpo (monastery)	Bkra shis lhun po
Tengyur	Bstan 'gyur
Tenma	Bstan ma
Thangkya (monastery)	Thang skya
Thuken Chökyi Nyima	Thu'u bkwan Chos kyi nyi ma
Tokden Dingpopa	Rtogs ldan Sdings po pa
Tölungpa Rinchen Nyingpo	Stod lung pa Rin chen snying po
Tré (sometimes Pö)	Spre (sometimes Spos)
Tromsherwa	Khrom zher ba
Tsalpa Künga Dorjé	Tshal pa Kun dga' rdo rje
Tsang	Gtsang
Tsangpa Rinpoché	Gtsang pa rin po che
Tsongkhapa	Tsong kha pa
Tsuklak Trengwa	Gtsug lag phreng ba
Tsültrim Gyalwa	Tshul khrims rgyal ba
Tumtön Lodrö Drak	Gtum ston Blo gros grags

Ü	Dbus
Uru	Dbu ru
Ütsang	Dbus gtsang
Yangchen Gawai Lodrö	Dbyang can Dga' ba'i blo gros
Yerpa	Yer pa
Yeshé Döndrup	Ye shes don grub
Yeshé Sung	Ye shes srung
Yongzin Yeshé Gyaltsen	Yongs 'dzin Ye shes rgyal mtshan

Notes

1 *The Book of Kadam* I, chap. 2. See p. 93 of the present volume.

2 In referring to these beliefs as "myths," I do not mean to contrast them with some kind of "reality" and suggest that they are somehow false. I am using the term in a sense suggested by Robert A. Segal (*Myth: A Very Short Introduction*, pp. 4–6), who defines myth broadly as a story whose main figures are personalities—divine, human, or even animal—who accomplish something significant for their adherents.

3 See, for example, Leonard van der Kuijp's "The Dalai Lamas and the Origins of Reincarnate Lamas" in Martin Brauen, ed., *The Dalai Lamas: A Visual History*, pp. 14–31.

4 Hubert Decleer makes this comparison in his paper, "Master Atiśa in Nepal: The Tham Bahīl and Five Stūpas according to the *'Brom ston Itinerary*,'" p. 43. The full text of this *Itinerary* is found in volume I of *The Book of Kadam*, pp. 229–90. For a succinct account in English of Atiśa's life in general and the Ngari rulers' efforts in bringing Atiśa to Tibet, see Pabongka Rinpoche, *Liberation in the Palm of Your Hand*, pp. 28–58.

5 Chim Namkha Drak, *Biography of Master Atiśa* in *The Book of Kadam* I, p. 135.

6 *Las rgyu 'bras kyi ston pa*. Ibid., p. 136.

7 For a contemporary discussion of the stages of the doctrine *(bstan rim)* genre and its distinction from the texts of the stages of the path *(lam rim)* proper, see David Jackson, "The *bsTan rim* ('Stages of the Doctrine') and Similar Graded Expositions of the Bodhisattva's Path" in José Ignacio Cabezón and Roger R. Jackson, eds., *Tibetan Literature: Studies in Genre*, pp. 229–43.

8 Although these lamrim notes appear to be no longer extant, extracts from some of these are provided in Yeshé Döndrup's *Treasury of Gems*, pp. 199–219. Lechen Künga Gyaltsen, *Lamp Illuminating the History of the Kadam Tradition*, p. 4a:2, refers to two interesting interpretations of the distinctions between *lamrim* and *tenrim* teachings, though he personally disapproves of such an understanding. He reports that some say those teachings that were given in public were referred to as *tenrim*, while those that were taught in a concealed manner were called *lamrim;* others say that those presented in the form of guided instruction are *lamrim*, while those presented in the form of their supporting explanations are referred to as *tenrim*.

9 This date is based on Panchen Sönam Drakpa's *History of Old and New Kadam Schools*, p. 5a:5, where he gives Earth-Horse and Wood-Sheep as the years of Ngok's birth and death.

10 The *Lam rim chen mo,* Tsongkhapa's classic work, is today available in English translation in three volumes under the title *The Great Treatise on the Stages of the Path to Enlightenment* (Ithaca: Snow Lion Publications, 2000–2004).

11 This text is mentioned in Sönam Lhai Wangpo's *A History of the Precious Kadam Tradition,* p. 383. This historian of Kadam fuses the stages of the path and the stages of doctrine teachings together and identifies what he calls the "three lineages of lamrim." They are: (1) the lamrim lineage stemming through Potowa, (2) the lineage stemming through Chengawa, and (3) the lineage stemming through Sangphuwa (i.e., Ngok Lekpai Sherap).

12 Selected extracts from these early stages of the doctrine texts can be found in Yeshé Döndrup, *Treasury of Gems,* pp. 106–28, 136–45.

13 See my introduction in *Mind Training: The Great Collection,* volume 1 of *The Library of Tibetan Classics.* The fifteenth-century historian Sönam Lhai Wangpo (*A History of the Precious Kadam Tradition,* p. 383) refers to the mind training teachings as "scattered sayings" *(gsung sgros thor bu).*

14 There is no consensus on Saraha's dates among contemporary scholars, and the Tibetan sources provide conflicting evidence. I have chosen to follow the tentative period suggested by Hajime Nakamura in *Indian Buddhism: A Survey with Bibliographical Notes,* p. 340.

15 A list of works in the Kangyur and Tengyur for which Atiśa is a translator, author, and both author and translator can be found in Alaka Chattopadhyaya's *Atiśa and Tibet,* appendix B: "The Works of Dīpaṃkara," pp. 442–502. The Tibetan tradition also identifies a collection known as "Atiśa's Cycle of One Hundred Short Texts" *(Jo bo'i chos chung brgya rtsa),* although it is not clear who first compiled the collection.

16 Gö Lotsāwa Shönu Pal, *The Blue Annals,* vol. I, p. 543.

17 Chim Namkha Drak, *Biography of Master Atiśa, The Book of Kadam,* vol. I, p. 179.

18 Lechen Künga Gyaltsen, *Lamp Illuminating the History of the Kadam Tradition,* pp. 2b–4a.

19 Jamgön Amé cites this verse and states that it is from Dromtönpa's "Short Version of Sevenfold Divinity and Teaching" *(Lha chos bdun ldan chung ba).*

20 Pawo Tsuklak Trengwa, *Joyful Feast for the Learned,* vol. I, p. 720.

21 For example, Nyangral Nyima Öser's (1124–92) early historical work *A History of Dharma: Pure Honey Extracted from the Essence of a Flower* (p. 469) lists only these two Kadam lineages of transmission and explicitly states that Phuchungwa did not cultivate any students of his own. Thuken Chökyi Nyima (*Crystal Mirror of Philosophical Systems,* p. 101) writes that, although essential instructions *(gdams ngag)* and oral instructions *(man ngag)* may generally be seen as synonymous, in the context of identifying the distinct transmission lineage of Kadam teachings, "oral instructions" refers specifically to the secret teachings of *The Book of Kadam.*

22 This is according to Thuken Chökyi Nyima (*Crystal Mirror,* p. 100). However, Tsalpa Künga Dorjé (*The Red Annals,* p. 65) identifies Naktso Lotsāwa (1011–64) as the source of the Kadam lineage of the stages of the path.

23 Sönam Lhai Wangpo, *A History of the Precious Kadam Tradition,* p. 372.

24 Gö Lotsāwa Shönu Pal, *The Blue Annals,* vol. I, p. 395. The alternative translation of the passage appears on p. 326 of Roerich's *The Blue Annals.*

25 For a brief account of the individual colleges of Sangphu and their conversion to Sakya and Geluk Schools, see Shunzo Onada, "Abbatial Successions of the Colleges of gSang phu sNe'u thog Monastery," in *Kokuritsu Minzokugaku Hakabutsukan kenky euhe okoku* 15, no. 4 (1999): 1049–71.

26 Thuken Chökyi Nyima, *Crystal Mirror*, p. 89.

27 A brief summary of the first twenty birth stories of Dromtönpa, the content of the Son Teachings, was produced in German in Dieter Schuh's *Tibetische Handschriften und Blockdrucke*. Sarat Chandra Das also prepared partial translations of the first, second, and sixth birth stories of the Son Teachings in "The Lamaic Hierarchy of Tibet," *Journal of the Buddhist Texts Society of India* 1 (1893): pt. 1, pp. 31–38 and pt. 2, pp. 44–57.

28 *The Book of Kadam*, vol. I, chap. 2. See p. 93 of present volume.

29 The brief description of the visualization practice of the sixteen drops presented here is based on Yongzin Yeshé Gyaltsen's *The Rite of the Mandala of the Sixteen Drops of Kadam*, pp. 60b:1–65a:2.

30 *The Book of Kadam*, vol. I, chap. 3. See p. 108 of this volume.

31 *Lha chos kyi sgom tshul.*

32 The full story can be found in chapter 15 of the *Jewel Garland of Dialogues*.

33 *Bodhisattva's Jewel Garland*, v. 16; also *The Book of Kadam*, vol. I, chap. 16. See p. 311–12 of present volume.

34 *Bodhisattva's Jewel Garland*, v. 23.

35 *The Book of Kadam*, vol. II, chap. 2. Lechen Künga Gyaltsen (*Lamp Illuminating the History of the Kadam Tradition*, p. 84a:6) gives Kushen Yaksher Phen as the name of Dromtönpa's father and Khuö Salenchikma as the name of his mother.

36 Thuken Chökyi Nyima (*Crystal Mirror*, p. 87) states that Dromtönpa was prophesized as the Upāsaka Dharmavardhana (Genyen Chöphel; *dge bsnyen chos 'phel*) both in the *Flower Ornament Scripture* and the *White Lotus Sutra*.

37 *The Book of Kadam*, vol. II, chap. 2.

38 *The Book of Kadam*, vol. II, chap. 5.

39 *The Book of Kadam*, vol. II, chap. 5, p. 163. Both this and the earlier stanzas are quoted by Desi Sangyé Gyatso in his *Yellow Beryl: A History of Ganden Tradition*, pp. 364–65.

40 *The Book of Kadam*, vol. II, chap. 19, p. 485.

41 *The Book of Kadam*, vol. II, chap. 19, p. 487.

42 *The Book of Kadam*, vol. II, chap. 19, p. 490. *Mantrikas* are tantric adepts.

43 For discussion of this second identification, see Franz-Karl Ehrhard, "The Transmission of the Thig-le bcu-drug and the Bka' gdams glegs bam," pp. 29–30 and 51. Lechen Künga Gyaltsen (*Lamp Illuminating the History of the Kadam Tradition*, p. 2a:2) also briefly mentions this tradition of identifying the three Kadam brothers with the three Avalokiteśvara icons in Tibet that are traditionally believed to be self-arisen, that is they arose naturally as icons rather than being fabricated by artists.

44 In the testament, Atiśa visits Lhasa cathedral with his attendant Naljorpa and does not mention Dromtönpa by name. Leonard van der Kuijp ("The Dalai Lamas and the Origins of Reincarnate Lamas," p. 24) argues that since the testament does not mention Dromtönpa, it may have evolved in an environment where Dromtön and the tradition growing out of his teachings initially had no stake. This suggests,

according to van der Kuijp, that the nineteenth chapter of Dromtönpa's birth stories can be seen as a means to establish Songtsen Gampo as one of Dromtön's previous births. Whatever the truth of this suggestion—which can only be determined once we have accurate dates for the two texts—the two texts are clearly intimately connected.

45 The *Kakholma Testament,* p. 319. This testament, as well as *The Book of Kadam,* especially chapters 5 and 19 of the Son Teachings, need to be studied carefully alongside another important treasure text, the *Sacred Collection on Maṇi [Mantra] (Ma ṇi bka' 'bum),* the discovery or revelation of which is traditionally attributed to Nyangral Nyima Öser (1124–92). Together, these texts appeared to have played a key role in propagating many aspects of the myth of Avalokiteśvara and his special destiny with Tibet, beliefs that became deeply ingrained and widespread among the Tibetan people. My own feeling is that the *Kakholma Testament,* at least in its archaic form, predates both *The Book of Kadam* as well as the *Sacred Collection on Maṇi.* In fact, the two latter texts represent subsequent attempts to connect the myth of Avalokiteśvara's special role in Tibet with two important figures in the development of Buddhism in Tibet—the first with Dromtönpa and the second with Padmasambhava. For a brief yet insightful study of the *Sacred Collection on Maṇi,* see Mathew Kapstein, "Remarks on the Maṇi bka' 'bum and the Cult of Avalokiteśvara in Tibet," in Steven D. Goodman and Ronald M. Davidson, eds., *Tibetan Buddhism: Reason and Revelation,* pp. 79–93, as well as chapter 8 of his *Tibetan Assimilation of Buddhism.*

46 The distinction between main book and ancillary texts presented here is based on Sönam Lhai Wangpo's *A History of the Precious Kadam Tradition,* pp. 379–80. Ehrhard discusses the division of *The Book of Kadam* into fifty-four sections ("The Transmission of the *Thig-le bcu-drug* and the *Bka' gdams glegs bam,*" pp. 31–34 and 37–38). The overall structure of *The Book of Kadam* and the sequence in which the various texts are organized are analyzed in Amy Sims Miller's doctoral dissertation, "Jeweled Dialogues: The Role of *The Book* in the Formation of the Kadam Tradition within Tibet."

47 These two texts appear in *Mind Training: The Great Collection* as selections 2 and 3.

48 Hubert Decleer, in "Master Atiśa in Nepal," presents a series of arguments that, to his mind, support the traditional attribution of this important historical text to Dromtönpa. For a critical analysis of these traditional biographies of Atiśa, see Helmut Eimer, "The Development of the Biographical Tradition Concerning Atiśa (Dīpaṃkaraśrījñāna)."

49 Khenchen Nyima Gyaltsen, "Chapter on Auspiciousness," *The Book of Kadam,* vol. II, p. 835.

50 The term "archaic version" of *The Book of Kadam* was, as noted by Franz-Karl Ehrhard ("The Transmission of the *Thig-le bcu-drug* and the *Bka' gdams glegs bam,*" p. 31), first suggested by Helmut Eimer in "Zur Faksimile-Ausgabe eines alten Blockdruckes des Bka' gdams glegs bam" in *Indo-Iranian Journal* 27, no. 11 (1984): 45 and 47.

51 Franz-Karl Ehrhard refers to this early transmission as the "legendary transmission" and the subsequent transmission from Phuchungwa as the "local transmission."

52 Tapka Namkha Rinchen wrote a twenty-Āve-stanza salutation to the lineage masters of *The Book of Kadam,* which is cited in full at the beginning of Khenchen

Nyima Gyaltsen's "Liberating Life Stories of the Lineage Teachers of the Seven-fold Divinity and Teaching." See *The Book of Kadam*, vol. I, pp. 299–302. The dates 1214–86 were suggested for Namkha Rinchen by Franz-Karl Ehrhard (op cit., p. 43), who gives Khenchen's "Liberating Life Stories" as his source. Judging by Khenchen's account in the "Liberating Life Stories" as well as by Lechen's account of Namkha Rinchen, especially with respect to the manner in which he transmitted the teachings of the book to Drom Kumāramati, it seems that Namkha Rinchen died when Drom Kumāramati was young. If Namkha Rinchen had indeed lived until 1286, Khenchen, our compiler, would have met him and would have mentioned his meeting, but he does not. Therefore, whether the Fire-Dog year provided as the year of Namkha Rinchen's death is not 1226 rather than 1286 is a question that can only be resolved with additional evidence.

53 See Franz-Karl Ehrhard (op cit., p. 44), who cites Yongzin Yeshé Gyaltsen's *Liberating Lives of the Lineage Teachers of Lamrim*, pp. 918–19. One possible way in which we can interpret this shift from a one-to-one direct transmission to a wider dissemination is as the beginnings of a written text. That there can be a highly successful transmission of oral texts of great length is attested by the early history of many of the Buddhist sutras, which were memorized, retained, and transmitted entirely orally for several generations, as well as the much-earlier transmission of the Vedas.

54 Khenchen, "Liberating Life Stories," *The Book of Kadam*, vol. I, p. 491.

55 Ibid.

56 *The Book of Kadam*, vol. I, pp. 294–97.

57 Ibid., p. 297.

58 "Liberating Life Stories," *The Book of Kadam*, vol. I, p. 327.

59 Ibid., p. 345.

60 That it was authored by Namkha Rinchen is explicitly stated by Khenchen in his colophon to the "Liberating Life Stories," p. 504. Earlier, Khenchen also states that the details of Namkha Rinchen's life, including the manner in which he received the transmission of the book, was based on an oral account that Drom Kumāramati heard from Namkha Rinchen himself ("Liberating Life Stories," p. 482).

61 Ibid., p. 302.

62 *The Rite of the Mandala*, pp. 12a:4–29b:1.

63 Ibid., p. 13a:1.

64 Ibid., p. 28b:6.

65 Ibid., pp. 29a:1–29b:4. This explicit, first-person statement of the authorship at the end of this short work lends considerable support to Phuchungwa as its author. Perhaps this short text is what Lechen Künga Gyaltsen (*Lamp Illuminating the History of the Kadam Tradition*, p. 4a:6) refers to as "Phuchungwa's supplement to the book, the Sevenfold Divinities and Teachings of Kadam."

66 "Liberating Life Stories," p. 351.

67 *Lha chos bdun ldan gyi man ngag.*

68 Yongzin Yeshé Gyaltsen, *The Rite of the Mandala*, p. 28b:6.

69 *Joyful Feast for the Learned*, vol. I, p. 709. Pawo Tsuklak Trengwa also suggests, given the almost identical nature of *Bodhisattva's Jewel Garland* and Atiśa's letter

to a Nepalese nobleman by the name of Nīryapāla, that this nobleman and Drom might share the same continuum of consciousness. It appears that Tsuklak Trengwa treated Atiśa's letter to the Nepalese nobleman and his *Bodhisattva's Jewel Garland* as being one work, a position the Fifth Dalai Lama (*River Ganges' Flow: A Record of Teachings Received*, vol. 1, p. 44a:4) rejects as naïve.

70 "Staircase to Liberation," p. 101.

71 See, for example, Sumpa Yeshé Paljor, *Excellent Wish-Granting Tree*, p. 398, and Thuken, *Crystal Mirror*, p. 103.

72 Ngawang Lobsang Gyatso, Fifth Dalai Lama, *River Ganges' Flow*, vol. *kha*, p. 45a:2.

73 Panchen Sönam Drakpa, *History of Old and New Kadam Schools*, p. 18a:3.

74 Ibid.

75 *Tshad ma yin min ni mi shes/ sems la ni phan po 'dug//*. Although I have personally heard this statement from His Holiness the Fourteenth Dalai Lama, I have failed to locate its textual source.

76 Pawo Tsuklak Trengwa, *Joyful Feast for the Learned*, vol. 1, p. 710. *Māra* is a personification of delusion, tempting practitioners from paths of virtue.

77 Ibid., p. 710.

78 Yeshé Tsemo, *Wondrous Garland of Excellent Jewels*, p. 84b:5.

79 Lechen Künga Gyaltsen, *Lamp Illuminating the History of the Kadam Tradition*, p. 396a:6.

80 See, for example, Taklung Ngawang Namgyal's *History of the Taklung Tradition*, p. 713, and Pema Karpo, *Sun Enhancing the Lotus of the Buddha's Teaching*, p. 285.

81 Strictly speaking, the Great Fifth was not the first to relate the two books—*Kakholma Testament* and *The Book of Kadam*—outside the texts belonging to the Kadam collection. For example, we see the following comment in Yeshé Tsemo's biography of Gendün Drup (p. 4b:6): "Furthermore, there are many similar statements. Later, too, numerous indirect indications will come to light. As for the details, however, one needs to understand them from *The Precious Book* and *The King's Testament*."

82 Desi Sangyé Gyatso, *Yellow Beryl: A History of Ganden Tradition*, for example, p. 365. This project of equating the Great Fifth with Avalokiteśvara, and with previous successive emanations of the Buddha of Compassion, especially with figures like Dromtön and the previous Dalai Lamas, is extensively developed in Desi's voluminous supplement to the Great Fifth's autobiography, *Fine Silken Robe*.

83 The four divinities and three teachings, also known as the *sevenfold divinities and teachings (lha chos bdun ldan)*, later came to be a defining characteristic of the Kadam tradition. The seven refer to the Kadampa masters' choice of four divinities—the historical Buddha as the teacher, Avalokiteśvara as the divinity embodying great compassion, Tārā as the divinity embodying enlightened activities, and Acala as the divinity guarding against all obstacles—and the three teachings—the three scriptural baskets of discipline, sutras, and higher knowledge. See the introduction for more on this subject.

84 Dīpaṃkaraśrījñāna is another name for Atiśa.

85 The term *conqueror*, an epithet for a buddha, here refers to Atiśa. The phrase *departure to liberation* is a euphemism for his death.

86 The four everyday activities are (1) walking toward a destination, (2) going for a stroll, (3) sleeping, and (4) sitting, as listed in the earliest Buddhist scriptures, especially those relating to the monastic vows.

87 Gyalwai Jungné *(Rgyal ba'i 'byung gnas)*—literally, "the source of the conquerors"—is Dromtönpa's name.

88 Whereas the verses previous to this line serve as a preliminary invoking of Atiśa and a request for him to bear witness, the actual text of the self-exhortation begins from here. By calling out to the son of Dīpaṃkaraśrījñāna, the author Dromtönpa is referring to himself.

89 "Extract the essence of this body" *(lus la snying po len pa)* is an expression that means to make the most of the rare opportunity to practice the Dharma as a human being, the type of rebirth that provides the ideal conditions for realization. The expression probably alludes to the analogy of extracting the juice or "essence" of a fruit or extracting the grain out of its husk.

90 "Four sessions" *(thun bzhi)* refers to engaging in sitting meditation practices during four formal periods during the day, one roughly from around 4–7 A.M., second 8–11 A.M., third 2–5 P.M., and finally 7–10 P.M. These formal sitting sessions are observed during an intensive retreat context.

91 The four immeasurable thoughts are (1) immeasurable compassion, (2) immeasurable loving-kindness, (3) immeasurable joy, and (4) immeasurable equanimity.

92 The Tibetan word translated here as "insects" is *srin bu*, which refers to bacteria-like organisms thought to be naturally present in the human body according to traditional Indian and Tibetan medical systems.

93 The term *corresponding causes* refers to the idea that we reap what we sow. According to the law of karma, our experiences in this life each correspond in character to the actions we performed in a past life to create them. For instance, a causally concordant effect of killing in a previous life would be a short lifespan in this life.

94 This alludes to a well-known analogy in the early sutras. The Buddha tells the members of his order that just as the ocean never keeps a corpse but pushes it to the shore, in the same manner, monks disassociate from those who commit evil. Candrakīrti also uses this analogy in *Madhyamakāvatāra*, 2:8.

95 This is probably a reference to Nāgārjuna, who is recognized as an emanation of the Buddha of wisdom, Mañjuśrī. Although I have failed to locate the source referred to here, the same analogy is used in *Mind Training: The Great Collection*, pp. 446–47, to characterize the precarious nature of our existence.

96 The *ten masteries* are mastery of: (1) lifespan, (2) mind, (3) material resources, (4) karma, (5) birth, (6) convictions, (7) aspiration, (8) supernatural feats, (9) phenomena, and (10) gnosis. The bodhisattvas on advanced levels are said to gain these masteries.

97 The critical Tibetan edition gives *gse tshags* here, which I think should be corrected to *gseb tshags*. Among other definitions, the Tibetan dictionaries give "seedless," "in between," and "cracks" as diverse meanings of *gseb*. I have chosen "seedless" since it connotes barrenness, which is the most appropriate meaning in the context here.

98 This is a reference to the heart instructions of *The Book of Kadam*, whose main

meditation practice is related to the Buddha, Avalokiteśvara, Tārā, Master Atiśa, and Dromtönpa.

99 These refer to Master Atiśa, the Buddha, the Perfection of Wisdom Mother, and the bodhisattvas.

100 In *The Book of Kadam*, the key elements of meditative practices are often referred to by the word *drop (thig le)*, as in "the sixteen drops."

101 The following paragraph is somewhat obscure, especially its opening sentence "The sequence [of the practices] appears as follows" *('di la'ang 'brel ba byung tshul)*, which literally translates as "here, too, the sequence is this." This paragraph is best read as a summary, probably inserted by the editor of *The Book of Kadam*, which brings together all the practices covered in Dromtönpa's *Self-Exhortation*. For convenience, I have numbered the individual practices.

102 "He" here refers to Dromtönpa, whose words are being cited once again in the verses that follow.

103 This is a reference to the three Kadam brothers: Potowa, Chengawa, and Phuchungwa. For brief biographical information on these three Kadam brothers and other Kadam masters, see my annotations to *Sayings of the Kadam Masters*, entry XI in this volume.

104 *Dungkar Tibetological Great Dictionary (Dung dkar tshig mdzod chen mo)* lists the following as the seven attributes: (1) excellent family, (2) physical beauty, (3) long life, (4) good health, (5) good fortune, (6) wealth, and (7) intelligence. Unfortunately, Dungkar provides no source for this enumeration.

105 The "ten levels" are the ten levels of the bodhisattva while the "accumulation" and so on refers to the five stages of the path to enlightenment. They are, in their respective order: the path of *accumulation*, the path of *preparation*, the path of *seeing*, the path of *meditation*, and the path of *no more learning*.

106 A "retention" *(gzungs;* Sanskrit, *dhāraṇī)* is a highly developed memory that is immune to forgetfulness. Four such retentions are listed among the Buddha's enlightened attributes. "Absorptions" *(ting 'dzin;* Sanskrit, *samādhi)* refers to a series of progressively more advanced meditative concentration states.

107 This is a reference to the well-known *Vows of Good Conduct Sutra (Bhadracaryā-praṇidhāna,* Toh 1095, Kangyur, gzungs bsdus, *vam)*, which is also part 4 of the *Flower Ornament Scripture (Avataṃsaka Sūtra)*.

108 This line is missing in the critical Tibetan edition, which is based on the Tashi Lhünpo edition of *The Book of Kadam*. Since it appears in the Dergé edition and, moreover, the reading of the text seems more complete with the addition of this line—coming immediately after the invocation of the auspiciousness of the noble Sangha and the sublime Dharma—I have chosen to include this line in the translation.

109 The four factors are: (1) giving what is needed, (2) speaking pleasantly, (3) working toward the aim, and (4) behaving consistently. Different texts give slightly different interpretations of the third and fourth factors and their relationship. A discussion of these four factors based on the important Mahayana sutra, the *Bodhisattvapiṭaka*, and Asaṅga's *Bodhisattvabhūmi* can be found in Ulrich Pagel, *The Bodhisattvapiṭaka: Its Doctrines, Practices and Their Position in Mahāyāna Literature*, chap. 4. For a later Tibetan understanding of these four factors and their functions within the overall bodhisattva ideal, see Tsongkhapa, *The Great Treatise on the Stages of the Path to Enlightenment*, vol. 2, chap. 15.

110 Although *Bodhisattva's Jewel Garland* exists in the Tengyur (Toh 3951), there are some variations between the Tengyur edition and the one found here as the root text of "Father Teachings" in *The Book of Kadam*. The version found here is, however, except for minor typographical variations, identical to the one found in *Mind Training: The Great Collection* (volume 1 of *The Library of Tibetan Classics*). The translation presented here is therefore the same, unless otherwise noted. The variations in the readings between this version and that in the Dergé Tengyur are fully annotated in the critical Tibetan edition of the text. For those variations in reading that are significant, see my notes to the text in *Mind Training*.

111 Given that this short work of Atiśa, *Bodhisattva's Jewel Garland*, is used in *The Book of Kadam* as the root text of the "Father Teachings," I have introduced numbers in parenthesis at the beginning of each line where the root text of a new chapter of the "Father Teachings" begins. This numbering is different from the stanza number introduced in my translation of the same text in *Mind Training*.

112 In *Mind Training: The Great Collection*, I have translated this line as "With mindfulness, vigilance, and conscientiousness." I now feel that "awareness" (or "meta-awareness" to be more correct) and "heedfulness" are preferable for the Tibetan terms *shes bzhin* and *bag yod*.

113 "Faith" here refers to faith in the law of karma.

114 The term *khenpo (mkhan po)*, translated here as "preceptors," often means an abbot of a monastery, but here the term refers to spiritual masters who have conferred vows upon you.

115 In *Mind Training* I translated this line as "Dispel hostility and unpleasantness." Reading the text more carefully and, especially taking into account the fact that the English term *unpleasantness* connotes more the notion of being unpleasant to others, I feel that this line is better translated as "Discard hostile and unhappy mental states." Since hostile and unhappy mental states undermine the conditions for a successful Dharma practice, the practitioner is urged to seek a place or a state of mind where happiness and joy dominate.

116 In *Mind Training* I translated these two lines as, "When you encounter the factors of happiness,/ In these always persevere."

117 To better suit the text of chapter 18 of the *Jewel Garland of Dialogues*, I have translated the first and last lines of the stanza more literally than in *Mind Training*.

118 "Seven limbs" refers to a popular Mahayana Buddhist rite of worship that includes the following elements: (1) paying homage, (2) making offerings, (3) confessing and purifying negative karma, (4) rejoicing in the virtuous deeds, (5) supplicating the buddhas to turn the wheel of Dharma, (6) appealing to the buddhas not to enter into final nirvana, and (7) dedicating the merit of your practice. This practice of seven limbs goes back to the earliest development of Mahayana Buddhism. It is found, for example, in the well-known sutra, *Vows of Good Conduct (Bhadracaryāpraṇidhāna)*, which is part 4 of the *Flower Ornament Scripture (Avataṃsaka Sūtra,* Toh 44) and also self-standing in Toh 1095. The second chapter of Śāntideva's *Guide to the Bodhisattva's Way of Life (Bodhicaryāvatāra)* also uses the seven limbs.

119 The two defilements are the obscuration of afflictions and, once the afflictions have been removed, the subtle latent propensities toward afflictions, including all subtle dualistic delusory perceptions.

120 Mount Potala is the pure realm of Avalokiteśvara, the buddha of compassion, and

should not be confused with the well-known Tibetan architectural wonder by the same name that was the winter residence of the Dalai Lamas. Potala is also the pure realm of Tārā, the buddha of enlightened activities. She was one of the principal meditation deities of Atiśa, hence the reference to Tārā at the beginning of this text.

121 One of the three principal types of awakening mind, the other two being the *king-like* and the *oarsman-like*. The *king-like* awakening mind is the altruistic wish to first attain full enlightenment oneself so that one can then help relieve all beings from cyclic existence. By contrast, the *oarsman-like* bodhisattva wishes that both he and others attain full enlightenment simultaneously, just as an oarsman crosses to the opposite shore together with his passengers. Finally, *shepherd-like* bodhisattvas aspire to lead all other beings to full enlightenment *before* themselves, like the shepherd who brings home his flock by herding them from behind.

122 This is a standard division of a day and night in the classical Indian and Tibetan texts as conveyed in the expression "the six periods of day and night" *(nyin tshan dus drug)*.

123 There is a tradition of listing seven past buddhas: three buddhas of the previous eon and the four past buddhas of the present eon, with the historical Buddha Śākyamuni being the last. Here, however, the reference is most probably to the seven buddhas of the Medicine Buddha mandala, who are believed to have a special connection with the beings of our degenerate era.

124 Mañjuśrī, Vajrapāṇi, Avalokiteśvara, Kṣitigarbha, Sarvanivaraṇaviśkamvin, Ākāśagarbha, Maitreya, and Samantabhadra. These eight bodhisattvas figure prominently in the Mahayana sutras as the Buddha's principal bodhisattva disciples who are in celestial form.

125 This is a reference to the second volume of *The Book of Kadam*, the tales of the former lives of Dromtönpa.

126 This is a reference to the mythical Mount Meru, which stands towering at the center of the classical Indian world system, surrounded by four continents and eight subcontinents.

127 An account of Atiśa's meeting with this Vajrayana master is found in *Mind Training: The Great Collection*, pp. 45–46.

128 This is most probably Ratnakaraśānti, who is the author of the well-known *Instruction on the Perfection of Wisdom* (*Prajñāpāramitopadeśa*, Toh 4079). Chim Namkha Drak's *Biography of Atiśa* (p. 80), citing a stanza from Naktso Lotsāwa's *Eighty Stanzas of Praise*, lists Śāntipa as one of the four main teachers of Atiśa, the other three being Serlingpa, Bodhibhadra, and Jétāri. Hajime Nakamura (*Indian Buddhism: A Survey with Biographical Notes*, p. 311) places Śāntipa around 1040, which would make him a contemporary of Atiśa.

129 This may be Dharmarakṣita, one of Atiśa's the three main teachers on the awakening mind. He is attributed with having authored several mind training verses, the most well-known being *The Wheel of Sharp Weapons*. Atiśa's other two awakening mind teachers are Serlingpa and Kusali Jr., known also as Maitrīyogi. On the identity of these three Indian masters and their relationship to Atiśa, see my introduction in *Mind Training: The Great Collection* and my notes to the individual mind training texts attributed to these three masters.

130 This is probably the well-known author of numerous epistemological works. His name is also written sometimes as Jītāri. Nakamura (p. 309) gives ca. 940–80 as the possible dates for Jetāri, which would place him fairly close to Atiśa. Since Naktso Lotsāwa, who was not only Atiśa's contemporary but also visited Vikramaśila Monastery in India, lists Jetāri as a principal teacher of Atiśa, one must accept this as credible.

131 The following seven are the seven buddhas of the Medicine Buddha mandala.

132 This is the historical Buddha Śākyamuni. He is the "fearless teacher" because he is said to have vowed to appear in the world during the most degenerate era in order to help lead sentient beings to liberation.

133 This is an allusion to the eight bodhisattva disciples of Buddha Śākyamuni. See note 124 above.

134 The five poisons are: (1) attachment, (2) aversion, (3) delusion, (4) jealousy, and (5) conceit.

135 The five wisdoms are: (1) mirror-like wisdom, (2) wisdom of equanimity, (3) discriminative awareness, (4) accomplishment of aims, and (5) expanse of reality. According to Vajrayana Buddhism, these five dimensions of the Buddha's enlightened mind represent the perfected states of the five mental poisons.

136 According to Monier-Williams, *A Sanskrit-English Dictionary*, 1993 edition, a *kīnāra* literally means "a cultivator of the soil" and can have the alternative meaning of "a vile man."

137 The chapter commences with Atiśa speaking. The opening Sanskrit sentence means "I pay homage to all the teachers."

138 This repeated name Kusalī refers to the two Kusalī brothers, the younger of which is Maitrīyogi.

139 Earlier, when paying homage to a similar group of teachers, it read, "To Maticāla and Tilopa the yogi,/ To Catipāla and Mañjuśrībhadra…" The difference is intentional.

140 This is Maitrīyogi to whom the mind training work, *Melodies of an Adamantine Song* (*Mind Training: The Great Collection*, entry 10), is attributed, while Rakṣita in the following line refers to Dharmarakṣita to whom is attributed the well-known *Wheel of Sharp Weapons* and *The Peacock's Neutralizing of Poison* (*Mind Training: The Great Collection*, entries 8 and 9). Together with Master Serlingpa, they are known as "the three awakening-mind teachers of Atiśa." See my introduction in *Mind Training: The Great Collection*.

141 Although the text states that there are five precious benefactors, only four are listed. This discrepancy is in the original text.

142 *Bstan pa blo gros.* This is probably supposed to be Sthiramati, the student of Dignāga, whose name in Tibetan is normally written as Lodrö Tenpa (*Blo gros brtan pa*). Tibetan writers, when reconstructing Sanskrit names, sometimes mistakenly write them in reverse order.

143 These are the four divinities of the Kadam [tradition] (*bka' gdams lha bzhi*).

144 *Oṃ, aḥ,* and *hūṃ,* which respectively represent the body, speech, and mind of the enlightened ones.

145 *Oṃ maṇi padme hūṃ.* This is the well-known six-syllable mantra of Avalokiteśvara, the buddha of compassion.

146 This is Dromtönpa who is now being addressed by Atiśa as an emanation of Avalokiteśvara.

147 Phuchungwa Shönu Gyaltsen, Potowa Rinchen Sal, and Chengawa Tsültrim Bar, who are Dromtönpa's primary disciples and lineage holders.

148 In the context of the teachings on the four divinities, Śākyamuni Buddha is referred to as the "Sage" *(thub pa)*.

149 The four are Dharma, wealth, liberation, and desire. The first two are causes, while the last two their fruits—i.e., Dharma leads to liberation, while wealth leads to the fulfillment of one's desires. Together, these four factors embody all the mundane and spiritual aspirations of an individual. This concept, if not exactly the same, probably shares the same origin with the Hindu idea of the four aims: the pursuit of (1) wealth as a means to fulfillment of (2) desire, and the pursuit of (3) Dharma as a means for attaining (4) liberation.

150 Dorlek is the abbreviation for Dorjé Lekpa *(Rdo rje legs pa)* and refers to a protector deity by this name. Similarly, Pekar *(Pad dkar)*, often written as Pehar *(Pe har)*, refers to a protector deity by that name. Pehar is the principal protector of Tibet's first monastery, Samyé. One of his main manifestations includes the present Tibetan state oracle, Nechung, who is believed to have hailed from Persia. The early Kadampa masters were highly critical of the Tibetan religious practice of propitiating worldly protectors and emphasized the alternative approach of entrusting one's faith more in the Three Jewels and the law of karma.

151 Acala is the fourth of the Kadam's four divinities; his name connotes "unwavering" or "immutability."

152 It is difficult to determine whether this is a reference to a specific icon of Maitreya in Tibet or an allusion to some canonical description of the height of the future buddha Maitreya. There evolved in Tibet the tradition of creating giant statues of Maitreya. In some cases, entire temples were devoted to the icon. For example, there is the famous Maitreya temple in Shigatsé in the Tsang province where the temple's three stories are divided according to three different sections of the Maitreya's body—his lotus seat and legs, his main torso, and finally his face.

153 Tuṣita is described in the Buddhist scriptures as a celestial realm that has a special connection with the future buddha, Maitreya. For example, the first of the twelve great deeds of Śākyamuni, the historical Buddha of our era, was his descent from Tuṣita into the human world. In similar fashion, Maitreya, being the next buddha to appear in the human world, is the buddha associated with this celestial realm at present.

154 In the Tibetan original, this second line is written in the instrumental case, thus giving the reading "Has not the Sage looked after the teachings?" *(thub pas bstan pa ma bskyangs sam)*. However, I have chosen to read this in the genitive case, which, to my mind, gives a clearer sense.

155 The Tibetan text reads *'o na 'khor ba stongs su bsha'*, which literally reads "If this is so, this will split open samsara into nothingness." However, I have chosen to read the opening phrase as "if the law does so exist" *(yod na)*, which seems to suit the flow of the narrative better.

156 *Lnga po de yi skya bar nas.* These together are known as *the five recollections,* in other words, (1) bringing to mind your teachers, (2) visualizing your body as a deity, (3) recognizing your speech as mantra, (4) contemplating all beings as your parents, and (5) experiencing the nature of mind as emptiness.

157 "The three spheres" *('khor gsum)* are the three key elements of an act—the object of the act, the agent, and the act itself. In this context, the text is referring to the act of dedicating one's virtuous deeds toward the attainment of buddhahood for the benefit of all beings.

158 As noted in the introduction to this volume, *dohā* (Sanskrit) refers to a genre of spiritual poems best described as spontaneous songs of deep religious experience. Written by mystics, who often lived as wandering hermits, these songs characteristically employ a style of writing that is closer to vernacular songs than high poetry. The most noted examples of dohās in the Buddhist tradition are those attributed to the Indian mystic Saraha (ca. ninth or eleventh century). It is interesting to see the text attribute to Atiśa a statement advocating that Dromtönpa take the dohās to heart as his main practice if he wishes to enter a swift path to buddhahood. For translations of Saraha's dohās, see Michele Martin's translation in Thrangu Rinpoche, *A Song for the King*, as well as Roger Jackson, *Tantric Treasures*.

159 A *damaru* is a small hand drum made from two small drums attached back to back. Two strings, each with a knot at the end, are affixed to the instrument such that, when you twist the instrument back and forth with your right thumb and index fingers, the knots strike the drums.

160 It is difficult to determine whether the text here should be read as suggesting Atiśa's actual meeting with Saraha or as suggesting some kind of mystic encounter. Sahara's historicity in general and his dating in particular remain uncertain. Some place him in the later half of the ninth century (Guenther), while others (Nakamura) place him in the eleventh century. If the second dating is accurate, chronologically at least, it makes it possible for Atiśa to have actually met with Saraha. Furthermore, the geographical proximity of Vikramaliśila, Atiśa's monastery in Bihar, to Bengal, the region where Saraha was thought to have been active, makes this even more probable.

161 The Tibetan expression translated here as "concepts of solid objects with mass" is *rnam rtog phang phung*. It refers to the belief that external objects exist inherently, independent of the mind that conceives them.

162 These lines relate to the practice and realizations of the ten perfections—giving, ethical discipline, forbearance, joyful perseverance, concentration, wisdom, skillful means, power, aspiration, and transcendent wisdom. According to the Mahayana doctrine of the bodhisattva ideal, the perfection of these ten practices is associated with the attainment and transcendence of the ten bodhisattva levels on the way to attaining full buddhahood. This list is an elaboration on the six perfections that constitute the core of the bodhisattva's path to enlightenment.

163 These and the subsequent lines echo concerns similar to those expressed in the mind training text "Peacock's Neutralizing of Poisons" (stanzas 48–56, *Mind Training: Great Collection*, pp. 163–65). They severely criticize those who, using the rhetoric of the superiority of Mahayana, especially tantra, denigrate the basic ethical norms outlined in the Buddha's teachings.

164 A Tibetan myth says that lion's milk is so powerful that only a container made of precious metals can contain it. It is difficult to determine whether this myth is indigenous to Tibet, with some pre-Buddhist folk traditions as its origin, or instead comes from classical Indian literarature.

165   The original Tibetan here is highly obscure, which is aggravated further by the use of several archaic Tibetan terms. However, the point being made is that Dromtönpa felt that he could serve the overall well-being of the Buddha's teaching best by keeping the secret mantra teachings hidden while propagating the three scriptural baskets.

166   Again, this entire paragraph in the Tibetan original is quite obscure. The key point is that the teachings of the three scriptural baskets are highly beneficial with virtually no risk involved, while the teachings of the secret mantra are for many practitioners extremely risky with questionable long-term benefit.

167   That is, with the basic Buddhist injunction to adopt positive actions and reject harmful ones.

168   The key Tibetan word here is the archaic *rme 'khrug*, which could be an abbreviation of *dme ba 'khrug pa*. I have read this as referring to the old Tibetan concept of *rme grib*, a curse that manifests as perpetual strife within the members of the same clan. According to Tsenla Ngawang Tsültrim's *Golden Mirror Unraveling the Terms* (p. 678), a lexicon on archaic Tibetan terms, the term *sme* can mean suffering or uncleanliness.

169   *Sems kyi bslab pa*, the second of the three higher trainings, the other two being the higher training in morality and the higher training in wisdom. This second higher training is known also as the higher training in concentration *(bsam gtan)* or in meditative absorption *(ting nge 'dzin)*.

170   The metaphor of shallow crossing points appears to be popular among the early Kadam masters, the most famous example being Potowa's saying, "There is no need to lift your clothes twice to walk across one shallow crossing point [of a river]."

171   In these verses attributed to the four divinities, "master" refers to Atiśa and "son" to Dromtönpa.

172   The "two welfares" *(don gnyis)* are one's own welfare and the welfare of countless other sentient beings, the fulfillment of which marks the attainment of complete buddhahood.

173   *Grogs ngan gyi byur bshal*. The Tibetan term *byur* connotes a kind of negative energy that attracts misfortune. This is often contrasted with *gdon*, or "malevolent forces." Unlike *gdon*, *byur* typically refers to human-related misfortunes or "inauspiciousness"—disrepute, unjust lawsuits, and so on. Hence the expression, "A bad person is a harbinger of misfortune" *(mi ngan byur gyi sna 'dren yin)*.

174   If the text is not corrupt here, which I think it is, the word *Khu* refers to Khutön Tsündrü Yungdrung, who later became one of the principal students of Atiśa from central Tibet.

175   As discussed in the introduction, this refers to practitioners of three levels or capacities—initial, intermediate, and great. This distinction between three capacities of practitioners—and the stages of the path related to them—were first systematically developed in Atiśa's *Lamp for the Path to Enlightenment (Bodhipathapradīpa)*, which later provided the framework for the *stages of the path (lamrim)* literature.

176   For a description of the seven limbs, see note 118.

177   Although *lung* can mean scriptural authority, it can also mean a "handle" or a "ring" that can be connected to a hook, as in the Tibetan expression, "If you have the ring of faith, the buddhas have the hook of great compassion" *(dad pa'i a lung yod na/ thugs rje'i lcags dkyu yod)*.

178 The following six paragraphs describe the practice of the seven limbs, for a listing of which see note 118.

179 *Khong skran. Skran* is the name of a specific illness in the Tibetan medical diagnostic system. The *Extensive Tibetan-Chinese Dictionary* (p. 176) gives the following definition: "A sickness resulting in the formation of hard lumps, either inside or outside the body, caused by indigestion of the unrefined part of food or by the dissolving of refined parts. If further delineated, there are around eighteen different types."

180 "Nonabiding middle way" is an epithet for what later came to be called Prāsaṅgika-Madhyamaka. This is the standpoint of Indian masters such as Buddhapālita, Candrakīrti, and Śāntideva that is espoused also by Atiśa himself. Similarly, the expression "the great middle way" *(dbu ma chen po)* is used here to suggest that the middle way standpoint of these Indian masters represents the highest understanding of the teaching of emptiness, for it marks the transcendence of all conceptual elaborations.

181 This refers to the whole set of practices, such as supplication, the seven-limbed worship, and so forth, that were presented in relation to the meditation on the teacher earlier.

182 The eight terrors are those of lions, elephants, fire, snakes, thieves, captivity, drowning, and spirits. The first Dalai Lama Gendün Drup, in his *Praise to Tārā*, associates these respectively with their internal counterparts of conceitedness, delusion, anger, jealousy, pernicious views, miserliness, attachment, and lingering doubts.

183 The "five drops" here refers to the five stages of meditation practice described earlier: visualizing (1) your teacher, (2) the Sage, Buddha Śākyamuni, (3) Tārā, (4) Avalokiteśvara, and (5) the guardian Acala. You visualize each of the latter as seated within the heart of the former.

184 This is most probably a citation from scripture, the source of which remains unknown.

185 Drom is here dividing up the well-known twelve links of dependent origination, often depicted as the "wheel of life," into causes, conditions, and effects with respect to a sentient being's karmically conditioned birth in the cycle of existence.

186 Here the text uses the Tibetan term *khrims*, which means "law," "rule," "regulation," or a "norm." Admittedly, the usage of this term here is somewhat peculiar. Perhaps it should be read as meaning "rules of usage in language" or "established linguistic convention." Thus, speaking of tasting the mind as if it were a food would violate normal linguistic convention.

187 The five heinous acts are (1) patricide, (2) matricide, (3) killing an arhat, (4) creating a schism within the monastic community, and (5) causing blood to spill from a tathāgata's body out of negative intent.

188 The Tibetan text in all available editions here gives the reading "There shall be eighty thousand or twenty-five thousand [trainees]." *(brgyad khri dang stong phrag nyi shu rtsa lnga'o).* This, I feel, is an orthographical error, and the line should read *brgya khri dang...* In the Tibetan numerical system, each decimal has an independent name, and the text here lists three of these decimal units—hundred, ten thousand, and thousand.

189 The expression "engaging in an unchaste conduct" *(mi tshangs par spyod pa)* is

being used here as a shorthand for "engaging in unchaste conduct out of perverted desires," which refers to an act of sexual misconduct, rather than to sexual activity in general. In Buddhist ethics, sex is not itself unethical; however, it becomes so for those who have taken the vow of celibacy, such as the members of the monastic order. Sexual misconduct, on the other hand, is unethical whether or not one has taken a vow of celibacy.

190 Here the text is alluding to an important aspect of the bodhisattva ethics, according to which highly evolved bodhisattvas can creatively engage in the seven nonvirtuous actions—the three bodily acts of killing, stealing, and sexual misconduct and the four verbal deeds of telling lies, divisive speech, harsh speech, and frivolous speech—on the basis of the principle of skillful means. In fact, if the situation demands a deliberate violation of the ethics of restraint from any of these seven nonvirtuous acts, such as when the well-being of a large number of other sentient beings is involved, refraining from the act is actually a transgression of the bodhisattva's vows. For a detailed discussion of this important aspect of the bodhisattva ethics, especially with reference to their key scriptural sources in the Mahayana sutras, see Mark Tatz's *Asanga's Chapter on Ethics with the Commentary of Tsong-Kha-Pa,* pp. 211–17.

191 In other words, when samsaric pleasures abound, our afflictions mushroom, and the promise of enlightenment becomes so remote as to be nonexistent, like a flower growing in the sky.

192 Although the Tibetan original reads "All these bursting bubbles are extremely *stable*" *(shin tu brtan no sbu ba sdos pa kun),* I have read this line in the negative as dictated by the context.

193 The core of a banana tree is empty and therefore insubstantial. The child of a barren woman is another analogy to convey the idea that the remnants of past karma too have no substantial reality.

194 An allusion is being made here to the Mahayana sutra *Dispelling Ajātaśatru's Remorse* (Toh 216 Kangyur, mdo sde, *tsha,* pp. 211b–268b), where the Buddha refers to craving and grasping (the eighth and ninth of the twelve links of dependent origination) as parents and admonishes king Ajātaśatru to slay them. The subsequent lines similarly advise the practitioner to commit the ten nonvirtues against these afflictions, thereby transforming the actions into virtues.

195 The Tibetan text reads here as *'jig rten gyi gtam dpe kha 'ug ma dang ma de ma'i tshul byung.* This expression, probably well known in certain parts of central Tibet at a certain time, remains totally obscure to me. I have read the Tibetan word *'ug ma* as a female owl and *de ma* as *de mo,* which is hen. We know from the context that Dromtönpa is suggesting that if the teachings are not given in accord with the mental level of the spiritual trainees, they will not be understood. This is akin to the offspring of a hen talking like an owl—she won't be understood by the rest of her species. I must emphasize that, given the opaqueness of the Tibetan text here, my translation must remain only suggestive.

196 This is probably an allusion to the story of prince Viśvāntara (Vessantara) in the *Jātaka Tales,* the collection of stories of the Buddha's previous births. In the Tibetan Buddhist canonical collection, or *Kangyur,* there is no specific category of texts under the title of *Jātaka Tales,* and the stories are found scattered in numerous scriptures, especially those belonging to the discipline basket. In commentar-

ial collection, or *Tengyur*, however, there are five volumes in the *Jātaka* cycle, among which is Āryaśūra's well-known *Garland of Birth Stories (Jātakamālā)*. This work contains thirty-four tales, Viśvāntara being number 9, and was later supplemented by the fourteenth-century Tibetan master Karmapa Rangjung Dorjé, thereby bringing the collection to one hundred tales. This prince's life is seen as a highest example of the practice of the perfection of giving.

197 "Faith" here refers to faith in the law of karma.

198 *Sbyangs pa'i yon tan bcu gnyis;* Skt. *dvādaśadhūtaguṇa*. One of the earliest sources for this list of twelve qualities, in the Sanskrit texts, can be found in the *King of Meditation Sutra (Samādhirājasūtra)* and *Sutra of the Ten Levels (Daśabhūmika-sūtra)*. The qualities are ascetic virtues, such as owning little, living in isolation, begging for alms, and restricting one's food and sleep. For a complete list of these twelve qualities, including their descriptions, see Dayal (1932), pp. 134–40.

199 In the Tashi Lhünpo edition, this line reads "Free of distraction, practice the four doors of concentration" *(g.yeng med bsam gtan sgo bzhi mdzod)*.

200 *'Khar gsil*. A *khakkhara* staff is a mendicant's staff held in the right hand by the monk disciples of the Buddha. For a drawing of the monk's staff along with a brief description of the various parts and their symbolism, see Willson and Brauen, *Deities of Tibetan Buddhism*, p. 568.

201 The reference to this walking staff as a cooler probably derives from a custom in India whereby Buddhist monks use the staff as a pole and place their yellow robes over it in order to provide shade when they pause to rest during their walks on a hot day.

202 This Dīpaṃkara should not be confused with Atiśa, who sometimes goes by the same name. This is instead the Buddha who came before Śākyamuni in the era prior to our own. Maitreya, mentioned in the next stanza, is said to be the Buddha of the coming era.

203 *Sems kyi bslab pa*. This "training in mind" refers to the higher training in concentration and not to "mind training" *(blo sbyong)*.

204 This is probably a reference to one of the "eight great cemeteries" mentioned in the Vajrayana texts that were reputed to be places of great terror.

205 In the following lines Atiśa is presenting the numerous qualities that characterize the attitude and lifestyle of the ideal practitioner who will uphold the monk's staff. In many ways, most of these qualities pertain to such a person's steadfast commitment to leading a simple life whereby, insofar as one's own personal needs are concerned, the individual has the minimum of everyday chores. Hence, the reference is to the fear of being caught up in a way of life that entails excessive chores.

206 The Tibetan term *mi chos,* which I have translated here as "social norms," refers to everyday social etiquette that Tibetan spiritual masters define as revolving around protecting one's friends and family and combatting one's enemies. Often, *mi chos* is contrasted with *lha chos,* the latter referring to spiritual norms that relate to the well-being of the practitioner in the future lives. For further explanation on this distinction, see note 315.

207 *Kog ste langs pas gzhi rdzogs pa*. This is one of the most well-known lines from *The Book of Kadam* and encapsulates the principle of simplicity in a most vivid manner. The idea here is that a true monk practitioner will own nothing other than the items necessary for leading a monk's way of life, such as the robes, alms bowl,

and walking staff, so that when he stands up, all his worldly possessions stand up with him.

208 This paragraph, especially the last few lines, is somewhat obscure. In essence, it seems to say that even the meditator who has forsaken home and embraced life in wilderness, if he is still beholden to social norms, will be held hostage to the various demands from his family. They may argue that his devotion to a meditator's life is selfish and that he should think more of looking after his parents and so on, thus undermining his commitment to Dharma practice.

209 *Sdig 'dzub* refers to a specific hand gesture or *mudrā (phyag rgya)*. This gesture is performed by stretching out the right hand, with the thumb pressing on the middle and ring fingernails and the index and the little fingers extended. Numerous such formalized hand gestures exist in Buddhist rites as well in classical Indian dance.

210 "Pristine melodies" *(tshangs dbyangs)* is one of the thirty-two exemplary marks of a Buddha. Described in terms of sixty different melodies of perfection, *tshangs dbyangs*, which literally means the "melodies of Brahmā," relate to the gentle and pleasing qualities of the speech of a fully enlightened being.

211 Here the term *disciple (śrāvaka;* Tib. *nyan thos)* is probably being used as a generic term for those who uphold the Vinaya discipline, which is the key component of the scriptural collections of the Disciple's Vehicle.

212 This stanza is one of the most quoted from *The Book of Kadam*. It underlines in a beautiful way Atiśa's insistence that the threefold pursuits of a spiritual trainee— learning, critical reflection, and meditation—must be undertaken in an integrated way and not in isolation from each other.

213 The Tibetan text of the last two lines of this stanza is somewhat obscure and my translation presented here must remain only a suggestion. I have read the lines to state that, given that Atiśa's approach toward the threefold pursuit of learning, reflection, and meditation is not a partial but a thoroughly integrated one, he understands perfectly how the referents of all our descriptions—that is, the world of cause and effect—resemble optical illusions. They may seem real but in fact they are devoid of inherent existence.

214 *Nga kha sgor gang byung rtog med zo.* Here I have translated the Tibetan term *rtog med* as "without discriminating." Dromtönpa appears here to be critiquing those who interpret the teaching of emptiness to imply the rejection of any evaluative judgment of right and wrong. This discussion is reminiscent of the key philosophical, epistemological, and soteriological issues raised in the Samyé debate, which, according to the Tibetan accounts, took place in Tibet between the proponents of the simultaneist followers of the Chinese Ch'an master Mohoyen and the gradualist followers of the Indian master Kamalaśila during the ninth century.

215 A yojana is a unit of measurement for distance in classical Indian texts. The value of this measurement varies according to different sources. In the standard *Abhidharma* system, which is the one most familiar to the Tibetans, a yojana *(dpag thsad)* is equivalent to about five miles. For a discussion of the conflicting values of this unit of measurement, see McGovern, *A Manual of Buddhist Philosophy*, pp. 39–48.

216 In other words, if someone perverts the teaching on karma by a misunderstanding of emptiness, the problem is with the person's view, and has no effect on how things actually are.

217 This refers to the fulfillment of one's own ultimate welfare and that of others.

218 The three qualities referred to here are: (1) erudition *(mkhas pa)*, (2) diligence *(btsun pa)*, and (3) kindness *(bzang po)*. In the Tibetan Buddhist tradition, these three are perceived to be the key qualities of a truly accomplished spiritual teacher.

219 Judging by the preceding exchanges, the "two" here refers to the two acts of: (1) admitting one into the order of the Buddha's teaching—in other words, introducing one to the Buddha's teaching—and (2) conferring empowerment.

220 This stanza presents the well-known seven-limbed practice. Interestingly, the order here is slightly different from the standard formula, with the making of offerings appearing last instead of second.

221 Here as well as in the subsequent lines, Drom is speaking to himself in the form of a self-exhortation.

222 This stanza illustrates the suffering of the realm of hungry ghosts, and the next stanza, on the "delusion-ridden," is a commentary on the animal realm.

223 This is a reference to goddess Tārā, one of Atiśa's principal meditation deities, who is believed to have prophesized Atiśa's meeting with his key disciple, Dromtönpa.

224 In the critical Tibetan edition, this line reads as *Jo bo mkhas pa khu yis mchod*, which translates as "Learned Atiśa shall be entertained by Khu." This, I feel, is an orthographical error and should be read as *Jo bo mkhas pa bu yis mchod*.

225 This is the principal buddha of the Medicine Buddha mandala, who is depicted as blue, symbolizing the color of blue beryl, a medicinal fruit.

226 These two lines are found in Atiśa's *Bodhisattva's Jewel Garland*, stanza 10c–d.

227 This is a protection mantra associated with the protector deity Acala.

228 I have failed to discern what significance this number fifty has here.

229 The Tibetan term *brdzes bcangs byed pa* literally means "to hoist one's robes and tuck them under the sash," as when crossing a river. Here Atiśa is alluding to the next chapter of the *Jewel Garland of Dialogues*, "How to Hoist Your Robes to Cross the Mires of Desire."

230 *Na yi me tog.* I have not been able to identify what this flower is.

231 A somewhat miraculous event is being described in the next few lines. It begins with Atiśa being astonished to see flowers blossoming in winter in the grounds of Nyethang Or. When Drom states that the falsely solid forms of the flowers have just about survived intact, Atiśa suspects that Dromtönpa may have conjured these flowers and asks to see the tongue that made the statement. Atiśa miraculously sees a lotus growing on Drom's tongue, as if a flower were growing in a pond in a meadow. Next Atiśa sees a miniscule replica of himself on that lotus, which, when touched by Atiśa, causes much laughter in both the replica and the real Atiśa.

232 In these lines Dromtönpa is first speaking to the flowers growing on the ground, asking them not to vanish, for this would reveal him to be a con artist. He then admits that in Tibet as a whole it is extremely cold, and that in the region of Uru in Central Tibet in particular, much of the ground freezes. He then goes on to say that if flowers blossoming in winter in Tibet pleases Atiśa, then it doesn't matter whether the flowers are real or not, so flowers might as well grow on Drom's tongue.

233 The "mother" here refers to the perfection of wisdom *(prajñāpāramitā; shes rab phar phyin)*. The four noble *(ārya)* beings are (1) the disciple noble, (2) the self-enlightened

noble, (3) the bodhisattva noble, and (4) the buddha noble. "Nobility" here connotes those beings who have attained the level of path of seeing (that is, the direct insight into the ultimate truth of all phenomena) or higher on their respective paths. This stanza echoes the salutation verse of Maitreya's *Ornament of Clear Realizations* (*Abhisamayālaṃkāra*, Toh 3786, Tengyur, shes phyin, *ka*, pp. 1c–13a), where the author pays homage to the perfection of wisdom for giving birth to the four noble sons.

234 The "irreversible ones" *(phyir mi ldog pa)* here refer to the bodhisattvas who have attained the eighth level (Skt. *bhūmi*), on which they totally eradicate all mental afflictions and their propensities.

235 In the critical Tibetan edition this line reads "Stands ten million crystal reliquaries" *(Shel gyi mchod rten bye ba gnas)*. I have chosen to follow the Dergé edition, the reading of which is more consonant with the subsequent stanzas.

236 In the lines that follow, the text is explaining the symbolism of the celestial mansion of Avalokiteśvara. The description of the mansion appears to follow the standard mandala architecture of a square structure with parapet walls and so on.

237 In the perfect symmetry of the mandala, the height of the celestial mansion is exactly the same size as its length and width.

238 The reference to "son" and "servants" in these two lines remains obscure to me.

239 At this point in the narrative, Dromtönpa's appearance changes and he assumes the form of the syllable *bhrūṃ*. Consequently, he is then referred to as Bhrūṃ Jé.

240 This is probably a reference to the crystal youth holding a staff who earlier appeared on the stamen of the large lotus.

241 These two epithets *conqueror (rgyal ba)* and *source ('byung gnas)* are allusions to Dromtönpa's name, Gyalwai Jungné *(rgyal ba'i 'byung gnas)*.

242 It is unclear whether this reference to *ati* is to be taken as an allusion to the Atiyoga of the Great Perfection *(rdzogs chen)*, where *ati* connotes something that is complete, perfect, or the highest, or whether it refers to the first part of Atiśa's name. My own sense is that it is the latter.

243 This is a reference to the Tathāgata, namely Buddha Śākyamuni, who was described earlier as composed of refined gold.

244 Tib. *me shel*. This same term is used also for magnifying glasses, since they can be used to make fire.

245 This is probably an allusion to some well-known story from classical Sanskrit literature. I have not been able to locate its source.

246 Literally, "Lion's Roar," Siṃhanāda is an ascetic form of Avalokiteśavara depicted seated on a lion. He is white with one face and two arms, his right hand in the gesture of granting higher attainments, his left resting on the seat at his back. For a detailed description, see Willson and Brauen, p. 270.

247 In the next few stanzas, Dromtönpa presents the practice of the seven limbs, minus the limbs of prostrating and paying homage. He begins the presentation with the limb of offering and proceeds to the limbs of confessing and purifying, rejoicing, requesting the buddhas to turn the wheel of Dharma, appealing them not to enter into final nirvana, and finally, dedicating merit.

248 This is the moon appearing as Dromtönpa, referred to earlier as Bhrūṃ Jé.

249 "Great Compassion" is Avalokiteśvara in his thousand-armed form.

250 *Jaḥ hūṃ baṃ hoḥ* are the four syllables with which the invoked "wisdom beings"

are dissolved into the visualized "commitment beings," thus making them inseparable. This act of uniting, an essential part of a standard meditation practice involving the visualization of deities, signifies that the practitioner's visualization has become inhabited by the actual deities.

251 Although I have not been able so far to find a source for the analogies of the twelve links of dependent origination as presented here in the sutras, Vinītadeva's commentary, *Clear Exposition of the Words of "Clear Differentiation of the Discipline [Basket]," Vinayavibhaṅgapadavyākhyāna* (Toh 4114 Tengyur, 'dul ba, *tshu*, 146a6) explicitly gives all these analogies.

252 From this point onward, beginning with ignorance, the text gives a detailed explanation of the twelve links of dependent origination and the manner in which they resemble their corresponding metaphors.

253 In the Tibetan *thangka* (painted scroll) of the wheel of life, which illustrates the twelve links of dependent origination, there is a rooster, a snake, and a pig inside the innermost circle. The rooster represents attachment, the snake represents aversion or anger, and the pig represents delusion. Each animal is grabbing another animal's tail in its mouth, thus forming an interlocking cycle, symbolizing the interlocking relationship among the three poisons of the mind. The stanzas here present the function and negative effects of attachment.

254 *'Bru dang tshigs pa bsnabs lud sogs/rang gi grogs la ster byed cing.* These two lines are somewhat obscure. Judging by the context, especially in relation to what follows immediately after, the reference seems to be to friends drinking grain alcohol from the same bowl. The suggestion seems to be that, in doing this, friends share with each other not only the grains from which the beverage is made, but also the fermented refuse as well as nasal mucus. In reading these lines in this manner, I have treated *tshigs pa* as a spelling error and corrected it as *tshigs ma*, which according to the lexicographical work *Golden Mirror* (*Brda dkrol gser gyi me long*, p. 721) refers to the fermented grains left over after the alcohol has been extracted.

255 Beginning here, the text describes the function and negative effects of aversion, or anger.

256 *Rkan sgra tog,* which literally means making noises by clicking one's tongue on one's upper palate. The idea here is that the pig is enjoying what it is eating so much that it makes continuous loud chewing noises.

257 Dergé edition: "Soften and seize the handle of the conscienceless heart" *(khrel med snying gi lung thag bsgrungs).* To "pull up the strings of one's heart" may be an expression for cultivating a sense of determination to do something.

258 "Foulness meditation" refers to a systematic meditation, found in classical Buddhist texts, that is specifically practiced as an antidote to craving and attachment. For a detailed explanation of the Buddhist meditation on foulness, whose primary purpose is to help overcome lustful attachment to others' bodies, see Buddhaghoṣa's *Visuddhimagga* (translated by Bhikkhu Ñāṇamoli as *The Path of Purification*), chap. VI. See also Śāntideva, *Bodhicaryāvatāra*, 8:40–70.

259 This is an act of paying respect, somewhat equivalent to bowing one's head in the custom of other cultures.

260 *Re sdug gyu rna ci phyir gcod.* A literal translation of this line would be "Why do you cut off the turquoise-adorned ears of hope and pain?" It is difficult to surmise what the allusion to hope and pain in this line signifies. One guess, perhaps a long

shot, is that these turquoise earrings are a family heirloom of such monetary value that they are seen as a potential asset to liquidate during times of hardship. In my translation I have chosen to keep the line simple by omitting this reference to hope and pain.

261 "Jowo" *(jo bo)* is a respectful term for one's elder brother; it can also mean "chief" or "principal" among humans or gods. The term also came to be applied to icons of buddhas in their enjoyment body *(saṃbhogakāya)* forms, such as the principal statue inside the central cathedral in Lhasa. Here the term probably refers to Avalokiteśvara.

262 These three allusions refer to different varieties of animal rebirths.

263 The specific sufferings and the characteristics of birth as a hungry ghost are described in the following lines.

264 From this point onward, the text describes the specific sufferings of the hell realm.

265 A monkey is the metaphor for consciousness in the wheel of life, where consciousness is the third of the twelve links of dependent origination.

266 In the critical Tibetan edition these two lines read: "If threatened by humans he jumps to the ground/ If threatened by birds he escapes to the treetops" *(mi yis 'jigs tse sa la bros/ bya yis 'jigs tse shing rtser bros).*

267 Form, feelings, discriminations, mental formations, and consciousness are of course the five psychophysical aggregates *(skandhas)* that constitute the existence of a person.

268 "Enemy" here refers to death and the owner who is slain refers to the consciousness.

269 This is the well-known fourfold emptiness as presented in the *Heart of Wisdom.* For a translation of this famous Mahayana text and a Tibetan commentary, see The Dalai Lama, *Essence of the Heart Sutra* (Boston: Wisdom Publications, 2002).

270 The opening two lines of this stanza appear as the following in Khenchen's "Elucidation of the Heart-Drop Practice," which cites the *Jewel Garland of Dialogues.* "Like mist, clouds, and light,/ I, the monk Dīpaṃ of appearance and emptiness,/..." Although this version found in Khenchen's text seems to be more valid, I have left the original as it is.

271 This is a paraphrase of a stanza from chapter 9 of the *King of Meditation Sutra, Samādhirājasūtra,* Toh 127 Kangyur, mdo sde, *da,* 26b2.

272 This is a paraphrase of a stanza from the *Meeting of Father and Son Sutra (Pitāputrasamāgamanasūtra),* which is part of *Ratnakūṭa* collection of sutras. Toh 60 Kangyur, dkon brtsegs, *nga,* 50b1.

273 The terms "victorious" *(rgyal),* "emerging" *('byung),* and "abiding" *(gnas)* refer to three parts of Dromtönpa's name, Gyalwai Jungné *(Rgyal ba'i 'byung gnas).*

274 This is a reference to Radreng, Dromtönpa's monastery in central Tibet.

275 It is difficult to determine which five names are being prophesized here.

276 This is probably a reference to the five recollections recommended by Tārā earlier in the text: (1) calling to mind your teachers, the source of refuge, (2) calling to mind your body as the meditation deity, (3) calling to mind your speech as mantra repetitions and recitations, (4) calling to mind all beings as your actual mothers, and (5) recollecting your mind as the ultimate nature.

277 Jñāna here refers to Master Atiśa, whose full name is Dipaṃkaraśrījñāna.

278 "White Lotus" (Skt. *Puṇḍarīka;* Tib. *Pad ma dkar po*) is an epithet of Ava-

lokiteśvara. Here it refers to Dromtönpa, who is seen as a human manifestation of Avalokiteśvara.

279 "Sahor" here refers to the city over which Atiśa's father ruled in the eastern part of India. Alaka Chattopadhyaya (*Atiśa and Tibet*, pp. 63–64) provides a brief analysis of the term and suggests that it may be a corrupt form of the Persian word *śahor*, which simply means city.

280 This is a paraphrase of the famous opening salutation verse of Nāgārjuna's *Fundamental Wisdom of the Middle Way (Mūlamadhyamakakārikā)*, where Nāgārjuna describes the world of dependent origination to be devoid of eight defining characteristics. For an accessible English translation of Nāgārjuna's classic, see Jay L. Garfield, *Fundamental Wisdom of the Middle Way* (New York: Oxford University Press, 1995).

281 "Son of space" *(Nam mkha'i bu)* is being used here as another epithet of the crystal youth, who is actually a manifestation of Drom himself. In fact, this current "collection on appearance" within chapter 12 began with Atiśa calling Dromtönpa "Stainless space" *(Nam mkha' dri med)*, an epithet in which the term *space* clearly connotes the emptiness and nonsubstantiality of all things.

282 The Tibetan text of this line is somewhat obscure and my translation must be regarded as suggestive. I have read this line as a reference to Dromtönpa as Avalokiteśvara. The Tibetan name for Avalokiteśvara, Chenresik *(spyan ras gzigs)*, connotes someone looking at beings compassionately with his eyes cast down. The main point of the stanza seems to be to demonstrate that even Dromtönpa himself is devoid of substantial existence.

283 This is clearly a citation from a tantra. However, the source remains unknown.

284 Source likewise is unknown.

285 This is probably a paraphrase of a citation from one of the Perfection of Wisdom sutras, the specific source of which was not found.

286 *Dharmasaṃgītisūtra*, Toh 238 Kangyur, mdo sde, *zha*, 39b2. This exact citation can also be found in *Saṃyutta Nikāya*, part III, 95(3) (translated by Bhikkhu Bodhi in *The Connected Discourses of the Buddha*, p. 952).

287 I have failed to locate the source of this citation exactly as it appears here. Most probably it is a paraphrase of the following stanza from *Commentary on the Awakening Mind (Bodhicittavivaraṇa*, 67bc–68ab), which is attributed to Nāgārjuna: "Independent of the conventional/ No [ultimate] truth can be found./ The conventional is taught to be emptiness;/ The emptiness itself is the conventional." (Toh 1800 Tengyur, rgyud 'grel, *ngi*, 41a).

288 "Four sessions" refer to four formalized meditation sessions, which are recommended for someone engaged in a single-pointed meditative practice during a retreat setting. The four are: (1) early dawn to sunrise, (2) morning to midday, (3) early afternoon to late afternoon, and (4) evening to late night.

289 *Lhan cig skyes pa'i lha 'dre gnyis/ rang dang rang gi bla gnyis so.* These two, the simultaneously born "god" and "demon," represent, respectively, the individual's conscience and lower impulses.

290 *Bla* (pronounced *la*), translated here as "life force," refers to the vital energy of an individual life.

291 In this collection, the text explains the procedures of the application of the method

of transferring one's consciousness at the point of death. This is the well-known Vajrayana Buddhist practice of "transference of consciousness" (*'pho ba;* pronounced *powa*), which is one of the "Six Yogas of Naropa."

292 These are *oṃ, aḥ,* and *hūṃ,* which respectively mark one's crown, throat, and heart. In Vajrayana Buddhism, these three letters represent the body, speech, and mind of the enlightened beings.

293 The "normal color" of Vajrasattva is white, Ratnasaṃbhava below is golden, Amitābha is red, and Amoghasiddhi is green.

294 This is a reference to a earlier stanza of this section where it has been stated if the dying person recognizes the appearances for what they are, he will experience joy. In contrast, if he fails to do so, he will then experience fear.

295 Despite all efforts I have not been able to discern what *ūbhi* means. Most probably, it's part of or a degenerated form of a Sanskrit term.

296 *Rnal 'byor spyod pa'i dbu ma pa/ dbu ma'i dbyings su dbu ma 'gro.* The expression *rnal 'byor spyod pa'i dbu ma pa* is Tibetan for Yogācāra-Madhyamaka, a subdivision of the Indian Madhyamaka school. Here, however, the term is used in a general sense to connote the upholders of the Madhyamaka (Middle Way) school who practice tantra as well.

297 *Phyi mi ldog la dung 'khyil te.* The Tibetan word translated here as "conch" is *dung 'khyil.* This is probably an abbrevation of *dung dkar g.yas 'khyil,* which is a rare conch on which the lines curl in the opposite direction. This "right-curling" conch is considered by Tibetans a precious object endowed with auspicious omens. Such a conch is the crowning ornament in the depiction of the eight auspicious symbols.

298 This is probably an allusion to the traditional Tibetan belief that, when highly evolved spiritual figures die and are cremated, their tongue and heart will often remain unburned.

299 This is a reference to the five heinous acts, which result at death in immediate rebirth in the hell realms without an intervening passage through the intermediate state just described. See note 187.

300 This is a form of Avalokiteśvara with one face and two arms who sits in a seated posture with his right leg extended. This particular aspect of Avalokiteśvara has special significance for relieving the sufferings of the beings in the hungry ghost realm. For a description and a short meditation practice on this deity, see Willson and Brauen, 2000, p. 266.

301 *Rigs gsum nyid kyi sprul.* The term *rigs gsum* is an abbreviation of *rigs sgum mgon po,* which literally means "the lords of the three classes." They are Avalokiteśvara (the embodiment of the compassion of all the buddhas), Mañjuśrī (the embodiment of their wisdom), and Vajrapāṇi (the embodiment of their power).

302 "Lady" and the "white youth" here refer, respectively, to Tārā and Avalokiteśvara.

303 What follows in the subsequent lines is almost the entire instruction found in the mind training work entitled "Leveling Out All Conceptions" (*Mind Training: The Great Collection,* root text, entry 12, and commentary, entry 32). Interestingly, here Atiśa attributes the instruction to his teacher Avadhūtipa, whereas in *Mind Training,* it is attributed to Serlingpa.

304 In the root text of "Leveling Out All Conceptions" in *Mind Training,* this line reads slightly differently as "Carry forth the force of all antidotes" *(gnyen po thams cad bcom theg yin).*

305 *Dpa' bo chen po la sdig sgribs kyis bsdad pa'i glags med.* In the Tibetan original, this sentence appears to be corrupt, so the translation provided here is only suggestive.

306 This is most probably an oral instruction of Avadhūtipa being cited by Atiśa.

307 In this instance, I am translating the Tibetan word *srid pa*, which literally means "possible," as the modal verb "can." I have read the expression "dejection is possible" *(zhum pa srid)* as an abbreviation of the full sentence "It is possible that dejection will arise" *(zhum pa skye ba srid).*

308 *De la srid pa mi khegs lags.* This line can also be translated as "Its possibility cannot be ruled out." However, I feel that the term *srid pa* should be translated here as "existence" in the sense of cyclic existence, rather than as "possible."

309 A translation of the story on illusion that appears here can be found in Geshé Wangyal's *Jewelled Staircase*, pp. 142–47.

310 Although this line is somewhat obscure, it probably means that Śrīman did not believe in magical illusions before but, having experienced an illusion, he was then brought face to face with their lack of reality later on. In the same manner, though the experience of wandering in cycle of existence may seem real, it, too, is devoid of substantial reality.

311 This is a reference to the Tibetan translator Naktso Lotsāwa whose personal name is Tsültrim Gyalwa. Not only was he the main Tibetan who successfully brought Atiśa to Tibet, he also became one of Atiśa's important students and a collaborator on numerous translations of Indian Buddhist texts into Tibetan. Naktso Lotsāwa is the author of the well-known verse biography of Atiśa known as the *Hundred and Ten Stanzas of Praise (Bstod pa brgya bcu pa),* the full text of which can be found in Yeshé Döndrup's *Treasury of Gems* (pp. 26–35).

312 In this exchange, Atiśa is reported as stating that the instruction on the meditative practice of *tong len* (giving and taking) on the basis of the respiration process was first taught to him by Serlingpa. The complete instructions on this practice can be found in the well-known *Seven-Point Mind Training (Mind Training: The Great Collection,* entry 6) and *Root Lines of Mahayana Mind Training* and its annotated version *(Mind Training,* entries 4 and 5), which together form the basis for the *Seven-Point Mind Training.* For the relationship between these three texts, see my introduction in *Mind Training: The Great Collection* and the annotations to the individual texts.

313 The Tibetan expression *mgo mjug log pa* literally means "head and tail reversed," and in general usage, simply means "upside down." Here I have chosen a literal translation so that Atiśa's rhetorical question in the next line retains its pun in English as well.

314 In the Dergé edition, this line reads "Master, how does one extend this to other ornaments" *(rgyan gzhan dag la ji ltar sbyar).* However, here I have chosen to follow Tashi Lhünpo edition, which appears to be more accurate.

315 The Tibetan term *mi chos,* which I have translated here as "worldly social norms," literally means the "human dharma," with *dharma* in its broader sense of a "way," "law," or a "norm." Often this term is contrasted with *lha chos* (literally, the "celestial Dharma"), the deeper spiritual and religious norms that pertain to the fate of future life. Sometimes, in the context of teachings on transcending mundane concerns, *mi chos* is used in a slightly pejorative sense with connotations of cunning and lax ethics.

316 For a female monastic practitioner, this line should be read as "It is men and so on, so forsake them." It becomes evident later on in the text that these pertain primarily to male monastic practitioners.

317 This image of dying like an injured wild animal in the wilderness has a profound appeal for serious practitioners who devote their entire lives to single-pointed meditation practice. This kind of sentiment is echoed extensively in Tibet's most famous meditator-poet, Milarepa, in his *Hundred Thousand Songs*. The present Dalai Lama has also expressed that one of his regrets in living the life of the Dalai Lama is his inability to fulfill his deep yearning to be able to spend his last years as an "injured wild animal" in the wilderness.

318 This is probably a reference to a death ritual, which, in the case of highly revered religious practitioners, would include the washing and cleansing of the bones following the cremation.

319 The three "white" ingredients are milk, yogurt, and butter, and the three "sweet" ingredients are honey, sugar, and molasses.

320 *Drug cu rtsa re'i sdug byas pas.* It is difficult to discern whether this number refers to a specific list of pains or it is simply an expression for many.

321 The five fields are: (1) Sanskrit grammar, (2) logic and epistemology, (3) arts and crafts, (4) medicine, and (5) inner science, this latter field referring to Buddhist thought and practice. These are the five fields of classical knowledge according to Indian Buddhism.

322 Having described the negative consequences of indulging in alcohol, meat, and so on in the previous stanzas, Dromtönpa then goes on to criticize what he perceives to be the excesses of those who indulge in such things under the pretext of possessing advanced spiritual realizations of "nonconceptuality," "nonclinging," "pure vision," and so forth. He asserts that, when caught in the afflictions, such things become nothing but expressions of basic afflictions like delusion, attachment, conceit, jealousy, and aversion.

323 *Ltong ltong zer zhing rdo rje 'gros.* This line is somewhat obscure, and the translation provided is only suggestive.

324 This is probably a reference to the following statement found in *Perfection of Wisdom in Twenty-Five Thousand Lines* (Toh 9 Kangyur, shes phyin, vol. *kha*, 245b1): "O son, Śāradvatīputra, it is thus: This profound perfection of wisdom will perform the task of the Buddha in the future, at a later time, in the southern and northern regions." The "conquerors' mother" is the perfection of wisdom in female form, who is metaphorically understood as the mother of all buddhas.

325 Since Radreng Monastery was founded by Dromtönpa in 1056, just over a year after Atiśa's death, this stanza is traditionally recognized as a prophesy pertaining to the founding of Radreng Monastery, which became the seat of the Kadam school.

326 The svāstika, though infamous in the West due to its association with Nazi Germany, is an ancient Indian symbol that represents stability and auspiciousness.

327 The "four foundations of mindfulness," the "four perfect endeavors," and the "four factors of supernatural feats" refer to the first three sets from the thirty-seven factors of the path to enlightenment. For a succinct description of these from the Sanskrit and Tibetan sources, see His Holiness the Dalai Lama, *The World of Tibetan Buddhism*, pp. 20–22.

328 From this point onward, the text gives symbolism for the different aspects of the the landscape at Radreng. It begins with reference to seven mountains that surround Radreng to the north, northeast, southeast, south, southwest, west, and northeast, and which are compared to the seven royal emblems.

329 This might be an allusion to an old Tibetan myth of cosmic creation according to which the entire universe is supported on the back of a giant turtle. Alternatively, it could be an allusion to a specific rite of geomancy where a drawing of a turtle with relevant inscriptions is buried in the foundation when constructing a temple.

330 This is a reference to the well-known "three scopes"—initial, intermediate, and great—presented in Atiśa's *Lamp for the Path to Enlightenment*. For more on this, see my introduction to this volume.

331 In Tibet, being well oiled or greased is considered a sign of being looked after with care. This relates to both one's skin, especially the face, as well as household furnishings, especially the wooden floor inside one's house.

332 *'Phan yul rig pa bsam grub.* I have read the Tibetan word *'phan yul* as referring to the region of Phenpo, which is in the southwestern part of Tibet. This is the region in which the Yerpa retreat, the site where all the dialogues contained in *The Book of Kadam* are supposed to have taken place, is located.

333 *Snum rtsi.* It is difficult to discern what substance is being referred to here by this Tibetan word. Generally, *snum* is used to refer to oil, while *rtsi* refers to some kind of glue-like substance that helps things adhere to the surface on which the substance is applied.

334 Jinasāgara, a Sanskrit epithet meaning "conqueror ocean" (Tib. *rgyal ba rgya mtsho*), is the name of a specific form of Avalokiteśvara. For a brief description of the iconography of this deity, see Willson and Brauen, p. 270.

335 *Sla nga.* This is a wok-like metal container without a handle used in Tibet to roast barley in hot sand. Roasted barley flour is a staple of the Tibetan diet.

336 The names in parentheses are found in the Tibetan original and were probably added by a later editor to identify the key disciples of Dromtönpa who are being prophesized here by Atiśa. Our editor writes *Potowa* as *Putowa*, which, although not a common spelling, is found elsewhere as well.

337 This and the following lines echo the well-known debate between the "sudden" and "gradual" approaches to enlightenment. The term used in this text is *one-stroke approach (gcig chod)*, which has the same meaning as *sudden (gcig sbyar)*. This was the principal issue at the famous Samyé debate, which is thought to have taken place between the Indian master Kamalaśila and the Chinese Cha'n master Hoshang Mohoyen in the eighth century. Most interestingly, here the two standpoints are placed in the voices of two students of Atiśa, with Dromtönpa as a proponent for the gradual approach and an Indian yogi as the proponent for the sudden approach.

338 *Rhugs dombhi kyed dang kyad mi mnga'.* Here, Atiśa calls the Indian yogi who had been debating with Dromtönpa Dombhi. Most probably, the yogi who appeared in a pure vision to partake in the discussion with Dromtönpa is to be recognized as the mahāsiddha Dombhīpa, one of the eighty-four mahāsiddhas, or "perfected ones," of classical India.

339 From this point on in this chapter, Atiśa cites the instructions of numerous

masters, beginning with his principal teacher, Serlingpa. In addition, he cites: Avadhūtipa, Jetāri, Dharmarakṣita, Śāntipa (known also as Ratnākaraśānti), Ḍombhīpa, Vidyākaukila, Nāropa, and Tilopa. Although the instructions attributed to the individual teachers appear as block quotes, they do not appear to be citations from these masters' written works. Rather, the text gives the impression that Atiśa received such teachings personally.

340   *Rgyu ma gnye ma mchin pa dang.* I have translated the Tibetan *gnye ma* as tendons based on the *Extensive Tibetan-Chinese Dictionary*, which defines it as part of the fibrous tissue between the joints.

341   This is the first story in the *Hundred Birth Stories*, or *Jātaka Tales*, that narrate the Buddha's previous lives. See note 196 above.

342   In these stanzas, it is difficult to discern which texts of Saraha and yoginī Nāgī are being alluded to in the instructions attributed to them.

343   *Gangs can mtsho.* Literally meaning the "Lake of the Snow Mountains," this probably refers to Lake Manasarovar, which is at the base of the sacred Mount Kailash in western Tibet.

344   Despite efforts I have failed to determine which text of Candrakīrti is alluded to in this instruction. It may be that only the first line of the stanza, i.e. "Jealousy destroys one's own roots of virtue," is being attributed to Candrakīrti here.

345   This is probably a paraphrase of a stanza from the root tantra of Cakrasaṃvara, although I have not been able to locate it.

346   The Tibetan terms I have translated here as "superficial friendliness" and "flattery" are *ngo dga'* and *phye 'thor* respectively. The first term literally means "happy face" while the second term translates as "sprinkling flour," suggesting that one is showering someone with friendly statements, the whiteness of the flour representing something positive.

347   This distinction between "divine spiritual norms" *(lha chos)* and "mundane human norms" *(mi chos)* appears to be very old, probably dating back to pre-Buddhist period in Tibet. Generally speaking, divine spiritual norms refer to some kind of religious or spiritual norms that pertain to one's well-being beyond the present life. By contrast, mundane human norms relate primarily to cultural, social, and civic values of decency, prudence, and collective responsibility. The most well-known enshrinement of these two sets of norms is found in the so-called "ten virtues of divine norms" *(lha chos dge ba bcu)*, which refers to the morality of refraining from ten negative actions, and the "sixteen mundane human norms of pure conduct" *(mi chos gtsang ma bcu drug)*, which refers to a set of sixteen values. The seventh-century Tibetan emperor Songtsen Gampo is credited with having established these two lists of norms.

348   "Endurance world" is a technical name used in the classical Buddhist scripture to refer to our world. For an explanation of this name, see note 418.

349   *Ma tha'ang khrom rgyal sdes khas 'byed pa yin.* The Tibetan original of this sentence is extremely obscure, and the translation I have provided is only a suggestion.

350   This is a reference to one of Atiśa's teachers, who is simply referred to as Vajrāsana *(rdo rje gdan pa),* literally, the one from Bodhgaya.

351   This is most probably a reference to Nāgārjuna. However, the source of this citation remains unidentified.

352   Although our author attributes this citation to Vasubandhu, the stanza comes

from the *Madhyāntavibhaṅga,* which is attributed to Maitreya (*Madhyānta-vibhaṅga,* 5:9–10, Toh 4021 Tengyur, sems tsam, *phi,* 44a4). The verse is included, however, in Vasubhandu's commentary on Maitreya's text, *Madhyāntavibhaṅga-ṭīkā,* chap. 5, Toh 4027 Tengyur, sems tsam, *bi,* 21a7.

353 It is clear from the text that the following stanzas from Vasubandhu are being cited from a visionary experience that Atiśa had in India. "Kaśmiri seats of learning" refers to the monastic centers of a branch of the Vaibhāṣika school of Indian Buddhism that was active in the region of modern-day Kashmir.

354 *Blo snying brang gsum.* In a more liberal translation, this expression could be translated as "one's mind, heart, and soul." Given the loaded meaning of the word "soul," I have opted to keep my translation literal.

355 The Tibetan text of these last five sentences appears somewhat obscure and the translation provided here is only suggestive.

356 *Seng ldan.* Monier-Williams (*A Sanskrit-English Dictionary,* p. 836) gives the following explanation for the Sanskrit word *khadira:* "*Acacia catechu* (having very hard wood, the resin of which is used in medicine, called Catechu, Khayar, Terra japonica)."

357 This is probably an allusion to Dharmarakṣita, one of Atiśa's three masters on the awakening mind. According to the tradition, Dharmarakṣita is a follower of the Mahāsāṃghika branch of the Vaibhāṣika school of Indian Buddhism. For a brief discussion of Dharmarakṣita and his teachings, see the introduction to *Mind Training: The Great Collection.*

358 *Stugs po bkod pa;* Sanskrit, *Ghanavyūha.*

359 Here, I have followed the Dergé edition. In the critical Tibetan edition, this line reads "So, not selling me as merchandise…"

360 The term "training in mind" *(sems kyi bslab pa)* is another name for the training in meditation, which is second of the three higher trainings, the other two being the training in morality and the training in wisdom.

361 The three spheres are (1) the *agent,* the person making the dedication, (2) the *object* to whom the dedication is made, and (3) the *material,* the substance being dedicated.

362 "Wheel of feasts" (*tshogs kyi 'khor lo;* Sanskrit, *gaṇacakra*) refers to a ritual ceremony in the highest yoga class of Vajrayana practice. In its original context, the practice involved a gathering of various male and female tantric practitioners for a feast of celebration. This ceremony is particularly popular in the so-called mother tantras, such as Cakrasaṃvara.

363 The "four pairs of personages" *(skyes bu zung bzhi)* are four classes of individuals on the disciple's path. They are (1) stream-enterers, (2) once-returners, (3) nonreturners, and (4) arhats. Each of these has two stages, the first the stage of entering and the second the stage of abiding in the result, thus making eight types of individuals altogether.

364 In general *torma* refers to a ritual cake, customarily made of roasted barley dough and decorated with butter at the front, that is consecrated and ritually offered to all classes of objects, such as buddhas, meditation deities, and protectors, including the local guardian spirits.

365 The two supports mentioned are the power of the basis. Together with the other three powers listed here we find what are called the *four powers,* or *four opponent*

powers. These four are the key ingredients in a successful purification of negative karmic imprints.

366 Although the Tibetan text of this preamble is somewhat obscure, it seems obvious from the context that it refers to one of the traditional understandings of the origin of the *The Book of Kadam.* According to this view, it is Mañjuśrī who, after having heard the entire dialogue that took place between Atiśa and Dromtönpa at the retreat of Yerpa, appears to Ngok Lekpai Sherap (the student being referred to as resembling Mañjuśrī) and incites him to go to Yerpa to receive the entire instructions. So, upon his arrival at Yerpa, Ngok requests Atiśa to give an oral transmission of the entire dialogue, and Atiśa complies by repeating everything once again for his benefit. A similar reference to the origin of the teachings of *Jewel Garland of Dialogues* appears later in the colophon.

367 This is probably a reference to the twin aims of bringing about one's own welfare and the welfare of others.

368 "Chariot" is being used here as a metaphor for Dromtönpa's Kadam tradition, suggesting that this tradition is like a great carrier that can transport many people to buddhahood. This resonates with the Tibetan custom of referring to Nāgārjuna and Asaṅga as the "two great chariot leaders" *(shing rta'i srol 'byed chen po gnyis),* meaning the two seminal figures of Mahayana Buddhism. In this epithet, the two Mahayana schools—Middle Way and Mind Only—are being compared to two great carriages.

369 These three exact lines appeared earlier in chapter 8. See note 207.

370 Known as the "twelve Tenmas" *(bstan ma bcu gnyis),* these are a group of twelve female protectors, all of whom are associated with different mountain ranges in Tibet.

371 Atiśa is stating here that he will die within a year and fortnight's time. The reference to Maitreya here is to indicate that he is being called to Maitreya's buddhafield, which is the heavenly realm of Tuṣita.

372 This "central land" probably refers to India, the birthplace of Buddhism. If this reference is correct, the text here is suggesting that it was Atiśa who "brought" the twelve Tenma protectors to Tibet from India.

373 In the critical Tibetan edition as well as in the Derge version, this line reads, "Conceited speech and speech of untamed horses." This is definitely an orthographical error. The context makes it clear that it is the afflicted views that are being referred to here. Instead of *lta* it has been misprinted as *rta.*

374 *Byams brtse bskyed gsal lhod de bshig.* The Tibetan text of this line is somewhat obscure and my translation should, therefore, be taken only as a suggestion.

375 These lines do not appear to be presented in the text as being spoken by Dromtönpa. They seem to be added by an editor who compiled the teachings together as a single text. Although the Tibetan text of these particular stanzas is somewhat obscure, after paying homage to Dromtönpa as Avalokiteśvara (hence the reference to Buddha Amitābha on his crown), the editor makes the following interesting points. First, he states that the root-text summary that encapsulates all the themes of the dialogue is without doubt Master Atiśa's own work. He then goes on to say that the collected dialogues between Atiśa and Dromtönpa stand apart *(logs su bkol ba)* as a collection in their own right, though no title was given to them by Atiśa. The editor then asserts that the teachings contained here are clearly

dialogues on Atiśa's *Bodhisattva's Jewel Garland,* although in this root text no queries and responses have been specified. This is followed by the remark that, upon embracing the words of Master Atiśa, the teachings were instantly written down. This is probably an allusion to the story of Ngok Lekpai Sherap being the scribe when Atiśa repeated to him the entire dialogue once again. Finally, the editor says that it was written in "the Bodhgaya style"; it is difficult to discern whether the editor means that it was originally written in some central Indian script or whether he is referring to a specific style of composition.

376 In some ancient Tibetan texts, Tibet is referred to as Purgyal (spelled *pur rgyal* or *spur rgyal*), which literally means, "the kingdom of Pu." In his encyclopedic dictionary *(Dung dkar tshig mdzod chen mo),* the Tibetan scholar Dungkar Lobsang Thrinlé asserts that, although there exist numerous explanations of the meaning of this expression, "the kingdom of Pu," it may have originally evolved as the name of the dominion ruled by the Tibetan king Pudé Gungyal, who is traditionally listed as ninth in a line of Tibetan kings starting from Nyatri Tsenpo. The historian Christopher Beckwith (*Tibetan Empire in Central Asia,* p. 8), states that in the *Old Tibetan Chronicle,* the Tibetans of the Namri Songten period refer to their king as "the king of Pu" (spu).

377 Dergé: "Negative friends are of inferior fortune;/ They recognize only the practioners."

378 The "twenty birth stories" here refer to the first twenty stories of Dromtönpa's former lives as narrated in the "Son Teachings" of *The Book of Kadam.* These first twenty birth stories are called the "Ngok cycle of teachings" *(rngog chos),* as they were told in response to requests from Ngok Lekpai Sherap. The remaining two birth stories are known as the "Khu cycle of teachings" *(khu chos),* as they were requested by Khutön Tsöndru Yungdrung.

379 For an explanation of the enumeration of the Father Teachings, see my introduction. In this "collection on the story of the origin" we are told that, of the twenty-three core chapters of the Father Teachings, the first twenty-one were actually revealed to Ngok Lekpai Sherap by Mañjuśrī in the forest, while the two remaining chapters were taught by Atiśa upon Ngok's arrival at the retreat of Yerpa.

380 This and its immediately preceding line together state that the chapter on the sacred seal and the diamond songs were taught after the twentieth of the Ngok cycle of teachings—namely, the first twenty birth stories of Dromtönpa—had been given. For the listing of the chapters of the Father Teachings and the Son Teachings of *The Book of Kadam,* see my introduction.

381 In this line, the "conqueror" refers to Atiśa, "his source" refers to Dromtönpa (which is the translation of the second part of his name, Gyalwai Jungné), and the "the Sherap pair" refers to Ngok Lekpai Sherap and Ngari Sherap Gyaltsen. These last two figures are closely associated with the development, dissemination, and sustenance of the unique teachings related to the *Jewel Garland of Dialogues.*

382 The three Gyaltsens referred to here are: Phuchungwa Shönu Gyaltsen, Rinchen Gyaltsen, and Dharma Gyaltsen, all three of whom are associated with the transmission of the Kadam lineage of inspiration. Namkha Rinchen, the author of a versified account of the lineage of the teachers responsible for early transmission of the *Jewel Garland of Dialogues,* lists Dromtönpa, Ngok Lekpai Sherap, Ngari Sherap Gyaltsen, Phuchungwa Jangchup Gyaltsen, Rinchen Gyaltsen, Dharma

Gyaltsen, and Jangchup Namkha, as the "seven precious individuals" *(skyes bu rin chen bdun)*. See "Biographies of the Lineage Masters of the Jewel Garland of Dialogues" in *The Father Teachings of The Book of Kadam (Bka' gdams glegs bam las pha chos)*, p. 300.

383 Here, *The Book of Kadam* refers to the *Jewel Garland of Dialogues*, which is considered the core text of *The Book*.

384 Kawa Shākya Wangchuk was a senior student of Atiśa and later also became a devout student of Dromtönpa as well. Referred to often as the "great elder" *(gnas brtan chen po)*, Kawapa was among the important lamas who went to western Tibet to formally welcome Atiśa when he first arrived in Tibet (Lechen, *Lamp Illuminating the History of the Kadam Tradition*, p. 81b4).

385 Clearly, Serlingpa's words are being spoken here in the context of a visionary experience. Despite efforts, I have not been able to identify what source our author, Khenchen, is using for this long citation attributed to Serlingpa.

386 "Infinite light" is probably a reference to Amitābha (literally meaning "infinite light"), whose head crowns the other ten heads of Thousand-Armed Great Compassion Avalokiteśvara.

387 The Tibetan original is *dri med chos kyi mchos rten rab mdzes pa*, which translates as "They adorn the beautiful unblemished golden stupa." Here, I have instead chosen the reading in the Dergé edition.

388 This is probably a reference to the Dharma protectors who employ all four means of activities—pacifying, wealth-increasing, influencing, and wrathful—to carry out their oath as protectors.

389 This line is partly a word play on the meaning of Dromtönpa's name, Gyalwai Jungné, which translates as "source of conquerors."

390 "Fame of the Dharma" (Chökyi Drakpa; Sanskrit, Dharmakīrti) is the personal name of Serlingpa, Atiśa's principal teacher on awakening mind.

391 It is difficult to discern the source of Khenchen Nyima Gyaltsen's citations from Avadhūtipa provided here.

392 This stanza and the three stanzas that follow are from chapter 12 of the *Jewel Garland of Dialogues*.

393 This and the next four stanzas are from chapter 9 of the *Jewel Garland of Dialogues*.

394 This and the subsequent stanza are from chapter 12 of the *Jewel Garland of Dialogues*.

395 This and the subsequent two long stanzas are from a separate section of chapter 12 of the *Jewel Garland of Dialogues*.

396 This and the last two stanzas are from another section of chapter 12 of the *Jewel Garland of Dialogues*.

397 In this line in the *Jewel Garland of Dialogues*, Drom is referred to as Bhrūṃ Jé.

398 This stanza is also from chapter 12 of the *Jewel Garland of Dialogues*.

399 This excerpt comes from chapter 10 of the *Jewel Garland of Dialogues*.

400 In the *Jewel Garland of Dialogues* itself, this line reads "Knives rain down from trees which they confused for cooling shade."

401 The first three lines of this stanza are from chapter 12 of the *Jewel Garland of Dialogues*.

402 The remaining stanzas of this section are from a separate section of chapter 12 of the *Jewel Garland of Dialogues*.

403 This excerpt is from chapter 12 of the *Jewel Garland of Dialogues*.

404 This and the two subsequent stanzas come from chapter 12 of the *Jewel Garland of Dialogues.*

405 The stanzas from this to the end of the stanzas cited in this section are from chapter 16 of the *Jewel Garland of Dialogues.*

406 This entire section in verse is from chapter 12 of the *Jewel Garland of Dialogues.*

407 These three stanzas are from chapter 9 of the *Jewel Garland of Dialogues.*

408 The following stanzas are from chapter 16 of the *Jewel Garland of Dialogues.*

409 These two stanzas are from chapter 2 of the *Jewel Garland of Dialogues.*

410 This and the two subsequent stanzas are from chapter 22 of the *Jewel Garland of Dialogues.*

411 This entire extract is from chapter 9 of the *Jewel Garland of Dialogues.*

412 In the *Jewel Garland of Dialogues,* this line reads: "What is illuminated is conception-free and devoid of substantial reality." Most probably, the reading found here in Khenchen's text is corrupt.

413 This is entry I of our present volume.

414 The text referred to here is the stanzas on the seven-limbs practice found toward the end of Dromtönpa's *Self-Exhortation,* which is entry I of our present volume.

415 The "three representations" refers to physical representations of a buddha's body, speech, and mind by means of statues, scriptures, and stupas respectively.

416 The following three auspicious stanzas are widely recited in Tibetan Buddhist rituals even to this day. They can be found in numerous earlier Indian Buddhist texts, especially those of Vajrayana class. See, for example, Prājñendraruci's *Rin chen 'bar ba zhes bya ba'i sgrubs thabs* (Toh 1251 Tengyur, rgyud 'grel, *nya,* 223a.)

417 This rite of expelling the interfering forces *(bgegs gtor)* by means of offering them a torma ritual cake is a standard ritual performed at the beginning of many important religious undertakings, such as at the beginning of a long meditation retreat or when conducting an empowerment ceremony.

418 *Endurance World* is a technical term and the translation of the Tibetan term *mi mjed 'jig rten gyi khams* (Sanskrit, *sahālokadhātu*). It refers to our particular world. Changkya's lexicography (*Source of Becoming Learned,* p. 561) takes the Tibetan term *mi mjed pa* to be an archaic term for "endurance" or "forbearance" *(bzod pa),* which is consonant with *Golden Mirror Unraveling the Terms* (p. 630). In the latter, the author cites Shüchen Tsütrim Rinchen's *Catalogue of the Tengyur,* which gives a slightly different take on the meaning of "endurance." According to this second view, which is based on the *White Lotus Sutra,* this world is called Endurance World because the sentient beings of this world endure or defy the three primary afflictions of attachment, aversion, and delusion. Monier-Williams (*Sanskrit-English Dictionary,* p. 1192) provides the following meanings for the Sanskrit term *sahā*—bearing, enduring, withstanding, defying, or equal to.

419 The Tibetan text of this line is quite obscure and contains the strange word *lo brtubs.* In Yongzin Yeshé Gyaltsen's *The Rite of the Mandala of the Sixteen Drops of Kadam* (p. 52a4), where he cites these stanzas on the drawing of the mandala in their entirety, this word is written as *logs btubs.* I have not been able to find this word in any of the Tibetan lexicons, including the various "elucidation of archaic Tibetan terms" I have at my disposal. Judging mainly by the progression in the instructions for drawing the mandala, I have guessed that this word means "main lines."

420   In drawing a mandala, two units of measurement are used prominently: "door size" *(sgo tshad)* and "micro unit" *(cha chung)*. The first refers to the size of the main door of the mansion, while the second unit refers to one fourth of the door size.

421   This is probably a reference to the members of the youth among the lay congregation that have come to participate in the celebration of the mandala.

422   This is a reference to Atiśa's three principal awakening mind teachers: Serlingpa, Dharmarakṣita, and Maitrīyogi.

423   *Shes rab mchog ldan.* This is most probably Ngok Lekpai Sherap, whose name is followed by Sherap Gyal (Sherap Gyaltsen). In this stanza Khenchen lists, following Atiśa and Dromtönpa, the names of the "seven precious beings" who are closely associated with the transmission of the teachings of *The Book of Kadam* in its earliest stages.

424   *Karaṇḍavyūhasūtra ('Phags pa za ma tog bkod pa'i mdo),* Toh 116 Kangyur, mdo sde, ja, 200a–247b.

425   These stanzas on the seven limbs are from chapter 16 of the *Jewel Garland of Dialogues.*

426   This and the subsequent stanza are cited from chapter 12 of the *Jewel Garland of Dialogues.*

427   Uru *(dbu ru)* is one of thirteen principalities of Tibet according to a system of classifying the different regions of Tibet that predates the current system of dividing the country into the three provinces of Ütsang, Kham, and Amdo.

428   This is a reference to Phuchungwa, one of the three Kadam brothers, whose personal name, Shönu Gyaltsen, is composed of two words that translate respectively as "youthful" and "victory banner." Phuchungwa became the custodian of the Kadam lineage of pith instructions, at the heart of which are the practices associated with *The Book of Kadam.*

429   This is Ngok Lekpai Sherap, one of the three principal disciples of Atiśa and the founder of Sangphu Monastery in central Tibet.

430   This is Khutön Tsöndrü Yungdrung, one of the three principal disciples of Atiśa.

431   This is the fifth chapter of the "Son Teachings" from *The Book of Kadam.*

432   *Maitri* here refers to the mantra *Oṃ maitri maitri mahā maitrīye svahā. Pāragate* is the Perfection of Wisdom essence mantra given above.

433   It is difficult to tell whether Khenchen is citing this stanza from somewhere or whether it is his own composition.

434   The Tibetan text of this sentence is quite obscure. I have read it to mean that, however close one might zoom in or out during the sixteen-drops meditation, the drop of great awakening is the final point, and that everything is contained within the bounds of this drop.

435   This and the three subsequent stanzas are from chapter 21 of the *Jewel Garland of Dialogues.*

436   This and the subsequent five stanzas are also from chapter 21 of the *Jewel Garland of Dialogues.*

437   This and the next stanza are also from chapter 21 of the *Jewel Garland of Dialogues.*

438   This stanza is also from chapter 21 of the *Jewel Garland of Dialogues.*

439   This stanza is from chapter 21 of the *Jewel Garland of Dialogues.* Here the first person voice has been used in my translation since Khenchen is clearly citing this stanza as part of an aspiration prayer.

440 This and the next three stanzas are from chapter 11 of the *Jewel Garland of Dialogues*.

441 Except for these two lines, the remaining lines of this stanza and the next are from the last part of chapter 11 of the *Jewel Garland of Dialogues*.

442 This and the last two stanzas of the aspiration prayers are from chapter 21 of the *Jewel Garland of Dialogues*.

443 All the stanzas of the proclamation of auspiciousness are from the chapter entitled "Sealing the Text," which is one of the three supplementary chapters of the *Jewel Garland of Dialogues* found in the Son Teachings, the second volume of *The Book of Kadam*. The Tibetan for these verses can be found in *The Book of Kadam: The Son Teachings*, pp. 603–5.

444 This is probably a reference to the six perfections—the perfections of generosity, morality, forbearance, joyful perseverance, concentration, and wisdom.

445 The stanzas in this extract are from chapter 21 of the *Jewel Garland of Dialogues*.

446 All the stanzas in this section are from chapter 22 of the *Jewel Garland of Dialogues*.

447 The Tibetan term *khrid,* which has been translated here as "manual" or a "guide," normally refers to texts that are composed in the style of a guided instruction on the various steps of the related meditation practice. Sometimes, the term can also be used to refer to a teacher's live instruction.

448 Stanza 3 of *Bodhisattva's Jewel Garland,* which is the root text for both the Father Teachings and the Son Teachings of *The Book of Kadam*. For the full text, see entry II of this volume. The numbering of the stanzas here is based on their correspondence to the chapters of the *Jewel Garland of Dialogues*, which differs from their numbering in *Mind Training: The Great Collection*.

449 This is Ngok Lepai Sherap, the same person who is requesting Atiśa to speak of Dromtönpa's previous lives. He is referred to here as Sangphuwa (the one from Sangphu) because he founded the famous Kadam monastery of Sangphu in central Tibet.

450 *Dad pa'i zhing sa log rtog gi bud kyis khyer ba.* The Tibetan term *bud pa* in its noun form refers to a bellow, an instrument used for blowing on coals. In its verb form, *bud pa* means to "expel," "to lose" in the sense of losing one's tooth, or to "undo" (i.e., to twist) in the sense of twisting an ankle. *Extensive Tibetan-Chinese Dictionary* defines several related terms such as *bud grong,* meaning a deserted town and *bud rnying,* a deserted house or a field.

451 The Vedas are a collection of ancient Sanskrit religious texts. Modern scholars date the earliest of the Vedas, the *Ṛg Veda,* to 12,000 B.C.E. and the second earliest, the *Atharva Veda,* to around 900 B.C.E. See *Hindu Myths* (translated by Wendy Doniger O'Flaherty), Penguin Classics, p. 17.

452 Sarat Chandra Das reconstructs the name *gsal ba* as Tviśya. See "The Lamaic Hierarchy of Tibet" in *Journal of the Buddhist Texts Society of India* 1 (1893): pt. 1, p. 33.

453 *Bram ze'i khye'u snang ba zhes bya bar gyur to.*

454 These refer to the two Mahayana schools of classical Indian Buddhism: Madhyamaka (following Nāgārjuna) and Cittamātra (following Asaṅga).

455 These two divisions of the Middle Way (or Madhyamaka) school roughly correspond to the later Tibetan division of this school into Svātantrika (Autonomous) and Prāsaṅgika (Consequentialist) camps. The division of the Middle Way school into "mere appearance" *(snang tsam)* and "utter nonabiding" *(rab tu mi gnas pa)* is found in numerous early Kadam writings.

456 These are the two main divisions of the Mind Only school known as Satyākarā-vādin (*rnam bden pa*, "true aspectarian") and Alīkāravādin (*rnam brdzun pa*, "false aspectarian"). The former maintain that the aspects of the objects that appear to sense perceptions are true or real existents, whereas the latter reject this, saying the aspects are mere constructs.

457 "Expanse of sky gliders" is a poetic epithet for the sky, wherein "sky glider" refers to the mythical *garuḍa* birds.

458 A krośa *(rgyang grags)* is one eighth of a yojana, or about a kilometer. For explanation of yojana, see note 215.

459 This is a reference to the classical Buddhist conception of time cycles during which the Buddha's teaching will survive in the world. According to this view, the duration of the Buddha's teaching is estimated at five thousand years, which is divided into ten five-hundred-year cycles.

460 The Tibetan equivalent of Sujata, which is *legs skyes,* means "well born"; it could also mean "gift," or "bringer of luck," which is probably being invoked here in this line.

461 This is probably a reference to the magical goose surrounded by eight geese.

462 This is the same person as Ujjvala, although this is the first time he is referred to as Ratna Ujjvala, which can be rendered as "Illumination of the Three Jewels."

463 Sarat Chandra Das reconstructs the name *phyags pa med pa* as Arāga. See "The Lamaic Hierarchy of Tibet," vol. I, pt. I, p. 51.

464 This is the translation of the king's name, Prabhāśrī *('od zer dpal)*. Asaṅga is the Sanskrit reconstruction of the Tibetan name Chakpa Mepa *(chags pa med pa)*.

465 The name of the younger prince, Asaṅga, literally connotes someone who is free of attachment, so there is a literary device of iteration used here in this line, which, when translated literally, would yield the following: "Attachment-Free will journey to freedom from attachment."

466 This is a reference identifying the monk with the goddess Tārā.

467 *Yab bzher sku gshen 'brom du gda'.* Lechen (*Lamp Illuminating the History of the Kadam Tradition*, p. 84a6) gives Kushen Yaksher Phen as the name of Dromtönpa's father and Khuö Salenchikma as his mother's name.

468 This Upāsaka Dharmavardana *(dge bsnyen chos 'phel)* is probably the former incarnation of Dromtönpa that was said to have been prophesized in the *Sublime Dharma of the White Lotus.* See, for example, Thuken Chökyi Nyima's *Crystal Mirror of Philosophical Systems,* p. 87.

469 Potowa Rinchen Sal, Phuchungwa Shönu Gyaltsen, and Chengawa Tsültrim Bar are the three Kadam brothers who were the principal students of Dromtönpa. Here the three are explicitly associated with the lords of the three buddha families, Mañjuśrī, Avalokiteśvara, and Vajrapāṇi.

470 The historical Buddha Śākyamuni (Skt., *mahāśramaṇa;* Tib., *dge sbyong chen po*).

471 On Kawa Shākya Wangchuk, see note 384.

472 *Bodhisattva's Jewel Garland*, stanza 16.

473 In all editions of the Tibetan text, the following note appears at the beginning of this chapter: "This is the second teaching of Khu and the twenty-second and final chapter of the Son Teachings."

474 This is a reference to Mount Lhari Nyingpo, which, according to the beginning of the *Jewel Garland of Dialogues*, is located upon Tārā's right leg.

475 This is Naljorpa Amé Jangchup, who served Atiśa as a personal attendant and later succeeded Dromtönpa as the head of Radreng Monastery.

476 This is an allusion to Khutön's reputation as a somewhat proud and conceited teacher. It is said that when Dromtönpa wrote a letter (the text of which is cited in its entirety in Chim Namkha Drak's *Biography of Master Atiśa; The Book of Kadam*, vol. 1, pp. 152–54) inviting the great figures of the Tibetan Buddhist world from central Tibet to come to formally receive Atiśa, he failed to include Khutön's name. This offended Khutön, who is reputed to have exclaimed, "I am not someone who is to be counted in the 'and so forth's,'" and went ahead to meet Atiśa (*The Book of Kadam*, vol. 1, pp. 152–57).

477 This line is missing in the critical Tibetan edition. I have added this from the Dergé edition.

478 Lotsāwa, or "translator," refers here to Ngok Lekpai Sherap.

479 In all the redactions of *The Book of Kadam*, a sentence or two appears to be missing here. Because of this, the connection between this reference to a paṇḍita and the story that follows is not immediately apparent.

480 There are several different redactions of these animated-corpse *(ro langs)* stories in Tibetan, most of which are attributed to Nāgārjuna. Nakpa Tsering (*Research on Ancient Tibetan Literature*, p. 557) lists the following redactions. The Kokonor handwritten collection has thirteen to sixteen stories; the Dergé blockprint edition has twenty-one stories; the Tashi Khyil Monastery blockprint has twenty-one stories; and the Lhasa handwritten edition has twenty-one stories. Although Indian animated corpse stories exist, Nakpa Tsering asserts that all the collections of such stories in Tibetan are indigenous, despite their attribution to Nāgārjuna.

481 *Bodhisattva's Jewel Garland*, stanzas 20–23.

482 Born in Tsang province in 1476, Gendün Gyatso was recognized as the reincarnation of Gendün Drup (retrospectively identified as the First Dalai Lama) at the age of ten. He studied at Tashi Lhünpo and Drepung monasteries and acquired great fame as a scholar. Gendün Gyatso's lifetime coincided with a deep political turmoil related to the allies of the Karma Kagyü school taking control of the city of Shigatsé and later Ü (central Tibet), including the capital Lhasa. His establishment of a close patronage relation with the Gugé rulers led to the successful spread of Geluk in the Ngari regions of western Tibet. Gendün Gyatso founded Chökhor Gyal Monastery and Ngari Monastery, the former becoming a personal monastery of the successive Dalai Lamas, and also held the abbotship of Tashi Lhünpo, Drepung, and Sera monasteries. His principal teachers include the reputed Geluk master and meditator Khedrup Norsang Gyatso, the author of *Ornament of Stainless Light* (*The Library of Tibetan Classics*, vol. 14). Gendün Gyatso was instrumental in disseminating the teachings of *The Book of Kadam*, especially within his own Geluk school. A succinct biography of Gendün Gyatso in English, based on his own autobiography, can be found in *The Dalai Lamas: A Visual History*, edited by Martin Brauen, pp. 43–50.

483 *Mtsho skyes rdo rje*. This is an epithet of Padmasambhava, the tantric master who is credited with the introduction of numerous Vajrayana teachings in Tibet in the eighth century.

484 The story of Prince Könchok Bang is the fifth in Dromtönpa's twenty-two birth stories (*The Book of Kadam*, pp. 97–205). Depa Tenpa's story is the sixth (pp. 206–303).

485 "Heat rays," a poetic name for the sun, refers here to Khenchen Nyima Gyaltsen, whose first name, Nyima, means sun. Nyima Gyaltsen is the Kadam master who finalized *The Book of Kadam* in its present form.

486 The "hundred and fifty" refers to the hundred and fifty teachers from whom Atiśa is said to have received teachings.

487 "The state of eight proficiencies" *(dbang phyug brgyad kyi go 'phang)* is an epithet of fully awakened buddhahood. The eight proficiencies are of: (1) body, (2) speech, (3) mind, (4) supernatural power, (5) pervading everywhere, (6) granting whatever is wished for, (7) enlightened activities, and (8) enlightened attributes.

488 In the critical Tibetan edition, these two lines read "When withdrawn, may the twenty-one drops that are the reality/ Of emptiness and compassion remain unwavering in my mind" *(bsdus tshe stong nyid snying rje dgnos gyur pa'i/ thig le nyer gcig yid la gyo med shog//).* I think this is an orthographical error.

489 "Definite goodness" here is an epithet for nirvana, the freedom from samsara and suffering that is the goal of the intermediate scope of the path.

490 Yongzin Yeshé Gyaltsen was born in Kyirong in western Tibet. At the age of eight he joined Tashi Lhünpo Monastery, where he studied the great Buddhist classics for seventeen years and became recognized as a highly learned scholar. From age twenty-three, when the great Geluk meditator Drupwang Lobsang Namgyal passed away in Kyirong, Yeshé Gyaltsen spent most of his life in the western part of Tibet meditating as a hermit, founding new monasteries like Samten Ling and Drip Tsechok Ling, and giving teachings to numerous students. When he was sixty-two, Yeshé Gyaltsen became the principal tutor of the Ninth Dalai Lama, Jampel Gyatso, and moved his residence to the Potala Palace. Because of his profound learning, deep meditative experience, and skill as a great teacher, Yeshé Gyaltsen became one of the most important masters and custodians of the ear-whispered teachings of the Geluk school.

491 The "two Senas" are Vimuktisena and Bhadanta Vimuktisena, both of whom are important masters in the lineage of transmitting Maitreya's teachings related to the exposition of the perfection of wisdom sutras.

492 This stanza is a salutation to Atiśa, acknowledged here by Yongzin Yeshé Gyaltsen as an "initiator of a chariot way" *(shing rta'i srol 'byed),* an appellation commonly reserved for the Buddhist masters Nāgārjuna and Asaṅga.

493 This is a reference to the great Tsongkhapa, who is recognized as an emanation of Mañjuśrī. The original Tibetan *'jam mgon,* which literally means the "gentle lord," is an abbreviation of the two words *mgon po,* lord, and *'jam dpal,* Mañjuśrī.

494 This is an allusion to the views of those Tibetan teachers who the author sees as propounding standpoints that resemble those of the so-called "nonmentation" of the Chinese teacher Hoshang Mohoyen. The views of this Chinese master had been a focal point of critique in Kamalaśīla's *Stages of Meditation.*

495 This is an abbreviation of Guhyasamāja, one of the principal tantras of the highest yoga class.

496 "This instruction" here refers to *The Book of Kadam,* especially the *Jewel Garland of Dialogues* in the Father Teachings.

497 Here, the author is referring to his own personal teacher Phurchok Jampa Rinpoché as an embodiment of Buddha Śākyamuni and Vajradhara.

498 The story of Forbearance Preaching Sage is number twenty-eight in the hundred

birth stories of the Buddha and can be found in Karmapa Rangjung Dorjé's *One Hundred Birth Stories*, pp. 207–20.

499 The "most excellent one" is Tsongkhapa, and this stanza paraphrases one in his "Three Principal Elements of the Path," which can be found in volume *kha* (2) of his Collected Works.

500 This appears to express the essence of Atiśa's teachings rather than citing a particular text.

501 This *fourfold practice* is a set of four practices recommended in the *Seven-Point Mind Training* in the line "The fourfold practice is the most excellent method." The four practices are (1) accumulating merit, (2) purifying negative karma, (3) making offerings to the malevolent forces, and (4) offering torma to the Dharma protectors. For an explanation of these four practices in the context of mind training practice, see *Mind Training: The Great Collection*, pp. 110–11.

502 *Jewel Garland of Dialogues*, chapter 20, e.g. p. 346.

503 This is also a reference to the above chapter of *Jewel Garland of Dialogues*.

504 This, too, is an allusion to Atiśa's instruction to Dromtönpa as found in *Jewel Garland of Dialogues*.

505 This is also a reference to chapter 20 of the *Jewel Garland of Dialogues*.

506 For explanation of the "three general points" and the "three inseparable conditions," see *Mind Training: The Great Collection*, p. 118 and pp. 125–26.

507 This is an epithet for Dromtönpa, whose name, Gyalwai Jungné, literally means "source of conquerors."

508 This is a reference to Phurchok Jampa Rinpoché (1682–1762), whose name "Jampa" is the Tibetan equivalent of the Sanskrit name Maitreya. Phurchok Rinpoché was an important Geluk master of the eighteenth century and one of the main teachers of the author of our text, Yongzin Yeshé Gyaltsen.

509 This entire citation is found in chapter 20 of *Jewel Garland of Dialogues*, with slight variations in the opening comment and right at the end of the quotation.

510 This is a reference to the Eighth Dalai Lama, Jampel Gyatso (1758–1804), whose teachers include the author of our text.

511 Chegom Sherap Dorjé is the author of the well-known trio of texts collectively referred to as "the three heaps" *(spungs pa rnam gsum)*. They are (1) *Heap of Jewels of Teachings through Similes (Dpe chos rin chen spungs pa)*, (2) *Heap of Jewels of Pith Instructions (Man ngag rin chen spungs pa)*, and (3) *Heap of Jewels of Practices (Lag len rin chen spungs pa)*. According to Yeshé Döndrup (*Treasury of Gems*, p. 383), Chegom was a student of Jangchup Nangwa of Phen, who was in turn a student of Potowa. Although not many details on Chegom are found in Lechen Künga Gyaltsen's *Lamp Illuminating the History of the Kadam Tradition* or in Yeshé Döndrup's *Treasury of Gems*, the latter provides extensive extracts from numerous writings of Chegom.

512 Although no section titles are provided in the original Tibetan text, the divisions of the miscellaneous sayings into three main parts—the sayings of Atiśa, the sayings of Dromtönpa, and those of other Kadam masters—is clearly evident in the text. Thus, for the convenience of the reader, I have inserted these section headings. An English translation of the main part of the *Sayings of the Kadam Masters* (excluding the two supplements) can be found in Geshe Wangyal's *The Door of Liberation*, part III. There the sayings are referred to as the "Kadampa Precepts,"

and the translation provided appears to be more free than literal. In my own approach, I have chosen to stay close to the text so that the archaic literary style of the Tibetan text and, more importantly, the tone of the authors, can be better retained in the translation.

513 Khutön Tsündrü Yungdrung (1011–75), Ngok Lepai Sherap (1018–1115), and Drom Gyalwai Jungné (1004–64).

514 This is a reference to Āryadeva's *Four Hundred Stanzas on the Middle Way*, 8:5, Toh 3846 Tengyur, dbu ma, *tsha*, 9a7.

515 This is a reference to the three key elements of an action: namely, the object of the action, the agent of the act, and the act itself, which together form the basis of grasping at the substantial reality of actions and events.

516 This is probably a reference to the diverse epistemological theories of the Indian schools such as Nyāya and Vaiśeṣika among the non-Buddhists and Sautrāntrika and Cittamātra among the Buddhists. No details can be found on the identity of these three teachers referred to here.

517 This is the Ngari ruler who, together with his uncle Lha Lama Yeshé Ö, was instrumental in bringing Atiśa to Tibet. It was, in fact, at the behest of Jangchup Ö, as testified by the opening lines in the text itself, that Atiśa composed the famous *Lamp for the Path to Enlightenment*. For a brief account of the Ngari rulers' efforts to bring Atiśa to Tibet, see Alaka Chattopadhyaya's *Atiśa and Tibet*, pp. 291–306.

518 Known also as Shangtsün of Yerpa, he was a student of Atiśa and later took teachings from the three Kadam brothers as well. In accordance with Atiśa's instruction, Shangtsün dedicated his entire life to meditative practice and was believed to have experientially realized the truth of impermanence. For a brief account of Shangtsün's life, see Lechen Künga Gyaltsen (*Lamp Illuminating the History of the Kadam Tradition*, pp. 80a5–81b3), and for extracts from Shangtsün's teachings, see Yeshé Döndrup (*Treasury of Gems*, pp. 133–34).

519 *Snying rus 'don pa*. A vernacular Tibetan expression for making strenuous effort.

520 Potowa Rinchen Sal, Chengawa Tsültrim Bar, and Phuchungwa Shönu Gyaltsen.

521 This is the first of the four stages of the path of preparation, the other three being "peak," "forbearance," and "supreme Dharma."

522 *Spre*. In the Dergé edition, the name of this region is written as Pö *(spos)*.

523 *Bodhicaryāvatāra*, 8:129–30, Toh 3871, Tengyur, dbu ma, *la*, 28b3.

524 Radreng Monastery, founded in 1056 by Dromtönpa near Lhasa in central Tibet, became the main center of the Kadam tradition.

525 Gönpawa (1016–82), whose personal name is Wangchuk Gyaltsen, was a prominent student of both Atiśa and Dromtönpa and held the abbotship of Radreng Monastery for five years after Naljorpa. His students include Neusurpa, Kharak Gomchung, and Shawo Gangpa, all well-known early masters of the Kadam tradition. A succinct biography of Gönpawa can be found in Lechen Künga Gyaltsen's *Lamp Illuminating the History of the Kadam Tradition*, pp. 109b6–114a4.

526 On Shangtsünpa, see note 518.

527 Potowa Rinchen Sal (1027–1105), as has already been mentioned, was one of the "three Kadam brothers" who were the three principal students of Dromtönpa. He is the initiator of the Kadam lineage of treatises and the author of the well-known *Blue Udder (Be'u bum sngon po)* and *Teachings through Similes (Dpe chos)*. After Dromtönpa's death, Potowa held the abbotship of Radreng Monastery (after

Naljorpa and Gönpawa), where he established the tradition of taking Atiśa's *Lamp for the Path to Enlightenment* as the principal text of practice and complementing it with six Indian Buddhist texts: Śāntideva's (1) *Compendium of Trainings* and (2) *Guide to the Bodhisattva's Way of Life;* Maitreya's (3) *Ornament of Mahayana Sutras;* Asaṅga's (3) *Bodhisattva Levels;* and Āryaśūra's (4) *Garland of Birth Stories* and (5) *Collections of Aphorisms.* These six texts came to be known as *the six classics for the Kadam school (bka' gdams gzhung drug).* He also founded Poto Monastery, and his students include such luminaries of the Kadam school as Dölpa Sherap Gyaltsen, Langri Thangpa (the author of the famed "Eight Verses of Mind Training"), Sharawa, and Drakarwa. A succinct biography of Potowa can be found in Lechen's *Lamp Illuminating the History of the Kadam Tradition,* pp. 215b4–224a1.

528 Despite efforts, I have not been able to identify this person. Furthermore, different editions of the Tibetan text give slightly different spelling of this name.

529 On the Buddhist meditation on foulness, see note 258 and below note 531.

530 For a woman practitioner, the object of this meditation would be that of a man's body, the key point being that one should take whatever happens to be the object of one's sexual attachment as the focus of foulness meditation.

531 Buddhaghoṣa's *Visuddhimagga* gives a list of ten aspects of foulness meditation, which are, in addition to the seven mentioned here: (1) scattered, (2) hacked and scattered, and (3) bleeding. The order of the visualization of these aspects presented in Buddhaghoṣa's text is slightly different from the one presented here. See *Path of Purification,* chap. VI, pp. 179–90.

532 As before, if one is a nun, the practitioner should relate all of this meditation to a man.

533 Chengawa Tsültrim Bar (1033–1103) was the youngest of "the three Kadam brothers." Chengawa attended a teaching of Atiśa on the awakening mind, during which Atiśa is said to have placed his right hand on Chengawa's head and predicted that he would be a great upholder of Atiśa's lineage. In a visionary experience, Chengawa met with the Indian master Nāgabodhi and received instructions from him, which he summarized into four sets of four practices. The set of four practices that is most well known is: (1) the yoga of recognizing all appearances as illusions by means of the analogy of sleep and dreams; (2) the yoga of recognizing the indivisibility of appearance and emptiness by means of the analogy of water and ice; (3) the yoga of recognizing all phenomena as being of a single taste by means of the analogy of the taste and mass of molasses; and (4) engaging in the conduct of the six perfections (Yeshé Döndrup, *Treasury of Gems,* p. 189). Chengawa is the initiator of the Kadam lineage of instructions, and his students include such luminaries as Jayülwa Shönu Ö and Tölungpa Rinchen Nyingpo. A succinct biography of Chengawa can be found in Lechen's *Lamp Illuminating the History of the Kadam Tradition,* pp. 164b1–68b3.

534 *Bodhicaryāvatāra,* 6:106, Toh 3871 Tengyur, dbu ma, *la,* 18b6.

535 *Bodhicaryāvatāra,* 6:42, Toh 3871 Tengyur, dbu ma, *la,* 16a5.

536 *Bodhicaryāvatāra,* 6:37–38, Toh 3871 Tengyur, dbu ma, *la,* 16b2.

537 These four lines can be found in *Bodhicaryāvatāra,* 9:151 and 152, where the first two lines and the last are part of verse 151, while line three is part of verse 152. It is conceivable that Chengawa is citing from a slightly different redaction of the Tibetan text of *Bodhicaryāvatāra.* For a discussion of the various redactions of

Śāntideva's *Guide to the Bodhisattva's Way of Life* in Tibetan, see the translator's introduction to Śāntideva, *The Bodhicaryāvatāra,* trans. by Kate Crosby and Andrew Skilton.

538 It is important to appreciate the right context for statements such as this. Many of the thought processes suggested here are relevant principally to those practitioners who have chosen to lead a single-pointed, celibate life of a hermit, for whom the issue of gaining total freedom from attachment to the concerns of this life is of cardinal importance.

539 Tsang is a region in central Tibet. *Btsan,* translated here as "ghost," refers to spirits of dead people that are described as aggressive.

540 Phuchungwa Shönu Gyaltsen (1031–1106), one of the "three Kadam brothers," dedicated his life to single-pointed meditative practice and did not cultivate many students. Phuchungwa is most recognized as the initiator of the Kadam lineage of pith instructions and the inheritor of Atiśa and Dromtönpa's teachings as enshrined in *The Book of Kadam.* Yeshé Döndrup (*Treasury of Gems,* p. 191) identifies Phuchungwa as the source of the mind training practice known as the "Heart of Dependent Origination," entry 36 in *Mind Training: The Great Collection.* A succinct biography of Phuchungwa can be found in Lechen's *Lamp Illuminating the History of the Kadam Tradition,* pp. 267a–270a.

541 The Tibetan text of this sentence is oblique, and my translation here is merely suggestive.

542 I have read the Tibetan *zho re* as an abbreviation of *zho gang re.* A *zho gang* is an old Tibetan coin made of copper.

543 Nyukrumpa Tsöndrü Bar (1042–1109) was a student of Chengawa and is in the Kadam lineage of pith instruction. He founded two Kadam monasteries, Lungshö Nyukrum and Thangkya, in central Tibet.

544 As its name implies, a wish-granting cow fulfills the wishes of its owner, like the genie in Aladdin's lamp. The wish-granting cow, along with the heavenly horse and treasure vase mentioned below, are mythical objects that are often imagined in standard Buddhist rites of offering, especially the mandala offering, whereby the entire cosmos is offered to the object of refuge.

545 According to Lechen's *Lamp Illuminating the History of the Kadam Tradition* (p. 292a4), Khamlungpa Shākya Yönten (1025–1115) was, together with the three Kadam brothers, a recipient of Atiśa's mind training teachings from Dromtönpa. He is also identified as the source of the instructions on "mind training in eight sessions," whereby the practitioner learns to relate all key aspects of everyday life to the mind training practice of cultivating and enhancing the awakening mind. For a succinct instruction on this special mind training, see *Mind Training: The Great Collection,* entry 22. Both Lechen (*Lamp Illuminating the History of the Kadam Tradition,* p. 106b5) and Yeshé Döndrup (*Treasury of Gems,* p. 195) list Khamlungpa as the fourth of the Kadam brothers and state that Khamlungpa met Atiśa in person.

546 This is probably a reference to the Kadam hermit Ben Gungyal, who was famed for his colorful rejections of worldly norms. Ben Gungyal, whose personal name is Tsültrim Gyalwa, was a student of Gönpawa (1016–82). Suffering from poverty as a young man, he is said to have lived the life of a robber before going on to become a revered yogi.

547 Kharak Gomchung Wangchuk Lodrö (ca. eleventh century), also known as Kharakpa, was born in Tsang province. He was one of the principal disciples of the Kadam teacher Gönpawa, who was, in turn, a student of both Atiśa and Dromtönpa. Kharak Gomchung is most known for his highly practical and concise teachings, most of which pertain to the central issue of overcoming attachment to the mundane concerns of this life. These teachings later became known collectively as the "three cycles of Kharak" *(kha rag skor gsum)* (1) the Twelve Points of the Stages of the Path, (2) the Seventy Exhortations, and (3) the Training in the Awakening Mind. Although Kharak Gomchung's complete first and the last cycles appear to no longer be extant today, large sections of the author's work on the first cycle can be found in Chenga Lodrö Gyaltsen's *The Initial Mind Training: Opening the Door of Dharma.* Kharakpa's text on the second cycle of teachings can be found in Yeshé Döndrup's *Treasury of Gems*, pp. 257–64.

548 This is probably a senior student of Dromtönpa who is known as spiritual mentor Jolek *(jo legs)*, a monk from the Drakgyap region. According to Lechen (*Lamp Illuminating the History of the Kadam Tradition*, p. 106a4), Jolek met Atiśa in person and was later to become a key student of Dromtönpa alongside the three Kadam brothers.

549 Neusurpa Yeshé Bar (1042–1118) was one of the principal students of Gönpawa and the main inheritor of Gönpawa's teachings on the stages of the path instructions. Notes compiled by Neusurpa's students on his stages of the path instructions were widely disseminated. Lechen (*Lamp Illuminating the History of the Kadam Tradition*, pp. 120a5–128b1) provides detailed biographical information on Neusurpa, including citations from his teachings. Yeshé Döndrup (*Treasury of Gems*, pp. 203–38) also provides extensive extracts from Neusurpa's own compositions as well as from the notes compiled by his students, especially those by Gezé Jangchup.

550 Langri Thangpa (1054–1123), a prominent student of Potowa and the author of the famous "Eight Verses on Mind Training," was the founder in 1093 of Langthang Monastery in Phenpo, which attracted around two thousand monks. His principal student was Shawo Gangpa, and the Kagyü master Phakmo Drupa also received teachings from him. Because of his constant contemplation of the sufferings of all sentient beings, Langri Thangpa is said to have been in tears most of the time and came to be known as "Langthangpa with a weeping downcast face" *(Lang thang ngu nag pa)*. His "Eight Verses on Mind Training" and a succinct commentary to this text by the Kadam master Chekawa can be found in *Mind Training: The Great Collection.* Lechen (*Lamp Illuminating the History of the Kadam Tradition*, pp. 228a3–229b1) provides a brief biography of Langri Thangpa.

551 Sharawa Yönten Drak (1070–1141), a principal student of Potowa, is responsible, along with his student Chekawa, for codifying Atiśa's scattered teachings on mind training into the well-known "Seven-Point Mind Training." He founded the monastery of Shara in the Tré region of Phenpo, which attracted three thousand monks (Yeshé Döndrup, *Treasury of Gems*, p. 338). His principal students were Chekawa, Tapkapa, Tumtön Lodrö Drak (founder of Narthang Monastery), and Naljorpa Sherap Dorjé. Lechen (*Lamp Illuminating the History of the Kadam Tradition*, pp. 236a6–240b4) provides a very useful biography of Sharawa, while Yeshé Döndrup (*Treasury of Gems*, pp. 338–74) gives extensive extracts from numerous writings of this important Kadam master.

552   The primary audience for these instructions is monk practitioners living as hermits in solitary places.

553   Jayülwa Shönu Ö (1075–1138) was an important student of Chengawa, one of the three Kadam brothers. He founded the monastery of Jayül, and his students include Gyergompa, Tromsherwa, Tsangpa Rinpoché, Drakmarwa, and Gampopa (the author of well-known *Jewel Ornament of Liberation* and a principal student of Milarepa). Lechen (*Lamp Illuminating the History of the Kadam Tradition*, pp. 171b2–178b3) provides an extensive biography of Jayülwa followed by the names of the successive abbots of Jayül Monastery.

554   Tölungpa Rinchen Nyingpo (1032–1116) was an important student of Chengawa and the great Naljorpa Amé. Lechen (*Lamp Illuminating the History of the Kadam Tradition*, pp. 168b3–70b5) provides a useful biography of this Kadam master, giving some details of his first meeting with Naljorpa at Radreng Monastery. His students include Tokden Dingpopa, Geshé Lhaso, and Ja Dülzin.

555   Lechen (*Lamp Illuminating the History of the Kadam Tradition* , p. 177a4) lists Nambarwa as one of the "eight great outer students" *(phyi yi chen po brgyad)* of Jayülwa Shönu Ö (1075–1138) as well as one of the "four senior sons" *(bu chen bzhi)* of the spiritual mentor Laksorwa (Yeshé Döndrup, *Treasury of Gems*, p. 106), who was, in turn, a student of the translator Naktso Lotsāwa (1011–64). Nambarwa founded the monasteries of Nambar and Rampa Lhading and held the abbotship of Sangphu Monastery for eight years (*Lamp Illuminating the History of the Kadam Tradition*, p. 337b2).

556   The reading of this line is slightly different in the critical Tibetan edition. Here I have followed the Dergé edition as found in Yeshé Döndrup's *Treasury of Gems*.

557   Both Lechen (p. 337b2) and Yeshé Döndrup (p. 106) list Chimphupa, known also as Rok Chimphupa, as one of the four senior sons of Laksorwa. Each of these four sons of Laksorwa is said to have compiled notes from Laksorwa's teachings. Jadülzin compiled a condensed collection of notes that contain both stories and instructions; Chimphupa's notes contain few stories but extensive instructions; Nambarwa's notes contain only instructions with no stories; while Shulenpa's notes contain extensive stories and extensive instructions.

558   Shawopa Pema Jangchup (1067–1131) was an important student of both Potowa and Phuchungwa, two of the three Kadam brothers. According to Lechen (*Lamp Illuminating the History of the Kadam Tradition*, p. 129b2), he was a key student of Langri Thangpa (author of "Eight Verses on Mind Training") as well. He founded the monastery of Shawogang, where thousands of monks congregated. Shawopa or Shawo Gangpa is sometimes written as Shawowa. In Geshe Wangyal's *The Door of Liberation*, however Shawo Gangpa is identified incorrectly as Sha-wo-gay-pa.

559   This echoes the well-known Kadam saying that was earlier attributed to Chengawa. See p. 586 above.

560   The original Tibetan text reads *tshe 'di'i 'dod pa'i skam sha 'tshal tsa na*, which literally translates as "If one seeks to find the dry meat of this life's desire,…" Probably, the author is evoking the analogy of eating dry meat, which, because of its dryness and also its salty taste, makes one thirsty, and which, when quenched with drinking water, probably leads to further craving for eating dry meat.

561   *Yar bskyed pas mar bskyed che ba'i bong ba'i rbab.* I have read this expression as referring to a slope made of clumps of earth, where there are more growths on

the lower level than on the higher parts. As I have not been able to find the expression *bong ba'i rbab* in any of the lexicons at my disposal, the translation here is only a suggestion.

562 On this Kadam master, see note 547. Although, as the brief colophon makes it clear, it was Lhopa who compiled these sayings into a single collection, it is not evident who included these sayings as a supplement here. Neither this nor the next supplement are translated in Geshe Wangyal's *The Door of Liberation.*

563 Both the Lhasa Shöl edition, the basis of the critical Tibetan edition on which the present translation is based, and the Dergé edition found in Yeshé Döndrup's *Treasury of Gems* are missing one item from this list. Although this is supposed to be part of a set of four, there are only three items.

564 In both the Lhasa Shöl edition and the Dergé edition, this line reads *spyod pa'i gso bo kha snyen sgrub pa'o,* which does not make much sense. I feel that there must be a typographical error, that *kha snyen* should be read as *lha snyen,* which means "rites that enable the practitioner to cultivate closeness with his or her meditation deities."

565 In both the Shöl and Dergé editions, one item is missing from this set. The "wisdom-knowledge empowerment" is the third main empowerment of the highest yoga class of tantra and involves offering a consort to the initiates for entering into sexual union as part of the empowerment rite. Typically, this empowerment is only visualized by the initiate.

566 This last item probably refers to articles belonging to the monastic community. If such items are inappropriately used for one's personal benefit, it is said to be like consuming burning fire.

567 There are actually six rather than five sets in this section. However, since all available versions of the Tibetan text lists the following section as "Five sets of six," I have left this caption as it is.

568 This is probably an epithet for the Buddha, in whose presence a Mahayana practitioner takes the bodhisattva vows.

569 The Tibetan term *mngon du rgyu ba,* which I have translated here as "manifest movement," is probably equivalent to the term *mngon du phyogs pa,* "approaching." The latter is the standard name of the sixth bodhisattva level, which marks a critical stage in the practitioner's direct realization of emptiness of all phenomena.

570 The expression "innate path" *(lhan skyes kyi lam)* probably refers to the Vajrayana path, in which the concept of innateness, especially the fundamental innate mind of clear light, occupies a significant place in the understanding of the nature of the path to full awakening.

571 The *"imputed nature,* the *dependent nature,* and so on" here refers to the three-natures theory central to Yogācāra analysis of the ultimate nature of reality.

572 The spiritual mentor Lhopa was a principal student of Kharak Gomchung. None of the historians of Kadam—Sönam Lhai Wangpo, Lechen, Paṇchen Sönam Drakpa, and Jamgön Amé—nor Yeshé Döndrup, give Lhopa's personal name. According to Lechen (*Lamp Illuminating the History of the Kadam Tradition,* p. 120a2), Lhopa was already deeply learned in the works of Maitreya and specialized in the teachings of tantra before meeting Kharak Gomchung, at whose feet he studied and practiced for eight years.

573 At the level of "heat," the first of the four stages of the path of preparation, the practitioner gains meditatively derived insight into emptiness on the basis of

yoking together tranquil abiding and penetrative insight. This is not the direct perception of emptiness, but it goes beyond mere intellectual understanding and serves as a condition for the later nondual experience.

574 Yeshé Döndrup (*Treasury of Gems*, pp. 410–16) provides a list of eighty scattered instructions of Chegom. Among these, a similar list gives only three perfect factors, all pertaining to the *view* of the practitioners of three levels of mental facility, with no reference to *meditation* and *action*. It is not evident who is responsible for including these sayings of Chegom as a supplement to the *Sayings of the Kadam Masters*.

Glossary

advice *(gdams ngag, upadeśa)*. A core prescription of the Kadam school is to relate to all the teachings of the Buddha as personal advice, especially to help overcome one's mental afflictions. In fact, the very name "Kadam" *(bka' gdams)* underlines this point, wherein the syllable *bka'* stands for the Buddha's sacred words while *gdams* literally means "advice." *Upadeśa* is also sometimes rendered as *man ngag* in Tibetan, which has been translated as "pith instructions" or simply as "instruction." *See also pith instructions*

afflictions *(nyon mongs, kleśa)*. Dissonant mental states, both thoughts and emotions, that have their root in ignorance. They are called "afflictions" because they disturb the individual from deep within. The classical Abhidharma texts list six root afflictions—attachment, aversion, conceit, afflicted doubt, ignorance, and afflicted view—and twenty afflictions that are derivative of these root afflictions.

antidote *(gnyen po)*. Just as specific medicines are seen as antidotes for specific illnesses, specific mental states such as compassion, loving-kindness, and so on are identified as antidotes against specific mental ills. The Tibetan term *gnyen po* is sometimes translated also as "remedy" or "counter force" as well.

arhat *(dgra bcom pa)*. Literally (in Tibetan), "foe destroyer," this Sanskrit term refers to a highly evolved spiritual person who has eliminated all the afflictions—the "foe"—and has thus gained victory over them. An arhat is no longer compelled to take rebirth in samsara under the force of karma and afflictions.

aspiration prayer *(smon lam, praṇidhāna)*. In the literary context, aspiration prayers in Tibetan are easily recognizable by the presence of their ending particle *shog*, which is translated as "may such and such be." The Tibetan term *smon lam* is sometimes translated simply as "prayer."

awakening mind *(byang chub kyi sems, bodhicitta)*. An altruistic intention to attain buddhahood for the benefit of all beings. The awakening mind is characterized by an *objective*, the full awakening of buddhahood, and a *purpose*, the fulfillment of others' welfare. Often another term, *mind generation (sems bskyed),* is used to refer to awakening mind as well. *See also two awakening minds*

awareness *(rig pa, vidyā; shes pa, jñā).* As a verb both Tibetan terms *rig pa* and *shes pa* mean "to know," "to be cognizant of," and "to be aware." When used as a noun, *shes pa* is often translated as "consciousness" or "mental state" while *rig pa* is translated as "awareness," suggesting a most basic quality of subjective experience. *Rig pa* can also mean a "knowledge discipline" or "science," such as in the case of *gso ba rig pa,* the "science of healing." In addition, the term can refer to "intelligence" or "mental aptitude," such as the quality of sharp intelligence *(rig pa rno ba).* In the Dzokchen teachings, the term *rig pa* can also refer to "pure awareness." It is in the sense of *rig pa* as a basic quality of awareness that the term is primarily used in *The Book of Kadam,* especially in chapter 12 of the *Jewel Garland of Dialogues.*

bodhisattva *(byang chup sems dpa').* A person who has cultivated the awakening mind and is on the path to buddhahood.

cherishing *(gces 'dzin).* The texts related to the teachings of *The Book of Kadam* and the mind training tradition speak of two kinds of cherishing, namely *self-cherishing* and the *cherishing of other's welfare.* An important element of the meditative practices based on the Kadam teachings is to reverse our deeply ingrained tendency to cherish our welfare alone above everything else and train our mind instead to cherish others' welfare more than our own.

compassion *(rnying rje, karuṇā).* A mental state that wishes for others to be free from suffering. *Compassion* is often used in the Kadam texts as a synonym for *great compassion (rnying rje chen po),* a universal, nondiscriminatory compassion that wishes all beings to be free of suffering.

conceptual elaborations *(spros pa, prapañca).* Conceptual elaborations include all forms of dichotomizing conceptualization, such as subject-object duality, as well as grasping at objects and their characteristics. The direct realization of emptiness, which is the ultimate nature of all things, is marked by total freedom from all such conceptual elaborations.

conceptualization *(rnam rtog, vicāra).* The Tibetan term *rnam rtog* has been translated as "conceptualization" and carries numerous connotations. (1) It can refer simply to thoughts, which unlike sensory experiences are mediated by language and concepts. (2) However, it can also refer specifically to dichotomizing thoughts that lead to the objectification and reification of things and events. (3) Sometimes, the term may be used in the negative sense of "false conceptualization." In the context of this volume, *rnam rtog* (conceptualization) carries more the second and third meaning.

conqueror *(rgyal ba, jina).* A common epithet used to refer to the fully awakened buddhas. When capitalized in this volume, it generally refers to the historical Buddha. The term also serves as a frequent epithet for Atiśa in *The Book of Kadam.*

cyclic existence *('khor ba, saṃsāra).* The perpetual cycle of birth, death, and rebirth conditioned by karma and afflictions. Freedom from cyclic existence is characterized as *nirvana,* the "transcendence of sorrow."

daylong precepts *(bsnyen gnas, upavāsa).* Eight precepts taken by lay practitioners for a period of twenty-four hours beginning prior to sunrise.

definite goodness *(nges legs, niśreyasaḥ).* A technical term used often to refer to the states of liberation from cyclic existence as well as the full awakening of buddhahood. The term is contrasted with "higher birth" *(mgnon mtho, abhyudaya),* which refers to birth in the more fortunate realms within the cycle of existence.

dharmakāya *(chos sku).* One of the three embodiments of buddhahood. *Dharmakāya,* which literally means "truth body" or "buddha body of reality," refers to the ultimate reality of a buddha's enlightened mind— unborn, free from the limits of conceptual elaborations, empty of intrinsic existence, naturally radiant, beyond duality, and spacious like the sky. The other two buddha bodies, the *enjoyment body (longs sku, saṃbhogakāya)* and the emanation body *(sprul sku, nirmāṇakāya),* are progressively grosser bodies that arise from the basic dharmakāya nature. Thus the two latter embodiments are referred to collectively as a buddha's "form body" *(gzugs sku, rūpakāya).*

Diamond Vehicle *(rdo rje theg pa, Vajrayāna). See tantra*

disciple *(nyan thos, śrāvaka).* Followers of the Buddha whose primary spiritual objective is to attain liberation from the cycle of existence. The Sanskrit term and its Tibetan equivalent are sometimes translated as "hearers" (which stays close to the literal meaning) or as "pious attendants." *Disciples* are often paired with *self-enlightened ones (pratyekabuddhas),* who seek liberation on the basis of autonomous practice as opposed to listening to other's instructions.

dzo *(mdzo)*. A crossbreed between a yak and a cow; a very strong animal prized in Tibet for long-distance transportation of goods.

emanation body *(sprul sku, nirmāṇakāya)*. One of the three embodiments of a fully awakened buddha according to Mahayana Buddhism. *Emanation Body* refers to the form body of a buddha, such as the historical Buddha Śakyamuni, that is visible to mundane beings. *See also dharmakāya; enjoyment body*

emptiness *(stong pa nyid, śūnyatā)*. According to the Perfection of Wisdom scriptures of Mahayana Buddhism, all things and events, including our own existence, are devoid of any independent, substantial, and intrinsic reality. This emptiness of intrinsic existence is phenomena's ultimate mode of being—the way phenomena actually are. The theory of emptiness's earliest systematic proponent was the second-century master Nāgārjuna, whose writings provide the philosophical foundation for the Mahayana tradition. Seeing emptiness, the ultimate nature of all things, is the indispensable gateway to liberation and enlightenment.

enjoyment body *(longs sku, saṃbhogakāya)*. The subtle form body of a fully awakened buddha. According to the Mahayana theory of the buddha bodies, the enjoyment body is perceptible only to advanced bodhisattvas. In contrast, the emanation body of a buddha can be seen even by ordinary sentient beings. *See also dharmakāya; emanation body*

essence mantra *(snying po)*. A key mantra associated with a meditation deity repeated many times as part of the practice of cultivating that deity. For example, the well-known mantra *oṃ maṇi padme hūṃ* is the essence mantra of Avalokiteśvara.

five fields of knowledge *(rig gnas lnga)*. (1) Sanskrit grammar, (2) logic and epistemology, (3) arts and crafts, (4) medicine, and (5) inner science, this latter field referring to Buddhist thought and practice. These are the five fields of classical knowledge according to Indian Buddhism, which came to be adopted as a formal division of knowledge disciplines in the Tibetan tradition.

five poisonous afflictions/five poisons *(dug lnga)*. Delusion, aversion, attachment, jealousy, and conceit. Sometimes, avarice is listed together with conceit as one class of poison.

five precious materials *(rin chen sna lnga)*. Often translated as either "five precious metals" or "five precious jewels" since there are two different systems of the five precious materials. One system lists gold, silver, copper, iron, and tin, while the other system lists gold, silver, turquoise, coral, and pearl.

five recollections *(rjes dran lnga)*. (1) Recalling your teachers, the source of refuge, (2) recalling your body as the meditation deity, (3) recalling your speech as mantra repetitions and recitations, (4) recalling all beings as your actual mothers, and (5) recalling your mind as the ultimate nature. *The Book of Kadam* repeatedly emphasizes that one's meditative practice must not be divorced from these five recollections.

four divinities *(lha bzhi)*. The four chosen divinities of the Kadam teachings: (1) the Buddha, the teacher of the doctrine, (2) Avalokiteśvara, the divinity embodying compassion, (3) Tārā, the divinity embodying enlightened action, and (4) Acala, the protective divinity.

four fearlessnesses *(mi 'jigs pa bzhi, caturvaiśāradya)*. (1) Fearlessness with respect to the perfect fulfillment of the powers, (2) fearlessness with respect to the perfect fulfillment of the abandonments, (3) fearlessness with respect to revealing the obstacles, and (4) fearlessness with respect to revealing the path to definite freedom. These are qualities of an enlightened buddha.

four immeasurable thoughts *(tshad med bzhi, caturapramāṇa)*. (1) Immeasurable compassion, (2) immeasurable loving-kindness, (3) immeasurable sympathetic joy, and (4) immeasurable equanimity.

four means of attracting (or gathering) others *(bsdu ba'i dngos po bzhi, saṃgrahavastu)*. (1) Giving what is immediately needed (such as material goods), (2) using pleasant speech, (3) giving sound spiritual advice, and (4) living in accord with what you teach. These four factors are identified as the primary means by which a bodhisattva attracts others and enhances their minds. In contrast, the *six perfections* are said to be the primary factors for the development and enhancement of the bodhisattva's own mind.

four perfect discernments *(so rig bzhi, caturpratisaṃvid)*. The perfect discernment of (1) words, (2) their meaning, (3) their etymologies, and (4) the perfect discernment through confidence. These are qualities of an enlightened buddha.

four powers *(stobs bzhi)*. The four key elements necessary for successful purification practice. The four powers are (1) the power of support, which refers to the objects of refuge, such as the Three Jewels, (2) the power of regret, (3) the power of the actual purification rite, and (4) the power of the resolve not to commit the act again.

four pure empowerments *(rnam dag dbang bzhi)*. The four empowerments of a highest-yoga-class tantra: (1) vase empowerment, (2) crown empowerment, (3) wisdom-knowledge empowerment, and (4) word empowerment.

four pursuits *(so nam rnam bzhi)*. (1) Farming, (2) trade, (3) monetary investment, and (4) raising cattle.

gandharvas *(dri za)*. Literally "smell eaters," *gandharvas* are sky-born gods of the classical Indian belief system.

garuda *(khyung, garuḍa)*. A mythical bird said to be the mount of the god Indra. In classical Indian and Tibetan Buddhist texts, the garuḍa is often depicted as a powerful counterforce to the nāga spirits.

giving and taking *(tong len)*. An important spiritual practice of the Kadam school wherein one visualizes taking upon oneself all the suffering, misfortune, and the negative karma and afflictions of others, while giving to others all that is positive, such as one's happiness, virtuous karma, and spiritual realizations. Traditionally, this meditation on *tong-len* is done in tune with one's respiratory process, where giving is visualized when one exhales and taking visualized when one breathes in.

Great Compassion *(thugs rje chen po, mahākaruṇā)*. When capitalized in this work, it is an epithet for Avalokiteśvara, the buddha of compassion, specifically in his thousand-armed manifestation.

guruyoga *(bla ma'i rnal 'byor)*. A Vajrayana meditative practice that primarily involves imagining one's personal teacher as inseparable from one's meditation deity.

hero/heroine *(dpa' bo, dpa' mo)*. These terms "hero" and "heroine" are used in *The Book of Kadam* to refer to powerful male and female protector deities. Sometimes, the term is also used to refer to the male and female bodhisattvas.

higher knowledge *(chos mngon pa, abhidharma)*. The Buddhist teachings that detail the diversity of the phenomenal world and the factors of the path. Among the three higher trainings, the teachings on higher knowledge are correlated to wisdom. *See also three scriptural baskets*

hoisting your robes *(brdzes bcangs)*. The Tibetan term *brdzes bcangs* literally means "to hoist one's robes and tuck them under one's sash" and refers to such an act when crossing a river or a stream. The expression is used in *The Book of Kadam* in the sense of a practitioner bracing him or herself against the "mires" or "swamps" of sensual desire so that he or she can successfully guard the mind. This idea and its associated practices are presented in great detail in chapter 12 of the *Jewel Garland of Dialogues.*

individual liberation vows *(so so thar pa, prātimokṣa).* Of the three sets of vows (the others being bodhisattva vows and tantric vows), those concerned primarily with restraining outward activity. Includes the monastic discipline and the vows for lay Buddhists.

irreversible state *(phyir mi ldog pa).* Bodhisattvas on the eighth level and above are referred to as having attained the irreversible state, because at this point all the afflictions as well as their seeds are totally eliminated.

khakkhara staff *('khar gsil).* A *khakkhara* staff is a mendicant's staff held in the right hand by the monk disciples of the Buddha. It is made of iron and wood. *See also note 200*

khaṭvāṅga staff *(kha ṭvāṃ ga).* A ritual hand implement in the shape of a trident. Depending on the associated meditation deity, some features of the trident slightly differ.

krośa *(rgyang grags).* An ancient Indian unit of length generally thought to measure around a thousand yards or one kilometer. One eighth of a yojana.

kumbhāṇḍas *(grul bum).* A class of beings in the classical Indian belief system.

Mahāsāṃghika tradition *(phal chen sde pa).* The ancient Buddhist monastic discipline lineage to which the Indian master Atiśa belonged. The mainstream monastic lineage current in the Tibetan tradition is that of Mūlasarvāstivāda.

Mahayana *(theg chen, mahāyāna).* Literally, "Great Vehicle"; refers to the Buddhism prominent today in the Himalayan countries and in East Asia. The Mahayana tradition is distinct from non-Mahayana Buddhism in idealizing the path of the altruistic bodhisattva, who practices in order to free all suffering beings rather than merely in order to secure his own personal nirvana. The Mahayana tradition is also philosophically determined by understanding the highest reality to be the emptiness of all phenomena rather than simply selflessness of personal identity.

method *(thabs, upāya). Method* refers to the altruistic deeds of the bodhisattva, including the cultivation of compassion and the awakening mind, the practice of the first five of the six perfections, and the accumulation of merit through making offerings, prostrations, and prayers to the enlightened beings and through serving one's teacher. In

Mahayana Buddhism, the union of method and wisdom is central to understanding the path.

nāgas *(klu)*. Literally, "snake," nāgas are demigods with the head of a human and the body of a snake who generally live underground or in lakes and rivers. They are sometimes considered part of the animal realm.

negative action *(sdig pa'i las, pāpakarma)*. Harmful actions of body, speech, and mind. Negative actions are motivated by any of the three poisons of the mind—attachment, aversion, and delusion. The classical Buddhist texts list ten classes of negative actions: three physical actions (killing, stealing, and sexual misconduct), four actions of speech (lies, divisive speech, harsh words, and senseless gossip), and three actions of the mind (covetousness, ill will, and wrong views). The last of these refers primarily to a deluded understanding of karma and its effects. Restraining from these ten nonvirtuous actions constitutes the basic level of the practice of morality in Buddhism. *See also nonvirtuous action*

noble one *('phags pa, ārya)*. A being on the path who has gained direct realization of the truth of emptiness. Noble ones are contrasted with ordinary beings *(so so'i skye bo, prthagjana)*, whose understanding of the truth remains bound by language and concepts.

nonvirtuous action *(mi dge ba'i las, akuśalakarma)*. Although in most Buddhist texts the term *akuśalakarma* (nonvirtuous action) is used interchangeably with *pāpakarma* (negative action), etymologically the Sanskrit term *akuśala* connotes an act that is unskillful rather than negative. The Tibetan equivalent, *mi dge ba'i las,* connotes an act that is not auspicious or virtuous.

pañcalika silk. Five-colored fabric of the god realm.

patrimony *(pha phogs)*. The archaic Tibetan term *pha phogs* is composed of two words, *pha* (father or paternal) and *phogs* (annuity, emolument). This term has been translated variously as "patrimony," as "heritage," "legacy," and at times also as "inheritance." In this volume, the expression is used to indicate the idea that the Kadampa's pure way of life is a legacy bequeathed to Dromtönpa by Master Atiśa, a theme most developed in chapter 13 of the *Jewel Garland of Dialogues*.

Pekar *(pe dkar)*. Sometimes referred to also as "Pehar," Pekar is a powerful protector deity who is the principal guardian of Tibet's first monastery, Samyé.

penetrative insight *(lhag mthong, vipaśyanā)*. An advanced meditative state where the meditator has successfully attained physical and mental pliancy because of having applied analytic meditation on a basis of tranquil abiding. Sometimes the term is also used to embrace all analytic, as opposed to absorptive, meditation practices.

perfection of wisdom *(sher phyin, prajñāpāramitā)*. One of the six perfections that lie at the heart of the practice of the bodhisattva. The term refers also to a specific subdivision of the Mahayana scriptures that outline the essential aspects of the meditation on emptiness and their associated paths and resultant states. *The Perfection of Wisdom in Eight Thousand Lines*, the *Heart Sutra*, and the *Diamond Cutter* are some of the most well-known Perfection of Wisdom scriptures. In *The Book of Kadam* the term is often used as an epithet for Perfection of Wisdom Mother, a feminine divinity that embodies the perfection of wisdom of a fully awakened buddha. To indicate this last usage, the term is capitalized.

pith instructions *(man ngag, upadeśa)*. Sometimes translated simply as "instructions," *man ngag (pith instructions)* connotes a specialized kind of advice, such as an instruction suited only to a select class of practitioners. Often, the Tibetan term *man ngag* also refers to an oral tradition. *See also advice*

pristine cognition *(ye shes, jñāna)*. Often contrasted with ordinary consciousness *(rnam shes, vijñāna)*, *pristine cognition* refers to a buddha's fully awakened wisdom and also to the uncontaminated gnosis of the noble ones that is characterized by the direct realization of emptiness. Some translate the Sanskrit term and its Tibetan equivalent as "wisdom" or "gnosis."

reality *(chos nyid, dhamatā)*. Translated also as "reality itself," "the very nature," and also as "essence," the Sanskrit term and its Tibetan equivalent refer to the ultimate mode of being of things. As such, the term is often used as a synonym for *emptiness* and *suchness*.

remedy *(gnyen po)*. *See antidote*

Sage *(thub pa, muni)*. An epithet for the Buddha. The Tibetan term *thub pa* literally means "the able one."

samsara. *See cyclic existence*

secret mantra *(gsang sngags)*. A term used often as a synonym for *tantra*. Its etymology underlines the importance of the pledge of secrecy on the part of the initiate practitioner of tantra. *See also tantra*

secure ground/secure base *(btsan sa).* A level of attainment on the Buddhist path wherein one can no longer slide back into the lower realms under the sway of karma and afflictions and wherein one's eventual enlightenment is assured.

self-enlightened one *(rang sangs rgyas, pratyekabuddha).* Sometimes called a "solitary realizer," a *self-enlightened one* is a Buddhist adept who seeks liberation on the basis of autonomous practice. *See also disciple*

self-grasping *(bdag 'dzin, ātmagrāha).* Instinctively believing in the intrinsic existence of your own self as well as of the self-existence of external phenomena. *Self* here means a substantial, truly existing identity. The wisdom that realizes emptiness eliminates this self-grasping. *Self-grasping* is a synonym for *ignorance.*

seven limbs *(yan lag bdun).* A popular Mahāyāna Buddhist rite of worship made up of the following seven elements: (1) paying homage, (2) making offerings, (3) confessing and purifying negative karma, (4) rejoicing in virtuous deeds, (5) supplicating the buddhas to turn the wheel of Dharma, (6) appealing to the buddhas not to enter into final nirvana, and (7) dedicating one's merit.

seven riches of a noble one *('phags nor bdun).* The wealth of (1) faith, (2) morality, (3) giving, (4) learning, (5) conscience, (6) shame, and (7) insight.

six perfections *(phar phyin drug, ṣaṭpāramitā).* The perfections of (1) giving, (2) morality, (3) forbearance, (4) joyful perseverance, (5) concentration, and (6) wisdom. These six perfections constitute the heart of the bodhisattva's practice, especially with respect to the perfection of his or her own mind. *See also four means of attracting others*

six sense bases *(skyed mched drug, ṣaḍāyatana).* (1) Visible form, (2) sound, (3) smell, (4) taste, (5) texture, and (6) mental objects. The Sanskrit and the Tibetan terms connote an entrance, and as such, these six are entrances through which the afflictions arise in our mind.

sixteen drops *(thig le bcu drug).* The meditation on the *sixteen drops* lies at the heart of the practice based on the teachings of *The Book of Kadam.* In the fashion of a highly powerful camera lens zooming in from the widest angle possible to a progressively smaller focus and, finally, to a tiny point, the meditation becomes increasingly focused, moving from the entire cosmos, to your world in particular, to the realm of Tibet, to your own dwelling, and finally culminating within your own body. Once you have zoomed in on your own body, then within your heart, there are in sequence—one inside the heart of the other—Perfection of Wisdom Mother, the Buddha, Great Compassion, Wisdom Tārā, Wrathful Tārā, the protector Acala, Atiśa, and Dromtönpa, inside of whose heart are the drops of the three lineages—Vast Practice, Profound View, and Inspirational Practice—finally culminating in the drop of Great Awakening. Entry IV of this volume, the *Elucidation of the Heart-Drop Practice,* presents a detailed guide to this meditation practice.

suchness *(de bzhin nyid/ de kho na nyid, tattva/tathāta).* The reality of things as they are; often used as a synonym for *emptiness.* The term is also translated as "thatness."

sugata *(bde bar gshegs pa).* Literally, "one gone to bliss"; an epithet for a buddha.

supplication *(gsol 'debs).* An appeal or a request written often in verse and directed to an object of veneration, such as the Three Jewels or your spiritual teacher.

tantra *(rgyud).* Literally, "continuum," *tantra* refers to a highly advanced system of thought and meditative practice wherein the very aspects of the resultant states of buddhahood are brought into the path right from the start. Unlike the practices of general Mahayana, the engagement in the meditative practices of tantra requires prior initiation into the teachings. The term *tantra* can also refer to the literature or tantric texts that expound these systems of thought and practice. Often the term is used as a shorthand for *Tantrayāna,* the "vehicle of tantra," or *Vajrayāna,* the Diamond Vehicle, where it is contrasted against the Sutra Vehicle *(Sūtrayāna)* or Perfection Vehicle *(Pāramitāyāna).*

tathāgata *(de bzhin gshegs pa).* Literally, "thus-gone one"; an epithet for a buddha. When capitalized, refers to Buddha Śākyamuni.

ten directions *(phyogs bcu, daśadik).* The four cardinal directions, the four ordinal directions, plus up and down.

ten powers *(stobs bcu, daśabala).* The powers of (1) knowing what is lawfully appropriate or inappropriate, (2) knowing the fruitional effects of karma, (3) knowing the diverse aspirations of sentient beings, (5) knowing the diverse mental dispositions, (6) knowing the level of mental faculties of sentient beings, (7) knowing the paths that lead to all destinations, (8) knowing the concentrations, liberating paths, meditative stabilizations, and absorptive states, (8) knowing the states of sentient beings' past lives, (9) knowing the future deaths and rebirths of sentient beings, and (10) knowing the cessation of all contaminants.

three dairy products and three sweet substances *(dkar gsum mngar gsum).* Translated also as "three white ingredients and three sweet ingredients," the expression refers to milk, yogurt, and butter (the three white ingredients) and honey, sugar, and molasses (the three sweet ingredients).

three doors *(sgo gsum).* Body, speech, and mind—the three avenues for activity, whether enlightened or worldly.

three ethical disciplines of the Supreme Vehicle *(theg mchog tshul khrims rnam gsum).* (1) The ethic of restraining from the nonvirtues, (2) the ethic of gathering the virtues, and (3) the ethic of working for the benefit of other sentient beings.

three (higher) trainings *(bslab pa gsum, triśikṣā).* The higher trainings in morality, meditation, and wisdom. Each constitutes, respectively, the principal subject matter of the scriptural collections on discipline *(vinaya),* discourses *(sūtra),* and higher knowledge *(abhidharma).* The entire Buddhist path is subsumed into these three higher trainings.

Three Jewels *(dkon mchog gsum, triratna).* The Buddha Jewel, the Dharma Jewel, and the Sangha Jewel. Together, these three constitute the true object of refuge in Buddhism. You take refuge in the Buddha as the true teacher, in the Dharma as the true teaching, and in the Sangha (the spiritual community) as the true companions on the path.

three scopes *(skyes bu gsum).* The *three scopes* refer to the practitioners of initial, intermediate, and advanced scopes or capacities. Atiśa's *Lamp for the Path to Enlightenment* presents the entire Buddhist path to enlightenment in terms of meditative practices appropriate to these three differing capacities—the initial, who seeks only a refuge from the fears of rebirth in the lower realms; the intermediate, who principally seeks freedom from cyclic existence; and the advanced, who seeks full awakening for the benefit of all beings.

three scriptural baskets *(sde snod gsum, tripiṭaka).* Refers to a threefold classification of all the teachings attributed to the Buddha: (1) the discipline basket *(vinaya piṭaka),* (2) the discourses basket *(sūtra piṭaka),* and (3) the higher knowledge basket *(abhidharma piṭaka). The Book of Kadam* emphasizes the need to subsume all the teachings of the Buddha within this threefold collection of scriptures and undertake their practice. The expression the "Kadam tradition endowed with sevenfold teaching and divinities," refers to the three scriptural collections along with four meditation deities.

three spheres *('khor gsum, trimaṇḍala).* This is a reference to the three key elements of an action: namely, the object of the action, the agent of the act, and the act itself, which together form the basis of grasping at the substantial reality of actions and events.

three syllables. *Oṃ, āḥ,* and *hūṃ.*

tīrthika *(mu stegs pa).* A proponent of any of the classical Indian non-Buddhist philosophical tenets.

torma *(gtor ma).* In general *torma* refers to a ritual cake, customarily made of roasted barley dough and decorated with butter at the front, that is consecrated and ritually offered to all classes of objects, such as buddhas, meditation deities, and protectors, including the local guardian spirits.

tranquil abiding *(zhi gnas, śamatha).* An advanced meditative state where the meditator has attained a physical and mental pliancy derived from focusing the mind. It is characterized by stable single-pointed attention on a chosen object with all mental distractions calmed. Tranquil abiding is an essential basis for cultivating *penetrative insight.* Sometimes, the term is applied also to the actual meditative practice that leads to the state of tranquil abiding.

transference *('pho ba).* An advanced tantric practice whereby the meditator deliberately directs his or her consciousness out of the body. According to the texts, this is to be applied when the practitioner perceives unmistakable signs of approaching death but the actual dying processes has not yet begun. Advanced practitioners can apply such transference to others as well.

true existence *(bden par grub pa/ bden par yod pa).* A real existence definable in terms of elementary constituents—or essences—or in terms of characteristics like true causes, conditions, and effects.

Tuṣita *(dga' ldan).* The buddhafield, or pure land, of the future Buddha, Maitreya.

twelve cultivated qualities *(sbyangs pa'i yon tan bcu gnis, dvādaśadhūtaguṇa).* This term is sometimes also translated as the *twelve ascetic virtues. See note 198*

twelve links of dependent origination *(rten 'brel bcu gnyis, dvādaśāṅgapratītyasamutpāda).* (1) Ignorance, (2) volition, (3) consciousness, (4) name and form, (5) sense bases, (6) contact, (7) feeling, (8) craving, (9) grasping, (10) becoming, (11) birth, and (12) aging and death. According to the Buddha's teaching on the law of cause and effect, it is through an unending interwoven chain of these twelve links that an individual revolves within the cycle of existence conditioned by karma and afflictions.

two awakening minds *(sems bskyed gnyis).* Following the Indian Mahayana Buddhist classics, the Kadam texts such as *The Book of Kadam* speak of *two awakening minds,* or *two bodhicittas*—conventional and ultimate. The former refers to altruistic intention as defined above under *awakening mind,* while the latter refers to a direct realization of the emptiness of the fully awakened mind. In general usage, *awakening mind* is a synonym for the conventional awakening mind.

two truths *(bden pa gnyis, satyadvaya).* Conventional truth *(kun rdzob bden pa, saṃvṛtisatya)* and ultimate truth *(don dam bden pa, paramārthasatya).* According to the Middle Way school (the perspective adopted in *The Book of Kadam*), *ultimate truth* refers to emptiness—the absence of intrinsic existence of all phenomena. In contrast, *conventional truth* refers to the empirical aspect of reality as experienced through perception, thought, and language.

ultimate expanse *(chos dbyings, dharmadhātu).* A synonym for ultimate nature. Calling it "expanse" invokes the space-like quality of the ultimate mode of being of all things.

ultimate nature *(gnas lugs).* Refers to the ultimate mode of being of things, which for a Mahayana Buddhist is *emptiness.*

ultimate truth *(don dam bden pa, paramārthasatya). See two truths*

upāsaka *(dge bsnyen).* A Buddhist practitioner who has taken the layperson's vow. The *upāsaka* vow consists of a deliberate adoption of a disciplined way of life whereby the practitioner commits to observing the five principal precepts against (1) killing, (2) stealing, (3) sexual misconduct, (4) telling lies, and (5) alcohol. Depending upon one's level of commitment, a practitioner can take all five precepts, including a vow of total celibacy, or choose to take one or several of the five precepts. Dromtönpa chose to remain as a lay practitioner and is often referred to in *The Book of Kadam* as the upāsaka. An *upāsikā (dge bsnyen ma)* is lay female practitioner with such a vow.

utpala *(utpala).* A blue flower belonging to the lotus family.

Vajrayana. *See tantra*

virtuous action *(dge ba'i las, kuśalakarma).* Actions of body, speech, and mind motivated by wholesome states of mind, such as nonattachment, nonaversion, and nondelusion; these are actions that result in happiness for others and one's own self. *See also nonvirtuous action*

wisdom *(shes rab, prajñā)*. The Sanskrit term *prajñā* and its Tibetan equivalent *shes rab* have different applications depending upon the context. In the Abhidharma taxonomy of mental factors, *prajñā* refers to a specific mental factor that helps evaluate the various properties or qualities of an object. The term can refer simply to intelligence or mental aptitude. In the context of the Mahayana path, *prajñā* refers to the wisdom aspect of the path constituted primarily by deep insight into the emptiness of all phenomena. Hence the term *prajñā* and its Tibetan equivalent *shes rab* are translated variously as "wisdom," "insight," or "intelligence."

yakṣa *(gnod sbyin)*. A specific class of beings that includes many of the well-known Buddhist protector deities, such as Vajrapāṇi. A *yakṣa* is generally depicted as possessing a stout heavy body with a round belly and short thick limbs.

yoga *(rnal 'byor)*. Literally meaning "union," yoga refers to advanced meditative practices, especially in the context of Buddhist tantra. The Tibetan term *rnal 'byor* has the added connotation of "uniting one's mind with the nature of reality."

Yama *(gshin rje)*. The lord of death.

yojana *(dpag tshad)*. An ancient Indian unit of distance, which, according to one system, measures about four and half miles or seven and half kilometers.

Bibliography

WORKS CITED IN THE TEXTS

Kangyur (*Canonical Scriptures*)

Clear Differentiation of the Discipline [Basket]. *Vinayavibhaṅga*. *'Dul ba rnam par 'byed pa*. Toh 3, 'dul ba *ja*. P1032, *che*.

Dispelling Ajātaśatru's Remorse. *Ajātaśatrukaukṛttyavinodana*. *Ma skyes dgra'i 'gyod pa bsal ba*. Toh 216, mdo sde *tsha*. P882, *tsu*.

Jewel Casket Sutra. *Karaṇḍavyūhasūtra*. *'Phags pa za ma tog bkod pa'i mdo*. Toh 116, mdo sde *ja*. P784, *chu*.

King of Meditation Sutra. *Samādhirājasūtra*. *Ting nge 'dzin rgyal po'i mdo*. Toh 127, mdo sde *da*. P795, *thu*.

Meeting of Father and Son Sutra. *Pitāputrasamāgamanasūtra*. *Yab sras mjal ba'i mdo*. Toh 60, dkon brtsegs, *nga*. P760, *zhi*. This is part of the *Ratnakuṭa* collection.

Perfection of Wisdom in Twenty-Five Thousand Lines. *Pañcaviśatisāhasrikā-prajñāpāramitā*. *Shes rab kyi pha rol du phyin pa stong phrag nyi shu rtsa lnga pa*. Toh 9, shes phyin *kha*. P731, *nyi*.

Perfectly Gathering the Qualities [of Avalokiteśvara]. *Dharmasaṃgītisūtra*. *Chos yang dag par sdud pa'i mdo*. Toh 238, mdo sde *zha*. P904, *vu*.

Vows of Good Conduct. *Bhadracaryāpraṇidhāna*. *Bzang po spyod pa'i smon lam*. Toh 1095, gzungs bsdus *vam*. P716, *ya*. This is also part 4 of the *Flower Ornament Scripture*.

Tengyur (*Canonical Treatises*)

Āryadeva. *Four Hundred Stanzas [on the Middle Way]. Catuḥśatakaśāstra. Bstan bcos Bzhi brgya pa.* Toh 3846, dbu ma *tsha.* P5246, *tsha.* An English translation of this work with extant fragments of the Sanskrit original can be found in Karen Lang's *Āryadeva's Catuḥśataka* (Copenhagen: Akademisk Forlag, 1986). A translation of the root text from the Tibetan edition with Gyaltsap Je's commentary can be found under the title *The Yogic Deeds of Bodhisattvas: Gyel-tsap on Āryadeva's Four Hundred.* Ruth Sonam, trans. and ed. Ithaca: Snow Lion Publications, 1994.

Āryaśūra. *Garland of Birth Stories. Jātakamālā. Skyes rabs kyi rgyud.* Toh 4150, skyes rabs *hu.* P5650, *ki.*

Atiśa Dīpaṃkara. *Bodhisattva's Jewel Garland. Bodhisattvamaṇevalī. Byang chub sems dpa' nor bu'i phreng ba.* Toh 3951, dbu ma *khi.* P5347, *ki.* An English translation is found in the present volume (entry II).

————. *Lamp for the Path to Enlightenment. Bodhipathapradīpa. Byang chub lam gyi sgron ma.* Toh 3947, Tengyur, dbu ma *khi.* P5343, *ki.* For an English translation, see Geshe Sonam Rinchen's *Atisha's Lamp for the Path to Enlightenment.* Ruth Sonam, trans. Ithaca: Snow Lion Publications, 1997.

Candrakīrti. *Exposition of "Entering the Middle Way." Madhyamakāvatāra-bhāṣya. Dbu ma la 'jug pa'i bshad pa.* Toh 3862, dbu ma '*a.* P5263, '*a.*

Jagaddarpaṇa ('Gro ba'i me long). *Compendium of the Tasks of a Vajra Master. Vajrācāryakryāsamuccaya. Rdo rje slob dpon gyi bya ba kun las btus pa.* Toh 3305, Tengyur, rgyud 'grel *bu.* P5012, *thu.*

Maitreya. *Clear Differentiation of the Center and Extremes. Madhyānta-vibhaṅga. Dbus dang mtha' rnam par 'byed pa'i tshig le'ur byas pa.* Toh 4021, sems tsam *phi.* P5522, *phi.*

Nāgārjuna. *Commentary on the Awakening Mind. Bodhicittavivaraṇa. Byang chub sems kyi 'grel pa.* Toh 1800, rgyud 'grel *ngi.* P2665, *gi.* An English translation is in Lindtner 1982.

————. *Fundamental Wisdom of the Middle Way. Mūlamadhyamaka-kārikā. Dbu ma rtsa ba'i tshig le'ur byas pa shes rab.* Toh 3824. Tengyur, dbu ma *tsa.* P5524 *tsa.* One English translation (among many) can be found in Jay Garfield, *Fundamental Wisdom of the Middle Way* (New York: Oxford University Press, 1995).

Prājñendraruci. *Ratnajvalasādhana. Rin chen 'bar ba zhes bya ba'i sgrubs thabs.* Toh 1251, rgyud 'grel *nya.* P2380, *zha.*

Śāntideva. *Guide to the Bodhisattva's Way of Life. Bodhicaryāvatāra. Byang chub sems pa'i spyod pa la 'jug pa.* Toh 3871, dbu ma *la.* P5272, *la.* English translations include Stephen Batchelor's *Guide to the Bodhisattva's Way of Life* (Dharamsala: Library of Tibetan Works and Archives, 1979), the Padmakara Translation Group's *The Way of the Bodhisattva* (Boston: Shambhala Publications, 1997), Alan and Vesna Wallace's *A Guide to the Bodhisattva's Way of Life* (Ithaca: Snow Lion Publications, 1997), and Kate Crosby and Andrew Skilton's *The Bodhicaryāvatāra* (New York: Oxford University Press, 1995).

Vasubandhu. *Commentary on "Clear Differentiation of the Center and Extremes." Madhyāntavibhaṅgaṭīkā. Dbus dang mtha' rnam par 'byed pa'i 'grel pa.* Toh 4027, sems tsam *bi.* P5828, *bi.*

Vinītadeva. *Clear Exposition of the Words of "Clear Differentiation of the Discipline [Basket]." Vinayavibhaṅgapadavyākhyāna. Dul ba rnam par 'byed pa'i tshig rnam par bshad pa.* Toh 4114, 'dul ba *tshu.* P5616, *wu.*

Tibetan Works

The Father Teachings of The Book of Kadam. Bka' gdams glegs bam las pha chos kyi skor. Reproduced from the Tashi Lhünpo woodblock edition by Lokesh Candra in New Delhi, 1982. Typeset edition based on the Dergé edition was published as *Jo bo rje dpal ldan a ti sha'i rnam thar bka' gdams pha chos bzhugs so.* Xining: Nationalities Press, 1994. This is volume 1 of *The Book of Kadam.*

The Son Teachings of The Book of Kadam. Bka' gdams glegs bam las bu chos kyi skor. Reproduced from the Tashi Lhünpo woodblock edition by Lokesh Candra in New Delhi, 1982. Typeset edition based on the Dergé edition was published as *'Brom ston rgyal ba'i 'byung gnas kyi skyes rabs bka' gdams bu chos bzhugs so.* Xining: Nationalities Press, 1993. This is volume 2 of *The Book of Kadam.*

Chegom Sherap Dorjé (ca. twelfth century), comp. *Sayings of the Kadam Masters. Bka' gdams gsung bgros thor bu.* Lhasa Phunkhang xylograph edition from the personal library of Kyabjé Zemey Rinpoché. Typeset edition of the entire text, based on Dergé edition, in Yeshé Döndrup's *Treasury of Gems,* pp. 562–615. This is entry XI of our volume.

Chekawa Yeshé Dorjé (1101–75). "Seven-Point Mind Training." In *Mind Training: The Great Collection*. Trans. by Thupten Jinpa. Boston: Wisdom Publications, in association with the Institute of Tibetan Classics, 2005, pp. 83–85.

Dromtönpa (1004–64). *Self-Exhortation Entitled "Tree of Faith." Rang rgyud la skul ma 'debs pa dad pa'i ljon shing*. Full text in *The Book of Kadam*, vol. 1. Typeset edition, Xining: Nationalities Press, 1993, pp. 566–90. This is entry I of our volume.

Khenchen Nyima Gyaltsen (1223–1305). "Liberating Life Stories of the Lineage Teachers of the Sevenfold Divinity and Teaching." *Zhus lan nor bu'i phreng ba lha chos bdun ldan gyi bla ma brgyud pa'i rnam thar*. Full text in *The Book of Kadam*, vol. I. Typeset edition, Xining: Nationalities Press, 1993, pp. 299–504.

Tsongkhapa (1357–1419). *The Three Principal Elements of the Path. Lam gyi gtso bo rnam pa gsum. The Collected Works of Tsongkhapa*, vol. *kha*. Lhasa Shöl edition reproduced by Guru Deva in Delhi, 1978.

TRANSLATOR'S BIBLIOGRAPHY

Akya Yongzin Lobsang Döndrup (1759–1823), a.k.a. Yangchen Gawai Lodrö. *Elucidation of the Terms of "A Heap of Precious Jewels on the Teaching through Similes." Dpe chos rin chen spungs pa'i brda bkrol*. Typeset edition in *Gangs can rig brgya'i sgo 'byed lde mig* 17. Beijing: Nationalities Press, 1991.

———. *Explanation of Some of the Difficult Terms in the "Blue Udder." Be'u bum sgon po'i brda go dka' ba 'ga' zhig bshad pa*. The Collected Works of Akya Yongzin, vol. *ka*.

Beckwith, Christopher. *Tibetan Empire in Central Asia*. Princeton, NJ: Princeton University Press, 1987.

Bhikkhu Bodhi, trans. *The Connected Discourses of the Buddha: A New Translation of Saṃyutta Nikāya*. Boston: Wisdom Publications, 2000.

A Biographical Dictionary of the Tibetan Scholars and Adepts. Gangs ljongs mkhas grub rim byon gyi ming mdzod. Kansu: Nationalities Press, 1992.

The Book of Kadam. Bka' gdams glegs bam. 2 vols. Typeset edition, Xining: Nationalities Press, 1993.

Brauen, Martin, ed. *The Dalai Lamas: A Visual History.* Chicago: Serindia Publications, 2005.

Buddhaghoṣa. *The Path of Purification (Visuddhimagga).* 5th ed. Trans. by Bhikkhu Ñāṇamoli. Kandy: Buddhist Publication Society, 1991.

Candrakīrti. *Entering the Middle Way. Madhyamakāvatāra. Dbu ma la 'jug pa'i tshig le'ur byas pa.* Toh 3861, dbu ma '*a*. P5262, '*a*. An English translation of the Tibetan version of this work can be found in C.W. Huntington, Jr., *The Emptiness of Emptiness.* Honolulu: University of Hawaii, 1989.

Chandra, Lokesh. *Tibetan-Sanskrit Dictionary.* Compact ed. Kyoto: Rinsen Book, 1990.

Das, Sarat Chandra. "The Lamaic Hierarchy of Tibet." *Journal of the Buddhist Texts Society of India* 1 (1983): vol 1, part I, pp. 31–38; part II, pp. 44–57.

Changkya Rölpai Dorjé. *Source of Becoming Learned: A Lexicon. Dag yig mkhas pa'i 'byung gnas.* In *Beautiful Ornament of Mount Meru: A Presentation of the Philosophical Systems. Grub mtha' lhun po'i mdzes rgyan.* Typeset edition, Kansu: Nationalities Press, 1989.

Chattopadhyaya, Alaka. *Atīśa and Tibet.* Delhi: Motilal Banarsidass, 1967; reprint ed. 1999.

Chenga Lodrö Gyaltsen (1402–72). *Initial Mind Training: Opening the Door of Dharma. Thog ma'i blo sbyong chos kyi sgo 'byed.* Xylograph edition reprinted in *Three Texts on Lamrim Teachings.* Dharamsala: Library of Tibetan Works and Archives, 1987.

Chim Namkha Drak (1210–85). *Biography of Master Atiśa. Jo bo rje'i rnam thar rgyas pa yongs grags.* In *The Book of Kadam,* vol. I, pp. 44–228. Typeset edition, Kansu: Nationalities Press, 1993.

Cleary, Thomas, trans. *The Flower Ornament Scripture: A Translation of the Avatamsaka Sutra.* Boston: Shambhala Publications, 1993.

The Dalai Lama. *Essence of the Heart Sutra.* Trans. by Geshe Thupten Jinpa. Boston: Wisdom Publications, 2002.

———. *The World of Tibetan Buddhism.* Trans. by Geshe Thupten Jinpa. Boston: Wisdom Publications, 1995.

Dayal, Har. *The Bodhisattva Doctrine in Buddhist Sanskrit Literature.* Delhi: Motilal Banarsidass, 1932; reprinted 1999.

Decleer, Hubert. "Master Atiśa in Nepal: The Tham Bahīl and Five Stūpas according to the '*Brom ston Itinerary.*" In *Journal of the Nepal Research Centre* 10 (1996): 27–54.

Desi Sangyé Gyatso (1653–1705). *Yellow Beryl: A History of Ganden Tradition. Dga' ldan chos 'byung bai dru rya ser po.* Typeset edition, Xining: Nationalities Press, 1989.

Dromtönpa (1004–64). *Biography and Itinerary of Atiśa. Jo bo'i rnam thar lam yig chos kyi 'byung gnas.* In *The Book of Kadam,* vol. I, pp. 229–90. Typeset edition, Kansu: Nationalities Press. 1993.

Doniger O'Flaherty, Wendy, trans. *Hindu Myths.* London: Penguin Books, 1975.

Dungkar Lobsang Trinlé (1927–1997). *Dungkar Tibetological Great Dictionary. Dung dkar tshig mdzod men mo.* Beijing: China Tibetology Publishing House, 2002.

Ehrhard, Franz-Karl. "The Transmission of the *Thig-le bcu-drug* and the *Bka' gdams glegs bam.*" In Helmut Eimer and David Germano, eds. *The Many Canons of Tibetan Buddhism,* pp. 29–56. Leiden: Brill, 2002.

Eimer, Helmut. "Zur Faksimile-Ausgabe eines alten Blockdruckes des Bka' gdams glegs bam." *Indo-Iranian Journal* 27 (1984): 28–56.

———. "The Development of the Biographical Tradition Concerning Atiśa (Dīpaṃkaraśrījñāna)." In *The Journal of the Tibet Society* 2 (1982): 41–51.

The Extensive Tibetan-Chinese Dictionary. Bod rgya tshig mdzod chen mo. 2 vols. Compact ed. Beijing: Nationalities Press, 1984.

Gendün Drup, First Dalai Lama (1391–1474). *Praise to Tārā. Sgrol ma'i bstod pa mkhas pa'i gtsug rgyan. The Collected Works of the First Dalai Lama.* Tashi Lhünpo edition, xylograph, vol. *ca, sna tsogs,* pp. 21b2–24a2.

Gendün Gyatso, Second Dalai Lama (1476–1542). *Summary Points of The Book of Kadam. Bka' gdams glegs bam gyi bsdus don.* The Collected Works, vol. 3. Old xylograph edition from the personal library of His Holiness the Fourteenth Dalai Lama.

Geshe Wangyal. *The Door of Liberation.* Boston: Wisdom Publications, 1995.

————. *The Jewelled Staircase.* Ithaca: Snow Lion Publications, 1986.

Gö Lotsāwa Shönu Pal (1392–1481). *The Blue Annals. Deb ther sngon po.* 2 vols. Typeset edition, Sichuan: Nationalities Press, 1984. English translation by George N. Roerich in *The Blue Annals.* Calcutta: Royal Asiatic Society of Bengal, 1949–53. Latest reprint Delhi: Motilal Banarsidass, 1988.

Guenther, Herbert. *Royal Song of Saraha.* Seattle: University of Washington Press, 1969.

Jackson, David. "The *bsTan rim* ('Stages of the Doctrine') and Similar Graded Expositions of the Bodhisattva's Path." In José Ignacio Cabezón and Roger R. Jackson, eds. *Tibetan Literature: Studies in Genre,* pp. 229–43. Ithaca: Snow Lion Publications, 1996.

Jackson, Roger. *Tantric Treasures.* New York: Oxford University Press, 2004.

Jamgön Amé (1597–1659). *Ocean of Wonders: A History of the Kadam Tradition. Bka' gdams chos 'byung ngo mtshar rgya mtsho.* Typeset edition, Kansu: Nationalities Press, 1995.

Jinpa, Thupten, trans. *Mind Training: The Great Collection.* Boston: Wisdom Publications, in association with the Institute of Tibetan Classics, 2005.

————. "Introduction." *Sngon gleng ngo sprod. Bka' gdams glegs bam las btus pa'i chos skor. Bod kyi gtsug lag gces btus,* vol. 2. Delhi: Institute of Tibetan Classics, 2005.

The Kakholma Testament. Ka chems ka khol ma. Typeset edition, Kansu: Nationalities Press, 1989.

Kamalaśila. *Stages of Meditation. Bhāvanākrama. Sgom pa'i rim pa.* Toh 3916, Tengyur, dbu ma *ki.* P5311 *a.*

Karmapa Rangjung Dorjé (1284–1339). *One Hundred Birth Stories. Skyes rabs brgya pa.* Typeset edition in *Gang can rigs brgya'i sgo 'byed lde mig,* vol. 22. Beijing: Nationalities Press, 1995.

Kapstein, Mathew. "Remarks on the Maṇi bka' 'bum and the Cult of Avalokiteśvara in Tibet" in Steven D. Goodman and Ronald M. Davidson, eds., *Tibetan Buddhism: Reason and Revelation.* Albany: State University of New York, 1992.

————. *The Tibetan Assimilation of Buddhism.* New York: Oxford University Press, 2000.

Khagang, Tashi Tsering, ed. *Research on Ancient Tibetan Literature. Bod kyi yig rnying zhib 'jug.* Beijing: Nationalities Press, 2003.

Lechen Künga Gyaltsen (fifteenth century). *Lamp Illuminating the History of the Kadam Tradition. Bka' gdams chos 'byung gsal ba'i sgron me.* Xylograph edition published under the instruction of the Fifth Dalai Lama. Text scanned by the Tibetan Buddhist Resource Center (TBRC), New York, at the request of the Institute of Tibetan Classics.

Lindtner, Christian. *Nagarjuna: Studies in the Writings and Philosophy of Nagarjuna.* Delhi: Motilal Banarsidass, 1982.

Longdöl Ngawang Lobsang (1719–94). *Staircase to Liberation: A Memorandum of Initiations, Oral Transmissions, and Commentaries Received Pertaining to Sutra and Tantra,* part I. *Mdo sngags kyi dbang lung khrid gsum thob pa'i gsan yig thar pa'i them skas,* stod cha. *The Collected Works of Klong rdol Ngag dbang blo bzang;* vol. 2, pp. 1–176. *Gangs can rig mdzod* 21. Xinhua: Tibetan Press for the Printing of Old Texts, 1991.

————. *A Useful List for Those Who Uphold the Geden Tradition and Aspire to Vast Learning* in *The Collected Works of Klong rdol Ngag dbang blo bzang;* vol. 2, pp. 307–29. *Gang can rig mdzod* 21. Xinhua: Tibetan Press for the Printing of Old Texts, 1991.

McGovern, William Montgomery. *A Manual of Buddhist Philosophy.* London: Routledge, 2000. First published, London: Kegan Paul, Trench, Trübner, and Company, 1923.

Maitreya. *Ornament of Clear Realizations. Abhisamayālaṃkāra. Mngon rtogs rgyan.* Toh 3786, Tengyur, shes phyin *ka.* P5184, *ka.*

Miller, Amy Sims. "Jeweled Dialogues: The Role of *The Book* in the Formation of the Kadam Tradition within Tibet." Ph.D. diss., University of Virginia, 2004.

Monier-Williams, Monier. *Sanskrit-English Dictionary.* Delhi: Motilal Banarsidass, latest reprint 1993.

Nāgārjuna. *The Precious Garland: An Epistle to a King.* John Dunne and Sara McLintock, trans. Boston: Wisdom Publications, 1997. (Commemorative volume produced for a public teaching given by His Holiness the Dalai Lama in Los Angeles.)

Nakamura, Hajime. *Indian Buddhism: A Survey with Biographical Notes.* Delhi: Motilal Banarsidass, 1987; reprinted 1989.

Naktso Lotsāwa (1011–64). *Hundred and Ten Stanzas of Praise. Bstod pa brgyad cu pa.* Full Tibetan text in Yeshé Döndrup, *Treasury of Gems*, pp. 26–35.

Ngawang Lobsang Gyatso, Fifth Dalai Lama (1617–82). *River Ganges' Flow: A Record of Teachings Received. Gsan yig gang ga'i chu rgyun. The Collected Works of the Fifth Dalai Lama*, vol. *kha.* Lhasa Shöl xylograph edition, reproduced by Sikkim Research Institute of Tibetology, Gangtok, 1991–95.

Nyangral Nyima Öser (1124–92). *A History of Dharma: Pure Honey Extracted from the Essence of a Flower. Chos 'byung me tog snying po sbrang rtsi'i bcud. Gangs can rig mdzod 5.* Xinhua: Tibetan Press for the Printing of Old Texts, 1988.

Onada, Shunzo. "Abbatial Successions of the Colleges of gSang phu sNe'u thog Monastery." *Kokuritsu Minzokugaku Hakabutsukan kenky euhe okoku* 15, no. 4 (1999): 1049–71.

Paṇchen Sönam Drakpa (1478–1554). *History of the Old and New Kadam Schools: Beautiful Ornament for the Mind. Bka' gdams gsar rnying gi chos 'byung yid kyi mdzes rgyan.* Xylograph edition of Potala Library reprinted in *Two Histories of Kadam School* published by Gonpo Tseten in Delhi, 1977.

Pabongka Dechen Nyingpo (1878–1941). *Record of Teachings Received. Gsan yig. The Collected Works of Pha bong kha*, vol. *ka.* Xylograph edition. Delhi: Chophel Lekden, reprinted 1973.

Pabongka Rinpoche. *Liberation in the Palm of Your Hand.* Edited by Trijang Rinpoche. Translated by Michael Richards. Second edition, Boston: Wisdom Publications, 2006.

Pagel, Ulrich. *The Bodhisattvapiṭaka: Its Doctrines, Practices and Their Position in Mahāyāna Literature.* Tring: The Institute of Buddhist Studies, 1995.

Pawo Tsuklak Trengwa (1504–66). *Joyful Feast for the Learned: A History of Buddhism. Chos 'byung mkhas pa'i dga' ston.* 2 vols. Typeset edition, Beijing: Nationalities Press, 1985.

Pema Karpo (1527–96). *Sun Enhancing the Lotus of the Buddha's Teaching. Chos 'byung bstan pa'i pad ma rgyas pa'i nyin byed. Gangs can rig mdzod* 19. Typeset edition, Xinhua: Tibetan Press for the Printing of Old Texts, 1992.

Sacred Collection on the Maṇi [Mantra]. Maṇi Bka' 'bum. Reproduced from a print of the no longer extant Spungs thang (Punakha) blocks by Trayang and Jamyang Samten. 2 vols. New Delhi, 1975.

Śāntideva. *The Bodhicaryāvatāra.* Kate Crosby and Andrew Skilton, trans. New York: Oxford University Press, 1995.

Segal, Robert. *Myth: A Very Short Introduction.* New York: Oxford University Press, 2004.

Schuh, Dieter. *Tibetische Handschriften und Blockdrucke sowie Tonbandaufnahmen tibetischer Erzählungen,* Teil 8. Wiesbaden: Sammlung Waddell der Staatsbibliothek Preussischer Kulturbesitz Berlin, 1981.

Sönam Lhai Wangpo (fifteenth century). *A History of the Precious Kadam Tradition: Sun Illuminating the Liberating Lives. Bka' gdams rin po che'i chos 'byung rnam thar nyin mor byed pa'i 'od stong.* Xylograph edition of Potala Library reprinted in *Two Histories of Kadam School,* published by Gonpo Tseten in Delhi, 1977.

Sumpa Yeshé Paljor (1704–1840). *An Excellent Wish-Fulfilling Tree: A History of Buddhism. Chos 'byung dpag bsam ljon bzang.* Typeset edition, Kansu: Nationalities Press, 1992.

Sutra of the Ten Levels. Daśabhūmikasūtra. Mdo sde sa bcu pa. Toh 44, Kangyur, phal chen *kha,* chap. 31. P761, *li.*

Taklung Ngawang Namgyal (1571–1616). *History of the Taklung Tradition. Stag lung chos 'byung. Gangs can rig mdzod* 22. Xinhua: Tibetan Press for the Printing of Old Texts, 1992.

Tatz, Mark. *Asanga's Chapter on Ethics with the Commentary of Tsong-Kha-Pa: The Basic Path to Awakening, the Complete Bodhisattva.* Lewiston, NY: Edwin Mellen Press, 1986.

Thrangu Rinpoche, Khenchen. *A Song for the King: Saraha on Mahāmudrā Meditation.* Translator of the song and editor, Michele Martin. Oral commentary translated by Peter O'Hearn. Boston: Wisdom Publications, 2006.

Thuken Chökyi Nyima (1737–1802). *Crystal Mirror of Philosophical Systems. Grub mtha' shel gyi me long.* Typeset edition, Kansu: Nationalities Press, 1985. English translation forthcoming as volume 25 of *The Library of Tibetan Classics.*

Tsalpa Künga Dorjé (1309–64). *The Red Annals. Deb ther dmar po.* Typeset edition with extensive annotations by Dungkar Lobsang Trinlé. Beijing: Nationalities Press, 1981.

Tsenla Ngawang Tsültrim. *Golden Mirror Unraveling the Terms. Brda bkrol gser gyi me long.* Beijing: Nationalities Press, 1997.

Tsering, Nakpa. "Initial Discussion on the Relation between the Corpse Stories and Some Ancient Tibetan Folk Stories Discovered at Tunhang." In Tashi Tsering Khagang, ed. *Research on Ancient Tibetan Literature. Bod kyi yig rnying zhib 'jug.* Beijing: Nationalities Press, 2003.

Tseten Shapdrung (1910–98). *Compendium of Chronologies. Bstan rtsis kun las btus pa.* Xining: Nationalities Press, 1982.

Tsongkhapa (1357–1419). *The Great Treatise on the Stages of the Path to Enlightenment,* vol. 2. Translated by the Lamrim Chenmo Translation Committee; Joshua W.C. Cutler, editor-in-chief; Guy Newland, editor. Ithaca: Snow Lion Publications, 2004.

van der Kuijp, Leonard. "The Dalai Lamas and the Origins of Reincarnate Lamas." In Brauen, ed., *The Dalai Lamas: A Visual History* (Chicago: Serindia Publications, 2005).

Willson, Martin, and Martin Brauen. *Deities of Tibetan Buddhism: The Zürich Paintings of the Icons Worthwhile to See.* Boston: Wisdom Publications, 2000.

Yeshé Döndrup (1792–1855). *Treasury of Gems: Selected Anthology of the Well-Uttered Insights of the Teachings of the Precious Kadam Tradition. Legs par bshad pa bka' gdams rin po che'i gsung gi gces btus legs bshad nor bu'i bang mdzod.* Typeset edition, Kansu: Nationalities Press, 1995.

Yeshé Tsemo (b. 1433). *Wondrous Garland of Excellent Jewels: A Biography of the Glorious All-Knowing Gendün Drup. Thams cad mkhyen pa dge 'dun grub pa'i dpal gyi rnam thar ngo mtshar rmad 'byung nor bu'i phreng ba. The Collected Works of the First Dalai Lama*, xylograph, Tashi Lhünpo edition, vol. *ka;* TBRC scanned version, vol. *ca.*

Yongzin Yeshé Gyaltsen (1713–93). *The Rite of the Mandala of the Sixteen Drops of Kadam. Bka' gdams thig le bcu drug gi dkyil chog bka' gdams gsal byed. The Collected Works of Yongzin Yeshé Gyaltsen*, vol. *tsa*. Xylograph edition. Tsechok Ling woodblock edition reprinted by Tibet House, New Delhi, 1977.

———. *Heart Instructions of the Book of Kadam. Bka' gdams glegs bam gyi snying po'i man ngag. Collected Works*, vol. *tsha*. New Delhi: Tibet House, 1977.

———. *The Liberating Lives of the Lineage Masters of Lamrim. Lam rim bla ma bryud pa'i rnam thar*. Typeset edition, Lhasa: Nationalities Press, 1990.

Index

About the Translator

GESHE THUPTEN JINPA was trained as a monk at the Shartse College of Ganden Monastic University, South India, where he received the Geshe Lharam degree. Jinpa also holds a B.A. honors in philosophy and a Ph.D. in religious studies, both from Cambridge University, England.

Jinpa has been the principal English-language translator for His Holiness the Dalai Lama for nearly two decades and has translated and edited numerous books by the Dalai Lama. His own works include *Songs of Spiritual Experience* (coauthored), *Self, Reality and Reason in Tibetan Philosophy*, and *Mind Training: The Great Collection* (translated). He is currently the president of the Institute of Tibetan Classics and is also an adjunct professor at McGill University, as well as a research scholar at Stanford University. He lives in Montreal with his wife and two daughters.

The Institute of Tibetan Classics

THE INSTITUTE OF TIBETAN CLASSICS is a nonprofit, charitable educational organization based in Montreal, Canada. It is dedicated to two primary objectives: (1) to preserve and promote the study and deep appreciation of Tibet's rich intellectual, spiritual, and artistic heritage, especially among the Tibetan-speaking communities worldwide; and (2) to make the classical Tibetan knowledge and literature a truly global heritage, its spiritual and intellectual resources open to all.

To learn more about the Institute of Tibetan Classics and its various projects, please visit www.tibetanclassics.org or write to this address:

Institute of Tibetan Classics
304 Aberdare Road
Montreal (Quebec) H3P 3K3
Canada

The Library of Tibetan Classics

"THIS NEW SERIES edited by Thupten Jinpa and published by
Wisdom Publications is a landmark in the study of Tibetan culture in general and Tibetan Buddhism in particular. Each volume contains a lucid introduction and outstanding translations
that, while aimed at the general public, will benefit those in the
field of Tibetan Studies immensely as well."

—Leonard van der Kuijp, Harvard University

"This is an invaluable set of translations by highly competent
scholar-practitioners. The series spans the breadth of the history
of Tibetan religion, providing entry to a vast culture of spiritual
cultivation."

—Jeffrey Hopkins, University of Virginia

"Erudite in all respects, this series is at the same time accessible
and engagingly translated. As such, it belongs in all college and
university libraries as well as in good public libraries. *The
Library of Tibetan Classics* is on its way to becoming a truly
extraordinary spiritual and literary accomplishment."

—Janice D. Willis, Wesleyan University

Following is a list of the thirty-two proposed volumes in *The Library of
Tibetan Classics*. Some volumes are translations of single texts, while others are compilations of multiple texts, and each volume will be roughly the
same length. Except for those volumes already published, the renderings of
titles below are only tentative and are liable to change. The Institute of
Tibetan Classics has contracted numerous established translators in its
efforts, and progress is proceeding on multiple volumes simultaneously,
with several near completion as of this writing.

1. *Mind Training: The Great Collection*, compiled by Shönu Gyalchok and Könchok Gyaltsen (fifteenth century). NOW AVAILABLE

2. *The Book of Kadam: The Core Texts*, attributed to Atiśa and Dromtönpa (eleventh century). NOW AVAILABLE

3. *The Great Chariot: A Treatise on the Great Perfection*, Longchen Rapjampa (1308–63)

4. *Taking the Result As the Path: Core Teachings of the Sakya Lamdré Tradition*, Jamyang Khyentsé Wangchuk (1524–68) et al. NOW AVAILABLE

5. *Mahāmudrā and Related Instructions: Core Teachings of the Kagyü School*

6. *Stages of the Path and the Ear-Whispered Instructions: Core Teachings of the Geluk School*

7. *Ocean of Definitive Meaning: A Teaching for the Mountain Hermit*, Dölpopa Sherap Gyaltsen (1292–1361)

8. *Miscellaneous Tibetan Buddhist Lineages: The Core Teachings*, Jamgön Kongtrül (1813–90)

9. *Sutra, Tantra, and the Mind Cycle: Core Teachings of the Bön School*

10. *The Stages of the Doctrine: Selected Key Texts*

11. *The Bodhisattva's Altruistic Ideal: Selected Key Texts*

12. *The Ethics of the Three Codes*

13. *Sādhanas: Vajrayana Buddhist Meditation Manuals*

14. *Ornament of Stainless Light: An Exposition of the Kālacakra Tantra*, Khedrup Norsang Gyatso (1423–1513). NOW AVAILABLE

15. *Lamp Thoroughly Illuminating the Five Stages of Completion*, Tsongkhapa (1357–1419)

16. *Studies in the Perfection of Wisdom*

17. *Treatises on Buddha Nature*

18. *Differentiations of the Profound View: Interpretations of Emptiness in Tibet*

19. *Elucidation of the Intent: A Thorough Exposition of "Entering the Middle Way,"* Tsongkhapa (1357–1419)

20. *Tibetan Buddhist Epistemology I: The Sakya School*

21. *Tibetan Buddhist Epistemology II: The Geluk School*

22. *Tibetan Buddhist Psychology and Phenomenology: Selected Texts*

23. *Ornament of Higher Knowledge: A Exposition of Vasubandhu's "Treasury of Higher Knowledge,"* Chim Jampalyang (thirteenth century)

24. *A Beautiful Adornment of Mount Meru: Presentation of Classical Indian Philosophies,* Changkya Rölpai Dorjé (1717–86)

25. *The Crystal Mirror of Philosophical Systems: A Tibetan Study of Asian Religious Thought,* Thuken Losang Chökyi Nyima (1737–1802). forthcoming next

26. *Gateway for Being Learned and Realized: Selected Texts*

27. *The Well-Uttered Insights: Advice on Everyday Wisdom, Civility, and Basic Human Values*

28. *A Mirror of Beryl: A Historical Introduction to Tibetan Medical Science,* Desi Sangyé Gyatso (1653–1705)

29. *Selected Texts on Tibetan Astronomy and Astrology*

30. *Art and Literature: An Anthology*

31. *Tales from the Tibetan Operas*

32. *Selected Historical Works*

To stay receive a brochure describing all the volumes or to stay informed about *The Library of Tibetan Classics,* please write:

Wisdom Publications
Attn: Library of Tibetan Classics Information
199 Elm Street
Somerville, MA 02144 USA
or send a request by email to info@wisdompubs.org.

The complete catalog containing descriptions of each volume can also be found online at www.wisdompubs.org, where you can sign up for an email newsletter dedicated to LOTC news.

Become a Benefactor of the Library of Tibetan Classics

The Library of Tibetan Classics' scope, importance, and commitment to quality make it a tremendous financial undertaking. Please consider becoming a benefactor. Contributors of US$2,000 or more will receive a copy of each volume as it becomes available and will have their names listed in all subsequent volumes. Simply send a check made out to Wisdom Publications or credit card information to the address below.

Library of Tibetan Classics Fund
Wisdom Publications
199 Elm Street
Somerville MA 02144
USA

Please note that contributions of lesser amounts are also welcome and are invaluable to the development of the series. Wisdom is a 501(c)3 nonprofit corporation, and all contributions are tax-deductible to the extent allowed by law.

To keep up to date on the status of the *Library of Tibetan Classics,* visit the series page on the Wisdom website, wisdompubs.org. Sign up for the email news list for the *Library of Tibetan Classics* while you are there.

About Wisdom Publications

Wisdom Publications is dedicated to making available authentic Buddhist works for the benefit of all. We publish translations of the sutras and tantras, commentaries and teachings of past and contemporary Buddhist masters, and original works by the world's leading Buddhist scholars. We publish our titles with the appreciation of Buddhism as a living philosophy and with the special commitment to preserve and transmit important works from all the major Buddhist traditions.

Wisdom Publications
199 Elm Street
Somerville, Massachusetts 02144 USA
Telephone: (617) 776-7416
www.wisdompubs.org

Wisdom is a nonprofit, charitable 501(c)(3) organization affiliated with the Foundation for the Preservation of the Mahayana Tradition (FPMT).

Mind Training
The Great Collection
Translated and edited by Thupten Jinpa
720 pages, cloth, ISBN 0-86171-440-7, $49.95

"The practice of mind training *(lojong)* is based on the essential Mahayana teachings of impermanence, compassion, and the exchange of self and other that the eleventh-century master Atisha brought to Tibet from India. The *lojong* teachings are a source of inspiration and guidance shared by masters of all Tibetan traditions. This makes Thupten Jinpa's translation of *Mind Training: The Great Collection* a natural choice for publication as part of the *Library of Tibetan Classics* series. For the first time, this early collection of the instructions of the great Kadampa masters has been translated in its entirety. The clarity and raw power of these thousand-year-old teachings are astonishingly fresh, whether studied as a complete anthology or opened at random for inspiring verses on the heart of Buddhist practice."
— *Buddhadharma: The Practitioner's Quarterly*

"Thupten Jinpa has done us all a great service by editing and translating this marvelous volume. In an era when Buddhist meditation is largely equated with simply calming the mind and developing mindfulness, this compendium of methods for training the mind gives a glimpse of the tremendous richness and depth of the Buddhist tradition for enhancing mental health and balance and realizing the full potential of consciousness in terms of wisdom and compassion. With the current rise of positive psychology, in which researchers are seeking a fresh vision of genuine happiness and well-being, this volume can break new ground in bridging the ancient wisdom of Buddhism with cutting-edge psychology. Such collaborative inquiry between spirituality and science is especially timely in today's troubled and divisive world."
— B. Alan Wallace, author of *The Attention Revolution*

Taking the Result as the Path

Core Teachings of the Sakya Lamdré Tradition
Translated and edited by Cyrus Stearns
His Holiness Sakya Trizin, Foreword
784 pages, cloth, ISBN 0-86171-443-1, $59.95

"The Sakya school of Tibetan Buddhism has been the most conservative in maintaining the secrecy of its lineage's special practices. *Taking the Path as the Result* represents a major breakthrough by bringing these teachings to light with the full blessings of the Sakya masters. In nearly seven hundred pages of translation, the indefatigable Cyrus Stearns presents an anthology of essential texts on Lamdré. This collection will be an invaluable resource for practitioners of the Lamdré system."

—Buddhadharma: The Practitioner's Quarterly

"No one is better suited than Cyrus Stearns to offer the first major translation of Lamdré teachings to the world. He has studied intimately with the most revered leaders of the Sakya tradition for decades. Beyond this, Stearns possesses a quality that sets him apart from most translators today—he is a poet. Few have transmuted the verse or the prose, the earthy imagery or the celestial style of Tibetan Buddhist teachings, with comparable eloquence and inspiration; few are endowed with the capacity to inspire students of Tibetan Buddhism through force of the sheer beauty of the translated word. The Sakya tradition will henceforth be known to English audiences in all its splendor thanks to this new translation."

—Kurtis R. Schaeffer, University of Virginia

"In this volume, Stearns makes available for the first time a selection of key texts from the highly prized esoteric transmission of the great Tsarpa masters, translated with enormous effort and care. Students of the Lamdré will rejoice to see these often enigmatic Tibetan yoga manuals transformed into such lucid English."

—David P. Jackson, University of Hamburg

Ornament of Stainless Light
An Exposition of the Kālacakra Tantra
Khedrup Norsang Gyatso
736 pages, cloth, ISBN 0-86171-452-0, $49.95

"A radiant gem drawn from the vast ocean of Tibetan literature on the Kālacakra tantra. It provides a clear, comprehensive summary of the basic structure and essential features of this important system of mysticism. Also, Khedrup Norsang Gyatso's interpretations of controversial issues in the Kālacakra contribute to our understanding of the evolution of Tibetan theories of mysticism. Gavin Kilty's faithful translation makes this work easily accessible—it is a fitting inaugural volume for the *Library of Tibetan Classics*."

—John Newman, MacArthur Professor of
Asian Religions, New College of Florida

"When the Dalai Lama performed the Kālacakra initiation for a crowd of 20,000 at Madison Square Garden in 1991, a page was turned in the history of tantra. It was perhaps because of the popularity of this event and the success of others like it that when he was asked to select a text for the inaugural volume of the important new *Library of Tibetan Classics* series, the Dalai Lama chose a commentary on the Kālacakra tantra. The inaugural volume, *Ornament of Stainless Light,* is an important resource for anyone who has attended or will attend one of the many public performances of the Kālacakra initiation around the world."

—*Buddhadharma: The Practitioner's Quarterly*

A Note About Dust Jackets

In response to readers' requests, Wisdom has elected to change the dust jackets on the *Library of Tibetan Classics* series from the vellum covers initially produced to conventional paper jackets. If you have purchased either of the first two releases in the series, *Ornament of Stainless Light* or *Mind Training*, and would like to receive a replacement jacket free of charge, please email us at info@wisdompubs.org with your mailing address. You can also send your request to Wisdom Publications, 199 Elm Street, Somerville MA 02144.